Arctic Ocean

Pacific

Ocean

Indian

Ocean

Comparative Criminal Justice Systems

Second Edition

Erika Fairchild

Harry R. Dammer
Niagara University

WADSWORTH

THOMSON LEARNING   Australia • Canada • Mexico • Singapore • Spain • United Kingdom • United States

WADSWORTH

THOMSON LEARNING™

Executive Editor, Criminal Justice: Sabra Horne
Development Editor: Terri Edwards
Assistant Editor: Ann Tsai
Editorial Assistant: Cortney Bruggink
Marketing Manager: Jennifer Somerville
Project Editor: Jennie Redwitz
Print Buyer: Karen Hunt
Permissions Editor: Joohee Lee

Production Service: Vicki Moran
Copy Editor: Tom Briggs
Illustrator: Lotus Art
Compositor: ColorType, San Diego
Cover Designer: Qin-Zhong Yu
Cover Images: Globe: PhotoDisc, Inc.: Scales:
    John A. Rizzo/PhotoDisk, Inc.
Text and Cover Printer: Von Hoffmann Press, Inc.,
    Custom Printing Company

Wadsworth/Thomson Learning
10 Davis Drive
Belmont, CA 94002-3098
USA

For information about our products, contact us:
Thomson Learning Academic Resource Center
1-800-423-0563
http://www.wadsworth.com

International Headquarters
Thomson Learning
International Division
290 Harbor Drive, 2nd Floor
Stamford, CT 06902-7477
USA

UK/Europe/Middle East/South Africa
Thomson Learning
Berkshire House
168-173 High Holborn
London WC1V 7AA
United Kingdom

Asia
Thomson Learning
60 Albert Street #15-01
Albert Complex
Singapore 189969

Canada
Nelson/Thomson Learning
1120 Birchmount Road
Scarborough, Ontario M1K 5G4
Canada

Library of Congress Cataloging-in-Publication Data
Fairchild, Erika.
    Comparative criminal justice systems / Erika Fairchild, Harry Dammer.—2nd ed.
        p.   cm.
    Includes bibliographical references and index.
    ISBN 0-534-51480-4
        I. Dammer, Harry R., 1957-   II. Title.
HV7419   .F35 2000
364—dc21   00-043252

Contents

Chapter 9 Courts 188

Chapter 10 After Conviction: The Sentencing Process 214

Preface

Undertaking to write a textbook that deals with any aspect of comparative government is a daunting task. Serial treatment of systems, while useful and informative, gives little basis for comparison. Process-oriented comparison, on the other hand, may prove to be too abstract for the undergraduate or even for the beginning graduate student. In this text on comparative criminal justice systems, an attempt is made to effect a compromise between the approaches. While the book is organized according to process, and there is a strong emphasis on comparison among systems, the dangers of this approach are mitigated by the use of six model countries, each exemplifying a different family of law or a different governmental arrangement that affects the criminal process. The use of the model countries brings the material to a concrete level and gives it a degree of interest that would be difficult to achieve in a purely comparative text. The model countries are: England, exemplifying a Common Law system; France, exemplifying a unitary Civil Law system; Germany, exemplifying a federal Civil Law system; The People's Republic of China, exemplifying a Socialist Law system; Saudi Arabia, exemplifying an Islamic Law system; and finally Japan, exemplifying a hybrid system made up of elements of various others but distinctive in its own right.

Ideally the student in a course on comparative criminal justice will have taken at least an introductory criminal justice course and an introductory government course. However, for those who have not, the book tries to introduce all criminal justice topics in clear and simple language. After a general introduction that includes the discussion of the importance of comparative study, and an exposition on comparative crime data, the book introduces not only each family of law in some detail but also each model country.

This sets the stage for a comparison of criminal process among these countries. The approach is historical and political; but the book does not ignore economic and social factors, however, since they are inevitably important in the history and politics of the various countries.

In addition to its comparisons of the modern countries in terms of various stages of the criminal process, the book addresses certain pressing issues of criminal justice that provide a challenge to policy-makers as well as justice officials worldwide. These issues are terrorism, international organized crime and drug trafficking. It is acknowledged that other issues could have been chosen; the choice of issues was determined largely by the rich literature on the international aspects of each of these issues.

This book was primarily written and updated to meet the needs of students in their final year of undergraduate studies, but also can be used for graduate students. The style of writing is meant to be accessible to all levels of student, however, and the book contains a large number of examples, cases, and other materials that bring the subject to life for undergraduate students.

New to This Edition

The second edition of this book includes many revisions and updates, including:

- Use of the People's Republic of China as a model country in the Socialist Law perspective.

- Expanded material about international crime, transnational courts, and drug trafficking.

- Introductory information about "new" crimes such as cybercrime, smuggling, and corruption.

- Addition of numerous student study features, including key terms, maps, charts, and questions at the end of each chapter that should provide a basis for lively class discussions.

Acknowledgments

The second edition of this book was written without the assistance and advice of Erika S. Fairchild. Dr. Fairchild passed away in 1992. I am extremely grateful that I was given the opportunity to write the second edition to this book. Having the opportunity to be co-author with Dr. Fairchild is truly an honor that I will cherish for years to come. Although I did not know Dr. Fairchild prior to her untimely death, I feel that rewriting this book has created a special bond between us. I sincerely hope that she would approve of the second edition, although I am sure it would be even better with her expertise and wise counsel.

The writing of this second edition was greatly assisted by numerous people who merit special recognition. I would like to acknowledge the administration at Niagara University for the general atmosphere of support for scholarly endeavors. To my colleagues in the Criminal Justice and Criminology program, our student assistants Eryn Morris and Tracy Hensler, our competent secretary Barbara King, and especially my exemplary graduate assistant Janet McMahon, I thank you very much for your support and invaluable assistance. As with all of my projects, I am grateful for the assistance of Phyliss Schultze, librarian of the Rutgers University School of Criminal Justice—NCCD Library.

Acknowledgments should also be given to Sabra Horne and her competent staff at Wadsworth/Thomson Learning and the valuable contributions of numerous reviewers and editors who provided advice for the second edition:

Eugene E. Bouley, Georgia College and State University

James T. Green, St. Thomas Aquinas College

David M. Horton, St. Edward's University

Roger D. Thompson, University of Tennessee at Chattanooga

Nancy Travis Wolfe, University of South Carolina

Finally, my most heartfelt thanks to my loving and beautiful wife Eileen Sulzbach-Dammer for being extremely patient throughout the entire book revision process.

Dedication

This edition of the book is dedicated to a few special friends and mentors who have helped me immeasurably along the way. Among the most notable: Fr. James Heft, S.M., University of Dayton, Dr. Todd Clear, John Jay College of Criminal Justice, and especially Professor Gerhard O.W. Mueller, Rutgers University, who nearly twenty years ago enticed me to learn more about comparative criminal justice and then supported my professional endeavors in recent years. I am only one in a worldwide group of students, scholars, and researchers who are indebted to Professor Mueller.

And finally, to you Erika. . . . Thank you and may God bless you and your family.

HRD

Part I ∼ Setting the Stage

1 Introduction

Key Terms and Concepts

criminal justice system
comparative criminal justice
cybercrime
ethnocentrism
globalization
international criminal justice
transnational crime

Consider the following:

- In Mexico, carjackers often drive victims to cash machines and force them to empty their bank accounts. Other new forms of extortion and robbery have also proliferated, and the crime rate has doubled since 1994 (Robinson, 1999).

- Responding to a survey, 72 percent of South African citizens said what they feared most was being attacked at home. The murder rate in South Africa is 53.5 per 100,000 population, the highest in the world (Burkins, 1995).

- In early 1999, two Libyan citizens were handed over to Scottish authorities for legal proceedings concerning their alleged involvement in the December 1988 bombing of PAN AM flight 103 over Lockerbie, Scotland.

- In the Tihar Central Jail in New Delhi, India, 8,000 inmates are crowded into a facility built to hold 2,400 (Sen, 1996).

The study of crime and the criminal justice system illuminates some of the basic problems faced by a society. One is how to provide a safe environment in which citizens can lead their lives without fear that they or their property will be threatened. Another is how to devise a fair and expeditious way to deal with those accused or suspected of disrupting the safety and security of the community. Still another is how to provide the citizenry with a sense that justice is being administered fairly, without regard to wealth, status, ethnicity, or gender.

The ways of dealing with crime may vary considerably in different societies due to a variety of factors, including different political arrangements, historical developments, and social and economic conditions. In the United States, for example, it is not uncommon for prison inmates to bring legal action against the state or federal government for what they claim are unfair prison conditions. But this kind of legal action is highly unusual in countries in which prison conditions are far worse, and, especially, in which there is less emphasis on the democratic process. In Communist China, minor crimes are disposed of in neighborhood courts presided over by neighborhood volunteers; in contrast, in Germany, professional judges trained over a period of years handle legal matters in a plethora of specialized courts.

As the preceding list suggests, the problems of crime and justice are not uniquely American, but are faced, to a greater or lesser degree, by all societies in the world. Although international criminal justice issues may seem far removed from our own lives, they can affect us all on a daily basis. For example, when drugs are smuggled from Colombia to Mexico, the next step is for them to be carried across the border into Texas. When authorities determine that there is a threat of a terrorist attack, embassies and airports are placed on alert, and security becomes paramount. And when Russian women, victims of human trafficking, are illegally brought to the United States, they often become prostitutes in New York. In each case local, state, and federal criminal justice system officials are called to intervene; these are no longer "someone else's problem." Clearly, ignoring criminal activity originating in other countries is short-sighted and a possible recipe for future societal problems.

This book deals with the criminal justice systems of countries other than the United States and with issues related to crime throughout the world. We will consider basic philosophies of law and justice, arrangements for crime prevention and law enforcement, legal settlement structures, methods of dealing with convicted offenders, and selected other issues related to crime and criminal justice. Although the focus is on other nations, we will often compare their processes of justice with those in the United States. Before proceeding, it is important to clearly define some terms that are often used in discussion of criminal justice issues and that will be used frequently throughout this book.

DEFINING TERMS

Comparative criminal justice is a relatively new discipline that applies the comparative methodologies used in law and political science to the social science of criminology and criminal justice. The term *comparative criminal justice* is often used interchangeably with *international criminal justice,* but these terms are not exactly alike.

International criminal justice involves the study and description of one country's law, criminal procedure, or justice process. **Comparative criminal justice** is different in that it attempts to build on the knowledge of criminal justice in one country by investigating and evaluating, in terms of another country, culture, or institution. This distinction is important because, when criminologists inaccurately interchange the terms *comparative* and *international,* they lose the distinctive meaning of "comparative analysis" in the related fields of comparative law and politics (Becker, 1970).

The origins of the comparative method in areas other than criminal justice actually can be traced back to ancient times. But the kind of comparative analysis that will be employed in this book is more closely aligned with scholarly methods developed in political science in recent decades. Specifically, we borrow the methods that systematically compile data, identify relationships within the data, and suggest why certain relationships exist (Brown and Macridis, 1996).

The **criminal justice system** involves the people and agencies that perform criminal justice functions. The three basic divisions of the criminal justice system are police, courts, and corrections.

International crimes have been defined as "crimes against the peace and security of mankind" (Adler, Mueller, and Laufer, 1994). Such acts become "crimes" based on agreements between countries, called conventions, or based on legal precedents that develop over time. Among the international crimes that have been identified by the United Nations are those listed here (Adler, Mueller, and Laufer, 1994).

Aggression (by one state against another)

Threat of aggression

Intervention (in the internal or external affairs of another state)

Colonial and other forms of foreign domination

Genocide (destroying a national, ethnic, racial, or religious group)

Apartheid (suppression of a racial or ethnic group)

Systematic or mass violations of human rights

Exceptionally serious war crimes

Recruitment, use, financing, and training of mercenaries (soldiers of fortune)

Terrorism

Drug trafficking

Willful and severe damage to the environment

It is important to keep in mind, however, that these are not the only forms of international crimes. Others have been identified by various legal conventions (e.g., human trafficking) while some are not yet formally recognized by international agencies and agreements.

Transnational crimes is a term that has been used in comparative and international criminal justice study in recent years to reflect the complexity and enormity of global crime issues. Formally, it has been defined by the Fourth UN Survey as "offences whose inception, proportion and/or direct or indirect effects involve more than one country" (1995, p. 4). Many transnational crimes have been identified by criminal justice officials and by international organizations such as the United Nations. Among the most problematic for the criminal justice system are the following:

Money laundering

Theft of art and cultural objects

Drug trafficking

Terrorism

Economic crimes (e.g., insurance fraud, fraudulent bankruptcy)

Illegal corporate practices

Environmental crimes

Illicit arms trafficking

Sea piracy

Illicit human trafficking and trade in human body parts

Computer crimes

Aircraft hijacking

Land hijacking

Infiltration of legal businesses

Theft of intellectual property

Corruption and bribery of public officials

Organized crime (which can include one or a combination of any of the above)

Transnational crimes are often referred to as international crimes, and vice versa. Although there may be some overlap with some of the crimes in the two categories, such as international drug trafficking or terrorism, they are technically not the same. Transnational crimes always involve at least two countries while some international crimes can occur only within the boundaries of a country, as with genocide or apartheid. The term *transnational crime* will be used consistently throughout this book to describe the illegal activities that occur across international boundaries. The most common and problematic of these crimes will be discussed in more detail in Part III.

WHY COMPARE SYSTEMS OF AND ISSUES IN CRIMINAL JUSTICE?

There are many reasons to study and compare issues in and systems of criminal justice. From a broader perspective, the process of comparing is itself essential to our daily functioning and the way we view the world. In reality, everything we perceive is based on comparison. As stated by political scientist Karl Deutsch:

> The differences which we perceive in certain aspects of any two events, are perceived against a background of similarity with others, and so is the relative uniqueness of an event. We call an event unique if it is similar in very few aspects or dimensions, and different in very, very many from others. Without attempting comparison, how could we know that something was unique? If something were truly unique in any aspect, how could we discuss it? We should have no words for it. We could only talk about it in negatives, calling it ineffable, unmeasurable and so on, and then we would be very close to magic or religion and well away from science. (1996, p. 31)

So, then, thinking is really comparing. It is what we do every minute of every day. Comparing reflects how we make decisions, and it provides the impetus for how we act. Comparing is also a key element in critical thinking.

Critical thinking is simply purposeful mental activity. In many ways, the ability to think critically helps us avoid embarrassment, solve daily problems, and even make important life choices. Critical thinking actually involves a three-step process. First, we determine what we know about an issue and ask ourselves why we think that way. For example, maybe we feel that the death penalty is a legitimate way to punish offenders because we believe that it is less costly than life imprisonment. Second, we find out the opposite side of the story. In the case of the death penalty, we may learn about the volume of research indicating that life imprisonment is cheaper than implementing the death penalty. Finally, we objectively weigh the evidence, or compare the diverging opinions, and then make a decision based on the available evidence. Again, using the example of the death penalty, we may determine that, based on our findings, we no longer believe the death penalty is viable or we need to reserve judgment on the issue until we learn more about it. The process of critical thinking, like that of comparing, is something we tend to do without even realizing it. In comparative criminal justice research and study, both are essential mental processes that we must learn to identify and improve upon.

For the purposes of this book, there are three practical reasons we should compare systems of and issues in criminal justice: (1) to benefit from the experience of others, (2) to broaden our understanding of different cultures and approaches to problems, and (3) to help us deal with the many transnational crime problems that plague our world today.

To Benefit from Others' Experience

"The reason for comparing is to learn from the experience of others and, conversely, that he who knows only one country knows none." This profound statement by George Sartori (1996, p. 20) was made to illustrate the importance of international comparative study in the field of political science. But his remarks are equally relevant to criminal justice study. Comparative work in criminal justice is an excellent vehicle for learning more about how others practice criminal justice. With this information, we can begin to solve the many problems related to crime and justice.

In all areas of the criminal justice system—police, courts, and corrections—there are many examples of how nations have adapted others' methods of criminal justice implementation. For example, people wonder why Japan has a much lower crime rate than the United States or, indeed, most Western nations. The Japanese themselves give some of the credit for their low crime rates to their police methods—most notably, community policing. Many countries have become interested in adapting the Japanese police practices, including the use of Kobans (small local police stations). Some U.S. cities, including Detroit and Houston, have modified the Japanese methods and use them in their local police operations (Bayley, 1991).

Many countries have also adopted rules of criminal procedure that were pioneered by oth-

ers. In fact, some criminal procedure rules, like the right to counsel at an early stage of the criminal process, are becoming universal in Western systems of justice. And many countries have even adopted entire legal codes from the codes of others. The Napoleonic Code of civil law, developed in France in the early nineteenth century, was one such export, as was the French penal code, also developed under Napoleon. Another export in the late nineteenth century was the German Civil Code. These codes have had an enormous influence on the development of legal systems and criminal justice systems throughout the world (Merryman, 1985).

Corrections strategies also tend to spill over borders. For example, the idea of day fines (see Chapter 10), which was first developed in Scandinavian countries, has been adopted by Germany and, more recently, by Great Britain and the United States. And New Zealand, Australia, Canada, and the United States all have implemented different kinds of restorative justice programs. Restorative justice, which will be discussed in more detail in Chapter 10, is an idea that was cultivated by many victims' rights advocates in the United States, but it has its roots in the justice practices of many indigenous cultures.

There are many other examples of countries borrowing or adapting criminal justice practices from the United States. In the nineteenth century, many European countries, especially France, copied American methods of incarceration—specifically, the Auburn system and the Pennsylvania system. More recently, former Communist countries in eastern Europe have called upon the FBI to help train them in the fight against organized crime. Many countries have also improved their ability to collect and disseminate crime statistics using the U.S. models of the Uniform Crime Reports (UCR) and National Crime Victimization Surveys (NCVS).

However it is essential to remember that specific practices can be adopted only after serious thought and planning. Criminal justice system reformers are aware that it is naive to try to import institutions that are very much bound to local cultural values, without modifying them to conform to the new context. For example, it would be shortsighted for U.S. policymakers to think that we could easily implement a strict corporal punishment system like that found in Islamic societies. The separation of church and state, the heterogeneity of our society, and the democratic basis for our laws would preclude such an idea. Similarly, it may not be feasible to expect the leaders of China to accept and implement U.S. ideas about freedom of speech and the right to assemble to protest specific governmental decisions.

To Broaden Our Understanding of the World

A second reason for studying the administration of justice in other countries is to broaden our understanding of other countries and cultures. This is imperative because the multicultural world we now live in has entered the stage of **globalization,** whereby the world has become interdependent in terms of the events and the actions of people and governments around the world (Mueller and Adler, 1996, p. vii). In short, globalization is the idea that the world is "getting smaller." Reflecting on the globalization of crime is a recent trend in criminal justice (McDonald, 1997, p. 3), and many countries, concerned with transnational crime, are developing a serious interest in globalization issues.

Globalization has occurred as a result of a number of events in the twentieth century. Two of the most prominent are the end of the Cold War and the growth in technology. The end of the Cold War—more specifically, the demise of the former Soviet Union—has led to the opening of many previously regulated borders and, in turn, to an increase in international trade and travel. Over the past thirty years, the number of international passenger flights has increased twentyfold, and the number of global imports has increased tenfold. Along with these increases has been a concomitant increase in crime.

Ease of travel by air has enabled criminals to do their work in other countries or easily escape to a safe haven. As air and sea trade has increased, so has the smuggling of illegal goods such as drugs and guns. Strong evidence suggests that some individuals have even engaged in the illegal smuggling of human body parts to wealthy persons in other countries who need medical assistance. In countries that are in economic or political turmoil, many persons attempt to flee, causing problems such as international criminal activity, refugee flows, the spread of contagious disease, and nuclear weapons and drug trafficking (Cusimano, 2000, p. 4). When refugees enter a country, either legally or illegally, they experience difficulties adjusting to new language and cultural norms, and many find themselves in some kind of legal trouble.

Technological growth also has contributed directly to the vast increase in the kind and volume of transnational crime, with computers and telecommunications playing a key role. **Cybercrime,** crime committed with the use of computers, now ranges from relatively minor acts of consumer fraud, to more serious crimes in which drug traffickers move billions of dollars of illegal drug money, to major crimes that can paralyze entire financial networks and national security systems. In sum, "the very networks that legitimate businesses use to move goods so cheaply are the same networks that criminals use to move illicit goods so easily" (Winer, 1997, p. 41).

It is also important to broaden our understanding of other countries because, as globalization occurs, we are more likely to fall prey to the problem of **ethnocentrism**—the belief that one's own country or culture does things "right" and all other ways are "wrong" or "foreign." Ethnocentrism is a common phenomenon, as people often think their country, culture, or religion is better than all others. In terms of crime and criminal justice, ethnocentrism is a problem because it can lead to crime within and across borders. For example, the failure to quell ethnocentrism has led to endless terrorist activity in Northern Ireland and the Middle East and, more recently, to ethnic strife among the peoples of the former Yugoslavia.

Americans are frequently astonished to hear about practices related to crime and punishment in other systems. Why does one country, Saudi

Arabia, cut off a hand or a foot or stone a person to death as punishment for certain criminal acts? Why is lengthy pretrial detention without bail condoned in some countries, such as France, as a way to ensure greater justice? Why does Japan have so few lawyers compared to most countries, especially the United States? The fact is that a nation's way of administering justice often reflects deep-seated cultural, religious, economic, political, and historical realities. Learning about the reasons for these different practices can give us insight into the values, traditions, and cultures of other systems. Such broadening of perspective helps us see our own system in more objective terms.

To Deal with Transnational Crime Problems

A third good reason to study criminal justice from a comparative perspective is the increasing need to address transnational and international crime problems. In the next chapter, we will deal more extensively with the issue of comparative crime statistics; here, we can make some general statements about the need to deal with the global crime problem.

First, crime is universal—there is no country without crime (*Global Report,* 1999, p. 64). Second, because of globalization, there are more kinds of crimes that are of international concern than was the case twenty years ago, as the transnational crimes listed earlier in this chapter indicated. Third, the number of crimes committed worldwide or at least reported to criminal justice agencies, on average, increased throughout the 1980s and 1990s. Between 1975 and 1990, the total amount of reported crime grew at an average of 5 percent each year (Reichel, 1999, p. 37). President Bill Clinton, in an address to the United Nations about global crime, implicitly stated the need to address the issue. He said, "In the global village, progress can spread quickly, but trouble can too. Trouble on the far end of town soon becomes a plague on everybody's house" (Harris, 1995).

Dealing with, and hopefully solving, the problems of transnational crime and criminal justice can only be accomplished through cooperation of the countries involved. The following case underscores the complexity of international and transnational crime and the reason cooperation is so important. In July 1999, Samuel Sheinbein, age 19, pleaded not guilty in a court in Tel Aviv, Israel, to murder of another teenager—an unfortunate but not unusual crime in countries throughout the world. What is peculiar about this case is that the murder took place in the state of Maryland in the United States but Sheinbein was arrested in Israel, where he had fled. U.S. officials asked Israeli officials to return him to Maryland to stand trial. But Israeli officials refused to extradite him to Maryland for trial, stating that Sheinbein was technically an Israeli citizen because his father had been born in Israel. An Israeli court ruled that Sheinbein is a citizen of Israel and can be tried there.

This is but one example of the many issues—in this situation related to the court of jurisdiction and to extradition—that criminal justice authorities must face in our modern world of rapid communications and easy passage from one nation to another. Other, more complicated cases, such as those involving terrorists or drug cartel leaders, are far more complicated and can include multiple criminal justice systems. In the Sheinbein case, sensitive negotiations about jurisdiction, power, and plans of action were required. At these times, a basic knowledge about the organizational makeup and operational traditions of criminal justice agencies in other countries is invaluable. Sensitivity to the values of and problems faced by agencies in other systems also helps in resolving conflicts or overcoming barriers to cooperation across borders. Developing cooperative relations with particular individuals in other systems is important, but understanding these systems facilitates such personal relations.

THE HISTORICAL-POLITICAL APPROACH

The general approach in this book with regard to comparative crime and justice might be characterized as historical and political. Particular national arrangements for the administration of justice do not exist in a void and do not result from simple acts of rational planning. They develop over the course of centuries in response to local needs, efforts by individual leaders, and historical events. Institutions and practices that may seem peculiar to an outsider often can be readily understood if their own history, as well as the larger context, is examined. Therefore, this book contains some measure of historical information that bears upon the systems of justice we are examining.

Related to historical context is the political context of systems of justice. Criminal justice structures are, after all, governmental institutions, and they reflect the nature and culture of politics in their societies. In the United States, it would be difficult to understand the development of criminal procedure the past thirty years if we did not have a good understanding of the role of the Supreme Court in government. In this book, then, criminal justice arrangements are examined in a historical context with attention to the political developments that affected the process.

This is not to deny that social and economic forces are also extremely important in shaping attitudes and developments related to administration of justice; such other forces will not be ignored in the book. For example, it is important to keep in mind the economic reasons for the rise and power of drug trafficking in Colombia or organized crime in Russia. The focus, however, will be on the historical and political environment in which systems of justice evolve.

MODEL SYSTEMS

This book will describe and compare six model systems of justice, associated with six different nations, within a general criminal justice process orientation. There are over 191 independent states in the world. "Independent state" refers to people who are politically organized into a sovereign state with a definite territory. A "sovereign state" is an internationally recognized unit of political authority. In addition, there are seventy-five "dependencies" or "areas of special sovereignty" that

are associated in some way with an independent state (*World Factbook,* 1998). Two examples are Puerto Rico, which is a dependency of the United States, and Hong Kong, which is politically tied to China.

To make matters more complex, there are even more "nations" than independent sovereign states. Nations can be any group with a common cultural, ethnic, racial, or religious identity, such as the different Native American groups present in North America (Cusimano, 2000, p. 3). Each sovereign state or nation has its own unique system of law and justice. The student of comparative criminal justice cannot learn all the facts about all these systems in depth. In fact, such information gathering does not necessarily result in better understanding of the nature of crime and justice in any particular systems. But by describing in some detail the particular arrangements in model systems, we can keep the discussion of criminal process in better focus and on a more concrete level than would otherwise be possible. At the same time, organizing chapters according to the stages of the criminal process helps us compare systems more closely.

Our model systems are found in the countries of England, France, Germany, China, Japan, and Saudi Arabia. These systems are "model" in the sense that they closely reflect the workings of particular historical families of law within various political frameworks. From this point on, we will use the terms *model countries* and *model systems* interchangeably. Chapter 3 will introduce these systems and their respective families of law. The choice of these six model countries does not imply that they are superior in any way to other countries that may have a similar legal background. To be sure, information about a number of other countries would have been equally informative for comparative purposes. Notable in exclusion are the developing countries in Africa and countries in flux after the breakup of the Soviet bloc. However, the turbulent political situations in many of these countries, coupled with the dearth of material written in English, makes their inclusion in this edition problematic.

Be forewarned that this book does not provide a complete description of all facets of criminal justice in any particular system or claim to give a complete account of any transnational/international crime issue. This task would require volumes. We hope that, after reading this book, you students will be inspired to study particular systems and issues more thoroughly.

BASIC VALUES IN THE CRIMINAL JUSTICE SYSTEM

The values of any system of justice may be classified as professed values and underlying values. Professed values are those that are proclaimed as values by the participants in the system. For example, equal justice under law—the ideal that all individuals, regardless of social status or background, will be treated equally and according to an existing rule—is a professed value of most established systems of justice. In the British and American systems of justice, another professed value is that the government has an obligation to prove an individual's guilt without any requirement that the individual cooperate with the prosecution. This value lies at the heart of the adversary process.

Underlying values are those that are not openly proclaimed but that nevertheless govern actions within the criminal justice system. Efficiency, or expeditious handling of cases, is one such value that may conflict with the value of equal justice under law. Affirmation of local culture, such as tolerance or intolerance of certain kinds of substance abuse or prejudice against certain groups of individuals, are other underlying values in the criminal justice process. For example, in the Chinese criminal justice system, there are numerous situations in which, by law (a professed value), individuals have certain rights that may protect them from governmental intrusion and abuse. However, because according to the underlying values of Chinese society societal needs are more important than individual rights, the latter may become secondary during a legal proceeding.

Underlying values are harder to understand and distinguish than professed values, and they require lengthier and more intense study. This presents a problem for students of comparative justice, as such values and the practices they engender are easy to miss in a superficial description. Although examples of research in comparative criminal justice that focus on underlying values in various systems are limited (see Berman, 1963; Rosch, 1987), it is still important that we begin to appreciate their significance within the total setting of a justice system. The student of comparative justice must beware of acquiring facile knowledge of professed values without understanding the dynamics in a system that reveals the underlying values. In this book, underlying values will be illustrated as we discuss particular practices and particular systems.

POLITICAL CULTURE VERSUS POLITICIZED JUSTICE

Administration of justice is a governmental function. As such, it is bound to reflect the political culture of a nation. When we speak of culture, we are talking about deep-seated patterns of behavior and thought that have developed over the course of a society's history. A nation like Germany, with a political culture that emphasizes legalism, or close adherence to rules, is bound to reflect that concern in its justice system. A nation with a political culture that values community welfare over individual rights, as does Japan, will reflect those values in its justice system. In the Chinese legal system, independence of the judiciary is not valued to the extent that it is in the United States. This is because the political culture in China emphasizes the needs of the collective (the entire society) and discourages independent action by citizens. In the United States, by contrast, the fear of centralized power that dominated the discussion at the Constitutional Convention in 1787 was reflected in a federal judiciary whose insulation from political influence was supposed to be guaranteed by a life term. Revolutionary or postrevolutionary societies and settled societies will have different approaches to justice. A political system that is founded on religious principles will ensure that those principles are reflected in its system of justice, as is the case in some countries of the Middle East, such as Iran and Saudi Arabia.

The fact that administration of justice in a given country reflects the political culture does not mean that justice is politicized. Politicization of justice, however, happens in all countries on occasion and in some countries on a regular basis. Politicized justice involves perverting the judicial or criminal justice process in order to achieve particular political ends. These ends are generally to punish enemies of the regime in power or to deter others from joining those enemies. Politicized justice may also involve an attempt to get publicity for causes that are supported by a regime's opponents. The trials of Stalin's opponents in the Soviet Union of the 1930s and of the Chicago 7 in the United States of the 1960s are often cited as examples of politicized justice (Danelski, 1971; Juviler, 1976). Although politicized justice is hard to demarcate exactly, since it is usually mixed with real violations of conventional law, it is a common occurrence and the object of concern by human rights activists throughout the world.

THE PLAN OF THIS BOOK

In the remainder of this book, we will consider each stage of the criminal process, from arrest to punishment, as it exists in the model countries chosen. We will look at legal cultures, trial preparations and processes, sentencing philosophies, and penal systems.

Because of the tremendous variety of practices and institutions, it would be confusing (even impossible) to discuss all of them. Fortunately, major systems can be classified according to historically based families of law. These are the Common Law family, Civil Law family, and Socialist Law family. All modern legal systems are based at least partially on one or another of these historical legal arrangements. In addition, Islamic Law, based on religious tenets, plays an important role in the legal systems of many Muslim countries and is the dominant legal structure in a few countries, including Iran, Saudi Arabia, and the Sudan. Describing these families of law before we examine criminal justice processes, as well as grouping countries according to their major orientation toward one or another family, will simplify the task of considering all systems.

The other tactic used to provide a measure of continuity and coherence to this book is to describe in summary form the rules and practices in our six model countries: England, Germany, France, China, Japan, and Saudi Arabia. These countries were chosen as model systems because they represent varying governmental and legal structures, as well as different cultural traditions, all of which have an effect on the criminal process.

England has a unitary centralized government and historically has been the prototype of a Common Law system. France, also with a unitary centralized government, is a model of a Civil Law system and, indeed, was the leading nation in developing the modern Civil Law tradition. Germany, a federal nation with both state and national levels of government, has implemented its own version of Civil Law since the latter part of the nineteenth century. Germany's defeat and occupation after World War II have also affected its legal system, especially in that it has taken on some of the characteristics of the American legal and constitutional system. China, the most populous country in the world, is one of the few that still uses the Socialist legal system. And although Socialist systems actually practice a variant of Civil Law, they have enough distinctive characteristics to warrant classification as a separate family. Japan has a truly hybrid system. At various times in its history, Japan has adopted Chinese law, French law, German law, and American law, all of which continue to influence and inform Japanese law and justice. The product, however, is distinctly Japanese and is attuned to the particular culture and social needs of the Japanese people. Finally, Saudi Arabia adheres to religious Islamic Law. This fact makes its justice system distinct from those of the other model nations, all of which have secular systems.

Because of the familiarity of the American system to most readers, it will be referred to frequently in this book to provide points of contrast with other systems. Although its law is based on English Common Law, the federal structure of the United States has required extensive development of written constitutional law that supercedes all other law.

Part I of this book, which presents an introduction, some international crime statistics, and a description of the legal systems of the model nations, is essential as background for the remaining chapters. Part II is organized according to process. Chapter 5 deals with law enforcement functions and organization. Chapter 6 deals with constitutional arrangements that affect the criminal justice process, and Chapter 7 with basic criminal procedure. Chapters 8 and 9 address trial processes and the personnel involved in these processes, while Chapters 10 and 11 deal with sentencing and corrections. Part III considers some of the major issues that affect transnational criminal justice systems. Chapter 12 is about terrorism, Chapter 13 organized crime, and Chapter 14 drug trafficking. Finally, in Part IV, we draw a few conclusions about criminal justice in the world today and discuss some of the international crime issues that may come to the forefront in the next decade.

SUMMARY

We compare crime and justice across national borders so that we can benefit from what other nations have learned, increase our understanding of other cultures, and deal with the increasing global crime problem. In this book, we use the historical–political approach to explain crime and criminal justice, and to fully understand the causes of, impact of, and solutions to crime. We can augment our understanding of how criminal justice is practiced around the world if we grasp the basic values inherent in six model systems and explore the sociopolitical context of those values.

DISCUSSION QUESTIONS

1. How do international and transnational crime differ?

2. Why should we study comparative criminal justice?

3. Using newspapers, magazines, or the Internet find one example of "borrowing" in criminal justice.

4. Discuss one transnational crime problem that affects your community.

5. In the case of Samuel Sheinbein, what might be the reasons Israel does not wish for him to be extradited back to the United States? How should this matter be resolved?

6. What are some of the underlying values that are present in the U.S. criminal justice system?

7. Have someone in your class or a guest speaker who is not from the United States discuss criminal justice in a foreign country. How is it different? The same?

8. What are the advantages of using a historical-political approach to the study of comparative justice systems?

FOR FURTHER READING

Findlay, M. (1999). *The Globalisation of Crime.* Cambridge: Cambridge University Press.

McDonald, W. F. (ed.). (1997). *Crime and Law Enforcement in the Global Village.* Cincinnati: Anderson.

Ragin, C. C. (1987). *The Comparative Method: Moving Beyond Qualitative and Quantitative Strategies.* Berkeley: University of California Press.

2 Measuring and Comparing Crime in and Across Nations

Key Terms and Concepts

dark figure
International Crime Victim Surveys (ICVS)
INTERPOL
National Crime Victimization Surveys (NCVS)
self-report survey
triangulation
Uniform Crime Reports (UCR)
United Nations Surveys of Crime and Trends and
    Operation of Criminal Justice Systems (UNCJS)

As noted in the first chapter, crime is a worldwide problem that either directly or indirectly touches each and every one of us. This should hardly be surprising given all the news reports we hear about crime and its negative impact on our society. Armed with this information, we may wish to know more: How great is the risk that we will be victimized? How should we adjust our behavior to account for known instances of crime?

When we want to know about crime in a global context, an entirely new set of questions may surface: What is the risk of crime in a certain country? How safe is country A as compared to country B? How does the crime rate in the United States compare with rates in other countries?

Because of our fear of crime victimization, we may consider extreme precautions such as moving out of a certain area, purchasing expensive home security devices, or even carrying a weapon when we go out to buy a quart of milk. We might even decide to stay locked up in our homes, never venturing far from home, let alone to other cities or countries.

Internationally and transnationally, the fear of crime may have other repercussions as well. The fear of terrorist attacks may curtail air travel and tourism. Governments that refuse to cooperate in curbing drug trafficking or political corruption may be threatened with economic and political sanctions from other nations. But are all these responses to perceived crime problems reasonable and necessary?

What we really need is a way to effectively assess the true amount of crime in our own town or country, or maybe a foreign locale we would like to visit. Probably the most logical way to answer these questions is to learn more about crime statistics. From crime statistics, we can judge more effectively whether we live in a safe place, what kind of crime we should be most concerned about, what locations we should avoid, and what behaviors we should change to mitigate our chances of being a victim of crime.

In this chapter, we will explore many of the issues related to crime data on the global level.

We will address the historical background and kinds of international crime data, ways to improve crime data, the rates of crime in different countries, and, finally, the ranking of the United States in the global crime scene. But first, we must clarify the reasons it is important to measure crime and compare crime data.

WHY MEASURE CRIME AND COMPARE CRIME DATA?

For the purposes of understanding crime and criminal justice systems, measuring crime and comparing crime data in other countries serve at least two purposes. First, collecting data about crime allows us to determine the kind and extent of crimes reported in any one country and, more importantly, to distinguish long-term patterns from year-to-year trends. This is in contrast to the practice of looking at crime data for one period of time, like in a snapshot, and then making limited observations and drawing limited conclusions about the data.

An example may clarify the matter and show the importance of looking at data over a period of time. Suppose there have been 1,000 car thefts in a country during the year with a rate of 5 per 100,000 persons. This figure by itself means little; it may or may not be cause for alarm. However, if we can show that the number and rate of car thefts increased 50 percent from last year, and 75 percent over the last three years, then we may consider the problem to be more serious and worthy of further consideration.

Understanding crime trends can be important both domestically and internationally. If they know more about crime trends, federal and local governments can make better decisions about how to allocate criminal justice resources. Evidence that indicates an increased crime risk to citizens will often prompt public officials to deal with crime problems. For example, if the United States determines that the main entry point of illegal drugs is through its southern borders, officials may wish to devote more effort on improving relations with Mexican criminal justice officials and to spend more money on border patrols and immigration control.

Second, measuring crime and comparing crime data provide clues as to why some nations are more successful than others in controlling crime rates. In this way, we can learn from the success of another country. To illustrate, suppose we review the criminal justice system of a country and find that a lower crime rate is the result of a specific policy. We may then study the policy and try to adapt it to our own situation. For example, we might learn something from Switzerland, which recently has attempted with some success to isolate drug offenders in certain urban areas with the goal of reducing some of the effects of illegal drug use (e.g., thefts, the spread of AIDS).

THE HISTORICAL BACKGROUND OF INTERNATIONAL CRIME DATA

The first attempt to collect data on crime at the international level occurred in 1853 at the General Statistical Congress in Brussels. Soon thereafter, in 1872, another attempt was made at the International Congress on the Prevention and Repression of Crime in London. The major issue discussed at both of these meetings was how to define certain crimes, for the comparability of definitions clearly was to be a major stumbling block in the collection of crime data.

The problem of definitions still was an issue in 1946 at the conference of the International Penal and Penitentiary Foundation (IPPF), which soon handed over most of its functions to the newly formed United Nations (UN) organization. In the early years of the UN, attempts were made to develop a mechanism for collecting criminal data at the international level. The Economic and Social Council Branch of the UN

passed several resolutions from 1948 and 1951, but they met with little success. Only one crossnational crime survey was conducted over the period 1937–46 (Burmham, 1997). Between the 1940s and the early 1970s, crime data collection was limited to the International Police Association (INTERPOL), which tried to collect data from as many of its member nations as cared to report them.

In 1970, a breakthrough occurred when the UN General Assembly resolved through its Crime Prevention and Criminal Justice Branch to develop a survey that would collect information from member countries about crime rates and the operations of criminal justice systems. The first survey, covering the years 1970–75, appeared in 1977, with 64 nations reporting, but 14 provided no data (Fields and Moore, 1996, p. 17). The UN has recently completed its Fifth UN Survey, with 103 nations responding. Currently, the survey is administered by the UN Centre for International Crime Prevention (CICP) and is called the United Nations Surveys of Crime and Trends and Operation of Criminal Justice Systems (UNCJS).

Over the past thirty years, many intergovernmental organizations, as well as private researchers, have attempted to collect crime data. In most instances, however, they record only crime data, whereas the UN surveys provide valuable information about criminal justice system operations and processes.

The development of data to measure the incidence of transnational crime has been less successful than the efforts mentioned previously. In 1995, the UN Secretariat attempted for the first time to assess the prevalence and extent of transnational crime as part of the Fourth UN Survey of Crime Trends and Operations of Criminal Justice Systems. However, because penal codes of nations do not include categories of transnational crimes, no official data were available. What did result from the Secretariat's efforts was the clarification of eighteen categories of transnational crimes, all of which were identified as forms of organized crime (Mueller and Adler, 1997). (For a complete list of these and other transnational crimes, see Chapter 1.)

THE DIFFERENT KINDS OF CRIME DATA

Technically, there are close to 200 ways to collect crime data—and each of them is slightly different. That figure reflects the number of countries that actually collect crime data (currently, at least 185 do so), as well as the many international agencies and private research groups that attempt to measure crime. Fortunately, this chapter will *not* detail each of them, and you will most likely *not* be held responsible for knowing the differences between them. But this statement about the large number and kinds of crime data highlights some important points to keep in mind throughout this chapter.

Crime data collection, analysis, and comparison is a very diverse and sometimes complicated endeavor. There is no right or wrong way to collect and compile crime data, and any method can be open to considerable subjective interpretation. Most importantly, because of the many limitations of international crime data collection and analysis, one must interpret any such data with extreme caution. Any comparison between two or more countries should be done only after serious consideration of the many variations and subtle nuances in the crime data. For example, suppose that, in observing the crime data in the Netherlands, we see that there is a high rate of theft and thus conclude that it is unsafe to travel there. However, what we might not know is that the high theft rate in the Netherlands is due in large part to the many bicycle thefts in the city of Amsterdam—where the bicycle is a primary means of transport. This information may change our minds about personal safety in the Netherlands.

In the remainder of this section, we will discuss the different kinds of crime data used throughout the world. We begin by summarizing the three major forms of data implemented in the United States: the Uniform Crime Reports, the National Crime Victimization Surveys, and self-reports of crime. An explanation of these methods is necessary because the American models have been adopted in some form in many countries around the world and thus provide a comparative framework to study methods used in other countries.

The Uniform Crime Reports

The **Uniform Crime Reports (UCR)** are crime data collected by over 16,000 city, county, and state law enforcement agencies about twenty-nine types of crimes that have been brought to their attention with or without an arrest. The law enforcement agencies then voluntarily send the data to the Federal Bureau of Investigation (FBI), which compiles them into an annual published report.

The UCR, which dates back to 1930, provides a good overall picture of the incidence of crime. However, it is not without serious methodological flaws. The UCR is limited in that it measures only crimes reported to police, often counts only the most serious crime committed in a series of crimes, does not differentiate between completed and attempted acts, and does not cover white-collar or federal crimes. Furthermore, the UCR fails to take into account the effect that police themselves might have on crime data. For example, police might be politically motivated to overreport or underreport crime statistics.

The past ten years have seen some improved methods of crime data collection by police. In 1991, the FBI began implementing an updated version of the UCR called the National Incident-Based Reporting System (NIBRS). This more detailed method counts each incident reported and collects additional information on each. More recently, criminal justice agencies have borrowed from the field of geography a method called geographic information systems (GIS), which in law enforcement is also called crime mapping. In GIS, locations of crime are displayed on maps to help develop more information about crime trends and crime prevention strategies. It is likely that use of these newer methods will spread to the international community in the near future.

The National Crime Victimization Surveys

In an attempt to learn more about the amount of unreported crime, in 1973 the U.S. Census Bureau began conducting nationwide victimization surveys for the Department of Justice. The best known of these surveys are conducted for the National Institute of Justice by the Census Bureau and are called **National Crime Victimization Surveys (NCVS).** The NCVS is a survey of more than 101,000 people from 49,000 households nationwide in which respondents are asked to report anonymously whether they have been the victim of certain crimes over the past year. The NCVS covers the crimes of rape, robbery, assault, larceny, burglary, and motor vehicle theft. The NCVS has shown that the total number of crimes committed in the United States is at least double the number reported to the police in the UCR.

The NCVS improves our knowledge of the true extent of crime and thereby reduces the **dark figure** of, or the amount of unknown, crime. But like the UCR, the NCVS has limitations. Among the most problematic are that the NCVS is expensive to administer and counts only a limited number of crimes. Also, because the NCVS and other victimization surveys rely on the memory and honesty of citizens, the validity of the data may be questionable. Finally, victimization data are collected by hundreds of interviewers across the country, and their recording styles may vary considerably. The result can be different ways of recording the same information. Table 2.1 compares the UCR and NCVS.

Self-Report Surveys

The third most common source of crime data in the United States is **self-report surveys,** in which people are asked to report their own delinquent and criminal acts in an anonymous questionnaire or confidential interview. Self-report surveys are used mostly with young persons in the school setting but have also been used with adult offenders under corrections supervision. Because of this, self-report surveys have limited utility in understanding the overall crime rate and so are less likely to be used in cross-national comparisons. And like victimization studies, they are prone to validity problems because they require that interviewees be totally honest and aware of their involvement in criminal activity.

(Note: The previous sections provide only a brief overview of the three main methods of collecting crime data in the United States. For a more detailed analysis of the methods, we encourage you to explore some of the many fine resources on the topic. For example, see F. Hagan, *Research Methods in Criminal Justice and Criminology,* 5th ed. [Boston: Allyn & Bacon, 2000].)

International Police Data

Over a two-week period in May 1999, these three crime stories were in the international news:

- In the city of St. Petersburg, in Russia, the crime rate increased 27 percent as compared to the previous year, according to city police officials (Itar-Tass News Agency, 1999).

- In the South American country of Colombia, a report was posted by the Board of Judicial Police (DIJIN) stating that during 1998 there was a 9 percent increase in the number of homicides (Inter Press Service, 1999).

- In the United States, according to preliminary figures from the FBI, serious crime in the United States dropped for the seventh consecutive year (Associated Press, 1999).

Each of these news stories presents an example of the use of police data. The information is collected by individual officers at the scene of a complaint, arrest, or criminal activity; compiled at the police station; and later usually forwarded

Table 2.1 How Do the UCR and NCVS Compare?

	Uniform Crime Reports (UCR)	National Crime Victimization Surveys (NCVS)
Offenses Measured	Homicide Rape Robbery (personal and commercial) Assault (aggravated) Burglary (commercial and household) Larceny (commercial and household) Motor vehicle theft Arson	Rape Robbery (personal) Assault (aggravated and simple) Household burglary Larceny (personal and household) Motor vehicle theft
Scope	Crimes reported to police in most jurisdictions; considerable flexibility	Crimes both reported and not reported to police; all data are available for a few large geographic areas
Collection Method	Police department reports to FBI or to centralized state agencies that then report to FBI	Survey interviews; periodically measures the total number of crimes committed by asking a national sample of 49,000 households encompassing 101,000 persons age twelve and over about their experiences as victims of crime during a specified period
Kinds of Information	In addition to offense counts, provides information on crime clearances, persons arrested, persons charged, law enforcement officers killed and assaulted, and characteristics of homicide victims	Provides details about victims (such as age, race, sex, education, income, and whether the victim and offender were related to each other) and about crimes (such as time and place of occurrence, whether reported to police, use of weapons, occurrence of injury, and economic consequences)
Sponsor	U.S. Department of Justice, Federal Bureau of Investigation	U.S. Department of Justice, Bureau of Justice Statistics

SOURCE: Bureau of Justice Statistics, 1988, p. 11.

to state or federal agencies. Most countries use police data as the primary and official measure of crime. In the United States, the equivalent of police data are the Uniform Crime Reports, which, as mentioned previously, are statistics collected by police agencies and forwarded to the FBI to be compiled in the Uniform Crime Reports. The United Nations Surveys and INTERPOL rely on police data that are voluntarily forwarded to them to develop their own data.

In most countries, the use of computers has made the process of crime data collection and analysis much more efficient. Some countries, like the United States and England, provide individual officers on the street or in the police cruiser with portable computers that can be used to enter data and search for information about suspects, stolen property, and so on. By speeding up the recording process, officers can more quickly return to the street to perform law enforcement functions.

United Nations Surveys

Previously, you were introduced to **United Nations Surveys of Crime and Trends and Operation of Criminal Justice Systems (UNCJS).** Since its first survey covering the years 1970–75, the United Nations Centre for International Crime Prevention (CICP) has conducted the survey every five years to provide a source of statistical information on crime and justice in UN member countries.

The crimes that are measured in the UNCJS are the "traditional" crimes of murder, rape, robbery, assault, and theft. Information on other crimes such as fraud, bribery, and drug offenses are included in the UNCJS but are much more difficult to interpret. The main features of the UNCJS are as follows:

- It is a survey of official data for individual countries.
- It provides standard definitions and classifications of crime and justice categories.
- It provides for ongoing and regular participation of UNCJS member countries.
- It helps develop a universal methodology for countries to follow when collecting crime data.
- It, in effect, provides different kinds of political statements about crime and criminal justice in member countries (*Global Report, 1999,* pp. 3–10).

The UNCJS can be an effective comparative tool if the interpreter adheres to some basic principles. First, the data should be viewed over time rather than at a cross-section. This allows for a clearer and more reliable perspective on crime trends over a period of time. Second, the UNCJS can be useful if the countries viewed are similar relative to geographic region or economic status. Keep in mind, however, that countries may differ greatly within these categories due to cultural, religious, and ethnic differences.

INTERPOL and INTERPOL Crime Data

One of the world's greatest sources of information on crime data and criminals is the International Police Association, more commonly called **INTERPOL.** The idea behind an international police organization was first proposed during the First International Police Congress of 1914 in Monaco. The original goal was to improve investigation and apprehension of fugitives (Fooner, 1989). Because of World War I, operations were dismantled, but the organization resurfaced in Vienna in 1923 as the International Criminal Police Commission (ICPC). With the outbreak of World War II, the commission again halted operations

but resumed them in 1946 in Paris. In 1956, the organization was renamed INTERPOL, and the General Secretariat (main headquarters) are currently located in Lyon, France.

As of July 1999, INTERPOL was composed of 177 member countries. They must all apply for membership, appoint delegates, pay dues, and follow organizational rules. Article 3 of its Constitution sets forth INTERPOL's aims:

> *(a) to ensure and promote the widest possible mutual assistance between criminal police authorities within the limits of laws existing in the different countries and in the spirit of the Universal Declaration of Human Rights; and, (b) to establish and develop all institutions likely to contribute effectively to the prevention and suppression of ordinary law crimes. (www.usdoj.gov/usncb/aboutint.htm)*

It is important to understand that INTERPOL is not an operational police force that works across borders. It does not have powers of arrest or search and seizure. INTERPOL relies upon local and national police forces to conduct investigations, collect and compile data, and carry out other activities such as delivery of arrest warrants ordered by courts of law.

INTERPOL does not intervene in religious, political, military, or racial disagreements in any member countries. This policy ensures that the agency can continue to access information about crime and criminals in member nations even during international conflicts and internal political instability. Only in the last fifteen years has INTERPOL investigated international terrorism and, more recently, drug trafficking (Bresler, 1993).

So what exactly does INTERPOL accomplish? Simply stated, INTERPOL acts as a clearinghouse (or central location) for information on offenses and subjects believed to operate across national boundaries. INTERPOL has been publishing crime statistics since 1950. The data are based on data collected by police in the 177 INTERPOL member countries. Published in four languages (English, French, Spanish, and Arabic), the data relate to seven major crimes that are reported to or detected by law enforcement officials: murder, sex offenses, serious assault, thefts and robbery, fraud, counterfeit currency, and drug offenses.

Over 5 million files are currently held by the organization. Through INTERPOL's computer information system, called the Lyon Criminal Information System, any member can, for example, perform searches on international criminals, access fingerprints and photos of criminals, call up indexes on stolen works of art and passports, and search for stolen vehicles, planes, and boats (*Law Enforcement Technology,* March 1997, pp. 60–61).

Many countries have created a special agency to work exclusively with INTERPOL. For example, U.S. INTERPOL is housed in the National Central Bureau, an agency within the U.S. Department of Justice. In some regions of the world, countries have developed specialized agencies to work on gathering and sharing law enforcement data. For example, in the early 1990s, a group of European nations formed EUROPOL to share crime information about drug trafficking among members of the European Union.

The following brief news item illustrates the work of INTERPOL, as well as the limits of its power:

> On July 31, 1999 the United States received notice through INTERPOL of China's request for the arrest, detention and extradition of the U.S. based leader of the Falun Gong spiritual movement, a movement which is being scrutinized and suppressed in Beijing. The leader, Li Hongzhi, leads the movement from his home in Queens, New York. There is currently no extradition treaty between China and the USA. (Reuters News Service, 29 July 1999)

As this story shows, INTERPOL is asked to relay information about criminal matters around the world. Yet INTERPOL relies on the cooperation of member countries to complete the tasks of law enforcement.

International Victimization Surveys

Additional information about crime can be obtained through the use of international victimization surveys. Although the initial modern crime victimization survey was conducted in the United States in 1965, the first national study was carried out in Finland in 1970. Soon thereafter, international studies were undertaken in Denmark, Sweden, and Norway (Jousten, 1994). Many countries now survey citizens about their crime victimization experiences, including the extensive British Crime Survey (BCS), which samples 10,000 citizens of England and Wales.

The first major comparative victimization survey was developed and carried out in 1988 by three European criminologists: Jan van Dijk, Pat Mahew, and Martin Killias. The second was conducted in 1992–94, and the third in 1996–97. These surveys, now formally called the **International Crime Victim Surveys (ICVS),** are conducted in approximately fifty-five countries through the coordinated efforts of the Ministry of Justice of the Netherlands and the United Nations Interregional Crime and Justice Research Institute, located in Rome (Schmalleger, 1999, p. 683).

As in the United States, international crime victimization surveys have shown that the total number of crimes committed is about double the number reported to the police (Miyazawa, 1981; Stephan, 1976).

The primary collection tool used in the ICVS is computer-assisted telephone interviewing, which randomly selects and calls a sample of at least 1,000 individuals in each country. In some countries, smaller samples are used because of logistical difficulties; and where telephone ownership is limited, in-person interviews are conducted.

The ICVS asks representative samples of individuals about selected offenses they have experienced over a certain period of time, usually five years. The ICVS is interested in incidents both reported and not reported to the police and in the reasons people do or do not choose to notify the police. It provides a count of how many people are affected by crime. Those who mention an incident of any particular type are asked some additional questions about what happened (van Dijk, 1997, p. 15).

The results of three ICVSs are shown in Table 2.2. The table provides the percentage of respondents victimized by car crimes, burglary, other

Table 2.2 ICVS Results, 1989–1996

	Number of Countries Responding	Number of Cases in Each Country	Car Crimes[a] 29.7%	Burglary and Attempts 20.4%	Other Thefts[b] 32.3%	Contact Crimes[c] 20.4%	Assaults (Women)[d] 7.4%	Assaults (Men)[e] 6.2%	Any Crime 63.7%
All	55	67,364							
Western Europe									
Austria		413	28.7	6.5	28.5	16.2	6.5	6.3	53.9
Belgium		345	33.1	14.6	25.0	10.6	3.9	1.0	56.1
England & Wales		1,700	42.3	22.5	21.1	16.7	4.5	6.6	63.4
Finland		1,660	27.2	4.6	28.4	18.5	10.0	10.0	55.8
France		482	43.6	21.0	31.8	15.9	3.6	4.5	69.5
Germany (West)		1,389	36.8	11.7	30.2	18.0	3.6	3.7	62.4
Italy		554	45.0	20.1	26.9	15.4	3.4	1.2	65.9
Malta		549	46.1	7.1	10.0	12.3	2.7	4.0	55.3
Netherlands		1,225	40.5	25.2	48.7	22.3	5.7	6.9	77.0
Northern Ireland		176	33.1	10.9	19.8	13.8	3.3	8.1	54.8
Norway		164	35.9	15.3	20.1	16.3	10.4	3.4	56.2
Scotland		821	38.2	18.9	16.0	13.8	4.7	5.7	58.2
Spain		2,615	43.8	11.7	20.9	19.2	3.1	4.0	63.5
Sweden		548	34.8	15.1	42.0	18.7	6.7	7.4	67.2
Switzerland		187	23.1	11.0	36.8	9.1	2.9	1.6	59.0
New World									
Australia		2,174	42.8	25.6	22.2	18.3	5.5	9.2	64.1
Canada		2,282	41.6	19.7	28.9	18.5	7.7	6.0	64.3
New Zealand		554	48.6	24.6	26.9	24.0	12.9	11.2	68.7
USA		941	45.4	23.4	28.5	19.8	5.7	7.0	64.1
Central and Eastern Europe									
Albania		983	9.6	15.5	35.0	12.7	6.0	1.6	52.6
Belarus		999	17.4	10.5	25.7	16.6	5.5	7.2	50.1
Bulgaria		1,076	44.9	31.4	35.8	21.5	6.9	6.4	77.2
Croatia		930	29.9	8.1	20.0	15.2	5.3	5.4	53.4
Czech Rep.		1,010	35.9	18.8	38.5	14.0	8.3	6.6	68.8
Estonia		842	26.8	27.1	31.7	22.3	6.4	8.7	64.0
Georgia		567	32.6	25.1	29.3	22.7	5.4	4.5	66.2
Hungary		756	34.6	16.6	24.2	10.3	1.8	3.6	57.4
Kyrgyzstan		1,494	14.0	19.6	36.1	22.4	13.1	8.3	60.4
Latvia		1,011	21.5	18.7	31.4	15.7	4.4	5.0	58.6
Lithuania		654	32.8	21.2	28.5	16.0	5.4	7.3	62.1
"Former Yugoslav Rep. Macedonia"		700	35.0	11.8	23.0	11.6	3.8	5.6	52.6
Mongolia		1,053	12.3	28.1	44.0	18.7	5.8	8.7	68.2
Poland		1,622	30.2	13.4	31.9	16.3	4.8	7.2	61.3

	Number of Countries Responding	Number of Cases in Each Country	Car Crimes[a]	Burglary and Attempts	Other Thefts[b]	Contact Crimes[c]	Assaults (Women)[d]	Assaults (Men)[e]	Any Crime
Romania		1,000	20.7	10.7	29.8	18.1	7.3	9.7	56.1
Russia		2,020	23.9	17.1	32.6	22.2	8.4	8.2	62.8
Slovakia		1,126	37.8	16.5	38.4	7.2	2.0	1.4	66.1
Slovenia		2,035	40.7	15.6	29.1	18.1	7.2	6.2	64.6
Ukraine		1,000	15.6	18.6	42.8	19.5	5.6	7.4	64.8
Yugoslavia		1,094	40.5	14.8	29.9	24.2	7.5	9.9	72.2
Asia									
China		2,000	1.9	9.1	44.2	12.9	3.7	2.7	52.2
India		2,039	6.6	9.9	28.5	14.6	8.7	2.2	43.7
Indonesia		3,928	15.6	16.7	25.5	13.0	5.5	2.8	43.8
Philippines		2,523	5.8	9.8	23.1	11.3	1.2	2.1	40.1
Africa									
Egypt		1,000	20.0	22.0	35.5	32.0	8.9	3.6	68.9
South Africa		1,994	24.2	23.1	24.7	28.7	11.5	12.8	64.2
Tanzania		1,002	25.4	46.4	47.4	29.8	17.9	2.9	76.5
Tunisia		1,086	25.9	32.0	46.0	31.4	7.2	7.6	76.5
Uganda		2,020	24.3	56.1	53.7	39.8	21.2	7.8	87.8
Zimbabwe		1,006	14.9	32.7	42.7	29.4	8.8	12.4	70.1
Latin America									
Argentina		2,000	44.1	28.2	53.0	36.8	18.6	8.8	86.7
Bolivia		999	15.7	43.6	45.0	30.0	5.2	10.2	76.6
Brazil		2,017	22.4	13.5	30.5	44.9	23.1	10.4	68.0
Colombia		1,000	44.5	39.1	54.0	50.6	15.9	8.3	87.1
Costa Rica		1,412	24.6	33.7	35.5	30.7	13.6	5.7	71.5
Paraguay		587	28.2	36.3	36.5	23.7	9.1	4.4	69.9

[a]Car theft, theft from car, and car damage.

[b]Motorcycle theft, bicycle theft, and other personal theft.

[c]Robbery, sexual offenses, threats, and assaults.

[d]Sexual assault and nonsexual assault.

[e]Assault.

SOURCE: *The Global Report of Crime and Justice*, 1999, pp. 283–284. United Nations Office for Drug Control and Crime Prevention. Reprinted with permission of the United Nations.

theft, contact crimes, violence against women, violence against men, and any crime over a five-year period in the urban areas of six global regions. The data have been combined from three ICVSs conducted in different countries at different points in time from 1989 through 1996. Four of our model countries—France, Germany, England and Wales, and China—are represented in the table, as well as the United States. Saudi Arabia and Japan did not participate in the surveys. Later in the chapter, we will discuss the overall results of the survey. In the meantime, note that according to the ICVS data, the United States has a similar victimization rate to other Western countries.

International victimization surveys, however, do not provide a final solution to the underreporting problem. Like the NCVS in the United States, the ICVS has methodological problems. For example, certain population groups, such as children, the homeless, and the very poor, may be excluded because they are difficult to survey. The ICVS also excludes commercial properties, which means it may report less crime than actually exists. Again, the accuracy is dependent on the memory and objectivity of respondents. For instance, a victim may err in the time frame of the occurrence of a crime. Overreporting may occur if people mistakenly report an event as criminal (e.g., an item was lost, not stolen). Underreporting is possible because some crimes may involve people close to the victim, and they choose not to divulge that information. A final major problem with victimization surveys throughout the world is the limited sample size—usually around 2,000 per nation. With such small samples, it is difficult to create detailed crime classes such as robbery and burglary (Lynch, 1995).

While the ICVS has its problems, it is still a valuable tool for studying comparative crime trends. One must be aware of its limitations and use the information in addition to other sources of data.

Other Sources of Crime Data

As mentioned in the summary of crime data in the United States, self-report surveys are a third primary method of international crime data collection and analysis. The use of this method internationally has grown in recent years as an alternative to police and victim surveys (Graham and Bowling, 1996). The most common use of self-report studies in other countries, as in the United States, is with juveniles. One such study compared juvenile rates of crime in twelve European locations and Omaha, Nebraska. An interesting result was that in participating countries between 80 and 90 percent of juveniles had committed either one or a combination of property, violent, and drug crimes (Junger-Tas, Terlouw, and Klien, 1994). However, the use of self-report measures outside the United States will not be discussed in detail here because of the limited information available about such studies and because the lack of a common methodology for conducting the surveys limits their utility for purposes of comparison.

In addition to the major kinds of international crime data mentioned so far, some less recognized forms are used for different purposes throughout the world. For example, the World Health Organization (WHO) collects and distributes national and global information about health and mortality issues. For purposes of criminal justice, the WHO provides valuable information about homicide rates based on death certificates issued by medical examiners (Huang and Wilson, 1993).

Two other major statistical attempts to measure crime, conducted by private researchers in the late 1970s and early 1980s, provide us with additional ways to measure and compare crime across boundaries. Dane Archer and Rosemary Gartner compiled the Comparative Crime Data File (CCDF) (Archer and Gartner, 1984), which revealed crime data for the period 1900–72 for five crimes in 110 nations. The Correlates of Crime (COC), developed by Richard R. Bennett, contained both crime data and social, economic, and political information relevant to crime for 52 nations for the period 1960–80 (Bennett, 1990). Both of these efforts used INTERPOL data and other sources to develop their findings and are valuable resources for longitudinal studies about crime.

With all these different kinds of crime data, can we accurately compare crime rates within and across borders? Yes and no. If we wish to study trends and make some general observations about crime, then the use of international crime data can serve us well. However, we must be more skeptical and cautious if we want to use international crime data to help us make definitive statements about and comparison between countries or to develop policies in the criminal justice arena. The next section explores some of the major limitations related to international crime data.

LIMITATIONS OF INTERNATIONAL CRIME DATA

Researchers have documented many limitations of the different kinds of international crime data. These limitations are understandable given the differences in language, methodological sophistication, technological resources, and culture across borders. This section will describe three of the major problems that plague most international crime data: (1) underreporting, (2) nonstandard definitions, and (3) differences in collection and recording practices. You will notice that the limitations discussed are sometimes related to those mentioned previously for crime data used in the United States. Those limitations may be briefly mentioned here to place them in context with international crime data.

Underreporting

Since the inception of international crime surveys, one of the major problems for researchers has been the underreporting of crime data. This underreporting actually takes two forms. First, as with the UCR and NCVS in the United States, citizens fail to report many crimes. Since most official aggregate crime data are based on crimes reported to the police, these data will be affected by the failure of victims or observers to inform police when a crime has occurred. This may be be-

cause they have little confidence in the police, are afraid of reprisals, or wish to protect the perpetrator. Other social factors such as limited telephone access and whether property is insured may also come into play; for instance, insured victims must file reports to collect their benefits. Table 2.3 lists reasons respondents in the ICVS gave for failing to report crime to police.

The second form of underreporting involves the limited number of countries that report international crime data. This has been a problem for all forms of international crime surveys for a number of years. Even in the first UNCJS survey in 1970, the number of member nation respondents was only sixty-four. There are many reasons a country might not wish to report its crime statistics. For example, the former Soviet Union and other socialist countries would often fail to report crime data because they felt that to do so would indicate the existence of crime and thus reveal a weakness in their political philosophy.

In research conducted by G.O.W. Mueller, a distinguished professor of criminal justice at Rutgers University and former chief of the UN Crime Prevention Branch, it was determined that countries fail to report crime statistics for a number of reasons. Mueller found that, although all countries do collect some form of crime data, many do not participate in the international crime surveys. Among the reasons are the following:

- Countries are so small that administrative staffs may not be able to handle the requests.

- Some countries are too involved in civil war to keep track of crime problems.

- "New" countries have not developed a system of collection and dissemination of crime data.

- Some countries lack the technical resources and knowledge necessary to report crime data.

- Some countries have the resources but still refuse because they are concerned that crime data will negatively affect the nation's world standing or tourist trade (Mueller, 1992).

Table 2.3 Reasons for Not Reporting Crimes[a] to the Police, ICVS, 1989–1996

Reasons for No Report	All	Africa	Asia	Central and Eastern Europe	Latin America	New World	Western Europe
Number of countries	55	6	4	20	6	4	15
Number of cases	35,484	3,494	2,089	10,101	4,514	4,917	10,369
Not serious	31%	19%	21%	30%	23%	44%	43%
Solved it	11	13	13	11	12	11	8
Inappropriate	11	11	10	11	13	11	7
Other authority	3	5	7	1	1	4	2
Family	4	5	6	5	4	1	1
No insurance	2	1	2	3	4	1	2
Could do nothing	21	21	24	29	23	12	18
Will not do anything	16	11	13	19	37	6	9
Fear/dislike	5	2	9	5	13	2	1
Did not dare	5	7	4	4	4	8	2
Other	9	6	7	6	4	18	14
Do not know	2	1	.4	2	2	5	28

[a]Five crimes combined: theft from cars, burglary with entry, robbery, sexual incidents, and assaults/threats.

SOURCE: Jan J. M. van Dijk, 1997. "Criminal victimization and victim empowerment in an international perspective: Key results of fifty nations of the international crime victims surveys 1989–1996." Keynote address at the opening session of the Ninth International Symposium on Victimology, Amsterdam, August 25–29. Reprinted with permission.

Nonstandard Definitions

A more complicated problem in comparing crime rates across nations is that of nonstandardized definitions of crime. At the root of the problem of nonstandardized definitions is the issue of determining what is a *crime* versus what is *legal*. All nations agree that major predatory actions like murder, robbery, and burglary should be illegal. When it comes to certain other actions, however, we may find that what is criminal in one country is acceptable behavior in another. Here are a few examples:

- Prostitution, largely illegal in the United States, is sanctioned and licensed in Japan and parts of Germany.
- Gambling, largely illegal in the United States, is legal in many other countries, including Japan, Germany, and France.

- Drinking alcoholic beverages, legal in most countries, is illegal in certain Muslim societies, including Iran and Saudi Arabia.
- Cases that would constitute minor traffic offenses in the United States are often classified as "professional negligence" in Japan on the theory that a driver's license constitutes a kind of professional certification.
- Sexual acts like adultery, fornication, and homosexuality, which are not usually handled as criminal cases in Western countries, may result in very grave sanctions, including death, in fundamentalist Muslim countries like Iran and Saudi Arabia.

What a country decides is illegal tells us something about that nation's social, economic, and political situation. For example, the determination of the need for a sober and reasonably docile working class in the early stages of the industrial revolution led to criminalization of acts like vagrancy, loitering, drunkenness, and brawling. Religion-based governments tend to criminalize acts that dishonor the religion or violate its moral code. Socialist governments criminalize incursions against property belonging to the state (e.g., educational, government, or military buildings). Slave-holding societies criminalize efforts to educate or otherwise raise the aspirations of slaves. Nations that, for economic reasons, wish to segregate people along racial or ethnic lines pass laws against miscegenation or other kinds of social contact between groups. In each case, actions that are perfectly legal in one country are defined as crimes in another.

Nonstandardized definitions are a particular problem in the case of data gathered by INTERPOL and the United Nations. For the sake of uniformity and comparability, these agencies request that countries report their crime data according to categories established by the agency rather than by the country itself. This practice, although making it easy to compile data, lends itself to confusion and controversy. To improve the situation and ensure that crimes are defined in a similar fashion, the United Nations has developed standard definitions for all countries to follow when compiling crime data. Member countries are encouraged to use these definitions to make crime counting more standardized across borders. (See the accompanying box on page 28 for a list of the definitions.)

Differences in Collection and Recording Practices

A third major problem with international crime data is the inconsistency of the actual collection and recording of crime data. These problems can arise in many ways. One is when private researchers collect the data through citizen surveys or an examination of public records to determine the extent of crime. In this case, the problem is that the styles of the different interviewers and

recorders may vary considerably, which may lead, in turn, to inconsistent data entry and analysis.

Another and more common inconsistency involves crime data collection and recording by the police. Police departments in many parts of the world often lack the resources, technical ability, and even the interest to effectively collect crime statistics. A number of structural, political, and personnel problems may contribute to the inability of police to collect valid crime data.

The structure of police agencies and their reporting measures vary considerably. The most obvious structural difference is the resources used in the fight against and recording of crime. Many countries, especially those in developing areas of the world, lack the manpower and the computers to efficiently collect, record, and report crime data. Countries that have more police and whose forces use more advanced technology tend to report a higher proportion of actual crime.

Many countries do not possess a unified criminal justice system and so may not be able to collect crime statistics on a national level. For example, in some countries, private security guards are not encouraged to report crimes to a central location. In other countries, police count crimes when they are reported and when they choose to pass details on to prosecuting authorities. In still others, local counting rules may mean police have already recorded an associated, more serious offense (Lewis, 1997).

Politics also plays a role in the collection and reporting of crime data. As mentioned previously, it was not uncommon during the Cold War for the former Soviet Union and other Socialist countries to underreport crime data so as to make their political system appear superior to democracy and capitalism. This policy was hardly surprising, since the existence of crime is an embarrassment in a Communist society; its extent is generally hidden from the citizens of those societies, as well as from outsiders. According to Karl Marx, the leading philosopher of communism, crime is a by-product of the acquisitiveness and unequal distribution of resources found in capitalist societies.

Definitions of Recorded Crimes Used in the Fifth UN Survey of Crime Trends and Operation of Criminal Justice Systems (UNCJS)

Intentional homicide refers to death deliberately inflicted on a person by another person, including infanticide. Countries were asked to indicate whether certain categories were charged or prosecuted as "aggravated assault."

Nonintentional homicide refers to death not deliberately inflicted on a person by another person. This includes the crime of manslaughter, but excludes traffic accidents that result in the death of persons.

Assault refers to physical attack against the body of another person, including battery but excluding indecent assault. Some criminal or penal codes distinguish between aggravated and simple assault depending on the degree of resulting injury. Countries were asked to provide the major criterion for this distinction if it applied in their country.

Rape refers to sexual intercourse without valid consent. Countries were asked to indicate whether statutory rape was included in the figures provided.

Theft refers to the removal of property without the property owner's consent. Theft excludes burglary or housebreaking. It includes the theft of a motor vehicle. Shoplifting and other minor offences (e.g., pilfering and petty theft) may or may not be included as thefts. Countries were asked to provide details.

Robbery refers to the theft of property from a person, overcoming resistance by force or threat of force.

Burglary refers to unlawful entry into someone else's property with an intention to commit a crime.

Fraud refers to the acquisition of the property of another by deception. Countries were asked

to give details of whether the fraudulent obtaining of financial property was included.

Embezzlement refers to the wrongful appropriation of property of another which is already in one's possession.

Drug-related crimes refers to intentional acts that may involve cultivation, production, manufacture, extraction, preparation, offering for sale, distribution, purchase, sale, delivery on any terms whatsoever, brokerage, dispatch in transit, transport, importation and exportation of drugs and isotropic substances. Separate statistics on possession and traffic were requested.

Bribery and corruption refers to requesting and/or accepting material or personal benefit, or promise thereof, in connection with the performance of a public function or an action that may or may not be a violation of law and/or promising as well as giving material or personal benefit to a public officer in exchange for a requested favor.

Other refers to serious types of crime completely different from those listed above and regarded as serious and frequent enough to require a separate category in the criminal statistics of a particular country. Countries were asked to provide details.

Crimes recorded by the police refers to the number of penal code offences or their equivalent (i.e., various special law offences) but excluding minor road traffic and other petty offences, brought to the attention of the police or other law enforcement agencies and recorded by one of those agencies.

SOURCE: United Nations Office at Vienna, Crime Prevention and Criminal Justice Division. Questionnaire of the Fifth UNCJS (1990–1994). Reprinted with permission of the United Nations.

What crime remains in Communist societies is therefore a sign of the imperfect transition to communism. Combined with the fact that both the former Soviet Union and China traditionally have been secretive and suspicious of outsiders, it is no wonder that we have not obtained official crime data, however incomplete or imperfect, for these countries.

Similarly, police departments in any number of towns, cities, and countries may manipulate data for their own political reasons. For example, to improve their records, police may decide not to record some crimes unless they also have solved them. Police may wish to show their area to be a safe place to visit, so they alter statistics accordingly. In some cases, police may even inflate crime data to highlight their need for more resources in the "fight against crime."

Decisions made by police administrators also affect crime data. For example, police activity focused on a particular kind of crime, like drug dealing, may lead to an apparent increase in that particular crime. This is not a true increase, since it is based on a greater expenditure of police energy rather than an actual increased incidence of crime, but in police reports it may show up as a dramatic increase. In this instance, crime data would reflect more about the activity of the formal criminal justice system than the crime rate or police competence.

Finally, personnel issues can affect crime data collection. Because some police personnel are either untrained, incompetent, or simply lazy, they sometimes neglect to report crimes in any coordinated fashion. Individual officers may use their own discretion in deciding that the matter was not serious enough to record officially. They may feel that it is too much work to do the paperwork or that the victims involved are not worthy of assistance from the criminal justice system. And even when officers have the manpower and technological resources to do the job, they may lack the requisite knowledge to utilize crime data in an effective manner.

HOW TO COMPARE INTERNATIONAL CRIME DATA

One could conclude, in light of the many problems associated with reporting, collecting, and recording crime data, that it is impossible to accord any legitimacy to comparative crime information. But this is clearly not the case, for as we discussed earlier in this chapter there are many

benefits to international crime data. Still, at least five tactics can be implemented to improve their usefulness and comparability.

Ways to Improve the Comparability of Crime Data

First, to improve the comparability of crime data, we should be more selective in our choice of analysis. Rather than try to make comparisons among numerous countries across some larger group of offenses, we would do better to analyze only a limited number of offenses and countries. For instance, instead of comparing crime rates among countries based on the total number of crimes or the total crime rate, we might compare only one category of crime such as homicide, bank robbery, or even the incarceration rate. Furthermore, we should try to limit our comparisons to similar nations (MacCoun et al., 1993). Because the social, economic, and political situations vary so greatly in the different nations, it is unwise to make comparisons between totally different nations and regions of the world. For example, comparing the crime rates and system functions of United States with Canada, Australia, or even England would be more beneficial than a comparison between the United States and Cuba, China, or South Africa. The many cultural differences between the United States and these latter countries would preclude any relevant comparison.

A second possible solution to the comparability problem involves reformulating the terms of reference—that is, using ratios rather than whole numbers when comparing crime data. Using ratios such as crimes per 100,000 persons rather than total number of crimes is a common practice for the obvious reason that it levels the playing field when comparing any two sets of large numbers.

Third, we could practice a form of triangulation whenever possible. **Triangulation** is the implementation of multiple measures as a way to improve the validity or truthfulness of what one is trying to measure. To use triangulation in international criminal justice data, we would refer to supplemental sources of data and varying statistical methods to make better judgments about crime rates in different countries.

Fourth, we should study crime data over a period of time rather than at one time to gain a more valid picture of the subject we are studying. Imagine the difference in the amount of information we receive from reviewing a thirty-minute video as opposed to a single picture. The same can be said for viewing crime data.

Finally, when we try to compare different kinds of international crime data, we should be aware of the limitations of our comparison. We must be aware of the specific information the crime data can provide as well as what that information does not tell us.

To best explain the need to understand limitations and adjust accordingly, we turn to an actual cross-national study by Richard Bennett and James Lynch (1990). In an analysis of crime rates as reported by four major sources (INTERPOL, United Nations, Comparative Crime Data File, and, for homicide, the World Health Organization), they conclude that, for certain types of analysis, it is possible to reconcile the differences among the various kinds of crime data. They distinguish between descriptive studies, in which figures are compared at points in time across nations and the actual accuracy of the data is in question, and analytical studies, in which differences in crime rates across nations are tied to other national characteristics. Analytic studies are able to cope with inaccuracies in data as long as the inaccuracies themselves are consistent.

Bennett and Lynch also distinguish between longitudinal and cross-sectional studies. Longitudinal studies, which describe crime trends, may give us a better picture of crime developments than cross-sectional studies that focus on one point in time. Through some collapsing of crime categories and statistical manipulation of the data reported by the various organizations, Bennett and Lynch conclude that, in the cases of longitudinal and analytical studies, it is possible to reconcile the differences among the four kinds of crime reports and to use these data with some confidence.

While Bennett and Lynch do not solve all the problems of international crime data, such as underreporting and nonstandard indicators, their research suggests that a carefully circumscribed use of contradictory data can be undertaken with some confidence by researchers into crime rates and trends.

Cautions in Comparing Crime Data

What all this means is that, in order to assess the true relationship between crime rates and societal factors at any one time in history, we must try to understand the many criminal justice system variables and definitional variables that will affect rates. And we must remember the following caveat: Crime rates should be studied and evaluated in terms of their makeup and their inclusiveness rather than taken at face value. In most cases, trends within individual countries will be more valid indicators of crime than cross-national comparisons at any one time.

Even if we adopt the suggestions presented previously about how to properly compare international crime data, we must still be aware of the dangers in doing comparative work. When we make comparisons of groups of countries over time, a method that is more likely to produce reliable information, we still may encounter problems due to changes in legal definitions, national borders, and recording practices. It is especially problematic to make comparisons between individual countries and then rank those countries from "best" to "worst." As a result, the best policy is to proceed with caution when interpreting international crime statistics.

INTERNATIONAL CRIME RATES

Overall Crime Rates

One form of international crime data that provides us with information about overall crime trends is the International Crime Victim Survey. The findings from the ICVS that were conducted from 1989 to 1996 are given in Table 2.2. Recall that in these surveys people were asked if they had been victimized by crime over the past five years. Those interviewed were living in cities with more than 100,000 inhabitants, so the results reflect urban rates of crime. Some interesting findings surface from a perusal of the data.

More than half of respondents reported being victimized by crime—a finding that is relatively consistent across regions of the world. The highest rates are in Latin America and Africa, and the lowest in Asian cities. A review of the specific forms of crime shows that car theft is more prevalent in Western countries. Contact crimes (robbery, sexual offenses, assault) are most prevalent in Africa and Latin America but are also prominent in North America, Australia, and New Zealand. Theft rates are extremely high in many areas of the world, but especially in Africa. It is also interesting to note that in many areas of the world, especially in Latin America, Africa, and even Asia, women are at an equal or even greater risk of being victims of crimes.

You may be surprised to observe that, although the United States may have relatively high rates of crime in a number of categories, in comparison with countries that are similar in economics and politics, there is less of a difference than one might suspect. For example, in the United States, rates of contact crimes are only slightly higher than in Canada, Germany, and England. And the burglary rate in the United States is reportedly lower than in Australia and the Netherlands and only slightly higher than in England and France.

Table 2.4 lists the 1990 and 1994 rates of five crimes in selected countries based on data compiled by the United Nations (UNCJS). As mentioned previously, the UN obtains this data with the assistance of law enforcement agencies worldwide. Table 2.4 shows that the most commonly reported crimes throughout the world are robbery and burglary. However, when studying Table 2.4, keep in mind two significant shortcomings of the data. First, the data reported here do not include three categories of crimes that are more difficult to detect and gain detailed information about than the common crimes mentioned. These are organized, transnational, and environmental crimes.

Second, the data in Table 2.4 actually fail to include the *most* commonly committed and reported crime—theft. According to 1994 UNCJS data, theft rates vary greatly, from under 100 to over 26,000 per 100,000 population, with over 60 percent of countries reporting a rate of under 1,000. Theft rates are lowest in Arab countries; moderate in Saharan Africa, eastern Europe, and Latin America; and highest in western Europe and North America (Lewis, 1999).

We can determine from the UNCJS data that, although many countries experienced an increase in crime between 1990 and 1994, others witnessed a stabilization or even a slight decrease in crime rates. Table 2.5 gives the percentages for countries reporting a decrease in crime from 1990 to 1994.

Table 2.6 shows the 1994 crime rates for five major offenses as compiled by INTERPOL. The main difference between the INTERPOL and UNCJS data is that the latter provide information about drug crimes while the INTERPOL substitutes auto theft for drug crimes. The findings by the UNCJS and INTERPOL are very similar because both organizations rely on data collected by police. For example, the UNCJS data reflect the fact that in Sweden the rape rate in 1994 was 20.64 per 100,000 persons while INTERPOL reported a rate of 20.6. In other cases, the numbers are less similar. For example, the UNCJS showed the burglary rate in Zimbabwe to be 519.67 per 100,000 while INTERPOL reported a rate of 445.3.

We supply the INTERPOL data so that you can compare them with the UN and ICVS data. You may find some of the figures to be similar and some to be slightly different. Take the time to pick some countries, assess which have more crime according to the various data, and then hypothesize about why they are different.

Homicide Rates

Homicide rates are of particular interest, not only because homicide is the ultimate offense against the social order but also because figures on homicide rates are more reliable than those for other

Table 2.4 UNCJS Crime Rates per 100,000 Population in Selected Countries, 1990 and 1994[a]

Country	Homicide	Rape	Robbery	Burglary	Drug Crimes
Austria	(3.1) 3.52	(12.3) 6.89	(24.4) 30.41	(1,155.1) 1,122.67	(68.7) 29.83
Azerbaijan	8.93	1.03	3.95	15.83	—
Bahamas	82.85	78.47	198.54	161.31	—
Belarus	9.94	6.49	67.73	198.21	—
Bermuda	(3.3) 12.70	(26.4) 30.16	(80.8) 147.62	(303.4) 1,800.00	(1,182.2) —
Bolivia	23.31	31.24	159.50	—	0.22
Bulgaria	(4.1) 11.23	(5.8) 10.70	(13.6) 78.14	(351.2) —	—
Canada	(5.9) 2.04	(104.7) 108.35	(105.7) 98.77	(1,426.0) 1,326.17	(228.0) 78.37
Chile	(3.0) 4.47	(5.7) 6.87	(582.3) 514.92	—	(0.2) 13.48
Colombia	78.59	5.59	82.52	24.72	—
Costa Rica	(14.9) 9.70	(8.6) 9.57	(438.7) 523.18	(290.2) 413.68	(10.4) 7.26
Croatia	8.15	2.09	8.64	404.80	—
Cyprus	(1.7) 1.63	(0.1) 0.95	(1.7) 1.91	(169.1) 175.89	(7.1) —
Denmark	(4.7) 5.05	(9.5) 9.24	(41.4) 93.76	(2,380.8) 2,043.00	(270.9) 17.21
Ecuador	18.47	8.33	194.40	70.56	7.69
Egypt	(13.9) 1.51	(0.0) 0.02	(0.7) 0.65	(7.9) 9.98	(14.5) 7.86
England and Wales	1.41	9.85	116.19	2,445.44	35.96
Estonia	25.68	198.87	—	—	—
Finland	(8.6) 10.46	(7.6) 7.60	(52.7) 41.65	(1,432.0) 1,936.33	(51.1) —
France	4.67	11.30	126.95	839.70	15.09
Georgia	14.44	0.90	6.01	—	3.48
Greece	(2.6) 2.86	2.47	(4.0) 7.79	356.06	(29.1) —
Hong Kong	(2.6) 1.62	(1.9) 1.65	(138.4) 103.43	(219.0) 222.88	(62.1) 15.89
Hungary	(3.3) 4.65	(7.2) 8.07	(27.6) 25.05	743.6) 768.71	(0.4) —
India	(8.0) 7.90	(1.2) 1.44	(4.4) 2.61	(15.9) 13.23	(1.7) —
Indonesia	0.79	0.87	3.53	21.80	—
Israel	(2.5) 7.23	(7.9) 10.22	(15.4) 8.36	(943.6) 54.86	(167.4) 33.87
Italy	(7.2) 5.32	(1.2) 1.52	(63.9) 52.42	—	(53.2) 66.95
Jamaica	29.77	42.87	218.79	58.53	81.41
Japan	(1.5) 1.40	(1.2) 1.29	(1.3) 2.15	(183.8) 198.46	(17.8) 0.18
Jordan	(2.5) 5.73	(0.7) 0.69	(108.5) 9.62	(72.5) 31.20	(3.4) —
Kazakstan	15.65	10.94	70.00	0.91	5.12
Kuwait	58.02	0.56	10.00	95.80	21.36

[a]Rates for 1990, for selected countries, appear in parentheses when available.

SOURCE: Data from the UN Crime and Justice Information Network.

crimes. Without a doubt, many homicides are masked as accidents and suicides, and there are cases in which individuals disappear and we can only guess whether they have been murdered. In general, however, the reality of a dead body forces the state to make a determination as to the cause of the individual's demise, and most homicides can be identified as such.

Homicide data are collected along with other mortality data by the World Health Organization (WHO), as well as by the United Nations and INTERPOL. Table 2.7 shows homicide figures

Country	Homicide	Rape	Robbery	Burglary	Drug Crimes
Kyrgyzstan	(13.7) 12.27	8.70	(34.2) 43.23	203.26	(19.8) 54.44
Latvia	(9.8) 16.17	(5.0) 5.06	(77.4) 44.82	(165.8) —	(3.9) —
Lithuania	(6.8) 15.05	(5.3) 4.43	(9.0) 21.66	(140.1) 197.66	(2.0) —
Madagascar	0.44	0.35	0.22	9.01	1.85
Malaysia	(1.8) 1.93	(3.6) 4.95	(32.7) 31.16	(104.9) 110.59	(61.7) 4.05
Malta	3.02	2.75	9.07	524.45	13.46
Morocco	1.78	3.51	—	—	34.45
Nicaragua	25.63	30.06	302.77	2.66	2.75
Northern Ireland	20.90	12.75	96.03	1,035.77	9.56
Philippines	(14.6) 9.45	(3.0) 3.72	(25.3) 13.68	—	—
Qatar	2.22	2.59	—	54.63	3.15
Republic of Korea	(1.5) 10.15	(9.9) 13.89	(11.1) 10.30	2.32	(5.2) 3.88
Republic of Macedonia	3.73	1.77	6.16	444.96	4.30
Republic of Moldova	9.52	6.14	52.60	198.44	0.94
Romania	(10.7) 7.62	(4.1) 6.12	(7.7) 18.30	(5.9) 133.65	(0.0) 1.17
Russian Federation	23.18	9.43	100.37	—	—
Sao Tome and Principe	142.40	—	—	4.80	—
Scotland	(1.7) 2.20	(9.7) 11.09	(91.2) 103.21	(1,993.7) 1,722.27	187.5) 119.53
Singapore	(1.8) 1.74	(4.1) 2.76	(58.3) 27.71	(140.1) 83.92	8.77
Slovakia	3.83	3.98	23.27	805.48	0.28
Slovenia	5.72	12.36	15.14	536.66	13.44
Spain	(1.6) 1.64	(4.6) 3.09	(1,505.1) 142.24	359.51	(65.2) 30.41
Sudan	3.46	2.11	2.92	269.54	—
Sweden	(7.9) 11.96	(16.5) 20.64	(69.7) 60.72	(1,799.7) 1,609.09	(309.8) 96.75
Switzerland	2.30	3.93	27.93	950.19	115.97
Syrian Arab Republic	1.26	0.72	0.13	11.73	4.24
Turkey	2.93	0.82	2.52	—	—
Ukraine	(6.2) 9.65	(4.1) 3.30	(34.3) 62.71	(80.4) —	(12.4) 3.17
United States	(9.4) 8.95	(41.2) 39.22	(257.0) 237.46	(1,235.9) 1,040.78	—
Uruguay	5.87		97.00	—	2.94
Western Samoa	6.10	5.49	1.22	24.39	0.00
Zambia	15.83	3.66	35.74	141.87	3.70
Zimbabwe	15.96	27.72	111.01	519.67	17.60

reported by individual nations to all three data-gathering agencies. In many cases the numbers are relatively similar while in others they vary considerably; for example, note the differences in data for the newly formed Russian Federation. The WHO reported a homicide rate of 32.4 per 100,000 population in 1994 as opposed to 20.2 for INTERPOL and 23.18 for the UN.

We can only assume that the variation is related to differences in the reporting agencies and in the time periods covered. Nevertheless, we can generalize that the United States has one of the

Table 2.5 Percentage of Countries Reporting a Fall in Crime, 1990–1994

Crime	Percentage
Robbery	43
Theft	41
Burglary	37
Rape	30
Fraud	27
Homicide	25
Assaults	21
Drug-related crime	11
Total crime	25

SOURCE: *Global Report,* 1999, p. 52. Used with permission of the United Nations.

highest homicide rates among Western nations although the rate is declining. Other countries with high rates include Mexico, Panama, Chile, and some of the eastern European countries. The Russian Federation has the highest homicide rate and Japan has the lowest.

Crime Rates in Model Countries

If we want to study and compare the crime rates in our model countries of France, Germany, Japan, Saudi Arabia, England, and China, we may find it difficult because few available data sets include all six nations. If we add the 1994 UNCJS statistics for England and Wales to the INTER-POL statistics in Table 2.6, we can see more easily how the six model countries compare against each other.

Table 2.6 INTERPOL Crime Rates per 100,000 Population in Selected Countries, 1994

Country	Homicide[a]	Rape	Robbery	Burglary	Auto Theft
United States	8.9	39.2	237.7	1,041.8	591.2
Austria	(1.1) 2.5	6.9	57.8	1,128.2	31.8
Bulgaria	5.9	8.8	78.5	1,174.9	207.9
Belgium[b]	(1.2) 3.2	8.9	56.6	1,546.6	314.2
Canada	(2.0) 5.2	—	98.8	1,326.2	545.9
Chile	11.0	9.5	35.1	—	13.1
China	0.2	3.4	—	45.2	6.9
Denmark	(1.4) 4.9	9.3	78.6	2,046.3	663.3
Ecuador	10.4	8.2	65.1	94.4	36.5
England and Wales[c]	1.4	9.8	116.2	2,447	—
Estonia	(20.1) 24.3	8.3	185.2	1,160.7	169.1
Ethiopia	(8.1) 14.5	1.1	9.2	5.6	2.1
Finland	0.6	7.6	44.2	1,934.9	359.5
France	(2.4) 4.7	11.3	126.9	839.3	639.6
Georgia	(8.5) 10.7	0.9	43.4	40.7	1.5
Germany	(1.7) 4.6	7.5	71.0	1,927.1	260.1
Greece	2.6	2.5	12.3	330.2	100.3
Guyana	(16.0) 19.9	20.6	—	509.5	—
Honduras	63.6	2.0	15.2	1.4	28.8
Hungary	(3.0) 4.3	4.2	25.0	767.4	51.1
Indonesia	0.8	0.7	3.6	24.8	8.0
Ireland	0.7	5.2	64.5	921.4	60.6
Israel	2.1	9.4	14.2	817.2	479.5
Italy	(1.7) 4.7	—	52.8	—	532.8
Jamaica	27.6	24.4	217.6	267.7	9.9

Country	Homicide[a]	Rape	Robbery	Burglary	Auto Theft
Japan	(0.9) 1.0	1.3	2.2	198.1	27.8
South Korea	1.4	13.6	10.1	6.7	—
Latvia	(13.6) 14.6	5.0	44.5	390.4	109.2
Lebanon	4.3	0.7	5.9	1.2	13.8
Luxembourg	1.5	6.6	73.7	943.8	227.3
Malaysia	(1.9) 2.1	4.9	30.6	108.7	12.4
Mongolia	19.0	16.8	21.9	204.5	—
Namibia	(33.3) 72.4	44.4	99.2	739.0	115.4
Nicaragua	(16.6) 25.6	30.0	109.8	—	—
New Zealand	(2.7) 3.9	34.7	48.8	2,352.90	788.6
Panama	13.9	—	38.2	—	77.7
Paraguay	(9.9) 15.6	4.1	—	—	50.3
Poland	(2.4) 3.1	5.3	61.2	789.5	109.1
Portugal	(3.0) 4.2	1.6	80.9	186.9	65.8
Romania	3.3	6.1	18.2	133.2	9.5
Russian Federation	(20.2) 21.8	9.4	126.0	262.3	55.1
Saudi Arabia	0.9	0.6	0.04	—	28.5
Singapore	1.7	2.8	32.9	83.9	7.2
Spain	(1.1) 2.6	4.1	233.2	555.4	253.0
Swaziland	88.1	89.3	270.6	941.4	71.4
Sweden	(1.8) 9.5[d]	20.6	60.5	1,610.1	616.1
Switzerland	(1.1) 2.3	3.9	27.8	946.7	—[e]
Thailand	7.7	6.1	—	9.9	3.3
Trinidad/Tobago	(9.9) 11.7	11.4	333.4	566.9	86.4
Ukraine	(8.0) 8.8	3.9	72.8	—	42.3
Venezuela	22.1	16.6	174.8	358.2	239.6
Zimbabwe	5.0	23.7	94.4	445.3	9.1

[a]Some countries combine murder and attempted murder statistics. In these cases the actual murder rate is given in parentheses. Where no parenthesized number appears, the rate given can be understood as the actual murder rate.

[b]Figures for Belgium were recalculated by Frank Hagan.

[c]Added to table by author.

[d]This figure is as given in the report. In 1984, the figure was 1.4 per 100,000. This 1994 figure (837.0) is for a population of 8,815,182.

[e]Excluded because Switzerland's auto theft figures include bicycle thefts.

SOURCE: From Frank E. Hagan, *Introduction to Criminology*, Fourth Edition. Nelson-Hall, 1998.

Even with missing values for Saudi Arabia, China, and England we can make some general statements about crime in the six countries. Apparently, the lowest crime rates for homicide and auto theft are found in China while rape and robbery rates are lowest in Saudi Arabia. Japan, for a country with a large capitalist economy, has an extremely low crime rate in all categories. France and Germany have the highest homicide rates—although much lower than the United States. (The accompanying box contains a 1998 Department of Justice press release comparing crime rates in the United States and Germany.) France appears to have the highest rates of rapes and robberies, while England does so burglary.

Table 2.7 Number of Homicides per 100,000 Population in Selected Countries

Country	World Health Organization (Year)	INTERPOL 1994[a] Attempted/Actual	United Nations 1990[b]/1993, 1994[c]
United States	9.9 (1992)	8.9/8.9	—/8.95[c]
Australia	1.8 (1993)	—	1.7/3.57[b]
Austria	1.2 (1994)	2.5/1.1	1.2/3.5[c]
Bulgaria	5.1 (1994)	5.9/5.9	2.5/11.25[c]
Canada	1.8 (1993)	5.2/2.0	2.2/2.04[c]
Chile	3.1 (1990)	11.0/11.0	—/2.40[b]
Costa Rica	—	—	4.6/9.70[c]
Denmark	—	4.9/1.4	4.6/5.05[c]
England and Wales	1.0 (1993)	—	1.4/1.41[c]
Finland	3.2 (1994)	0.6/0.6	3.0/10.05[b]
France	1.1 (1993)	4.7/2.4	—/4.67[c]
Germany	1.2 (1994)	4.6/1.7	2.2[d]
Greece	1.1 (1994)	2.6/2.6	1.1/2.86[c]
Hungary	3.5 (1994)	4.3/3.0	1.9/4.65[c]
Ireland	—	0.7/0.7	—
Italy	2.2 (1992)	4.7/1.7	3.1/5.32[c]
Japan	0.6 (1994)	1.0/0.9	0.5/1.4[c]
Latvia	22.9 (1994)	14.6/13.6	5.7/16.17[c]
Netherlands	1.1 (1994)	—	1.5
New Zealand	1.5 (1993)	3.9/2.7	—
Norway	3.1 (1991)	—	1.0
Mexico	17.8 (1993)	—	—
Panama	—	13.9/13.9	—
Romania	—	3.3/3.3	3.4/7.62[c]
Russian Federation	32.4 (1994)	21.8/20.2	9.3/23.18[c]
Spain	0.9 (1992)	2.6/1.1	0.7/1.64[c]
Sweden	1.3 (1993)	9.5/1.8	1.4/11.96[c]
Switzerland	1.3 (1994)	2.3/1.1	1.6/2.3[c]

[a]The UN homicide figures include attempted homicides, which brings the rate closer to that calculated by INTERPOL. Although INTERPOL also includes attempted homicides in its figures, some of the countries that report to INTERPOL submit only their actual homicide figures. Actual homicide rates were calculated by Frank Hagan from the data supplied by the secretariat.

[b]The UN statistics were given as actual numbers of homicides. Homicide rates were calculated by Frank Hagan.

[c]Second figure added to table by author.

[d]These statistics come from the former Federal Republic of Germany.

SOURCE: From Frank E. Hagan, *Introduction to Criminology,* Fourth Edition. Nelson-Hall, 1998.

Most Serious Crime Rates Far Higher in the United States Than in Germany

WASHINGTON, D.C.—Most serious crime rates are far higher in the United States than in Germany, according to a new study prepared for the Justice Department's Bureau of Justice Statistics (BJS). There are five murders and rapes per 100,000 population reported to police in the United States for every one in Germany, Europe's largest country. There are three or four robberies and felony assaults reported here per 100,000 population for every one in Germany.

For property crime the differences are smaller, but still substantial. There are one and a half times as many burglaries, two and a half times as many motor vehicle thefts and arsons and twice as many drug offenses reported to law enforcement agencies here for each one in Germany.

The number of crimes per 100,000 inhabitants reported to police during 1992 in the United States and Germany was as follows:

	U.S.	Germany*
Willful homicide	9	2
Rape	43	8
Robbery	264	71
Aggravated assault	442	120
Burglary	1,168	747
Serious theft	1,747	2,175
Arson	42	17
Drug offenses (arrests only)	418	187

*Former West Germany and all of Berlin but not including the remainder of the former East Germany.

THE EXCEPTIONS: COUNTRIES WITH LOW CRIME RATES

According to Manuel López-Ray, crime rates tell us something about a country's stage of development (López-Ray, 1970, p. 189). As urbanization, industrialization, increased gross national product, and increased higher education occur, crime also tends to rise. Developing nations in Africa, Asia, and Latin America have experienced this phenomenon. If this is true, perhaps we should stop worrying about crime and view it, instead, as an indicator of economic health! Unfortunately, crime and the fear of crime diminish the quality of life in these growing cities and industrial areas. These problems cannot be ignored, especially as more and more people migrate from the countryside and village to cities and outlying areas, where there are greater economic opportunities and employment possibilities.

Using United Nations data on crime and comparing them to various demographic variables, Freda Adler (1983) has confirmed the data on levels of crime and stage of development. She identified ten "nations not obsessed by crime," including countries in western Europe, Latin America, the Middle East, and Asia. Saudi Arabia and Japan, two of our model countries, are included in her list of low-crime societies. According to Adler, the demographic variables most associated with low crime rates are a rural population, low incidence of modern communications facilities such as telephones and radios, and high crude death rates. These are all characteristics of relatively nonindustrialized societies.

Adler related high crime rates to the condition of anomie (rough, social instability and personal alienation) that develops in societies with massive social change and dislocation. Some industrialized nations, however, have been able to avoid the social conditions that lead to crime. She cites Japan and Switzerland as two of the nations that fall into this category.

Japan

We look with fascination at those societies that seem to have "beaten the odds" with respect to increased industrialization and accompanying increased crime. Switzerland, landlocked and mountainous, and located in the heart of Europe, has remained aloof from foreign entanglements and has been a pacifist society for centuries in the midst of multiple European wars. Japan, by contrast, is an island nation, expansive and dynamic, with a history of warlike and imperialistic behavior prior to its defeat in World War II. With a population of 7 million, Switzerland is a rather small nation; in fact, after Luxembourg, Denmark, and Norway, it has the smallest population in western Europe. Japan's population is 120 million, half the size of the population of the United States. Much of Japan's land mass is mountainous and uninhabitable, so most of its people are crowded into coastal cities on Japan's two major islands, Honshu and Kyushu.

The fact that Japan is so often included in comparisons among Western countries reflects the fact that the degree of wealth accumulation, industrialization, and modernization that has occurred in that country makes it seem to be part of the Western world. In fact, however, Japanese industrial might masks the fact that Japanese culture is both highly peculiar to that society, and different from Western culture in many ways. For instance, Japanese culture stresses group norms, the suppression of individualism, suspicion of outsiders, harmony, and conflict avoidance. Japan practices a kind of modified capitalism in which the government is highly involved in industrial development and social welfare.

No really good explanation for the Japanese low-crime phenomenon exists. While it might be logical to assume that Japan would have lower crime rates than the abundantly heterogeneous and multicultural United States, this hardly explains the fact that these rates actually declined during the years of rapid urbanization and industrialization. The normal tendency in such a situation is to suspect that the statistics have been kept in different ways at different times or that police activity has changed, thus affecting the number of reported crimes. While this may be the case, it is not evidently so in Japan, as there appears to be uniformity in reporting and actual incidents are the basis for crime rate information.

How the Japanese police enter into the crime equation is an intriguing question. Police organization in Japan will be discussed in greater detail in Chapter 5. For now, with respect to crime prevention, it is worth noting that, in each neighborhood in Japan, police officers organize both crime prevention and traffic safety associations.

These crime prevention associations meet regularly with police, discuss strategies, and organize yearly festivals or other celebrations. The close surveillance over the Japanese population by the police may have some effect on the crime rate. Discretion not to arrest in local cases, in which police officers know all the citizens and can see better ways to deal with juveniles or other offenders, may also be a factor. Certainly, the close surveillance is a factor in the high apprehension rate of offenders in Japan, a rate far surpassing that of Western nations (Bayley, 1991).

Low crime rates in Japan cannot be attributed to high punitiveness in the criminal justice system. The incarceration rate is well below that of the United States, and prison sentences are generally short in comparison with those in Western nations. In fact, prison is seen as so much of a last resort in Japanese corrections that only hard-core criminals are sent there. Prison life itself is highly regimented and work oriented.

Saudi Arabia

Another of our model countries, Saudi Arabia, is also described by Adler as a country with a low crime rate (Adler, 1983, ch. 9). When we review the INTERPOL data, we do see significantly low crime rates in Saudi Arabia when compared to many countries, especially the United States (see Table 2.6).

Again, there are various explanations for the low crime rate. Saudi Arabia is not a highly developed country in some ways and is certainly not highly urbanized, despite its great wealth per capita. Also, a sizable portion of the population continues to be nomadic Bedouins, who are unlikely to resort to a formal legal system to settle their disputes and resolve their crime problems.

The Saudis themselves offer two explanations for their low crime rate. The first is that the harsh corporal punishments they employ, which are based on a philosophy of retribution, serve as effective deterrents to crime. The second, and contradictory, explanation is that Saudis commit fewer crimes not for fear of punishment but because of their devotion to the Qur'an and its teachings. According to the proponents of this argument, since the criminal law and the punishments for breaking that law are contained in the holy book and merely administered by the government, it is religious zeal that inhibits lawbreaking. One scholar claims that Saudi Arabia was a hotbed of banditry until the fundamentalist regime of King Abdul Assiz created the modern Saudi state in 1932 and the people became more law-abiding (Badr el din, 1985). This scholar thus concludes that it was the religious nature of the state that made the difference. Such a conclusion might well be described as a "post hoc" logical error—that is, that because the decrease in crime followed the regime change, we can attribute it to that change. In addition, few statistics exist that might reveal the true extent of crime in what is now Saudi Arabia prior to its creation as a state.

The puzzle remains. Why is it that some societies have been able to swim against the tide of ever-increasing crime and fear of crime that plagues so many European countries, as well as the United States? A closer look is needed, not only at crime data, but at the variations in the social fabric and criminal justice agencies of various countries to see what criminogenic and anticriminogenic forces are at work. (See the accompanying box for an overview of some possible causes of or reasons for crime.)

HOW DOES THE UNITED STATES MEASURE UP?

A review of international crime data clearly reveals the fact that the United States has a very high level of crime. But that is only part of the story. When we compare the United States to other countries, we see that the American crime problem is really one of violent crime—robbery and murder in particular. The murder rate in the United States is eight to ten times greater than that of other countries with similar economies,

like Japan and most of the western European nations. Robberies in the United States in 1994 were committed at the rate of 237.7 per 100,000 population. Contrast that with Germany at 71.0 and Japan at an extremely low 2.2 per 100,000 population (INTERPOL, 1997).

With other kinds of crimes, the story is not so distressing for those who live in and visit the United States. When it comes to property crime rates, the United States is similar to, and in some cases lower than, other industrialized countries (Lynch, 1995). For example, in 1994, the burglary rate in the United States (1,041 per 100,000 population) was even lower than that in Germany (1,927) and neighboring Canada (1,326) (INTERPOL, 1997).

Even though the United States may be safer than some countries in a few crime categories, crime is still undeniably a major social problem. Why does the United States have such a high crime rate, especially in the area of violent crime? We can only speculate about the historical and social reasons for this. Among the reasons that have been mentioned are the significant economic disparity between rich and poor, the heterogeneity of the population, the widespread urban areas, and even the extensive images of violence in the media. Many observers claim that the increase in crime is the result of a general disrespect for authority that began in the 1960s.

Some scholars have stated that the United States has historically been a violent nation, with Indian wars, race riots, frontier feuds, and vigilantism as savage norms at various periods of our history (Brown, 1979). Agrarian uprisings and labor conflicts have added to this background of violence. Reed (1974) described violence as one of the distinguishing characteristics of the American South. In addition, assassinations and multiple homicides are not unusual occurrences, at least since the Civil War. By contrast, European nations, with their older civilizations and more homogeneous populations, may have evolved beyond the stage of easy recourse to violence as a way to settle disputes or as a norm in the socialization of young boys.

Reasons for Crime

The struggle to understand the impulses that make one person willing to deviate from the norms of society while the large majority conform is a continuing one that has produced no definitive answers.

The causes of crime are no doubt varied; some of those most often mentioned are social conditions, economic conditions, family circumstances, and physical or mental health problems. More recently, with the rise in the number of random murders committed by young people in the United States—such as the school killings in Kentucky, Arkansas, and Colorado—we have added television, movies, and video games to the list of possible reasons for violent crime.

From a Western cultural or capitalist viewpoint, crime is the result of modernization. This argument holds that societies change and crime occurs as result of a progression in demographic, economic, and technology developments. These developments create structural change, which leads to more complex social norms and an increase in crime. For example, as technology has developed and demographics have changed, we have moved from a rural and farm-based economy to an urban-industrial economy. And as cities grow, the opportunities for crime increase, as does the number of persons who can be involved in criminal activity. (See Shelly 1981, 1986 for a more complete explanation of the theory of modernization and its relationship to crime causation.)

Dedicated Communists like to agree with Karl Marx that crime disappears once a true communist society has been established. The goal is to reduce the gap between the rich and the poor so that all members of society possess according to need, not want. They argue that the spoils of capitalism, such as materialism and greed, cause crime. Unfortunately, even those countries that have retained a Communist political orientation have developed crime problems.

Another perspective is that, when people lack religious values and fail to live a religious lifestyle, crime will proliferate in that society. This idea is generally shared in countries that have a "religious base" in laws and social control mechanisms. The most obvious examples of this line of thinking can be found in the Islamic nations of Iran and Saudi Arabia. In these countries, religious and secular (nonreligious) laws are not developed or practiced in isolation from each other. Other countries in which religious principles are deeply engrained in societal structures include India, where the majority of persons practice some form of Buddhism, and Japan, where Buddhism and Confucian thought form a spiritual foundation.

Whether religion does, in fact, reduce crime in a society is not scientifically supported. Some have argued that it is questionable to imply that an increase in a person's religiousness will cause a decrease in criminal behavior or delinquency (Sutherland and Cressey, 1974). Yet, some research has indicated that religion can at least decrease victimless criminality such as marijuana usage (Cochran, 1987) and that in "moral communities" (places where religion is paramount with community members) crime can be reduced (Stark, Kent, and Doyle, 1982). Examples of such communities in the United States include the Mormons in Utah and the Amish in Pennsylvania. However, most of the research on the topic of crime and religion has been conducted in the United States, and any form of transnational or comparative perspective is lacking.

The French sociologist Emile Durkheim proposed that crime actually serves a useful function in society. The commission of crimes by a few members of a society draws the rest of the group together in an affirmation of the values that have been breached by the deviant (Durkheim, 1947, ch. 2). However, Durkheim, speaking in the abstract, surely could not have envisioned the extent of the crime that plagues many Western societies today. Our current crime situation would seriously challenge his idea that crime can enhance social cohesion.

In some cases, crime can draw attention to flaws in the social structure. In this instance, people commit crimes because they feel it is their duty to expose injustices in society. This was the case in the 1950s when Rosa Parks and Martin Luther King refused to obey unjust segregation laws in the United States.

Easy access to guns is another factor that may contribute to the high homicide rates in the United States. In 1992, almost a million handgun crimes were committed, a 30 percent increase over the previous five-year average (Bureau of Justice Statistics, 1994). This is in sharp contrast to most Western countries, to say nothing of Socialist countries, where ownership of guns is strictly regulated (Bureau of Justice Statistics, 1991). However, even the excessive number of guns cannot be counted as a firm reason for violence in the United States. Gun advocates have recently gained some measure of support in research conducted by John Lott (1998). Lott, using UCR data for 3,054 counties, determined that more guns actually can lead to less crime because criminals may be deterred from physical confrontation if they fear the victim may be carrying a weapon.

Our discussion of the causes of crime, in the United States or throughout the world, is only a brief summary of what would take volumes to illustrate fully. Over the course of the relatively brief history of criminology, thousands of articles and books have been written on the subject. In the attempt to make sense of the reasons behind criminal behavior, one fact remains—that in most countries today crime is perceived to be a major and growing problem that seems to defy an easy solution.

SUMMARY

We measure crime and compare crime data across nations to determine the types and extent of crime, to identify long-term trends, and to learn why some countries are more successful than others in controlling crime. International crime data collection dates back to the mid-nineteenth century. Modern sources of crime data, both internationally and in the United States, include the UCR and NCVS, the UN and INTERPOL, and self-reports. However, these data may be limited due to underreporting of crime by both victims and law enforcement agencies, nonstandard definitions of various crimes, and differences in methods of measuring and reporting crime. Ways of improving international crime data collection and comparison include being more selective in the choice of topics or issues to analyze, reformulating the terms of reference, using triangulation, studying data over time, and recognizing the limitations of different data collection methods. Studying the crime rates in our model countries can help us to understand the underlying social factors that may cause crime and to find ways to mitigate the problem of crime.

DISCUSSION QUESTIONS AND EXERCISES

1. Which international crime data do you believe provide the most helpful information? Explain.

2. To what extent can we rely on crime data from other nations? How can we evaluate such data? How does the problem of nonstandardized indicators interfere with evaluation of crime data across countries?

3. What factors might contribute to the relatively low crime rates in Japan? To the relatively high rates in the United States? Overall, how does the United States crime rate compare with other countries?

4. Look up INTERPOL on the Internet, and find out more about how that agency works with law enforcement organizations in this country.

5. Study the tables in the chapter that provide crime data for selected countries, and discuss any major differences you notice. Why might there be such a disparity between certain countries?

FOR FURTHER READING

Adler, F. (1983). *Nations Not Obsessed with Crime.* Littleton, Colo.: Rothman.

Archer, D., and R. Gartner. (1984). *Violence and Crime in Cross-National Perspective.* New Haven, Conn.: Yale University Press.

Clinard, M., and D. Abbott. (1973). *Crime in Developing Societies.* New York: Wiley.

Lynch, J. (1995). Building Data Systems for Cross-National Comparisons of Crime and Criminal Justice Policy: A Retrospective. *ICPSR Bulletin,* XV (3).

3 ∿ Families of Law

Ancient and Lesser-Employed
   Legal Systems
Clarifying Terms
The Civil Law
The Common Law
The Socialist Law
The Islamic Law
Summary
Discussion Questions and Exercises
For Further Reading

Key Terms and Concepts

Canon Law
civil law
commercial law
Common Law
Corpus Juris Civilis
criminal law
habeas corpus
hybrid legal tradition
indigenous law
injunction
Islamic law
judicial independence
ombudsman
private law
procurator
public law
secular law
Shari'a
Socialist Law
stare decisis
writ of mandamus

According to the Book of Exodus, Moses went up to Mount Sinai, where God gave him a tablet of stone listing ten rules. These rules, called the Ten Commandments, are familiar to most of us; they include "Thou shalt not kill," "Thou shalt not steal," and "Thou shalt not commit adultery." The Ten Commandments have formed the basis of a code of ethics and, in some cases, a body of laws that have guided Western civilization for several thousand years. They are written rules that tell people what is and is not illegal and unethical behavior in the eyes of God. In the case of governments that have adopted religious pronouncements as part of their law, as was the case in the seventeenth-century Massachusetts Bay Colony, these rules also tell people what behavior will be punished by the state.

Some time later, another prominent Jewish leader in ancient times, the wise King Solomon, made it his practice to settle disputes among his subjects by having them appear and present their cases to him in person. According to a famous biblical story, two women claiming the same baby appeared before Solomon so that he could decide who was the real mother. Solomon ordered his guards to cut the baby in half and give each woman half. One of the women immediately spoke up and said that she would relinquish her claim to the baby rather than have the child killed. At this, Solomon awarded the baby to this woman, saying that the true mother would be more concerned with the baby's welfare than with her claim.

The Bible presents this story to exemplify the wisdom of Solomon. In contrast to the Ten Commandments of Moses, which represent rules that have been handed down for people to follow, the story of Solomon and the baby reflects a different kind of rule making, one based on responding to cases as they arise.

All legal systems of modern nation-states combine the kinds of rule making that are typified in the stories of Moses and Solomon. In other words, all modern legal systems combine written laws that place limits on behavior with rules that derive from decisions handed down in particular cases.

There is a difference in emphasis, however, as well as strong historical traditions that make it possible to classify legal systems into code-based systems and case-based systems. As we discuss different systems of the world, we will find that this difference between code-based systems and case-based systems tends to categorize legal arrangements around the world.

Throughout the book, we will also frequently refer to the different legal systems of the world as "legal families" or "legal traditions." These terms are instructive because they have broader meaning than the term *legal system*. This is important because, by placing specific systems within a family or tradition, we are making general statements about the law and process of justice in a country while allowing for overlap and individualism.

In this chapter, we examine the four major legal families in the world today. The largest and most common are Civil Law, Common Law, and Socialist Law. Because it has been adopted by several nations, Islamic Law is also included as a major family.

Unfortunately, this classification scheme tends to conceal more than it reveals, since each nation of the world has its own distinct family or tradition, often a hybrid one that incorporates elements of the Civil or Common Law with local customary or religious law. A **hybrid legal tradition** combines different aspects of more than one legal tradition. One could argue that the hybrid legal tradition is technically the most common legal system, seeing as how most countries borrow some aspects of criminal justice from other countries. The most typical form of borrowing is to combine some aspects of the Common Law and Civil Law systems. Among the countries that are considered hybrids are Japan, Egypt, Scotland, the Philippines, and South Africa. Japan may be the best example of this hybrid form. The Japanese began to inculcate Roman Civil Law into their legal tradition in the late 1800s, were strongly influenced by German law in the early 1900s, and added elements of Common Law after World War II.

In subsequent chapters, we will discuss the development of a hybrid legal tradition in Japan

Table 3.1 Sample Countries in the Four Main Families of Law

Civil Law Family
Belgium
France
Germany
Luxembourg
Spain
Portugal
Common Law Family
Canada (except Quebec)
England
India
Australia
United States
Socialist Law Family
China
Cuba
North Korea
Vietnam
The former Soviet Union
Islamic Law Family
Iran
Pakistan
Saudi Arabia
Sudan

in more detail. In this chapter, however, as well as in the book, we will concentrate on the four main traditions or families: Civil Law, Common Law, Socialist Law, and Islamic Law.

Table 3.1 lists several nations within the four main legal families. For a more complete list of countries and the legal families they most closely represent, see Appendix D.

ANCIENT AND LESSER-EMPLOYED LEGAL SYSTEMS

This chapter is not intended to be an all-inclusive discussion of all the different kinds of legal systems in history or even a complete description of those practiced in the world today. Many legal systems that were used for centuries or that are implemented today on a smaller scale than the four main families will be touched on only briefly—if at all. It is important that we mention some of these systems that are currently in practice so as not to imply that there are no variations beyond our four main traditions. We refer to some as "ancient" because they originated centuries ago and are now extinct. "Lesser employed" describes legal systems that are currently used somewhere in the world but are specific to only one or a limited number of countries and geographic regions.

Ancient/Historical Legal Systems

Many ancient and now extinct legal families have been recorded in history. According to John Henry Wilmore, who conducted the most comprehensive study of the evolution of the different legal families, there have been sixteen major forms of legal systems in the world; Table 3.2 lists these ancient/historical legal systems. Four of these ancient systems—Egyptian, Mesopotamian, Chinese, and Hebrew—are discussed here because they helped to form much of the foundation for our modern legal families.

The oldest known formal legal system was the Egyptian system, which is believed to date back as far as 4000 B.C. Egyptian rulers developed an extensive system for handling legal procedures that included codes to direct citizen behaviors and a judicial system to handle disputes (Wilmore, 1936).

Around the same time, the Mesopotamian system emerged in the Near East; it lasted until approximately the time before the birth of Christ. The Mesopotamian system is best known for the development of the Code of Hammurabi, king of Babylon. Hammurabi's code sought to prevent the strong from oppressing the weak. The code contained 282 laws covering such matters as property rights, renting, and medical treatment. The most famous passage in the code was the law stating "an eye for any eye, tooth for a tooth," which was later adopted into the Old Testament (Grove, 1997).

Table 3.2 Legal Systems in History

Egyptian
Mesopotamian
Chinese
Hindu
Hebrew
Greek
Roman
Maritime
Japanese
Mohammedan
Celtic
Germanic
Slavic
Ecclesiastical
Romanesque
Anglican

SOURCE: Wilmore, 1936.

Some 1,500 years after the Egyptian legal system began, the Chinese developed their own legal system, much of it rooted in the philosophy of a man popularly known as Confucius (c. 551–479 B.C.). Confucianism is, in fact, more of a moral and religious system than a philosophy, and it has influenced Chinese governmental and educational practices, and individual attitudes toward correct personal behavior and duty to society.

Hebrew Law, which was developed around 1200 B.C., was the result of the birth of Judaism around 2000 B.C. Hebrew Law was extracted from the Hebrew Bible, which includes the Torah, and the Talmud, which is a guide to civil and religious laws, as well as from other writings. Judaism began before the time of Christ with Moses receiving the two tablets of stone and the subsequent recording of the first five books of the Bible.

Religious Law

Throughout this book, we refer to a legal family that is currently rooted in religious tradition, the Islamic family. But Islamic Law is not the only legal tradition that is strongly influenced by religion. The country of India, although deeply infused with English Common Law principles, is rich in religion-based Hindu Law. Much of Hindu Law has been influenced by early Hindu doctrine, which stated that adherence to the Veda, or scriptures, was more important than adherence to the edicts of any king or ruler. Even today, devout Hindus believe that faithful adherence to correct behavior will move them up the ladder in a new incarnation.

In Israel, the legal codes are influenced by English Common Law and Israeli secular laws, but they also include Jewish and non-Jewish religious laws. Israeli religious laws generally apply in personal matters such as marriage, divorce, and alimony. In Israel, different religious courts represent the various religious groups, including Rabbinical, Muslim, Christian, and Druze (Bensinger, 1998).

India and Israel are but two examples of countries with laws that continue to be important in religious communities. In each of these countries, the religious laws depend on voluntary consent and do not have the force of government behind them. In this way, they differ from our model country of Saudi Arabia where religious and secular (nonreligious) laws are intertwined.

Indigenous Law

In addition to religious laws practiced in religious communities, many forms of indigenous law are observed throughout the world. **Indigenous laws** are native laws of persons who originate from or live in a particular area. There are literally thousands of indigenous laws that have influenced legal systems throughout the world. In some isolated areas, indigenous laws have contributed to the formation of small, private legal societies. Just as we speak of Common (U.S.), Socialist (Chinese), or Islamic (Saudi Arabian) law, anthropologists speak about Tongan, Tiv, or Zapotec Law in the South Pacific Islands, African bush, and Mexican mountains, respectively. In each of these societies, the definition of what is a crime and how to settle disputes and punish criminals varies considerably (Lubman, 1983).

In the United States, indigenous laws are practiced by Native Americans on reservations; similarly indigenous laws are practiced by the aboriginal populations of Australia and in many regions in Africa. For example, in Nigeria, the most serious crimes are tried in federal courts that are run according to the British-imposed English Common Law. However, all other offenses are still heard by tribal (indigenous) courts of justice based on native laws and customs. In southern Nigeria these laws are unwritten while in the northern regions they are available in written form (Ebbe, 1996).

CLARIFYING TERMS

Before proceeding with the discussion of the main legal families present in the world today, a few terms that will be used with some frequency from now on need to be explained. These are public law, private law, civil law, and criminal law.

Public law is the law that is developed by modern states in their legislatures or through their regulatory processes. It deals largely with the relations between governments and citizens. It includes constitutional law, criminal law, tax law, environmental law, and the myriad other laws that bodies like Congress pass each year. Most statutory law today is public law.

Private law, by contrast, is the law that regulates behavior between individuals within the state. It involves contracts, torts, inheritances, wills, marriage and family matters, and general private property matters. Although private law is promulgated and enforced through the state either in codes or in case law, it tends to evolve slowly and in general does not have the political dimensions or implications of public law.

Another term for private law is *civil law,* especially in Anglo-Saxon legal systems. Civil law is distinguished from criminal law because, at least in modern times, **criminal law** is defined as an offense against the state rather than a dispute between individuals. Thus, if Jones kills Smith in the state of Ohio and is brought to trial, the case

will be known as *Ohio v. Jones* rather than *Smith v. Jones.* (To be sure, since Smith is dead, he can hardly bring a case against Jones!)

In earlier times, Smith's survivors would have brought the case. Today, however, in all criminal cases, whether major or minor, the state, and not the victim, is technically the aggrieved party, and it is the state that has the obligation to see that justice is done. In this way, the state supposedly fulfills its obligation to maintain the public order and to minimize episodes of private vengeance. Because of the potentially severe consequences for an accused of being convicted of a crime, standards of proof and details of procedure in criminal cases are usually more stringent than in noncriminal cases.

There are exceptions in Islamic Law, which distinguishes between crimes against God (Hudud), which the state is obligated to punish, and crimes against others (Quesas and Tesar), which allow for retribution or blood money for the victim or the victim's family. Crimes against God are those that are particularly likely to endanger the social order, including theft, highway robbery, and most sexual crimes. Crimes against others are those that threaten a family's livelihood, including murder or manslaughter, and assault. In practice, the distinction is not as great as it seems, since all criminal cases in Islamic countries are decided in government-run courts, and most punishments are fixed by the courts in accordance with religious or traditional rules (Lippman, McConville, and Yerushalmi, 1988).

Noncriminal cases, or civil cases, are disputes between parties that do not involve the potential of criminal sanctions. These cases typically bear the names of the two disputing parties. Thus, if Jones' car runs into Smith's car in a parking lot, causing a crushed fender, and Smith decides to sue Jones for damages, the case would be called *Smith v. Jones.* Although most civil cases involve two private parties, the government may also be a party to a civil case. The defining element is not the plaintiff or defendant but the nature of the case, with criminal cases falling in a separate category.

The distinction between civil law and criminal law, which exists in all modern systems of law, creates a certain amount of confusion when one is talking about families of law. The confusion arises because one major family of law is known as the Civil Law family. Although there are some historical reasons this family of law has the same name as the branch of law that is distinguished from criminal law, the term *Civil Law family* is used to denote the entire legal culture of a nation that uses that tradition, not just the noncriminal aspects of that nation's law. These terms may seem confusing at present, but their meaning will become clearer as we consider issues like criminal procedure in Civil Law systems.

The Civil Law family is sometimes called the Romano-Germanic family (David and Brierly, 1978; Ehrmann, 1976) because its origins are in the old Roman Code of Justinian and the laws of the Germanic tribes, such as the Franks and the Bavarians, that bordered the Roman Empire in central Europe and eventually conquered most of Europe. While use of the term *Romano-Germanic* avoids the problems of confusion between the Civil Law family and civil law in general, it presents another problem, because most texts and histories continue to use the term *Civil Law* to distinguish that family of legal systems from the other major families. To make the matter less complicated in this book, we will capitalize *Civil Law* when it denotes the family of law and lowercase *civil law* when it refers to noncriminal law.

We must remember that legal systems deal not only with criminal law and criminal process but also with other matters that require official involvement in dispute resolution, such as divorce, property matters, and civil injuries. Nevertheless, to understand criminal justice, one needs to have some appreciation of the context in which this specialized branch of law operates. Furthermore, criminal procedure, an essential element of criminal law, is intertwined with features of the various legal families.

Historically, the Civil Law, Common Law, and Islamic Law developed over the course of centuries, while Socialist Law is a twentieth-century phenomenon. As a result, the Civil Law and Common Law have changed quite radically over time, while Socialist Law, until recently, had not undergone major transformations. With the breakdown of Communist governments in eastern Europe and the Soviet Union, and the efforts to modernize the economy in China, we can anticipate some major changes in Socialist Law in the twenty-first century. Similarly, Islamic Law is based largely on the Qur'an, the holy book of Islam, but it has also been extended by the commentaries of major schools of Islamic scholars. In the remainder of this chapter, we will examine how these major legal systems arrived at their current place in history.

THE CIVIL LAW

The Civil Law tradition is the most pervasive legal tradition in the world. It is found throughout western Europe, in Latin America, and in parts of Africa and the Far East. Indeed, it was historically the basis of law in Socialist countries, and Socialist Law, while classified separately, has many elements of the Civil Law remaining. As explained earlier, the Civil Law is sometimes called Romano-Germanic law because of its historical roots.

The **Civil Law** is code law. It is like the Ten Commandments of Moses that were published so that all people could know and follow them. Four major codifications of law, each building on the previous one, are involved in the history of the Civil Law. These are the Roman Law of the emperor Justinian, the Canon Law of the medieval Catholic Church, the Napoleonic Code of early nineteenth-century France, and the German Law of the People (Buergerliches Gesetzbuch) that was compiled under Bismarck after the German Empire was established in 1870. In each case, the legal code derived from earlier laws, customs, and informal regulations (David and Brierly, 1978; Ehrmann, 1976; Glendon, Gordon, and Osakwe, 1985; Merryman, 1985).

Writing a set of laws is not as simple as it may sound. As in writing constitutions, the framers must be concise, must cover all contingencies, and must not depart radically from accepted custom. The laws must be at once general enough to allow for particular cases to be fit into the scope of legal rules and specific enough to provide adequate guidance for those whose job it is to administer the law. The various incarnations of the Civil Law met these requirements with varying degrees of success.

Roman Law

In the sixth century A.D., the Byzantine emperor Justinian arranged for the compilation and codification of the law then in force in the Roman world. The result was the **Corpus Juris Civilis,** also known as the Institutes of Justinian. Included in this code were laws pertaining to family, property, torts, and contracts.

Justinian's goal was to simplify the massive amounts of legal materials, understood only by legal counselors, and often contradictory or unclear, that made up the laws of the empire. After the code was compiled, Justinian ordered that all previous works of legal commentary and all previous law be disregarded. He also forbade commentary on his own code by legal scholars. (Obviously, lawyers who obfuscated the law and made themselves indispensable through their specialized knowledge of different branches of the law were a problem in Justinian's time as well as our own.) Although learned commentaries by legal scholars are very important in Civil Law countries today, the judicial tradition of referring to the law itself rather than to precedents established in prior cases remains an essential part of the Civil Law tradition and an important feature that distinguishes it from the Common Law.

The Institutes of Justinian, although gradually watered down and changed through contact with local legal traditions, especially Germanic tribal law, remained enormously influential. In fact, it became both the basis of legal study in medieval universities and the backbone of some national legal systems during the period of the development of nation-states in the sixteenth and seventeenth centuries. Even today, law students in countries that use the Civil Law must take a course in the Corpus Juris Civilis, or Roman Law.

Canon and Commercial Law

Although Roman Law remained a source of legitimacy in temporal law throughout Europe for many centuries, the Catholic Church developed its own law, **Canon Law,** that dealt with church and spiritual matters. Canon Law included provisions regulating family life and morals, as well as rules for church governance. It was administered by ecclesiastical, or church, courts.

It is hard for us today to realize that two systems of law, claiming authority over different matters and running separate court systems, could have coexisted in medieval Europe. In truth, however, this is no stranger than the dual court systems (state and federal) and dual law that exist in the United States. Although, as in the United States, there were jurisdictional disputes in specific cases, and the church tended to assume simultaneous jurisdiction in some matters regarding family relations, this dual court system seems to have worked quite well overall.

As trade and commerce among nations became more complex, an important new body of law, **commercial law,** developed in Europe during the Middle Ages. Commercial law is a body of legislation that deals with the exchange of goods between cities or nations. This law developed initially in the large merchant cities of Italy, but it was soon adapted by other countries and became, like Roman and Canon Law, a kind of internationally accepted law in Europe.

With the rise of nation-states, the Protestant Reformation, and the seemingly endless wars that wracked Europe in early modern times, much of the code law fell into disuse or was practiced only partially, in conjunction with local customary law. Various rulers made more or less successful efforts to codify the laws of their countries. It was not until the early nineteenth century, however, that a legal code rivaling that of Justinian in terms of influence and comprehensiveness was drawn up.

This was the famous French Civil Code of 1804, or Code Napoleon, named after the French emperor Napoleon, who ordered its development.

The Napoleonic Code

The Revolution of 1789 was a major turning point in French history. The revolutionaries abolished the hereditary monarchy, executed King Louis XVI and Queen Marie Antoinette and proclaimed a republic based on the principles of liberty, equality, and fraternity. A period of turmoil and confusion that featured several attempts at republican government ensued during the 1790s. Napoleon Bonaparte, a Corsican by birth, gradually became more powerful due to his military and administrative genius, his ambition, and his ability to take advantage of the deteriorating political situation in France. Eventually, Napoleon made himself the first emperor of France and enacted a series of governmental reforms that significantly changed the administrative and legal structures of that country. After numerous military adventures, Napoleon's career ended at the famous Battle of Waterloo in 1815. His governmental reforms, however, including the civil code, the administrative court structures, and the local governmental structures of France, have persisted.

The case of Napoleon and the civil code exemplifies what often happens when a postrevolutionary or postconquest government takes over in a country. One of the best ways to discredit previous governments and to consolidate the power of the new government is to throw out the old laws and create new ones. Legal and judicial personnel, those with a major stake in the prevailing system, are usually purged at the same time. As we will see, this is what happened in England at the time of the development of the Common Law. It is also what happened in the twentieth century in communist countries such as the former Soviet Union, China, and Cuba. Often, these radical changes eventually accommodate themselves to traditional practices and rules. They do provide a major break in legal history, however.

The Napoleonic Code was drawn up by legal experts and went into effect in 1804. These experts brought together in one code much of the law that was being practiced in various parts of France—some based on Canon Law, some on Roman Law, some on commercial law, and some on the feudal practices in existence before the Revolution. But they went much further, also incorporating into this code many of the new ideas about private property and relations between people fueled by the Enlightenment. Therefore, this code was the first truly modern set of laws.

The Napoleonic Code consisted of 2,281 rules, or articles, covering a variety of subjects: persons (including marriage, divorce, and family law), property, torts, and contracts (Schwartz, 1956). This body of law was to supersede all law that had been in use in France prior to the Revolution. Since part of the objective was to create a body of law that would not depend on interpretation by lawyers, the code makers aimed to create law that was simple, easy to understand, nontechnical, and accessible to the masses. In this they generally succeeded, and the Napoleonic Code has come down to us as a paradigm of a spare, well-written, well-conceived, and comprehensive code that somehow typifies the vaunted French spirit of rationalism. As Merryman says:

> *The French Civil Code of 1804 was envisioned as a kind of popular book that could be put on the shelf next to the family Bible. It would be a handbook for the citizen, clearly organized and stated in straightforward language, that would allow citizens to determine their legal rights and obligations by themselves. (1985, p. 28)*

Of course, women today would find many of the provisions of the French Civil Law to be nothing less than obnoxious. Husbands were given authority over their wives, who owed them obedience. Wives could not sell or buy property, or even receive free property, without their husband's permission. Husbands had control over community property and could administer any property a wife brought to a marriage (Tunc, 1956, p. 36).

Napoleon's influence on the criminal law was even more extensive than on the civil law. He fostered the Code Penale of 1810, a truly harsh criminal law. Napoleon had little sympathy for lawbreakers and believed in the deterrent effect of severe penalties. Postrevolutionary France was going through a period of lawlessness and high crime rates, and the French people were inclined to support a stern criminal code (Wright, 1983, ch. 2).

Throughout the nineteenth century, the Napoleonic Code exerted a major influence on other countries that sought to codify their laws. The earliest countries to adopt the French code were those that were conquered by Napoleon: Belgium, the Netherlands, Poland, and part of Germany. France also exported its codes to its colonies in Africa and the Near and Far East, and even to its former colonies in North America. Today, French civil law continues to influence many of these emergent countries, as well as the state of Louisiana and the Canadian province of Quebec (Schwartz, 1956).

The German Civil Code

Almost a century passed between the time that the Napoleonic Code went into effect and the time that Germany developed its own civil code. Whereas the French code was a model of simplicity, the German code was long, academic, and complex. And whereas the French code had been drawn up in the course of a few years, it took twenty years to put together the German code. Although the German code, like the French, also represented an attempt to pull together and control a new nation, the unification of Germany took place in 1871 while the code did not actually go into effect until 1900. The German code was the end result of a massive scholarly effort to study previous law, develop a philosophy of law, and provide a rational basis for legal development. Much local (indigenous) law was incorporated into the German code; it shared with the French, however, roots in Roman law and postfeudal ideas

about property and personal rights (Glendon, Gordon, and Osakwe, 1985).

The Importance of the French and German Civil Codes

Both the French and the German codes have been enormously influential in the development of law over the past two centuries, for several reasons. In the first place, both codes were developed during a time of constantly increasing industrialization and expansion of worldwide commerce and trade. Common rules governing contracts and property, as well as individual obligations and rights, facilitated such trade and thus were crucial in the development of modern industrial society. In addition, imperialism was at its height, fostering cross-national adaptation of laws and legal structures.

Further, in the postcolonial era, as new countries formed and older countries sought to modernize, and as revolutions and other political changes created a need for rules of development, importing a full code of laws simplified the process. Such a code also helped to unify new nations, just as it did in postrevolutionary France and postunification Germany and hopefully will do in the newly formed Russian Republics.

Development of an indigenous (local) code, or gradually defining law, as was done during the development of the Common Law, would take decades or even centuries. This does not mean that other countries have taken over the civil codes wholesale. Rather, they have adapted them to local circumstances and local legal traditions.

Even Iran, which had previously adopted the Civil Law but in 1979 rejected the system in favor of a return to Islamic Law, continues to be influenced by the Civil Law in some areas of endeavor, especially with regard to trade and commerce. It is probably no exaggeration to say that the Civil Law is a kind of common denominator for international private law transactions throughout the world today. Thus, the Civil Law will tend to grow in influence as multinational economic cooperation grows and as trade barriers fall in Europe and other parts of the world.

THE COMMON LAW

The Common Law is more ancient, more complex, and more difficult to deal with than the French or German Civil Codes. In Anglo-Saxon countries, its relative peculiarities have shaped not only the legal tradition but also a good part of the legal education, criminal procedure, and general approach to law and government. To understand the nature of the Common Law system, we need to look at a few major landmarks in the history of its development.

The King's Court

When William the Conqueror, a French (Norman) nobleman, defeated the English (Saxons) at the Battle of Hastings in 1066 and became king of England, he faced the usual problems of trying to rule a conquered nation. William insisted that French be spoken, but the Saxon language persisted throughout his new kingdom. In general, William found that it was easier to conquer the English than to rule them.

We must remember that this was happening in the eleventh century, some 800 years before Napoleon decided to strengthen his hold on the French people by developing a code of law that they would all have to follow. In William's time, the feudal system was in full sway on the Continent, and the law itself was a peculiar amalgam of Canon Law, feudal customs, and remnants of Roman Law that existed throughout Europe. In this era, the civil codes did not have the importance that they would assume in the Enlightenment Europe of Napoleon's time. Therefore, William could not simply call for a new code of laws to usurp the power of the local gentry. He was not without resources and imagination, however, and he found ways, including taxation and use of the French language, to impose his will on his subjects.

One of the ways that William and his Norman successors consolidated power was to set up courts, known collectively as the King's Court, or Curia Regis. The kings appointed the judges of these courts, and the judges traveled around the countryside, ruling on disputes that had not been settled in the local courts or hearing appeals from the local courts. King Henry II, known as the Father of Common Law, was the most prominent of the twelfth-century judicial pioneers. Thus, England was the first European country to set up a centralized system of courts available to all freemen in the kingdom. This system of courts actually built upon an English tradition of centralized kingly authority that existed before William's time and that contrasted with the prevailing system in Europe of many competing regional powers (Plucknett, 1940; Van Caenegem, 1973).

Like Solomon, however, the judges of the English courts did not refer to a specific body of laws as a standard for deciding cases. Presumably, they decided crucial political cases in a way that would benefit the king. For conventional cases, however, the judges typically based their decisions on a combination of common sense and local norms and laws.

Although the law itself was not previously defined, the jurisprudence of the King's Court came to be characterized by common procedures, or rules for handling cases. (To this day, procedural matters are crucial to the Common Law.) Over time, a body of law developed that was based on the decisions of the judges of the King's Court. As new cases arose, the judges referred to similar previous cases as authority for their decisions. This established the importance of the precedent as a way of deciding cases. The Latin term **stare decisis** (literally, "it stands decided") is used in Common Law countries to signify the legal force of precedent. Adherence to precedent resulted in the gradual development of rules that were uniform throughout the kingdom. These rules came to be known as the **Common Law** because they were common to all

Englishmen, and thus distinguished from the rules and laws that existed in each local region.

The early kings set up the King's Court as a way to strengthen their power. But over time (after William's and Henry's time, to be sure), the force of the rules and precedents developed in the Common Law courts was so great that a tradition of **judicial independence** arose. In other words, judges of the Common Law courts saw themselves as bound by the law rather than by the desires of the ruler. Judicial independence is something that we take so much for granted these days that we forget the long history of political regimes in which absolute rulers (what we would call the executive branch today) made rules, enforced them, and decided cases that arose under them.

Equity Courts

Judicial independence was not really a welcome development to William's successors on the English throne. In addition, the Common Law itself became increasingly cumbersome and rigid in application. Therefore, the practice arose of appealing directly to the king to rule on cases that did not fit well into the Common Law structure. By the fifteenth century, a new set of courts, known as chancery courts, or equity courts, had developed.

As the name implies, equity courts and the law that they administered dealt with efforts to obtain justice, or fairness. The courts did this by developing a set of practices known as equity procedures that helped people bring their cases to court without hazarding the use of the complex Common Law system. Some equity procedures are familiar to us even today. For example, the **writ of mandamus** orders public servants to perform the duties that are part of their jobs. **Injunctions** are court orders designed to prevent harms that would occur before a case could work its way through the regular court systems.

The United States and England no longer have separate equity courts to handle equity cases; instead, equity cases are now handled by the regular courts. Originally, however, these equity courts

were a major innovation, once again making the king more powerful in legal matters.

As the equity courts became entrenched, they became as rule-bound as the Common Law courts. Further, the judges of the equity courts developed the same inconvenient habit of judicial independence that their Common Law brethren had before them. Thus, English kings again had to set up new courts to do their personal bidding. Star Chamber courts and Courts of High Commission became notorious in the seventeenth century for their ruthless persecution of the kings' enemies (Prall, 1966).

The Modern History of the Common Law

With the decline in the power of the monarchy and the ascendancy of Parliament, the English court system stabilized; judicial independence was taken for granted and no longer considered a problem by the English rulers. Even Oliver Cromwell and his Puritan followers, who overthrew the Stuart kings and established a commonwealth in England between 1648 and 1660, feared the possible destabilizing effects of sweeping changes in the law. Cromwell thus made no major effort to supersede the Common Law (Prall, 1966). The English legal system remained a complex system of rules and precedents, interpreted with small shades of meaning and requiring a body of legal experts to deal with it. These legal experts had to serve long apprenticeships to become familiar with the vast number of cases and precedents that would govern their decisions.

The Development of Criminal Procedure. The fact that the Common Law is based on precedent does not mean that this law is not written down in one place. In the eighteenth century, William Blackstone set out to compile all the laws in effect in England up to that time. His monumental work *Blackstone's Commentaries* constituted a major step forward in English legal history. Since Blackstone's time, the Common Law has continued to be compiled and brought up to date in various collections.

For most of its existence, the Common Law addressed all matters likely to need settlement in court—not only private concerns such as contracts, property disputes, family questions, and torts against individuals but also criminal offenses (Holmes, 1923). But more important than the actual delineation of criminal offenses was the development of Common Law criminal procedure. Most of the criminal procedure rules that are set forth in the Fourth, Fifth, Sixth, and Eighth Amendments to the U.S. Constitution, as well as the rules about bringing the accused before a judge to question his incarceration **(habeas corpus),** were adapted from Common Law rules and from Parliamentary decrees based on the Common Law. The concern in U.S. courts with criminal procedure, which often seems excessive to people in Civil Law countries, has its origin in the English Common Law criminal procedure.

The Definition of Crimes. The definition of crimes, as opposed to the procedure for processing those accused of crimes, has gradually become part of public statutory law rather than the case law of Common Law countries. For example, when we say that murder is a crime in the state of New York, this is as a result of a law passed by the legislature of that state making murder a crime and prescribing a penalty for the commission of this crime. Of course, murder was also a crime under the Common Law, so it may seem unnecessary to have a statute that outlaws the act. The chief difference that has developed is in the penalties attached to various crimes. Thus, when the state of New York passes a law outlawing murder, it has prescribed different penalties at various times in its history, and these penalties are not the same as those that were usually imposed under the Common Law.

With the rise of legislative democracy in both England and the United States, the actual rule-making power of the Common Law was eclipsed by the rule-making power of the legislatures. Indeed, in a constitutional system such as that of the United States, the very fact that all laws must be in conformity with state or federal constitutions

suggests that a "pure" Common Law, in which judges make the law, no longer exists. Criminal law has been codified for many years, and much law-making is concerned with administrative agency regulations and even such formerly private regulations as those dealing with marriage, divorce, and other family concerns.

The Current Status of the Common Law. Does this mean that the Common Law is dying out or dead in the modern world? To answer this question, we need to consider the continued importance of judge-made law in the United States. Constitutional law, in which judges interpret the Constitution based on the precedents of previous interpretations of this document, is a good example. For example, the Supreme Court, in the 1961 case *Mapp v. Ohio,* interpreted the Constitution's guarantee against unreasonable searches and seizures to mean that evidence obtained by state authorities through an illegal search may not be used at trial. This decision meant that the Exclusionary Rule, formerly required in federal cases, was extended to the states. Subsequent to that decision, the Supreme Court handed down many further interpretations of the dimensions of illegal searches, in each case building on its previous decisions—sometimes extending the scope of police power to search, and other times restricting it. In effect, the judges are continuing to make law built on precedent, in the tradition of the Common Law, even though the source of this law is a fixed statutory or constitutional prescription.

In the Common Law countries, the traditions of the Common Law—its use of precedent, its historically developed procedural forms—continue to be a vital part of the legal process despite the fact that most law has become statutory in modern times. Ironically, the United States, with its need for constant interpretation of constitutional provisions to establish the parameters of state and federal relations and of relations between individuals and the state, has become a nation that is more deeply wedded to the Common Law tradition of judge-made law than England, where Parliament is supreme. U.S. judges have much

Table 3.3 Differences Between the Civil (Roman) and Common Law Systems

Civil (Roman) Law	Common Law
Law and procedure are governed by separate, comprehensive, systematized codes, which are forward-looking, wishing to anticipate all new problems.	Law and procedure are governed by laws and precedents, which, if codified at all, simply organize past experiences.
Codes are based on scholarly analysis and conceptualizations.	Laws reflect the experience of practitioners, on a case-by-case basis.
Supreme Courts interpret nuances of law.	Supreme Courts develop law.
Legal proceedings must establish the entire truth.	Truth-finding is strictly limited by pleadings and rules of evidence.
Judges are free to find and interpret facts.	Rules of evidence limit the fact-finding process.
There is very little lay participation.	Grand and petit juries play a strong role.
There is no presumption of guilt or innocence.	There is a presumption of innocence.

SOURCE: Adler, Mueller, and Laufer, 1995. Used with permission of The McGraw/Hill Companies.

more discretionary, lawmaking power than English judges.

The Common Law tradition also continues to have a major influence in legal education. In Common Law countries, legal education traditionally occurred through apprenticeship, with the budding lawyer learning large numbers of cases that formed the various precedents necessary for understanding the law. Law schools have largely replaced apprenticeships in the United States, but law school education focuses chiefly on the case law method, thus emphasizing the Common Law tradition and preparing the lawyer to operate within that tradition. In England, trial lawyers are trained at the Inns of Court, essentially continuing the apprenticeship tradition. Civil Law legal education is a less practical, more academic course of study that includes a good deal of philosophy, history, and general education. Apprenticeships in Civil Law systems follow formal legal education. Case precedents will not be binding on the practicing lawyer and are thus not emphasized in legal education.

Table 3.3 lists the major differences between the Civil (Roman) and Common Law systems.

THE SOCIALIST LAW

Socialist Law has its origins in socialism, which is a system characterized by the absence of classes and by common ownership of the means of production and livelihood. The political, economic, and social term used to describe socialism is *communism*. Karl Marx (1818–1883) was the prophet of Communist ideology. Marx believed that the current economic system (capitalism) was one that exploited the masses (the proletariat) and supported those who controlled the economic resources (the bourgeoisie). Eventually, Marx predicted, the proletariat would revolt and eliminate the bourgeoisie, and socialism would replace capitalism as the economic system of choice.

Marx addressed the issue of crime when he stated that, after a true Communist society was established, the state would "wither away" and there would be no further need of criminal law or sanctions to deal with lawbreakers. In this ideal society, cooperation and concern for community welfare would replace individualism and competitiveness. Property would belong to all, thus eliminating the incentive to rob or steal, and people would not be subject to the pathological urges that make them criminal in conventional societies.

Although Marx's utopian vision has not been realized in any country of the world, Communist countries have adhered to one or another version of what is known as Socialist Law (Berman, 1963; David and Brierly, 1978; Glendon, Gordon, and Osakwe, 1985). The former Soviet Union was for decades the most prominent of the Socialist Law nations. Nations that currently retain major aspects of Socialist Law are Cuba, North Korea, Vietnam, and China.

Socialist Law needs to be considered in any study of comparative criminal justice because it has enough distinct characteristics to warrant being categorized as its own family of law and because we can learn much about the nature of law in systems that emphasize communal values at the expense of individualism.

The Historical Background of Socialist Law

To understand Socialist Law, we must take a look at legal developments in the former Soviet Union following the Russian Revolution of 1917. Again, we are faced with a new regime, a post-revolutionary government dedicated to the destruction of the institutions and laws of the hated old order. As in France, a king and queen (in this case Czar Nicholas and his wife Alexandra) were executed to break the bonds with the past and symbolize the destruction of the old ruling class. And as in France, where the Revolution, despite its atrocities and excesses, came to represent the triumph of a new ideology of enlightenment and rationalism, the Russian Revolution represented the triumph of a more recent ideology, that of Karl Marx.

It is important to note that even Socialist Law is historically grounded in the Civil Law. For centuries, eastern European countries, including Russia, used recorded codes as a means to rule the populace. Prior to the Revolution, Russia's legal system had combined elements of the Civil Law, Canon Law, and traditional Russian customs. Imperial Russian law, however, was chiefly statute law that had gone through various phases of codification. The major influence on imperial law was the Germanic law of the Middle Ages, the same Germanic law that had had such an important influence on the two great nineteenth-century codes, the Napoleonic Code and the German Civil Code.

After the Revolution, Russia went through a chaotic period in which there was no formal legal structure and revolutionary tribunals dispensed revolutionary law. Vast discretion resided in the judges of these tribunals. However, these judges were not legally trained, since the lawyers and judges of the old regime had been eliminated along with the law. Ultimately, however, with the realization of the need to make the Soviet Union into a viable trading partner and the relaxation of revolutionary fervor during the time of the "New Economic Policy," Russia moved again to develop a code of laws. The result was the "new" Russian Civil Code, which drew from the earlier Russian code, the German Civil Code, the French Civil Code, and the Swiss Civil Code (Glendon, Gordon, and Osakwe, 1985, ch. 13).

With the rise to power of Joseph Stalin (1879–1953), in the latter part of the 1920s, a new period of Communist zeal began. Stalin tried to institute a "pure" Communist approach, without great concern for legalism. He soon decided, however, as had William the Conqueror and Napoleon before him, that the law could be used to consolidate and strengthen his power. The Soviet Union entered into a period of "Socialist legalism," rule making that tried to encompass every aspect of the Russian citizen's home and work life. A huge bureaucracy and a highly developed legal system became part of the Soviet state apparatus.

Although the Russian legal system continued to owe much to the civil codes of western Europe and could easily be identified with them through an examination of rules of procedure, especially criminal procedure, it gradually became such a distinctive system that it is now possible to speak of a Socialist Law family, as distinguished from the Civil Law or the Common Law. With the breakup of the Soviet Union, major changes in the Socialist Law governmental form and ideology have taken place in eastern Europe. Many countries such as the former East and West Germany have now adopted the Civil Law system. However, this does not mean the total demise of all remnants of Socialist Law for two key reasons.

First, even the countries that have rebuked socialism as their main political ideology will surely retain some principles of the legal system. History tells us that, when countries encounter political upheaval and significant change in their legal system, they often find it difficult to totally eschew all aspects of the previous form of law. This is understandable seeing as how the basic principles often remain in the collective psyche of the citizens who lived under the previous kind of law. In the case of the former Soviet Union, for over fifty years citizens lived under the auspices of Socialist Law.

Second, Socialist Law will undoubtedly remain as a significant legal and political system because it is still practiced by the most populous country in the world—the People's Republic of China. For this reason, we chose China as a model country to be discussed throughout this book.

Socialism and the People's Republic of China

To understand the formal origins of Socialist Law in China, one must first learn about the history of the country immediately prior to the implementation of socialism. For over 4,000 years, China was ruled by a series of feudal dynasties, which limited any significant attempts to modernize the political, economic, or social structures in the country. The majority of people who lived in the vast regions of China were poor peasant farmers.

The most recent dynasty, the Qing dynasty, was overthrown in 1911. In 1912, the democratic ideals of the Kuomintang (Nationalist party) dominated. However, between 1911 and 1949, the Chinese political situation was chaotic and prone to warlordism, corruption, civil war, and invasion by Japan.

It was during this tumultuous time that the ideals of socialism were introduced into Chinese society. The birth and early growth of socialism in China was directly influenced by the Soviet Union and its Socialist leader Vladimir Lenin (1870–1924). Lenin, a firm believer in the ideas of Karl Marx, visited China in the 1910s, espousing the ideals of Marxism/Leninism, and the Communist party in China was formed in 1921.

However, the Socialist government, called the People's Republic of China, was not officially established until October 1949 when Mao Zedong (1893–1976) and his fellow Communists gained full control of the government over the Nationalist party. The Communist government abolished all laws of the Nationalist regime, claiming that these laws represented only the interests of the bourgeoisie, landlord classes, and feudal society (Situ and Liu, 1996).

During the first thirty years of communism under Mao, the government replaced the Nationalist laws not with new codes but with a combination of statutes, rules, and regulations based on the ideals of the ruling party. Large, bureaucratically structured courts were held in disdain; whenever possible, local lower-level courts and ad hoc tribunals made legal decisions. This rather informal and almost random method of settling legal disputes eventually led to the creation of an extensive committee system in China. Committees were set up in neighborhoods, communities, and workplaces to act as systems of surveillance, control, and sanctioning. In this era, more consideration was given to developing a formal legal system, legal decisions in China were made based solely on political needs and ideals.

Mao's major contribution was to adapt Communist principles to the Chinese political, economic, and social situation. By gaining the support of the large numbers of peasants throughout agrarian China, he was able to develop an army and mobilize the masses, thereby furthering the objectives of communism (Terrill, 1999).

The People's Republic of China is currently in the process of attempting to develop a legal and criminal justice system that will accommodate its needs as a Socialist nation, a nation with a long Confucian tradition, and a modern commercial power. In the next chapter and throughout this book, we will continue to discuss the history and current structure of the legal system in China.

Socialist Versus Civil Law

How does Socialist Law differ from a conventional legal system such as exists in other Civil Law countries? Six characteristics of **Socialist Law** distinguish it from Civil Law:

- The public law/private law distinction
- The importance of economic crimes
- The educational or "social engineering" function of law
- The distinctive role of the procurator
- The distinction between political and non-political justice
- The mitigated independence of the judiciary

The Public Law/Private Law Distinction.
Laws regarding private property, inheritance, and personal relations between individuals continue to be important in Socialist Law systems. The ideal of collectivization of property and ownership of the major means of production by the state, however, has resulted in immoderate importance being attached to public law—that is, to statutory laws and regulations of the state. The amounts and kinds of rule making that are involved in centralized, noncompetitive economic production are tremendous, and the Socialist state is often choked with bureaucratic regulations because so little of economic life is left to open-market competition. To be sure, governmental regulation of the economy through laws controlling trade, production, banking, and other economic matters is familiar in all Western societies today, but Socialist and non-Socialist systems continue to place a different emphasis on public versus private law.

Economic Crimes.
In a non-Socialist system, managers and employees are driven to a certain extent by a "bottom line" mentality. Workers who are chronically late for work, who abuse valuable machinery, and who fail to achieve a reasonable level of production usually will lose their jobs. And an enterprise that consistently fails to produce a profit will cease to exist. By contrast, in a Socialist system, in which all enterprises are owned by the government and full employment is guaranteed, failure to live up to working standards cannot be handled by dismissal of employees or bankruptcy of organizations. Without these kinds of private punishments, criminal law becomes a means for punishing unacceptable work behavior. Thus, the concept of economic crimes—obstruction of Socialist production—is a peculiar aspect of Socialist as compared to non-Socialist law.

The Educational Function of the Law. A legal system in which the people have no knowledge of the law would be an absurdity. How can one obey the law if one does not know what it is? But the reality is that most of us do not have much knowledge of the Common Law or of most of the public law to which we are subject. We tend to learn those parts of the law that affect us: basic criminal law, including traffic law; internal revenue law; and simple rules about property and contracts. Entrepreneurs or government administrators learn about the laws that affect their enterprises. For the most part, however, we have only a rudimentary knowledge of even the most basic criminal laws of our own states, and we depend on an army of attorneys to interpret the law for us.

In postrevolutionary societies, in which the law may have changed drastically, there is some urgency about having the citizens learn the new law. The Napoleonic Code was famous for its accessibility. It was relatively short, simple, and direct, without obscure phrasing and indecipherable language. The emperor Justinian, upon promulgating the new code of laws developed in his regime, abolished all previous law and refused to allow commentaries on his new law to be published. In this way, he hoped to negate the insidious influence of the lawyers who previously had been indispensable as mediators between the people and the law.

We might expect, therefore, that the Chinese government after 1949 would have made efforts to familiarize the people with the laws of the new regime. In fact, in post-1949 China, the masses did learn about the ideals of the Communist party through statements reported to the tightly controlled media and campaigns intended to popularize and implement certain policies. However, formally stated criminal and procedural laws were unclear and tenuous, depending on various shifts in political (Communist) philosophy. In many cases, unwritten and internal rules guided the police, courts, and ruling party in defining crimes and punishments (Lubman, 1983).

The educational or "social engineering" aspects of Socialist Law supposedly are another method of familiarizing the people with the new law. One of the basic tenets of Communist ideology is that socialism is a transitional stage on the way to a true Communist society in which people will have become transformed and will no longer be predatory and competitive in nature. Since coercive law is supposed to cease to exist in a true Communist society, it is especially important that those who are judged under the present law acquiesce in its reasonableness and justice. In order to achieve this Communist society, people need to become reeducated, and one of the prime agents of this reeducation must be the government and the legal system (Berman, 1963).

The Role of the Procurator. The procurator in Civil Law systems is roughly equivalent to the prosecutor in Common Law systems. The **procurator** works on behalf of the government, prosecuting crimes and making sure the proper indictments are served in the courts. However, in the Socialist Law family, the procurator is far more important than in either the Civil Law or Common Law family.

In the former Soviet Union, the head procurator general was actually one of the most powerful individuals in the government, becoming far more involved in governmental reforms and administrative decision making than most ministers of justice. Local procurators also were generally more powerful than judges in the Soviet system. They served the regime in political cases and generally had final say over decisions to prosecute. Soviet procurators have been described as having nine roles: "criminal investigator, grand jury, criminal prosecutor, judicial ombudsman, executive branch ombudsman, general ombudsman, prison ombudsman, military ombudsman, and propagandist of Soviet law" (Glendon, Gordon,

and Osakwe, 1985, pp. 819–820). An **ombudsman** in this sense is an individual who hears complaints and ensures that government agents are performing their functions correctly.

As in the former Soviet Union, the procuracy in China is among the most important and powerful positions in the criminal justice system. Located within a bureaucracy that contains different levels of influence, the office of procurator, according to the Chinese constitution, is "independent and not subject to interference by administrative organs, public organizations, or individuals." In fact, the office is a very complicated one in China because procurators must prosecute offenders, uphold lawfulness of prosecution, obey the law, and check the lawfulness of other security departments and the courts—all while following the leadership of the party without violating its own independence under the law (Organic Law, 1979).

Based on the Soviet model, Chinese procurators in the 1950s were also given the responsibility of prosecuting criminal offenders, supervising the entire criminal justice system, and ensuring that all citizens and state personnel carry out the laws and policies of the state. Since being redefined in 1978, the position now can be summarized to include supervisory, investigatory, and prosecutorial functions (Tanner, 1994). (See the accompanying box on p. 59 for a more detailed list of the duties of the procurator in the People's Republic of China.)

Political Versus Nonpolitical Justice. To speak of "political justice" implies that it is possible to have a kind of justice that departs from a norm of impartiality and engages in some form of partiality that is determined by politics—that is, the influence of those in power. Although we know that political influence often affects the outcomes of legal cases in the United States, the norm or ideal of Western law is definitely "equal justice under law." Therefore, one of the hardest things to explain about Socialist Law is its duality—a distinction between conventional cases and

Duties of the Procurator in the People's Republic of China

1. Investigate and prosecute treason and other criminal cases.
2. Review police cases and determine the appropriateness of arrest and prosecution.
3. Supervise the investigations of police to determine if they are in compliance with laws.
4. Conduct public prosecutions of officials.
5. Supervise judicial actions to determine if they are in compliance with laws.
6. Supervise judgments and court orders in criminal cases to determine if they are in compliance with laws.
7. Supervise all incarceration facilities to determine if they are in compliance with laws.

SOURCE: Organic Law, 1979.

cases in which the state has a particular interest that supersedes the interests of conventional justice. Such latter cases involve what is sometimes called "prerogative law," under which standard legal procedure is subverted through the intervention of those in power. Prerogative law was actually legitimated in the old Soviet system and was justified by its defenders as necessary to the evolution toward an ideal Communist society. If we read the novels of Aleksandr Solzhenitsyn, which describe the terror of life under Stalin, or various accounts by political dissidents in China, we might well find the concept of prerogative justice to mean no more than wanton disregard of matters of guilt or innocence under law. As a concept, however, it stresses the importance of the collective as opposed to the individual good, and it supposes that reasons of state may allow for setting aside normal criminal procedure to neutralize enemies of the state.

The Independence of the Judiciary. Independence of the judiciary means that judges are free to decide cases in accordance with the law and cannot be pressured to rule for any reason other than legality. This principle is highly valued in Western law, although it is honored only in theory in many cases. In the United States, for example, judges in most state court systems are elected and must answer to the voters for their decisions on the bench. One of the reasons the Founding Fathers guaranteed a life term for federal judges (except in rare cases of impeachment) was their hope that these judges could thereby act with total independence and without fear of losing their positions. Again, in reality, a great deal of politics is involved in the appointment and decision making of federal judges; the norm, however, is one of independence.

In the United States, an independent judiciary is tied to the idea of separation of powers, whereby excessive power of government is thwarted by distributing power among different branches. Separation of powers is not considered a desirable governmental arrangement in all Socialist countries, however, because it introduces an element of competition and conflict when promoting the public good should be the only goal. The idea of a benevolent state that rules for the good of its citizens thus replaced the idea of a government that must be curbed because of its tendency to become tyrannical and rule for the good of the rulers instead of the people as a whole. Therefore, even though in theory constitutional rights exist to protect individuals against governmental actions, in practice this ideal is often overshadowed. What is more important is the primacy of the Communist state over the needs of individuals. Similarly, China does not idealize separation of powers or a totally independent judiciary. In fact, judges in certain courts in China are appointed by a standing committee of that court and can be removed or even replaced by a substitute assistant judge by that same committee.

In practice, this does not mean that judges in all Socialist countries are tools of political leaders or that legal judgments in these countries are always arbitrary and determined exclusively by reasons of state. What it does mean is that, in the extraordinary case and according to the theory of law, reasons of state are a legitimate justification for deviance from conventional procedure.

THE ISLAMIC LAW

The three families of law described thus far in this chapter—Civil Law, Common Law, and Socialist Law—are pervasive in every part of the world today. There is hardly a country, region, or even tribe that has not been brought under the influence of one or the other, at least with respect to certain aspects of social life. A distinguishing characteristic of each of these systems of law is that it is secular in nature. **Secular law** is law that does not pertain to religion or any religious body—as opposed to laws in countries that have a strong religious basis, like Saudi Arabia.

In other words, none of the three major families of law claims to have the force of a religion behind it, despite the fact that many of the tenets of the laws are derived from religious teachings. In addition, religious courts or mediation agencies still exist for some religions and can exert moral influence rather than forced compliance through their decisions. However, since the decline of the Canon Law of the Roman Catholic Church, a law that coexisted with secular law during the Middle Ages, religion and law in large part have been separate. Since the latter eighteenth century the separation of religion and law has extended in many countries, including the United States, to complete separation of church and state.

In addition to the three major families of law described previously, however, other legal traditions persist in many countries of the world. Traditional law still plays an important part in dispute resolution in small communities in many countries. Some of these systems of law are derived from religious tenets. Hindu Law, which dates back to about 100 B.C., is still used in parts of India. The Confucian legal tradition, which goes back at least to the time of Confucius, continues to influence the Chinese legal system. Hebrew Law, derived from the Old Testament, is the source of some of modern Israeli laws. Most importantly, Islamic Law, which is known as Shari'a (literally, "the way"), plays a leading role in the legal systems of most Middle Eastern nations and some Asian nations (David and Brierly, 1978).

Islamic Law has become increasingly important in recent years after going through a period of decline in the nineteenth and early twentieth centuries. Saudi Arabia has been an Islamic state, adhering to Islamic Law, since its founding in 1926. Since 1979, Iran has adopted Islamic Law as its basic law. Under the influence of increasing Islamic fundamentalism, two other countries, Pakistan and Sudan, made Islamic Law the basis for their government in recent years. Other countries, including Egypt, Iraq, Syria, Bahrain, and Kuwait, have incorporated more and more Islamic elements into their legal systems (Amin, 1985a, 1985b; Bassiouni, 1982; Liebesny, 1975; Lippman, McConville, and Yerushalmi, 1988). (For a complete list of countries that consider Islamic Law a basis for their legal system, see Appendix D.)

Shari'a

Islamic law has two primary sources: the Shari'a and the Sunnah (or Sunna). What exactly does Shari'a consist of? **Shari'a** law may be defined as "the body of rules of conduct revealed by God (Allah) to his Prophet (Muhammad) whereby the people are directed to lead their life in this world" (Nader, 1990, p. 1). Nader lists six key characteristics of the Islamic Law (1990, p. 1):

- It is not given by a ruler but has been revealed by God.
- It has been amplified by leading Muslim jurists like Abu Hanafi, Shafi, and Malik.
- It remains valid whether recognized by the state or not.
- It originates not in customs and traditions but in divine revelation only.

- It is so comprehensive and all-embracing that it covers every aspect of a legal system—personal law, constitutional law, international law, criminal law, mercantile law, and so on.
- It is not in the nature of "should be" but lays down what the law is.

This list of characteristics requires some amplification. The most important source of Shari'a is the Qur'an, the Muslim holy book. The Qur'an (more commonly spelled Koran), however, is not in whole or even in part a code of laws. According to Amin, out of a total of about 6,000 verses in the Qur'an, only about 80 might be defined as legal rules (Amin, 1985a, p. 9). Therefore, other sources of law are included in Shari'a. Some of these are traditions derived from the statements and actions of the Prophet that were recorded in the Sunnah. The Sunnah (also called the Hadith), the second major source of Islamic Law, contains those decisions of the Prophet that deal with issues not directly addressed in the Qur'an (Moore, 1996). Other sources of law, developed by different schools of Islamic Law in the centuries after the death of Muhammad in A.D. 632, were common consent of Islamic jurists and judicial reasoning.

The Prevalence of Shari'a

As you can see, Islamic Law is truly distinctive among the families of law that we have considered. It does not represent the bringing together of traditions and customs into either a code law such as the Civil Law or a case law such as the Common Law. David and Brierly claim that Islamic Law is completely original "by its very nature," because it is based on divine revelation and is independent of all other systems that do not derive from that same revelation (1978, p. 429). At the same time, despite its basis in the Qur'an, Islamic Law depends on the compilation of cases and traditions from its early centuries. Therefore, it has some of the characteristics of case law: complex rules dependent upon interpretation and local developments.

When Nader tells us that Shari'a remains valid whether it has been adopted by the state, he illustrates an important aspect of the history of Islamic Law. Although this law was eclipsed by the laws of countries and colonial powers bent on modernization in the nineteenth and twentieth centuries, it remains in force for devout Muslims within those countries. An important distinction, however, is that Islamic Law is not the established law and so lacks the power of government to enforce its sanctions; thus, it depends on voluntary obedience. Moreover, in a country such as Turkey, which pursued modernization with a vengeance, the continuance of the Islamic Law was actively discouraged.

India, with its large Islamic minority, presents a peculiar situation. The desires of this minority cannot be ignored, and concessions to their beliefs are sometimes incorporated into Indian Law. In the famous Shah Bano case of 1985, for example, a Muslim citizen of India divorced his elderly wife, Shah Bano, according to Islamic rules, which do not call for alimony in the conventional sense. Shah Bano sued for and was granted economic support according to Indian law. This case caused a furor in the Muslim community, becoming a symbol of Hindu dominance and the repression of Muslims. In the end, the Indian Parliament passed the Muslim Women's Act, which provided for separate divorce regulations when the parties to the suit are Muslims. This law, in effect, acknowledges the power of Shari'a in a nation that otherwise practices separation of church and state (O'Donnell, 1990).

Today, in most predominantly Islamic countries, Islamic Law forms part of the legal system (often the part that deals with family law). In a few Islamic countries, including Iran, Saudi Arabia, Pakistan, and Sudan, it is proclaimed as the basis for all law, including the harsh Islamic criminal law based on the ideal of retribution. Even in these countries, however, certain concessions are made to modern exigencies of trade, banking (Islamic Law does not allow the payment of interest), and industry. In the other Islamic countries, part of a growing religious fundamentalism necessarily includes a push for greater incorporation of Shari'a into the national law.

Crime and Punishment Under Shari'a

There are four major schools of Islamic Law, derived from religious leaders living in different areas and facing different problems in the two centuries following the death of Muhammad. These schools are Hanafi, Hanbali, Maliki, and Shafi'i. The main differences between these schools are in matters of emphasis, whether on tradition, judicial reasoning, or the elaboration of the Qur'an. Different countries tend to follow one or another school of Islamic Law. Thus, for example, the primary legal tradition in Iraq is that of the Hanafi school, while in Saudi Arabia it is the fundamentalist Hanbali school, named after the great theologian and jurist Ahmad Ibn Hanbal (A.D. 780–855) (Amin, 1985b, p. 12).

In addition to the conventional issues of law, including property, contracts, and inheritance, Shari'a is concerned with many aspects of individual behavior, including dress, food, etiquette, and religious worship. For students of criminal justice, Shari'a presents an interesting contrast to Western systems. Crimes are categorized according to whether they are acts against God or private wrongs against individuals. In the former case, the state must initiate prosecution; in the latter, the victims or heirs theoretically must bring a complaint. In practice, however, the state usually initiates these proceedings as well. Crimes against God are very serious: They include apostasy (voluntary renunciation of Islam or its rules), rebellion, and defamation, as well as drug offenses and sexual crimes such as adultery, sodomy, and fornication (Lippman, McConville, and Yerushalmi, 1988, p. 41).

It is not only Shari'a law that makes Muslim legal systems different from those of Western countries. Shari'a courts are also different in makeup, procedure, and effect. Sanctions are prescribed in the Qur'an and are often harsh, with the emphasis on corporal and capital punishment. Theft is punished by imprisonment or by amputation of hands or feet, depending on the number of times

it is committed. Crimes against God, including adultery and acts of homosexuality, are usually punished by death. Thus, the death sentence for apostasy imposed on the Muslim novelist Salman Rushdie by the late Ayatollah Khomeini was peculiar only because Rushdie, as a British citizen, was not subject to Iranian criminal law. As a Muslim, however, he was subject to the Qur'an, and this fact was used as justification for the death sentence. Under Shari'a, imprisonment is the punishment of last resort.

Equality and Islamic Justice

A peculiarity of Islamic Law is the distinction between men and women in many matters. Although the Qur'an improved the status of women from what it had been previously, there are still aspects of Islamic Law that discriminate heavily against women. For example, women do not count as witnesses for certain crimes or may count only half as much as male witnesses (i.e., two women witnesses would be required where only one man was required) (Amin, 1985a, p. 36). Laws relating to property and to marriage and divorce also discriminate against women. Still, considering that much of the Western impetus for equal legal rights for women is of recent origin, these tenets of law that date back almost 1,500 years should come as no surprise.

In general, however, Islamic scholars assert that Islamic Law shows great concern for human rights with respect to freedom of religion (none but Muslims are required to follow the Muslim law), criminal procedure, and human development (Amin, 1985a, pp. 30–39). According to Muslim scholars, while particular countries, such as postrevolutionary Iran, may treat people arbitrarily and severely curtail their human rights, this is in spite of, rather than in keeping with, Islamic Law.

SUMMARY

Families of law have distinctive characteristics if seen as ideal systems. The Common Law places great emphasis on case precedents and fine distinctions of procedure. The Civil Law combines ancient Roman rules and the laws and customs of medieval Europe with regulations that address modern social and economic problems. The results have been codes of law that stand by themselves without the modifications of case law. Socialist Law espouses the idea that the law should be an instrument in the creation of a new Socialist society rather than simply a way of settling disputes or dealing with criminal deviance. Islamic Law is based on religious revelation combined with the traditional rules that emanated from the society of faithful Muslims in the early centuries following the death of the Prophet Muhammad.

None of these kinds of law is practiced in its "pure," or ideal, form in today's world. Countries that practice the Common Law are actually closely regulated by statutory law. In countries that practice the Civil Law, attorneys are not unmindful of the decisions that higher courts have handed down in previous cases. Therefore, precedent, while not formally acknowledged, plays a part in the law. In countries that formerly or even currently practice Socialist Law, the law will probably resemble that in the Civil Law countries more and more as communism breaks down as an ideological force. Islamic Law is unique among the families of law considered because it is actually expanding in its original form as religious fundamentalism spreads in the Middle East. Even Islamic Law, however, must coexist with commercial and other laws required by modernization and industrialization. Indeed, worldwide, increasing transnational business, research, and other enterprises provide the impetus for increasing integration of laws. In the European Community, for example, a whole new body of law exists that, by agreement of the members of the community, supersedes national law.

The very real tendencies toward integration and amalgamation among legal systems will become more apparent as we consider the criminal process in various countries. Nevertheless, it is a mistake to assume that the heritage of the families of law is breaking down in large part. The fact is that the legal heritage in any country is closely tied to the political and administrative culture of that country, and these cultures continue to be distinctive in many ways. These distinctions will also become more apparent later in this book.

DISCUSSION QUESTIONS AND EXERCISES

1. What are the chief differences between the Common Law and the Civil Law families?

2. How did the Common Law courts develop?

3. What is the basis for the rules of Shari'a?

4. Which of the families of law has been most influential around the world?

5. Search your state laws to determine if any examples of indigenous law are present. If there is a nearby Native-American reservation, ask a resident to come to your class to talk about local indigenous laws.

6. If you were a political leader in a Socialist Law nation, how would you legislate to educate people about the law? What kind of behavior would be made illegal? Answer the same questions for an Islamic Law country.

FOR FURTHER READING

David, R., and J. C. Brierly. (1985). *Major Legal Systems in the World Today.* London: Stevens.

Glendon, M. A., M. Gordon, and C. Osakwe. (1985). *Comparative Legal Traditions.* St. Paul, Minn.: West.

Merryman, J. H. (1985). *The Civil Law Tradition.* Stanford, Calif.: Stanford University Press.

Milsom, S. F. C. (1969). *Historical Foundations of the Common Law.* London: Butterworth.

Mukherjee, S., and P. Reichel. (1999). Bringing to Justice. In *Global Report on Crime and Justice.* United Nations Office for Drug Control and Crime Prevention. Graeme Newman (ed.), New York: Oxford University Press, pp. 65–69.

Souryal, S. S., A. I. Alobied, and D. W. Potts. (1994). The Penalty of Hand Amputation for Theft in Islamic Justice. *Journal of Criminal Justice,* 22 (3): 249–265.

Wilmore, J. H. (1936). *A Panorama of the World's Legal Systems.* Washington D.C.: Washington Law Book.

4 Six Model Nations

England
France
Germany
China
Japan
Saudi Arabia
Summary
Discussion Questions
For Further Reading

Key Terms and Concepts

Annuaire statistique de la justice
Boryokudan
Bundesrat
Bundestag
Bundesverfassungsgericht
Confucian thought
Council of Ministers
Cultural Revolution
Diet
Laender
Legal pluralism
Monarch
National People's Congress (NPC)
Parliament
Prefect
Prefectural police (PP)
Prefectures
Procurator
Reichsstrafgesetzbuch
Republican government
Shoguns
Shura
Unitary government

To place in perspective the structures and operations of the criminal justice system in any one nation, we need to know something about that country's history, government, and social development. This chapter introduces the six nations that we will examine in depth in the rest of the book. These thumbnail sketches will make it easier to follow the material in subsequent chapters and will help you understand how the respective criminal justice systems have developed.

Our model nations are England, France, Germany, China, Japan, and Saudi Arabia (see Figure 4.1). These nations are designated as "models" not because they provide an ideal that might be copied by other nations, but because each exemplifies a distinct approach to criminal process. The distinctions are based on families of law, governmental arrangements, and historical traditions. England is a unitary Common Law country, while France typifies a unitary Civil Law country. Germany is a federal Civil Law country, while China is one of the few countries that typifies Socialist Law. Japan is a hybrid system that exemplifies the merging of foreign legal cultures with a strong and enduring national tradition. Saudi Arabia represents an application of Islamic Law as pure as can be found today. For each country, we will provide current background information, a historical sketch of the development of government, and summaries of the current crime situation, criminal law, and criminal justice system.

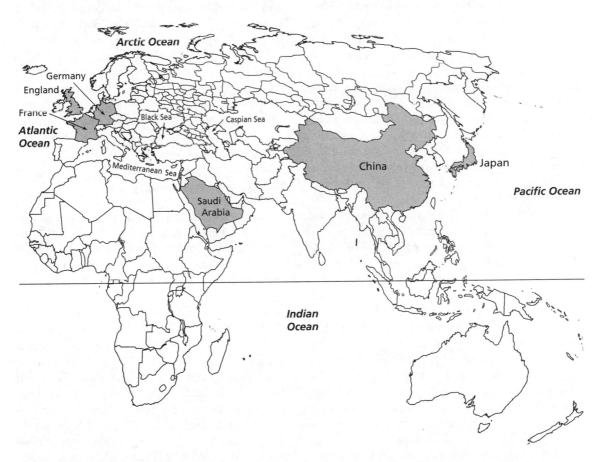

FIGURE 4.1 The Six Model Nations

ENGLAND

Overview

England is the largest political division within the United Kingdom of Great Britain and Northern Ireland and is the largest entity within the geographic area called Great Britain (England, Scotland, and Wales). England is the historical backbone of the Common Law legal tradition. Scotland, however, continues to operate under a Civil Law tradition mixed with Common Law elements. Therefore, we will consider only England and Wales rather than all of Great Britain or all of the United Kingdom.

England and Wales span 58,350 square miles and include forty-seven counties and seven metropolitan counties. England basically operates a capitalist economy, although various forms of socialism have made the country resemble a welfare state. England remains one of the world's great trading powers and financial centers, and boasts one of the four largest economies in Europe. It is also a world leader in the manufacture of heavy machinery, although it has lost much of the smaller industry that formerly was a major source of employment. During the late 1990s unemployment dropped slightly while the inflation rate remained moderate. For a summary of demographic information on the United Kingdom, see Table 4.1; for more detailed information, refer to Appendix C.

England is a **unitary government.** This means that governmental power is centralized rather than being divided between states and a central government, as happens in a federal system such as in the United States and Germany.

Parliament is the supreme power in England. What makes Parliament so powerful is that parts of the executive, judicial, and legislative branches are contained within it; thus, it can override both executive decisions and common law legal decisions by lower courts. Parliament consists of three parts: the monarch, the House of Lords, and the House of Commons.

A **monarch** is a person who is the sole and absolute ruler of a country, such as a king, queen, or emperor. However, in England, the influence of the monarchy has eroded, and today it serves a ceremonial rather than an executive function. The House of Lords has several important functions, including acting as the highest court of appeals and serving as a reviewer of legislation of the House of Commons. The House of Commons is the major component of Parliament because its 658 elected members discuss and vote on legislation proposed by the executive or by House members. The real leader of the nation is the prime minister, who is the head of the political party that possesses a majority of seats in the House of Commons. The prime minister acts as an advisor to the monarch and chairs of the cabinet. Cabinet ministers, in turn, are responsible for the administration of various government departments. For example, the lord chancellor administers the courts including appointing all judges, and the Home Secretary oversees the police and the correctional system.

England has always been similar to the United States in governmental and cultural traditions, to say nothing of their common language. English government and law have had a strong influence on U.S. government, and England and the United States are two of the major Common Law countries in the world today.

Historical Developments

From the time of the Norman Conquest of England in 1066 to the end of the seventeenth century, English history was marked by power struggles between the monarchs and their subjects, both nobles and commoners. For example, William the Conqueror centralized royal power at the expense of the local nobles. In 1215, the nobles retaliated by drafting the Magna Carta, or "great charter," forcing the king to recognize certain of their rights. In the sixteenth century, the Tudor monarchs, including Henry VIII and Elizabeth I, ruled with increasingly absolute powers. In the seventeenth century, the first two Stuart kings, James I and Charles I, tried to do likewise but faced an increasingly assertive Parliament and unhappy populace. After a civil war and the execution of Charles I in 1649, England came under the dictatorship of the Puritan leader

Table 4.1 Selected Demographics Summary

	United States	China	France	Germany	Japan	Saudi Arabia	United Kingdom
Geography							
Area (sq km)	9,629,091	9,596,960	547,030	356,910	377,835	1,960,582	244,820
Location	North America	Eastern Asia	West Europe	Central Europe	Eastern Asia	Middle East	West Europe
Capital	Washington, DC	Beijing	Paris	Berlin	Tokyo	Riyadh	London
People							
Population	270 mill. (98)	1.236 bill. (98)	58.8 mill. (98)	82.08 mill. (98)	125.9 mill. (98)	20.79 mill. (98)	58.97 mill. (98)
Growth rate	0.87%	0.83%	0.31%	0.02%	0.2%	3.41%	0.25%
Birth rate	14.4	15.73	11.68	8.84	10.26	37.63	12.01
Death rate	8.8	6.99	9.12	10.77	7.94	5.02	10.72
Life expectancy	76.13	69.59	78.51	76.99	80	70.03	77.19
Literacy	97%	82%	99%	99%	99%	62.8%	99%
Government							
Type	Federal Republic	Communist party led	Republic	Federal Republic	Constitutional Monarchy	Monarchy w/Ministers	Constitutional Monarchy
Divisions	50 states 1 district	23 provinces 5 regions 4 municipalities	22 regions 4 overseas dept. 5 overseas terr. 2 special terr.	16 states	47 prefectures	13 provinces	47 counties 7 metro counties 26 districts 9 regions 3 island areas
Constitution	Sept. 17, 1787	Dec. 4, 1982	Sept. 28, 1958	May 23, 1949	May 3, 1947	None	Unwritten
Legal system	Common law	Socialist	Civil law	Civil law	Civil law	Islamic	Common law
Suffrage	18 years	18 years	18 years	18 years	20 years	None	18 years
Economy							
GDP	$8.083 trill. (97)	$890 bill. (97)	$1.32 trill. (97)	$2.1 trill. (98)	$3.797 trill. (98)	$145.9 bill. (97)	$1.29 trill. (97)
per capita	$30,200 (97)	$700 (97)	$22,700 (97)	$25,000 (98)	$30,100 (98)	$7,200 (97)	$22,241 (97)
Growth rate	3.8% (97)	8.8% (97)	2.3% (97)	2.8% (98)	–2.5% (98)	7.1% (97)	3.5% (97)
Inflation	2% (97)	0.028% (97)	2% (97)	0.9% (98)	1.7% (97)	0.0% (97)	3.1% (97)
Labor force	136.3 mill. (97)	699 mill. (97)	25 mill. (97)	38.6 mill. (98)	67.23 mill. (97)	7.2 mill. (97)	28.2 mill. (96)
Exports	$625.1 bill. (96)	$182.7 bill. (97)	$275 bill. (97)	$539 bill. (98)	$421 bill. (97)	$54.3 bill. (97)	$268 bill. (97)
Imports	$822 bill. (96)	$142.4 bill. (97)	$256 bill. (97)	$467 bill. (98)	$339 bill. (97)	$26.9 bill. (97)	$283.5 bill. (97)
Debt—external	$862 bill. (95)	$131 bill. (97)	$117.6 bill. (96)	NA	NA	NA	$16.2 bill. (92)
Communications							
Televisions	1/1.26 ppl	1/16.49 ppl	1/2.01 ppl	1/1.83 ppl	1/1.26 ppl	1/4.62 ppl	1/2.95 ppl
Telephones	1/1.48 ppl	1/13.89 ppl	1/1.68 ppl	1/1.87 ppl	1/1.97 ppl	1/14.24 ppl	1/2.00 ppl
Radios	1/0.50 ppl	1/5.71 ppl	1/1.20 ppl	1/1.17 ppl	1/1.3 ppl	1/4.16 ppl	1/0.84 ppl
Transportation							
Railways	240,000 km	64,900 km	32,027 km	43,966 km	23,670 km	1,390 km	16,878 km
Highways	6.42 mill. km	1.18 mill. km	892,500 km	633,000 km	1.16 mill. km	162,000 km	372,000 km
Waterways	41,009 km	138,600 km	14,932 km	5,222 km	1,770 km	0 km	3,200 km
Airports	14,574	206	473	620	167	202	497

Oliver Cromwell—hardly an improvement on the monarchy. The restoration of the Stuart monarchy in the latter part of the seventeenth century was unsuccessful, again because of power struggles between king and Parliament. The Stuart lineage was permanently ended in 1689 when Parliament asked a Dutch ruler, William of Orange, and his wife, the English princess Mary, to take over the English throne.

A condition of the offer of the English throne to William and Mary was that they accept the Bill of Rights passed by Parliament in 1689. This Bill of Rights is another of the "great charters" of British constitutional development. It proclaimed certain important rights related to criminal procedure and freedom of expression. Although they do not have the force or scope that the U.S. Bill of Rights has today, the English Bill of Rights and the Magna Charta are of tremendous historical significance in that they pioneered a tradition of limited government, with rulers constrained in their actions by a compact with the ruled.

Since the eighteenth century, Parliament has been the supreme decision-making body in England. Because of the diminished role of the monarch in England, executive functions are performed by the prime minister and the cabinet ministers, who are generally members of Parliament. One function of the House of Lords in Parliament is to serve as the highest court of appeals. Consequently, there is little of the legal separation of powers between judicial, legislative, and executive functions that we have in the United States. Since the Act of Settlement of 1700, which took the power to appoint judges away from the king, England has had an independent judiciary, with Parliament also retaining the power to remove judges from office.

More recent historical developments in England have also had important effects on the legal and constitutional system. The rise of the British Empire resulted in the export of English law to the colonies. This export led, in turn, to **legal pluralism,** the mixing of more than one system of law within a particular country or region of a country. Colonies retained many of their customary laws and dispute settlement procedures while the English-style courts handled major crimes and civil matters. Thus, the expansion of the empire led to new legal challenges for both colonial legal personnel and legal personnel at home in England, where appeals from colonial courts were generally heard. And the breakup of the empire has led to new challenges relating to rights and citizenship status of former colonial subjects (Glendon, Gordon, and Osakwe, 1985, ch. 7).

Technically, England does not have a written constitution that can be read, cited, and interpreted. It does, however, have a strong constitutional tradition that has evolved over centuries. This phenomenon requires some explanation.

Written constitutions as we know them today are essentially compacts between people and their governments. These compacts describe the governmental machinery, the rights of the people, and the obligations and powers of the government. Such compacts for the governance of large nation-states did not exist until the late eighteenth century. They descend from eighteenth-century Enlightenment thought, which stressed natural rights, reason, and the idea of a "social contract." At that time, constitutions were developed in conjunction with revolutionary movements in the United States and France and reflected attempts to solidify and legitimize new systems that represented radical breaks with the past.

England, perhaps because it did not experience such a radical post-Enlightenment break with the past as France and the United States, has never had a comprehensive compact between government and people. Over the centuries, Parliament, especially its lower house, the House of Commons, has become the supreme decision-making agency in Britain. Although there are few formal governmental checks on this parliamentary supremacy, the weight of tradition and a sense of practical limits governs parliamentary exercise of power. The so-called Rights of Englishmen, although not set forth in a single document, are as sacred in England as any established rights in countries with written constitutions.

This does not mean there are no concrete elements in the English Constitution. Certain fundamental laws, doctrines, and customs are usually listed as part of this constitution. These are organic laws, great charters, constitutional traditions, and legal procedures, including Common Law and equity procedures.

The organic laws are those laws of Parliament that describe the machinery of government. In the twentieth century, for example, a series of laws known as Parliament Acts gradually reduced the power of the House of Lords, the hereditary upper house of Parliament. Organic laws also govern the electoral process.

The great charters of the English Constitution are those compacts and laws that have become thoroughly entrenched as part of British governmental tradition. These are the Magna Charta of 1215, the Petition of Right of 1628, the Bill of Rights of 1689, and the Act of Settlement of 1701. Although specific provisions of these earlier charters have often been superseded by later declarations, laws, and historical developments, they continue to represent major milestones in English constitutional history.

"English style" constitutional traditions are harder to explain to an outsider. Among other things, they cover relations between the monarch and the rest of the government. The king or queen, for example, always asks the leader of the opposition party to form a new government after a previous government has failed to get a vote of confidence in the House of Commons. Although no law requires this action, no monarch would fail to respect the tradition.

Finally, legal procedures, including criminal procedure, evolved within the Common Law as an integral part of the English Constitution. More so than in the United States with its fixed constitutional rights, the rights of the accused in England are subject to revision and have undergone some important changes in recent years.

In sum, English government and the English Constitution consist of a plurality of structures, laws, and customs, tied to certain basic values about representative government and individual rights. Relationships among parts of this whole are often subtle and complex, and the English criminal justice system reflects these complexities. Containing a peculiar mix of amateur and professional elements, it strives to bring justice closer to the people through lay participation at all stages of the process.

Crime

Immigration to England of former colonial subjects has created a problem of minority rights that has had important effects on the crime rate and on the law enforcement community, courts, and prisons in England. Likewise, the unrest in Northern Ireland, caused by a seemingly intractable conflict between Catholics and Protestants, has given rise to a serious problem with terrorism. Terrorism, in turn, has affected the criminal justice process and led to the abridgement of some cherished rights of the accused in recent years. In April 1998, a historic peace agreement was approved in Northern Ireland that, it is hoped, will reduce the violence in that region. Unfortunately, radical groups on both sides have shown some resistance to the peace process, and only with the passage of time will we be able to determine if the peace agreement was a success.

England and Wales have also witnessed the effects of the illegal drug trade. Cocaine from Latin America and heroin from Southwest Asia enter there for distribution to the European market, and a cottage industry has developed for the production of various synthetic drugs. Because of the large number of financial institutions in England, it is also a prime location for money laundering (CIA, 1998).

Crime statistics in England are collected and reported by the Research and Statistics Department of the Home Office. According to recent public opinion surveys in Britain, a quarter of respondents see crime as a major problem. Although the crime rate may be too high for many who live in England and Wales, it is low in comparison to other industrialized countries, especially the United States. In fact, the crime rate in England has declined in recent years: the overall crime rate for the year 1994 was approximately 10,250 crimes per 100,000 population (HEUNI, 1999), and the crime rate per 100,000 population in 1997 was 8,576 (INTERPOL, 1997).

Criminal Law

During the fifth century in England, law developed according to decisions made by judges in individual cases, and the Common Law legal tradition was born. The tradition became stronger after the Norman Conquest in 1066, when judges began to travel around the land ruling on cases as they arose, and these judicial circuit courts survive to the present. However, England and Wales still do not have a unified penal code; rather, the criminal law is a combination of statutes and Common Law practice. Statutes are approved by Parliament, and the Common Law is a body of precedent that has developed over centuries that is written in legal textbooks. The most important offenses, like murder, are under the Common Law, but their penalties are set by statute. Over time, Parliament has codified other Common Law crimes into statutes.

In 1967, Parliament passed the Criminal Law Act, which made all crimes in England and Wales either "arrestable" or "unarrestable" offenses. Arrestable offenses, which include all indictable offenses, are those that a person commits or attempts to commit and that are punishable by a fixed incarceration term—for example, murder, manslaughter, rape, burglary, and assault with intent to rob. All other offenses are nonarrestable, or "summary"; these include drunk and disorderly conduct, loitering, and most traffic offenses. These crimes are generally tried in magistrates' court without a jury. Some summary offenses are more serious in nature, such as carrying a weapon or driving while intoxicated, and thus can be indictable, brought before a higher court, and receive a jury trial.

The Criminal Justice System

England and Wales have a long history of allowing local counties and towns to administer and supervise their own affairs. However, the national government remains very active in the administration of justice, and it retains total control of the judiciary. The lord chancellor, who is appointed by the prime minister and is a member of the cabinet and the House of Lords, appoints all judges and supervises the court system of England.

Keeping order in England is a shared responsibility between the national and local government. The police are accountable to the Home Secretary, who is also a member of the cabinet. The Home Secretary sets standards and provides the majority of funding for the police, who are then administered on the local level. Yet local governments retain the right to hire employees and must financially contribute to maintaining the local office (Terrill, 1999). The prison service is also under the control of the Home Secretary; however, most administrative power is given to the wardens, who are in charge of the daily operations of the institutions.

Criminal justice in England is strongly influenced by decisions made in Parliament. Each year, Parliament enacts laws defining more offenses, and every few years, it develops legislation, called Criminal Justice Acts, that make changes in the system. For example, the Criminal Justice Act of 1991 changed how England deals with sentencing offenders, and more recent acts have impacted the police, courts, and correctional systems (HEUNI, 1999).

A further influence on English criminal justice, as well as on Continental justice, has been the gradual "Europeanization" of the separate nations of Europe. England has become part of the European Union (EU) and is thus responsible for developing economic and human rights policies that fit the goals of that organization. Members of the union must adhere to EU law, which can override English legislation and common law decisions.

FRANCE

Overview

The French Republic, with a population of over 58 million, is divided into twenty-two administrative regions. The French also retain control over eleven regions outside metropolitan France.

France boasts one of the four strongest western European economies, mainly because of its fertile farmland and highly developed industrial sector. In addition to being the leading agricultural producer in western Europe, France also is a major producer of steel, chemicals, electronics, and nuclear power energy. The economy achieved modest gains in the late 1990s, but a high unemployment rate poses a major problem for the French government and people. For a summary of demographic information on France, see Table 4.1; for more detail, refer to Appendix C.

Like England, France is a unitary state that has always prized a highly centralized form of government, in which all major decisions are made through a national bureaucracy situated in the capital city of Paris. Parisians distinguish between Paris and the rest of the country, with the implication that anything that is not Parisian is provincial in the sense of being somewhat backward and lacking in sophistication. France also maintains a strong **republican government** style, in which a president heads the government but the main power remains in the hands of citizens, who vote for representatives who are then responsible to the electorate.

France's twenty-two administrative regions are further divided into ninety-six provinces that act as conduits to the central government. Each province is administered by a **prefect** selected by the government to enforce the laws of the nation. During the presidency of François Mitterand (1981–1995), the government proposed modifying this 200-year-old system of total centralization. Legislation has attempted to decentralize authority, giving a broader range of powers to local elected officials. The prefect still retains general power over law and order, but local governments can now hire their own officials, including police officers (Terrill, 1999).

Unlike England and Wales, which have never clarified their governmental arrangements through a written constitution, France has had fifteen constitutions since 1789. The constitution of the Fifth Republic, formed in 1958, provides for an independently elected president who is the chief of state. Duties of the president include presiding over the cabinet, which is called the **Council of Ministers,** and selecting the prime minister, who is the actual head of the government. Like England and the United States, France has a two-house legislature consisting of the National Assembly (lower chamber) and the Senate (upper chamber). Although the constitution calls for an independent judicial system, France does not have an equivalent of the U.S. Supreme Court to consider the constitutionality of cases. Instead, it has a Constitutional Council that gives advisory opinions about legislation that has been passed but has not yet gone into effect. (This council will be described in greater detail in Chapter 6, in which we consider judicial and constitutional review.)

Historical Developments

In the centuries prior to the 1789 Revolution, France was ruled by a series of Bourbon kings, the most famous of whom was Louis XIV. Under Louis XIV, who ruled from 1643 to 1715 (the same period when England was going through the major upheavals that ended the absolute power of the Stuart monarchs), royal power in France became increasingly strong and centralized. His successors, however, were unable to deal with the economic and social change that characterized the eighteenth century. After borrowing heavily to finance France's wars with England, the monarchy collapsed under the pressure of internal revolutionary forces. King Louis XVI and his wife, Marie Antoinette, were executed in 1792, and the 1790s remained a period of turmoil.

From the standpoint of governmental philosophy, the passage of the Declaration of the Rights of Man and of the Citizen by the French parliament in 1789 was a defining moment in the revolutionary period. The declaration asserted the right to resist oppression, the rights to both liberty and equality, and the need for separation of powers to avoid a tyrannical government. Although not primarily concerned with the administration of justice, three of the seventeen articles addressed this subject. Most importantly, the declaration asserted the right to a presumption of innocence and to freedom from arbitrary detention.

The republican spirit in France was marred by the excesses of the Reign of Terror that followed the Revolution. It was brought to an end by a renewed absolutism, that of Napoleon Bonaparte, a general in the French army who seized power in 1799. Napoleon's dictatorship brought about major changes in the French government, especially the administrative and legal structures. In 1804, Napoleon declared himself emperor, and France became an empire. In that same year, the French Civil Code, or Napoleonic Code (described in Chapter 3), went into effect.

After a series of wars that involved most of western Europe and part of eastern Europe, Napoleon himself met final defeat in 1815 at the Battle of Waterloo. The rest of the nineteenth century was characterized by successive attempts at renewed monarchy, republican governments, and even another empire under a nephew of Napoleon. In 1875, following a period of turmoil that included war with Germany and the revolutionary Paris Commune movement in 1871, France again established a republic. This Third Republic lasted until World War II, although the average life of a ruling parliamentary coalition during that time was only six months. Following the postwar downfall of the Vichy government, which had collaborated with the Germans, the Fourth Republic was established. In 1958, the Fourth Republic gave way to the Fifth Republic, a brainchild of the military and political leader Charles de Gaulle (1890–1970). General de Gaulle became prime minister in June 1958, became president later that year, and remained in office until 1969.

Crime

Like the English, the French must deal with problems related to drugs, terrorism and immigration. With the collapse of its North African colonial empire, France has experienced a large immigration of Arabs from the former colonies of Algeria, Tunisia, and Morocco. Racial tension and cultural conflict have resulted, with attendant problems for law enforcement and judicial operations. France is also a crossroads for terrorist activity, from both internal and external sources. Politically motivated acts of violence are a major concern for citizens, with many of the problems stemming from labor unions protesting government cutbacks of services and benefits. Several violent riots have taken place recently, and attacks on police officers and other public officials are not uncommon.

Drugs are also a major social problem. Like England, France is both a trans-shipment point for and consumer of South American cocaine and Southwest Asian heroin. According to crime statistics from 1993, 17 percent of all crimes and misdemeanors were linked to drugs (Minister of the Interior, 1993).

Crime statistics in France are derived from the Directory of Justice statistics and are called the **Annuaire statistique de la justice.** The total recorded crime rate in France remained relatively stable during the 1990s, with evidence suggesting a slight decline in the overall crime rate. In 1994, the crime rate, according to the UN, was 6,786 per 100,000 (United Nations, 1997). In 1996, it dropped to 6,173 per 100,000 (HEUNI, 1999), and in 1997, to 5,972 (INTERPOL, 1997).

Criminal Law

The basic principles of criminal law in France come from the 1789 Declaration of the Rights of Man and of the Citizen. The first penal code was devised in 1810, but it has been revised many times, most recently in 1992. The penal code distinguishes crimes based on their seriousness, from serious felonies, to less serious felonies and misdemeanors (called delit), to violations (called contraventions). These categories are important because they determine what court the case will be heard in and the kind of punishment that will be implemented.

The French penal code is divided into five books. Book I explains the general provisions in the penal law, including criminal liability and responsibility, lengths of sentences, and kinds of punishments. Book II describes crimes (felonies) and delits (serious misdemeanors) against persons, including crimes against individuals and against human rights. Book III deals with crimes and delits against property. Book IV is devoted to crimes and delits against the nation, the government, and the public order. Book V addresses other crimes and delits not associated with categories included in the other books. The new penal code also distinguishes between completed and attempted acts of crime; addresses recent issues such as corporate crime, alternatives to incarceration, and punishment for serious offenders; and defines new crimes like ecological terrorism, sexual harassment, crimes against humanity, and genocide (Borricand, 1999).

The Criminal Justice System

Through all the political instability of the past 200 years, French administrative structures have provided an element of continuity that has helped hold the country together. The French bureaucracy has a reputation of being extremely powerful, rule bound, and inaccessible. Within criminal justice, particularly in the court system, France has developed a highly sophisticated (and complicated) system of administrative courts to fill in the gaps where the legislature has not functioned well and to deal with relations between citizens and bureaucracy. In short, the administrative courts supervise the government. The two most influential administrative courts are the Constitutional Counsel Court and Council of State.

The Constitutional Counsel Court (Conseil Constitutionnel) reviews legislation proposed by the legislature, prime minister, or president and determines whether it comports with the constitution. The Council of State (Conseil d'Etat) is the supreme administrative court. Originally set up to aid the rulers in their contacts with citizens, it has become a leading advocate of citizens' rights in dealing with the government. The Council of State has been especially valuable since the French Constitution makes no provision for challenging the constitutionality of government action, and only in recent years has the Constitu-

tional Council Court extended its mandate to some cases of human rights abuses.

In addition to administrative courts, France has a number of ordinary courts that deal with civil and criminal law cases, the highest of which is the Supreme Court of Appeals (Cour de Cassation). A unique feature of the French legal system is the unity of the civil and criminal courts—the same court can hear both criminal and civil cases.

The police in France are divided into two bodies. The largest of the two, the Police Nationale, operates under the supervision of the Ministry of the Interior and is responsible for policing any town with a population exceeding 10,000. The Gendarmerie Police, operating under the Ministry of Defense, is responsible for policing towns in rural areas in France with populations under 10,000 persons. Correctional services in France are under the supervision of the Ministry of Justice. (We will discuss the courts, police, and correctional systems in more detail in subsequent chapters.)

It is possible that, in light of the historical and political forces that are present in the country, the criminal justice system in France will change considerably in the next few decades. France historically has had an unstable political environment and has been prone to revolution. Ideological debates over the importance of individual rights versus community interests remain heated, and recent attempts have been made to decentralize governmental authority.

GERMANY

Overview

As of October 1990, Germany includes the formerly separate Federal Republic of Germany (West Germany), German Democratic Republic (East Germany), and the city of Berlin. The formal name of Germany remains the Federal Republic of Germany, or Bundesrepublik Deutschland. Germany is a densely populated country, with over 82 million people occupying an area about the size of California. The country is divided into sixteen states, called **Laender** (singular land), and as discussed in Chapter 3, the Civil Law legal tradition is strongly entrenched.

By any measure, Germany is one of the richest nations of the world, with average per capita income of over $25,000. However, high taxes, high wages, and increasing unemployment have limited the post–World War II growth and caused some economic troubles in Germany. This situation is exacerbated by the task of rebuilding the former East Germany, which costs the Germans roughly $100 billion a year (CIA, 1999b). For a summary of demographic information on Germany, see Table 4.1; for more detailed information, see Appendix C.

Germany is a federal republic in which power is distributed between the federal government and state (Laender) governments. The government contains executive, legislative, and judicial branches, much like the United States. However, the presidency is largely a ceremonial post, and true executive power lies in the hands of the chancellor, who is the leader of the party that gained the largest number of votes in the most recent elections, and his chosen cabinet. Generally, no party wins a majority of seats, so the cabinet is usually a coalition; that is, it contains both members of the chancellor's party and some members of at least one other party that joins with the chancellor's party to create a majority in the legislature.

Germany has a bicameral legislative branch that contains a lower house and principal chamber, known as the **Bundestag,** and an upper house or federal council, called the **Bundesrat.** The Federal Constitutional Court, the **Bundesverfassungsgericht,** stands at the apex of a hierarchy of state and lower federal courts. Half of its judges are elected by the Bundestag, and half by the Bundesrat. (We will discuss the different levels of courts in Germany in Chapter 9.)

Historical Developments

The nation of Germany actually did not exist until 1870, when most of the German states in central Europe were unified in a federation under Emperor William I. Otto von Bismarck, who became chancellor of the new nation, was the architect of German unification. Like Napoleon in France, Bismarck left his imprint on the German administrative apparatus.

During Bismarck's term as chancellor, Germany was experiencing a belated industrial revolution, as well as adjusting to centralized governmental power. Bismarck was careful to involve the German nobility in administration at the state level even as he was consolidating policymaking power at the central level. The culture of a strong, elite civil service that was established through these actions survives to this day in Germany. This civil service includes the personnel of all police, judicial, and sanctioning agencies in Germany.

As we learned in Chapter 3, one of the most important changes in German law in modern times was the German Civil Code, developed under Bismarck. This code of laws helped to consolidate and legitimate the new state.

Imperial Germany lasted only until 1918 when, following its defeat in World War I, a federal republic with a model democratic constitution was established. This republic was known as the Weimar Republic after the city where its constitution was promulgated. The Weimar Republic was short-lived, ending with the ascent to power of Adolf Hitler and his National Socialist, or Nazi, party in 1933. The Nazis abolished federalism and made Germany a centralized, absolutist, and essentially arbitrary and lawless state.

Hitler restored Germany's economic and military strength, but his nationalist themes and aggressive policies, most notably the attempt to eliminate the Jewish population in Europe, led Germany into World War II. The war led to the political and economic destruction of Germany, which surrendered unconditionally in May 1945. At the Yalta Conference in 1945, Germany was split among the "big three" allies of the war: the United States, Britain, and the Soviet Union. Soviet forces assumed control over the eastern half of Germany while the western half came under the supervision of Britain and the United States.

The city of Berlin, although it was within the Soviet territory, also was divided up among the three powers. This situation remained until October 1990, when the nation of Germany was reunited after forty-five years of postwar division.

The former East Germany was a Communist state, with a Socialist Law orientation. Since reunification, the nation has operated under the constitution of the former West Germany. This constitution, called the Basic Law, was first promulgated in May 1949.

The constitution's framers tried to avoid some of the weaknesses of the earlier constitution that made the Weimar Republic unstable and unable to deal effectively with radical opposition. One of the changes was the establishment of a lawmaking constitutional court, such as exists in the United States, to settle disputes and establish the parameters of power between state and federal governments and between the government and the people. The Basic Law, which contains 146 articles, describes the composition and functions of the various organs of government including the system of checks and balances, the distribution of power between the federal government and Laender, the administration of federal law, government finances, and government administration in emergency conditions. The first seventeen articles spell out the rights of Germans. Some of these rights are familiar, such as freedom of religion, freedom of speech and press, and freedom from unreasonable searches and seizures. Other rights, such as the right to "free development of . . . personality," the provision of special state protection for families and illegitimate children, and the right to choose one's own trade or profession, are different from the rights enumerated in the U.S. Constitution, although they are certainly amenable to interpretation as being implied in the Bill of Rights.

Crime

A perusal of crime statistics for Germany shows that in the first few years following reunification the country experienced a sharp increase in crime. Between 1990 and 1994, the total number of persons prosecuted for crimes increased from 576,338 to 637,531. However, toward the end of the decade, there was a drop in, or at least a leveling off of, the crime rate in Germany. According to INTERPOL, in 1994, the overall crime rate per 100,000 population was 8,030.6 (HEUNI, 1999). In 1997, the same agency reported the relatively unchanged rate at 8,030.7 per 100,000 population (INTERPOL, 1997).

By international standards, Germany appears to have a very low rate of burglary, an average rate of petty crimes, and a high rate of offenses related to motor vehicle theft (HEUNI, 1999). As in much of the Western world, drug offenses have become a major problem in Germany, and they account for the significant increase in the incarceration rate since 1991. Germany is a source of chemicals for South American cocaine processors and a trans-shipment point for and consumer of Southwest Asian heroin and hashish, Latin American cocaine, and European-produced synthetic drugs (CIA, 1999b).

In addition to the problem of drugs and crime, the extensive immigration from bordering countries, the integration of Germans from the east, and related ethnic violence are three of the most important contemporary influences on the criminal justice system in Germany.

Immigrants from the former Yugoslavia, Greece, Italy, and Turkey, as well as a new wave of ethnic German immigrants from neighboring countries, have strained the German capacity to assimilate new people. The attendant problems of economic disparity, culture clash, discrimination, and even overt racism are creating cleavages in the formerly homogeneous German society, and these problems carry over into the criminal justice process. Similarly, the integration of former East Germans into a united Germany has created many difficulties for the criminal justice system. One of the most obvious ones is how to educate former East German police, judges, lawyers, and even private citizens about the "new" German laws and democratic principles. Another problem involves the potential for civil unrest and crime arising from the unemployment and social dislocation occurring in the former East Germany. Because of economic uncertainty, some right-wing extremist groups blame the hardships on foreigners. Harassment and violence towards foreigners, conducted by a small minority of Germans, has caused an increase in the incidence of hate crimes in Germany.

We can expect that, as Germany continues to deal with the assimilation of east and west, as well as its role in the changing central Europe, there will be some fluctuation in the rate and nature of crimes committed.

Criminal Law

In earlier times, German criminal law was a combination of Common Law principles and local indigenous law. In the late seventeenth century, criminal law became codified in most territories, and in the late nineteenth century, under Bismarck, a unified criminal code was enacted. This code, called the **Reichsstrafgesetzbuch,** has generally remained in effect despite the many changes that have happened in Germany over the past 125 years. Major reforms in the German criminal code have been implemented on several occasions since the 1960s; the most recent was in 1998, when the criminal code was revised to clarify sanctions for and definitions of violent and property offenses (HEUNI, 1999).

German law is a combination of statutes (Gesetz), ordinances and administrative rules (Rechtsverordnung), and customs (Gewohnheitsrecht). Two kinds of statutes comprise the largest portion of German law. The first, called Bundesgesetz, are federal statutes enacted by the Bundestag. The second are state (Laender) laws, called Landesgesetz, that are enacted by state legislators. Ordinances are issued by the federal government, federal ministers, or state governments. Customs are not formally considered a formal source of law, but for centuries they provided direction in legal matters because they were habitually practiced and informally acknowledged as having the rule of law.

The criminal codes are carefully integrated bodies of general principles arranged in a highly systematized manner and phrased in abstract language. This enables lawyers and judges to liberally apply the principles of the law to assist them in resolving particular cases. Previous court decisions are used not as sources of law, as in Common Law countries, but as guides by lower-court judges, and so they have an influence on legal norms (Herrmann, 1987). The German criminal code distinguishes between felonies and misdemeanors. Felonies (*schwerverechen*) are punishable by imprisonment of at least one year; misdemeanors (*vergehen*) are punishable by a fine or a shorter minimum prison term.

Even though Germany is a federal republic that allows individual Laender to attend to their own criminal court matters, almost all criminal and procedural laws are subject to federal legislation. In practice, this means that federal law is applied to the state courts.

The Criminal Justice System

Because Germany is a federalist country, it generally allows individual Laender to handle their own affairs related to policing, corrections, and lower-court administration. For example, Article 30 of the federal Basic Law provides legal authority for the Laender over police matters within their own territory. However, this does not mean that the Laender may do whatever they please in the administration of justice; rather, their decisions must be legally within the provisions stated in the federal Basic Law. An example may help to clarify this situation. In the Prison Act of 1976, rehabilitation was identified as a major philosophical principle in German penal law and correctional practice. So, even though the individual Laender are allowed to administer their own correctional facilities, they must adhere to the major principles of the Prison Act (Dammer, 1996).

The criminal justice system of Germany reflects the influence of both the Civil Law tradition as it was redefined in imperial Germany and the Common Law tradition as it was applied during the U.S. occupation after World War II. Like the U.S. Supreme Court, the German Federal Constitutional Court has been active in defining the balance of powers between states and the federal government. It also has interpreted the constitutional rights included in the Basic Law. Criminal procedure as practiced in Germany reflects some U.S. influence, but it is still largely a Civil Law process. (Criminal procedure in Germany will be discussed in more detail in Chapter 7.)

CHINA

Overview

China, the third largest country in the world after Russia and Canada, is only slightly larger than the United States with a geographic area of about 3.7 million square miles. As of July 1998, the population of China was over 1.2 billion, which makes it more populous than Europe, Russia, and the United States combined. For a summary of demographic information on China, see Table 4.1; for more detailed information, refer to Appendix C.

China is a unitary, multinational Socialist country with twenty-three provinces (including Taiwan), five autonomous regions (including Tibet), and four municipalities directly under the authority of the central government. The country is also divided into over 450 autonomous prefectures, 458 cities, and 1,904 county and city districts. (Guo et al., 1999).

The primary organs of governmental power in China are the presidency, the State Council, and the **National People's Congress (NPC).** The NPC, theoretically the most powerful, meets annually to review and approve the budget and major new policy directions, laws, and personnel changes. However, in reality, all levels of the Chinese government are subordinate to the Chinese Communist party (CCP), so the real role of government is to implement party policy. For example, all initiatives proposed by the NPC must have been previously endorsed by the CCP's Central Committee.

For thousands of years, China was primarily a peasant-based society. In the years following the Communist takeover in 1949, the government essentially owned all industry and commercial land holdings. Since 1979, China has sought to convert its economy from a Soviet-type centrally planned economy to a Socialist market-based one. What this really means is that China is trying to adapt modern economic practices while retaining the right to oversee policies so they meet Communist ideologies. Reforms have included reducing the role of the government in economic policy, promoting household responsibility in agriculture, increasing the power of local officials in industrial plant management, and introducing small-scale enterprise in the service and light-manufacturing areas. These reforms worked very well into the 1980s, spurring tremendous growth in agricultural and industrial output. However, recent problems with inflation have caused public officials to retighten central controls of the economy. The growth rate of the 1980s has slowed, and unemployment in China has reached 13 million according to official figures, with the real number perhaps twice that number (Fang, 1999, p. 35). With the shift from a purely Socialist to more eclectic economic system, China has encountered some of the problems associated with such a change, including an overall increase in crime.

Historical Developments

The Chinese traditionally have struggled with the formulation of their law and criminal justice system. A succession of dynasties ruled during most of China's 4,000-year-long history with various systems of bureaucratic controls. The last dynasty, the Qing, endured from 1644 through the first decade of the twentieth century. Some of the more enduring written laws and statutes that surfaced during these times were the Yuxing criminal laws of the Xia dynasty, Hanlu laws of the Han dynasty, and the Daquing Luli criminal code of the Qing dynasty. In reality, however, the codes of laws developed during dynastic rule were no more than rules implemented to protect the totalitarian governments in place at the time (Terrill, 1999, p. 564).

Because the concept of equal rights before the law for all persons was absent, disrespect for the law was commonplace, and there was minimal acceptance of any formal codes proposed by the ruling class. What resulted was the adoption of an informal social control system, rooted in Confucian and Taoist thought, that began to take hold in China during the Han dynasty (206 B.C.–A.D. 220).

Confucius (551–479 B.C.) was a philosopher who believed that social order can be achieved through moral and political reforms and that humans are by nature good or capable of goodness. What is essential is that individuals treat one another with kindness and propriety. When individuals act contrary to these virtues, they bring shame to themselves, family and friends. Thus, the idea of "group consciousness" or "collectivity" is the main force motivating people to avoid illegal or immoral activity. In **Confucian thought,** written laws and formal social control may be important, but they are not nearly as important as strong individual moral virtue. As Confucius stated, "The superior man is concerned with virtue; the inferior man is concerned with law" (Confucius, 1989).

Taoist philosophy, which was developed in Asia a century after the introduction of Confucianism, proposed that all forces of nature are connected and that it is necessary for individuals to become "one" with those forces. If a person is in a state of "harmony" or "oneness" with nature, then conflict will cease to exist. Together, Confucian and Taoist thought have permeated Chinese society, with the goal of getting citizens to be in consonance with those around them, to be in harmony with others and the rules of society. It was believed that the best way to accomplish this was through social persuasion and informal social control. Informal social control mechanisms include family members, neighbors, and fellow workers, as well as local town, city, or countywide boards that point out deviant behavior and provide sanctions.

Within the ideals of Confucian and Taoist thought, the Chinese have often rejected legal-

ism, and relied on mediation and compromise to settle disputes and conflict. In fact, under Confucianism, people were discouraged from using litigation to protect themselves or their rights.

For thousands of years, this informal system of social control dominated in China's vast regions. Between 1911 and 1949, the democratic Kuomintang regime attempted to install a legal system rooted in six basic written laws. However, efforts to formalize the legal system were often subverted by civil unrest, invasions from Japan, and continuing political chaos.

The mentality of distrust of formal law also continued into the twentieth century, serving as a catalyst for the reconstruction of the law and social order under the Communist party of the People's Republic of China. From 1949 through 1979, the Chinese government developed a Soviet-style criminal justice system with overall control in the hands of the Communist party. Meanwhile, all formal criminal law codes were rejected, and all forms of written codes of law were eliminated. Instead, a series of edicts, rules, and regulations based on the ideals of the ruling party were used to control behavior and punish deviance. These documents were highly politicized, based as they were on the edicts of the CCP. The goal of the Communist law was to destroy economic classes and construct a social order based on the rule of the people rather than the rule of law. The belief was that formal written laws served only those in power and the bureaucracy, which was abhorred by Chairman Mao (1893–1976) and the Communist party.

However, a shift away from total acceptance of unwritten codes and informal social control mechanisms occurred as a result of a series of events that began in 1966. In that year, Mao tried to reform the party, which he saw as becoming "old in thought, culture, customs and habits." This "reform" period, called the **Cultural Revolution,** lasted until 1976. Mao and his followers encouraged direct opposition to those in power—most notably, the police and any person who was considered "bourgeois"—and bands of young supporters called the Red Guard were formed to implement and oversee the reform policies. The goal was to move Chinese society from socialism to a purer form of communism.

But the Cultural Revolution was a significant failure. Economic, political, and social institutions were seriously disrupted throughout China. The police, procuracy, and courts were often simply handed over to political activist organizations as tools to harass and arrest those opposed to Mao and his followers. The public order was disrupted, and crime and violence became so prevalent that the army was called in to restore order. By 1976, the year Chairman Mao died, the government was able to declaw supporters of the Cultural Revolution and bring some semblance of order to China.

Under the leadership of Deng Xiaoping (1904–1997), the government sought to promote law as part of an ordered society, in contrast to the chaotic environment of the Cultural Revolution (Lawyer's Committee, 1994, p. 5). Under Xiaoping, the Chinese changed from their previous ideals of the "rule of man" to the principles of the "rule of law." The movement toward a more formal legal system with codified laws was also necessary to Xiaoping's goal of modernizing the economy and increasing contact with the outside world.

Crime

It is difficult to assess crime in China because, for the first thirty-eight years of Communist rule, crime statistics were rarely available and even less reliable. In 1987, the Ministry of Public Security presented the first set of "official" crime statistics in the *China Law Yearbook* (Guo et al., 1999). These data revealed that in the early 1980s the country experienced its first "crime wave"; in 1980, the overall crime rate was reported to be 77.2 per 100,000 population. In response to the problem, the government initiated a new crime policy that dealt harshly with street crime such as theft, robbery, drug violations, and prostitution. Law enforcement officials were allowed to implement sharp strikes against certain types of crimes,

the death penalty was made available for more offenses, and the rights of criminals were curtailed to make it easier to arrest, detain, and prosecute.

In the short run, these policies seemed to work. By 1985, the overall crime rate had dropped to 49.7 per 100,000 population. However, the decrease was short-lived as, in 1990, the crime rate rose to a new high of 200 per 100,000 (Ma, 1995). While some of the crime increase has occurred in the areas of juvenile and violent crime, a considerable amount of illegal activity is directly linked to organized crime and drug trafficking. Organized crime in China has flourished since the modernization of the economy in the 1980s; activities include selling guns, smuggling, gambling, prostitution, and drug trafficking. Drug abuse and drug trafficking in general have increased since the late 1970s, with China a major trans-shipment point for heroin produced in the Golden Triangle region of Thailand, Laos, and Burma.

There has been considerable speculation as to why the crime rate has increased in China. As the cities have become crowded with people who migrated from rural areas looking for work, there has been a diminished capacity for social control. In some cases, individuals have turned to crime because they are frustrated that they cannot obtain the wealth and prosperity of others around them (Ma, 1995). Many people in China, especially the young, have grown cynical about the politics of the Communist party while becoming infatuated with capitalism and the idea of individual wealth (Rojek, 1996). Apparently, the economic and social changes in China have inculcated Chinese society with the Western ideals of individualism, independence, and self-assertiveness—traits that are in conflict with the Confucian ideals of collectivism, conformity, and self-restraint.

Over the past decade, the Chinese government has tried to combine strict law enforcement and punishment with preventive measures to reduce the crime rate in the country. Harsh sentences have been implemented for violent crimes and drug offenses. In addition, neighborhood watch committees report suspicious activities to police, mediation committees deal with civil disputes to prevent assaults or homicides, and security committees in the workplace work with police to reduce theft and fraud. The government has also worked to educate citizens on different facets of law and to develop offender rehabilitation programs that focus on educational and vocational needs (Ma, 1995). In 1997, the overall crime rate in China decreased to 133.82 per 100,000 population (INTERPOL, 1997). Thus, the combined efforts of crime control and rehabilitation seem to have helped stabilize the crime situation in China. As we enter the twenty-first century, it will be interesting to see how China deals with economic and political turmoil and the social problems associated with change.

Criminal Law

In 1979, the Second Session of the Fifth National People's Congress adopted codes of criminal law and procedure, as well as other laws. The criminal law, which took effect in January 1980, consisted of 192 articles divided into two sections—general (*zongze*) and special (*fenze*) provisions. The general provisions gave the basic principles underlying the application of the criminal law. The specific provisions included chapters addressing eight classes of offenses: (1) counterrevolutionary offenses, (2) offenses endangering public security, (3) offenses against Socialist economic order, (4) offenses infringing upon the personal and economic rights of citizens, (5) offenses of encroachment of property, (6) offenses against public order, (7) offenses against marriage and the family, and (8) dereliction of duty and corruption (Lawyers Committee, 1998).

In March 1997, the criminal law of the People's Republic of China received a major overhaul. The new law is significantly larger than the old law, with 452 versus 192 articles, and in general is broader in coverage and contains more specific definitions of crimes. An attempt has also been made to unify the criminal law, depoliticize the correctional system, and lessen discretion for officials (Lawyers Committee, 1998). Additional

efforts have been made to modernize and professionalize lawyers, judges, and prison personnel.

At first glance, it might seem that the Chinese government is "softening" to the idea of increased individual rights for citizens. However, the law still neglects to include provisions for some basic human rights enjoyed by citizens in many other countries, such as freedom of speech and freedom of association. The impact of the new criminal and procedural laws will only be determined over time. And even with the new emphasis on the rule of law in China, the Communist party remains the major decision-making body in China, and the government is still unrestrained by the rules of law—unlike the situation in most Civil and Common Law legal systems.

The Criminal Justice System

China's centrally monitored criminal justice system has four components: police, procuratorate, courts, and corrections. Each operates under the guidance of its respective national agency while maintaining offices on numerous levels, including provinces, regions, prefectures, counties, and municipalities.

The Ministry of Public Security is responsible for the police, while the correctional system is under the direct supervision of the Ministry of Justice. The courts are hierarchically organized; the highest court is the Supreme People's Court of China, which deals with matters of national importance, while most criminal cases are dealt with at the county level under the auspices of the Basic People's Court. The procuratorate, directed by the Supreme People's Procurate, is responsible for supervising criminal justice throughout the country, including investigating and prosecuting crimes and overseeing the courts, police, and correctional facilities (Jiahong and Waltz, 1995).

In theory, the Chinese criminal justice system has a built-in system of checks and balances to curb abuses of power. Arrests by police are approved by the local procurators, and prosecution can be deemed unnecessary by the courts. However, in practice, the courts and procuratorate are typically in collaboration with local political leaders and will generally operate to meet the ideals of the Communist party.

In addition to the formal system outlined here, China operates an extensive informal system of justice. This informal system supplements the formal system with political, economic, educational, cultural, and judicial methods to help keep social order. Informal justice in China depends on different county and municipal agencies acting as social control agents, including neighborhood public security committees, people's mediation committees, and the numerous security departments within businesses, schools, and public agencies (Situ and Liu, 1996). (We will discuss more about Chinese informal social control mechanisms in Chapter 10.)

JAPAN

Overview

Japan is slightly smaller in area than California but has a population of almost 126 million. The country is divided into forty-seven administrative divisions, called **prefectures.** Japan is one of the most homogeneous countries in the world, with over 99 percent of the people being native Japanese. And it is actually the only non-Western industrial giant in the world. Excellent government-industry cooperation, a strong work ethic, mastery of high technology, and a small defense budget have enabled Japan in the years following World War II to become the second most powerful economy in the world. Its industries are among the world's largest and most technologically advanced. From the 1960s through the 1980s, the country was a model for other capitalist economies. However, during the early 1990s, the economy slowed considerably, and a recession has further dulled the enthusiasm of investors at home and abroad (CIA, 1999a). For a summary of demographic information on Japan, see Table 4.1; for more detailed information, see Appendix B.

Japanese society, government, and legal processes present an interesting mixture of Eastern and Western ideas and institutions. There is still something of the tribal—secret and closed—in Japanese society that makes this modern, highly industrialized, and wealthy nation seem rather mysterious to outsiders. The Japanese language itself, one of the most difficult in the world to speak and write fluently, constitutes a barrier to communication with outsiders. And the 264 years of self-imposed isolation from foreign influences during the time of the Tokugawa shoguns (1603–1867) seem to have fostered a suspicion of outsiders that continues to this day. However, observers are struck by the ability of the Japanese to integrate both Western technology and Western industrial culture with typically Japanese behavior patterns and values.

The Japanese legal tradition is modeled after the European Civil Law, but it is influenced by English-American legal traditions as well. The U.S. occupation of Japan after World War II resulted in a new constitution that mandated three branches of government. Legislative government in Japan is based on a bicameral (two-house) legislature called the **Diet,** which includes a House of Representatives and a House of Councillors. An executive branch consists of the prime minister, a cabinet that is appointed by the prime minister, and a hereditary emperor. Because the emperorship is primarily a ceremonial position, Japan is technically a constitutional monarchy. The judicial branch is headed by a Supreme Court whose members are appointed by the cabinet.

Like France and Britain, Japan is a unitary state; that is, it does not have a federal system of government with division of powers between states and the federal government. Most of the forty-seven prefectures depend on the central government for financial subsidies.

Historical Developments

An important peculiarity of Japanese history is the period of isolation from other cultures that started in 1603 and lasted until 1867. During that time, the warlord (shogun) family of the Tokugawas ruled Japan from what is now Tokyo. **Shoguns** were military leaders who exercised absolute rule in Japan. The emperors, who lived in the holy city of Kyoto, were venerated as deities but had little real power.

The Tokugawa shoguns, alarmed by the increasing influence on Japanese society of missionaries and traders from the West, closed the entire country to outsiders during these years. They allowed only a small amount of trade with Dutch merchants in the port of Nagasaki, and missionary efforts to penetrate Japanese society were ruthlessly suppressed. Thus, at a time when other countries were going through a major period of exploration, invention, and international interchanges, Japan was entering a period of introspection and cultural inertia.

Prior to this time of isolation from foreign influence, Chinese civilization represented the major external influence on the Japanese. Much of Japanese civilization today, including the writing, the Buddhist religion, and general social values, is adapted from the Chinese. The Chinese influence was even greater in the years before Western ideas were introduced into Japan.

The years of isolation allowed for a strengthening and consolidation of Japanese culture and mores that would keep the culture distinct even after outside ideas began to penetrate the country. The period during which Japan was opened to Western ideas and trade was called the Meiji Restoration, named after the emperor at that time. Meiji was the winner in a power struggle with the last of the Tokugawa shoguns, and the imperial family ostensibly resumed the leadership of Japan that it had relinquished about a thousand years earlier. In reality, however, a military junta ruled Japan in the twentieth century until the end of World War II, with the emperor serving as a father figure and national idol but hardly a strong ruler.

Following Japan's defeat of Russia in the Russo-Japanese War of 1904–5, Japan became increasingly imperialistic and militaristic, hoping to establish Japanese hegemony over all of East and Southeast Asia. Japan's defeat in World War II brought about a major change in Japanese government and society. Japan lost all of its overseas possessions, and the victorious Allies gained full control of the government. Only with the 1972 reversion of the island of Okinawa to Japanese control were the full powers of governing returned to Japan. Since World War II, industrial development has replaced militarism as the chief driving force in the new Japan.

Japan's new constitution, called the Showa Constitution, which took effect in May 1947, is modeled after the U.S. Constitution and mandates a parliamentary system similar to Great Britain's. It includes a bill of rights similar to that in the United States and provides for a Supreme Court with the right of judicial review.

Crime

By any standard, crime rates in Japan are remarkably low compared to crime rates in other industrial countries. There are many cultural reasons Japan has such a low crime rate, and much has been written on the subject (see, e.g., Bayley, 1996). However, understanding Japanese culture and the effect it has on crime and criminal justice is not an easy task. Japanese culture has many subtleties and contradictory elements that make it difficult for outsiders to understand.

The Japanese have traditionally valued harmony, group ideals, and conformity as opposed to individualism and individual rights. These attitudes and behaviors impact the system in many ways. For example, because of the value of harmony, bringing legal action against a neighbor is frowned upon. People from the United States, who are accustomed to the use of litigation as a way to redress grievances—and, indeed, who are often accused of excessive litigiousness—would find this peculiar.

While group values and group cohesion remain paramount in Japanese social life, they often are at the expense of individual expression or self-development (Nakone, 1973). Authority and status relationships are complex and important. Despite this fact, Japanese society in general does not have the strong social class or wealth distinctions that one finds in many Western societies, including those of the United States, England, and France. Some people locate the roots of modern

Japanese culture in village life during the Tokugawa years or even earlier. In these villages, grounded in a rice culture, people were forced to work together for the good of the community and were not permitted to seek their fortunes elsewhere. Outsiders were regarded with suspicion.

The Japanese emphasis on harmonious and nonconflictual relationships is also reflected both in private industry, where unions are seen as a cooperative force for industrial development, and in government, where the ruling Liberal Democratic party has been the only party to hold office in the postwar years. Employees in particular industries often wear a "uniform" that distinguishes them from outsiders. The kimono itself, the Japanese national garment, tends to envelop people in a uniform way and does not require separate sizes, since all adults fit into adult-size kimonos. In such a society, the pressure to conform rather than to stand out is overwhelming.

According to Robert Bellah (1985), another strong social value of the Japanese is particularistic loyalty, whereby loyalty to specific leaders becomes almost a religious ritual. The old Japanese folk tale of Chushingura epitomizes this kind of loyalty. In this story, Lord Asano, who is publicly humiliated by Lord Kira, draws a sword on the latter in the shogun's palace. Because of this illegal act, he is forced to commit ritual suicide. His forty-nine followers, known as ronin, or masterless lords, decide to avenge him by killing Kira. After a series of adventures, the group finally succeeds in its plot to kill Kira. Because of this murder, all forty-nine of the ronin are ordered to kill themselves. The devotion of the forty-nine retainers to their lord is a prime example of the virtue of loyalty to one's lord or superior in Japanese society.

Japanese society is also bound by important rules of propriety regarding the proper relationships among individuals, including father-son, nephew-uncle, husband-wife, and merchant-customer relationships. These are usually hierarchical relationships that involve rituals of deference reflected in the Japanese language itself. All of these linguistic and social conventions create a certain formality in Japanese life and make it difficult for outsiders to penetrate the society.

Loyalty to one's superior and its corollary, a certain paternalism toward inferiors, as well as strong group identities, suggest that Japanese society, despite its advanced technological and educational status, retains some feudal characteristics. For example, harmony, conformity, and loyalty are feudal characteristics that contribute in a relatively benign fashion to a cohesive and homogeneous culture void of serious crime problems. Additional factors that may contribute to the low crime rate include a low unemployment rate, lack of urban ghettos, a strong family structure, and strict gun control laws.

Keep in mind, however, that the low crime rate comes with concomitant social costs. One could argue that a darker side of this culture is manifested in the suppression of individuality, subordination of women, and suspicion of non-Japanese people—even those who have lived in Japan for generations. In addition, Japanese society is changing, just as other modern societies are changing, and generalizations based on cultural patterns of even a few decades ago may not be as relevant today. These changes are reflected in the increasing crime rates and crime problems in Japan.

Crime statistics in Japan are compiled by individual criminal justice agencies and then summarized by the Ministry of Justice into a statistical yearbook called the *White Paper on Crime.* Between 1950 and 1975, the Japanese crime rate dropped from around 1,900 per 100,000 population to as low as 1,100 per 100,000 (Reichel, 1999). Since 1975, however, there has been a steady increase in the total crime rate, with a rate of 1,750 per 100,000 as of 1997 (INTERPOL, 1997). In comparison, the United States experienced an overall crime rate increase from 1,900 per 100,000 population in 1950 to over 5,200 per 100,000 in 1975 and remained at around 5,100 per 100,000 in 1997 (Schmalleger, 1999, p. 42).

Two types of crimes that seem to be especially troubling to the Japanese people are drug crimes and organized crime. The rate of drug crimes per

100,000 people increased from 17.8 in 1990 to 23.1 in 1997 (INTERPOL, 1997), with many of the drug arrests attributed to visitors to Japan. The main form of drug abuse in Japan is the use of amphetamines imported from other Asian countries. Unlike in the United States and western Europe, the illegal sale and use of other kinds of drugs, such as cocaine and heroin, has not reached serious proportions in Japan.

Organized crime, or **Boryokudan** in Japanese, is the number-one crime problem in Japan and the main reason for crime increases in recent years. Organized crime groups are heavily involved in the production and distribution of amphetamines and in a plethora of other illegal activities. Their activities include extensive and violent infighting, many violations of gun laws, gambling, loan-sharking, prostitution, and trafficking in guns and human organs (Bayley, 1996).

Criminal Law

Attempts at developing a code of laws in Japan can be traced back as far as A.D. 604 with the Seventeen Maxims of Prince Shotoku, and in the 700s with the Code of Taiho and Code of Yoro (Wilmore, 1936). But since the 1800s, Japan has developed highly structured legal codes that have been influenced by French, German, Chinese, and U.S. law. At the time of the Meiji Restoration in 1868, Japan adapted the French Penal Code for its criminal justice transactions.

In the latter nineteenth century, after the Germans developed their comprehensive civil code, Japan adopted many of the elements of the German code. Even today, the Japanese legal code is predominantly German in character despite the adoption of much of U.S. criminal procedure. Many Japanese legal scholars, especially of the older generation, have spent time studying in Germany.

U.S. law has influenced Japan with respect to constitutional and human rights law. The U.S.-inspired Japanese Constitution, with its listing of constitutional rights and its provision for a Supreme Court to secure these rights, has introduced a new element in Japanese justice, an element that is becoming more influential as time goes on.

Chinese law had the most influence on the Japanese system prior to the closing of Japan in 1603. Much of the subtlety of the Japanese approach to conflict, as well as much of Japanese aversion to formal legal processes, can also be found in Chinese society. The two social orders have much in common despite the fact that the Chinese civilization is more ancient than that of Japan.

The Japanese criminal code actually consists of three integrated codes: (1) the penal code, which defines crimes and punishments; (2) the code of criminal procedure, which sets legal standards for prosecution and sentencing; and (3) prison law, which regulates correctional matters. In many ways, the criminal code articulates many of the same basic principles as in the criminal and prison law code that was developed in 1907.

The penal code itself is divided into two books. The first deals with general provisions such as criminal intent, age of responsibility, and types of sanctions; the second lists the major crimes and the elements of those crimes. Interestingly, the Japanese penal code makes no formal distinction between felonies and misdemeanors, although there is a body of laws that pertain to minor offenses called the Minor Offense Laws. Instead, crimes are divided into three categories: (1) crimes against the state—(e.g., bribery, crimes against the imperial family), (2) crimes against individuals—(e.g., homicide, assault, bodily injury, rape, indecent assault, kidnapping, theft, fraud, robbery, embezzlement) and (3) crimes against society—(e.g., indecent behavior in public, arson, gambling).

The Criminal Justice System

The use of the law or the criminal justice system to settle disputes between individuals in Japan is minimal in comparison to most other countries, especially those with a developed economy and legal structure. In Japan, dispute settlement processes emphasizing compromise, mediation, and consensus are the norm. Further, informal procedures used by police, neighbors, or families are preferred to formal criminal processes for dealing with offenders.

This does not mean, however, that the Japanese lack a formal and organized system of justice. In fact, Japanese criminal justice is largely centralized and in many cases tightly controlled by the national government.

The Ministry of Justice generally oversees the correctional system, including the Prison Bureau, which is the primary agency responsible for juvenile and adult correctional facilities. The courts in Japan are hierarchical in nature, with two appellate courts and two trial courts. The Supreme Court is the highest-level appellate court, right above the high courts. District courts and summary courts are the trial courts, each with jurisdiction in its own prefecture.

The two national police organizations are the National Police Safety Commission (NPSC) and the National Police Agency (NPA). The NPSC makes policy and administers all police affairs, including police education, communications, and criminal statistics. The NPA actually runs the police through the **prefectural police (PP),** autonomous agencies that carry out police duties within the boundaries of the forty-seven prefectures.

Ultimately, Japanese law and criminal justice is hybrid, having borrowed from the Chinese, the French, the Germans, and the Americans. The final product, however, is peculiarly Japanese and certainly not analogous to any of the systems of origin. Thus, understanding Japanese justice is a real challenge to the student of comparative justice.

SAUDI ARABIA

Overview

Saudi Arabia is mostly uninhabited desert, with a population of approximately 21 million people. Prior to the 1960s, most of the population was nomadic or seminomadic, but due to rapid economic growth and urbanization, most of the population is now settled.

The economy of Saudi Arabia is primarily based on oil. Saudi Arabia has the largest reserves of petroleum in the world and ranks as the world's largest exporter of oil, which accounts for 75 percent of government revenues. The country plays a leading role in the Organization of Petroleum Exporting Countries (OPEC), which regulates the flow and price of oil in the Middle East. Because of its heavy reliance on oil, Saudi Arabia has been highly affected by the fluctuation in oil prices. In the late 1990s, with the increase in the number of oil fields around the world and the general decrease in the demand for oil, the economy faltered and budgetary problems arose. As a result, the Saudi government has begun efforts to diversify the petroleum economy and encourage private economic activity. For a summary of demographic information on Saudi Arabia, see Table 4.1; for more detailed information, see Appendix B.

Thirteen provinces, called mintaqah (singular, minaqat), make up the country's administrative divisions. Each of the provinces is run by a governor who is under the responsibility of the minister of the interior, but in practice, the governors often report directly to the king.

Saudi Arabian government is characterized as a nonconstitutional monarchy. The king is the chief of state and head of government, and he rules with the help of a twenty-five member **Council of Ministers,** chosen by him. The council serves as an advisory panel, assisting the king in bureaucratic and policy matters. Many high officials in Saudi Arabia, including the highest ones in the police and judiciary, are related to the king.

Saudi Arabia is not a democracy, and there is no system of election and representation, so there is no legislative branch. Legislation is enacted by resolution of the Council of Ministers and ratified by royal decree. In 1992, however, the king made some concessions to the westernized elements in his population by providing for a new sixty-member Consultative Council, appointed by him, to advise the cabinet on laws and decrees. The Consultative Council, or **Shura,** is an all-male advisory body with no legislative functions. Its meetings are closed to the public, and members are forbidden to take any documents out of the council offices (Human Rights Watch, 1998). In 1997, the membership of the Shura was expanded from sixty to ninety members.

Historical Developments

The modern nation of Saudi Arabia dates back only to 1926. However, the territory of present-day Saudi Arabia includes the holy cities of Mecca and Medina, where the Prophet Muhammad lived, and thus has been central to Islam ever since its founding in the seventh century A.D. This territory was ruled by Islamic caliphs until the rise of the Ottoman Empire in the thirteenth century. The empire, headquartered in modern Turkey, lasted until the end of World War I, but Islamic Law became much attenuated during the nineteenth century, when Ottoman rulers began to integrate European codes into the legal system.

In the period following World War I, the Arabian peninsula, and indeed most of the Middle East, went through a period of turbulence, with the British, the French, and local hereditary rulers vying for power. The kingdom of Saudi Arabia resulted from the conquest of warring factions by Sheikh Abdul Assiz, with the support of the British. Since his death in 1953, a succession of Saudi kings have ruled the nation.

Prior to the discovery of large oil deposits in 1932 and their major development after World War II, Saudi Arabia was a poor country populated largely by nomadic tribes. Its economy revolved in large part around the pilgrims who traveled to Mecca and Medina, and it spent a good deal of its scarce revenues providing facilities for these pilgrims, restoring the holy places, and protecting them from environmental and human damage.

Oil has been both a blessing and a curse to Saudi Arabia. On the one hand, it has become a rich nation, and its people are extremely prosperous. On the other hand, it has struggled to maintain the degree of Islamic piety that its position in the heart of Islam and its historical legacy demand. The corruption of wealth, the importation of large numbers of foreign workers (not only for the oil fields but also for most hard labor), and the problems attendant upon industrial development have all clashed with Islamic fundamentalism as oil production has come to dominate the economic, social, and even political life of the kingdom. Further, the fields of Saudi Arabia, which produce a large proportion of the world's oil, have become a military target of powerful Middle Eastern rivals.

Because the country is governed according to the Shari'a, there is no separate and formal constitution although some Saudis consider the Qur'an, the holy book of Islam, to be the constitution. In 1993, a document called the Basic Law (*nizam*) was introduced that articulates the government's rights and responsibilities. Although not a formal constitution and lacking some of the basic principles of other nation's constitutions, such as the rights of assembly and diverging religious expression, it fulfills many of the same purposes of such a document.

Crime

It is somewhat difficult to summarize the nature and extent of crime in Saudi Arabia. Ali (1985) and Souryal (1987) identify at least two difficulties in comparing crime statistics for Saudi Arabia with those for other countries. First, crime is often underreported in Saudi crime statistics because the Shari'a promotes informal and nonlegalistic responses to criminal behavior. As a result, less cases are handled by the police and courts (Souryal, 1987). Second, there is the problem of determining crime rates over the course of the calendar year. The Arabic lunar calendar is based on the Islamic year, which has only 354 days rather than the Gregorian standard of 364. This slight difference over time makes crime comparisons problematic (Ali, 1985). In addition, much of what goes on in the area of social policy and government in Saudi Arabia is not always released as public information.

Yet, in spite of the obstacles to measuring crime in Saudi Arabia, we can still state with confidence that it is very low in comparison to most countries. Even in comparison to other Islamic countries, Saudi Arabia has a minuscule crime rate (Souryal, 1987).

Crime statistics compiled by INTERPOL for 1994 revealed that Saudi Arabia had a homicide rate of less than one (0.9) per 100,000 population. Rape, robbery, and auto theft were also rare occurrences in Saudi Arabia, with rates of 0.6, 0.04, and 28.5, respectively. To compare, even Japan, with an extremely low homicide rate of 1.0 and low rape and robbery rates of 1.3 and 2.2, ranked higher.

Drug crimes are not a serious problem in Saudi Arabia although recently there has been some increase in the consumption of heroin and cocaine. Apparently, harsh punishments for drug traffickers, including the death penalty, have helped to control the drug problem.

The reasons for the low crime rates in Saudi Arabia, as in other countries with low rates, are probably related to a combination of factors. In Saudi Arabia, the low crime rate likely reflects the way the Islamic religion, most notably the Shari'a, permeates every aspect of society. The Shari'a prescription of both prosocial behaviors and strict punishments has helped make Saudi Arabia create a "spiritual and peaceful" society (Souryal and Potts, 1994).

Criminal Law

The Saudi government has not published or disseminated a penal code, code of criminal procedure, or code of judicial procedure, and only a limited number of other laws exist in published form. Any legal decision must be made under the auspices of Islamic Law, and all are subject to the approval of government-appointed religious leaders (Human Rights Watch, 1998). Recall from Chapter 3 that the Shari'a is the totality of law that results from the Qur'an, the Sunnah, and other traditional sources from the early centuries of the Muslim faith. Of the four major schools of Islamic jurisprudence that developed at that time, the Hanbali school is the most strict in its efforts to return to pure Qur'anic principles. It is to this school that the Wahhabi sect favored by Sheikh Abdul Assiz adhered, and thus Saudi Arabia's law is based on the Hanbali version of Islamic Law. Under the influence of modern development, for which no clear Hanbali precedent exists, Saudi Arabia allows for some variation on the texts. These variations are based first on the precepts of other schools of Islamic jurisprudence and second on the reasoning of contemporary jurists (Amin, 1985b, p. 314). A Judicial Council, including large elements of religious leaders, reconciles conflicts between traditional Islamic Law and modern requirements. In addition, the king may supplement Shari'a through decrees when conditions require such extension.

Although Islamic Law is the basis for criminal law in Saudi Arabia, commercial transactions are based on laws that were largely put into effect after World War II. In addition, laws regarding civil service, social insurance, mining, labor relations, and various other social and economic issues form part of the whole of Saudi law. A Board of Grievances acts as a supreme administrative court to hear cases against administrative agencies and state officials (Nader, 1990, p. 4).

In each case, the issuance of new codes and royal decrees to meet the challenges of commerce and industry was not undertaken lightly and without concern for reconciliation with Shari'a. When rules for incorporating companies were issued, the Ministry of Commerce and Industry explained in some depth that, although modern development in Saudi Arabia required such rules regarding establishment, dissolution, and conduct of business, these companies were in keeping with the tradition of the Sunnah, in which the Prophet spoke about having partners and allowed companies that existed to continue. Further, according to this directive, "Any such rules or provisions [regarding companies] as were inconsistent with the orthodox Shari'a were excluded, and due regard was given to the various forms of companies established by Muslims in the past" (Amin, 1985b, p. 317). Again, we see the pervasiveness of Shari'a influence in Saudi law.

One of the most difficult aspects of economic development to reconcile with Shari'a is that pertaining to banking. The Qur'an explicitly forbids the charging or paying of interest on money loaned to others. Despite this fact, the Saudis allow traditional banks to exist, and according to some observers, they may avoid the proscription against interest by adding a charge equivalent to interest to financial transactions. However, the Saudis have also developed an Islamic banking system that concentrates on developing aid for the poor through investment (in keeping with the religious duty to devote a portion of one's income to the poor and needy) and providing interest-free loans for various purposes, including the stimulation of agriculture and the building of private homes (Amin, 1985b, pp. 318–319).

Why has Saudi Arabia followed Islamic Law ever since its establishment in 1926, while other Muslim territories at that time adopted a hybrid of European and Islamic Law? To understand this, we need to look at the father of Abdul Assiz, Muhammed ibn Sa'ud. This earlier Saudi sheikh, who ruled in the nineteenth century, came under the influence of a fundamentalist Islamic sect known as the Wahhabis. The Wahhabis were devoted to a return to pure Islamic principles and the purging of Western influences from Islamic society. One of the reasons King Abdul Assiz was so successful in his campaign to unite the Bedouin tribes of the territory and drive out some of the other claimants to the land was his piety and general nobility of character. He lived modestly and adhered strictly to religious practices and principles. Thus, Islam was at the foundation of the modern Saudi state. Since Saudi Arabia does not have representative government, but is ruled by royal decrees of the king and his advisors, the religious hegemony in government is not likely to change without a major upheaval. In any case, the piety of the rulers reflects the strong faith of much of the population (Al-Farsy, 1986).

The Criminal Justice System

Islamic Law as stated in the Shari'a is the basis for all criminal justice functions in Saudi Arabia. The Ministry of Justice presides over the Shari'a-based judicial system. The system is administered according to the Shari'a through religious courts whose judges are appointed by the king on the recommendation of the Supreme Judicial Council, which is composed of twelve senior jurists. The independence of the judiciary is protected by law. The king acts as the highest court of appeal and has the power to pardon.

Saudi Arabian police are also highly centralized. Police are under the authority of the director of public safety, who is supervised by the minister of the interior. The minister controls all police forces throughout the kingdom. Local police are commanded by the provincial governors, who answer to the director of public safety. The correctional system in Saudi Arabia is also under the authority of the director of public safety within the office of the Bureau of Prisons (Murty, Roebuck, and Almolhem, 1991).

As you can see, the Saudi Arabian law and criminal justice system is unique in many ways and cannot be as readily compared to those of England, France, Germany, Japan, or China as those systems can sometimes be compared to one another. Nevertheless, as we proceed, we will see many similarities in institutions and processes among the various countries, including Saudi Arabia.

SUMMARY

Out of a total of 191 independent states in the world, 6 countries may not seem like a very large sample. In addition, this book has not included any information about criminal justice in either Africa or Latin America, both continents that demand further study. Although the nations of Latin America are Civil Law nations and base their legal processes on the traditions of that family, there are variations in style and substance that may make these systems distinctive. In Africa, we find many examples of legal pluralism, in which local customary laws coexist with those derived from the colonial powers that once ruled. The traditional conflict resolution mechanisms are particularly functional in small villages and rural areas. They are a kind of arbitration process that tends to keep minor cases out of the formal, westernized legal system.

A student of comparative law should take the time to explore other criminal justice systems in addition to those covered in this book. The usefulness of those that are included, as explained previously, is that they exemplify broad kinds of legal processes within different cultural settings. Each is a model system that can be used as a reference for comparison with other systems throughout the world.

DISCUSSION QUESTIONS

1. If the English lack a formal constitution, what do they use as a foundation for determining criminal law and criminal justice procedure?

2. In addition to the cultural reasons for the low crime rate in Japan stated in the chapter, can you hypothesize about any other factors that may contribute to the low crime rate in that country?

3. Within each of the six model nations, what particular historical developments may have had a major effect on their formation of criminal law and criminal justice administration?

4. Compare and contrast the model countries, and identify one distinct approach to criminal justice that each of the model countries exemplifies.

5. Review the data in Table 4.1 and in Appendix B. What demographic characteristics help to explain the crime rates in the model countries? Then compare your findings with data about the United States. Do you find any significant differences that would account for the high crime rate in the United States?

FOR FURTHER READING

Barclay, G. (1995). *The Criminal Justice System in England and Wales,* 3rd ed. Croydon, U.K.: Home Office Research and Statistics Department.

Dando, S. (1997). *The Criminal Law of Japan: The General Part,* Vol. 19. Littleton, Colo.: Rothman.

Knapton, E. (1971). *France: An Interpretive History.* New York: Scribner.

Lawyers Committee. (1994). *Criminal Justice with Chinese Characteristics.* New York: Lawyers Committee.

Merryman, J. H. (1985). *The Civil Law Tradition,* 2nd ed. Stanford, Calif.: Stanford University Press.

Moore, R. (1996). Islamic Legal Systems: Traditional (Saudi Arabia), Contemporary (Bahrain), and Evolving (Pakistan). In C. B. Fields and R. H. Moore, Jr. (eds.), *Comparative Criminal Justice: Traditional and Nontraditional Systems of Law and Control.* Ill.: Waveland Press.

Westerman, T., and J. Burfeind. (1991). *Crime and Justice in Two Societies: Japan and the United States.* Pacific Grove, Calif.: Brooks/Cole.

Part II $\sim$ # Criminal Justice Processes

5 # Law Enforcement: Functions, Organization, and Community Involvement

Functions of Police
Policing in Model Countries
Community Policing and Its
    Implementation in Model Countries
International Police Cooperation
Summary
Discussion Questions and Exercises
For Further Reading

Key Terms and Concepts

Bereitschaftspolizei (Bepo)
chusai-san
chuzaisho
community policing
civil order control
deviance control
Gendarmerie Nationale (GN)
kidotai
koban
Kontachbereichsbeamter (KoB)
Kriminalpolizei (Kripo)

mubahith
mutawa
National Police Agency (NPA)
Police Authority Board
Police Nationale (PN)
prefectural police
Public Security police
residents' committees
Schutzpolizei (Schupo)
Ujama

"A policeman's lot is not a happy one," sings a chorus of English constables in Gilbert and Sullivan's comic opera *The Pirates of Penzance*. These particular constables, a kindly if rather cowardly and unintelligent band, are filled with sympathy for the felons and other wrongdoers whom they encounter. They hate having to cause them grief in the course of carrying out their "constabulary duties," as they refer to their work. In some ways, Gilbert and Sullivan's constables reflect the image that English people were said to have of their police in the latter nineteenth century: well meaning, earnest, and not overly bright.

While most modern police officers do not have the same problem with their work as these legendary constables, there is no doubt that the police officer's lot today is not an easy one. Police are asked to perform a variety of functions: crime prevention, apprehension of lawbreakers, riot control, community service, and protection against internal security threats. Particular police organizations may perform one or more of these functions; few do them all.

The term *police* is derived from the Greek word *polis,* which in ancient Greece was used to describe the group responsible for maintaining health, safety, and order in the community. Later, the Romans redefined the police into an authoritative arm for those in power.

Police must be both responsible and responsive. That is, they should be true to the law and at the same time adaptable to the needs of the public they serve. We must remember that police work is at the threshold of the criminal process and that it may determine whether justice is done in a particular case. Rules of criminal procedure often govern encounters between police and citizens who are suspected or accused of crime.

The police task is particularly difficult in a democracy, in which the two mandates of responsibility and responsiveness may be contradictory in certain situations. In times of prosperity and peace, however, this task is immeasurably easier than in times of tension, conflict, and civil disorder. In difficult times, the police tend to become the focus of public discontent. They begin to see themselves as victims, and confrontations between police and citizens become surrogates for confrontations between government and dissidents.

In nondemocratic societies, police are expected to be responsive chiefly to the ruling elite. The degree to which they are also law-abiding and responsive to the public depends on the nature of that ruling elite. Examples of this kind of policing can be found in our model countries of the People's Republic of China and, in some respects, Saudi Arabia.

In all societies, policing is the most basic function that a government performs to make community life tolerable. At the same time, it is the most problematic function, in that police have both the power and the obligation to respond with force if the occasion requires. This power to use force in the name of the government raises critical questions about police discretion and oversight of police operations by nonpolice institutions. No legitimate government can allow misuse of power by a rogue police organization to continue unchecked.

In this chapter, we examine police functions, organizational structures, interactions with the community and issues related to professionalism. The emphasis is on the arrangements that police departments make to deal with both deviance control and maintenance of civil order. This emphasis reflects the importance that many nations place on police arrangements to control civil disorder. As we look at the police structures of the six model nations, we will begin to evaluate how they respond to the needs of modern societies for responsible and responsive police agencies. We will see that particular police structures have developed in different countries in response to historical developments and political needs.

FUNCTIONS OF POLICE

Police perform two major functions, or tasks, in modern societies; (1) deviance control and (2) civil order control. Both of these functions are necessary to ensure that people feel secure and able to carry out their everyday business without fear and major disruption. Indeed, failure to perform either one of these functions means that a society is not adhering to the most basic tenet of the social contract: avoiding the predatory relations that would exist in a "state of nature."

Deviance Control

Deviance control refers to the police mission to reinforce community values and laws and typically involves several tasks. Police personnel must protect citizens against lawbreakers. In addition, the police seek to discourage alarming or threatening behavior that tends to make people uneasy or insecure. They must also ensure that people can move around freely and exercise their various rights as citizens without fear, harassment, or undue impediments. For example, police are carrying out this mission when they work with troubled juveniles or remove drunks from the streets.

This function is profoundly conservative in nature, protecting the community against nonconformists and trying to keep violators of community norms under control. Community service and community contact may be a part of this function of reinforcing community values and discouraging criminal or other deviant behavior.

Civil Order Control

Civil order control activities are also an important aspect of the police function in any society, although they are often performed by agencies other than the police or by specialized units within police forces. **Civil order control** differs from deviance control in that there often is a strong political component to the activities being controlled—actions that disturb the civil order may be extremely threatening to a government. There is always the possibility that police will overreact to or exacerbate the situation. Police may end up being adversaries of the citizens rather than part of the citizenry, and this can be a very uncomfortable role.

Training police for minimal use of force in confrontations with citizens is truly of a different order of complexity than is training them for conventional police work of law enforcement and order maintenance. For these reasons, there is international interest in civil order control and maintenance, and efforts have been made to convene police leaders from different parts of the world to discuss and learn about civil order control. For example, in July 1999, representatives from twenty countries met in Hyderabad, India, to exchange ideas about how to handle public disorder (Kratcoski, 1999).

The Functional Organization of Police Forces

It must be emphasized that, when we discuss civil order control, we are not talking about the kind of police forces that are established as personal armies for authoritarian leaders and that have few qualms about ruthless suppression of dissent in their societies. Such forces, while still too common in the world today, cannot be classified as modern police agencies in the sense that we describe others in this book.

The two police functions—deviance control and civil order control—require different kinds of training and even different kinds of organizational arrangements to be effective. Finding some kind of organization that can perform both tasks optimally is a major challenge for police departments in modern societies.

In performing deviance control activities, police officers act by themselves or in pairs, generally unsupervised at the street level. They have to make important decisions about tactics, community needs, levels of enforcement, and priorities in dealing with the many duties they perform. The "military model" of organization may not be optimal in such work.

In performing civil order control work, however, police use paramilitary formations, moving in troops and obeying the orders of a field commander. Close control of police action becomes necessary both for handling volatile confrontations with citizens and for coordinating actions in various locations. Nevertheless, police must not adopt a purely military attitude, since their chief function is to protect people, not to kill them.

One of the first things the student of comparative law enforcement must do is examine the basic organizational structures in each nation. And one of the first questions to ask is: What arrangements are in place for dealing with the two major police functions? This basic information provides the groundwork for asking further important questions regarding organization and operations: How democratic is the organization? How militaristic is it? What kinds of individuals become police officers, and how are they recruited and trained? How accountable are the police to the public?

David Bayley tells us that "the structures of national police systems display remarkable permanence over time" (1985, p. 60). We will find that actual organizational arrangements, despite extensive modern reform efforts, reflect historical developments in particular nations. Nevertheless, new generations of police have had to adapt their organizations to meet modern challenges, especially with regard to human rights issues and technological changes.

POLICING IN THE MODEL COUNTRIES

Modern police forces generally organize to accomplish the functions of civil order control and deviance control in one of two ways. By far the most common arrangement is to have these functions performed by different divisions within the larger organization. Among our model countries, this is the arrangement favored by Germany, France, China, Japan, and Saudi Arabia. By contrast, in England and the United States, civil order control is not organizationally separated from deviance control but is performed by regular street police. Military units may also be used in extreme cases on an ad hoc basis. Although no democratic country wants to use its military to maintain

order internally, the military remains the last resort in a civil order crisis in any country.

Countries like France and Germany that separate the functions organizationally differ among themselves with respect to these arrangements. These differences reflect particular historical developments. Even countries with separate civil order control divisions have had limited success in creating structures that reconcile disparate organizational needs and at the same time are both responsible and responsive. None of the model countries has been truly satisfied with its own success in dealing with the major problems of student uprisings and other civil order control crises that have occurred in recent decades.

A look at the basic police organization in our model countries will illustrate these various points. As a general frame of reference, Table 5.1 lists the police per 100,000 population in our model countries; Table 5.2 summarizes the amount of training, variations in training, and police qualifications in these countries.

England

The modern English police force dates back to 1829, when the prime minister, Sir Robert Peel, urged Parliament to establish the London Metropolitan Police. Previously, because of the general British repugnance toward the idea of a police agency (such as existed in France) that might be used by the government to stifle dissent, Parliament had refused to set up a police agency.

Table 5.1 Police per 100,000 Population, 1994

England and Wales	346.69
France	349.28
Germany	311.91
China	74.0[a]
Japan	207.62
Saudi Arabia	n/a
United States	300.06

[a]1990 figure.

SOURCE: *Global Report*, 1999, p. 124; Ministry of Public Security, 1994.

Table 5.2 Police Standards in the Model Countries

Country	Amount of Training	Type of Training	Qualifications
England	2 years	Classroom, field, and physical fitness training	Unavailable
China	6 months	Unavailable	High school or college, at least 25 years old
Germany	Varies—generally 2–3 years	Physical fitness, classroom, and field training	Varies—generally midlevel education
Japan	1 year for prefectural police	Classroom, field, and physical fitness training	National qualifying exam, high school
France	For National Police, 1 year	Classroom, field, and physical fitness training	Written and physical test, 19 years old
Saudi Arabia	3 months for lower officers, 3 years college for higher officers	For higher officers, extensive academic training	Unavailable
United States	2–40 weeks, with an average of 10	Physical fitness and classroom training	High school; in some jurisdictions, some college

SOURCE: UNCJS, 1999, pp. 333–334; Terrill, 1999, pp. 23, 214, 371; Alobied, 1989, pp. 80–84.

The unrest, crime, and disorderliness that accompanied urbanization and industrialization in nineteenth-century London led to the establishment of the Metropolitan Police. From the beginning, the English police have tried to develop the image of being "civilians in uniform": friendly, helpful, capable. Traditionally, they have not carried firearms and in violent confrontations have had only the truncheon as a means of protecting themselves and asserting their power. Traditionally, also, the English police have been decentralized, with each city or town making rules and providing funds for its own police operations and controlling the hiring, firing, and compensation of police personnel. Although the traditional view of English police may have been somewhat romanticized, the general impression has been of a police force that established a comfortable relationship with and won the respect of the English people (Miller, 1977).

Organization and Training. Over time and through a series of Police Acts, Parliament has changed the police organization, consolidating departments and providing subsidies in exchange for certain uniform policies regarding training and professionalism; Figure 5.1 charts the basic police hierarchy. At present, there are forty-one large provincial police forces in England and Wales, plus two in greater London. The two in London are called the Metropolitan Police Force (the largest, with 28,000 officers) and the London City Police. Other kinds of police, like the British Transport Police, the Ministry of Defence Police, and the Port of London Authority Police, have responsibility in specific locales or over specific activities. For the provincial police, the local districts provide 50 percent of the funding for the police in their regions, while the central government provides the other 50 percent.

Each region (county) contains a **Police Authority Board,** a uniquely English committee made up of local elected officials and judicial officials appointed by the Home Secretary. The Police Authority hears citizen complaints about alleged police abuses and consults about police practices. It is also involved in hiring the local chief constable and setting his or her compensation (Gregory, 1985). The chief constable is the main administrator for each of the forty-one provincial forces. For the Metropolitan Police, the overseeing body is the UK Government Ministry,

FIGURE 5.1 Organization of the English Police

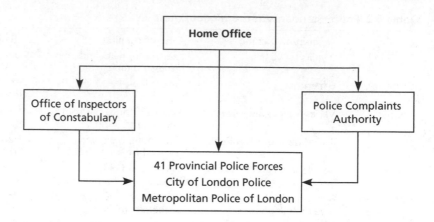

which is generally responsible for crime control in England. The national government and the Home Office is very influential in promoting the unity of police practices throughout England.

Many have heard of the famous English police term *Scotland Yard*. Scotland Yard is actually the location for the Metropolitan Police Force of London; it serves as a national repository for crime statistics, information on criminal activity, missing persons reports, fingerprints, and juvenile delinquent data.

Training for English police, called constables, entails a 14-week course during which recruits learn theoretical and practical information on a variety of topics, followed by a 10-week field experience under the supervision of an experienced constable. After that 24-week period, the new constable remains on probation for the first two years of service while gaining additional classroom training and supervision. Those who aspire to become police administrators attend the police staff college at Bramshill, the central police leadership training college in Britain.

Civil Order Control.   The English police, as presently organized, predominantly carry out the deviance control function of police. However, private security companies are used extensively in England; it is estimated that there are now more private security officers than sworn police officers (Southgate, 1995).

There is actually no separate agency or even well-defined way to deal with civil order control problems in England. This does not mean that England has no such problems. In the twentieth century, there have been many occasions of major social upheavals, including labor troubles, student protests, and riots of various kinds. Always the first line of defense has been the local police agency, acting in a civil order control rather than a deviance control capacity. Although police training has always included some aspects of crowd control, it has not traditionally been a major part of training or practice.

England on occasion has used the military to back up its police civil control efforts. The last time this happened, however, was in 1926, during a general strike. Even then, the military were used chiefly to help transport foodstuffs to the cities. In effect, there is a strong tradition against the use of the military in less-than-regime-threatening situations.

The English system, or rather nonsystem, for civil order control seemed to work well as long as there was some consensus about the proper parameters of social protests and about the relations between the police and public. As long as demonstrators did not see the police as the enemy, it was possible to work with disorderly elements or at least to maintain their respect for the police. During the student antiwar demonstrations of 1968, for example, students and police treated each other with respect and even "sang a chorus of Auld Lang Syne together outside the undamaged American Embassy, which the extremists had threatened to bomb" (Gregory, 1985, p. 52).

Participants in the 1980s riots in Liverpool, Birmingham, London, and other cities showed a different attitude toward police, however. In these confrontations, an alienated minority expressed deep resentment toward the police, angry at what it perceived to be police discrimination against foreigners and minorities. Many feared that police authority was breaking down in slum areas of some cities. For the first time in English history, police used tear gas in dealing with crowds (Reiner, 1985).

Discussion followed about whether to train special riot control troops such as those used by continental European nations. Although this has not yet happened, investigatory commissions have recommended major reforms in police training and operations to defuse some of the hostility toward police held by minorities and poor people (Alderson, 1985; Fowler, 1979). Additional training and strategic planning with respect to riot control and weapons use has also been implemented, partly in response to the British Crime Surveys of 1983 and 1988, which revealed a declining support for British police (Mayhew, Elliot, and Dowds, 1989). In particular, police leaders now are given fairly extensive training in dealing with civil disorder situations. For example, in the three-month Intermediate Command Course at Bramshill, police administrative trainees receive instruction in civil order maintenance. Likewise, the three-month Senior Command Course, which trains the highest-ranking police officials, emphasizes "policing in a changing society, with particular reference to the delicate task of maintaining the peace in an inner-city environment" (Watt, 1988, p. 11).

In addition to improved training, another initiative aimed at reducing the problems of civil unrest is the hiring of more minority officers. Nowhere is this more needed than in London, which has a substantial minority population but only 865 minority officers in the 28,000-member Metropolitan (Met) police force. The Met has addressed this issue with a policy calling for financial rewards for minority college students who pledge to become police officers and with an enhanced recruitment drive (Mason, 1999, p. 32). Moreover, chief constables now must develop their own programs for recruiting, monitoring, and retaining minority officers (Holdaway, 1990).

Today, the police in England are known for their ability to use advanced technology, including DNA testing and closed circuit television, to do daily police work. This has been very helpful in reducing the threat of terrorism and apprehending suspects (Johnson, 1999, p. A8).

France

The police organization of France has its roots in the Napoleonic system of internal spying and policing that consolidated the power of the nineteenth-century dictator. Despite reform efforts, its reputation as a repressive force that has little concern for procedural rights persists to this day.

In addition, the conception of police agency power in France (as in Germany) historically has been much broader than in England. Police power traditionally involves both regulation of society and maintenance of order. In France, all police power rests in one agency, with the police involved in such additional tasks as public health regulation, housing regulations, population registration, and other general regulatory activities (Stead, 1983).

Organization and Training. The organization of the French police is an unusual one by U.S. standards, with both military and civilian bureaucracies. Figure 5.2 shows the various divisions of responsibility in the French police. There are really two French police organizations, the **Police Nationale (PN),** and the **Gendarmerie Nationale (GN).** The PN operates within the Ministry of the Interior while the GN operates within the Ministry of Defense. The leadership of both is highly centralized in Paris.

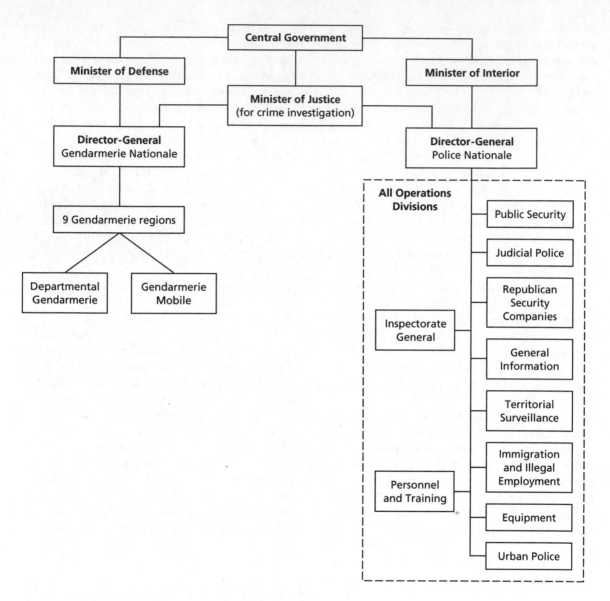

FIGURE 5.2 Organization of the French Police

Both have conventional deviance control responsibilities, although in different places, with the PN responsible for Paris and other urban areas and the GN responsible for small towns and rural areas.

The GN oversees ten geographical regions with two main administrative divisions: the de-partmental and the mobile gendarmerie. The Departmental Gendarmerie, with a total strength of over 100,000, perform all basic police tasks for nearly half of the French people. The Gendarmerie Mobile are assigned to civil disorder and other large-scale problems that involve the possibility of violence. In addition, a number of specialized units within the GN provide assistance in areas like security of public officials, maritime and overseas support, airport security and transport, and training.

The PN is the largest police force with over 133,000 personnel divided into nine different departments. The Division of Information controls the flow of information of political, economic, and social significance. The Division of the City Police (also called Public Security) is responsible for urban law enforcement. The Central Branch of the Judicial Police coordinates searches for dangerous juvenile delinquents and investigates serious offenses. The Division of Territorial Surveillance is responsible for state security. The Republican Security Companies (CRS) are the equivalent of the Gendarmerie Mobile in that they respond to civil disorder. The Inspectorate investigates complaints against the police. The Division of Immigration oversees illegal movement of people and materials. The Personnel and Training Division and the Equipment Division are self-explanatory.

Recruitment and training for the PN and GN are handled separately by each organization. The PN requires police recruits to take written and physical agility tests. If selected, the recruit attends an eight-month training period at one of the eight regional National Police Schools, followed by a four-month in-the-field training period. The recruit then is assigned to a town, city, or Republican Security Company. Longer periods of training and additional schooling are required for those interested in being police inspectors or administrators (Terrill, 1999, p. 214). GN training is slightly different, with more emphasis on the military aspects of police work. For this reason, the GN feels that as a law enforcement agency it is more disciplined than and superior to the PN (Terrill, 1999, p. 215).

Civil Order Control. When it comes to civil order control, the GN and the PN each have specialized forces that perform this task. In the PN, the Republican Security Companies assume responsibility; in the GN, the Gendarmerie Mo-

bile does so. Both of these specialized civil order control branches operate independently of conventional police work of patrol and criminal investigations. Their employees live in barracks and undergo paramilitary training, with emphasis on crowd control techniques. Curiously, working for the GN, the police arm of the military, carries greater prestige than working for the PN under the Interior Ministry (Roach, 1985; Stead, 1983).

The French police organization is closer to the way that policing worked in the days before large urban police departments were developed in the late nineteenth century. In earlier times, policing the countryside and controlling citizen unrest were the responsibility of a militia allied to the military. Policing in urban areas, the task of local watchmen or watch societies, did not have the comprehensive nature of modern police work. The smaller cities of those times generally found such an arrangement adequate for their needs.

However, as mentioned in the previous chapter, changes in governmental policy during the Mitterand presidency have led to a new idea in French policing—local self-management. Recent legislation has allowed local governments to hire their own police officials and officers. These police forces, called Police Municipale, are usually small and exercise police powers relative to arrest and crime prevention (Horton, 1995). Although this concept has not taken root throughout France, and the attendant roles and responsibilities have not yet been clarified, the numbers of these officers are growing, with over 10,000 currently employed (Journes, 1993).

The French police organization may seem unusual and even threatening to us, since a good portion of its work is done centrally through the Defense Ministry. Another way to look at this organization, however, is to regard the GN as a separate force that helps offset the highly centralized nature of the PN, which takes all its orders from the Interior Ministry in Paris. Thus, an element of pluralism is introduced into an otherwise monolithic police organization.

Germany

German police strength grew from 200,000 to 1.5 million between 1933 and 1945, the years when Germany was under the domination of Hitler and the National Socialist party. This force, which included the Gestapo, much of the SS, and other notorious Nazi agencies, acted as a private army for Hitler, ruthlessly stamping out dissent, running death camps in the occupied territories, and otherwise acting in a way that made the organization synonymous with evil in the modern world. Little wonder, then, that one of the first items of business for the occupying authorities after the defeat of Germany in World War II was a thorough overhaul of the police apparatus.

Organization and Training. The German police were organized during the postwar period in response to the new realities of a democratized Germany. The basic police structures, however, were quite familiar to Germans since they were essentially the same as those that existed during the Weimar Republic, the democratic government that took power following the fall of the German Empire in 1918 (Berkeley, 1969; Thomanek, 1985; Fairchild, 1988).

Each of the sixteen states (Laender) of Germany has its own police organization. The police forces for each Laender are controlled from that state's Interior Ministry and are not decentralized to municipalities or other units of local government. Thus, the German system occupies a middle level of decentralization between the highly centralized French system and the highly decentralized and fragmented U.S. system.

Within each Laender are several kinds of police. The **Schutzpolizei (Schupo)** are the equivalent of municipal police; they are the first to arrive at the scene of most crimes and handle all general aspects of law enforcement and simple investigations. The **Kriminalpolizei (Kripo)** are plainclothes police who handle serious crime investigations and situations that require developing a case against a suspect. The **Bereitschaft-spolizei (Bepo)** are actually officers-in-training living in barracks, but they serve as civil order police when the situation arises.

The German federal government also has some police agencies at its disposal. The Federal Border Police (Bundesgrenzschutz, or BGS) are organized along military lines but are under the supervision of the Ministry of the Interior, not the Ministry of Defense. Their major functions include border control, sea patrol, and airport and railroad security; they also may assist in major civil disturbances beyond the scope of the Laender police. Included within the BGS is a special task force, called Special Group 9 (BGS-9), that handles terrorist incidents. This task force was formed after the terrorist attack on Israeli athletes at the 1972 Olympics in Munich.

Germany also has an agency similar to our FBI called the Federal Criminal Investigation Office (Bundeskriminalamt, or BKA). This agency acts as a clearinghouse for criminal records and provides support to the Laender relative to criminal investigations, forensics, and research.

An individual who aspires to a career of policing usually joins the German police at the young age of sixteen or seventeen, straight out of vocational secondary school. The first two and a half to three years are spent living in barracks and undergoing basic training. A large part of this training focuses on riot control; the rest involves conventional school subjects, the law, and law enforcement. After one year in the training schools, the young officers may be used for civil order control work either in their own states or, if the need arises, in other states of the Federal Republic. Again, these are the training/civil order units, called the Bepo police.

After the years of basic training and civil order control work, the Bepo officers spend about six months in general law enforcement training prior to beginning street patrol work. With few exceptions, recruits must go through the street patrol experience for at least a few years. After that time, some of them will undergo several more years of training to become either criminal investigators or middle-management supervisors. Candidates for the top 1 percent of police jobs go through still another two years of training, with one year at the central police academy, where they meet and mingle with top management candidates from other states.

Civil Order Control. Thus, almost all German police recruits are trained to do civil order control work at the earliest stage of their careers. Once they move on, their primary responsibility during their early years is patrol work, although they may be called upon to back up some of the Bepo troops during particularly difficult confrontations with citizens or in other emergencies. Their training during the Bepo years puts heavy emphasis on crowd control techniques and nonlethal weaponry use in encounters with citizens.

According to German police authorities, using the recruits in military-like duty is a way to provide discipline and order and to socialize the young officers into the police profession at a time when they are impressionable and malleable. By the time they are graduated to street work, with all its discretionary responsibilities, they are more mature and capable of handling emergencies on their own.

As you can see, the German division between civil order control structures is different from the French system, although both have separate units that handle this kind of work. In Germany, all officers live in barracks and handle civil order control incidents before going on to do street patrol work. In France, civil order work is performed by special units in both the National Police and the Gendarmerie. Presumably, the French system actually produces officers who are more experienced in handling demonstrations and riots since they are both older and more specialized. In practice, however, the German structures seem to work quite well, with few instances of police losing control in the highly charged and provocative atmosphere that exists at many demonstrations.

Problems Following Reunification. The reunification of Germany in 1990 posed some organizational problems for police since East Germany at that time was broken up into its former states,

and police organizations had to be decentralized to the state level. The process was facilitated by the fact that the new organizations were essentially similar to those of West Germany. Personnel issues were more problematic, since many East German police had collaborated closely with the brutal East German secret police, the Stasi, and were thus discredited. Some police, especially among the leadership ranks, were purged. In general, however, most of the rank-and-file East German police were incorporated into the new organizations. Undoubtedly, the anticipation of problems of civil order control in the wake of the social and economic dislocations caused by reunification prompted the rather easy acceptance of the new police.

China

Like many other countries, China has experienced periods in its history when crime and disorder were a major social problem and other times when it was less of a problem. And as in other countries, Chinese law and order functions have adjusted to those times. Prior to the twentieth century, crime was not a serious problem in China, which was predominately poor and agrarian. After the Qing dynasty was overthrown in 1911, the Kuomintang (Nationalist party) presided over the country. Between 1911 and 1949, the Chinese political situation was far from stable, with crime and social upheaval resulting from warlordism, corruption, civil war, and invasion by Japan. However, it was between 1945 and 1949 that China experienced its most serious civil strife when frequent battles took place between rival political factions. The Kuomintang, which espoused democratic ideals, was often in violent conflict with the Communist party and those who wanted to establish a Socialist political system. After gaining power in 1949, the Communist party handed over policing to three groups: (1) public security forces, which provided basic police services, (2) militia groups, which monitored the border regions, and (3) the People's Liberation Army (PLA), which was the military wing of the Communist party (Terrill, 1999, p. 531).

In the 1950s, the Communist party became more entrenched, and formal mechanisms for law enforcement were developed based on the principles outlined in the first constitution of the People's Republic of China in 1954. Basically, the Chinese government formulated a Soviet-style criminal justice system with overall control in the hands of the Communist party.

From the mid-1950s until 1966, there was little crime or civil disorder in China. But in 1966, the Cultural Revolution changed all that. Along with Mao's attempt to reform the Communist party came attacks on police officials and police stations and seizures of courts by the followers of Mao and the Red Guard. Local police were placed under the control of local Communist party officials. Eventually, Mao had to call on the PLA to restore some semblance of order. This period of lawlessness and disorder continued until 1976 with the death of Mao and the arrest of his principal followers, the "Gang of Four."

In the late 1970s, Deng Xiaoping reestablished the rule of law and restored the police as the main enforcers of law. This return of law and order to the police was reinforced by the Police Law of 1995, which replaced the previous law of 1957. The new law outlined the organizational structure, authority, and duties of police in China and defined the roles of police in a more modern, citizen-oriented, and realistic fashion (Yisheng, 1999). Table 5.3 summarizes the key provisions of the two laws as they pertain to police functions.

Organization and Training. As mentioned in Chapter 4, China's police are under the centrally monitored guidance of the Ministry of Public Security. The ministry formulates policies and regulations, coordinates police work and operations among the twenty-three provinces, and provides technological and specialized assistance to local police (Jinfeng, 1997).

Chinese police consists of five main components: **Public security police,** state security police, prison police, judicial procuratorates police, and judicial people's courts police. We will concentrate our discussion on the Public Security police because they make up 86 percent of all police personnel in China (Li, 1997).

Public Security police in China provide not only basic uniformed patrol but also twelve other specialized functions including criminal investigations, fire control, border patrol, and monitoring of all modes of transportation (Wang, 1996, p. 155). State security police, established in 1983, are responsible for preventing espionage, sabotage, and conspiracies. Prison police supervise convicted offenders in prisons. The judicial procuratorates police escort suspects in cases investigated by the procuratorates (similar to prosecutors). Finally, the judicial police in the people's courts maintain security and order in the various courts and also may carry out death sentences (Xiancui, 1998).

Although this organization may seem straightforward, what obfuscates an understanding of the

Table 5.3 Police Functions in China According to the Police Acts of 1957 and 1995

1957	1995
Punish counterrevolutionaries according to the law	Safeguard state security
Prevent and stop other sabotaging activities of other criminal elements	Maintain social order
Maintain public order and social security	Protect personal safety
Protect public property	Protect the personal freedom and lawful property of citizens
Protect the rights and lawful interests of citizens for the smooth progress of the country's socialist construction	Guard against and punish law-violating activities

SOURCE: Yisheng, 1999.

Chinese police is the myriad of levels under which they operate. Although the five police agencies are directly answerable to the Ministry of Public Security, they are also under the authority of the 23 individual provinces, 450 prefects, and 1,904 county security bureaus and local police stations (Guo et al., 1999). Consequently, in theory, the police fall under the leadership of the Ministry of Public Security; but in practice, the day-to-day administration is governed by the corresponding agency. In many cases, local levels of government can determine their own policing priorities and appoint and promote their own officers (Xiancui, 1998).

Most Chinese police graduate from one of the 298 police universities, colleges, or police academies located in the individual provinces, all which are coordinated by the Ministry of Public Security (Ministry of Public Security, 1994). Recruits with special skills may be hired without this training but all must be at least twenty-five years of age and have a strong physique. Training lasts for an average of six months, but it will vary depending on officers' future positions and specialization. Provincial police directors are trained directly by the Ministry of Public Security while other officers are trained by their respective governmental offices: province, county, prefect, or municipality (Guo et al., 1999). Apparently, the Chinese have become very serious about education for police. In 1980, less that 10 percent of officers were college graduates or postgraduates; in 1997, this proportion increased to 37.6 percent.

Civil Order Control. When there is a civil order dispute in China, the Ministry of Public Security generally calls upon the main public security police in that jurisdiction. However, when the matter requires strength in numbers, the ministry may turn to the Chinese People's Armed Police, which serve as part of the army with dual responsibilities to the Central Military Commission and the Ministry of Public Security.

There is significant controversy over the way in which the Chinese handle the police function of civil order control. In the early days of Com-

munist rule, in the 1950s and 1960s, there were few confrontations between police and the public, and confidence and trust in the police were high. However, since the Cultural Revolution, public attitudes toward the police have shifted. The Chinese people now seem to view police with more distrust and to see them as bullies or tyrants. The number of complaints against police has increased considerably, and physical confrontations with citizens have become more frequent (Cao Guanghui, 1995).

There appear to be many reasons for this shift in attitude toward police. Since the end of the Cultural Revolution, the government has implemented significant reforms in many social and economic areas. With a free market economy and an increase in individual wealth have come the social ills of crime and corruption. As a result, the Communist party, fearing a total breakdown of control, has called on the police to crack down on crime and on the courts to severely punish offenders of all types. Citizens have responded with calls for increased civil rights and democratic participation. However, these requests have not been received well by the Communist party, and there have been frequent and sometimes violent confrontations between police and citizens. The most famous occurred in 1989 in Tiananmen Square, Beijing, when over 800 people died in a hail of gunfire from the Red Army in response to a mass demonstration in favor of democracy and freedom. Despite the international furor that followed, Chinese officials to this day defend their actions, stating that they were necessary to maintain public order.

Japan

Prior to the Meiji Restoration of the late nineteenth century, Japanese village and community culture monitored the behavior of citizens very closely—not only to keep them from committing crimes but also to keep them from "laziness, neglect of business, quarreling, scandal mongering, etc." (Clifford, 1976, p. 75). After the Meiji Restoration, and with the gradual development of Japan as a militaristic society in the early decades of the twentieth century, formal police forces carried on this tradition. Many of the now unemployed samurai warriors who had served the feudal lords in the prerestoration Tokugawa period were integrated into the new police, thus assuring that this force would have a large degree of prestige in Japan (Westney, 1987, ch. 2).

Organization and Training. The actual model of police organization for crime prevention and control was borrowed from nineteenth-century France. Japanese authorities hoped that, by setting up a European-style police organization, they would rid themselves of the treaties of extraterritoriality imposed on them by Western powers. These treaties provided that citizens of the treaty partner would not be subject to the criminal justice system as it existed in Japan at that time but would be processed through that nation's own system (Westney, 1987).

Under the new organization, a powerful, centralized administration controlled the various geographic divisions of the police. Local police officials, however, lived and worked within their own communities and were prominent in local affairs. Within a few years, Japan had established the vast network of tiny local police posts, called *kobans* in urban areas and *chuzaisho* in rural areas, that make the Japanese police a distinctive force. Such local posts did not exist in France and remain a peculiarly Japanese institution.

Japan returned to a centralized police organization after an abortive attempt by the U.S. occupation forces in the post–World War II years to institute community-controlled police based on the U.S. model. In today's organization, a civilian National Public Safety Commission supervises the National Police Agency with respect to most aspects of police organization and administration, including training, equipment, recruitment, communications, and criminal statistics. The **National Police Agency (NPA),** located in Tokyo with eight regional bureaus in various parts of the country, includes a number of special divisions to handle training, research, crime prevention, and public safety functions related to the environment and transportation. The NPA also provides funding for local police needs such as equipment, salaries, riot control, escorts, and natural disasters, and it handles all matters of national security and multiple jurisdictions. There are 47 **prefectural police** agencies, and 1,200 local police stations under them. In addition, a specialized riot police force lives in barracks in each prefecture, and a national police academy trains the highest supervisory officials. For a graphic summary of the Japanese police structure, see Figure 5.3.

To become a police officer in Japan, one must graduate from high school, pass a national qualifying exam, complete a physical exam, pass an aptitude test, undergo an extensive background check, and complete a series of personal interviews. After this process the recruit must attend the NPA Training School. If the recruit is a high school graduate, the training lasts one year; if he or she is a college graduate, it lasts six months. The training combines academic and legal courses with the martial arts. After completing school training,

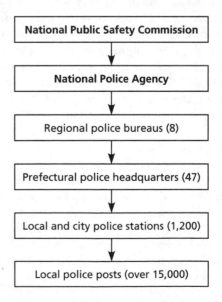

FIGURE 5.3 Organization of the Japanese Police

the recruit receives one year of field experience and then returns to school for six months for further training. As in other countries, officers who advance to higher ranks within the agency are required to undergo additional training to develop their leadership and administrative abilities. As you can see, the Japanese police are among the most highly trained police in the world.

The *Koban* and the *Chuzaisho*. It is the large network of local police posts—the *koban* and the *chuzaisho*—that makes the Japanese police organizations so distinctive. These tiny police posts, located in all neighborhoods, constitute the heart of the Japanese police operation.

The *koban* is a police post located in an urban neighborhood; in large cities, one finds a *koban* every few blocks. There are over 6,000 *koban*—many are storefront offices or tiny buildings resembling sentry stations. The officers in the *koban* account for about 40 percent of the total police strength in Japan.

Koban for the most part function as a "community safety center" for the local community (Hirota, 1999). The main duties of *koban* officers, according to Hirota (1999), are as follows:

- Administrative service. For instance, they give directions to visitors (the main task in big cities), handle lost and found articles, take charge of unaccompanied children, and provide counseling services for residents.

- *Initial response to incidents and accidents.* For example, when crimes or accidents occur, as needed, they rush to the scene, arrest suspects, locate eyewitnesses, care for victims, and secure the scene. Then they hand over the case to investigators.

- *Prevention of crimes and accidents.* For example, they routinely visit houses and workplaces to raise public awareness of crimes and accidents, meet with residents and workers to learn their concerns, and lead community relations meetings to discuss community problems.

The officer is supposed to know in great detail what is happening in his neighborhood. According to Ames:

> The koban has a wealth of . . . data on the jurisdiction . . . such as lists of people working late at night who might be of help as witnesses to crime, of people who are normally cooperative with the police, of people who own guns or swords, of all rented homes and apartments that might serve as hideouts for fugitives, of people with criminal records, and of people with mental illness; organizational charts of gangs in the police station jurisdiction and in the prefecture (sometimes complete with photographs of all the gangsters); lists of old people in the area living alone who should be visited periodically, of all neighborhood organizations in the jurisdiction and their leaders, and of all bars, restaurants, and amusement facilities in the jurisdiction; a short history of the koban; and a compilation of the total population, area, and number of households in the jurisdiction. (1981, p. 39)

Work in a *koban* is the first assignment in a typical Japanese police career, and officers later move on to detective work, traffic patrol, riot police, and other specialized police work (Bayley, 1991, ch. 2).

The *chuzaisho* is the rural equivalent of the urban *koban*. There are over 8,000 *Chuzaisho* although their numbers have declined in recent years as Japan has become more urbanized. These rural police officers are known as **chusai-san.** He (almost all are men) lives with his family in a small house provided by the government that also serves as an office for conducting police business. According to Ames (1981), the *chusai-san* ranks with the school principal and the village headman as the most prestigious officials in the local communities.

The *chusai-san* spends his time patrolling his district (usually on motorcycle), visiting the residents, or conducting business out of his office in the *chuzaisho*. He is required to visit each household twice per year, during which time he becomes acquainted with family members, neighborhood news, and problems that might be occurring. He is always available in case of emergencies, and his wife and children also get involved in keeping the office operating. The *chusai-san* is invited to local celebrations, drinks with the local farmers, and in other ways integrates himself into community life to keep informed about matters that might aid him in his task of crime prevention and control.

In some ways, the *chusai-san* resembles a local sheriff in a rural community in the United States. The *chusai-san,* although not dependent on the community for his job, is more effective if he earns approval from the local merchants and citizens by enforcing the law but not in an overly zealous manner. Ames describes one crime investigation in a rural area:

> I once visited a chuzaisho which had a burglary in its jurisdiction reported that morning. Someone had entered a home while the occupants were gone, and a couple of bottles of whiskey had been stolen. The woman living there sent her son to the chuzaisho to report the crime and the chusai-san and I went to the scene. He had the woman fill out some forms, and when she could not do it correctly, he did it. He spent a little over three hours there chatting, finishing the forms, eating food and drinking tea the woman brought out, and watching television. (1981, p. 29)

Obviously, there is some room for corruption in such a system. In order to cut down on this possibility, the *chusai-san* is transferred to a new post approximately every three years. In this way, he has the time to get to know his neighborhood but not to abuse his office by granting special favors and accepting more than the customary Japanese ceremonial gifts.

While *koban* service as a first step in a police career seems to be well entrenched in Japan, modern forms of communication, greater mobility through patrol cars, and other technological changes are resulting in some consolidation of small *koban* into larger ones and some changes in operation. The rural institution of *chuzaisho* appears to have a more fragile existence in modern

policing and may be heading for changes. Modern, highly trained professional police officers often do not wish to subject themselves to the working conditions characteristic of this kind of policing. The long hours, the entire family's constant involvement with the community, and the lack of a stable home no longer seems an attractive work situation for many Japanese police officers.

A Unique Police Culture. The Japanese are particularly proud of their police. They believe that the peculiar Japanese police culture is one of the main contributing factors to the low crime rate in Japan. In addition, they believe that the close relationship between the police and the public contributes to social harmony and good neighborhood relations. Whereas police of the Meiji Restoration period were largely ex-samurai and were seen as protectors of the public, in the post–World War II era police came to be seen as public servants (Ueno, 1986). Among the duties of Japanese police are to act as counselors to troubled individuals in the neighborhood, provide marriage and divorce counseling, offer money management tips, give advice to parents with rebellious children, and help with problems of alcohol addiction. These activities all are part of the police officer's routine.

Another task performed by police officers who work in the local police stations is organizing the neighborhood for both crime control and traffic safety. Volunteer crime control organizations exist in most neighborhoods. Most communities also have festivals or special occasions each year to celebrate their efforts.

The Japanese people are generally fond of their police and do not resent the close contact. Police stations provide opportunities for exchanging information and socializing at the neighborhood level. Obviously, however, the police organization also provides an opportunity for a government that has become tyrannical or hostile to the people to spy on the populace. The military dictatorship that ruled Japan for many years before World War II did, in fact, use the system of *koban* and *chuzaisho* as an internal security force that served the rulers rather than the people. Thus, the flip side of the model community relations practiced by the Japanese police is the capacity for control rather than service that is built into the system. Close accountability to the public can turn rapidly into accountability to the rulers alone.

Nevertheless, the success of the Japanese police in establishing excellent community relations, as well as the low crime rate in Japan, have caused many countries to consider adopting the Japanese style of policing. Even the United States has begun to look at Japanese police practices. According to Bayley (1991, p. 82), "Until ten years ago Japan and the United States followed fundamentally different philosophies in designing police practices. Now they are converging, and Japanese practices are being studied carefully by American police."

The Japanese system of local police stations illustrates an important principle about police effectiveness—that policing goes beyond a reactive response to crime and deviance on the part of public officers. According to Bayley, the Japanese experience emphasizes the importance of the police as an agency that works with the public to obtain a commitment to lawfulness: "American police officers fulfill their responsibilities when they bring people into compliance with law; Japanese police officers seek more than compliance; they seek acceptance of the community's moral values" (1991, p. 154). To be sure, without some large degree of citizen commitment to societal norms, any police efforts short of sheer terrorism are likely to be unsuccessful in any country. What the Japanese example suggests is that educating people for compliance can be promoted in a positive way by police efforts. A democratic society needs to be concerned about the degree to which police agents, who are carriers of the coercive force of a government, should be involved in the private lives of citizens. As presently constituted, however, the Japanese police exert a relatively benign influence in Japanese society.

Civil Order Control. Civil order control in Japan is handled through a separate division in each prefecture. The division is militarized in the sense that officers live in barracks, receive training in crowd control, and use military formations during civil order crises. There are around 15,000 of these officers, called **kidotai.** Young officers are used for this division and generally serve for three years before returning to conventional street police work.

The Japanese civil order control police have proved useful in the large demonstrations and student riots that occur periodically, as well as in national emergencies like earthquakes and floods. During any kind of violent disorder, the *kidotai* can be seen moving in closed formation, swathed in protective clothing and holding shields. They are very disciplined, use nonlethal force, and carry no firearms. In fact, police brutality is rarely an issue in Japan. In most cases, the Japanese police force is friendly and peaceful—but at the same time ever present in all levels of Japanese society.

Saudi Arabia

Organization and Training. Saudi Arabia's highly centralized police force was formally developed by royal decree in 1950 by King Abd al Assiz. The minister of the interior, who is appointed by the king, is responsible for the administration of all police matters. The main police force is actually called the Department of Public Safety. Police in the Department of Public Safety handle most of the daily law enforcement functions in the country. The department is divided into the regular police and the special investigative police of the General Directorate of Investigation (GDI)—the **mubahith,** or secret police. The *mubahith* conduct criminal investigations and handle matters pertaining to domestic security and counterintelligence.

Saudi Arabia is divided into fourteen provinces or amirates that make up the country's administrative divisions. Each of the provinces is run by a governor, but the police are directly administered by a general manager who controls the activities of the police within that area. The managers are responsible to the provincial governors, who are directly answerable to the director of public safety. The director is actually the head of the Saudi police and is a high-ranked official in the Interior Ministry. The director appoints most of the managers and officers of the local police forces. Under the provincial forces, there are also municipal forces. For a graphic summary of the line of supervision for the Saudi police, see Figure 5.4.

In addition to the Department of Public Safety police, Saudi Arabia also has a "morals force," the religious police known as **mutawa,** which ensures that Saudi citizens live up to the rules of behavior derived from the Qur'an. This 50,000-member agency maintains the strict separation of the sexes in Saudi public life, pressures women to wear the traditional long black robes and face coverings, and stops women from driving cars. The *mutawa* also ensures that businesses are closed during prayer hours and cover up ad-

vertising that depicts attractive women and alcohol use. One of the more surprising rules that the *mutawa* enforces is that women are not allowed to buy music from music stores; in fact, music in general is suspect in the highly puritanical Saudi society.

The *mutawa* came to Western attention in November 1990, when forty-seven Saudi women flouted the unwritten ban on driving by women and drove their cars through the capital city of Riyadh. The women became the subjects of a campaign of harassment by the *mutawa*, who publicized their names and phone numbers and branded them prostitutes and Communists. As a result, the women lost their jobs, and the ban on women's driving was officially proclaimed by the religious establishment (*Wall Street Journal*, 1991, pp. 1, 12).

The *mutawa* is organizationally separate from the regular police, with which it cooperates closely. Its actual leadership comes from the **Ujama,** the council of religious authorities who are deeply involved in most aspects of Saudi life, especially the administration of criminal justice.

Saudi police make a strong distinction between commissioned officers and rank-and-file police. The commissioned officers receive three years of training at King Fahd Security College and are promoted through the ranks from second lieutenant to general. The director of public safety, who heads the Saudi police, usually is a relative of the king (as are many heads of executive agencies in Saudi Arabia). Rank-and-file police personnel must be literate and spend three months in training. They are not eligible to become commissioned officers, however (Alobied, 1989).

Civil Order Control. With its relatively small population of 8 million people, many of whom continue to live and work as part of nomadic Bedouin tribes, Saudi Arabia has little need for a large civil order control division within its police force. However, when the situation does arise, Saudi Arabia has a separate "special forces" divi-

FIGURE 5.4 Organization of the Saudi Arabian Police

sion to handle civil order control functions. One use of these special forces, called the Pilgrims and Festivals Police Force, is used to control the large throngs that gather during the annual pilgrimage to the cities of Mecca and Medina. When civil order situations go beyond the control of the special police, the National Guard and Saudi Army are called in (Ross, 1996).

As the guardian of the holy cities, Saudi Arabia must maintain order, sanitary conditions, and food distribution channels among the approximately 2 million Muslims from other countries, as well as Saudi Arabia, who go on the pilgrimage each year. In past years, the pilgrimage has been marred by high crowd concentrations and riots resulting in many deaths and serious foreign relations problems among Saudi Arabia, Iran, and Pakistan.

Comparing the Different Styles of Policing

The structural arrangements that each model nation has devised accomplish two important police functions: civil order control and deviance control. Each nation has features of civil order control work that differ from the others. For example, France has specialized troops in both the national police and the military. Britain depends on its regular street police. Germany divides the functions according to stages of the police career, with its youngest officers doing civil order control work in conjunction with basic training and its more mature officers engaged in street work. Japan has specialized civil order police in each prefecture. During the Cultural Revolution, the Chinese government used the Red Guard to support the political agenda of Chairman Mao. More recently, civil order control in the People's Republic of China has worked through the powerful public security police with assistance from the army when the situation becomes more serious. Saudi Arabia, much like the United States, relies on the military (National Guard) to handle serious civil disorder.

We must remember that, even in countries with specialized civil order control units, the "front-line" responsibility for civil order, as well as for deviance control, rests with the street police who are in place to respond to all emergencies that arise, including ones of public order. This is true in all systems. In many cases, police authorities try to control situations through the local police rather than dramatizing them by sending in the riot police. Street police also supplement riot troops in most instances. Therefore, street police need to have some training and equipment for riot control.

In general, we can conclude that none of the described patterns of organization is ideal. In the British system, little attention is paid to civil order control forces, with the result that emergencies may be handled ineptly or through resort to some form of military force. In the French system, specialized units tend to be militaristic in nature and not amenable to the kind of public accountability that police should have in a democracy. In the German system, the use of relatively raw recruits may have detrimental effects on the police organization and may also result in a lack of perspective and cohesion in action situations.

The indigenous organization in each of these systems has evolved over the course of decades and even centuries, however, and seems to fit the peculiar organizational culture of that system. Although incremental reforms such as additional crowd control training for U.S. police forces are possible, major changes are not likely in the foreseeable future in any except the German system. There, the authorities, mindful of the criticism of the young officers who are used, may come to rely more and more on the Federal Border Police to handle crowds. Some states have also experimented with prolonging the tour of duty in the Bepo to four years and using only those officers in their last year in that force for crowd control work. Even these changes are not radical, although they do move the German police toward a more militarized response to civil order control.

COMMUNITY POLICING AND ITS IMPLEMENTATION IN THE MODEL COUNTRIES

What Is Community Policing?

One of the ways in which police deal with the tasks of deviance and civil order control is the development of community policing programs. **Community policing,** also called community-oriented or problem-oriented policing, is an umbrella term describing programs that represent collaborative efforts between the police and the public to identify crime problems and then find solutions.

Community policing plays an important part in police thinking today. At least two factors have contributed to this recent change in modern police departments. The first is the growing hostility between police and many segments of the public, as evidenced in violent clashes between police and citizens. The second is the fact that the ever-increasing crime rates that characterized the 1970s and 1980s seemed to be impervious to conventional police prevention and control activities. Although the number of police personnel increased steadily in most areas, and although modernization of forces through communications and other technology occurred in most large police agencies, the crime rate continued to rise and criminal violence appeared to be increasingly uncontrolled. The result has been a call for a return to an earlier era of policing, a time when officers on the beat knew their constituents and their neighborhoods in detail and developed ties to the community.

As mentioned previously, *community policing* is actually a catchall term for a variety of programs designed to bring police closer to the public. Skolnick and Bayley (1988, p. 5) describe four key elements of community policing:

- Community-based crime prevention
- Reorientation of patrol activities to emphasize nonemergency servicing

- Increased accountability to the public
- Decentralization of command, including, under certain circumstances, civilianization.

Models of Community Policing

Community policing has become the focus of attention in police departments in many countries. For example, Singapore has become a model in the development of community policing. Singapore, a city-state with a population of over 2.5 million that consists of Chinese, Malays, Indians, and others, embarked on a major reform of its police in 1981, using the Japanese police as an example. Ninety-one neighborhood police posts (NPPs) have become the basis for the new police. These *koban*-like structures, which are dispersed throughout the city, now employ a large proportion of Singapore's police force. At the same time, motorized patrol and other police divisions were sharply cut back to supply the personnel for the NPPs.

Like the Japanese police, the police in Singapore now regularly visit homes and businesses, organize crime prevention associations, and develop close ties with community groups and leaders. An NPP is usually staffed by five officers who work regular eight-hour shifts. Criminal investigations are carried out by specialized police, as is traffic control; these are not included in NPP work (Quah and Quah, 1987).

The NPP structure is borrowed directly from the Japanese, with some modifications regarding shifts and extent of jurisdiction. The interesting difference in Singapore's case, however, is that the population being policed is composed of many ethnic groups with different religious beliefs, customs, and economic status. The Singapore experience seems to belie the claim that the Japanese structures are peculiarly suited to Japan because it has a homogeneous population that has carried a village culture into its modern cities and economy. Whether the Japanese model, with its pervasive surveillance of the population, would also be successful in a more individualistic Western culture is not known.

In addition to Singapore and our model nations, a number of other countries practice some forms of community-oriented policing. The United States, where most decisions about police practices must be made at the city or town level, also moved toward community policing in the late 1990s. Experimentation in community policing in the United States goes back to the 1970s, and especially the 1975 community profile experiment in San Diego, in which officers were assigned to particular neighborhoods and asked to "profile," or study, the neighborhood in great detail and to prepare a plan for dealing with its problems. Team policing, in which the same officers remained in one neighborhood for at least six months to a year instead of being assigned randomly to different neighborhoods, also became quite prevalent during the 1970s.

These earlier programs presaged the present dominant community policing trend. The standards established by Bayley and Skolnick are a kind of yardstick for evaluating the degree of community policing that exists. Some cities have even set up *koban*-like storefront police operations in some neighborhoods. Although no other agency has copied the Japanese model to the extent that it was in Singapore, it has certainly been influential as a basis for planning in this country. Many feel that the implementation of community policing programs in the United States contributed greatly to the decreasing crime rate in the last half of the 1990s.

Community Policing
in the Model Countries

England. The origins of modern community policing can be traced back to the basic ideas of policing (locally based, local accountability) as set by Sir Robert Peel in 1829. But more recently, with legislative mandates in the Police and Magistrates' Court Act of 1994 and the Criminal Justice and Public Order Act of 1994, and upon the advice of the Home Office, England has reestablished its commitment to community policing (Richards, 1996). One example of a community

policing program, launched in 1993, is the parish constable scheme, whereby trained volunteer constables in specific local areas provide a foot patrol presence and address problems of nuisance and minor crimes. They try to improve communication between police and the community; offer victim support, crime prevention advice, and school liaison support; and assist crime watch programs (Southgate, 1995).

France. In the 1980s, France, like many other countries, began to realize that the maintenance of law and order and the prevention of crime are not the sole responsibility of the police. With this in mind, they began to develop crime prevention units in over 700 communities (Journes, 1993). These have become the springboard for community policing–type programs in areas such as senior citizen assistance, victim support, community services for offenders, drug prevention efforts, and juvenile delinquency programs. At the same time, the French police have begun patrolling high-crime areas on foot or on motorcycles (Terrill, 1999).

Germany. The police in Germany have traditionally held the role of a strong, disciplined, and organized force that is viewed more as a powerful organ of the state than as an organization hoping to "serve" the community. In this sense, the ideals of community policing might seem to be in conflict with the police culture in Germany. Although this may be true to a large extent, efforts have been made in various locations to bring the police closer to the people.

In the city of Berlin, police have been assigned to one of 756 beats or patrol areas. These officers, called **Kontachbereichsbeamter (KoB)** (contact officer), typically are at least forty years of age with a considerable amount of police experience, including at least three years as a senior sergeant and six months of special training. Each officer is responsible for policing a specified area over a forty-hour work week, whenever he or she feels it is necessary to patrol. Main job functions include contact with the public, crime suppression, traffic control, accident prevention, and assistance to other agencies. During the course of the day, this officer will receive information about crime in the area, ask citizens on the street about specific crimes, visit local businesses, and contact government agencies about when public services will be delivered or a hazard repaired (Brown, 1983).

This is just one type of a community policing program in Germany. Because each of the sixteen German Laender has its own police organization, the kinds of programs can vary considerably depending on the region.

China. It has been argued that community policing as described here cannot be practiced in China because the essence of such policing involves building a coalition between police and the public—a concept that cannot be accomplished in a totalitarian state (Jiao, 1995, p. 69).

The Western concept of community policing has not been fully accepted in China. What is practiced, however, is something called "beat policing," which entails "patrolling the community and being available for citizens who wish to turn to police when they are in difficulty" (Yisheng, 1999). This is different from the Western community policing model in that it is reactive rather than proactive in dealing with crime and community problems. However, if we broaden our definition of what community policing encompasses, we can see that policing in China, both historically and currently, reflects some of the core principles described earlier by Skolnick and Bayley.

For centuries, the Chinese have relied heavily on notions of "community mutuality." This means they believe that harmony, balance, and mutual dependence between police and the public are essential ingredients to social well-being At the same time, China used a self-checking system involving the home, workplace, and local community to self-police as to avoid the strong intervention of government (Dutton, 1992).

Since the 1950s, the national police force of the People's Republic of China has moved to decentralize police to thousands of neighborhood stations to help them control crime and build the Socialist welfare state (Jiao, 1995, p. 72). These neighborhood stations, called Paichu Suo, were possibly the forerunner of the Japanese *koban* system.

In the early 1950s the Chinese government also formed a series of organizations in neighborhoods, workplaces, schools, and rural areas called **residents' committees** (also called public security organizations). The purpose of these committees was to encourage the participation of all citizens in their community and to assist police in maintaining public order. Duties of the committees included mediating disputes, assisting in traffic control, monitoring sanitation conditions, distributing political and health information, organizing political meetings, and educating the citizenry about crime prevention and the legal system. In times of disorder in Chinese society, these committees served as a watchdog group to determine who was not in line with the Communist party philosophy. A number of these organizations still exist today although they are now called Community Service Commissions (Terrill, 1999, p. 539). There are over 12 million people participating in these organizations in China as of 1993 (Yisheng and Zu Yuan, 1993).

More recently, the Chinese have also developed a range of programs that reflect the values of community policing. In an effort to make police more accountable, they have asked citizens to evaluate their work. Also, as in many cities in the United States, most notably New York, the Chinese have implemented policies to reduce crimes that impact the quality of life. Finally, programs have been adopted that align with the problem-oriented approach, which is a model that tries to solve the problems of crime (Jiao, 1995, pp. 74–77). In each case, the Chinese have shown that they are listening to the needs of the citizenry and following current trends of policing throughout the world.

Japan. Japan, with its decreasing crime rates over most of the last forty years, has provided a model for effective community policing. Interest in Japanese police practices was fueled by U.S. studies of Japanese police, especially the work of David Bayley. At the same time, the U.S. Department of Justice, through the National Institute of Justice, and the Police Foundation, a private research agency supported by private and public funds, became involved in a series of controlled experiments on police practices. These experiments dealt largely with the effect of various police practices on crime rates. Some of the results of these experiments suggested that random preventive patrol, the cornerstone of police activity in the United States and in other industrialized nations, had little effect on crime rates. Likewise, massive increases in police personnel had little effect on crime. Increased foot patrols, while also having little effect on crime rates, had the positive result of a decrease in the fear of crime in neighborhoods with such protection. As a result, the Japanese storefront police stations, practice of home visits, and development of community ties through various kinds of team policing have all been investigated as new ways to deal with the old problems of police-community relations and crime prevention (Skolnick and Bayley, 1986, ch. 1). (The accompanying box on page 116 recounts a typical day in the life of a Japanese *koban* officer.)

Saudi Arabia. The Saudi Arabian police, because of their strong affiliation with Islamic traditions, do not often engage in the same police practices as our other model countries. The lack of any formal community policing programs is one example.

INTERNATIONAL POLICE COOPERATION

There is currently no police agency that we can call "international" in the sense that they perform the deviance and civil order control functions of police throughout the world. As mentioned in Chapter 2, we do have the International Police Association (INTERPOL). Since 1950, INTER-POL has worked with local and national police agencies to conduct crime investigations, collect and compiling statistics, and deliver arrest warrants ordered by courts of law. Yet the agency is not an operational police force that works across boundaries, and it has no powers of arrest or search and seizure.

But the impact of INTERPOL cannot be minimized. Because of the success of the agency, other kinds of cooperative efforts by police have begun to surface. Police have learned that, through collaboration and communication, much can be accomplished in the fight against crime. In the past few decades, we have begun to see many examples of international police cooperation.

In fact, the development of the European Union (EU) has spurred a number of arrangements for police cooperation on the continent. In 1976, a group of European countries concerned with the growth of terrorism formed the Trevi Group, which eventually included twelve EU countries. In 1985, the Schengen Group was formed by Belgium, France, Germany, Luxembourg, and the Netherlands. The original purpose of the group was to discuss treaties addressing constitutional and legal issues such as allowing police to pursue criminals across national borders and improving information exchanges between countries. Schengen has added several member countries and through computer technology has developed a central information system (Benyon, 1997, p. 110). In the 1990s, the EU created the European Police Office, which analyzes information on drug trafficking and money laundering and acts as an information clearinghouse (like INTERPOL) for EU countries (Benyon, 1997, p. 115). And more recently, in September 1999, police in the Netherlands, Belgium, and Germany began to administer the first cross-border police precinct. In a small town in Holland, only a couple of miles from the Dutch-German border, one can now see German and Dutch police working side by side in a multinational command.

Although these examples are limited to one continent, the cooperative efforts may be reflective of the future of policing throughout the

A Day in the Life of a Tokyo Police Officer

Mr. Yamada, a typical Koban officer, finished a ten month preservice training course at a prefectural police academy two years ago, and he was assigned to a police station. The station is made up of six sections: administration, crime prevention, criminal investigation, traffic, security, and community police. The total personnel numbers around 400. Almost half of them are assigned to the community police section, under which ten Koban and five patrol cars operate.

The working pattern of the Koban is based on the three-day rotation system. Officer Yamada, for example, works from 8:30 A.M. on the first day to 8:30 A.M. on the second day. After that, he works from 8:30 A.M. to 5:15 P.M. on the third day. This is the basic pattern, but the working hours a week are limited to 40 hours.

Officer Yamada lives in a dormitory attached to the police station. He shares his room with a colleague. He gets up at 6:30 A.M. and takes breakfast at the dining facility in the dormitory. At 8:30 A.M. he goes to an auditorium in the police station. About 40 officers in all, who will be assigned to each Koban on this day, assemble there. A chief of the station checks out their uniforms and equipment, and gives general directions. After the morning formation, Officer Yamada and two other policemen go to "Ekimae Koban" by bicycle, a kilometer away from the station.

At 9 A.M. Officer Yamada and his mates take over the responsibilities from members of an outgoing group. A police sergeant, Koban leader of the day, gives them specific instructions.

At 10 A.M. Officer Yamada goes out of the Koban to patrol. At 10:30 A.M. he gets a radio report of a traffic accident in the neighborhood. He rushes to the scene, rescues victims, and controls the traffic there, until traffic police officers come from the police station.

At 11 A.M. Officer Yamada goes back to the Koban and carries out his duties there until 12:00 noon. He orders a lunch box by phone from a restaurant that has delivery service. The lunch box comes in ten minutes. He eats it in a rear room of the Koban and takes a break until 1 P.M.

From 1 to 2 P.M., Officer Yamada stands just in front of the Koban and gives directions to more than ten strangers, while his mates are eating lunch.

At 2 P.M. Officer Yamada starts to make routine visits to houses and offices on his beat by bicycle. He visits eight houses and two offices for two hours, and tells the residents and the office workers about burglaries that recently occurred nearby. He also hears from them about what they want the police to do.

At 4:10 P.M. a little girl visits the Koban accompanied by her mother to turn in a wallet she found at a park. Officer Yamada receives the wallet from her, checks what is in it, and makes out the "Found Property Report." He explains to her mother that she can claim a reward of from 5 to 20 percent of its value if its owner is identified. In case the owner does not appear in 6 months and 14 days, the law says that the wallet will be awarded to her.

At 7 P.M. Officer Yamada goes out on foot patrol with his partner. Around 8:50 P.M. at a narrow street, a suspicious-looking man does an about-face and tries to run away as soon as the man recognizes the police. They dash up to the man and ask several questions. Consequently, they find the man carrying a handgun illegally. In Japan, the possession of a handgun is almost totally banned by the law. The man is immediately put under arrest for violating the Firearms and Swords Control Law. They take the suspect to the police station and hand him over to criminal investigators. After transferring the suspect to the detectives, they return to their patrol.

Officer Yamada is supposed to have a few hours of sleep in the rear room until 5 A.M. But at 3:15 A.M. there is a fire report from a nearby resident. He is awakened by his partner, rushes to the scene, and helps the people escape to safety. The fire is put out in 30 minutes and no one is injured. At 4 A.M. he returns to the Koban and takes a rest until 6 A.M.

At 7:30 A.M. Officer Yamada stands at a busy intersection to help school children cross the street on their way to school. He loves the school kids, because they always say to him, "Good morning, Officer! Thank you very much for the good job."

At 8 A.M. members of an incoming party arrive at the Koban and take over the duty. After some paper work at the police station, Officer Yamada goes back to the dormitory, takes a quick shower, and goes to bed.

SOURCE: T. Hirota, 1997. From National Police Agency of Japan. In *Global Report on Crime and Justice.* Reprinted with permission of the United Nations.

world. Clearly, the police are to learn that by working together, sharing information and ideas, they can better solve the problems related to crime and justice.

SUMMARY

The ideal police force is one that prevents crime, keeps order, respects the rights and dignity of citizens, is friendly and courteous, respects the laws, and does not abuse its power through corruption. Most modern police forces attempt to achieve this ideal through education, training, careful recruitment, and organizational regulations. The peculiarities of police work, however, including the need to keep public order in times of civil tension and the large amount of discretion exercised by individual officers on the street, may interfere with ideal operations. Furthermore, the organizational climate and structure are strongly influenced by historical developments and political realities in particular systems.

In the descriptions in this chapter, we have seen manifestations of this historical and political influence time and time again. In England, with its tradition of decentralization and resistance to government power, the police culture has emphasized local control and the idea of "police as citizens." This cultural emphasis continues despite increased central control and claims of police misconduct toward minorities and violations of due process. In France, with its tradition of centralization and bureaucratization, the entire police organization is directed from two ministries in Paris. Germany's police operations are highly influenced by twin fears: fear of the kind of public disorder that signaled the end of the Weimar Republic and fear of the excesses that characterized police in the Nazi years. In the People's Republic of China, police have always been under the close scrutiny of the Communist party. Recently, at least in public announcements, the Chinese government has begun to recognize the rule of law over the rule of those in political power. In the postwar years, the Japanese police have become a relatively benign, if intrusive, force for service and crime prevention. Saudi Arabia, a small country with few crime problems, and with no aspirations to democracy, has a police force that is modeled in some ways on the French; but its major challenge is policing the pilgrimages to the Muslim holy cities. Despite extensive reforms in recent decades in most of these countries, as well as extensive international cooperation among the Western countries of England, France, and Germany, the prevailing culture remains in these various agencies.

Social upheavals in a number of countries in the 1960s through the early 1980s, as well as a rising crime rate, have taught police agencies that they must be responsive to the citizenry and that they cannot be effective in crime prevention without citizen assistance. The response of police agencies has been an attempt to develop various forms of community-oriented policing, much of it inspired by the Japanese example of close and constant contact between police and citizenry. As we enter the twenty-first century, we can also expect that the police will work more closely not only with citizens but also with other police agencies in the international fight against crime.

DISCUSSION QUESTIONS AND EXERCISES

1. Which of the six model nations do you believe has the most effective police force? Why?

2. How does the United States deal with problems related to civil order control? How do these methods compare and contrast with our model countries?

3. How might the *koban* system contribute to a low crime rate in Japan? Would such a system be adaptable to the United States?

4. Using the Internet, find an example of a community policing program in the United States. Would it be possible to implement such a program in China? Support your conclusions.

5. How would you rank the model countries with respect to potential abuse of power by police agencies?

FOR FURTHER READING

Bayley, D. (1991). *Forces of Order: The Police in Japan.* Berkeley: University of California Press.

Fairchild, E. (1988). *German Police: Ideals and Reality in the Postwar World.* Springfield, Ill.: Thomas.

Goldstein, H. (1990). *Problem-Oriented Policing.* Philadelphia: Temple University Press.

Kelling, G. L. and W. J. Bratton. (1993). Implementing Community Policing: The Administrative Problem. In *Perspectives on Policing,* 17. Cambridge, Mass.: U.S. Department of Justice and Program in Criminal Justice Policy and Management, Harvard University, July.

Marenin, O. (ed.). (1996). *Policing Change, Changing Police: International Perspectives.* New York: Garland.

Stead, P. (1983). *The Police of France.* New York: Macmillan.

Tavaras, C., and A. Prout. (1995). *Digest: Information on the Criminal Justice System in England and Wales.* London: Home Office Research and Statistics Department.

6 | ∾ | Constitutional Review

Key Terms and Concepts

abstract review
ancien régime
Bundesverfassungsgericht
Conseil Constitutionnel
deputies
European Court of Human Rights (ECHR)
federal system of government
Grand Bench
International Court of Justice (ICJ)
International Criminal Court
judicial review
Petty Bench
Standing Committee of the NPC

With the following words, Chief Justice John Marshall set out the basis of the logical argument for judicial review that the U.S. Supreme Court advanced in 1803 in the famous case of *Marbury v. Madison* (2 L.Ed. 60).

> *A constitution is either a superior paramount law, unchangeable by ordinary means, or it is on a level with ordinary legislative acts, and like other acts, is alterable when the legislature shall please to alter it. If the former part of the alternative be true, then a legislative act contrary to the constitution is not law: if the latter part be true, then written constitutions are absurd attempts . . . to limit a power in its own nature illimitable.*

In this case, the U.S. Supreme Court asserted the right of the judicial branch to rule on the constitutionality of an act of Congress, thereby establishing the functions and prerogatives of the judiciary in relation to the legislative branch (*Black's Law Dictionary*, 1979). Marshall continued by making these points:

- If written constitutions establish limits on the powers of sitting governments, then governmental agents can act in ways that go beyond their allowed powers.

- If governmental agents, whether executive or legislative, overstep their allowed powers, there must be a way to curb their actions, or a written constitution would be a useless document.

- Since courts are set up to compare the adherence of particular actions to the law, they are the most likely bodies to interpret whether a particular action is contrary to a constitution.

- Since, in addition, United States judges take an oath to support the Constitution, they are particularly suited to act as judicial protectors of the constitution.

- It therefore follows that federal courts should have the power to decide whether particular actions of government or individuals are in accordance with constitutional law and to declare those actions unconstitutional if they are not.

Marshall's argument was a cogent one, and one that seemed to persuade both politicians and the public, since it was not seriously challenged. Indeed, the Supreme Court did not again wield its power to declare federal laws unconstitutional until 1854, when, in the Dred Scott decision, it held some portions of the Missouri Compromise of 1820 to be unconstitutional. Thus, there was little reason for a power struggle between the Court and other federal agencies over court power.

Likewise, the power of the Supreme Court to declare state laws and portions of state constitutions not in conformity with the U.S. Constitution, and therefore illegal, became well established during the first quarter of the nineteenth century through decisions of the Marshall court. These decisions included such well-known cases as *McCullough v. Maryland* and *Gibbons v. Ogden*. Collectively, these decisions regarding state powers suggested that in a *federal* system of government, in which two levels of government, state and national, have discrete powers assigned to them, it becomes necessary to make decisions about the locus of power in specific, often ambiguous, situations. In the United States, the power to make such decisions fell to the Supreme Court, which gradually became accepted as the arbiter of American federalism and, much later, as the arbiter in cases in which states were accused of violating minority rights as they are expressed in the Constitution.

In this chapter, we examine the ways that governments make ultimate decisions regarding both the constitutionality of criminal process rules and the behavior of agents in the criminal process. A knowledge of these governmental practices will help illuminate the significance of some of the cases and systems we consider in this book. Such knowledge will also help you appreciate the breadth of governmental protection of individual rights in the criminal process around the world.

JUDICIAL REVIEW: AN AMERICAN CONTRIBUTION TO THE SCIENCE OF GOVERNMENT

Judicial review truly can be described as an American institution that, because of its success, has been adapted by many other nations of the world. Over 40 percent of political systems have some form of judicial review today. Much of the push toward adoption of judicial review came after World War II, as many emergent nations broke away from the colonial powers that had controlled their governments and set up systems of their own. At the same time, the governments that had collapsed or been overthrown during the course of the war tried to rebuild their governmental institutions.

The U.S. Constitution became a model for these nations, for several reasons. For one thing, it represented an earlier break with a colonial past, a break that had proved to be highly successful over the course of 150 years. For another, the American contribution to the war effort made American institutions particularly popular among liberated nations. In sum, many countries were preoccupied with governmental forms, and U.S. institutions provided a particularly attractive model.

Another postwar development that helped bring about judicial review was the presence of U.S. occupying forces that monitored the constitutional development of the defeated Axis nations—Germany, Italy, and Japan—which all instituted constitutional courts at that time. The German and Italian courts differ in many ways from the American one, and Japanese constitutional history has followed a distinctively Japanese path since 1945. Nevertheless, the constitutional courts in these countries have proved to be enduring institutions that have actually grown stronger over the years.

OTHER POSSIBLE ARRANGEMENTS FOR CONSTITUTIONAL REVIEW

Is judicial review by a supreme court the only way that a constitution can be protected against legislative or executive encroachment? Is it even the most desirable mechanism for resolving issues of constitutionality? Supreme court justices, after all, are usually appointed officials who do not represent the public in a direct way and who do not have to answer for their decisions in any meaningful way. In the United States, in fact, they are appointed for life and thus constitute a strongly antimajoritarian faction in government.

There are at least three other ways to handle the problem of constitutionality: (1) no review, (2) nonjudicial review, and (3) judicial review with legislative approval. They are presented here and will be explained further as we consider constitutional review and its effect on criminal process in our model countries.

No Review

The most obvious alternative to conventional judicial review is no constitutional review. This is the alternative that John Marshall viewed as absurd in a constitutional government. Despite Marshall's belief, historically, many systems based on written constitutions, such as the series of French constitutions from 1792 to 1958 and the constitution of Germany's Weimar Republic, have not provided for constitutional review. In these cases, there was little inclination in postrevolutionary or postimperial times to give broad powers to judges, who previously had been part of an oppressive elite. A more recent example of a constitutional system without constitutional review, at least with respect to individual rights, is the former Soviet Union.

Britain is a special case: Since it does not have a written constitution, judicial review in the American sense is not possible.

How do countries without provision for constitutional review avoid the "absurdity," as Marshall called it, inherent in their arrangements? If they are unitary rather than federal nations, and thus do not have to worry about settling disputes over the respective powers of state and national governments, as the U.S. Supreme Court often has had to do, the task becomes easier. The task is also easier if the country has a homogeneous populace and does not have serious problems of discrimination against minorities. Of course, problems related to individual liberties occur in all systems and transcend the simple problem of ethnic or other discrimination.

In effect, however, a certain respect for basic constitutional arrangements exists in most democratic governments, so that, in broad terms, the problem may not be as great as it seems. In nondemocratic regimes, the matter is moot, since there is little concern for constitutionality in any case. Courts may also practice a constitutional protection function that involves deciding cases in ways that maximize fidelity to the constitution rather than to a dubious statute or executive action. In certain countries, such as Australia, judicial review has become a de facto reality although it is not provided for in their constitutions. This is, of course, also the case in the United States.

Nonjudicial Review

Another alternative to judicial review is the establishment of a nonjudicial constitutional review agency to resolve issues of constitutionality. France adopted this alternative in its 1958 Constitution, which provides for a nine-member Constitutional Council. The chief function of this council is to resolve disputes over constitutionality that are brought to it by the president, the heads of the houses of parliament, or by petition of at least sixty members of either house of parliament.

The French system is known as **abstract constitutional review** because the council decides on issues of constitutionality without hearing actual cases that have arisen under specific laws. Abstract review essentially means that the council gives advisory opinions rather than judgments in cases. Since it is not a court, it seems logical that the council would be engaged in abstract review. Abstract review may also be practiced by a court that also hears concrete cases, as is the case in Germany. However, there are some problems with abstract review, as we shall see when we discuss the French arrangement in some detail later in the chapter.

In theory, it would be possible to set up other arrangements for constitutional review. For example, subcommittees of parliaments, committees of elder statesmen, representatives of the various branches of government sitting as a constitutional committee—all are possible agencies for constitutional review. Nor do such bodies necessarily have to practice merely abstract review; it might be possible to let them do case-based review with respect only to the constitutional issues in particular cases. The fact is, however, that such agencies do not exist.

Judicial Review with Legislative Approval

Another form of judicial review is to have constitutional decisions by a supreme court subject to approval by a legislative body. This arrangement exists in India, where constitutional amendments may be passed with the approval of two-thirds of both houses of parliament. Thus, an unpopular or unacceptable decision of the Indian Supreme Court regarding the constitutionality of legislation may be nullified with relative ease (Cappelletti, 1971; McWhinney, 1965).

CONSTITUTIONAL REVIEW AND THE CRIMINAL PROCESS

One function of most constitutions is to proclaim the rights of individuals and protect them against governmental or other violations. Criminals are not usually popular individuals: For every Robin Hood who steals from the rich to give to the poor, there are millions of predatory criminals who rob, maim, rape, and murder innocent individuals. The public demands satisfaction in terms of stiff sentences or other punishments to ensure that the particular offender or future offenders will not commit other crimes. Procedural niceties designed to ensure that innocent people are not convicted of crimes may seem unnecessarily obstructive to those who want swift justice.

Governmental agents may also be willing to sacrifice scrupulous evidence collection in favor of rapid, if arbitrary, disposal of criminal cases. Frequently, governments eliminate political enemies and social outcasts through the criminal process. The accused, who is often poor, defenseless, and weak, has little chance against unbridled action by the government. The history of all nations has been marred by cruel and arbitrary treatment of those accused of crimes, whether political or predatory.

Some constitution makers, mindful of the history of persecution of the unpopular through the criminal process, have included provisions for redressing at least minimally the power imbalance between the accused and the state. This is done through rules of criminal procedure that provide guarantees of fairness with respect to searches, arrests, trial, and sanctions. In modern times, one of the key tasks of constitutional review has been the interpretation and, in many cases, the broadening of these procedural rules.

The U.S. Constitution's criminal procedure provisions are familiar to most of us and are found chiefly, but not exclusively, in the Bill of Rights. They include the right to be free from unreasonable search and seizure, the right to counsel during the pretrial process and at trial, the right to a speedy trial by jury, and the right to remain silent during a criminal procedure. In addition, the right not to be subjected to cruel and unusual punishments is an important postconviction guarantee. In each case, the original proponents of the Bill of Rights were adapting rights of Englishmen that had developed, painfully and over centuries, in the Common Law, expanding them and applying them to the new federal government.

Other nations may not have detailed criminal procedure rules incorporated into their constitutions to the degree that the United States does. In Germany, for example, most rules of criminal procedure are found in criminal procedure laws. Nevertheless, the Federal Constitutional Court does hear appeals related to criminal cases in which violations of basic constitutional rights (such as freedom of expression, freedom of movement, the right to liberty, and free development of one's personality) are involved. Most modern constitutions are concerned with basic human rights and cannot ignore mistreatment or unfair treatment of individuals accused of crime.

CONSTITUTIONAL REVIEW IN THE MODEL COUNTRIES

Four of the six model countries have written constitutions, with England and Saudi Arabia the exceptions. England claims to have an unwritten constitution and to be guided by a peculiarly English constitutional law, while in Saudi Arabia, the Qur'an has constitutional status. In each case, constitutional review takes on a more or less unique form; Table 6.1 summarizes the key components in each model country. Examining the process of constitutional review in these countries will lead to a better understanding of the criminal justice process and its legal foundations.

England: Indirect Judicial Review

As explained in Chapter 4, the supremacy of Parliament is the major source of British government. Since there is no written constitution, even the most sacred English traditions of government and human rights theoretically can be abrogated by an act of Parliament. This supremacy of Parliament came about over the course of centuries of struggle and even war. It constitutes a source of pride in government for most British citizens, just as separation of powers and checks and balances

Table 6.1 Constitutional Review Procedures

Country	Government/Legal System	Constitutional Review Arrangements
England	Unitary/Common Law	No formal review exists; the government and courts are expected to uphold the (unwritten) constitution.
France	Unitary/Civil Law	The Constitutional Council, not a court, reviews on request the constitutionality of legislation; abstract review only.
Germany	Federal/Civil Law	The Federal Constitutional Court has judicial review powers, both abstract and concrete.
Japan	Unitary/modified Civil Law	The Supreme Court has judicial review powers; no abstract review.
Saudi Arabia	Unitary/Islamic Law	The Qur'an as interpreted through the centuries by legal/religious scholars serves as basic law. Interpretation by religious leaders is possible.
China	Unitary/Socialist Law	National People's Congress (NPC) and Standing Committee Perform Judicial Review

are valued by Americans as integral to the government of the United States.

Does this mean that there is no judicial or constitutional review in England? The answer is a guarded yes. To be sure, even the highest appellate courts in England do not have the kind of political and decision-making power that American courts have. Judicial personnel are chosen more for their demonstrated competence or for their political loyalty to the party in power than for their ideological stances, as is the case with federal judges in the United States. British constitutional law scholars, however, maintain that there exists a kind of judicial review of basic constitutional tenets. According to one account, "A statute which is contrary to the reason of the common law or purports to take away a prerogative of the Crown is none the less valid, but it will, so far as is possible, be applied in such a way as to leave the prerogative or the common law rights of the subject intact" (Keir and Lawson, 1967, p. 9). In true Common Law fashion, Keir and Lawson give examples of cases in which judges have held to a "higher law," or Common Law tradition, rather than upholding an action of Parliament.

Rule of law, representative government, freedom of expression, an independent judiciary—these are immutable traditions that the courts are obligated to uphold despite the sovereignty of Parliament. In fact, the very idea that Parliament

is sovereign may be looked upon as an evolved constitutional tradition in England rather than some higher truth. Edward McWhinney calls this process of judicial oversight "indirect judicial review," or "braking" (McWhinney, 1965). He gives the example of the Married Women's Property Act of 1832, according to which a woman, even if married, could dispose of real estate belonging to her alone. The court interpreted this law to mean that, despite its face provisions, a woman could not dispose of lands of which she was active trustee, as opposed to outright owner, without the consent of her husband. In 1907, however, Parliament nullified the effect of the court decision through new legislation. This case illustrates the kind of give-and-take between the judiciary and Parliament that can result in gradual social and constitutional change.

In another case, *Rex v. Halliday, Ex parte Zadig* (1917), Zadig, a naturalized British citizen of German birth, was detained under the Defense of the Realm Act of 1914, which was designed to prevent subversion of the World War I war effort. The law allowed for preventive detention for those who appeared, because of "hostile origins or associations," to pose a danger to the government. Zadig's case was ultimately appealed to the House of Lords, which acts as the final court of appeal. The case involved important issues related to the writ of habeas corpus, under which a detainee has the right not to be detained indefinitely without having formal charges instituted. A majority ruled against Zadig on the grounds of the seriousness of the wartime emergency. However, the minority argued strongly against Zadig's detention on the grounds that Parliament itself did not literally make the rules that regulated such internments, but allowed the executive to carry out the intentions of the act through particular rules.

Lord Shaw of Dunfermine expressed his strong indignation at the interpretation of the law that was adopted by the majority:

> *The construction upheld implies a repeal of the ancient liberties and rights of our people. . . . No repeal like this, or in this manner, at once so sweeping and so covert, has ever been accomplished in the modern history of this island. That Parliament should have entertained such an intention of repeal I do not believe; that it would have recoiled from putting such an intention of repeal into words I can well understand. (Keir and Lawson, 1967, p. 43)*

Note that there is no question of unconstitutionality of an act of Parliament in this dissent by Lord Shaw. Rather, he is claiming that the act should be construed to conform to the basic tenets of English constitutional law. Obviously, then, the less explicit a law of Parliament is, or the more it delegates power to administrative agencies to carry out broad objectives, the more the English courts can become involved in issues of constitutionality.

The Zadig case has interesting parallels with the Japanese internment case (*Korematsu v. U.S.,* 323 U.S. 214) in which American citizens of Japanese extraction were interned as part of a wartime exercise of emergency powers. At issue in *Korematsu* was the basic written constitutional right not to be deprived of liberty without due process of law. At issue in Zadig was a parliamentary statute that could be construed to abrogate basic Common Law rights that had constitutional stature in the British justice system. Interestingly, both cases were decided in favor of prerogative state emergency powers and at the expense of individual rights.

The English system of constitutional law seems extraordinarily elusive to Americans, who are accustomed to a formal constitutional rationale for issues related to governmental powers. Much relies on accepted tradition and historical precedent that hardly seem to approach the status of law according to any commonly accepted definition. An American student of English government must get past a certain threshold of misunderstanding or even impatience before the subtleties of English government can be understood. In order truly to understand what is going on, it becomes necessary to study English history, and especially the great struggle for parliamentary supremacy that occurred in the seventeenth century.

France: The Conseil Constitutionnel

France, a model Civil Law nation, has never been comfortable with the concept of constitutional review, for two reasons. First, the revolutionary tradition in France was partially founded on distrust of the corrupt and cruel judiciary of the **ancien régime,** a judiciary body that served the rulers at the expense of the people. Second, in a Civil Law country, the idea that powerful judges can decide important policy questions on a case-by-case basis seems to run counter to the notion of the supremacy of the legal code and statutory law.

Thus, we have a peculiar contrast with England. In England, case-based law and the ideal that the law protects individuals from the government has a long history and is easily accepted along with the contrary notion of the supremacy of Parliament. In France, powerful lawyers and judges are antithetical to both the revolutionary and the Civil Law traditions.

Another factor to consider is that France, as a unitary state with no problems of balance and dual sovereignty between the states and the federal government, has not had to face the difficult and delicate questions about power and states' rights that a federal nation must face. (By contrast, in the early years of the United States, the Supreme Court played a crucial role in establishing the balance of powers between the states and the federal government, generally to the benefit of the federal government.) As a result, the first fourteen French constitutions that followed the Revolution of 1789 contained no effective mechanisms for deciding matters of constitutionality and few checks on legislative power.

At the same time, an elaborate system of administrative courts, originally designed by Napoleon to help him control the empire, evolved into a mechanism for upholding individual rights in the face of government violation. This mitigated possible public outrage at the lack of individual legal protections, and the courts have been able to check executive power, despite their impotence in the legislative sphere. At the apex of this network of administrative courts is the powerful Council of State, which has acted for many years as a check on the powers of government.

It was not until the advent of the Fifth French Republic, set up under the presidency of Charles de Gaulle and at his instigation, that France, in 1958, joined the ranks of nations that include organs of constitutional review in their basic scheme of government. As explained previously, constitutional review in France does not mean judicial review in the sense that it is employed in the United States. French constitutional review is carried out by a **Conseil Constitutionnel** (Constitutional Council), which is not a court and does not hear actual cases such as generally are brought to courts. Instead, the council, upon application by the president, the prime minister, the presiding officer of either house of the legislature, or sixty elected representatives to the legislature, considers the constitutionality of legislation before it goes into effect. Certain kinds of legislation that affect the structural components of the French government are automatically reviewed by the council. In addition, the council has certain other functions related to ensuring that elections are conducted properly and votes are counted correctly. Elections appeals, in fact, constitute a large proportion of the council's work.

The council consists of nine members. Three are appointed by the president, three by the president of the Chamber of Deputies, and three by the president of the Senate. Members of the council serve for nine years and are ineligible for reappointment, although former presidents of the republic may serve as life members ex officio if they have decided to give up political life. Council members are not required to be jurists or to have legal training. About half the members have been outstanding political personalities, with the other half professional judicial personnel (Mc-Whinney, 1986).

There is no appeal of the decisions of the council, so it has effective power to nullify legislation. In its early years, and in keeping with the French tradition, the council was conservative in its approach, rarely opposing Parliament in its decisions. Since 1970, however, it has ventured into the field of individual rights, deciding cases in which the constitutionality of legislation that infringes on basic rights included in the Preamble to the 1958 Constitution, is at stake.

With respect to criminal justice procedure, the council has also moved to assert basic constitutional rights. In January 1977, the council challenged the constitutionality of a law that allowed for extensive police searches of vehicles without probable cause. Following its practice of declaring portions of laws unconstitutional, it declared that "the provisions of the single article of the law authorizing the search of vehicles for the investigation and prevention of criminal infractions are therefore declared not to conform to the Constitution" (Cappelletti and Cohen, 1979, p. 71).

Almost inadvertently, the Constitutional Council has become involved in politics, just as constitutional courts can hardly avoid political considerations in their decisions. The council has favored the program of one or another party, depending on the appointees at any one time. Since all appointments are made by political leaders, and many appointments have emphasized political as opposed to judicial background, this politicization seems quite natural. It may also reflect the fact that the council, over the course of thirty years, has gradually matured, becoming more assured and confident about its jurisdiction, its powers, and its limits.

Recently, the council seems to be emerging as a major voice in French government. According to Morton (1988, pp. 89–110), the number of challenged laws has increased dramatically, with the opposition in parliament challenging every major piece of legislation that is passed. Between 1958 and 1974, only nine laws were sent to the council for consideration. Between 1974 and 1981, that number was forty-seven, and between 1981 and 1986, it rose to sixty-six. By 1987, 40 percent of the council's nullifications of laws had been in the area of fundamental rights (Morton, 1988, pp. 90–91).

Germany: The Bundesverfassungsgericht

Germany underwent three abrupt—in fact, cataclysmic—switches in regime type over the course of the twentieth century. People in the former East Germany actually went through four such switches, as they also abandoned a Communist authoritarian government for the liberal democracy of the West.

The first switch was from an authoritarian and paternalistic imperial order to the liberal, politically permissive Weimar Republic that followed Germany's defeat in World War I and the end of the empire in 1919. The second switch was from that same Weimar Republic to the ruthless and totalitarian Third Reich under Hitler's Nazi party. The Third Reich lasted from 1933 to 1945, when Germany was finally defeated in World War II. It was followed by the division of Germany into the Federal Republic of Germany in the west and the German Democratic Republic in the east. The Federal Republic's 1949 constitution, known as the Basic Law, again established a liberal democracy. This time, however, a more cautious and constrained democracy was set up, one that was designed to avoid the pitfalls of the Weimar constitution. With the reunification of Germany in 1990, the Basic Law has become the constitution of the entire nation of Germany.

One of the mechanisms developed in the 1949 Basic Law was the **Bundesverfassungsgericht,** or Federal Constitutional Court (FCC),

which was to be a major guardian of German democracy and the values of the new German government. It was given broad powers (1) to declare laws unconstitutional, (2) to clarify questions relating to division of powers between the federal government and the state, or Laender, governments, and (3) even to rule that extreme political groups might be outlawed because of their potential to undermine the constitutional order. It was also to be the determining force in the interpretation of Articles 1 through 17 of the Constitution. These articles constitute an enumeration of the basic rights of German citizens and are analogous to the Bill of Rights in the U.S. Constitution. Like the Bill of Rights, however, they are also open to many shades of meaning and thus require frequent court interpretation.

The Federal Constitutional Court may seem like a familiar institution to Americans, and, indeed, it performs functions similar to those of the U.S. Supreme Court. Remember, however, that Germany is a Civil Law country, concerned with adherence to statute law and not readily amenable to some of the more political, discretionary, and personalistic aspects of American judicial practice. Thus, there are certain structural differences that are immediately apparent in the two court systems. These have to do with personnel, jurisdiction, and access routes.

German judges are civil servants, trained for a lifelong tenured position in the judiciary. In contrast, American judges are usually prominent lawyers, appointed or elected to office, often with a view to their political record or ideological views. In Germany, as neutral civil servants, judges' political opinions are not at issue (although the German judiciary was notoriously conservative during the Weimar Republic and was bitterly criticized for its latent opposition to the regime and its willingness to cooperate with the Nazi government).

The Federal Constitutional Court has sixteen judges. They are chosen by Parliament, half by the lower house, or Bundestag, and half by the upper house, or Bundesrat. Eight of these judges generally are high-ranking career civil service judges while the other eight usually are prominent lawyers, law professors, or politicians. Thus, this court is exceptional in the German judiciary in that its political nature was acknowledged even at the time of its creation. At the same time, the inclusion of career judges is a reminder of the respect for legalism that has been so prominent in Germany in modern times (Kommers, 1976).

Each judge sits permanently on one of two panels, called "senates." The court rarely sits as a whole body, and then only to settle questions of jurisdiction between the senates. One senate handles the many cases dealing with civil and constitutional rights; the other handles all other constitutional cases. Judges serve for nonrenewable twelve-year terms. In this way, the Germans hoped to avoid the problem of senility that they felt occurred with lifetime appointments, such as exist in the American federal courts.

In the matter of jurisdiction, there is some difference between the U.S. Supreme Court and the German Constitutional Court. Whereas the U.S. court is the final appellate court for all federal cases, Germany has five supreme courts that handle final appeals in all cases except those in which a constitutional question is raised. Where constitutional questions arise in the course of regular proceedings, all German courts must bring the case to the Federal Constitutional Court. In practice, to be sure, the U.S. Supreme Court may restrict its workload through its power selectively to grant writs of certiorari and to refuse direct appeals. The German court has no writ of certiorari and must hear all cases that fall within its jurisdiction. However, in reality, the court actually turns down many cases as not falling within its jurisdiction.

In addition to its case-based jurisdiction, the Federal Constitutional Court has the power to give advisory opinions. Thus, it has abstract as well as concrete review powers. Abstract review may be called for by state or federal governmental agencies, and even by individual citizens if they believe that particular laws violate their constitutional rights.

One of the most famous of the cases involving abstract review was the Southwest Case of 1951 (Decision of October 23, 1951, Bundesverfassungsgericht [1952] 1 BVerfGE 14). In this case, the court, early in its existence, was petitioned by the state of Baden to rule on the constitutionality of a federal law that combined three small southwestern states into the one state of Baden-Wurttemberg. The court ruled in favor of the federal legislation, thus embarking on a course of strengthening the power of the fledgling federal government, just as the Marshall Court in the early nineteenth century strengthened the power of the U.S. federal government.

Since that time, some highly controversial public policy questions have been subject to abstract review by the Federal Constitutional Court. These include the party finance decision of 1966, the decision related to the treaty between two German states in 1973, and the abortion decision of 1975. Indeed, the court has been widely criticized for the lack of judicial restraint in its abstract advisory decisions.

A peculiar power of the court, granted in the Basic Law, is its right to declare unconstitutional political parties that "by reason of their aims or the behavior of their adherents, seek to impair or abolish the free democratic basic order or to endanger the existence of the Federal Republic of Germany" (Grundgesetz [GG] art. 21, §2). This provision was designed to guard against the resurgence of right-wing Fascist parties. It was used by the court in the early 1950s to outlaw both the Neo-Nazi Socialist Reich party and the Communist party. Outlawing of parties is not as easy as it may seem, however, since it is possible for the same group of people to reorganize under another name. This is what happened in the case of the Communists who, being outlawed as the Communist party of Germany (KPD), resurfaced as the German Communist party (DKP). The latest right-wing party to gain strength in Germany is the Republican party. Neither the federal government in Bonn, or the Federal Constitutional Court seems inclined any longer to go through the tedious fact-finding procedure involved in outlawing political groups. This suggests that postwar German democracy has reached a level of legitimacy and self-confidence that makes such action unnecessary.

As mentioned, access to the Federal Constitutional Court is by direct action of citizens, referral of cases by other courts, and appeal by officials of the states or the federal government. The most interesting route of access, from the American point of view, is direct appeal by German citizens for abstract review. Such direct access to the court was considered an important way to empower a third force to intervene in possible legislative violations of basic rights. This avoids the tedious and costly process of bringing a particular case to the court through litigation. The court was overwhelmed in its early years by requests from individuals for review of particular statutes, and it continues to receive most of its petitions in this way. A large proportion of these petitions are turned down as trivial or nonrelevant, and the court hears only those that involve important constitutional questions.

Compared to the U.S. Supreme Court, which has a large percentage of its caseload in the criminal procedure and criminal justice sphere, the German court's significance for criminal procedure is circumscribed. This is because most criminal procedure matters are regulated by statutory rather than constitutional provisions. Nevertheless, some important human rights issues come before the German high court involving questions of criminal procedure with respect to the articles of the constitution that allow for the free development of personality, the inviolability of the home, and liberty.

Japan

Japan, like Germany, was an occupied country after World War II. Also like Germany, Japan developed a constitution modeled in many respects on the U.S. Constitution. And like Germany, Japan established a supreme court designed to re-

inforce the separation of powers and to uphold individual rights through broad powers of judicial review. Furthermore, the Japanese legal culture falls into the Civil Law family and, indeed, was much influenced by the German law.

Despite these similarities, the end product in Japan is quite different from that in Germany. The Japanese Supreme Court has not become a leading institution in Japanese government. Its few major decisions regarding the unconstitutionality of laws passed by the Diet (the Japanese legislature) have been largely ignored, emphasizing that the courts, which have few means at their disposal to enforce decrees calling for positive action, often depend on respect and good will to carry out decisions that involve action by policymakers. The Japanese continue to deal with conflict in indirect and informal ways rather than asserting their rights through the legal system. Whereas Germany's Federal Constitutional Court has gradually become a major player in the German governmental system, the Japanese Supreme Court remains on the periphery in Japanese government and society.

Why Japan's Supreme Court Is Different. What accounts for these differences? On a structural level, we can postulate that a policy-making constitutional court tends to be more crucial to governmental operations in a federal system, such as the Germans have, than in a unitary system like that of Japan. In addition, certain structural characteristics of the Japanese legal system tend to make the high court conservative and bureaucratic. On a deeper level, however, the basic differences in the approach to law and legalism between the Germans and the Japanese may help explain the different development of their respective courts.

A closer examination of the Japanese legal structures and customs helps us understand the subtleties of the Japanese approach to judicial review. The Japanese Constitution itself is quite clear in this matter. Its Article 81 states that "the Supreme Court is the court of last resort with power to determine the constitutionality of any law, regulation, or official act." Between 1947, when the Constitution went into effect, and 1985, the Supreme Court used this power approximately ten times to declare actions or laws of the Diet unconstitutional. The first time was in 1973, when a section of the Criminal Code that called for greater punishment in the case of parricide (killing a parent) than for other kinds of murder was declared invalid.

Ten times is actually not an infrequent exercise of the power of judicial review when we consider that the U.S. Supreme Court used this power with respect to laws of Congress only once in the course of the first sixty-five years of the American republic. At that time, however, the U.S. court was quite busy establishing the supremacy of the federal government by dealing with issues relating to the constitutionality of state actions, legislation, or constitutions. The difference in the Japanese case is that its Supreme Court decisions have had little effect on governmental policy or social change. In some cases, such as the two decisions that found a serious malapportionment of seats in the legislature, the decisions were ignored by the Diet, the governmental body that would have had to deal with the problem (Luney, 1990).

The broad wording of Article 81, on the power of judicial review, naturally gave rise to questions about whether the court should give advisory opinions on the constitutionality of rules and laws that have been passed but have not been brought to the court in the form of justiciable cases. The other two Civil Law countries that we have examined, France and Germany, do allow for abstract constitutional review. In France, as we explained, it is the only kind of formal constitutional review that exists. The Japanese court elected to follow the American model in this respect, refusing to give opinions unless a concrete case existed. In this sense, it departed from the pure Civil Law tradition, which emphasizes the actual code or law rather than judicial interpretation and concern for precedent.

In other respects, however, the Japanese court has become more representative of the Civil Law

tradition than of the bolder and more political approach to law found in the United States and Germany. The court, according to scholars like Noriho Urabe (1990) and Hiroshi Itoh (1988), has not used its power to uphold individual rights against governmental power. Even the famous parricide case of 1973, regarding whether parricide should be treated as a more serious crime than conventional murder, was decided on a technicality rather than as an equal rights case. In other cases the court has deferred to the political branches of the government and to the administrative authorities. For example, when the issue of the constitutionality of the Japanese defense forces arose, the court chose not to deal with it, calling it an issue of national survival and thus not subject to court review. When parliamentary procedure was challenged in a taxpayer's suit, the court declared that it could not deal with internal parliamentary matters. And when the question of governmental payments related to welfare arose, the court declared that it could not interfere with bureaucratic processes (Itoh, 1988, pp. 209–210). According to Urabe, "In Japan, the Constitution is in most cases treated as important in principle, but of little importance in practice" (Urabe, 1990). He cites numerous cases, including the *Nishiyama* case, in which a reporter obtained and published a secret government document from a female official with whom he was carrying on a love affair. The court declared this action illegal because it violated "the spirit of the whole legal order." Urabe claims that this decision is typical of the Japanese Supreme Court's tendency to ignore the Constitution and its clear prescriptions regarding human rights and legal procedure.

When it comes to criminal procedure, the Japanese Constitution follows the U.S. Constitution almost slavishly, often using the same words found in the Fourth, Fifth, Sixth, and Ninth Amendments. This is in contrast to the German Constitution, which has few provisions that address criminal procedure directly, relying on general provisions and on the statutory law of criminal procedure. In Articles 31 through 38, the Japanese Constitution guarantees due process of law, access to courts, no warrantless searches or seizures, no cruel punishments, no self-incrimination, counsel upon arrest, habeas corpus, speedy public trial, no double jeopardy, and no ex post facto laws. Thus, we have the peculiar situation in which a Civil Law country, which normally uses an inquisitorial criminal procedure, adopts rules that are typical of the adversarial procedures of Common Law countries. There have been some changes in Japanese criminal procedure as a result, although hardly more than the changes in inquisitorial process that have occurred in Germany and other European countries. The Japanese courts are not preoccupied with the rights of the accused and convicted to the same degree as American courts. In addition, the continuation of the office of public procurator, dedicated to the interests of the public rather than the government in criminal cases, remains as a major legacy of Civil Law procedure.

Some important decisions of the Japanese Supreme Court have dealt with procedural rights of the accused and convicted in criminal cases. For example, capital punishment has been upheld, including hanging as a form of execution. Also, the guarantee against double jeopardy has been interpreted to mean that a prosecutor may ask for a harsher penalty than was imposed by the court or even ask for reversal of a "not guilty" judgment. And a prison term has been upheld in a case involving a guilty plea that followed statements about a more lenient sentence to follow if such a plea were entered (Tanaka, 1976, p. 820). (Criminal procedure will be examined in greater detail in Chapter 7.)

The Structure and Functioning of the Japanese Supreme Court. The Japanese Supreme Court serves two purposes: (1) to interpret constitutional issues and (2) to administer the larger Japanese court system. The Court actually is separated into two courts: (1) the Grand Bench and (2) the Petty Bench. The **Grand Bench** includes all 15 members of the Court and deals with matters related to new constitutional rulings and administrative responsibilities, including nominating lower-court judges and regulating attorneys and public procurators. The **Petty Bench,** divided into three separate benches of five justices each, handles all other legal matters, including cases of appellate level jurisdiction.

What kind of court are we talking about? Some writers claim that the Japanese Supreme Court has become increasingly bureaucratic over the course of its history (Itoh, 1988). This is partially because the judges of the Supreme Court are responsible not only for deciding cases involving constitutional interpretation but also for nominating all lower-court judges. These judges, however, are civil servants trained to be judges, and not political appointees or well-known lawyers, as in the United States. In addition, general matters of judicial administration in Japan are controlled by a judicial conference composed of all the Supreme Court judges.

The composition of the Supreme Court also fosters a conservative and bureaucratic approach to its work. There are fifteen judges, appointed by the cabinet, but ten of these judges must come from the career judiciary—prosecutors, practicing attorneys, and lower-court judges. Over the years, there has been increasing dominance of career judges sitting on the court (Tanaka, 1976, ch. 8).

Other factors that tend to produce a certain weakness in the Supreme Court include the tenure of judges, the manner of making decisions, and the parliamentary power situation in Japan. Judges are usually appointed when they are in their mid-sixties, but they face mandatory retirement at age seventy. This means that they do not have the time to develop individual reputations or even to become comfortable with the policy-making aspects of the court. For most decisions, the court is divided into three panels of five, but the panels are not stable and do not specialize in certain aspects of law. Thus, a case may be brought before any of the panels, and the same judges do not always sit together—which lends a certain anonymity to the process. With respect to parliamentary power, only one party, the Liberal Democratic Party, has ever been in power since the establishment of the present Japanese Constitution. Thus, all the judges owe their appointments to this one party, and it is not inconceivable that there may be a bias toward conservatism in dealing with elected representatives.

One distinctive feature of the Japanese Supreme Court is that judges are subject to recall by the public at the first parliamentary election after their appointment. Such a recall, however, has never taken place.

In general, with regard to judicial review in Japan, we find a large gap between this institution on paper and in reality. This is often the case when one examines Japanese institutions, for reasons that are deeply rooted in Japanese culture and history. For instance, recourse to the legal system, with its connotation of conflict and confrontation, is not highly valued in a society that emphasizes harmony and suppression of conflict. The abrupt imposition of the American model following World War II resulted in a certain lack of legitimacy for the idea of a powerful court that could overturn decisions of the political branches of the government. The reinforcement of the bureaucratic elements in the judiciary and the peculiar administrative powers of the court have tended to diminish the political instincts that might have developed and have fostered instead a basically introspective and conservative group.

With only a half century under the new Japanese Constitution, the final chapter of this story of judicial review obviously has not been written. Although the tendency until now has not been to strengthen the court, future judges and future regimes may well make the third branch of government a strong political force within Japanese society.

China

The ways in which the Chinese government makes decisions regarding the constitutionality of laws, criminal process rules, and the behavior of agents in the criminal justice system has been a controversial issue since the founding of the People's Republic in 1949. The present Chinese Constitution, which was adopted in 1982 and has

since been amended, includes a section on the rights and duties of citizens. In 1994, the Chinese government passed the Administrative Procedural Law, which allows citizens to sue officials for abuse of authority or malfeasance. Yet, although the Chinese Constitution and other legal documents provide for fundamental human rights of citizens, including rights related to due process, these rights are often ignored in practice.

Both individuals and international human rights groups have published numerous documents outlining these violations. Among the most vociferous of these groups is the Human Rights Watch. Since 1989, the Human Rights Watch has published an annual report evaluating the yearly progress or lack thereof of countries whose human rights procedures are in contrast with international standards. China has been cited for many violations, and the most recent 1999 report reflected this trend. Among the problems were serious restrictions on basic freedoms related to observances of anniversaries such as the fortieth anniversary of the Tibetan uprising, the tenth anniversary of the Tiananmen Square massacre, and the fiftieth anniversary of the founding of the People's Republic of China. Other apparent violations included the incarceration of members of political parties opposed to Communist rule, constraints on the use of the Internet and print media, and police detention of members of at least four religious sects (Human Rights Watch, 1999).

Similarly, the U.S. State Department issued a stinging report in March 1999 about human rights in China. According to the report, human rights abuses in China include "instances of extrajudicial killings, torture and mistreatment, forced confessions, arbitrary arrest and detention, lengthy incommunicado detention and denial of due process." Further, the judicial system denies criminal defendants basic legal safeguards and due process because "authorities attach higher priority to maintaining public order and suppressing political opposition than to enforcing legal norms" (Jackson, 1999).

These kinds of examples about the way the Chinese conduct their legal business have angered the international community and caused many to suggest that China should be refused entry into various world trade and economic organizations. In response, the Chinese have acknowledged, at least in principle, the importance of human rights through the signing of the International Covenant on Economic, Social, and Cultural Rights in 1997 and International Covenant on Civil and Political Rights in 1998. However, as of late 1999, they had failed to ratify the documents in the National People's Congress.

Human Rights in Chinese Context. Why have the Chinese apparently ignored international standards, and even their own legislation, when it comes to issues of human rights and means of redress for governmental abuse of authority? This question has no easy answer. Yet it is important for students of international justice to try to understand the reasons the Chinese minimize the importance of individual rights, especially for those who understand government from a Western, democratic mindset.

Understanding the historical context behind the Chinese mentality toward human rights may be helpful in this endeavor. Although the Chinese have recently made attempts to legitimize and formalize their written constitution, this was not always important to the Chinese—at least not to those in power. As we discussed in previous chapters, China and Japan were governed for centuries by feudal dynasties. During this period of dynastic rule, laws were sometimes made to control those in power and to provide protections for the governed. However, these laws lacked any strength and were primarily developed to give the false impression that rulers were benevolent or benign. Further, in most cases, any laws that protected citizens were ignored or manipulated to meet the needs of the rulers. As a result, the people living in the vast regions of China became used to abiding by the commands of a superior who could deviate from the law and to living with the reality that they could seek no redress from any higher authority (Terrill, 1999, p. 522). This mentality—that power and the immediate needs of the government can supersede law—

continued into the twentieth century with the development of Communist rule in China. While it can be said that efforts have been made over the past fifteen years to improve upon the "rule of law" in China, the fact remains that the needs of the Communist party remain paramount over individual rights.

We can also gain insight into the Chinese mentality concerning human rights if we look more closely at the contents of the Chinese Constitution. The Chinese Constitution, unlike other constitutions in the world, is not a list of rights designed to curtail the power of the central government or to protect citizens from intrusive actions of the government. Rather, its purpose is mainly to explain to the people the government's orientation to public policy (Terrill, 1999, p. 525). For example, Article 5 states that "no organization or individual may enjoy the privilege of being above the constitution or the law." This kind of wording allows the Chinese government officials considerable flexibility in interpreting the document to their own benefit when it comes to maintaining order and supporting Communist ideology.

Nonjudicial Review, Chinese Style. So, then, how do the Chinese handle matters that come before the courts relative to constitutional matters and actions of those in the legal system? A perusal of the legal system of China reveals that, within their highly structured and hierarchical court system, the Chinese have developed formal mechanisms to serve the functions of judicial review. At the apex of that system is the Supreme People's Court. This court is responsible for administration of justice by lower courts, and it handles major criminal cases of national importance, cases on appeal from two lower-court levels (the Higher People's Court and the People's Military, Railway, and Maritime Courts), cases brought by the procurator of the Supreme People's Court, and death penalty cases.

However, in reality, the Supreme People's Court does not have the power to conduct any serious form of judicial review of constitutional issues or inappropriate behavior of those in the system. This responsibility is solely under the baili-wick of the National People's Congress (NPC) and its **Standing Committee.** The NPC is the main source of state power and the principle legisla-tive body in China. Its 2,800 members, called **deputies,** are elected to five-year terms from smaller provinces, autonomous regions, or munic-ipalities. The NPC elects and oversees all major of-ficials in the government, approves the budget, develops economic and social development, makes laws, and amends and enforces the constitution. The NPC usually meets once a year, for around two weeks, unless an emergency arises, in which event it may convene for a special session.

Because of the short time the NPC is in ses-sion, the Standing Committee of the NPC han-dles the full-time governmental responsibilities. The Standing Committee consists of 135 full-time members, including the leading government officials and influential members of the Chinese Communist party. The NPC and Standing Com-mittee can annul any law or court decision if they find them to contravene the constitution, legal statutes, or administrative rules and regulations. Although this may seem rather benign, the fact is that all members of the Standing Committee are subordinate to the Chinese Communist party and all initiatives proposed by the NPC and Standing Committee must have been previously endorsed by the party. The real role of the NPC and Stand-ing Committee is to implement party policy. In summary, then, we can say that the Chinese prac-tice what most resembles a nonjudicial form of constitutional review.

Saudi Arabia

According to a leading text on the development of Saudi Arabia, "It is the fundamental assump-tion of the polity of Saudi Arabia that the Holy Qur'an, correctly implemented, is more suitable for Saudi Muslims than any secular constitution" (Al-Farsy, 1986, p. 96). Therefore, although there are "constitutional" documents (really, organic laws) that establish governmental structures, there is no constitution in the modern sense in Saudi Arabia.

This reliance on the Qur'an as the basis of law makes Saudi Arabia unique, even among Islamic nations, and is one of the things that Westerners find most difficult to understand about Saudi so-ciety. Even Iran, which now outdoes Saudi Ara-bia in terms of Islamic piety, has a constitution that outlines the organs of government and pro-claims Shari'a as the basis for the legal process. According to the Saudis, the Qur'an, written in Arabic and accessible to Arabs, deals with people's relationship not only with God but also with one another. There is therefore no need for a separate secular constitution. Thus, while we can see reli-gious influences in most legal systems, even adamantly secular ones, the Saudi system is inte-grally tied to Islamic scripture.

Constitutional review in the broad sense is particularly important in such a system. This is because scriptures written in the seventh century need to be interpreted to deal with a twenty-first century nation involved in major industrial and military projects. Qur'anic interpretation, how-ever, tends to fall to religious rather than secular leaders. As we learned in Chapter 3, the four basic schools of Islamic jurisprudence have al-ready added decision making based on tradition to the pure letter of the Qur'an. Latter-day Saudi judges and kings are bound by the traditional law, but they often interpret it in ways that allow for modern development. Royal decrees may supple-ment Shari'a law, but in cases of conflict, Islamic Law is supposed to prevail. According to Amin, laws of commerce, forgery, social insurance, set-tlement of grievances, and so on are supported by Saudi jurists through "a convenient legal fiction" (1985b, p. 315).

In criminal, family, private property, and per-sonal injury law, however, close adherence to Is-lamic Law is the norm. Newly fundamentalist Islamic nations such as Iran and Pakistan use ad-herence to Shari'a criminal law as a proof of seri-ous commitment to the Qur'an; in Saudi Arabia, this criminal law has been in use since the estab-lishment of the modern Saudi state in 1932.

The Supreme Judicial Council serves as both an administrative agency that runs the court sys-tem and a court of last resort with respect to some cases (including penalties involving death, stoning, and amputation) arising under Shari'a. In most criminal cases, however, the final appeal is decided in one of two regional courts of appeal, in which the judges act as the interpreters of the Qur'an and the traditional law. The king remains as the final decision maker in all cases, however.

The structures in Saudi Arabia hardly provide for constitutional review in the sense that it exists in Germany, France, or Japan. Of the model countries we consider, the Saudi arrangement is, in a formal sense, probably closest to the English one, with its concern for tradition and interpretation of the work of previous jurists. The Saudi emphasis on integration of the secular with the religious, however, gives its system a very different flavor from most modern countries, with their secular legal and constitutional systems.

BEYOND CONSTITUTIONAL REVIEW: SUPRANATIONAL COURTS OF HUMAN RIGHTS

What happens when a citizen within a particular country has exhausted all the legal means of redress but still feels that his or her rights have been violated by the criminal justice system? In some regions of the world, courts of human rights have been developed to address such situations. Because these courts and their decisions cross national boundaries and supposedly have a higher legal standing than decisions of courts in individual countries, they are often referred to as international or supranational courts. With the explosion in worldwide communications, the globalization of the economy, and the increase in international problems related to crime and justice, supranational courts are developing at a rapid pace.

The European Court of Human Rights

One example of a supranational court is the **European Court of Human Rights (ECHR).** The ECHR is unique in that it allows for individuals to bring cases directly to a judicial body

after they have been denied relief in their national courts. The mission of the ECHR in general is to interpret and uphold the European Convention on Human Rights and Fundamental Freedoms, a treaty that was prepared by the Council of Europe in 1950. The convention outlined a number of basic principles of justice including the right to life (Article 2), the prohibition on torture (Article 3), the right to liberty (Article 5), and the right of due process (Article 6), among others.

The Development of the ECHR

How did the ECHR develop? To answer this question, we need to realize that the matter of individual human rights was crucial in a world that had recently gone through the terrible experience of World War II. During that time, human rights were constantly violated, especially by the Germans, who ran the notorious extermination programs in the concentration camps and killed millions of civilians in the course of the war. In this atmosphere, both the fledgling United Nations and the newly created Council of Europe fostered the development of treaties regarding individual human rights. In the case of the United Nations, the Universal Declaration of Human Rights was the product, while in Europe it was the European Convention on Human Rights. Access to the ECHR is complicated and involves the prescreening of cases by the Commission on Human Rights and the Council of Ministers.

The European human rights review mechanisms gradually have become more assertive and self-assured and have built up a body of case law that has required responses from the governments involved. These responses are sometimes negative and sometimes positive. On the one hand, the nation involved may change its rules to conform to the court's decisions or may admit to a violation in particular cases. For example, in several Austrian cases dealing with excessively long pretrial detention, the ECHR found that the defendants' rights to speedy trial had been violated. As a result, the government of Austria changed its criminal procedure codes to provide, with some exceptions, for a maximum of six months of pretrial custody.

On the other hand, the nation may choose to ignore the court's decision. Take the case of the 1991 arrest of a drug trafficker in Paris, France. After being arrested, the accused drug trafficker claimed that he was abused and tortured by the French police. The five officers involved were convicted and sentenced to prison by a French Court. Soon thereafter, the verdict was partially overturned by an appeals court, and four of the officers were released. In July 1999, the ECHR ordered the French government to pay 500,000 francs ($83,000) in fines to the drug trafficker. The court ruled that the physical and mental damages done to the drug trafficker did constitute torture. However, the French Interior Ministry immediately rejected the verdict by the ECHR, stating that the earlier decision by a French court, one overturning a verdict of guilty against the police, would be directed for appeal to the French Supreme Court (Cour de Cassation). The French were adamant that the judgment of the ECHR not be imposed on a French judge who remained "a master of his decisions."

This case is an example of the difficulty of the mission of the ECHR, its constraints in carrying out this mission, and even of the complexity of the law that it is developing.

Often, political or mediated settlements of major controversies may occur while they are being considered by the ECHR. This was the situation in two cases, both called *Greece v. the United Kingdom* (1956 and 1957), in which Greece accused Britain of violations of human rights with respect to detention of prisoners on Cyprus (while Cyprus was still under British rule). The cases were dropped, and the results of the investigation of the European Commission that precedes the filing of a case with the ECHR were not published after a political settlement on the status of Cyprus was reached (Robertson, 1977).

The Dilemma of the ECHR

The ECHR faces a dilemma. As a supranational court charged with upholding a treaty, it does not have the legitimacy backed up by coercive force that most national courts have. Further, its status varies among the signatories of the European Convention of Human Rights. In some countries, like Austria, the Convention has the same status as the constitution itself. In other countries, such as the Federal Republic of Germany, it has the status of legislative law—that is, it is subconstitutional in rank. In Great Britain, with its ideal of parliamentary supremacy, most of the decisions of the ECHR have no status unless they are ratified by Parliament. Even where the convention has constitutional status, local authorities must be willing to implement its decisions, just as the Supreme Court in the United States depends on the executive to enforce its decisions.

At a time when Europeanization is becoming more and more a reality with respect to economic affairs, the Europeanization of human rights through the convention is also advancing. But the ECHR confronts a peculiar dilemma when it comes to matters of criminal process—namely, that it is dealing with two different concepts of this process: (1) the Common Law adversarial process and (2) the Civil Law inquisitional process. The actual provisions of the convention tend to favor the Common Law rules and are quite familiar to most Americans, because of the criminal procedure rules contained in the Bill of Rights. Most of the signatories of the convention are Civil Law countries, however, and the ECHR must reconcile cases that arise from individual codes of criminal procedure in a variety of countries to the general procedural requirements of the convention. In effect, a kind of Europeanization of criminal procedure is going on, albeit slowly.

Looking to the Future

Given the limited number of cases that have been decided by the ECHR to date, it is hard to see a clear pattern of decisions emerging. As the integration of Europe continues, however, and as ever greater cooperation among law enforcement and legal system authorities develops, we can expect that the influence on criminal process of the European Convention on Human Rights will continue to grow. More recently, other parts of the world have established regional human rights compacts and legal mechanisms to deal with issues related to human rights. In 1997, for example, the African Commission of Human Rights began with the charge of reviewing prison conditions in Zimbabwe.

In addition to the ECHR, which deals with violations related to human rights in the European Union, other supranational courts have been developed during this past century. The most famous of these was the International Military Tribunal at Nuremberg, Germany, which tried those accused of committing war crimes during World War II. In the 1950s, the United Nations attempted to create a permanent international criminal court but was unsuccessful.

More recently, the efforts of the United Nations have been revived. The Security Council of the United Nations has established a court with the power to adjudicate charges of international crimes by countries and individuals. This court, called the **International Criminal Court,** has been asked to rule on alleged criminal actions committed during civil wars in the former Yugoslavia and in Rwanda. In addition, the **International Court of Justice (ICJ)** has been established at The Hague in the Netherlands. The ICJ, also called the World Court, serves the United Nations in the capacity of adjudicating disputes among member countries. (These courts will be discussed in more detail in Chapter 9, which discusses court structures.)

SUMMARY

Concern for the "higher law," whether it be the law of a written constitution or the traditions of law in a particular legal system, exists in all systems. Mechanisms are established to maintain conformity with this higher law. These mechanisms may be relatively simple, consisting largely of higher courts that have the mandate to adhere to the higher law in actual cases, or they may be complex, requiring involvement by other structures of government or other judicial officials. What we are dealing with in all cases, however, is some semblance of the familiar notion of checks and balances. As we explained, in federal nations such as Germany and the United States, constitutional review is particularly crucial in defining the balance of powers between levels of government. Unitary countries like England, France, Japan, and Saudi Arabia use various latent or manifest forms of constitutional review to uphold the higher law. China is unique in that the NPC and Standing Committee of the NPC handle constitutional review while under the supervision of the Communist party.

Often, the higher law—whether it be constitutional law, as in Japan; a Common Law tradition, as in England; or sacred text, as in Saudi Arabia—is directly related to the administration of justice and the rights of accused individuals. For that reason, this review of the forms and functions of constitutional review is particularly appropriate before consideration of the very important matter of criminal procedural rights.

DISCUSSION QUESTIONS AND ACTIVITIES

1. What are the different methods of constitutional review? Which do you believe is best, and why?

2. Which of the model nations has a constitutional review system that is most similar to that of the United States?

3. Explain why the Chinese feel it is necessary to minimize the importance of human rights.

4. Should England set up some agency for constitutional review? How could it be organized?

5. How are Saudi Arabia and China similar in their views toward human rights? What has been the response of the international community? What can be done to "motivate" these countries to make some changes?

6. What challenges will the Saudi system face as it tries to deal with increasing modernization?

7. Use the Internet to search out what the international community feels about the human rights policies of the United States.

FOR FURTHER READING

Amin, S. (1985). *Islamic Law in the Contemporary World.* Glasgow: Royston.

Cappelletti, M. (1971). *Judicial Review in the Contemporary World.* New York: Bobbs-Merrill.

Cappelletti, M., and W. Cohen. (1979). *Comparative Constitutional Law.* New York: Bobbs-Merrill.

Human Rights Watch. World Report. (1998). New York: Yale University Press.

McWhinney, E. (1969). *Judicial Review,* 4th ed. Toronto: University of Toronto Press.

———— . (1986). *Supreme Courts and Judicial Law-making: Constitutional Tribunals and Constitutional Review.* Dordrecht: Martinus Nijhoff.

Morton, F. (1988). "Judicial Review in France." 36 *American Journal of Comparative Law,* 89–110.

Murphy, W., and J. Tanenhaus. (1977). *Comparative Constitutional Law.* New York: St. Martin's Press.

Tanaka, H. (1976). *The Japanese Legal System.* Tokyo: University of Tokyo Press.

7   Criminal Procedure

The Adversarial System
Common Law Criminal Procedure
The Inquisitorial System
Civil Law Criminal Procedure
Socialist Criminal Procedure
Japan: The Hybrid Situation
Islamic Criminal Procedure
The Convergence of Systems
Summary
Discussion Questions
For Further Reading

Key Terms and Concepts

adversary system
advocat
assessor
challenges for cause
courts of assize
dossier
inquisitorial system
juge d'instruction
justice of the peace
mixed court
PACE
peremptory challenges
plea bargaining
Schöffen
voir dire
yanda

The person accused of a serious crime is in a terrifying situation. Removed from home, family, and friends, he or she may be subject to humiliating, confusing, and painful treatment. Spending time in a jail or prison cell has its particular horrors. Worst of all, accused people are fundamentally helpless to act, with the whole power of a coercive, armed, authoritative government aligned against them. The accused who are innocent of the crimes charged to them may be especially vulnerable as they try to defend themselves against the superior power of the state.

Over the centuries, most legal systems have developed a series of rules, called criminal procedure rules, that are designed to redress to some extent the awesome imbalance in power between the accused and the state. In effect, the authorities are supposed to "play by the rules" rather than assert naked power when dealing with an accused person.

Protecting the rights of accused persons is not the only reason governments have rules of criminal procedure. Rules are necessary to guide the many people engaged in the criminal justice process, to provide a certain predictability to the process, and to legitimize the government's effort to maintain a criminal justice system. In the highly bureaucratized society of today, detailed rules are a familiar way to frame legal processes and reduce the discretionary power of law enforcement officials.

Many criminal procedure rules are familiar to Americans because they are listed in the Constitution, especially in certain provisions of the Bill of Rights. Mindful of past excesses against accused people, the Founding Fathers sought to ensure that the fledgling national government of the United States would not arbitrarily arrest, imprison, or kill those accused of crimes without giving them a chance to prove their innocence. Most of the American rights of the accused actually existed in England prior to the establishment of the American republic, and many had already been incorporated in state constitutions.

The criminal procedure rules found in the Constitution include the right of habeas corpus, according to which the state must inform accused persons of the charges against them and justify their imprisonment. The rules also include the right to be free from illegal searches and seizures, the right to an attorney at trial and at various pretrial stages, the right not to be tried twice for the same crime, the right to trial by jury, the right not to testify against oneself, and the right to reasonable bail.

The Founding Fathers' concern with potential abuse of prisoners and unfair legal proceedings, however, did not stem from a desire to protect conventional predatory criminals. It was a response to the English history of abuse of political and religious dissenters. Many of the rules of criminal procedure that gradually developed in the Common Law and then were incorporated into the state and national constitutions in the United States reflected America's role as a haven for those who had suffered persecution because of their beliefs.

In this chapter, our model countries serve as examples to show how criminal procedure is generally practiced within the different legal traditions. For instance, England and the United States practice the Common Law tradition, France and Germany the Civil Law tradition, and China the Socialist Law tradition. Japan and Saudi Arabia represent two unique traditions and will be explained separately. We will also examine the two major systems of legal procedure that have historically influenced how defendants are treated in our model countries and throughout the world. These are the adversary and the inquisitorial models of criminal procedure.

THE ADVERSARIAL SYSTEM

The **adversarial system** is often compared to a game or contest in which both sides are trying to win and a neutral umpire decides two things: (1) whether they are playing by the rules and (2) which side wins. Often, the judge acts as umpire for both these aspects of the contest. In some cases, the judge's chief responsibility is to make decisions that ensure a fair contest, while a jury declares the actual winner.

The analogy to a game is not inappropriate when describing an adversary system. Not only is the accused not obligated to cooperate with the government in a case, but the government may fail to disclose crucial elements of its case against the accused. This does not mean that the government has the right to ignore or suppress evidence that would help the other side in the case—only the accused has that right. But it does mean that the prosecutor, who represents the government, is expected to devote his or her efforts to proving guilt rather than potential innocence once an individual has been indicted and is moving toward trial.

Another way to understand the adversarial system is to compare it to its philosophical opposite—the nonadversarial or inquisitorial system. Advocates of the adversarial systems of justice believe that the competition between the two parties is the best process for obtaining truth. Advocates of the nonadversarial system, which we will discuss later, believe that judicial control of the investigative process is the best way to uncover the truth. These fundamental beliefs create the differences in the role of witnesses, attorneys, and judges found in the common and civil law systems (Spader, 1999, p. 119).

In the adversarial system, most of the procedural advantages are on the side of the accused. The right to an attorney, the right to remain silent, the right to be free of unwarranted searches and arrests, the right to compel witnesses to appear for the defense, the right to confront one's accuser, the right to appeal—these and other rules of criminal process help keep the prosecutor from automatically winning a case. These rules have been developed over centuries as a response to abuses of citizens by monarchs and governments in dealing with their citizens, and these rules recognize that arbitrary government action remains a real possibility.

There is concern that correct criminal procedure has become so extreme that predatory criminals who learn to manipulate the rules of the system are likely to win the game despite their obvious guilt. Such criticism often does not take into consideration mitigating factors that counteract excessive manipulation of criminal procedure. In the first place, a vast majority of cases that occur in Common Law countries are settled through guilty pleas rather than through court trials. Students of criminal justice in the United States are well aware of the importance of **plea bargaining** and sentence bargaining in the settlement of criminal cases. In these cases, the accused agrees to plead guilty in return for various concessions, such as a lesser charge or a reduced sentence. On an aggregate basis, it is estimated that over 90 percent of criminal cases are settled through plea bargains in the United States.

In Common Law jurisprudence, a prosecutor has the obligation not to accept a guilty plea if there is no evidence to support it. However, once a guilty plea is accepted and made before a judge, no further trial is held.

America's overt, and by now legitimized, plea bargaining seems unique in modern legal systems. Nevertheless, we find that most cases in other Common Law countries are also settled through guilty pleas, despite the claims of legal system personnel that no plea bargaining exists. For example, in a study of the lower criminal courts in Sheffield, England, it was found that over 80 percent of cases were settled through guilty pleas (Bottoms and McLean, 1976).

The decision to plead guilty rather than use the full weaponry of the adversary system to make the state prove one's guilt weakens the system in a significant way. The motivation for pleading guilty may be varied—honest remorse, overwhelming evidence of guilt, a desire to achieve a guaranteed outcome, a belief that a judge will deal more leniently with a person who does not go to trial—but the result is the same. Many more cases can be processed than could be under a "pure" adversarial system, and the intricacies of adversarial criminal procedure are largely evaded.

A further factor that must be considered in discussing the supposedly dysfunctional nature of the adversarial process is that this process is in no way as complex in most Common Law systems as it is in the United States. For example, the exclusionary rule, which is the target of much criticism in the United States, does not exist in England in the case of most violations of search and seizure rules. In the United States, illegally obtained evidence, no matter how incriminating or useful, may not be produced at trial. In England, by contrast, only evidence that has been obtained through undue pressure on the accused is barred.

COMMON LAW CRIMINAL PROCEDURE

Although there is some variation from country to country, the core practices of criminal procedure in Common Law countries are very similar. Among the most common and important procedures are the rights to counsel, to remain silent, to bail, and to a trial by jury. In this section, we discuss these criminal procedures, using England as the primary example and, when applicable, the United States as a comparison country.

Criminal procedure in England has been under some scrutiny in recent years and as a result has undergone some major changes. In 1984, the British Parliament passed the **PACE**—Police and Criminal Evidence—Act, a law designed to make arrest and prosecution procedures less cumbersome. This law replaced the Judges' Rules that had previously delineated English criminal procedure (Spencer, 1989; Zander, 1989).

Due to the terrorist actions in Northern Ireland and urban unrest in England, criminal procedure rules were modified by Parliament in 1988 to abrogate the right to remain silent in cases involving terrorism. Ironically, both police and civil liberties advocates claimed that the new law was detrimental to their causes. In the case of police, the new rules about arresting suspects and warning them of their rights make the limits of acceptable police conduct more explicit than previously. Civil liberties advocates condemn the

provisions that allow continued questioning of a suspect in the face of an expressed desire to remain silent and that make it possible to hold certain suspects for up to 96 hours without charges (Spencer, 1989, p. 220).

In the wake of this law and other developments with respect to criminal procedure, there is concern in England about abuses of the criminal process. In two much-publicized cases, those of the Birmingham Six and the Guildford Four, appellate judges reversed earlier unsuccessful appeals. The judges found that the appellants in both these cases, all of whom had been convicted of Irish Republican Army bombings of pubs and had spent many years in prison, were forced to confess under police pressure (Lawton, 1991; Longworth, 1990).

In the 1990s the Royal Commission on Criminal Justice was developed to assess the effectiveness of PACE and the overall criminal justice system. The result was the passage of additional legislation including the Criminal Justice and Public Order Act (1994) and the Police and Magistrates' Court Act (1994), which deal with reform in a number of criminal justice related areas. The overall effects of these laws are yet to be determined (Bridges, 1994).

The Right to Counsel

In England, under the PACE Act and previously under the Judges' Rules, any detained person not involved in a nonserious arrestable offense has the absolute right to see a lawyer, although police have the right to begin questioning before the lawyer arrives. The suspect can also agree to talk to police without a lawyer present.

Suspects detained for involvement in a serious arrestable offense have the same right to a lawyer, but access can be delayed up to 36 hours in most cases and up to 48 hours in terrorism cases. Reasons for the delays can be the belief that any delay in questioning or waiting for an attorney may cause harm or risk of danger to person or property. The right to an attorney during the pretrial process is an example of how English criminal procedure is not as highly developed as American procedure. In the United States, the famous *Miranda* ruling of the Supreme Court requires that a person being taken into custody be informed of his or her right to remain silent and to have an attorney. Further, in the United States, the right to remain silent includes a prohibition against an attorney commenting unfavorably on the exercise of that right during trial or pretrial proceedings. In England, by contrast, this kind of comment is allowable (Graham, 1983).

In fact, the right to remain silent provides the foundation for the adversary system of criminal process found in Common Law countries and is worthy of further discussion.

The Right to Remain Silent

Since passage of the Criminal Justice and Public Order Act in 1994, the status of the right to silence in England has been altered. Previously, the accused could not be required to incriminate him- or herself, and silence could not be taken to infer guilt. But since passage of the act, it is possible for guilt to be inferred by silence, and so there is pressure on the accused to waive the right to silence when being questioned by police (Dennis, 1995; Philips, Cox, and Pease, 1999).

Yet, the right to remain silent is at the heart of Common Law criminal procedure. The Fifth Amendment to the U.S. Constitution puts it this way: "No person . . . shall be compelled in any criminal case to be a witness against himself. . . ." Thus, the state must prove its case without the help of the accused if the accused chooses not to give that help. At its most basic level, the right to remain silent is designed to protect individuals against forced confessions obtained through torture, threats, or other undue pressures. It also means, however, that the accused can remain silent throughout the pretrial or trial phase of his or her criminal proceedings. In other words, the state must prove that an individual is guilty without the help of that individual.

Although its roots go back to the early years of the Common Law, the right to protection against

self-incrimination achieved its real definition during the period of religious conflict in the sixteenth and seventeenth centuries. At that time, those accused of crimes were required to take an oath to tell the truth without having been informed of the charges against them or of the identity of those who accused them. Religious dissenters called on to take the oath faced a serious problem. If they acknowledged their religion, they were subject to state sanctions. If they denied their religion, they were going against their conscience and, in their view, risking eternal punishment.

Some dissenters chose to deal with this dilemma by refusing to take the oath and refusing to testify, claiming that the authorities had no right to require individuals to testify against themselves. Unfortunately, many of them suffered severe punishments as a result of their refusal to take the oath. One of the most famous of these dissenters, the Puritan John Lilburne, defied both King Charles I and Oliver Cromwell and became a popular hero although he was tortured and spent a large part of his life in prison or in exile. Gradually, over many years and through the courage of many brave dissenters who incurred the wrath of the authorities by their intransigence, the custom of refusing to testify at all became common and was finally legitimized by Parliament in the latter seventeenth century. This hard-won right was especially precious to the American colonists, since so many of them were the progeny of religious dissenters, such as Quakers and Puritans, who had made a new home in the American wilderness (Levy, 1969).

The Right to Trial by Jury

Although the right to remain silent is the most basic element of the adversarial system, trial by jury is the most venerable of the Common Law procedures and is sometimes seen as the major English contribution to systems of justice worldwide. The origins of this right to be judged by a jury of one's peers goes back to the concessions made by King John to his nobles in the Magna Charta of 1215.

Trial by jury today is used less than previously in Common Law systems, with the United States using it more than any other. In England, people accused of an indictable offense have the right to trial by jury in crown courts, while summary offenses are heard in magistrates' courts without a jury. More than 90 percent of all criminal cases are tried as summary offenses before one professional (stipendiary) magistrate or before at least two, but not more than seven, lay magistrates. So, in reality, the trial by jury has all but disappeared in civil cases, and its use in criminal cases has been modified by the fact that, since 1967, a unanimous jury verdict has not been required. According to Baldwin and McConville, "trial by jury is now only a small part of the English criminal justice system. No more than about one in twenty of those eligible to be tried by jury are so tried" (1979, p. 130).

In the crown courts, a trial has three stages. First is the arraignment, during which the indictment is read and the accused is asked to respond to the charge. If the accused pleads guilty and he or she understands the consequences of that plea, the judge will impose a sentence. If the plea is not guilty, the trial proceeds to the second stage—selection of a jury.

Twelve persons are selected to serve on the jury from a list of registered voters. People are excused for a variety of reasons, and the prosecution and defense can disqualify an unlimited number of jurors if they use **challenges for cause.** Challenges for cause provide the opportunity to remove someone from a jury if there is a reason to believe that he or she would not be a fair or impartial juror. In England, there are no **peremptory challenges** that allow the defense counsel or prosecutor to remove a juror for no specified reason. These challenges are allowed in the United States but are limited in number.

The third stage of the trial in England is the oral arguments presented by the prosecution and the defense. These steps are listed in Table 7.1.

The responsibilities of the judge and jury are similar in England and the United States. The judge acts as a referee, maintaining order in the court, ruling on points of law, assisting the jury to come to a verdict, and determining the sentence.

Table 7.1 Steps in Trials in English Crown Courts

1. The prosecuting counsel gives opening remarks outlining evidence to be presented.
2. The prosecutor calls and examines witnesses.
3. The defense counsel cross-examines witnesses.
4. The prosecutor reexamines the witness.
5. The defense can make an opening statement and outline defense evidence.
6. The defendant can choose to be examined (not required).
7. The defense calls other witnesses.
8. The prosecution can cross-examine each witness.
9. The defense can reexamine the witnesses.
10. The prosecutor gives closing remarks.
11. The defense gives closing remarks.
12. The judge summarizes the case for the jury by discussing the specific law, its applicability to the case, and the burden of proof required to establish the accuser's guilt, and then summarizes the evidence presented by both parties.
13. The court is recessed for the jury to consider a verdict.

SOURCE: Adapted from Terrill, 1999.

The jury in England can return three different verdicts: general, partial, or special. A general verdict states that all of the charges in the indictment are valid. A partial verdict means the jury finds the accused guilty or not guilty on a limited basis—as when the jury finds the person not guilty of one crime but guilty of another. A special verdict is handed down when the defendant is found not guilty by reason of insanity. In each case, the jury may also reach a unanimous verdict or a majority verdict. A majority verdict is when 10 of the 11 or 12 jurors agree. Majority verdicts are accepted only if the jury deliberates for at least two hours or longer and the court believes the verdict is reasonable. If the jury is unable to reach a verdict, it is discharged, and the accused may be tried again (Terrill, 1999).

The Right to Bail

The right to bail is an interesting aspect of Common Law procedure. When the English Parliament in 1689 called upon the Dutch prince and princess, William and Mary of Orange, to assume the throne of England, it made the offer contingent upon their acceptance of a bill of rights that included, among others, the rights to free elections, to freedom of speech in parliamentary debates, to petition, and to a jury trial. Also included was the phrase "excessive bail ought not to be required, nor excessive fines imposed, nor cruel and unusual punishments inflicted" (Laing et al., 1950, p. 14). These words, which were echoed a hundred years later in the Eighth Amendment to the U.S. Constitution, exemplify the importance of bail to the concept of fair criminal procedure in Common Law history.

As stated in the Bail Act of 1974, bail in England is allowed for anyone who is not a fugitive from the law, who is accused of a crime that would require imprisonment, and whose prior record or history of absconding are not an issue. In 1994, under the Criminal Justice and Public Order Act, the police were empowered to set bail and provide conditions of bail prior to the first appearance of the accused in court.

The purpose of bail is to allow the accused to remain at liberty, while a trial is pending, by providing a cash bond that supposedly guarantees his or her appearance at trial. Bail is usually higher for serious crimes because the stakes are higher. For some crimes, such as most cases of murder, bail may not be available. Mindful of the problems that poor people may have in making bail, both England and the United States today have rules for allowing individuals in certain cases to remain free without posting bail if they meet certain criteria such as gainful employment and a stable home life.

The possibility of bail being discriminatory toward the poor has been cited as a potentially serious problem for Common Law systems. In Civil Law systems, the criteria for arrest are more stringent than in Common Law systems, but arrestees may be released "when the risk of release is worth taking . . . ; when the risk cannot be taken, release will not be ordered" (Mueller and LePoole-Griffiths, 1969, p. 24). In other words, bail is not emphasized (although it's an option in most Civil Law systems), and the accused is set free pending

trial if it seems reasonable to do so. In all systems, there is concern about the number of individuals who are detained "on remand" pending a trial. As we shall see, however, this is a greater problem in Civil Law systems because of the long periods of pretrial investigation.

The Differences in Criminal Procedure Rules in Common Law Countries

We should reemphasize that criminal procedure in Common Law countries is not always similar. For example, many differences of style and substance exist between the United States and England, with the English criminal trial more favorable to the prosecution than the American trial. Some of the differences in style in England include (1) placement of the accused alone in an area called the dock rather than next to counsel as in the United States (thereby making meaningful communication between the two impossible during trial), (2) the wearing of wigs and robes by counsel and judges, (3) the placement of defense and prosecution counsel next to each other, and (4) the generally detached and nonpartisan demeanor of the defense counsel are other style differences.

Differences in substance at trial include the fact that in English trials (1) there is no right to **voir dire** (the right of prosecution and defense to ask potential jurors questions in order to decide whether to challenge them for cause or peremptorily) or to re-cross-examination, (2) judges are more likely to offer personal views and to give the jury directions about evidence, (3) there are limits on the media in the courtroom, and (4) the defense has a reduced ability to attack the credibility of prosecution witnesses (Graham, 1983; Spencer, 1995).

If we extend the analysis to other Common Law countries, we find that even greater differences have evolved over the course of their political and institutional development. In India and some African Common Law countries, for example, trial by jury hardly exists, and the Civil Law practice of choosing lay assessors to assist a judge in deciding cases has become the norm in some states (McWhinney, 1965).

THE INQUISITORIAL SYSTEM

U.S. Supreme Court Justice Warren Burger once remarked that "if he were innocent, he would prefer to be tried by a civil law court, but . . . if he were guilty, he would prefer to be tried by a common law court" (Burger, 1968). This remark is in some ways an indictment of the Common Law procedure in its suggestion that it is less likely than the Civil Law procedure to arrive at the truth of a case. We can weigh the validity of this statement as we examine some of the details of Civil Law procedure.

One way to anger a scholar of the Civil Law is to claim that a major contrast between Common Law and Civil Law criminal procedure is that in the former the accused is innocent until proven guilty while in the latter the accused is guilty until proven innocent. This is indeed not necessarily true, since both kinds of procedure are theoretically based on a presumption of innocence. Nevertheless, the extensive pretrial investigation that characterizes Civil Law systems gives rise to the feeling that defendants who actually are brought to trial are most likely to be guilty.

Criminal procedure in Civil Law countries is characterized as inquisitorial, as opposed to adversarial, in nature. This characterization evokes unfortunate images of the Inquisition, that notorious and cruel institution that persecuted alleged heretics during the sixteenth and subsequent centuries in Spain and other Catholic countries, extorting confessions through brutal tortures and executing its victims, often by burning. In fact, however, confessions resulting from torture were the norm in both England and Continental Europe for secular as well as religious crimes until the right to remain silent became the distinguishing characteristic of the adversarial system of procedure.

In modern Civil Law systems, the **inquisitorial system** refers not to any legacy of the Inquisition but to the extensive pretrial investigation and interrogations that are designed to ensure that no innocent person is brought to trial. Even to this extent, *inquisitorial* is a misleading term that does not truly describe the rather hybrid procedure that developed in Civil Law systems, often in emulation of Common Law procedural rights, during the nineteenth and twentieth centuries. Miryan Damaska (1986, p. 3) describes the inquisitorial process as an "official inquiry" and compares it to the "contest" or "dispute" that characterizes the adversary process.

Many countries of the world can be classified as having inquisitorial systems, including our model countries of France, Germany, China, and even, in some respects, Japan. But there are important disparities in criminal procedure among them. France and Germany have long Civil Law traditions but differ from each other with respect to some aspects of criminal procedure, such as the use of a prosecutor in Germany and an examining magistrate in France. Italy, another Civil Law country, changed much of its pretrial process in 1988, and its system now resembles Common Law procedures in many ways. The Italians call this "Process Perry Mason."

Despite individual variations, certain aspects of criminal procedure in the Civil Law countries give this procedure a distinctive character. Among these are the relative ease with which procedural rules are adopted and changed and the relative length and importance of the pretrial process in determining the outcome of a case.

As we have explained on several occasions, an essential characteristic of the Common Law is the importance of precedent, form, and procedure in the passage of cases through the courts. Indeed, it was the "common" procedural rules that brought this rather amorphous body of law together in the thirteenth and fourteenth centuries. In the Civil Law, it is the substantive rules of the law—the rules that explain what is lawful and what is not—rather than how one makes a case in court, that have tended to predominate. The procedure for effecting legality is changed quite simply, usually through legislation. In England and the United States, by contrast, although criminal procedure rules are often modified by legislation, they have a certain continuity because of their constitutional and Common Law status.

CIVIL LAW
CRIMINAL PROCEDURE

Civil Law is the most common of all the legal traditions, but there are numerous variations of criminal procedure practiced within that tradition throughout the world. Here, we will use France as our model nation, because French criminal procedure presents us with a characteristic Civil Law process.

The Investigation

As mentioned in Chapter 4, the French divide criminal offenses into three categories: (1) crimes (felonies), (2) delits (serious misdemeanors), and (3) contraventions (minor crimes). This is important to remember because the category of offense affects the kind of investigation and the level of involvement by police and the courts. Minor crimes and misdemeanors are handled by police investigators and prosecuting attorneys. Felonies, however, are handled through the extensive process of pretrial investigation (called "instruction") that characterizes Civil Law systems. In this section, we trace the process for the more serious felony category.

After a crime has been committed and a preliminary investigation has been undertaken, a suspect can be brought in for questioning. In this initial questioning period, called the *garde a vue,* the suspect can be held for up to twenty-four hours without being formally charged or being told that he or she is the primary suspect. After the *garde a vue,* the suspect must be released unless the judicial police officer (a member of the criminal investigation branch of the French police) believes there is enough evidence against him or her. Since 1994, the French procedural law has ensured that suspects have immediate access to an attorney unless they are involved in terrorist activity. French suspects also have the right to remain silent, and the law requires that they be informed of that right during pretrial inquiries but not in police interrogations. Instead, defen-

dants have the right to withdraw any pretrial confession (Frase, 1990, p. 549).

After it is determined that the evidence is sufficient, the suspect is arrested and formally charged for the offense and then is bound over to judicial authorities. At this stage, the judicial police, the procurator, and the *juge d'instruction* proceed with the investigation. The *juge d'instruction* is the examining magistrate who is responsible for a complete and impartial investigation of the facts.

Judicial philosophy in France demands that the accused be a part of this process from the outset. In other words, suspects are not investigated by a prosecutor and then faced with charges to which they have not had an opportunity to reply in depth, as in the adversarial system.

The pretrial investigation in France involves the calling of witnesses on both sides, extensive gathering of facts and testimony, and careful questioning of the accused prior to a final decision to bring the case to trial. In France, as in many Civil Law systems, this pretrial investigation is conducted in secret by the *juge d'instruction,* with the help of police investigators and the procurator. The reason for secrecy in these proceedings is to protect the accused from adverse publicity prior to the determination that the government has a strong case for prosecution (Cappelletti and Cohen, 1979, pp. 381–387).

In some ways, the investigation is analogous to grand jury hearings in the United States, which are conducted in secret and in which evidence is weighed to decide whether the accused should be indicted. Grand jury hearings are usually short, however, dominated by the prosecutor and designed to make sure that the prosecution will not be frivolous or willful. Thus, they are really quite different from the careful and lengthy pretrial investigation that occurs in France.

After the investigation, the *juge d'instruction* forwards his or her findings to the Court of Appeals, also known as the Indicting Chamber. The function of the Indicting Chamber is to review the evidence and determine whether a trial is warranted. If warranted, in a serious criminal (felony) case, the matter is referred to the **courts of assize,** which is the court of original jurisdiction in criminal matters.

The purpose of the inquisitorial proceedings is to protect the accused against unwarranted accusations and trials. However, the potential for abuse in lengthy, secret pretrial proceedings is obvious. In effect, the accused may spend long periods of time in detention, often without possibility of bail, while these proceedings are going on.

The accused or defense counsel can apply for bail at any time during the case, and the examining magistrate decides whether bail will be granted. The magistrate can order the suspect to pay a cash security. This serves two purposes: (1) to ensure that the suspect will appear in court and (2) to pay fines or damages if he or she is found guilty. The problem with bail in France is that it is so infrequently given that most suspects spend a considerable amount of time in pretrial detention (Ingraham, 1987; Oberheim, 1985, p. 32).

Readers of detective novels about French investigators are usually introduced to the concept of the dossier. The **dossier** is actually a complete record of the pretrial proceedings, and it informs the judges, the defense attorney, and others about the testimony of key witnesses and the evidence to be presented. The judge who reads the dossier ahead of time knows fairly well what is going to happen during the trial. The accused, who has participated at each stage of the development of the dossier, also knows what is likely to happen at trial.

The Right to Counsel

The accused in France has the right to the assistance of an *advocat* (attorney), and if he or she cannot afford one, then one is appointed. Since 1897, French law has required that an attorney represent the accused during the process of pretrial investigation. The magistrate may not ask questions of the accused unless this attorney is present, and the accused may not refuse assistance of counsel.

The mandatory representation by an attorney, which predated the provision of attorneys to indigents in the United States by over half a century, is actually antithetical to the spirit of pretrial investigations within the inquisitorial process. These investigations were meant to be inquiries, similar to police investigations before a suspect is arrested, that would help to determine if charges should be brought against an individual. While this rule that an attorney be assigned to the accused was designed to ensure that no abuses would occur during the investigation, the result, according to some commentators, has been to lengthen the process and inject a note of formality that makes it far less useful as a preliminary investigation than was originally planned.

The Right to Remain Silent

In addition to requiring the presence of an attorney, French law requires that the accused be informed of his or her right to remain silent during the pretrial proceedings. This right, so integral to the adversarial system, represents another modification of the inquisitorial procedure. However, it does not have the stature that the similar right has in Common Law countries, and the presumption on the part of all parties is that the accused will cooperate in the investigation by answering questions and raising points that might help in the defense.

Despite the presence of an attorney, the pretrial investigation of the accused by a magistrate can be an intimidating process for one who is inexperienced in criminal cases. As Cappelletti and Cohen put it (1979, p. 385):

> *The French process of inquiry appears to be principally concerned with the attempt to obtain an admission of the truth of the charge from a person reasonably believed to be guilty; confession is self-evidently, surely, the most proper result of a properly conducted instruction which does not end in a discharge.*

At the same time, except in minor cases, the accused has to be proven guilty through the entire process of developing a dossier and going through a trial. If the accused chooses to make a statement at trial, he or she is not under oath, as in Common Law procedure, and is not subject to cross-examination. Any confession in the pretrial or trial process is treated as part of the evidence included in the dossier. This is a major difference from many Common Law countries, especially in the United States, where plea bargaining is the norm.

The Trial

In court, major crimes (felonies) are presided over by a judge, called a president. Juries are used only in the courts of assize. Juries, a concept borrowed from Common Law systems, have been used in felony trials since the nineteenth century, but in a modified form that allows for greater interchange between judge and jury members. There are nine jurors in the assize court trial. Potential jurors are first picked through a lottery and then randomly selected for the final panel after the procurator and defense counsel are allowed a minimal number of challenges (five for the defense, four for the prosecution). No reason is needed to challenge a juror selection (Terrill, 1999, p. 247).

The trial judge in France is less of an "umpire" than in adversary systems and more of a participant with a responsibility to discover the truth. At the court of assize level, in addition to the president judge, there are two **assessors,** who are professional judges selected from other courts to sit in on the trial. Judges question witnesses and defendants, call for further investigation if necessary, and ask to see additional witnesses. Jurors can also question witnesses and the accused if they ask permission from the president. While judges have many of these powers in Common Law systems, the tradition in these systems is for the judge to be disengaged and impartial, rather than proactive and involved as in Civil Law systems. For a summary of the steps of the typical French trial in a felony case or civil trial, see Table 7.2.

If the accused is convicted, he or she has the right to appeal in the courts of appeal and has the

Table 7.2 Steps in French Felony or Civil Trials

1. The clerk reads the names of all the witnesses present, and they are then sequestered until called upon.
2. The decree of demand is read, which includes a list of charges against the defendant, witnesses' evidence and the defendant's response, the personal history of the defendant, the results of any psychological or psychiatric examinations, and the criminal history of the defendant.
3. The defendant can make a statement and is questioned by the judge (president), assessors, jurors, and procurator.
4. Witnesses make uninterrupted statements and are examined by president, assessors, jurors, and procurator.
5. The defense counsel questions witnesses.
6. The procurator presents their case.
7. The accused or his or her counsel presents the defense.
8. The procurator is allowed a rebuttal.
9. The defense is allowed a final rebuttal.
10. The president suspends the hearing, and the judges and jurors begin deliberations.
11. After deliberation, the judges and jurors vote on secret written ballots regarding the charges against the accused. A majority of eight votes is required for a guilty verdict.
12. After conviction, judges and jurors vote on a sentence in a majority vote.

SOURCE: Adapted from Terrill, 1999.

right to an attorney at each stage of appeal. As in the United States, the highest appeal court, or Cour de Cassation in France, considers only issues of law; it does not review the facts of criminal cases. The intermediate courts of appeal may consider both questions of law and questions of fact.

Although France has not abandoned trial by jury, as have most other Civil Law countries, its practice on most levels resembles the system of lay judges found in most Civil Law systems (Cornish, 1968).

The most controversial aspect of criminal procedure in Civil Law countries is the examination phase of the proceeding, under the supervision of an examining magistrate. The secrecy and length of the proceedings, the sweeping powers enjoyed by the magistrates, and cases of abuse of powers have all brought the institution of examining magistrate under fire. Italy, in its criminal code revision of 1989, abolished the position of examining magistrate. In France, the power of individual magistrates to work in secret and to keep people incarcerated for long periods of time came under increasing fire. Reforms were designed to create greater oversight of magistrates' work and greater shared responsibility for arrest decisions. Several proposals, including the use of a team of magistrates to make decisions about arrest and trial of suspects, have been advanced. And it is now necessary in serious cases for the examining magistrate to present the charges to a panel of the courts of appeal.

Differences and Similarities Between the French, German, and American Systems

We haven't said much in this chapter about the practice of criminal procedure in Germany, mainly because much of the German system is very similar to the French system. However, it is important to mention here some of those important similarities, as well as the key differences. According to Frase and Weigend (1992), the French and Germans are most similar in at least the following ways:

- Less frequent use of custodial arrest and pretrial detention for most criminal defendants
- Strict control over prosecutorial discretion
- Broad use of pretrial discovery rights
- More use of noncustodial sanctions like fines
- Lay citizen input into verdicts and sentencing

At the same time, there are some differences between the Germans and the French. In fact, in many ways, the German system may more closely resemble the American. According to Frase and Weigend (1992), the German and American systems are similar in these aspects:

- Pretrial procedures
- Levels of courts that increase in level of formality and punishment as the crime severity increases
- Arrest and detention procedures
- Prosecutors' broad discretion whether to prosecute
- An adversarial trial process relative to examining witnesses
- The use of "*Miranda*-type" rights, exclusionary rules, and plea bargaining

Only time will tell if the Germans continue to transform more of their criminal procedures from the inquisitorial to the adversarial model. For now, they remain strongly aligned with the Civil Law/inquisitorial model.

Procedural Variations in Other Civil Law Countries

The major variation on the French procedure that is found in other Civil Law countries is in the use of a procurator, or prosecutor, rather than an examining magistrate, or *juge d'instruction*. Germany introduced the use of a prosecutor to prepare cases for trial during the early nineteenth century. In fact, although the prosecutor is responsible by law for the criminal investigation, it is almost always carried out by the police. Italy has also abandoned the position of examining magistrate. Japan uses a prosecutor rather than an examining magistrate. Indeed, essentially, only Spain, Portugal, and some of the Latin American countries continue to use examining magistrates in the traditional way.

A second, less common difference between French criminal procedure and other Civil Law countries is the use of jury trial. As mentioned earlier, the French use jury trials in the courts of assize. By contrast, Germany has no jury trials. All adjudication in Germany is handled by a judge or a panel of judges consisting of professional judges or a combination of professional and lay judges.

The Mixed Court

The **mixed court** is another variation of criminal procedure that is used primarily in Civil Law countries but that is also found in Socialist and Common Law legal systems. It is a method of adjudication in which one or more lay judges help the professional judge come to a decision. Lay judges are typical citizens, not professional legal personnel. They are usually elected (on the local level) or chosen by the government agency responsible for monitoring the courts. The lay judges either work as volunteers a certain number of days each year or serve a term prescribed by law. Their numbers vary depending on the seriousness of the case, the court level, and the laws of the country; they range from at least two to six. In effect, the lay judges replace the jury system, providing the balance between the state acting against the accused and the peers of the accused in considering the interests of justice and the community at large. It is possible in many systems for the lay judges to overrule the professional judge. However, in practice, lay judges often defer to the professional judge's knowledge and rarely muster a majority that overrides the professional judge's vote. Their main function seems to be a restraining one, to keep the judge from acting in an arbitrary or unreasonable manner.

The mixed court in Civil Law countries developed in the nineteenth century when some European countries attempted to imitate the Anglo-American criminal jury system. It reflects the importance that Civil Law countries place on nonprofessional participation in the court process (Spader, 1999, p. 122). One of our model countries, Germany, uses lay judges, called **Schöffen,** extensively in courts of appeal for cases of limited jurisdiction (minor offenses) and for first-level cases of general criminal jurisdiction (criminal offenses). Some countries employ all-lay tribunals.

In this form, the courts usually have one person who is legally trained to work with and provide advice to laypersons in matters that are considered less serious or during administrative or arbitration hearings.

China employs lay judges, called lay assessors, in its people's courts to serve as adjudicators in serious criminal cases of first instance. Lay assessors in China must be twenty-three years of age and eligible to vote; they are either elected or temporarily invited to sit on the court. The United States and England also use a derivation of this method in their lower courts. Many small towns in America have a person called a **justice of the peace,** who carries out many legal functions, including traffic violations, some misdemeanors, small civil claims, and some domestic matters. In England, in the lower magistrates' court, at least two lay judges must hear all summary (minor) offenses.

SOCIALIST CRIMINAL PROCEDURE

Criminal procedure in most Socialist countries is similar to, and derived from, criminal procedures in Civil Law systems. Thus, criminal procedures in these countries have generally reflected the Civil Law and inquisitorial systems in that state procurators investigate crimes, thorough pretrial inquiries are the norm, and judges take an active role in the trial process. However, there are many differences in the way criminal procedure is practiced in Civil Law and Socialist Law systems. To understand these differences in context, we turn to our model country of the People's Republic of China.

Chinese legal culture, like that of Japan, traditionally has been heavily influenced by Confucian philosophy, stressing informal means of settling disputes and valuing social harmony above individual justice. So, for years, China had little or no concern for individual rights, which would have limited the rights of the group or the power of the state (Baker, 1982). Given this philosophy, China operated without a code of criminal procedure for the first thirty years following the Communist takeover. However, the political upheaval of the Cultural Revolution forced the Chinese government to implement changes.

During the Cultural Revolution, the legal system was in shambles and the Ministry of Justice was abolished. Many people, including Communist party officials, were arbitrarily harassed, punished, and even executed. To control the excesses, as well as make the legal adjustments necessary to accommodate a new economic vision, the National People's Congress (NPC) adopted its first Criminal Procedure Law (CPL) in 1979. The CPL, developed over two decades, contained 164 articles covering all stages of the criminal process, from initial detention through investigation, prosecution, trial, appeal, and execution of sentence.

However, two important developments limited the implementation of the 1979 CPL. First, because of the unfamiliarity of the law and the inability of legal actors to deal with its many legal boundaries, police, prosecutors, and judges in China found it difficult to carry out the law. This resulted in numerous abuses of the law as it was first framed. Second, in the early 1980s, the Chinese were faced with a perceived rise in violent crime. As a result, the Communist party initiated a major anticrime campaign called **yanda** (strike hard) in the belief that this policy would stem the supposed rise in crime (Lawyers Committee, 1996).

These two developments led to changes in the CPL by the NPC. For example, many procedural safeguards were eliminated or amended by numerous government regulations. Legal requirements about notices of trial, controls on the severity of punishments, and the time allowed to file appeals all were modified to reflect the needs of the system and the *yanda* campaign against crime and criminals (Lawyers Committee, 1996, pp. 3–4). Although these changes were unpopular with some citizens and frowned on in the international community, they were viewed by the

Chinese government as necessary to maintain control of the populace and reduce the crime rate.

During the 1980s and early 1990s, it became increasingly clear to the Chinese that the 1979 CPL was an ineffective law. Despite the ongoing *yanda* campaign, crime continued to increase even as new and more sophisticated forms of crime developed. The economic reforms and "opening" to the outside world created new kinds of legal needs that were not addressed in the current criminal laws and criminal procedures. At the same time, international criticism of the Chinese relative to their human rights policies began to mount, especially after the events at Tiananmen Square in 1989.

In 1996, the NPC addressed the problem by adopting a new Criminal Procedure Law of the People's Republic of China (revised CPL). The 110-article document contains amendments and additions to the 1979 CPL. Of the original law, 70 articles were amended, eliminated, and 63 added (Lawyers Committee, 1996, p. 19).

In this section, we will examine some of the major elements of the CPL of 1979, as well as some of the changes in the revised CPL of 1996. However, two qualifications are necessary. First, remember that the procedural elements discussed here are those that are *stated* in the revised CPL. Whether they have in fact been *implemented* throughout the criminal justice system and are available for all Chinese citizens remains to be seen. Second, keep in mind that the criminal procedures in countries that employ the Socialist Law tradition, such as China, North Korea, and Cuba, may vary. The economics and politics of many Socialist Law systems are presently in a state of flux, and criminal procedures may well continue to change appreciably in the coming years.

Pretrial Investigation, Arrest, and Detention

Once a crime is committed or alleged, it is reported to the public service agency (police), the procurator, or the court. After a brief preliminary investigation, if it is determined that the matter warrants further state involvement, the case is filed, and an investigation conducted by the police (public service agency) or the procurator. If the police investigate, they submit an opinion whether to prosecute or to exempt from prosecute. They then transfer the case to the procurator, who reviews it and decides whether to prosecute. In the revised CPL, victims can ask the procurator to file the case if the police neglect to do so, or they can choose to privately prosecute if the procurator refuses to accept the case (Articles 83 and 88). In the latter situation, the victims, legal representatives, or close relatives have the right to prosecute directly in the people's courts.

If a suspect is arrested, a family member or living partner must be notified within twenty-four hours and informed of the reasons for the arrest and the place of custody. Police must conduct an investigation within twenty-four hours of placing a suspect in custody, and the person must be formally arrested within three days or be released if the procurator decides not to prosecute. Arrested persons should not be held during the investigation stage for longer than one month. However, according to the revised CPL (Articles 126 and 127), the time can be extended if circumstances justify. These circumstances include major criminal gang cases, complex cases involving multiple offenses and offenders, complex cases in remote areas, and cases in which the penalty for the crime would be more than ten years imprisonment.

Pretrial detention is one area in which China has gained a considerable amount of unwanted attention in the international community. The 1979 CPL authorized five forms of pretrial detention, each of which has come under fire as illegal or improperly implemented. However, the main problem over the years has not been with those five, but with a form of detention unauthorized and unstated in the CPL called "taking in for shelter and investigation." Shelter and investigation was originally developed in the 1960s as a policy to round up migrants and return them to rural areas. However, in response to their inability to juggle the procedural restrictions in the 1979 CPL with the provisions of the *yanda* (strike hard) crime campaign of the early 1980s, the police turned to shelter and investigation to control the social disorder problem (Lawyers Committee, 1996, p. 22). Over the past twenty years, the police have greatly expanded its use to detain other kinds of criminals and those suspected of political subversion. Reportedly, persons have been detained under this policy without formal arrest or procurator approval for months and even years. For example, many people have been detained under this policy for their involvement in the Tiananmen Square demonstration (Lawyers Committee, 1994, pp. 70–71).

The revised CPL addressed all five forms of pretrial detention and has also led indirectly to changes in the use of shelter and investigation. It has been stated in official government documents, and confirmed by numerous press reports, that shelter and investigation is no longer permitted as a method of detention. Although this is a cause for some optimism, some provisions in the revised CPL and other new government polices have partially negated this advance. According to the revised CPL (Article 60), arrest standards have been relaxed, and the categories of persons who can be detained prior to arrest have been expanded. Further, the period of pre-arrest detention has been increased from seven to thirty days.

Bail is also more restricted in China than in most other countries. The revised CPL provides that a detained suspect can apply for and receive bail, but he or she is not entitled to this right, and the police maintain complete discretion over whether to approve the application (Lawyers Committee, 1996, p. 33).

In short, there have been some positive advances in curtailing abuse in the area of pretrial detention in China. The revised CPL has addressed some major pitfalls of the 1979 law and has added some needed procedural elements. However, the changes in the revised CPL leave some gaping holes, and in practice they fail to meet various international standards (Lawyers Committee, 1996).

The Right to Counsel

The 1979 CPL stated that all defendants have the right to defend themselves or to appoint someone to defend them. Indigent defendants were not assigned defense counsel unless they had a physical disability (blind, deaf, mute), were a minor, or faced the death penalty. This was modified in the revised CPL, which states that "economic difficulties" are grounds for the "optional appointment of a defender" (Article 34). Another important modification is the time at which counsel is allowed to enter the case. Under the old law, the right to counsel held only during the trial stage. The current law states that the defendant is allowed counsel from the day when the case is transferred to the procurator for a decision to prosecute. Counsel is also allowed for defendants who are detained during the investigation stage.

Although these changes seem significant, they have some serious limitations. One problem is that the terms "economic difficulties" and "optional appointment of counsel" lack clarity, and implementation can be left to the discretion of those with the power to permit and provide free counsel. As a result, many Chinese may be unable to exercise this important right. Further, counsel at the investigation stage is limited and can be blocked if it is determined that the case may involve "state secrets." This restriction can lead to abuses by police, who may claim that a variety of defendant behaviors are suspicious in this sense. Unfortunately, the limitations stated within Article 34 that pertain to the right to counsel cause it to fall short of the UN Basic Principles on the Role of Lawyers, adopted in 1990 (Lawyers Committee, 1996, pp. 41–43). The UN document clearly states that all persons are entitled to a lawyer of their choice to protect them at all stages of criminal proceedings.

The Trial Process and Judicial Fairness

At the standard Chinese trial, the procurator represents the interests of the state, and the defendant or legal counsel represents the interests of the defendant. Most cases of first instance are heard in public unless the case involves state secrets or private disputes. Because jury trial does not exist, a panel of judges, whose number determined by the court level, comes to a verdict. Judicial decisions are determined by majority rule. There is no separate sentencing phase to a proceeding; sentences are handed down immediately after the verdict. The judge or judges have access to material about a defendant's previous criminal history, as well as the defendant's life situation.

In the trial, more emphasis is placed on the confession of the defendant than on the testimony of witnesses. Witnesses usually do not even have to appear before the court and thus are available for challenge from the defense. Instead, witnesses can submit a written testimony prior to the trial. This issue has been addressed but not changed in the revised CPL (Article 49). In a review of the actual steps to the typical Chinese trial, we can see a number of similarities to other Civil Law countries. The judge can take an active role in questioning and guiding the trial, the prosecutor and the defendants or their legal representative can present material and debate on their own behalf, and the decision is made by a panel of judges. A full list of the trial steps in the typical Chinese trial is given in Table 7.3.

Prior to the revision of the CPL, several problems were clearly evident with the trial process and judicial fairness, and whether these issues have been resolved is unclear. One interesting change involves the duties of the trial judge. Steps have been made to transfer the main examination of witnesses and the presentation of evidence from the judge to the procurator, defense attorney, and victim's attorney. In fact, past practice allowed the procurator merely to forward the investigation materials to the court. The judge would then try the case without the procurator being present. This is no longer the case because, as stated in Article 153 of the CPL, procurators must now be present to prosecute the defendant, question witnesses, and debate the defense (Liu and Situ, 1999).

Table 7.3 Steps in a Typical Chinese Trial

1. The procurator reads the bill of prosecution in court.
2. The defendant replies to bill of prosecution.
3. The victim can make a statement about the charges in the bill of prosecution.
4. The procurator can question the defendant.
5. With the permission of the presiding judge, the victim, as well as the plaintiff and defender in an incidental civil action, can question the defendant.
6. Judges can question the defendant.
7. With the permission of the presiding judge, witnesses and then expert witnesses are questioned by the procurator, parties, defendants, or defense counsel. The presiding judge may halt the line of questioning if he or she deems it irrelevant to the case. The parties and defendant have the right to request that new witnesses be summoned to the session, that new material evidence be collected, that a new expert evaluation be conducted, or that another inquest be held. The collegial panel rules on the merits of each request. If the request is granted and the hearing postponed, the procurator is granted one month to complete the supplementary investigation.
8. Judges can question witnesses and expert witnesses.
9. Procurators and defendants present material evidence in the court.
10. The statements of witnesses who are not present in court are read. If the court has any questions about the evidence presented, it can adjourn in order to verify the evidence.
11. The procurator, victims, defendant, or defense counsel present their opinions, which are heard by the judges. They all can debate the quality of the evidence and facts in the case.
12. After the presiding judge has declared the debate concluded, the defendant has a right to present a final statement.
13. The presiding judge announces an adjournment, and the collegial panel begins its deliberations. Potential decisions include these:
    a. If the facts are clear, the evidence adequate, and the defendant guilty by law, the court should pronounce a verdict of guilty.
    b. If the defendant is found not guilty by law, the court should pronounce a verdict of not guilty.
    c. If the evidence is insufficient, the defendant cannot be found guilty. The court would pronounce a verdict of not guilty on the grounds that there was a lack of evidence or that the charges were not substantiated.
14. Judgments are pronounced publicly in court. The judgment indicates the time limit for appealing the decision and the appellate court to which the appeal should be directed.

SOURCE: Adapted from Terrill, 1999.

Because the judge was the main investigator in the case, acting on the same side as the prosecution, there was a question as to whether the defendant was in fact receiving a fair trial. In reality, judges would reach a verdict and decide the sentence, and the trial was a mere formality reflecting this process. A common phrase used to explain the process was "decision first, trial later."

According to the revised law (Article 150) and subsequent interpretations by the Supreme People's Court, the trial judge(s) can only conduct a procedural review prior to the trial. As a result, the investigative duties of the judge now apply during rather than before the trial. The goal here is to eliminate a major problem with Chinese criminal procedure prior to 1996—the determination of guilt before the trial even begins.

The issue of the standard of determining guilt has also been emended. Article 162 of the revised CPL states that, in cases that do not have a preponderance of evidence, the defendant cannot be found guilty. This establishes the principle of presumption of innocence in cases that do not have "sufficient evidence." Although this is a welcomed change in Chinese criminal procedure, there is some question about what happens to the principle of presumption of innocence when sufficient evidence is present. Does sufficient evidence preclude the presumption of innocence? Because of the newness of the law and the difficulty in obtaining information about legal matters within China, it is impossible to answer this question at this time.

After the trial, under the 1979 CPL, the trial judge would submit his opinion to a chief judge (president), who would then review the report and give the final decision. In some cases, lower-court judges would ask for instructions from higher-court judges. But this would cause two procedural problems. First, asking for a review of the case by a higher judge (president) would cause a disjuncture between the judge who tried the case and the judge who decided the case. Second, if the lower-court judge asked for instructions from a higher court, that would create a possible bias for later appeals to that higher court. According to the revised CPL (Articles 149 and 162), trial judges now have the authority to determine the verdict and sentence based on majority rule except in difficult or important cases, which are decided by the Judicial Committee. This amendment was created to promote an essential system of checks and balances. However, we must remember that the members of the Judicial Committee are appointed by the NPC and nominated by the president of the court, who is usually a member of the Communist party. As a result, the independence of the court system is in question because ultimately any sensitive political decision will be controlled by the party (Liu and Situ, 1999).

Another controversial aspect of Chinese criminal procedure relative to adjudication is the concept of being judged by lawful verdict of the court, not by an agency outside the courts. Since the 1950s, the Chinese have practiced a policy called "exemption from prosecution" that, in effect, contradicts this basic concept. Exemption from prosecution is an alternative to bringing a case to trial or dismissing it altogether. With this policy, the procurator has the option not to initiate a prosecution if the matter involves a "minor crime." In the 1979 CPL, the policy was ex-

tended to all crimes for which the criminal law did not require criminal sanctions or that exempted the accused from punishment for reasons such as physical deficiency, self-defense, or show of remorse (Article 101). The use of this policy has been common in cases that involve economic crime and corruption. Research indicates that the policy has been used in over 10 percent of all cases involving the procuratorate (*China Law Yearbook,* 1995).

It would seem that exemption from prosecution is a policy that provides an alternative to penetration into the criminal justice system and permits some form of leniency. But actually there are many problems with the implementation of this policy. For one thing, it provides a tremendous amount of discretion to the office of the procuratorate. In effect, the procurator in the case becomes the judge and jury and is responsible for assigning punishment. Because the accused is exempt from formal prosecution, he or she does not receive the benefits of a legal defense and a court trial. And even though the procurator decides "not to prosecute," he or she still refers to the suspect as having committed a "minor crime." The sanctions that the person receives under this "exemption" are significant as well. In this policy, the procurator can recommend noncriminal sanctions against the suspect, such as confiscation of "illegal income." Finally, and probably most damaging, the procurator can publicly announce the suspects' involvement in his or her "minor crime" at the suspect's place of work. In China, this can result in the individual being labeled as a failure, a pariah, and a disgrace to family and society.

The term *exemption from prosecution* has been eliminated from the revised CPL, and the issue supposedly has been addressed in Article 12, which states that only a court and no other individual or institution can determine guilt. However, some vestiges of the old policy remain. For example, in cases of minor crimes for which the law does not require criminal sanctions, the procuratorate has the discretion "not to prosecute" (Lawyers Committee, 1996, p. 48).

The criminal procedure elements discussed here are just a few of the key issues and changes that have been promulgated by the revised CPL of 1996. For a further description of the revised CPL, we suggest that you refer to an English translation of the original law or an analysis by Fan (1997) or the Lawyers Committee for Human Rights (1996).

Distinctive Aspects of Socialist Law Procedure

What is it that distinguishes Socialist Law criminal procedure from Common and Civil Law procedure? In Common Law and most Civil Law systems, the tendency is to be protective of individual rights. In Socialist Law systems, by contrast, the major emphasis is on the public's interest. This is clearly reflected in Article 1 of the revised CPL, which states:

> *The Criminal Procedure Law of the People's Republic of China is formulated in accordance with the constitution of the People's Republic of China in order to correctly carry out the criminal law to punish crimes, protect the people, safeguard the state security, ensure the public safety, and maintain the social order of socialism.*

In other words, the collective is more important than any one individual, and individual rights are tempered by the need to further the cause of communism. As a result of this philosophy, the concept of separation of powers, with an independent judiciary, is subordinate to the ideal of the sovereignty of the state. Guarantees regarding rights of the accused are always subject to the needs of the state. Further, as we discussed earlier, in Socialist China, there are much broader pretrial detention possibilities, defendants have limited rights to counsel, and procurators enjoy extensive discretion.

Finally, another major difference is that in Common Law and traditional Civil Law systems all kinds of crimes are dealt with in the same procedural fashion. By contrast, in China, cases seem to be handled differently depending on whether it is a political or a criminal case. Political cases, which are often the only ones publicized in the West, appear to lack many procedural standards, giving the impression that the accused have few rights and that the criminal justice system in China is highly political. While this may be true, conventional criminals, those who commit violent and property crimes, typically are processed according to rules that are largely similar to those used in Western, Civil Law–type systems. The differences in *style,* in the basic objectives of the justice system, and in the courtroom atmosphere are more marked, and these will be discussed further in subsequent chapters.

JAPAN: THE HYBRID SITUATION

As we explained in Chapters 3 and 4, the Japanese system of criminal justice is distinct in that it has been so largely influenced by the Civil Law, the Common Law, and the Chinese Confucian traditions but at the same time has retained a distinctly Japanese flavor.

During its 250 years of isolation from outside influences, which ended only in 1858, a system of inegalitarian feudal relationships governed the Japanese criminal justice system and all other aspects of social life. There was no question of rights of the accused during that time. The Japanese found antithetical the whole notion of fixed laws that clarify the limits of state control. The substitute, in addition to arbitrary and often cruel use of power by superiors over inferiors, was a complex system of rules regarding relationships among individuals within and outside the family.

Rules of deference and obligation were particularly strong and provided the cement that held Japanese society together as no formal laws and sanctions could have done. Even today, Japanese society is characterized by strong adherence to patterns of deference, group norms, and group loyalties, as opposed to individualism and legalism. These norms are reinforced in the justice process through extensive use of discretion that diverts cases from the process, development of informal methods of settling disputes, and pressure on individuals to avoid the formal justice system in dealing with their problems. Therefore, describing the formal rights of the accused in Japan does not transmit the total picture regarding these rights. Nevertheless, the formal law is important in understanding the development of Japanese criminal process.

With the opening of Japan in 1858 and the period of the Meiji Restoration, the French penal code and code of criminal procedure were the major influences on Japanese criminal law; later the German codes were adapted to Japanese use. Criminal procedure was thus modeled on that of Civil Law countries. Although the post–World War II criminal procedure law instituted a process that is more adversarial than inquisitorial, there are some continuities with prewar procedure, especially in the process of pretrial investigation.

The Japanese Constitution of 1946 contains important provisions regarding criminal procedure. Articles 31–40 give the impression that Japanese citizens have all the constitutional rights of the accused that exist in the United States. Indeed, the language of several of these articles is very similar to that found in the U.S. Constitution. The differences indicate in some cases the different procedural practices that existed in Japan prior to the war and in other cases the progression of thought that has occurred in the two–plus centuries since the U.S. Constitution was written. For example, the Sixth Amendment to the U.S. Constitution states, in part:

> In all criminal prosecutions, the accused shall enjoy the right to a speedy and public trial, by an impartial jury of the state and district wherein the crime shall have been committed . . . ; to be confronted with the witnesses against him; to have compulsory process for obtaining witnesses in his favor, and to have the assistance of counsel for his defence.

Article 37 of the Japanese Constitution covers much of the same ground but includes the pro-

viso that counsel will be provided for those who cannot provide it for themselves. In the United States, this right to counsel for the indigent exists only through interpretation. It was not incorporated into the meaning of the Sixth Amendment until 1963, in the case of *Gideon v. Wainwright* (372 U.S. 335). Article 37 reads:

> In all criminal cases the accused shall enjoy the right to a speedy and public trial by an impartial tribunal.
>
> He shall be permitted full opportunity to examine all witnesses, and he shall have the right of compulsory process for obtaining witnesses on his behalf at public expense.
>
> At all times the accused shall have the assistance of competent counsel who shall, if the accused is unable to secure the same by his own efforts, be assigned to his use by the State.

Another point worth noticing in the language of Article 37 is that it makes reference to an "impartial tribunal" rather than an "impartial jury." This difference reflects the fact that trial by jury was abandoned in Japan in 1943 after an unsuccessful effort to institute it early in the twentieth century. To some extent, it also reflects the decreasing importance worldwide of trial by jury as a major cornerstone of due process of law.

Trials in Japan are very similar to those in the United States. They are open to the public, and after the judge provides the defendant with his or her rights, the procurator and the defense present their cases. After the trial is concluded, both parties (procurator and the defense) have the right to appeal to a higher court. The vast majority of trials in Japan end up with a guilty plea by the defendant. In Table 7.4, we list the steps of a typical trial in Japan in a case in which the defendant does not plead guilty.

Vestiges of inquisitorial procedure remain despite the elaborate American-style procedural rights found in the Japanese Constitution and in the 1948 Code of Criminal Procedure. The judge continues to be actively involved in questioning during the trial stage, and the prosecutor contin-

Table 7.4 Steps in a Typical Japanese Trial in Which the Defendant Does Not Plead Guilty

1. The procurator gives the indictment before the court.
2. The judge advises the defendant of his or her right to remain silent.
3. The defendant or defense counsel can make a statement.
4. The defendant admits or denies guilt.
5. After a denial, the procurator makes an opening statement and summarizes his or her case.
6. Evidence is presented by the prosecution.
7. Witnesses are examined and reexamined.
8. Evidence is presented by the defense counsel.
9. The procurator provides a statement about the defendant's prior record.
10. The defense provides character witnesses for his or her defense.
11. The defendant is questioned by the procurator, judge(s), and defense counsel upon waiver of the right to remain silent.
12. The procurator gives closing arguments.
13. The defense gives closing arguments.
14. A date is set for determination of guilt.

SOURCE: Adapted from Terrill, 1999.

ues to conduct a detailed pretrial investigation of the case. The Japanese prosecutor, however, has vastly greater discretionary powers to dismiss cases than his continental European counterparts. This power, similar to the power of the American prosecutor, actually allows for affirmation of the Japanese norm of avoidance of formal judicial processes.

An important check on the power of the Japanese prosecutor in each prosecutorial district is the Committee of Inquest of Prosecution. These committees, composed of laypeople, have the duty to investigate cases that the prosecutor has dropped and to recommend their prosecution as warranted. In effect, these committees respond to victim complaints (Tanaka, 1976, p. 482).

Japan's ability to borrow from the different legal traditions of the world while retaining its own social mores has apparently resulted in a very successful criminal justice system. But it is possi-

ble that Japanese criminal procedure, and the Japanese criminal justice system in general, will undergo some changes within the next decade. In a study of court challenges involving various social problems in Japanese society, including industrial pollution and denial of equality to women and Burakumin (a traditionally despised caste in Japan), Frank Upham (1987) found that interest group litigation and concern for individual rights is beginning to find greater acceptance in Japan. Institutional barriers to use of the justice system, which will be described in subsequent chapters, remain, but no doubt they will be subject to pressures for change to conform to a new approach to social ills.

ISLAMIC CRIMINAL PROCEDURE

In his discussions of law in society, sociologist Max Weber speaks of "*quadi* justice" as a distinctive kind of justice. What he is referring to is justice dispensed on a discretionary, case-by-case basis by an Islamic "*quadi,*" or judge, to whom parties bring their disputes for resolution (Weber, 1985). Although the implication is that the *quadi*'s decisions are purely personal (and, in minor matters, indeed may be), the fact is that the *quadi* derives his authority through adherence to the Qur'an and the legal traditions developed by the various schools of Islamic jurisprudence. Further, in Islamic countries today, there is a hierarchy of courts and formalized criminal procedure to deal with all important cases (Moore, 1996). There is little doubt, however, that the concept of "rights" of accused persons is not highly developed in terms of formal procedure in Islamic Law, but exists more in terms of the need for justice and community welfare.

Since Saudi criminal justice is informed by Qur'anic principles, legal officials must look to this source for guidance with respect to criminal procedure. In addition to defining crimes, Islamic Law sets penalties and provides guidance for developing proof of the commission of crimes (Belal, 1993). In general, however, details of criminal procedure are left to the particular jurisdictions and their court systems.

The standard of proof is high in Islamic Law, usually requiring a number of witnesses of particular kinds, and the accused is considered innocent until proved otherwise. For some Hudud crimes (acts against God), which include apostasy, rebellion, theft, adultery, defamation, and drug offenses, the standard of proof is especially high—so high that it is not often adhered to in Islamic courts. For example, proving adultery requires the testimony of four witnesses (who must be male Muslims) or a confession. But confessions can be easily retracted, so, as can be imagined, such a standard of proof is not easy to obtain. For apostasy, which is renunciation of Islam by a Muslim, two witnesses or a confession are required as proof (Amin, 1985b; Lippman, McConville, and Yarushalmi, 1988).

In the case of Salman Rushdie, the British author who was condemned in absentia in Iran by the Ayatollah Khomeini of apostasy for writing the novel *Satanic Verses,* the proof was found in his actual words. The penalty for apostasy in Islamic Law is death. Such a sentence of death without a trial and outside the jurisdiction of an Islamic country is by no means a usual one, and it has been condemned by many Islamic as well as Western jurists. In general, cases are brought to court, and a predetermined procedure is employed to find an outcome using the Shari'a and Islamic jurisprudence (Belal, 1993).

For crimes against persons, witnesses or confessions are also required as proof. Various types of homicide, assault, and fraud usually require two witnesses. Further, not just any witness is acceptable in the Islamic courts; the witness must be male (although in some cases two females can be substituted for one male) and have sound mind and character (Sanad, 1991).

Islamic jurists have argued at length about the kinds of guarantees that should be allowed for persons accused of crimes. An example would be the case of pretrial arrest. According to Awad (1982, pp. 102–103),

Shari'a jurists hold that in principle man is guaranteed the freedom to move as he pleases. Ibn Hazm cites the following Qur'anic verse as the source of this principle: "He it is Who hath made the earth subservient unto you, so walk in the paths thereof and eat of His providence." Jurists have condemned the violation of this principle by forbidding arrest except when necessary. . . .

[However] Preventive detention is recognized by Islamic jurists as . . . legitimate. . . . Saraksi, a Hanafi jurist, suggests that when witnesses accuse a person of adultery, the judge, if unfamiliar with the suspect, should keep him under arrest until the truth . . . is established. . . . Precautionary arrest is not limited to cases of adultery but applies to all cases where it is necessary to detain the accused in order to guarantee that he does not escape or in order to execute the judgment as soon as it is handed down.

That is, the judge should respect the right of an individual to be free but should limit that right if circumstances call for such restriction. This is essentially the same standard that is applied in Civil Law nations.

Rules regarding counsel for defense are somewhat muddier. In keeping with Islamic Law, in Saudi Arabia each person who is accused is entitled to defend him- or herself. This means that the accused must be informed of charges, must understand the nature of the proof, and must have the opportunity to reply to the charges. Although defense counsel are used in many cases, they may not be present at all hearings and are not involved by right. The accused is expected to take charge of his or her own defense. Under Shari'a law, however, the accused is not required to testify. According to Awad, if testifying, the accused does not have to tell the truth. Further, if an accused has confessed, he or she may retract the confession at any time, and it cannot then be used as evidence in a court. Here again, however, the true situation is not always clear, since confessions obtained by force or by deceit may be used (Awad,

1982, pp. 106–107). Nevertheless, the procedure approximates that used in Civil Law nations.

A contrast with Western systems is the requirement in the West for public trials in most cases. Trials in Saudi Arabia are held without jurors and are generally closed. The judge has no need to justify exclusion of outsiders—they may be excluded to protect the privacy of the parties or for the sake of morals (Moore, 1987).

The question of rights of the accused in Islamic Law has been debated by both Islamic and non-Islamic scholars. Saudi Arabia's reaction to the UN Universal Declaration of Human Rights was to argue that the universal principles of the Qur'an protect humans better than international treaties and conventions (Amin, 1985a, p. 30). According to Amin, "The prevalent opinion amongst contemporary Muslim lawyers is that traditional Islamic law affords human rights protections to criminally accused comparable to those recognized in modern international law" (1985a, p. 35). Organizations like the Humans Rights Watch would disagree. They have provided reports stating that Saudi Arabia has violated a number of international standards relative to criminal procedure, including the use of arbitrary arrest, the use of detention without trial, and a number of violations relative to cruel punishment (Human Rights Watch, 1999).

As we have seen, we must consider the application of Islamic Law within particular systems, rather than in general. Seen in this light, the Saudi system presents many protections for those accused of crime, but it does not emphasize this aspect of the justice process to the extent found in most Western systems.

THE CONVERGENCE OF SYSTEMS

Each country develops its own code of criminal procedure, at least partially as a result of its own history, and we would have to scrutinize them all to identify all the differences among them. The classification into adversarial and inquisitorial systems, however, seems to be increasingly a matter of style and history rather than major differences in procedure. Civil Law countries have adopted many of the rules of procedure that protect the accused from arbitrary action by the state. Common Law countries have modified the excesses of the adversarial system by allowing for pretrial investigations, by allowing judges to participate in trials if they choose to do so, and by making various arrangements for avoiding trial through the use of plea bargains.

Convergence can also be seen in Islamic and Socialist legal systems. In Saudi Arabia, Islamic Law reflects the inquisitorial system through strong cooperation between the judge and the investigator. In addition, the defense attorney is less adversarial than in Common Law trials. At the same time, Islamic Law includes provisions for the right to confront accusers and to remain silent and for the presumption of innocence (Reichel, 1999, p. 147). And with the changes in the role of judges and in the standard of proof, the Chinese may actually have moved from a strict inquisitorial to a semi-adversarial model (Liu and Situ, 1999).

The end result seems to be a certain homogenization of criminal procedure among the legal traditions. This process was predicted by legal scholar John Merryman, who over thirty years ago wrote of the blending of the inquisitorial and adversarial systems:

> In a sense, it can be said that the evolution of criminal procedure in the last two centuries in the civil law world has been away from the extremes and abuses of the inquisitorial system, and that the evolution in the common law world during the same period has been away from the abuses and excesses of the accusatorial system. The two systems, in other words, are converging from different directions toward roughly equivalent mixed systems of criminal procedure. (1969, p. 134)

SUMMARY

We have seen how all law systems gradually have developed a series of procedures designed to make certain that accused persons are not treated unfairly or arbitrarily by the government that has jeopardized their well-being by accusing them of breaking its laws. We have also seen how, over time, there has been a large degree of convergence among various families of law with respect to rights of the accused. By considering the different traditions in our model countries, we have been able to develop some sense of the way that criminal procedure controversies are handled in other modern systems of justice.

Questions of criminal procedure are often related to certain constitutional provisions. Nevertheless, a distinction in emphasis continues to exist between Common Law and Civil Law criminal procedure. In the Civil Law, criminal procedure is still largely defined by statute. If it has converged with Common Law procedure, it has done so as part of the evolution of the concept of human rights that occurred chiefly in the twentieth century. The inquisitorial process is concerned not with procedural intricacies but with truth finding in a fair and expeditious manner. In the Common Law, however, the guarantees of protection for the accused historically have been integral to the whole concept of adversarial procedure. Criminal procedure guarantees are designed to ensure that the state cannot call on the accused to help prove his or her innocence or guilt. The state alone must prove guilt beyond a reasonable doubt.

Socialist procedure is in many ways similar to Civil Law procedure. Although Socialist theory emphasizes the collective good rather than judicial independence or defendants' rights, the law of criminal procedure is designed to provide predictability and fairness in the criminal justice process, at least in nonpolitical cases.

Islamic criminal procedure is more like that of the Civil Law than that of the Common Law. Of the various families of law, Islamic Law has fewer formal guarantees regarding the rights of the accused than either the Civil Law or the Common Law. It relies instead on a criterion of fairness and justice to secure these rights.

Ultimately, we must judge a system's performance by studying the actual cases that arise. Even recognizing some difference in philosophy and procedure among governments, most nations want to have a criminal process that distinguishes fairly between the guilty and the innocent and that achieves its goals without abusing the accused.

DISCUSSION QUESTIONS

1. What is unique about Saudi criminal procedure as compared to most of the Civil Law countries of the world?

2. What are the major differences between Common and Civil Law criminal procedure?

3. Compare the criminal procedures in the model countries with the principles stated in the UN Basic Principles on the Role of Lawyers in Appendix A. What countries appear to comply with the standards? Which do not?

4. If you were on trial for a felony, in which of the model countries would you most like to be tried? In which would you least like to be tried? Why?

5. Why does China have such a significantly different attitude toward criminal procedure than our other model countries? Further, why would a policy like "exemption from punishment" be allowed in China and not in the United States?

6. Why are guilty pleas not accepted as such in the inquisitorial systems?

FOR FURTHER READING

Glendon, M. A., M. Gordon, and C. Osakwe. (1985). *Comparative Legal Traditions.* St. Paul, Minn.: West.

Ingraham, B. (1987). *The Structure of Criminal Procedure.* Westport, Conn.: Greenwood Press.

Jacob, H., et al. (1996). *Courts, Law, and Politics in Comparative Perspective.* New Haven, Conn.: Yale University Press.

Langbein, J. (1977). *Comparative Criminal Procedure: Germany.* St. Paul, Minn.: West.

Lawyers Committee for Human Rights. (1996). *Opening to Reform?: An Analysis of China's Revised Criminal Procedure Law.* New York: Lawyers Committee for Human Rights.

Lippman, M., S. McConville, and M. Yerushalmi. (1988). *Islamic Criminal Law and Procedure.* New York: Praeger.

Merryman, J. H. (1985). *The Civil Law Tradition.* Stanford, Calif.: Stanford University Press.

Spencer, J. R. (1989). *Jackson's Machinery of Justice in England.* New York: Cambridge University Press.

Tanaka, H. (1976). *The Japanese Legal System.* Tokyo: University of Tokyo Press.

Trouille, H. (1994). A Look at French Criminal Procedure. *Criminal Law Review:* 735–744.

8 ∿ Legal Actors

The Legal Profession
Key Issues in the Legal Profession
Bureaucratic and Political Organization of
    Legal Actors
The Legal Profession in the Model Systems
    of Justice
Summary
Discussion Questions
For Further Reading

Key Terms and Concepts

adjudicators
advocates
barrister
coordinate ideal
Crown Prosecution Service
empirical systems
hierarchical ideal
law lords
legal advisors
legal scholars
license
magister
notaries
quadi
queen's counselor
rational systems
Rechtsanwälte
referendar
solicitors
staatsexamen

Lawyer bashing is a favorite American pastime. In 1820, Thomas Jefferson called lawyers "that subtle corps of sappers and miners constantly working underground to undermine the foundations of our confederated republic" (Schmidhauser, 1963, pp. 145–146). Many people blame lawyers for obfuscating issues, creating undue delays in the legal process to enrich themselves, and manipulating rules to subvert the clear intent of legislators and other public officials. Indeed, the lawyer joke, a familiar part of American folk humor, voices in a humorous way the frustration, and even helplessness, that people feel about the power of lawyers in our society.

Such feelings are not uncommon in other parts of the world and in other historical eras. As mentioned in Chapter 3, two of the major legal codes developed in Europe over the course of centuries, the Code of Justinian and the Napoleonic Code, were specifically designed to be accessible to laypeople without the need for legal intermediaries. But somewhat naively, Justinian forbade the publication of commentaries on and analyses of his code (Merryman, 1985, p. 7).

In postrevolutionary societies, lawyers who served the old regime often are an endangered species. This is because much of the old legal framework has been discredited, and lawyers, as representatives of the rules of the old order, become objects of the feelings of anger and desire for revenge that follow the overthrow of a hated regime. Thus, in postrevolutionary France, the former Soviet Union, Cuba, and even Iran, adjudication and advocacy became the province of laypeople, usually trusted followers of the revolutionaries. An exception here was the period of the "Glorious Revolution" in seventeenth-century England. Although Oliver Cromwell and his followers deposed and executed King Charles I, Cromwell was determined that the Common Law should survive and be strengthened as a way to preserve some stability in the realm (Prall, 1966).

The legal profession, despite the expressed distrust of lawyers, actually holds a position of high status in modern societies. Leadership posts in governmental agencies are often filled by legally trained individuals. In the United States and, to a lesser degree, other Western countries, lawyers hold a disproportionate number of seats in legislatures.

Criminal law, however, is not as highly regarded as other aspects of legal work. Monetary compensation is not as great in this field as in other realms of legal work, and advocates may actually share in the general unpopularity of the accused criminals that they defend. It is small wonder, then, that criminal defense work is often the province of young, inexperienced attorneys or lawyers who spend most of their time doing civil work. Prosecutors and judges, however, who serve the state and are perceived to be less partisan than defense attorneys, even in adversarial systems, enjoy a high status in modern legal systems.

There has been frequent occasion to mention the role and functions of various legal actors in the earlier discussions of constitutional review, courts, criminal procedure, and other aspects of the criminal process. In this chapter, we will again touch on those roles, but we will focus primarily on the recruitment, training, and professional development of these legal actors. We will see that there is a major distinction between bureaucratic and political approaches to organizing for the legal process. This distinction is reflected in many aspects of the career path of the legally trained. It also is reflected in the general legal culture that we find in different societies. The chapter then goes on to describe in more detail the role of legal actors in the criminal process in each of our model countries.

THE LEGAL PROFESSION

There are generally four categories of legal professionals in developed societies: adjudicators, advocates, legal advisors, and legal scholars (Ehrmann, 1976, p. 56). **Adjudicators** are those individuals who decide the outcome of legal disputes; more commonly, these legal professionals are called judges. **Advocates** represent either the defendant or the prosecution in legal matters before the court. **Legal advisors** provide legal advice to advocates and citizens outside the court. **Legal scholars** study the law and discuss it in legal commentaries and professional journals. Advocates, legal advisors, and legal scholars are more generally called "lawyers," which is a comprehensive term used to describe anyone who gives legal advice, manages legal affairs, and pleads cases in court. In this section, we discuss each of these legal professionals in some detail.

Adjudicators

As we saw in Chapter 7, there are different methods by which various countries and courts determine the legal fate of citizens. Many countries rely on professional judges who are trained and paid to adjudicate legal matters; in others, lay judges, jurors, or a combination of lay and professional judges handle the adjudicatory functions of the courts. There is also variation throughout the world relative to judge selection, with three primary methods generally employed.

The most common method is by appointment. After gaining experience as a lawyer, the prospective judge is selected by an individual within the executive branch of the government or by a special committee. Of our model countries, appointment is the method of choice in England, where judges are appointed by the monarch, prime minister, or lord chancellor.

The second method of judge selection is by career choice path, whereby individuals decide on their own to become judges either during or immediately after their legal training. Exams and extensive apprenticeships follow the decision to become a judge. This kind of career choice system is found in many Civil Law countries and some Islamic Law countries, such as Saudi Arabia. It may seem odd, especially to Americans, for legal actors to decide so early in their careers to become judges before gaining any real legal experience. The need for legal experience may be necessary in the Common Law legal tradition, which necessitates that judges be more knowl-

edgeable so as to better handle the many legal subtleties of the tradition. But in the Civil and Islamic legal cultures, the interpretation of law is limited because of the nature of the law itself. Judges are not asked to make law or even to interpret law, but only to apply the law.

Finally, a less common method of judge selection involves citizen elections. Although this method has been criticized as highly political, it has been adopted by a number of state, county, and local jurisdictions in the United States. Some states have adopted a combination method called the Missouri Plan, which requires judicial candidates to be selected by a committee and then, after some time in office, to face the electorate. Another variation of this method is used in Switzerland, where judges are elected by the country's legislature. This method ensures that the judges have certain traits desirable to the needs of the country (Hitchner and Levine, 1981).

Of our model countries, China uses a combination of election and appointment. The leading judges, called presidents, are elected by the people's congresses at the different court levels while the remaining judges are all appointed by the corresponding standing committees. In the United States, a combination of methods is also employed for judge selection. Judges at the federal level are nominated by the president and then confirmed by the Senate. On the state level, judges are appointed by the governor. In most counties and municipalities, judges are elected by the citizenry.

Whatever the method of determining adjudicators, they are expected to be fair and independent in their judgments. Ideally, they should not be subject to political or economic pressures that might affect their efforts to match the facts of each case with the governing law. Allowing judges the freedom to make decisions without any form of outside pressure is called judicial independence. In countries that have a democratic government structure, judicial independence is essential for maintaining individual rights for all citizens. We have mentioned in previous chapters how China has eschewed judicial independence under the rationale that it is "better for the society" that all legal decisions be in sync with Socialist ideals. To some extent, Islamic countries such as Saudi Arabia have adopted the same approach to fit their religious values. (For a summary of the methods of judge selection in our model countries, see the accompanying box.)

The reality is that adjudicators do not live in a vacuum and are themselves shaped by the circumstances of their society, as well as their upbringing and training. But the ideal of fairness and independence in accordance with a rule of law is a strong socializing influence and a societal norm that should provide a framework for the work of adjudicators.

Advocates

Advocates are expected to be partisan, and a lack of zeal in pursuing the interests of their party is a serious violation of the norms of this category of legal actor. This is so even in Socialist systems, in which the interests of the state are considered paramount and may influence the degree of advocacy that can be exercised. Advocates are legal representatives, usually lawyers, who present the evidence and the arguments that allow adjudicators to make their decisions. Advocates work for the state (prosecution) or the criminally accused (defense).

Efforts have been made on the international level to ensure the quality of legal assistance throughout the world by standardizing the duties and responsibilities of lawyers and others providing legal assistance. In 1990, the Eighth United Nations Congress on the Prevention of Crime and Treatment of Offenders was held in Havana, Cuba; the result was the UN Basic Principles on the Role of Lawyers. The goal of the Basic Principles is to serve as a guide for member states of the United Nations as they promote and develop the proper role of lawyers. The Basic Principles addresses such topics as citizen access to lawyers, qualifications and training, duties and responsibilities, independence from interference, freedom of expression and association, freedom to develop

---

Methods of Judge Selection in Our Model Countries

- England: appointed
  In magistrate's courts, local committees are responsible for appointments; in other courts (generally), the lord chancellor has the responsibility.
- Germany and France: self-selected
  Candidates undergo an extensive apprenticeship period and then face rigorous civil service examinations.
- China: elected and appointed
  The heads of the courts, called presidents, are elected by the corresponding people's congresses while all other judges are appointed by the corresponding standing committee of the particular court.
- Japan: self-selected and then promoted by merit
  After passing a national-level judicial examination, candidates train for two years at the Legal Research and Training Institute and then move up through the ranks based on merit.
- Saudi Arabia: self-selected
  Candidates must first qualify for this position and then go through a period of apprenticeship before being allowed to decide cases.

---

professional (bar) associations, and methods for disciplining lawyers who fail to act in accordance with any ethical standards. (See Appendix A for the full text of the principles.)

Like adjudicators, advocates are subject to economic, social, and political pressures that affect their work. In two of our model countries, Saudi Arabia and China, advocates for both the prosecution and the defense are under considerable pressure to conform to forces beyond the courtroom. In Saudi Arabia, advocates must be schooled in classic Islamic Law because there is no distinction between religious and secular offenses. In China, lawyers must be approved by the Ministry of Justice and are expected to protect the rights of their clients while also promoting the interests of the state. Sometimes, this has proved to be difficult. One survey of 127 lawyers in China, published in 1993, stated that 94 percent of the lawyers experienced some form of interference in their work from either individuals, the government, or the Communist party (Xiangrui, 1993).

Advisors

Legal advisors are the many legally trained individuals who work outside the courtroom to advise and instruct individuals who have legal problems or needs, both civil and criminal. They handle a large proportion of the paperwork that is necessary for the functioning of large bureaucratic societies: wills, contracts, tax analysis, real estate transactions, and analysis of business regulations. Legal advisors are also the first point of contact in criminal cases. They do investigations and advise clients prior to the start of formal adjudication processes. The position of advisors is often viewed as less prestigious than that of advocates because they do not handle cases in the public arena. However, this is only a matter of perception. In reality, legal advisors handle many of the same legal tasks as advocates and usually possess the same qualifications and training, except that they lack courtroom expertise.

Legal Scholars

In every society, legal scholars have played an important role in shaping the law and clarifying its meaning. Their role has been much more prominent in Civil and Islamic Law than in Common Law systems, but people like Blackstone in England and Roscoe Pound in the United States represent milestones in the development of the Anglo-Saxon legal systems and legal thought.

Americans may be puzzled by the strong distinction between advocates and advisors. A German may be puzzled by the strong distinction between legal scholars and adjudicators. The fact is that in different societies the same individual may fit into more than one of these categories. Thus, in the United States, we do not distinguish clearly between trial lawyers and legal advisors, and a single attorney usually handles all aspects of

a case. In Germany, a professor of law who writes learned commentaries may also function as a judge, especially in the higher courts and the European courts. The categories, in other words, are functional ones rather than classifications of particular individuals.

KEY ISSUES IN THE LEGAL PROFESSION

In the modern legal world, most countries share some key issues. These include the trends toward specialization and stratification and the provision of legal aid.

Creeping Specialization

The categories of adjudicator, advocate, advisor, and scholar conceal another aspect of the modern development of legal actors. Legal actors traditionally were generalists rather than specialists, and adjudicators dealt with both criminal and civil aspects of the law. The law, being applicable to all citizens in a society, was administered by people whose general education and familiarity with the rules was enough to ensure the possibility of a fair and reasoned process.

In the twentieth century, the proliferation of laws and regulations and the complexity of the subjects involved made the generalist orientation more and more difficult to maintain. Lawyers now tend to specialize in certain areas of the law. Although judges in traditional courts in many countries, including the United States, continue to decide a large variety of cases, administrative law adjudicatory bodies are taking on more and more of the complex cases dealing with particular technologies and categories of regulation. Germany has four hierarchies of specialized courts (labor, social security, tax, and administrative), as well as generalist courts that handle criminal and other civil matters. Within the generalist courts in some countries, including France and Germany, different chambers are set up to hear criminal and civil cases. Specialized courts tend to reinforce the momentum that has propelled the legal profession toward specialization in modern times.

The drawback of greater specialization, a drawback that infuses not only the legal process but also the legislative process in a democratic society, is that the law becomes more and more remote from the average citizen. This enhances the prestige and value of the legal profession, but it also promotes distrust of and alienation from the profession. The importance of the rule of law can become diminished in such circumstances.

As we move more into a media-controlled governmental process, we might well reflect on the possible consequences of a failure of the law to be a force for evenhanded justice in modern societies.

Stratification Within the Profession

Specialization is not the only force that divides the legal profession. Status-based stratification is common among lawyers in most countries. In Great Britain, advocates, who are known as **barristers,** enjoy a higher prestige than advisors, who are known as **solicitors.** This is so even though solicitors are often more highly paid and work for large firms doing millions of dollars worth of business. Among barristers, appointment to be a QC (queens counselor) is coveted because of the higher prestige that this status confers. In fact, being a QC is generally a condition for becoming a judge, since most judges are appointed by the lord chancellor from within the ranks of this group. In the United States, attorneys who work in large firms, especially Wall Street firms, have higher status than the smalltown lawyer who hangs out a shingle and handles all kinds of cases. Status in the United States is also related to the law school that one attended, with schools like Yale and Harvard providing more prestige than lesser-known law schools. In Germany, professors of law have higher status than other legal professionals, no matter how much more money these other professionals may be making. In France, Japan,

and, to a lesser extent, Germany, a large corps of legal advisors supplements the body of higher-status attorneys. These advisers are known as **notaries** in France, but their work goes well beyond the kind of work done by notaries in the United States. Most basic legal work on wills, contracts, and other noncontroversial matters is done by these individuals.

A more obvious kind of status-based stratification is between judges of higher courts and judges of lower courts. One measure of the status difference here is that many judges of the lower courts in England are women. Another measure is that lower-court judges in some countries, including China, may not be required to be trained in the law. Another is the fact that lower-court judges may work for little or no compensation.

Legal Aid

Free legal aid for indigent defendants in criminal cases is understood to be a function of due process in most modern societies. Among our model countries, only Saudi Arabia and China do not provide such aid as a matter of course. This does not mean that there are no differences among countries with respect to the kind of aid that is provided or the stage of the criminal process at which such aid becomes mandatory. In Civil Law systems, a distinction is often made between the summary investigation that takes place in a police setting and the formal investigation that starts when an examining magistrate or prosecutor takes over the case. In most cases, the right to an attorney applies only at the latter stage. Another distinction is between the mandatory requirement of a defense attorney even if the defendant does not want one, as in France, and the voluntary use of this service, as in the United States. In some countries, such as Austria, attorneys have not always been paid for indigent defense work; in any case, this work generally results in less compensation than conventional private practice. In most countries that provide legal counsel for indigents, the judge is responsible for assigning counsel from a list of local attorneys.

Legal Aid in the Model Countries

- England: Free and independent legal advice is assured regardless of means. Persons must be notified of their right to legal advice by police from duty solicitors at the time of custody; or defendants can use their own private solicitor.
- France and Germany: All suspects have a right to be defended in court. They can choose their own attorney; if indigent, counsel will be assigned. In France, the defendant is required to have legal counsel.
- Japan: The state must provide legal counsel if the defendant cannot afford a private lawyer. Counsel is assigned from a list of lawyers provided by the Japanese Bar Association.
- China: Suspects have a right to defend themselves, or they can appoint someone to defend them. Indigent defendants are not assigned defense counsel unless they have a physical disability (blind, deaf, mute), are a juvenile, or face the death penalty.
- Saudi Arabia: Suspects have a right to defend themselves, or they can appoint someone to defend them. Indigent defendants not automatically assigned defense counsel.

The situation with respect to legal aid becomes more confused in civil cases. In general, however, Civil Law systems have traditionally been more generous in providing legal services to indigents in these kinds of cases than has the American judicial system. (For a summary of the kinds of legal aid in our model countries, see the accompanying box.)

BUREAUCRATIC AND POLITICAL ORGANIZATION OF LEGAL ACTORS

German sociologist Max Weber distinguished between rationally based and empirically based law (Weber, 1985). In essence, the distinction is between code-based law (rational systems) and case-based law (empirical systems). Weber further distinguished between a rational bureaucratic organization for administering the legal process and an organization based on such nonrational factors as appointment by political leaders and election by the people. The rational bureaucratic organization is found in the countries that have rational systems of law—that is, Civil Law systems. Such an organization has the general characteristics of a rational bureaucracy: (1) It is hierarchical in nature, (2) entry into the organization is based on merit alone, and (3) employees of the organization are highly trained for specific tasks.

Legal scholar Miryan Damaska makes a similar distinction between systems that adhere to the **hierarchical ideal** and those that adhere to the **coordinate ideal** (Damaska, 1986). The former are organized around routinization and specialization, with long periods of tenure in office. In such a system, institutional thinking tends to overshadow individual thinking, says Damaska (1986, p. 19). The coordinate ideal, however, stresses horizontal distribution of authority, an amorphous machinery of justice, and short terms of office, with extensive use of lay officials (Damaska, 1986, p. 40).

Keeping these various terminologies in mind, it might be clearer if we made a distinction between bureaucratic elements in organization for legal process and nonbureaucratic elements (which can conveniently be called political elements). Political elements include appointment or election of judicial system personnel. These individuals generally cannot divorce themselves from the people they serve. While trained in the law, they are not usually highly prepared for the specific tasks they must undertake. Such a distinction is roughly analogous to what Weber described. We must be careful from the outset, however, not to overgeneralize about these distinctions. The fact is that there is no "pure" bureaucratic legal organization and no "pure" political organization. Although a system may lean more or less toward one or the other, all systems have elements of both kinds of organization. When it comes to Socialist systems, in fact, we will encounter a confusing hybrid of the political and the bureaucratic.

Another caveat to keep in mind is the fact that the judicial branch of government, no matter how bureaucratically organized, is idealized in modern governments as a separate and independent branch. Therefore, a judicial bureaucracy—that is, an organization of adjudicators—does not fall within the executive branch of a government.

Finally, use of the terms *bureaucratic* and *political* is not meant to invoke any kind of value judgment about either kind of system. Both terms actually have a pejorative connotation to many Americans. In this chapter, however, they are used as a convenient way to distinguish between organizational arrangements that are closely related to the legal culture in their various systems. Just as these legal cultures are bound to historical and social circumstances, so the kind of organization for legal processes that a country has is the legacy of many years of evolution.

Bureaucratically Oriented Organization

Among our model systems, Germany, France, and Japan display the greatest degree of bureaucratic organization of the personnel of the justice system. In each of these countries, students interested in the law follow university programs that emphasize both a general liberal education and specific training in the code law. Upon graduation, many law school students go on to careers in business, public administration, or other nonlegal fields. Those who continue in the legal profession, however, must choose among training to be a judge, an attorney for the state, or an attorney in private practice. This training determines the kind of career that the individual will follow, unless he or she goes into legal scholarship and university teaching. Rigorous examinations and years of apprenticeship are necessary to become fully accredited in the particular branch of legal process that the individual chooses. Both prosecutors and judges have civil service status—that is, they are tenured and rise through the ranks gradually, with some possibility of more rapid advancement for particularly talented individuals.

Exceptions occur chiefly at the highest levels of judicial appointment, such as the Supreme Court

Table 8.1 Number of Professional Judges per 100,000 Population, 1994

China	3.48
Germany	27.19
Japan	2.29
England and Wales	1.91
France	14.88[a]
Saudi Arabia	n/a
United States	4.31

[a]1986 rate.

SOURCE: *Global Report,* 1999, p. 321. Reprinted with permission of the United Nations.

in Japan and the Federal Constitutional Court in Germany. In these policy-making courts, the legislature chooses a mixture of career judges, political figures, and legal scholars to serve for fixed terms. For a summary of the number of professional judges in our model countries, see Table 8.1.

While civil service status assures that judges in Civil Law systems are chosen on the basis of merit rather than ideology or politics, a judge's advancement to higher-court adjudication is usually controlled by those in political power. Despite efforts in some countries to mitigate this political influence, the system in Civil Law countries tends to reward conservatism and conformity rather than individualism and willingness to risk unpopularity in the cause of equal justice (Ehrmann, 1976, p. 78). As a corollary, bureaucratic systems do not generally produce celebrated judges whose opinions are widely read and cited. One does not find the equivalent of an Oliver Wendell Holmes or a Hugo Black in such systems. In fact, anonymity has been the general rule in opinions, although there are increasing exceptions to this rule, especially in Germany.

Law school education in bureaucratic systems does not actually prepare students to practice law in any practical sense. Rather, they are prepared through years of apprenticeship to be either practicing lawyers or state officials such as judges and prosecutors. Over the course of centuries, legal education in the Civil Law countries has developed along rather academic lines, with an emphasis on philosophy, political science, and legal history. These educational systems, in which case precedents do not have the force of law, naturally do not emphasize case law as American law schools do.

Politically Oriented Organization

Of our model countries, England and China, and to a lesser degree Saudi Arabia, might be classified as legal systems that are politically oriented in organization. The United States, as we mentioned earlier, also displays a clear political organization structure. English judges are chosen from among barristers, who are practicing lawyers rather than civil servants trained to be judges. The lord chancellor, a cabinet member who is somewhat analogous to the attorney general of the United States, makes judicial appointments, generally from among the most prestigious barristers, the queen's counsel (QC). The law lords, who sit in the House of Lords and act as the court of final appeal, are also appointed rather than achieving their position through a merit system.

In China, the head judges of the various people's courts are called presidents. The presidents are elected by the people's congresses of the respective court levels. For example, the president of the Supreme People's Court is elected by the National People's Congress, while the presidents of the local people's courts are elected by the people's congresses on the local level. All remaining judges are appointed by standing committees at the particular court levels. Politics greatly affect the judge selection process in China because the National People's Congress and the standing committees primarily consist of influential members of the Communist party.

Prosecutors, who are politically chosen in the United States, fall into different categories in both England and China. Although there have been some changes in recent years, English prosecutors have not traditionally specialized even in prosecuting cases. Instead, they are chosen for particular cases from among the ranks of the barristers. Thus, it is quite possible for an individual to be a prosecutor one day and a defense attorney the next. Prosecutors in China, called procurators,

are under the direct supervision of the office of the procuratorate. At the federal level, procurators are all appointed (and removed) by the Standing Committee of the National People's Congress. At the provincial, regional, and municipal levels, the chief procurators are elected or removed by the respective people's congresses, and the deputy procurators are selected by the standing committees of the respective level of government.

When we come to Saudi Arabia, our distinction between bureaucratic and political organization breaks down. However, since judges are part of the religious establishment and are chosen from a committee that is approved by that establishment or from the ranks of the royal family, this system tilts toward the political. Advocates and advisors in this system, however, follow the Civil Law model imported from France.

In sum, the distinction between bureaucratic and political arrangements is not always clear-cut. Nevertheless, a dominant style or orientation exists in each of our model systems, and awareness of this style helps us analyze and understand the details of the various systems as we examine them. This dominant style is related to the particular family of law to which a country adheres, with the rational, code-based systems having a rational bureaucratic hierarchy of legal professionals working for the state, and the empirical, case-based systems having a more mixed, even pluralistic culture of the legal profession. As we consider legal training, judicial recruitment, and career paths of prosecutors and defense attorneys in the model systems, these classifications of bureaucratic and political will provide a useful framework for the analysis.

THE LEGAL PROFESSION IN THE MODEL SYSTEMS OF JUSTICE

England

John Mortimer gives us an inside look at the legal profession in England in his stories about Rumpole of the Bailey Court. Horace Rumpole is an aging irreverent barrister who specializes in criminal cases (heard in the Old Bailey criminal court in London) and who describes in sarcastic detail the foibles and pretensions of the other barristers in his chamber. The chamber is the equivalent of a law firm for barristers, and each firm is within one of the four large clubs of barristers in London. The clubs are called the Inns of Court, and every barrister is a member of one of the clubs.

In one of Mortimer's stories, Rumpole's clerk, Albert, tells him that Rumpole's next case will be a robbery case and that the prosecuting barrister will be a gentleman named Guthrie Featherstone, M.P. (Mortimer, 1978, p. 15). Later, we encounter this conversation between Rumpole and Featherstone as they walk down to the Old Bailey together.

> We walked together down Fleet Street and into Ludgate Circus, Featherstone wearing his overcoat with the velvet collar and little round bowler hat, I puffing a small cigar and with my old mac flapping in the wind; I discovered that the gentleman beside me was quietly quizzing me about my career at the Bar.
> "You've been at this game a long while, Rumpole," Featherstone announced. . . . "You never thought of taking silk?"
> "Rumpole, Q.C.?" I almost burst out laughing.
> "I'm sure you could, with your seniority." . . .
> I gave [Featherstone] my view of Q.C.'s in general:
> "Perhaps, if I played golf with the right judges, or put up for Parliament, they might make me an artificial silk, or, at any rate, a nylon." . . .
> "Sorry, I forgot. You did put up for Parliament." (p. 16)

Upon arriving at court, Rumpole discovers who the solicitor in the robbery case is:

> "Ah, Bernard! You're instructing me."
> Mr. Bernard, the solicitor, was a thirtyish, perpetually smiling man in a pinstriped suit. . . .
> "I'm always your instructing solicitor in a Timson case, Mr. Rumpole." Mr. Bernard beamed

and Fred Timson, a kindly man and most innocent robber, stepped out of the ranks to do the honors.
> "Nothing but the best for the Timsons, best solicitor and best barrister going." (p. 18)

These excerpts tell us a good deal about the legal profession as it traditionally has been practiced in England. Rumpole, who specializes in and loves the practice of criminal law, is something of a maverick even within his own chambers. His practice is not regarded as highly as that of those who litigate the more lucrative civil cases, and Rumpole responds by dressing and acting in ways that do not conform to the conventions of the Bar.

The fact that his colleague Featherstone is acting as prosecutor in the case in which Rumpole is the defense attorney illustrates the traditionally peculiar situation of prosecuting barristers in England. While there have been many changes in recent years in the position of prosecutor, the government still can assign a practicing barrister to prosecute criminal cases. In other words, the clear distinction between prosecution and defense as professions that exists in Civil Law and Socialist Law countries, and even in the United States, does not obtain in England. Barristers are experts in courtroom advocacy; which side they are on is not really as important as the fact of their specialized training to perform in public. American prosecutors may also have practiced defense advocacy at some point in their career. During the time they are prosecutors, however, they operate only in that capacity.

"Taking silk" (being allowed to wear a silk gown and a more elaborate wig) is the popular term for appointment to the coveted status of QC, or **queen's counsel.** The QC is a group of preeminent barristers who serve as counsel to the British Crown. Featherstone, with his patrician manner, supercilious tone, and political connections through his position as a member of Parliament (MP), is a natural choice to be a QC. Appointment is by the lord chancellor, the cabinet officer who is the equivalent of a minister of justice in England or the attorney general in the

United States. In subsequent Rumpole stories, Featherstone becomes a judge, again a natural step since judges are almost always appointed by the lord chancellor from among the ranks of the QCs.

The division of labor between solicitors and barristers in England is also illustrated in the preceding excerpt from Rumpole. Bernard, the instructing solicitor, has all the preliminary contacts with the client and gathers the evidence in the case. He advises the barrister assigned to the case about his findings and his experiences with the client. He attends at court, but he does not have a "right of audience" before the court. However, solicitors are forbidden to participate only in crown court cases, that is, the more serious cases. They routinely appear in the lower criminal and civil courts.

Rumpole's chambers (law firm) are part of one of the four ancient Inns of Court: Middle Temple, Inner Temple, Gray's Inn, and Lincoln's Inn. These inns are large establishments, almost like fraternities or eating clubs, in which aspiring barristers are trained in the law and in courtroom behavior. The complex case law that is integral to the Common Law is learned slowly and through experience at the inns. Admission to one of the inns traditionally has assured a career as part of the elite company of barristers. Barristers are attached to their inns throughout their careers, even if they actually practice outside London.

Laypeople in British courts have an active role as adjudicators in the magistrates' courts, and as jurors who adjudicate issues of fact in the crown courts. However, this does not diminish the important role of professional judges in England. On the magistrates court level are two types of judges. The most common magistrate is the layperson who serves without financial remuneration; this person, called the justice of the peace, is chosen by the local advisory commission and serves for at least a six-year term. The second kind of magistrates' court judge is the professional or stipendiary magistrate who is trained in law and paid for his or her services. Magistrates' courts handle over 90 percent of all criminal cases, as well as some civil cases including renewal of licenses, marital separations, child custody, and some adoptions.

The role of judges in England in the development of Common Law has changed considerably over the years. For centuries, English judges took an active role in formalizing and creating law, but now most English law is created in the form of a statute passed in Parliament. Parliament is the supreme legal authority in England, and no English court can declare a law unconstitutional (Griffith, 1991).

Judges in the crown courts, as mentioned earlier, generally are selected by the lord chancellor. The judges in the crown courts are very active in questioning witnesses and delivering instructions and summations to the jury. They handle all major criminal cases and appeals from magistrates' courts. The Court of Appeals, the intermediate appellate court for England, handles both civil and criminal matters. The judges are selected from the High Court of Justice and the House of Lords and are assigned in groups of four or five to review cases. A unique feature of the Court of Appeals is that the judges can actually add time to the sentence (up to three months) if they feel the appeal made by the convicted was frivolous.

The High Court is both a court of original jurisdiction and a court of appeal for both criminal and civil matters. It consists of about eighty judges who are usually assigned cases based on their own expertise. Cases of original jurisdiction are handled by one judge, and appeals cases by two or three judges.

The House of Lords, the highest court in England, hears civil and criminal appeals from the Court of Appeals and a limited number from the High Court. The House usually consists of nine members who are selected from the Court of Appeals. **Law lords,** as they are called, must have been practicing barristers for fifteen years or have held a high judicial office for two years. (The different levels of English courts will be discussed further in Chapter 9.)

In recent years, discontent with the delays and inefficiencies of the legal process and with the stratification of the legal profession in England has led to two major changes: (1) the development of the Crown Prosecution Service and (2) a lessening of the distinction between barristers and solicitors in the practice of law.

The **Crown Prosecution Service** (CPS), constituted in 1986, was designed to improve the legal process by taking responsibility for the prosecution of cases away from police agencies and assigning it to an independent government agency similar to a prosecutor's office. Before the establishment of the CPS, the police engaged solicitors to take on cases. Larger police departments had a separate unit of solicitors to handle cases. Employees of the CPS now serve as solicitors for the prosecution, but the practice of appointing independent barristers continues. Some problems have surfaced with the implementation of the CPS. The service has been accused of discontinuing winnable cases and wasting police time by demanding full case dossiers before deciding to prosecute (Phillips, Cox, and Pease, 1999).

Another problem in the legal profession in England involves the pressure to break down the stratification within the profession and to permit solicitors to appear as advocates in the Crown Courts. This pressure has been building for some time as the educational and class differences between solicitors and barristers have narrowed. Gradually, solicitors have become more assertive in demanding an opportunity to present cases in the higher courts. On May 9, 1986, the judges of the High Court and the Court of Appeals decided that solicitors would be allowed to handle formal and uncontested cases. "Two working days later, three solicitors made legal history by being the first to appear in open court in the High Court as spokesmen for their clients, robed and in winged collars (though without the barrister's wig)" (Zander, 1989, p. 26). Although few solicitors seem to be taking advantage of their new opportunity to appear in court (Zander, 1989, p. 40), the gradual breakdown of the traditional system appears to be just a matter of time.

Zander points out that legal education is fueling much of the change. Barristers traditionally received a liberal arts education, starting in private preparatory schools and going on to one of two highly prestigious universities, Oxford or Cambridge. Training in the law was through junior work at one of the Inns of Court. Today, the preeminence of the two ancient universities is being challenged, and law schools based on the American model have been established at many British universities. Many graduates of these law schools choose to become solicitors because of the greater opportunity for specialization, the greater monetary rewards from working in a large law firm with corporate customers, and the generally more modern and dynamic quality of this branch of the legal profession. For many years, the concept of professionalism allowed lawyers in England to define standards and control entry into their ranks in order to maximize profits and social prestige. In the future, lawyers will increasingly become employees of large organizations or be subject to increasing free market forces, and the elitist nature of the English bar will change markedly (Abel, 1987).

The test of the extent of change will come as more judges are chosen from the median ranks of lawyers rather than from the QCs. At present, the English judiciary, because of the way members are culled from among the most prestigious barristers, is a conservative group. It has a strong tradition of independence going back to the Act of Settlement of 1701 and the abolition at about the same time of prerogative royal courts such as the High Commission and the Star Chamber. English judges serve for life; this also guarantees a certain amount of independence. Some reformers suggest a mandatory retirement age for judges, but Parliament has not yet acted on this recommendation.

In sum, the legal profession in England is undergoing some major changes. As it deals with the challenges of the twenty-first century, we can expect that the face of this profession will be quite different from what it was just a generation earlier.

France and Germany

The legal professions in both France and Germany fall into the category of bureaucratic systems, and both fall within the Civil Law family.

Thus, there are many similarities in the legal professions of the two countries, and it is convenient to group them together. Nevertheless, there are also important differences that reflect the differences in governmental structure and historical development and that provide a distinctive character to each system.

In most countries, including Common Law countries, judicial duties include finding the law in the codes, applying the law to the specific facts of the case, and interpreting the law if it is vague, has a gap, or is outdated. In Civil Law countries, judges have less power to create, interpret, and overturn law, but they have more power to investigate and determine facts. In France, the interpretive function is limited by legislation that curtails judicial powers. This legislation was developed following the French Revolution, when distrust of judges was the prevailing attitude. As a result, the French have established the Supreme Cour de Cassation to overturn any incorrect interpretations by judges. In Germany, there is less concern about improper interpretation, but if the situation arises appeal courts may sit as a court of revision (Spader, 1999, p. 128).

Because judges in Civil Law countries are freer to seek evidence and to control the nature and objectives of the inquiry they take on different roles than judges in Common Law countries (Merryman, 1985). Thus, trials in Germany and France are influenced more by judges, while in Common Law countries, like the United States, lawyers are the focal point of the trial. An example of the judicial actions in Germany is described here:

After the judge has questioned witnesses, the lawyers and the defendant may ask further questions. Except in political trials, however, it is rare for them to exercise this option, and it is almost unheard of that a lawyer would ask more than one or two questions. In part, this is because a lawyer who asked a lot of questions would be implying that the judge had not done a good job, a dangerous tactic, to say the least. The lawyers also submit written pleadings and make closing arguments. Beyond that they do nothing. (Luban, 1988, p. 95)

As in England, legal education in France and Germany is both a product of the legal culture and a major influence on the development of the legal profession. In both countries, legal education in its earliest stages consists of a basic university education that encompasses general liberal arts courses and some courses in the law. At the University of Paris, for example, law students, depending on which department of the university they enter, may elect to take courses in history, sociology, philosophy, and even various aspects of arts studies (Carbonneau, 1980). In France, this education is highly controlled by the Ministry of Education despite some efforts to decentralize law education following the student uprisings in 1968.

In Germany, with its federal structure, basic regulations for legal education are set by the central government, but each state is free to achieve the general objectives through individual structures. In practice, there has been some experimentation with increased "practical" training in German law schools, especially at the University of Bremen, but the rigorous federal examination requirements have dictated a fairly uniform system of legal education in the various states.

Upon receiving the academic secondary school degree (known as the baccalaureate in France and the abitur in Germany), students in both countries are eligible to enter the law school at one of the state universities. The large numbers of applicants in both countries have created problems for the quality of legal education, and the norm has become huge lecture classes and little or no teacher-student contact. Germany has attempted to deal with this problem by restricting the number of law school entrants at various universities and by assigning university seats throughout the country from one central admissions office. France continues to allow all students with baccalaureates to achieve a basic law school education. Both countries continue to have unacceptably large numbers of law students in the various universities (Glendon, Gordon, and Osakwe, 1985, ch. 3).

These students do not all go on to become legal professionals, however. In fact, a law school education in these countries also provides the basic liberal education for students who do not wish to go to professional schools of medicine, science, or various technologies.

With respect to duration of studies, the law student in France may graduate in three years with a general degree, known as the **license.** Those who plan to enter the legal profession generally go on to a fourth year, leading to the degree of **magister,** or master of law. Students must pass national examinations in order to obtain these degrees.

Germany also has a unified bar with a national examination, or **staatsexamen,** that follows three and a half years of university education. German experiments with a more "practical" legal education (often inspired by the case-based education that American students receive) have been limited by the national requirements regarding length and content of study. At Augsburg University, periods of study are interspersed with periods of apprenticeship. A more radical reform effort took place in the University of Bremen, where small groups of students concentrate on particular problems, thus learning the law sequentially on a more intense basis than is usual when taking a variety of courses in the traditional manner. This program lasts six years but replaces much of the three and a half years of apprenticeship training that prospective lawyers usually undergo in Germany (Geck, 1977).

University education is followed by an intensive apprenticeship and further training in both France and Germany. The countries differ in the objectives of this training, however. In France, the training is specialized, designed to introduce the student to the particular kind of law that he or she wishes to practice: adjudication, advocacy for the state (prosecution), private advocacy, or advisory. Those who want to become private attorneys must pass an exam, register with the local bar association, and then begin a three year apprenticeship. Those who wish to become judges or procurators must attend the Ecole Nationale de la Magistrature (National Magistrate's School).

After attending the school, which includes apprentice training, the graduate can become a judge or procurator (prosecutor).

In Germany, the decision to specialize is deferred, and the apprenticeship, known as the *referendar* period, rotates students among different specialties. In the end, however, students in both countries must take rigorous examinations to qualify for the civil service positions of judge or prosecutor or the advocacy positions in the law— known as *advocats* in France and **Rechtsanwälte** in Germany. Once embarked on a specialty, the student has little opportunity to change career paths. The only major exception to this rule is that in France prosecutors may switch to the judiciary, and vice versa (David, 1972; Reuschemeyer, 1973).

As we can see, then, the aspiring legal professional in both these countries must undergo both academic and practical training. The case method of education, so prevalent in American law schools, has no place in university education in the Civil Law. At the same time, the graduate of a law school in France or Germany, upon passage of a bar examination, may not "hang out a shingle" and practice all kinds of law, as is done in the United States. Despite the fact that the amount of training and education are the same (about seven years) in all three countries, the degree of specialization in training is greatest in France, followed by Germany and then the United States.

One peculiar thing about the results of the educational process in France and Germany that seems anomalous to an American is the fact that the adjudicators in those systems tend to be a good deal younger than their counterparts in the United States. Although elevation to a higher court generally occurs only after many years at the lower levels, this elevation in a civil service system is based largely on faithful and meritorious service rather than outstanding reputation or political influence, as is the case in the United States. Further, judges in the United States usually have little or no training for their position, whereas Civil Law judges go through lengthy apprenticeships. Thus, competence is the hallmark of the

Civil Law judge, whereas power and influence, and even idiosyncrasies, often characterize the Common Law judge. In keeping with the bureaucratic tradition, judges in Civil Law systems do not as a rule sign their opinions, and dissenting votes or opinions are not made known when appellate judges vote on a particular case.

A feature of Civil Law systems is the relatively large number of legal professionals who are judges. In Germany, for example, about 28 percent of those in the legal profession are judges (Luban, 1988). On a per capita basis, there are four to five times as many judges in Germany as in the United States (Reuschemeyer, 1973, p. 34). This proliferation of judges reflects to a large extent the specialized nature of the courts, described earlier in the chapter, and the fact that many matters decided by administrative agencies in the United States end up in the regular courts in Germany. If we add the fact that many lawyers in Germany become advisors in government agencies or businesses rather than practicing attorneys, we find the ratio of practicing attorneys to attorneys in government or business to be even smaller in Germany than in the United States (Reuschemeyer, 1973, p. 31).

Stratification of nongovernmental attorneys exists in both France and Germany. Although not as colorfully separated as barristers and solicitors in England, there is a distinction in France between *advocats* (advocates) and *avoués* (advisors) that is only slowly being erased. In Germany, a similar distinction between the Rechtsanwälte as advocates in court and other attorneys as advisors exists but is also undergoing changes. In both countries, law professors have both great influence and high prestige. Legal scholars in Civil Law countries generally have a higher status than judges. This is in contrast to England, where professors of law do not generally influence the interpretation of statutes or the path of the law. The influence of law professors is another function of the difference between a code law system and a case law system. Where judges actually make law, as in a case-based system, they are bound to be more powerful than in one where they do not. At

the same time, the interpretation of law from an abstract standpoint and a philosophical approach to legal questions are important not only to students but also to practicing professionals in a code-based system.

In keeping with the bureaucratic tradition, there is, in Germany and France, no question of using advocacy attorneys interchangeably as both prosecutors and defense attorneys, as is done in England. In both countries, a good deal of legal work, including wills and contracts, is done by local notaries, who are graduates of law schools and cannot be compared to the American notary public.

As in so many other aspects of the legal process, especially the criminal process, there is today a good deal of ferment and change with respect to legal education and practices in France and Germany, as in England. Some of the elitism and stratification of the profession is breaking down in all three systems. The rigidities of education and training are being softened—in England toward greater academic training, and in France and Germany toward greater "practicality" in university legal education. England is instituting reforms designed to increase the possibility of specialization in the legal profession. Precedent, while not having the legal force that it does in Common Law systems, is becoming more and more a factor to be considered in the Civil Law, especially where constitutional interpretation is at stake. At the same time, the proliferation of legislation has tended to negate much of the force of the Common Law as a case-based system.

Elements of convergence between the two kinds of legal systems do not suggest that their organizations will be indistinguishable within the foreseeable future. The generally bureaucratic culture of the Civil Law systems and the generally political culture of the Common Law systems result from long historical traditions and entrenched modes of thought. Such cultures change slowly, and reform efforts that involve adaptation of the institutions of other countries often develop an indigenous flavor. Even major upheavals, such as the French Revolution of 1789, that target legal organizations for extinction and manage to bring about some major changes usually do not succeed in changing deep-rooted organizational patterns and styles.

China

The legal profession traditionally has been viewed in a negative light in Chinese society. It was generally believed that overreliance in law and lawyers would lead to a litigious society, one full of self-indulgent people who would be unable to live in harmony with others. During the early nineteenth century, lawyers were often ridiculed and even jailed if they fought too vigorously for individual citizens (Bodde and Morris, 1967, p. 416). But despite the early aversion to the legal profession, the necessity for lawyers in China has grown as the society has become more advanced. The number of lawyers in China increased from less than 1,000 in the 1800s to more than 10,000 in 1935 (Conner, 1994).

Since the formation of the People's Republic in 1949, the legal profession in China has undergone a number of considerable changes. After the Communist Chinese came to power, the number of lawyers dwindled to below 3,000, and their influence was reduced considerably. Those who remained were highly regulated by a series of laws set forth by the Communist party concerning their purpose, responsibilities, and organization (Lawyers Committee, 1998, p. 14). During this time, lawyers were used in civil matters to draw up simple contracts and documents needed in the new economy, thereby assisting the masses while serving the Socialist state (Alford, 1995). In criminal trials, lawyers were even less influential, with justice being dispensed by administrative agencies and people's tribunals. The sole purpose of lawyers in criminal trials was often reduced to seeking leniency in punishment (Gelatt, 1991).

This situation turned from bad to worse in the political turmoil of the late 1950s. The Anti-Rightist Campaign attacked lawyers with considerable vigor, claiming that, by defending criminals and protecting economic interests of clients, law-

yers were in direct conflict with Socialist ideology. Many lawyers were labeled capitalists and rightists and were often persecuted, law offices were closed, and the Ministry of Justice was disbanded (Lawyers Committee, 1998, p. 15). After a short period of softening and some legal reforms, the Cultural Revolution of 1966–76 resumed the attack on the legal profession. In this decade, the legal profession was basically abolished, and no lawyers were trained (Leng and Chiu, 1985).

Following the Cultural Revolution, the Ministry of Justice was reestablished, and all law departments and schools were reopened. A change in attitude toward law and the legal profession in China was influenced by Deng Xiaoping, who actively promoted many economic, political, and legal reforms in the late 1970s. With Deng's broad reforms came massive amounts of legislation. The goal of much of the legislation was to transform the economy, prevent the legal abuses of the Cultural Revolution, and change the international image of China. As a result, the need for qualified lawyers became apparent.

Apparently, some efforts have been made by the government to address the shortage of legal professionals. In 1982, there were only 5,500 lawyers in China, but by the early 1990s, the number had grown to 50,000 (Situ and Liu, 1996). By the end of 1997, the number of law firms had doubled since 1993, and more than 100,000 lawyers were registered with the Ministry of Justice (*China Law Yearbook,* 1997, p. 1074). Although a drastic increase from only ten years earlier, the numbers of lawyers in China is still small in number considering the size of the population, the legal needs of citizens, and the fact that half of the lawyers work part-time as law teachers or legal researchers. Current figures show that, with a population of over 1.2 billion, China has one lawyer for every 10,909 people. In comparison, the United States has one lawyer for every 274 people.

Two pieces of legislation have been paramount in the development of the legal profession in China over the past twenty years. The first, a law called the Provisional Regulations of the

PRC on Lawyers, was passed by the National People's Congress in 1980. This law outlined the purpose, rights, activities, and qualifications of lawyers in China and called for an increase in the expansion of the legal profession (Lawyers Committee, 1998, p. 17). It also explicitly stated that lawyers in China were "to serve the cause of socialism" and to advance the interests of the state and the "collective" while protecting the legitimate rights and interests of the citizens.

Over time, however, the many weaknesses of the Provisional Regulations began to surface. Under this law, lawyers were defined as workers for the state and thus received little financial compensation for their work. Education and training were minimal and flexible, resulting in political appointments and a lack of quality control within the ranks. Because the government had full control of the process, lawyers lacked any protections from any formal professional bar association. Lawyers who tried to openly oppose the state or too vigorously defend their client against the state were highly criticized. Most strikingly, lawyers were shown to be incapable of handling the increasingly complex tasks required within the new economy initiated by Deng Xiaoping. It was apparent that changes in the legal profession were necessary and that new standards and qualifications for lawyers were needed. As a result, in 1996, the Lawyers Law was unanimously passed by the Standing Committee of the National People's Congress to address these issues.

The Lawyers Law consists of fifty-three articles within eight chapters that outline in skeletal form the operation of the legal field in China. Many laws in China are developed in this manner so that the Ministry of Justice and local jurisdictions can "clarify" the general principles and set specific regulations. The objectives of the Lawyers Law have been described by the Lawyers Committee for Human Rights in the following manner:

First, to bring China's regulatory framework more into compliance with reality by replacing the outdated Provisional Regulations with a legal structure that better accords with a socialist market economy, in particular by redefining the role of the lawyer and codifying the changes in organizational forms of law firms.

Second, to pacify the masses angered by the unethical behavior of lawyers by emphasizing the professional responsibilities of lawyers and strengthening the system for disciplining wayward lawyers.

Third, to protect the rights of lawyers and ensure that lawyers are not interfered with or subjected to physical or other forms of abuse when carrying out their responsibilities in accordance with law.

Fourth, to protect the rights and interests of individuals and parties served by the legal profession through a variety of channels, including: (i) promoting a more independent legal profession; (ii) improving the quality of lawyers by setting higher standards for qualification, holding lawyers to a higher standard of professional responsibility, and improving management over lawyers; (iii) clarifying the rights of lawyers to represent clients and the obligations of lawyers to their clients; (iv) protecting lawyers from interference and abuse; and (v) laying the foundation for a legal aid system. (1998, pp. 47–48)

The Lawyers Law appears to be a serious attempt to improve the quality of legal representation and rule of law. However, it is generally believed that, because of the strong political influence of Communist party, the Lawyers Law lacks some of the essential elements stated in the Basic Principles on the Role of Lawyers as outlined by the United Nations (see Appendix A). In comparison with the Basic Principles, the Lawyers Law fails to address lawyers' freedom of expression, due process concerns, and the duty of lawyers to uphold human rights as recognized in international law (Lawyers Committee, 1998, p. 46).

The term *lawyer* in China actually refers to a professional who is a legal representative or attorney-at-law and excludes judges, law teachers, and legal scholars. Law teachers and scholars devote most of their time to teaching and research and sometimes dabble in part-time law or legislative drafting. The role of defense counsel in China is very different than in most other countries. Individuals can represent themselves or allow another to represent them. The legal representative can be a lawyer, someone from an organization the defendant belongs to, or even a relative or friend. Chinese defense attorneys are "encouraged" to help the court render a just verdict. Although the job of the defense counsel is supposedly to prove that the defendant is innocent, the reality in China is that the defense counsel in most cases can only act to help mitigate the severity of the sentence. Until recently, defense attorneys in China were not allowed to meet with defendants until the trial, defense counsel had restricted access to information about the case prior to the trial, and, in some cases, trials began without defense counsel being notified about the case (Chenguang and Xianchu, 1997).

As we discussed in Chapter 4, the procuratorate in China is responsible for supervising the administration of the criminal justice system, including investigating crimes, monitoring the activities of the courts, overseeing the police and correctional institutions, initiating prosecutions, and upholding the lawfulness of the procuratorate itself. The procuratorate, in theory, is independent from outside influence, as stated in the 1979 Organic Law for People's Procuracy. Although this may seem straightforward, it is rather complicated by the fact that the procuratorate is also supposed to follow the policies and philosophy of the Communist party. The party provides general guidance through the provision of Communist ideology, principles, and policy while avoiding improper interference in the disposition of general cases (Nader and Parnell, 1983).

The role of judges in China is much different than in any of our other model countries. Except for minor civil cases, judges in China are unable to decide on cases individually. All cases are decided by a panel of judges and can be overridden by an adjudicatory committee. In civil cases (and until recently in criminal cases), judges are seen as part of the government, and in that capacity they are

not impartial adjudicators but play an active role in questioning and fact finding. In this way, judges in China are similar to those in other Civil Law legal systems (Lawyers Committee, 1998, p. 9).

Judges in China at most levels are poorly educated and lack any formal legal training. Until recently, many judges were selected from among former military officers. However, efforts have also been made to improve judicial qualifications and standards with passage of the 1995 Judges Law, which set new standards for judges. To improve the quality of judges at the lower-court levels, China has established a National University of Judges, and for senior judges, the Supreme People's Court has formed a special training center. The Judges Law also has attempted to strengthen the independence of the judiciary by providing that judges have the right to be free from external interference in their work. However, there is some skepticism as to whether this ideal will become a reality (Lawyers Committee, 1998, p. 9).

Legal training for advocates in China is tightly regulated by the Ministry of Justice and the Ministry of Education. The responsibilities of the Ministry of Justice include training legal personnel, improving legal education, supervising lawyers, conducting legal research, publishing materials on law, and disseminating legal information to the public. In recent years, law has become an important field of study in China, with the subject being studied in high schools and in numerous kinds of training courses. To pursue a formal career in law as a lawyer, court administrator, procurator, or law enforcement officer, one must first take a national exam to enter either a university law department or legal institute. In the university program, students take courses in Chinese legal history, political science, foreign languages, and various kinds of law. In the legal institutes, the training is more practical in nature, with courses in investigation, forensics, and criminology (Terrill, 1999, p. 562). To complete their legal training and become lawyers, students must complete two years of legal work, pass a national bar exam, and be approved by the Ministry of Justice.

The Chinese legal profession has been marked by considerable changes over the past fifty years. With the economic, legal, and cultural changes that are reverberating within China, we can surmise that more changes will soon follow. One constant, however, has been the strong influence of politics on the selection and daily functioning of those in the legal profession.

Japan

The most prominent feature of the Japanese legal profession is the relative rarity of these professionals in a nation as populous as Japan. In 1995, there were approximately 15,450 lawyers in Japan (Dean, 1997). The United States produces three times as many lawyers *each year.* To put it another way, the entire country of Japan has half as many lawyers as in the Washington, D.C., area alone. The stark contrast between the two nations in this respect is usually explained by the fact that the Japanese people are not as litigious as Americans. According to this analysis, the ideals of harmony and conciliation are so strong in Japan that few people will embark on the inherently conflictual process of formal adjudication.

While there is no doubt that formal conflict is eschewed by the Japanese and that consensus and concord are highly valued, the fact is that the government strictly controls the number of individuals who can enter the legal profession. The result is the increased use of "institutionalized mediation," in which legal disputes between parties are resolved informally with a mediator rather than through formal court involvement (Rosch, 1987). It is very difficult to become a lawyer in Japan. To show just how difficult, consider the story of a Japanese student named Fumito Kobayashi. Since graduating from law school, Kobayashi spends ten hours a day studying for the bar exam. He has taken the exam seven times in seven years but has yet to pass. Of course, he is not alone—that is about the average failure rate for lawyers trying to pass the bar in Japan. About 700 out of 20,000 individuals pass the exam every year.

After passing the exam, students spend another two years at the government-run Legal Research and Training Institute (Jordan, 1996). This means that the number of new lawyers in Japan each year is going to be less than 700. If we offset this figure by a presumably sizable number of retirements each year, we see that the total number of lawyers in Japan grows very slowly. The dearth of lawyers ensures that citizens will find informal ways to settle conflicts rather than taking these conflicts to court.

The 14,500 Japanese lawyers do not handle all the functions that legal advisors usually handle: doing legal research, drawing up legal papers, advising on tax problems, and dealing with inheritances, divorces, and commercial contracts. Instead, these functions are performed by an additional 70,000 quasi-lawyers. These quasi-lawyers include judicial scriveners who draft documents and handle real estate transactions, patent attorneys, tax attorneys, and law graduates not admitted to the bar (Tanaka, 1976, pp. 563–564). Not all of these quasi-lawyers are law school graduates. Tax attorneys, for example, may be accountants by profession. Of the many law school graduates not admitted to the bar (that is, the Legal Research and Training Institute), some go on to become specialists in some aspect of the law and act as advisors to business corporations or other organizations. Thus, the figures comparing lawyers in the United States and Japan are misleading in that they do not count the people in Japan who are performing the functions that in the United States would be performed by lawyers.

Only procurators (prosecutors) are allowed to initiate the prosecution of criminal cases and to direct enforcement of criminal sanctions. There are two major roles of prosecutors in Japan: (1) to investigate and collect evidence in the case and (2) to provide information to the judge about the suspect to assist in sentencing. One unique feature of criminal procedure in Japan is the ability to suspend prosecution even when the prosecutor can prove the offender committed a crime. According to the Japanese Criminal Procedure Code

(Article 248), if the prosecutor feels the crime or criminal represents or reflects some special situation, he or she can choose to suspend the matter. Among the special situations that can promulgate a suspended sentence are the age of the offender, an expression of remorse, the possibility of rehabilitation, and a desire to avoid the stigma attached to being formally processed through the criminal justice system. All prosecutors in Japan are appointed by the executive branch of government through the Office of the Minister of Justice (MOJ). This means that the MOJ has considerable control over the procurators although it is unusual for MOJ to control investigations or interfere with disposition of individual cases.

Defense attorneys, called private advocates, are provided for all those accused of a crime in Japan. If the accused is indigent, a lawyer is appointed from a list of attorneys from one of the fifty-two local branches of the Japanese Bar Association. Because of the high confession rate and low crime rate in Japan, there is little business for private advocates, and they must often do other kinds of legal work to make a living (Castberg, 1990). Taking legal action against another person is considered unnecessary in most cases in Japan—as well as being a social taboo. Thus, representing plaintiffs as a private advocate is not a highly respected position in Japanese society.

To solve minor disputes between two parties, mediation is used with police officers and lawyers acting as judges. Summary courts, which handle minor civil matters, often use untrained lawyers and court clerks for judges. However, the district courts and high courts and the Supreme Court are all staffed by professional judges who are selected by the cabinet upon recommendations of the Supreme Court. The way in which Japanese judges interpret the law has changed over the past two centuries. From the Meiji Restoration until the end of World War II, the law was viewed as sacrosanct—judges were not to interpret the law but only enforce the law that was passed by the legislature. As the twentieth century progressed, Japanese judges found this method to be inflexible and inadequate to meet the economic and legal changes in the society. As a result, judges have begun to find the need to adjudicate cases more on an individual basis and on judicial precedent (Terrill, 1999, p. 382).

In the Civil Law tradition, Japanese university law departments provide a basic education that can lead to any number of professions other than law. Many individuals who go to law schools, including the prestigious Tokyo University school, do not intend to become legal professionals. In the pre–World War II years, in fact, a career in law was not very highly regarded in Japan. The two public branches of the legal profession—prosecutors and judges—had little independence from the autocratic rulers. Nevertheless, they still had more prestige than the third branch, the private advocates. Tanaka describes the response of the private attorneys to this lack of prestige:

> *Practicing attorneys were in a lower position socially as well. Faced with humiliation and rejection by the members of the other branches of the legal profession, as well as from laymen, it was quite natural that practicing attorneys developed an esprit de corps of their own. . . . They emphasized what they called . . . "out of office spirit." They vigorously attacked the bureaucratic character of lawyers "in office," i.e., judges and procurators, and tended to be proud of not cooperating with these "bureaucratic lawyers." Judges and procurators, on the other hand, tended to look down on practicing attorneys. . . . (1976, p. 551)*

Despite the greater prestige attached to being a private attorney that developed after the war, especially as a result of the creation of the Legal Research and Training Institute, Tanaka notes the profession continues to be quite strongly divided: "For a typical Japanese lawyer, the feeling that he belongs to one of the three branches of the profession is much stronger than his sense of being a member of the whole legal profession" (p. 553).

As mentioned, those who pass the bar complete an additional two-year course of study at the Legal Research and Training Institute. This program combines academic work and apprenticeship training in various branches of the law.

Apprentices who have finished the training take a further examination and, if successful (actually, there are very few failures at this stage), are qualified to enter one of the three legal branches (Tanaka, 1976, p. 570). Those who become judges undergo a ten-year probation period as an assistant judge, after which they are generally appointed to successive ten-year terms.

One of the purposes of the American-inspired Japanese Constitution of 1946 was to create an independent and powerful judiciary based on the American model. The framers hoped that such a judiciary would provide a balance of powers that would help guarantee civil liberties for the Japanese people and counterbalance any tendencies toward renewed autocratic rule. The Civil Law tradition that existed in Japan before the war and the general legal culture in Japan have combined to thwart these ideals, at least up to this time.

The Supreme Court, which is appointed by the Cabinet, has not been particularly bold in asserting its power within the governmental framework. At the same time, the lower judiciary, although appointed for ten-year terms by the secretariat of the Supreme Court, has turned into a largely bureaucratic career judiciary on the French model. Judges are chosen upon finishing study at the Legal Research and Training Institute—that is, at a relatively young age—and are reappointed to successive ten-year terms throughout their careers. Since they start at the lowest level and their chances for elevation to higher courts depend on their winning the approval of their superiors, they tend to be conservative and cautious in their approach, rarely handing down unpopular or controversial opinions (Luney, 1990).

Comparison of the legal profession in Japan with that in our other model countries again shows some basic similarities and differences. It is very difficult to become a lawyer in Japan, and there are very few lawyers there. Essentially, advocates and public professionals have higher status than advisors, although Japan does not have the colorful differences that one finds in England.

Despite efforts by the postwar American occupation authorities to create a more political third branch of government in the sense that such a branch exists in the United States, Japan has largely reverted to the bureaucratic Civil Law model, with career judges and prosecutors chosen according to merit and rising through the ranks of a hierarchical organization.

Saudi Arabia

The legal profession in Saudi Arabia is most prominent in its role in civil rather than criminal cases. The peculiar nature of Saudi society, which combines premodern and nondemocratic political institutions with a modern and thriving commercial/industrial sector, requires the reconciliation of various aspects of law and justice with Qur'anic principles. Attorneys practicing in the commercial sector work chiefly in the administrative tribunals and through the Grievance Commission. These institutions are outside the Shari'a court hierarchy. In addition, there is a strong element of imitation of the French system of judicial process in the Saudi one (a peculiarity since Saudi Arabia was never colonized by the French). The French influence is particularly strong with respect to administrative law and courts and to judicial training. Saudi lawyers who practice in court, however, must be male Muslims, a requirement that not only reinforces elite status for this group but also highlights the importance of the religious tradition that infuses national life.

According to Islamic tradition, it is not necessary to have a trained advocate in criminal trials. In the Shari'a courts, in fact, the accused are expected to defend themselves, calling on legal counsel, relatives, friends, fellow employees, and others to advise them. Counsel by nonlawyers formerly was so prevalent, amounting to the practice of law without a license, that a Saudi law now allows lay counsel to handle no more than three cases at a time (Amin, 1985b, p. 325). Licensed attorneys may also be the advocates of choice. The Ministry of Justice issues licenses for those who wish to practice before Shari'a courts. The Ministry of Commerce issues licenses for practice before the administrative and commercial courts and for general work as a solicitor (Nader, 1990, p. 14). Thus, the dichotomy between these two types of courts is reinforced at the earliest stages of a lawyer's career. Foreign lawyers may act as advisors but not as advocates in Saudi courts.

The tradition of schools of law, with major scholars and their disciples interpreting the Qur'an and studying the interpretations of others, attests to the importance of training in the law in Islamic history. The training was religious training, however, essentially consisting of attempts to understand the Islamic scriptures and extend their interpretation to meet the needs of the particular era in Islamic society.

This religious tradition of legal scholarship continues in Saudi Arabia today. The Shari'a is taught at special religious training institutes, some of them loosely affiliated with the Saudi universities in Riyadh, Jeddah, Medina, and Mecca. According to Amin:

> The training of both advocates and judges is confined to the study of Islamic law in the Shari'ah institutes of learning. Generally the aspiring advocates and judges attend a preparatory religious school (which is equivalent to the secular secondary school) for five years. Having completed the preparatory schools, the would-be judges attend one of the Shari'ah colleges. After graduation the applicants for judicial appointments, if selected by the appropriate committee in the Ministry of Justice, embark on a three-year course of judicial training at the Higher Judicial Institute. (1985b, p. 326)

The Higher Judicial Institute, which is part of the Iman Muhammed Ibn Sa'ud Islamic University in Riyadh, confers a master's degree in judicial affairs and jurisprudence (Al-Farsy, 1986, p. 179).

We can see that legal training in Saudi Arabia involves a heavy emphasis on religious orthodoxy. A law graduate does not necessarily have a university degree. However, many Saudi law students prefer to undergo the secular law training that they get in other Arab countries, especially Egypt. Law degrees from other Arab countries are honored for the practice of law in Saudi Arabia (Nader, 1990), even though the law taught in these foreign universities is their own local law and not always appropriate to Saudi Arabia. To be sure, practice before Shari'a courts requires knowledge of Shari'a law.

The dichotomy between advocates and advisors that exists in our other model systems also occurs in Saudi Arabia in the distinction between licenses issued by the Ministry of Justice and those issued by the Ministry of Commerce. Notary work relating to preparation of legal papers, registration of documents, and the like, however, is performed within the Ministry of Justice by a special unit for Courts and Notary Public Affairs (Al-Farsy, 1986, p. 121).

The fact that aspiring judges must attend the Higher Judicial Institute (set up in 1965 on the model of the French Ecole Nationale de la Magistrature) shows how the Civil Law practice of bureaucratic development of career judges has influenced the development of the Saudi judiciary. Like the French or German aspirant to a judicial post, the Saudi must first qualify for this position and then go through a rather lengthy period of apprenticeship before he is qualified to decide cases. This is a large change from the Islamic tradition of the *quadi* judges who were only required to be a highly respected member of society and well versed in the Qur'an and religious law. **Quadi** is still the term used to describe Islamic judges who decide cases in the Shari'a courts based on the facts according to their own wisdom and the principles of the religious law. Since there is no lay participation in court judgments, however, the Saudi judges have a large degree of individual power.

Judicial independence has been proclaimed as an ideal of Saudi justice. A royal decree in 1975 declared that "judges are independent and, in their administration of justice, are subject to no authority other than the provisions of Islamic Law and Regulations in force" (Moore, 1987, p. 5). However, an independent and self-regulating bar association, such as exists in all our other model countries, even to a certain extent in China, does not exist in Saudi Arabia. This fact is a probable further consequence of the somewhat marginal role that lawyers play in the Islamic tradition.

SUMMARY

Legally trained professionals hold positions of high status and relatively high income in each system that we have examined, as they do in all modern nations. Looking back at the various systems of justice, however, we find important points of difference that allow us to make some broad generalizations about legal actors in different families of law. These generalizations deal with legal education and training, as well as with the four functional categories of legal actors: adjudicators, advocates, advisors, and scholars.

Legal education differs according to the dominant culture of each family of law. In the code-based Civil and Socialist Law countries, a legal education is a basic university education including a large element of general liberal studies. Students who enter into such a course of study may or may not intend to become legal professionals. In practice, only a minority of them do so. In recent times, France and Germany have strengthened this basic education with specific legal studies, as in the master of law degree program in France and the experimental programs in legal training mixed with education found in a few German universities. In general, however, students who study law are those who have not opted to go into specialized professional training in medicine, science, or technology. In Saudi Arabia, legal education is theologically based and occurs in Shari'a institutes that also train religious leaders. In China, students receive an education based on the political-historical ideals of communism.

In the case-based Common Law systems, by contrast, legal education puts a premium on the practical learning of cases. This is done in law schools that follow university education in the

United States and, despite the increasing possibility of legal training at some British universities, in apprentice-type training at the Inns of Court in England.

Even the code-based systems put a premium on apprenticeship training, however. Usually one cannot enter the practice of law without a period of practical training in a legal setting. An exception is the United States, although in practice few people start practicing law here without having had experience working with others in the field. The kinds of practical training vary from system to system, but the principle of apprenticeship before entry into the guild of lawyers is maintained.

Becoming an adjudicator, once entered into as part of a career in the law, tends to become a permanent assignment. The paths to a career in adjudication vary, however. Judges may be elected, as is often the case in the United States. They may be appointed, as in England and, sometimes, the United States. Most frequently, however, adjudication is a civil service career that is undertaken at an early stage and that involves special training and gradual promotion from summary courts to trial courts of the first instance and then to appeals courts at various levels. In Japan, despite the formal provisions for, respectively, an elected and an appointed judiciary, the bureaucratic Civil Law tradition tends to be followed in practice. English judges, although politically appointed, usually come from the elite ranks of queen's counselors, and thus are rather more conservative and less politically prominent than their American counterparts. Both American and English judges start their judicial work at a relatively advanced stage of their careers, and generally without formal training for the position. In these countries, a judgeship is a position of distinction based on legal and political excellence rather than a career choice made shortly after finishing law school.

Each of our model countries distinguish between advocates and advisors, with those admitted to advocacy status allowed to practice in major courts. Advisors do the bulk of legal work and practice before summary courts and administrative or commercial tribunals. The distinction between advocates and advisors appears to be breaking down in some countries, including England and France. In Japan, however, with its policy of strictly limiting the number of advocates, and in Saudi Arabia, with its insistence on religious education as a prerequisite for advocacy in the Shari'a courts of general jurisdiction, the distinction appears to be holding firm.

The role of prosecutors as advocates is a peculiar one in the various jurisdictions. In England, they are chosen from among the barristers on a case-by-case basis and do not specialize in prosecution work. In the United States, prosecutors, like judges, are chosen politically, either by appointment or by election. In the Civil Law systems and their offshoots, the prosecutorial office is related to the judicial office and involves a similar apprenticeship. There is also some interchange between judges and prosecutors in these systems. The prosecutor in China, chosen by committee, is part of the powerful government hierarchy associated with the procuratorate, the office that oversees the administration of the legal system, as well as prosecuting cases.

Finally, legal scholars occupy a highly important position in Civil Law countries because legal scholars are important interpreters and compilers of the codes and laws that form the backbone of the Civil Law. In case-based systems, judges, especially judges of appellate courts, are engaged in interpreting and making law in a way that is unknown in the Civil Law. Therefore, judges in the Common Law systems occupy the position of importance and respect that legal scholars occupy in code-based systems.

DISCUSSION QUESTIONS

1. What are the advantages and the disadvantages of having a bureaucratically organized legal profession?

2. What is the major difference between legal education in England and in the continental Civil Law nations?

3. Are there any advantages to continuing the distinction between barristers and solicitors in England?

4. Peruse the Basic Principles on the Role of Lawyers in Appendix A. Determine whether any of the model nations would have a compliance problem with the principles. What principles would be most problematic? For what countries?

5. Why are there so few lawyers in Japan?

FOR FURTHER READING

Abel, R. (1987). *The Legal Profession in England and Wales.* Oxford: Basil Blackwell.

Al-Farsy, F. (1986). *Saudi Arabia.* London: Routledge & Kegan Paul.

Ehrmann, H. (1976). *Comparative Legal Cultures.* Englewood Cliffs, N.J.: Prentice-Hall.

Jehle, Jorg-Martin. (1997). *Criminal Justice in Germany: Facts and Figures.* German Federal Ministry of Justice.

Jiahong, H., and J. R. Waltz. (1995). *Criminal Prosecution in the People's Republic of China and the United States: A Comparative Study.* Beijing: China Prosecutorial Press.

Lawyers Committee for Human Rights. (1993). *Criminal Justice with Chinese Characteristic.* New York: Lawyers Committee for Human Rights.

9 Courts

The Concept of a Court
The Development of Courts in Western
    Nations
The Study of Courts
Courts in England
Courts in France
Courts in Germany
Courts in China
Courts in Japan
Courts in Saudi Arabia
Supranational Courts
Summary
Discussion Questions and Exercises
For Further Reading

Key Terms and Concepts

Amtsgerichte

assize courts

basic people's court

Bundesgerichtshof

Bundesverfassungsgericht

Civil Liberties Bureau

collegial bench

correctional court

Council of State

court

Court of Cassation

court of appeals

crown courts

Federal Constitutional Court

High Court

High Court of Justice

higher people's courts

House of Lords

intermediate people's courts

International Court of Justice

International Criminal Court

International Criminal Tribunal for Rwanda

International Criminal Tribunal for Yugoslavia

judicial impartiality

jus cogens

Landgericht

lay magistrate

magistrates' courts

médiateur

Oberlandesgerichte

people's assessor

police courts

stipendiary magistrate

Supreme Court

Supreme Judicial Council

Supreme People's Court

Courtroom encounters provide a seemingly endless source of material both for fiction and nonfiction writers and for news reporters and media producers. Our newspapers, news magazines, and news programs are filled with stories of crime and punishment, with the trial typically the highlight of the story.

What is the reason for our fascination with courtroom drama? The element of suspense is certainly an ingredient: Will the accused be acquitted or convicted? The outcome of a criminal trial has a certain "zero-sum" quality whereby the defendant either wins or loses, despite whatever mitigating factors are brought to bear at the sentencing phase of the process. The accounts of intrigue, violence, depravity, and lawlessness that are central to court proceedings are also of intense interest to most people.

Most important, however, a public trial tends to affirm the community values that the government seeks to protect and promote through the criminal process. As such, it provides vicarious satisfaction that justice is being done, that those who choose to reject these values do not go unpunished. The community is strengthened through this public repudiation of deviance, even if the accused is exonerated. So, in the end, the court system provides us with a sense of security and a feeling that justice is highly valued in society.

In this chapter, we consider the subject of court organization and court operations. We will discuss the functions of courts in society, some characteristics of courts in general, and the organization of courts in our model systems, as well as supranational courts. We concentrate on criminal courts, but we must remember that courts, as dispute resolution agencies, also handle noncriminal, or civil, disputes between individuals or between the government and individuals. Often, as in the United States, the same courts handle both civil and criminal cases.

THE CONCEPT OF A COURT

What are courts, and what functions do they serve in a society? What is their role within the political framework of a nation?

A simple definition of a **court** is that it is an agency with power to settle disputes in a society. The word "court" is derived from the Latin term *co-hortus,* later shortened to *cohort* or *court,* meaning "being together in the same garden," such as being in the garden of a medieval castle or courtyard (Mueller, Adler, and Laufer, 1994). One of the parties in a court case presents the facts of the case and explains how these facts are related to some body of law or principles that are considered binding in the society. The other side disputes these facts and tries to show that the person or issue before the court is not within the jurisdiction of the proscribed law. The crucial word in this definition is "power." While there may be voluntary agencies that also mediate disputes and that may on occasion be called courts, a court by our definition is an agency of government that has the coercive power of government behind it.

According to Martin Shapiro (1981, ch. 1), there is a certain "triadic" logic that functions in the dispute resolution mechanisms of all societies. The three corners of the triad consist of two parties and an agent that settles disputes between them; a court is a special form of this triadic situation. In its ideal, or prototypical, form, says Shapiro, it has four characteristics: an independent judge, preexisting legal norms, adversarial proceedings, and dichotomous decision making (only one party "wins"). In reality, however, a powerful force for consensus exists in most court situations, and judges and other court agents find themselves spending a good deal of time as mediators.

Whatever the reality of court operations in a society, most people can agree that a court should have two basic characteristics to function properly: (1) judicial independence and (2) judicial impartiality. Judicial independence, as we discussed briefly in Chapter 8, implies that the court, while enforcing governmental norms, does so without being under the influence, direct or indirect, of other governmental or political agents. In the U.S. Constitution, the framers sought to ensure judicial independence by guaranteeing lifetime tenure to Supreme Court judges once they had been appointed by the president and approved by the Senate. To be sure, a president may be inspired by political motives in the choice of judges. Indeed, most presidents choose individuals who mirror their own philosophical and pragmatic preferences—former President Reagan was famous for his wholesale appointment of conservative Republicans to the federal bench—but the judge does not owe his or her future to any further political influence.

Pure judicial independence, to be sure, is an ideal that hardly exists, as innumerable studies of courts, including the U.S. Supreme Court, have shown. But blatant political influence on court operations can usually be recognized, and we say that courts that choose, or are forced, to carry out governmental wishes have become "politicized." Likewise, a court may operate in a politicized manner in particular trials, and we usually call these "political trials." There are many shades of ambiguity surrounding the concept of judicial independence. Nevertheless, it remains a basic ideal in most court structures.

Judicial impartiality may be tied to judicial independence in some cases, but it is a broader concept that calls for judicial authorities to treat parties in court as equals. "Equality before the law" is a cherished precept of modern justice systems. A judge who distinguished among plaintiffs by race, creed, or social class would not be practicing judicial impartiality. Of course, judicial impartiality, like judicial independence is an ideal that often is honored only in the breach. Thus, although these two concepts are important in studying and evaluating the operations of courts, we cannot claim that they must be present for a court to exist.

As mentioned earlier, the function of courts is to settle, authoritatively and according to prede-fined legal norms, the many disputes that arise in a society. In complex modern societies, in which communal ties may not be strong enough to enable disputes to be settled in informal ways, this is a crucial function. The disputes may be between two parties in a civil suit, or they may be between the state and a party accused of a criminal violation. In both situations, as we explained earlier, a latent function of courts is to affirm the values and rules of the society and to provide citizens with a sense that some measure of impartial justice is being done. To the extent that this latent function becomes part of the overt mission of courts in any society, we can say that the courts play a role as educators in the law and in the norms of a regime. This is the case in the People's Republic of China, where the courts educate the people in the law and philosophy of the Communist government.

In the second half of the twentieth century, the role of the courts was expanded beyond national boundaries. After World War II, the Nuremberg trials were held to try Nazi war criminals and to define how international tribunals would handle atrocities of war. More recently, the United Nations has revived the idea of courts with the power to adjudicate international crimes by countries and individuals. These courts have expanded the role of courts in our individual societies to the larger global context. Later in this chapter, we will discuss in more detail the background, purpose, and current status of these supranational courts.

THE DEVELOPMENT OF COURTS IN WESTERN NATIONS

The highest court of appeal in England is a group of judges known as law lords, who sit in the House of Lords. They are appointed as peers rather than being born into that status, but they constitute a typically English institution, one that adapts historical custom to modern governmental needs.

In earlier times, dispensing justice was the prerogative of the monarch. As kings found it too cumbersome to try to hear cases from all over their territories, they began to delegate the judicial function to others. As we learned in Chapter 3, William the Conqueror established a network of King's Courts to hear cases and develop a law common to the entire kingdom. These Common Law courts were to be an extension of the Curia Regis, or King's Council, which advised the king on matters of state, including settlement of disputes. At a time when legislative bodies were rudimentary or nonexistent, the King's Council served as a combination lawmaker and court. In each case, the monarch reserved the right to act as the final arbiter in case of appeals from the various courts.

As we also saw, courts in England soon began to assert their independence from the king and to develop laws that would be applied to all persons. British kings responded at various points by setting up new kinds of courts—equity courts and Star Chamber courts, for example—to do their will. At no time, however, did they give up the right of final appeal. Over the course of centuries, the court of final appeal became more and more of a governing chamber—first helping to administer the affairs of the kingdom and eventually, after monumental struggles with the monarchy, becoming the chief legislative body. The law lords in England sit as a reminder of the earlier times when separation of powers did not exist in England. Today, the royal power of pardon is carried over into the power of executive clemency that is enjoyed by most modern rulers, including, in the United States, the president and state governors.

In France, the king's courts were known as parlements and existed in all the major regions of the country. These parlements, acting as courts, administrative bodies, and regulatory agencies, did not achieve the independence from the king that their English counterparts had achieved in the thirteenth and fourteenth centuries until the eve of the French Revolution. In 1788–89, when Louis XVI hoped to use the parlements as deliberating bodies to help him achieve fiscal and ad-

ministrative reforms rather than calling the larger constituent assembly, the Estates-General, into session, the parlements refused to cooperate. Some say the French Revolution was precipitated by this refusal (Stone, 1986).

The word *parlement* itself suggests the origins of today's parliaments in the courts of earlier times. Although courts have developed in different stages and at different times in other jurisdictions, the examples of France and England show the progression from dispute resolution by one ruler to the modern courts of today. At the same time, they show how the development of government has been from a relatively simple form to complex and differentiated structures. Peculiarly, however, the modern practice of judicial review of legislation in many countries, including the United States and Germany, return the courts in some ways to the earlier practice of the French parlements and the English House of Lords, which claimed the right to review acts of the monarch and make policy in certain matters.

THE STUDY OF COURTS

There are many ways to study courts and their role in a society. We can look at litigiousness, or the tendency to take cases to court, in various societies, which can tell us a great deal about the levels of consensus or complexity in a society. We can also look at patterns of decision making by judges, as has been done in great detail by scholars of the U.S. Supreme Court. We can look at judicial recruitment, training, and tenure in order to understand more about the personnel who make up the apex of the court triad. At the most basic level, we can look at the arrangement and organization of courts within a society. The United States, with its dual federal and state court hierarchies and with its many different court organizations in the fifty states, is a typically complex model of court organization. Finally, we can look at the passage of cases through particular courts in order to contrast the reality of justice in various systems. With respect to criminal justice, basic issues involve the organization of the courts and the passage of defendants through these courts. These are the realities that we look at in the model systems.

COURTS IN ENGLAND

England, which gave the United States its system of law, presents many contrasts to its former colonies in actual judicial process. The American observer visiting the Old Bailey, the major criminal court in London, would be struck by two things: (1) the difference in style between English and American courts and (2) the differences in details of procedure.

Magistrates' Courts

Figure 9.1 shows the general structure of the English courts. England has established two levels of trial courts for criminal cases: magistrates' courts for minor crimes and crown courts for serious crimes. Magistrates sit singly or in groups of two or three and decide large numbers of cases in the

course of an ordinary court session. Over 98 percent of English criminal trials are conducted in the 900 magistrates' courts (Schmalleger, 1999).

There are both **stipendiary magistrates,** who are attorneys by trade and are paid by the state for their work, and **lay magistrates,** who are appointed to serve as volunteer judges. Lay magistrates vastly outnumber stipendiary ones, although the numbers of the latter are increasing. Lay magistrates receive a minimal amount of training (about one week in aggregate). Stipendiary magistrates usually sit alone, while lay magistrates usually sit in pairs or groups of three.

Appointment as a lay magistrate is an honor often bestowed on those who belong to the majority political party in a region. Many of them are women, a natural phenomenon since professional men usually do not have the time to devote to this volunteer service. Lay magistrates may serve until age 70, and they are obligated to sit in court at least twenty-one days each year.

Magistrates' courts also conduct preliminary hearings in major criminal cases, with the magistrates deciding whether to bind the case over to the crown court. Thus, they serve in lieu of the

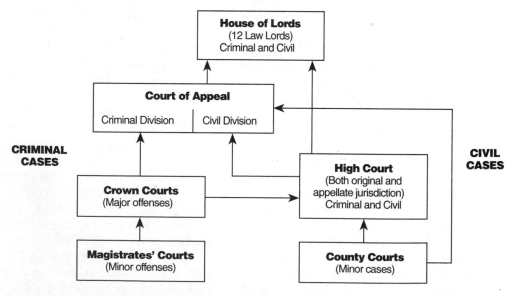

FIGURE 9.1 Structure of the British Courts

grand juries or other devices for pretrial hearings that exist in the United States. In addition to trials for petty crimes and preliminary hearings, certain magistrates' courts are designated to handle some minor civil cases and juvenile cases involving defendants under 18 years of age.

Magistrates' courts are a prime example of the continued influence of laypeople in the British criminal justice system. Magistrates are heirs to the justices of the peace, local judicial officials who existed in England until well into the nineteenth century. In the United States, justices of the peace have also largely been abolished, with their functions taken over by magistrates. American magistrates are paid, however, and perform minor judicial functions, including the issuing of warrants. They do not settle the large number of minor criminal cases—traffic violations, disturbances, minor thefts and assaults—that constitute the bulk of criminal cases in any jurisdiction. Handling these cases is the function of the various local courts of first instance.

Crown Courts

The trial courts for serious crimes in England are known as **crown courts.** To an American observer, one of the most noteworthy sights in English court proceedings at the level of crown court and above is attire. Judges and attorneys alike wear gowns (red for judges, black for attorneys on both sides), decorated in some cases with signs that the wearer has achieved the coveted status of queen's counsel, QC. Becoming a QC gives a barrister the right to wear a silk gown and is thus known popularly as "taking silk." In addition to the gowns, English lawyers and judges must wear wigs to court. The attorneys' wigs, gray and curled, sit like hats on the backs of their heads, while judges wear a more resplendent full wig that comes down to their shoulders.

The physical appearance of the courtroom is also formal and often is ornate. Judges sit on an elevated dais that emphasizes their distance from the other courtroom personnel. The judge is addressed as "my Lord" or "your Lordship." The ac-

cused, however, also sits in a high position, the "dock," where he or she can be seen by all. With the accused in the dock is a uniformed constable. Contrary to practice in the United States, counsel for the accused do not sit with them but rather sit at a separate table near the center of the courtroom.

Cases in crown courts are decided by juries. This is in contrast to the various civil trial courts, such as the county courts and the High Court of Justice, in which jury trial is all but obsolete. A major difference between jury selection in England and the United States is the rapidity and ease with which juries are chosen in England. In theory, counsel on both sides can challenge jurors for cause, and the defense counsel may use up to three peremptory challenges. In practice, however, jurors are rarely challenged since, given that there is no questioning of jurors, it would be difficult to formulate grounds for a challenge. The voir dire process in the United States, whereby jurors may be questioned at length by the defense and prosecution, does not exist in England. Nor is a unanimous verdict necessary for conviction in England. If at least ten jurors of a twelve-person panel agree that guilt has been established beyond a reasonable doubt, then the accused may be convicted.

As we explained in Chapter 8, a peculiar aspect of English justice at the level of the crown courts or higher is that both prosecution and defense counsel are part of a select group of attorneys known as "barristers." Barristers conduct trials in major cases. They do not do preliminary investigations or take depositions from witnesses as American attorneys do; that is the job of solicitors. In effect, both the prosecution and the defense engage solicitors to prepare a case. The solicitors on both sides then engage barristers to conduct the trial. Often, the barristers do not even see the case file until the day before the trial. This arrangement has the advantage that experienced trial lawyers conduct both prosecution and defense. It has the disadvantage for the defense that the barristers are rather detached from the case and have not built up the kind of relationship with the accused that typifies an American trial. Since barristers are engaged to argue the case by both sides, both prosecution and defense attorney may come from the same "chambers," as barristers' offices are known. According to Michael Graham, who studied the progress of cases in the English courts in some depth,

> some barristers describe the atmosphere of chambers as that of an officer's club. There is a silent respect for each other's talents and an understanding of the need for all to comply with the rules of custom if the trial process is to continue to function well. This understanding has over the years resulted in the development of practices concerning both pretrial preparation and trial which make it possible for a barrister to prepare for a trial the night before and try a case solely from a Brief and accompanying documents. (1983, p. 67)

The actual conduct of a trial is similar in England to the trial process in the United States, although there are some differences in rules that tend to make the English process more formal. Barristers tend to avoid emotional appeals to the jury. In keeping with the adversarial nature of the process, prosecution counsel may not comment on a defendant's failure to testify, and the prosecution must prove guilt rather than the defendant having to prove his or her innocence. Sentence is usually passed right after a trial and without separate sentencing hearings. (For a full list of the trial steps in England, see Table 7.1.)

Until recently, the function of prosecution was in the hands of police, and larger police agencies had prosecution divisions as part of their organizational structure. In minor cases, police officers actually were the only prosecution representatives in court. For crown court cases, police appointed barristers to conduct the cases in court. In 1985, Parliament passed a law setting up the Crown Prosecution Service, taking responsibility for prosecution away from the police and placing it in the hands of an independent agency. In doing so, Parliament hoped to make the courts more independent and impartial in their operations. The Crown Prosecution Service has had difficulties getting established, largely due to a

lack of resources, confusion about how to proceed, and the inertia of well-established traditions of judicial process. It is too soon, however, to evaluate the ultimate success or failure of this institution. (Spencer, Zander, 1989). Although courts in England are by no means as politically involved and powerful as courts in the United States, appointments to judgeships in crown courts and other courts are made by the politically appointed lord chancellor, who is equivalent to the U.S. attorney general. Thus, inevitably, there is some trace of partisan politics involved in these appointments. In addition, since the Common Law accords judges the power to make and modify law through their decisions, they occupy a unique station in the development of the law and its interpretation.

For minor civil cases, the court of first jurisdiction is the county court. If the matter is appealed, it is brought to the **High Court of Justice,** which is the first level of appeal for the county court but which primarily acts as a court of original jurisdiction for serious civil cases and some criminal cases (see Figure 9.1). The High Court of Justice is actually divided into three branches: (1) the Queen's Bench Division, which handles the majority of civil and criminal matters of original and appellate jurisdiction, (2) the Chancery Division, which is responsible for matters involving property, trusts, and wills, and (3) the Family Division, which deals with matrimony and guardian issues.

Appeals Courts

A convicted criminal offender may appeal to the criminal division of the **Court of Appeals.** This court hears appeal cases from the crown courts and the High Court of Justice. The civil division of the Court of Appeals handles all civil matters.

The next level of appeal, which handles only those cases that include an important point of law involving general public importance, is the **House of Lords,** which is technically the highest court in England. The House of Lords has a long history in England, going back 1,000 years to when English kings summoned religious leaders to council meetings called "witans." The House of Lords, which is actually the upper chamber of the British Parliament, has approximately 1139 members. There are currently three different kinds of lords: Some are chosen based on heredity (634), some are political appointments (479), and a small number (26) are religious leaders selected from the Church of England. In October 1999, the House of Lords voted to change the system considerably by limiting the number of heredity lords to 90 (Krose, 1999, p. A24).

Although legal matters technically are the responsibility of the entire House of Lords, they actually are handled by a small group of nine to eleven law lords, selected mainly from the Court of Appeals. This group handles a limited number of cases, typically around fifty a year (Terrill, 1999). An even smaller group of law lords, usually three to five, hears final appeals in a restricted number of cases. Thus, the British government, in this as in so many other matters, creates a compromise arrangement between modern distributions of power with venerable traditions dating back many centuries.

The House of Lords is different than the Supreme Court in the United States in that it cannot rule that acts of Parliament are invalid or in violation of a written constitution. And although the right of appeal is well established in England, appeals are rarely accepted by the courts, and convictions are rarely overturned. Therefore, the trial itself assumes a larger importance in major cases than it does in the United States, where appeals are often heard and indeed anticipated in the course of the trial proceedings (Graham, 1983). In fact, few convicted persons appeal sentences in England. This is undoubtedly because of the ability of the Court of Appeals to add up to three months to a sentence if the appeal is deemed frivolous.

COURTS IN FRANCE

The court structure in France is relatively complicated when compared to that of the English. Continental Europe is the realm of the bureaucratized system of courts and state attorneys. The rather formal and rational nature of the Civil Law, compared to the case- and tradition-bound Common Law, is reflected in the court structure, with its prominent administrative courts, which are themselves part of the government bureaucracy, and its other specialized courts.

In France, almost all judges are civil servants, rising through the judicial bureaucracy based on merit and after long years of study, examinations, and apprenticeship. Consequently, French courts, as well as most courts in other Civil Law nations (the German Federal Constitutional Court is definitely an exception here), do not have the prominent role in the political system that they do in the United States and even in England.

Accounts by participants and observers are rarely complimentary to French criminal justice. Whereas in England the courts have gradually developed some credibility as impartial arbiters of cases and are capable of tempering pure justice with a degree of common sense and even compassion, the French courts have maintained some of the reputation for high-handedness and arbitrariness that characterized them in the times before the Revolution of 1789 (Hayward, 1983, ch. 5). For example, in Sybille Bedford's popular account of criminal trials in England, France, Germany, Austria, and Switzerland, her depiction of French courts, both summary courts and major criminal courts, presents a picture of remote judges little concerned about the realities of the lives of the defendants before them (Bedford, 1961, pt. 4). Nevertheless, because of their lesser concern with procedural detail and because of the large number of courts throughout the country, both administrative and regular, French courts are accessible and fairly inexpensive for defendants in criminal trials and for parties in civil suits.

Figure 9.2 presents a simplified chart of the structure of the French courts. Not depicted there, however, are separate hierarchies of administrative courts. Administrative courts deal with cases in which the acts of government officials are at issue. For example, if a citizen believes that he or she was given false information about social security entitlements, redress may be sought against

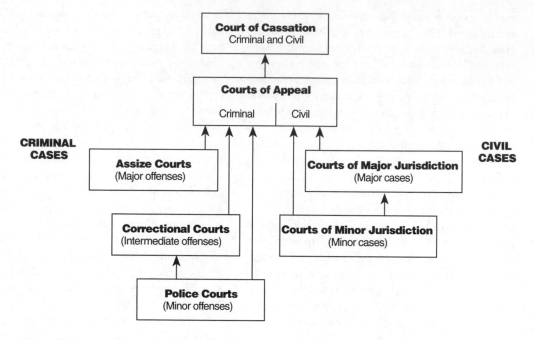

FIGURE 9.2 Structure of the French Courts

the government in an administrative court, where the process is simple and attorneys are not required. An exception to the kind of redress available in administrative courts, however, involves cases of police abuse of power or criminal procedure lapses. Consequently, these courts are of little use for defendants whose rights have been violated in the criminal process.

Trial Courts

Criminal cases in France move up a hierarchy of courts much as they do in Common Law countries. The major difference is that there are three levels of trial courts that hear cases according to the seriousness of the crimes involved. At the bottom are the **police courts** (Tribunaux de Police), which handle more than half the criminal cases that arise. The maximum sentence in police court is two months in jail, and the maximum fine is approximately $1000. Judges in police courts are generally younger and less experienced and are just starting up the hierarchy of judicial

positions. Matters in these courts are often dealt with outside the courtroom, and when a trial does occur, it is usually very brief (Frase, 1988).

At a somewhat higher level are the **correctional courts** (Tribunaux Correctionnels), in which more serious (up to five years in prison) crimes are heard. Three or more judges hear the cases in these courts, and the verdict is by majority vote. The accused has the right to appeal the judgment and demand a new trial in a higher court, the assize court.

In addition to hearing appeals from lower courts, the **assize courts** (Cours d'Assise), have original jurisdiction in major felony cases. The tribunal in these cases consists of three professional judges and nine lay judges or jurors. Unlike the English judge and jury system, in which the jury decides matters of fact and the judge decides matters of law, the French tribunal considers both matters as a group. Further, decision is by a plurality of eight votes rather than by the unanimous or (in some jurisdictions) near-unanimous vote required in the U.S. system for conviction in major criminal cases. Decisions on the sentence, which are made at the same time, are by majority vote. Both verdict and sentence are announced after the deliberations of the tribunal.

The French courtroom presents a different aspect from the English one. As a legacy of revolutionary tradition, there are fewer signs of pomp or status. The professional and lay judges seem almost huddled together in the front of the courtroom, which is not raised as prominently as the bench in English courts. However, prosecutors and defense attorneys do wear black gowns with starched white collars when appearing in court.

The case file, or dossier, is available to all the judges prior to the trial. Nevertheless, in cases before the assize courts, the "principle of orality" requires that all evidence be brought out in open court. In the correctional and police courts, it is not necessary to go through each step of the case and each piece of evidence at the actual trial, as is the case in England and the United States. Although spectators may not get the complete recounting of all the facts and circumstances of the case, the judges have all the information at hand (Ingraham, 1987, pp. 86–87).

Appeals Courts

For civil and criminal cases that are decided at a level lower than that of the assize courts, appeals go to one of the twenty-seven judicial districts and the **courts of appeal** (Cours d'Appel). These courts hear appeals from the lower civil and criminal courts and from a plethora of special courts, including the commercial court and the juvenile court. Three to five judges rule on cases and decide on points of law and of fact (Abraham, 1986). Disputes over points of law can be appealed to the next court level.

The highest level of appeal is the **Court of Cassation** (Cour de Cassation), which hears appeals from the assize courts and the courts of appeal. The Court of Cassation sits in five chambers with fifteen judges in each, although only seven need be present to hear a case. Criminal cases are heard in only one of these chambers. In criminal cases, as opposed to civil cases, the Court of Cassation must hear appeals. Therefore, it does not have the authority to turn down cases, as the U.S. Supreme Court does in most instances through its power to grant or deny a writ of certiorari.

The Court of Cassation has a peculiar history tied to France's revolutionary tradition, with its suspicion of judges and lawyers as advocates of the entrenched prerevolutionary regime. As explained previously, the French parlements were, in the prerevolutionary period, courts that also assumed consultative and legislative duties. The judiciary that made up these parlements was essentially conservative and protective of its own status and prerogatives. According to Mauro Cappelletti (1971), many of these judges lost their heads in the revolution. After the revolution, the legislature sought to guard against the judiciary assuming too much power by setting up the Court of Cassation as an agency of the legislature, just as in later years the Constitutional Council, which has the right to review legislation for constitutionality, was not set up as a court. The function of the Court of Cassation originally was to review judicial actions at lower levels to guard against usurpation of legislative power and to ensure that judges decided cases only by matching facts to written law, and not by considering political expediency or other factors. This prerevolutionary attempt to disempower the judiciary was in sharp contrast to the American experience, in which, despite the constitutional separation of powers, the judiciary, and especially the Supreme Court, soon became embroiled in a large number of public policy issues. The American federal system, with its provision of an arbiter of wielders of power at the state and national levels, highlights some of the difference between the emphases in the two countries. Some of it, however, can probably be explained by a consideration of the less-threatening tradition of the judiciary in Anglo-Saxon, as opposed to French, history.

By the early nineteenth century, however, the Court of Cassation had become what it essentially is today: the final court of appeal in both civil and criminal cases. Since the Constitutional Council does not hear cases but decides the constitutionality of laws only at the request of high government officials, the Court of Cassation becomes by default an organ for interpreting the constitutionality of certain kinds of legislation.

Administrative Courts

A strong system of administrative courts distinguishes the French judicial system. These courts hear cases brought by citizens against agents of the government for violations of the citizens' rights under the law. There are thirty-one such courts in the various regions of France. At the apex is the renowned **Council of State** (Conseil d'État), which has earned the reputation of being the primary guarantor of the rights of French citizens.

Like the Court of Cassation, the Council of State was not designed to protect citizens against the government. Indeed, it was set up by Napoleon to advise him and act on his behalf and on behalf of various public agencies in developing administrative regulations and dealing with internal disputes. To this day, the majority of the 180 members of the council do not act as a court. Only one of its five sections hears cases, but it is this section that has gradually evolved into the highly developed organ for protecting the rights of the French that exists today.

In some ways, the process of championing citizen rights through administrative courts in France serve the same function as appealing to one's elected representative in the United States. It is a peculiarity of the American system that congresspeople and senators spend a large proportion of their time dealing with the constituents' problems, many of which are related to dealings with government agencies. While the agency response to congressional inquiries does not have the formality of an administrative court proceeding, the fact of congressional interest does require some kind of response from the governmental agency. In France, access to administrative courts is cheap and easy, with few of the procedural and legal encumbrances that make the average court case so daunting for most individuals. A simple petition is filed, no attorneys are required, and the court provides the machinery for investigation of complaints. However, the backlog of cases in the administrative courts has become so great that France has established the office of **médiateur,** a kind of intermediary agent, who hears minor complaints against the government and makes recommendations for redress.

The jurisdiction of the administrative courts is not very clear with respect to rights of the accused (Cappelletti and Cohen, 1979, p. 42). In general, however, administrative courts do not hear cases of abuse of power by police or judicial personnel. Therefore, the relevance of these courts for the criminal process is not as great as for other matters of individual rights.

According to J. E. S. Hayward (1983, p. 147), "the public standing of the courts in France is low. The number of those who consider that the judicial system works badly has consistently exceeded by a wide margin those who believe that it works well." Further, Hayward states, a majority of those involved in a 1977 survey believed that the courts were subject to political pressure.

Why do the French have so little confidence in their courts? There are historical reasons for these sentiments, including (1) the establishment of special courts to deal with matters of internal security in times of crisis, (2) the bad experience during the German occupation, when the courts of Vichy France collaborated with the Germans, and (3) the general distrust and fear of courts that have their origins in prerevolutionary times. The office of the examining magistrate, which investigates cases and develops the dossier for trial, is also a focal point for distrust and calls for reform in the French system. This is because the examining magistrates have such great power to detain people for long periods of time and to work in secret, which has led, in turn, to celebrated scandals involving abuse of powers by these officials.

In general, the judicial process in France bears the weight of a public image that is less than ideal, and the reform efforts that are made must counter the lingering effects of a reputation that has developed over many centuries.

COURTS IN GERMANY

German trial courts are similar in style and tradition to the French courts. Procedure is based on the inquisitorial model, including extensive pretrial investigation with which the accused is expected to cooperate. As in France, however, procedural safeguards based on the adversarial model, such as the right to an attorney at the trial and pretrial stages of the criminal process, dilute the inquisitorial nature of the process.

There are some major differences between the German and French systems, however, as Figure 9.3 shows. Germany is a federation, and this affects court arrangements. The **Federal Constitutional Court,** which has the final word in cases of basic rights, including some criminal procedure cases, has become a strong political force and has important functions in protecting the German Basic Law and preserving the federal balance. Germany, however, does not have a dual court system like that of the United States, in which there are both state and federal courts at the trial and appeal levels, with the U.S. Supreme Court as a final arbiter of constitutional and other legal questions. Rather, all cases in Germany are tried in the state courts and may move through various levels of state jurisdiction before being brought to a federal court of final appeal. Further, the five federal supreme courts in Germany are technically the final courts of appeal. The Federal Constitutional Court has the last word in interpreting the constitution, but it remands cases to the lower courts for disposition based on its opinions.

Another peculiarity of the German system is the proliferation of courts and judges. By American standards, German courts are highly specialized, with different tribunals at both the trial and appellate levels hearing cases related to social security, labor, tax law, administrative law, and conventional civil and criminal law. In addition, Germany, with about one-third the population of the United States, has more than twice as many judges overall. Although the volume of litigation handled would make the Germans seem exceptionally litigious when compared with Americans, who are themselves considered highly litigious, the fact is that many of the disputes that are handled

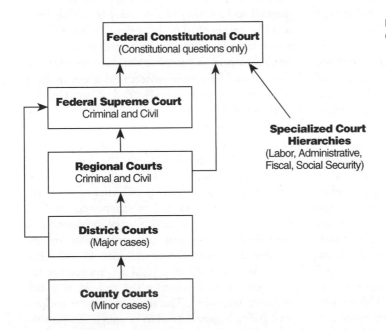

FIGURE 9.3 Structure of the German Courts

in the specialized courts are handled through regulatory procedures in the United States.

Criminal Court Organization

The judicial system in Germany consists of three types of courts: (1) ordinary courts, which handle criminal and most civil cases, (2) specialized courts, which hear cases related to administrative issues, and (3) constitutional courts, which deal with judicial review and constitutional interpretation.

At the ordinary level are four tiers of courts. The **Amtsgerichte** courts hear minor criminal and civil cases at the local level. Many of these courts are staffed by a single judge, but in some criminal cases, lay judges provide assistance. Above this is the **Landgericht,** which is the regional court trying major criminal and civil cases and hearing appeals from the Amtsgerichte courts. At the top level of the state (Laender) court system are the **Oberlandesgerichte** courts, which primarily hear points of law raised in appeals in the lower courts and hold original jurisdiction in cases of treason and anticonstitutional activity. The fourth ordinary court, called the **Bundesgerichtshof,** or Federal Supreme Court, handles final appeals in all cases from the lower courts except those involving constitutional interpretation.

The Germans are known for their many specialized courts that deal with five areas: social security, labor, tax law, administrative law, and patent law. These courts are organized on the local, Laender, and federal levels, and within their own subject area.

With regard to the constitutional courts, any judge in Germany who believes that a constitutional question is involved in a case may refer that question to the **Bundesverfassungsgericht,** the Federal Constitutional Court. However, individual appellants who believe that their constitutional rights have been violated generally may not appeal to the Federal Constitutional Court until they have exhausted all other avenues of petition and appeal. The Federal Constitutional Court consists of sixteen judges and does not actually decide the outcome of cases; rather, it rules on the constitutional question involved and then returns the case to the lower court for final disposition.

A large proportion of cases in Germany are disposed of through summary procedures at the police and prosecutorial level. Minor crimes such as routine traffic offenses are handled through administrative procedures at the level of police agencies. Prosecutors have the power to dismiss charges when the defendant agrees to pay a fine to the state or to a nonprofit organization. A large majority of criminal cases in Germany are settled through the payment of fines. This procedure, which is not without its critics because of the vast discretionary powers it gives to prosecutors, diverts a great deal of case pressure from the criminal courts. The prosecutor also has the power to handle criminal cases through summary procedures, in which a disposition is offered to a defendant and the case proceeds no further if the disposition is accepted. An accused may always assert the right to trial rather than accepting the summary actions of either police or prosecutor.

There is a certain irony in the fact that so large a proportion of cases in Germany are handled in a nontrial manner. German jurists and many German and even American legal scholars have pointed to Germany as a country in which there is little prosecutorial discretion, a country in which the prosecutor may not enter into any kind of plea bargain or sentence negotiations with the accused and in which prosecution is compulsory once an offender is apprehended. Thus, German legal scholar Joachim Herrmann says, "Compulsory prosecution, except where otherwise provided by law, is regarded as a German constitutional requirement based on the equal rights clause" (1976, p. 18). While such assertions may give voice to the ideals of the German system, the reality is that a good deal of sanctioned, or *legal,* discretion is evident, and a large proportion of cases do not go to trial. In keeping with the inquisitorial tradition, however, once an individual is formally accused in a judicial proceeding, the case goes to trial whether the individual pleads guilty or not guilty. The trials of those who have pled guilty, however, tend to be much shorter than the trials of those who maintain their innocence.

The jury system, which has never found a hospitable environment in inquisitorial systems, does not exist in Germany. As we mentioned in Chapter 7, lay judges in Germany serve in courts of limited jurisdiction and in higher-level courts with general criminal jurisdiction (crimes involving potential sentences of three or more years in prison) (Holland, 1988, p. 88). In the lower criminal courts, we find two lay judges and one professional judge. In the courts in which more serious crimes are tried, there are three professional judges but only two lay judges. The verdict in a trial is by majority vote, so the lay judges theoretically can have an important voice in deciding guilt or innocence. In reality, however, the professional judges dominate both the questioning of the accused and witnesses and the deliberations about the verdict. Since there is no separate jury, the judge does not instruct a jury formally in matters of law, but instead informs the lay judges about the law as part of the general deliberations leading to a verdict. Appeals in criminal cases are heard by professional judges and are restricted to matters of law (Holland, 1988; Wolfe, 1983).

In contrast to the United States, expert witnesses are called and paid for by the state. In practice, this usually means the police or prosecutor. Therefore, the German trial does not have the peculiarity of opposing expert testimony about matters like insanity and ballistics that one finds in adversarial proceedings. Attorneys may challenge the testimony of experts, however, and the court may choose to employ additional experts if it seems warranted.

A further contrast with American procedure is that it is possible to appeal acquittals in criminal cases. The law does not allow an increase in severity of sentence, however, when an acquittal is successfully appealed.

COURTS IN CHINA

The structure of the formal court system in China, first developed in 1949 after the establishment of the People's Republic of China, is outlined in the Constitution and Organic Law of the People's Courts. Chinese courts are highly centralized and organized along four levels: (1) basic (also called primary) people's courts, (2) intermediate people's courts, (3) higher people's courts, and (4) the Supreme People's Court. Except for the Supreme People's Court, each of these courts operates in different geographic territories that include provinces, autonomous regions, municipalities, prefectures, cities, county and city districts (Guo et al., 1999).

The lowest level of the formal Chinese court system is the **basic people's court,** which is found in each county and municipal area. These courts, around 3000 in number, handle most criminal, civil, and economic matters of first instance unless the matter is a special case. Factors that can make a case "special" include severity and provincial or national importance. Another important purpose of the basic people's courts is to coordinate the people's mediation committees.

People's mediation committees (PMCs) are one of the three informal social control mechanisms implemented throughout China and the only one under the control of the court system. The other two—public security committees and security departments of commercial enterprises and institutions—are supervised by the police branch and serve as crime prevention measures. PMCs are found in the workplace, schools, rural areas, and city neighborhoods. Over 8000 of these committees handle more than 8 million cases annually (Zhang et al., 1996).

The PMCs have a 2000-year history in China, going back to the early days of Confucianism. The general idea behind the PMC is that harsh punishment does not necessarily control behavior and that moral education is the most prudent method of correcting behavior. A PMC has five to seven members who use the force of public opinion and education to persuade those involved in minor disputes and misdemeanors to resolve their problems without formal court intervention. Therefore, only the most serious crimes are dealt with by the formal court system, with less serious criminal behaviors and civil matters disposed of locally through people's mediation (Situ and Liu, 1996, p. 135).

The parties involved must agree beforehand to mediation. During mediation, the parties discuss the offense, relevant laws, and the public interest in the matter, and then reach an agreement. The agreement has the force of law and, if violated, could result in further legal action (Ai, 1989). The PMC has remained an important part of Chinese society to this day because it is so entrenched in the culture and legal history of the country.

Two formal courts have legal jurisdiction equal to the basic people's courts. The first are people's tribunals, which handle the duties of the basic people's courts in both rural areas and large urban districts like Beijing. The decisions of these 18,000 tribunals are equal in weight to those of the basic people's courts, and any appeal goes directly to the next level, the intermediate people's courts. The second group of formal courts, the special people's courts, are also equal in the court hierarchy to the basic people's courts: these courts handle military, railway, and maritime matters.

The **intermediate people's courts** handle serious criminal, civil, and economic cases of first instance at the municipal and prefectural levels. They also deal with serious cases that might be transferred from basic people's courts, including murder, rape, robbery, bombing, arson, and grand larceny, as well as special cases related to counterrevolution or involving the death penalty or life imprisonment and cases involving foreigners. These 380 courts also handle appeals from the basic people's courts, and protests from procurators from the lower courts about the decision of a case.

The next level in the formal Chinese court system is the **higher people's courts.** These thirty courts handle criminal, civil, and economic matters of first instance that may affect the entire province, autonomous region, or municipality, and matters of second instance (appeal) from the intermediate courts. Like the intermediate courts, it also handles first-instance crimes transferred from lower courts, and cases protested by the procurator.

As mentioned briefly in Chapter 4, the highest court is the **Supreme People's Court** of China, which deals with matters of national importance. Most of the cases that come before this court are appeals from the next lower level, the higher people's courts. It is divided into seven permanent divisions: two criminal divisions and a single division each for administrative issues, civil matters, communications and transport, complaints and petitions, and economic matters (Terrill, 1999). The criminal courts mostly handle appeals of serious felony crimes, including death penalty cases. The Supreme People's Court also provides explanations and advice to lower courts, interprets laws, and supervises the administration of the military courts.

Every court at every level must consist of a president, two or more vice presidents, one chief judge, and several deputy judges and assistant judges. The president is elected by the people's congress at the corresponding level, while other members are appointed by the standing committees of those congresses. Every court must also set up a judicial committee, whose members are selected by the National People's Congress, to deal with the most difficult or most important cases (Davidson and Wang, 1996).

However, the actual trying of cases in the basic people's, intermediate people's, and higher people's courts is done either by one judge if it is a minor criminal matter or by a **collegial bench.** The collegial bench is composed of one to three judges and two to four **people's assessors** depending on the case and court level. The people's assessors are citizens who must be elected, at least 23 years of age, and eligible to vote (Situ and Liu, 1996, p. 129).

Although people's assessors are an important component of trials and involve the public in judicial proceedings, and although technically they may represent a majority when it came to a verdict, they are not likely to disagree with professional judges on matters of either fact or law. In this way, lay assessors are similar to lay judges in Germany, who follow the leadership of the professional judge in almost all cases. The professional judges are chosen for individual trials by the president or vice president of the respective court.

If we compare the court system of the People's Republic of China with our other model countries, we see a number of both similarities and differences. All of our model countries, including China, have a hierarchical court structure with certain jurisdictional limits; that is, they only handle cases within their own bailiwick. The different levels also handle appeals from the lower levels. Another similarity is the use of laypeople as adjudicators. In China, the collegial panel consists of professional and lay assessors. Lay judges are also used in Germany, and laypeople serve as jurors in serious crimes in England and the United States.

Differences also are clearly evident. Unlike in Common Law countries, Chinese judges are unable to make law. As a result, they often handle cases very flexibly and in accordance with the needs of the government (Leng, 1982). Another significant difference is the extensive system in China that prevents cases from moving level by level through the formal court system. The people's mediation committees handle thousands of minor civil and criminal matters every year. The Chinese courts are also averse to the implementation of many procedural rights that are available in other countries. The presumption of innocence, the exclusionary rule, protections against self-incrimination, the right to trial by jury, and protection against being tried twice for the same offense (double jeopardy) are absent in Chinese criminal justice (Situ and Liu, 1996).

Finally, there are clearly serious questions relative to the issue of judicial independence in China. Verdicts in important legal cases are reviewed by the president of the court, and the most difficult cases are dealt with by the judicial committee. This may at first seem to constitute an extensive method of checks and balances. But after review, one finds that the president and members of the judicial committee are, in effect, political appointments, selected by the National People's Congress, which means that the principle of judicial independence essentially is absent in China.

COURTS IN JAPAN

Americans accused of crime in Japan would do well to acquaint themselves with the cultural underpinnings of Japanese procedure, rather than trying to play by American or even European rules in the ostensibly Western process of Japan. In *The Japanese Legal Advisor,* written by George Koshi (1970) to acquaint American visitors and businesspeople with the vagaries of Japanese law, we find the hypothetical case of *Japan v. Jones.* In this case, Jones, an American businessman, finds himself in serious trouble when a Japanese bicyclist swerves in front of his car and is struck and killed. Jones, who was driving well within the speed limit, is dismayed when he is accused of driving at an excessive speed and of criminal negligence in causing the death of the bicyclist. Despite the politeness of the Japanese police officials and the assurances that he does not have to make a statement without consulting an attorney, Jones is frightened and upset by the proceedings in Japanese, a language that he does not understand, and by the fact that he is asked to sign a statement that he cannot read, although it has been interpreted for him.

A business colleague assures Jones that the best thing to do is to pay a visit to the widow of the deceased, apologize for the crime, make a small payment of amends, and attend the funeral of the victim. Although Jones finds this process highly irregular from an American point of view, he complies, bringing flowers and money to the wife of the victim, stating his regret about the accident, and attending the funeral. With the help of his colleague, he hires a Japanese attorney to represent him. The attorney tries to deal with Jones's misgivings about making a payment to the widow. He explains that such a gesture is a social obligation that

> *falls upon any person who has been the agent through whom others have suffered, however innocently and unavoidably he may have become involved. . . . This moral obligation is completely isolated from legal concepts of criminal guilt or civil law obligations. When the social obligation has been satisfied in proper form and in good spirit, the legal effect ranges from neutral to favorable. If either ignored or rendered with bad grace, however, the legal effect could be only unfavorable. (Koshi, 1970, p. 22)*

At Jones's trial, held before a single judge and consisting of a series of short sessions held over the course of eight months, the widow testifies that he had paid a visit of condolence and that the family bears him no ill will. Although Jones is found guilty of a crime that in the United States would be equivalent to manslaughter, his sentence is a fine of 50,000 yen (about $200 at the time of Jones's trial), suspended for three years. Jones is relieved about the lightness of the sentence, but he is also upset at being convicted of a crime for what seemed to him to be obviously an accident (Koshi, 1970, ch. 1).

As we can see, persons not versed in the mores and customs of Japanese society could make disastrous mistakes in asserting their rights or their innocence when accused of a crime in Japan, no matter how much the law allows for such assertions.

The extent to which Japanese judicial institutions reflect Japanese culture is also illustrated by the **Civil Liberties Bureau** (Rosch, 1987). This bureau was set up in 1949 to hear complaints and provide remedies for individuals whose civil liberties had been infringed. It had roughly the same mission as the Civil Rights Section of the U.S. Department of Justice and undoubtedly was a brainchild of post–World War II reconstructionists in Japan. Unlike the Civil Rights Section, however, Civil Liberties Bureau personnel are unpaid commissioners who are nominated by their localities and confirmed by the Ministry of Justice. There are over 11,000 commissioners, operating in every town and neighborhood. The position of commissioner is an honorary one, and candidates go through both an elaborate local screening and a national investigation before being appointed. Over the course of a year, over 300,000 complaints about violations of fundamental human rights are heard.

From an American point of view, however, many of the cases would seem strange and would not fit our conventional categories of violations of human rights. Many of them would be handled through tort processes in this country. Many others would not be seen as causes for litigation or

official complaint, no matter how sad or angry they might make one feel. Here are a few typical cases as described by Rosch:

> *A family in a rural area was ostracized by its neighbors for a number of years because its members were said to be uncooperative. They were not invited to any weddings and funerals. Their children were bullied at school. CLB officials convinced the other members of the community that their behavior was inappropriate.*
>
> *An elderly woman was very lonely and felt that she did not see her son, daughter, and grandchildren enough. A CLB Commissioner contacted the offending children.*
>
> *Workers at a drug company were forced to take a drug the company wanted to test. A number became ill and one died. The company was persuaded to cease such practices and compensate the injured parties. (1987, pp. 246–247)*

These cases address fundamental questions about social harmony and relations within groups. They have little to do with the relations between government and citizens, or with denial of rights of free expression, or with unfair practices directed at particular minority or ethnic groups. The Civil Liberties Bureau acts chiefly as an agency of mediation rather than as a legal advocate for the civil rights of the people. In effect, an institution that represented an attempt to bring American-style bureaucracy and democracy to a country eventually adapted to the peculiar legal and social traditions of the Japanese people.

Court Organization

Figure 9.4 depicts the Japanese court hierarchy. Japanese court structures, like those of other modern countries, form a hierarchy that begins with the lower courts, known as **summary courts,** which have original jurisdiction in minor criminal and civil cases. Procedures in these courts are usually truncated, with very few formal trials (Research and Training Institute, 1996). If the defendant agrees, the judge, who is not necessarily a trained lawyer, can decide the

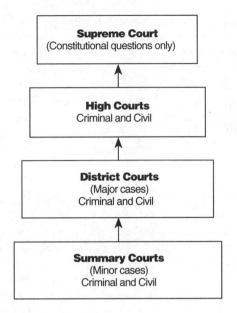

FIGURE 9.4 Structure of the Japanese Courts

case based on the evidence in the case file and on the prosecutor's sentence recommendation. Neither side appears before the judge. If the prosecutor or the defense is unhappy with the ruling, they can ask for a formal trial (Castberg, 1990). If the criminal case before one of the over 500 summary courts would result in a prison term of more than three years or if the civil case would result in a fine of more than 900,000 yen, then the case would be handled by the district courts level.

The fifty district courts handle civil and criminal cases and matters that have been appealed from the summary courts by the prosecution or the defense. At the same level as district courts are the family courts, which handle most domestic and juvenile cases.

A single judge presides over most district court cases. In important criminal cases, a three-judge court may be convened. Three judges are always necessary when the sentence would result in imprisonment of more than a year or a death sentence or when civil cases are heard on appeal from the summary courts. Most cases at this level

are handled quickly because many defendants confess to the charges brought before the court. When the defendant does contest the charges, a formal trial ensues. (See Table 7.4 for a summary of the steps in a typical Japanese trial.)

The **High Courts** in Japan generally handle cases that are appealed from the district or family courts, but they also deal with appeals that come directly from summary courts and with cases of initial jurisdiction when a person is charged with insurrection or sedition. Each of the eight High Courts has a president and a group of judges, from which a panel of three are chosen to hear an appeal. Although High Court cases normally have three judges, in extraordinary cases there may be five. After individual cases are decided, a written majority opinion is provided. If the decision is appealed, it is brought before the **Supreme Court.**

The Supreme Court is the highest court in Japan and is the final court of appeal in civil and criminal cases. In addition, the Supreme Court, according to the Japanese Constitution (Article 81), determines "the constitutionality of any law, order, regulation, or official act." It is also responsible for nominating judges to the lower courts, determining judicial procedures and training, and supervising of the judicial system.

In cases dealing with constitutional questions, all fifteen members of the bench preside; eight justices must agree for a law to be declared unconstitutional. For all other cases, the court divides into panels of five justices. Unlike in the High Court, both opinions of the court are provided, and the justices can express their personal views on the case (Terrill, 1999).

The judges of the Supreme Court are chosen by the Japanese cabinet. In practice, a mix of professional judges, practicing attorneys, and other personnel, including law professors and career civil servants, are appointed to this court. Judges of the district courts and courts of appeal are nominated by the Supreme Court and approved by the legislature. They come from the highly trained career judiciary, all of whom, in the Civil Law tradition, are civil servants. Summary court judges and family court judges, however, do not have to be trained jurists, but may be legal practitioners or otherwise respected individuals.

All judges in Japan must retire at age seventy. Since Supreme Court appointees are rarely under age sixty, this requirement means that the Supreme Court historically has had little opportunity to develop as a collegial group that articulates a philosophy of law, as often happens in the U.S. Supreme Court. At the same time, the frequent turnover in the Supreme Court tends to ensure a politically more responsive body than the American court, in which many justices are holdovers from earlier administrations. The Supreme Court of Japan has not developed as the potent political force that the U.S. Supreme Court and even the German Supreme Court have during their histories. This may reflect the fact that Japan has not traditionally been a nation in which the assertion of individual rights and recourse to litigation have been culturally accepted. An important function of the Japanese Supreme Court is general oversight of court administration throughout the country. This is a function that the U.S. Supreme Court exercises for the federal system and the state supreme courts exercise for their systems, usually through a separate administrative office.

Citizen Participation in the Judicial Process

The Japanese judicial process seems to allow little opportunity for the citizen involvement in court decisions, either through juries or lay judges, that is found in Western and Socialist systems. In fact, of all the court systems that we have considered so far, the Japanese system is the only one that does not have a formal requirement for lay decision-making participation in major crime cases. However, courts in Japan may call on laypeople to form conciliation groups in order to settle disputes prior to formal adjudication.

Japan had a short-lived experiment with juries between 1928 and 1943, during which time a defendant in a felony case could request a jury trial. Jury trials were compulsory in cases in which death or life imprisonment were possible outcomes, and the verdict was by majority vote. As time went on, and despite the fact that cases that were decided by jury resulted in "not guilty" verdicts in far larger numbers than those heard by judges, there were fewer and fewer requests for jury trials in elective cases. In 1943, the Japanese legislature formally discontinued the use of juries.

Why did this manifestation of lay participation die after only fifteen years? The organization itself had some structural defects that inhibited its use. Defendants who requested jury trials had to pay for the costs involved; judges did not have to acquiesce to jury verdicts; and jury trials were not allowed in a variety of cases, including elections and public order cases.

More importantly, however, the course of Japanese history at that time, as well as general Japanese cultural realities probably led to the disuse of juries. The country was moving toward an extreme militarism that culminated in war, first against China and other Asian countries and finally against the Allied nations in World War II. The Japanese tradition of respect for authority and agents of government gave decisions by professional judges greater respectability than those by juries. Even after the war, when the possibility of reinstituting jury trials was considered, many judicial leaders opposed the system as being "un-Japanese," or not suited to the Japanese concept of authority (Maruta, 1989; Tanaka, 1976, pp. 483–491). The result is that Japan, despite the fact that it fashioned its legal system in large part on the Civil Law tradition, and despite the additional postwar influence of American legal practices, has not found it desirable to institute any semblance of the lay participation that is so valued in these other systems. We must remember, though, that citizen participation often occurs at the pretrial stage or through dispute resolution agencies such as the Civil Liberties Bureau.

Further, Japan makes a unique contribution to efforts to control prosecutorial power through its committees of inquest of prosecution. These eleven-member committees are chosen by lot from voter lists in each district. Their function is to examine the conduct of prosecutors with respect to nonprosecution of cases and to make recommendations, if necessary, to the chief district prosecutor that a case be pursued. This oversight of prosecutorial discretion is in great contrast to the U.S. system, in which there are few limits on the power not to prosecute specific cases. It also presents a contrast to the German system, in which compulsory prosecution of felony cases is the rule and the prosecutor ostensibly has little discretion.

The Nonlitigious Japanese:
Myth or Reality?

As we discussed in Chapter 8, Japan is a country with few lawyers, especially when compared to the United States. This differential is often attributed to the Japanese culture, in which social harmony is prized above individual wants or needs and in which confrontation and conflict are avoided as much as possible. In such a culture, litigiousness, or the tendency to settle disputes through court cases, would tend to be disapproved. The result would be less need for the services of lawyers.

In recent years, challenges have been offered to this prevailing assumption that nonlitigiousness is simply explained by cultural dynamics. Scholars like John Owen Haley (1978) suggest that this cause-and-effect relationship is not all that clear and that there are actually strong *institutional* as well as cultural barriers to litigation. These institutional barriers include the strict limitation on the number of students admitted to the Legal Training Institute in Tokyo each year. Since admission to this institute is the only path to a legal career in Japan, the number of lawyers is automatically restricted by the government. These lawyers, being in short supply, charge high fees, in itself a barrier to litigation. In addition, barriers related to extremely high standards of proof, prohibition of class actions, and little means for effective discovery tend to discourage litigation. At the same time, more highly developed institutions of mediation provide alternatives for dispute settlement that are more in keeping with the Japanese culture and that result in settlements similar to or even better than those coming out of court proceedings. In short, the limited use of litigation in Japan stems not only from culturally based reluctance but also from the fact that in many cases it is easier, cheaper, and more profitable to pursue other avenues of dispute settlement.

Although nonlitigiousness refers chiefly to the propensity not to initiate court proceedings in civil matters, it also has effects in the criminal process in cases in which charges are not brought or pursued by victims, in which police settle cases at the local level, or in which prosecutors or courts use mediation or conciliation rather than criminal procedures. In all these situations, we can predict that social change in Japanese society, as well as the force of centuries of tradition, will continue to combine to affect the nature of the criminal process, resulting in a peculiarly Japanese product.

COURTS IN SAUDI ARABIA

Traditional Islamic societies such as Iran and Saudi Arabia mold their court systems to assure that Islamic Law is the basis for court proceedings and decisions. This is especially so for criminal law, in which Qur'anic principles are clearly developed and are not as complicated with respect to the demands of modern life and commerce as in the civil law. Traditionally, an unusual feature of Islamic justice has been the absence of appeals courts (Shapiro, 1981, ch. 5). In Western nations, appeals courts serve not only to assure that the trial at the lower level was fair and according to law but also to guard against the possibility of disparate interpretations of law or idiosyncratic legal development at the lower-court levels. In other words, appeals courts make the law uniform and centralized where a given law applies. From a political standpoint, we can also say that the appeals process is an agency of central control in a particular nation or area. Fortunately, contemporary courts in Saudi Arabia do include an appeals process.

Islamic Law is highly decentralized in nature and is not tied to any particular nation-state. Thus, the kind of secular law that is usually interpreted by courts in other legal traditions does not exist in Muslim countries, and the need for uniformity is not as great as it is in other kinds of law. Appeals against injustice can always be directed to administrative officials, including the ruling caliphs, so individuals have some recourse against arbitrary judges without appealing on matters of law to higher courts.

In today's nation-states that incorporate Islamic Law, further avenues of appeal have developed, not only for the non-Islamic elements of the law but also for some cases under Islamic Law. Thus, we find once again that it is possible to adapt Islamic Law, using more or less of it depending on the circumstances and the culture of each country.

Saudi Arabia is one of the few countries that claims to be ruled by Shari'a—in this case, the Hanbali school of Muslim jurisprudence. However, because much industrial and economic development in this sparsely populated but wealthy country is conducted by foreigners, a parallel system of justice is needed to handle contracts, commercial disputes, and other matters not covered by traditional Islamic Law. As a result, there is a dual system of justice, with Shari'a courts to handle criminal cases, family law, and some civil law, and additional courts and administrative tribunals (called committees) to handle other matters.

Court Organization

The Shari'a court system in Saudi Arabia is a four-tiered hierarchy. There is no formal division between civil and criminal cases, with the same judge hearing cases in both areas on the same day (Karl, 1991, p. 144). The courts of first instance, called either lower or general courts, are presided over by one Islamic judge, or *quadi*. Lower courts, found in every town, deal with minor domestic matters, misdemeanors, small civil claims, *tazir* (discretionary) crimes, and the Hudud crimes of intoxication and defamation. These courts have

no power to hand down a sentence of mutilation or death.

At the same level are the general courts that have original jurisdiction over all criminal and civil cases (Moore, 1996). The general courts also have one judge for most matters. In cases in which sentences of stoning, amputation, or death are possibilities, however, a three-judge panel must hand down the sentence (Karl, 1991, p. 145).

Any decision that is appealed at the lower- or general-court levels is brought before the high courts of Shari'a law. The high courts have exclusive jurisdiction to hear appeals from the lower courts and to handle Hudud and Quesas crimes. One judge presides over these cases, except in cases involving death, stoning, or amputation, for which a three-judge panel is required (Moore, 1996).

If judgments from the high courts are appealed, they are brought before the courts of appeal. There are two first-level appeals courts in Saudi Arabia, with their jurisdiction divided geographically. Three-judge panels hear most appeals in these two courts. Five judges are necessary, however, in cases involving death, stoning, or amputation. These courts provide the final appeal in all cases except, again, those involving death, stoning, or amputation.

The **Supreme Judicial Council** provides the final avenue of appeal. This council is also the agency that makes regulations and policies for administering the court system of the country as a whole. In reality, the Supreme Judicial Council cannot alter a verdict but can only refer the case back to the court of appeals for reconsideration. The court is composed of eleven members, and any final verdict is subject to the review of the king, who determines whether it was in consonance with the Shari'a (Moore, 1996). For a graphic depiction of the Shari'a court structure, see Figure 9.5.

In addition to the Shari'a court structure, Saudi Arabia has a number of administrative tribunals, called committees, that make decisions about regulations in a number of specialized areas relative to business, traffic, labor, and so on. Each

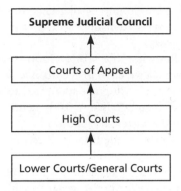

FIGURE 9.5 Structure of the Shari'a Courts

committee includes Shari'a or former Shari'a judges. The most important of these committees is the Board of Grievances, which, like the French Council of State, hears cases involving government rulings and actions. Disputes involving relations of foreign businessmen to the Saudi government are generally handled by the Board of Grievances as well.

In both Iran and Saudi Arabia, foreigners are subject to Shari'a law, court procedure, and punishments in the case of criminal actions. This includes the various sexual crimes that would not be punished severely, if at all, in their home countries.

Procedure in Saudi Shari'a courts is quite informal by Western standards, perhaps because of the long tradition of *quadi* justice, in which the *quadi,* an agent of the caliph, heard and decided cases on an individual basis. Courtrooms may simply be small rooms in a government building, and proceedings may be held in secret if the judge determines that the interests of morality demand it. Journalists are not permitted in court, and spectators are rarely present. Defendants are expected to participate in the proceedings, and there often is no defense attorney. The burden of proof, however, is on the prosecution.

In cases involving possible sentences of death or mutilation, appeal is automatic; in other cases, the losing party, whether defendant or prosecutor, must file an appeal within fifteen days of the judgment. Courts of appeal cannot overturn

judgments; they can only return them for reconsideration to the lower court. Appeals are considered by judges only, with no representatives of either side present during an appeals proceeding (Moore, 1987).

SUPRANATIONAL COURTS

In Chapter 6, we discussed one option that is available in the European community for individual citizens who have exhausted all the legal means of redress and yet still feel their rights have been violated by the criminal justice system. This organization, called the European Court of Human Rights (ECHR), allows for individuals who live in countries that have signed international human rights conventions to bring cases directly to a judicial body after they have been denied relief in their national courts.

But what happens when a legal solution is required *between* two countries? And how is justice meted out to an individual or individuals responsible for illegal acts that are in violation of international standards or treaties? Although some regions, such as Europe, have developed methods to address abuses of human rights, other problems of global crime and justice have become too complicated for regional courts to handle. In response, the international community has developed judicial mechanisms that direct their decisions across boundaries, and they supposedly have a higher legal standing than decisions of courts in individual countries. These institutions are called international or **supranational courts.**

The Background of Supranational Courts

The idea of developing courts to handle legal matters across boundaries and for violations of international standards is not a novel idea. In the late nineteenth century, in the country of Crete, two military courts prosecuted and tried individuals for "crimes against humanity" in the aftermath of the Candia massacres of September 1898. After World War I, some 3000-odd war crimes trials were conducted by the French and Belgians. Also at that time, an unsuccessful attempt was made by the League of Nations to establish an international tribunal to deal with war crimes. Tribunals are generally temporary bodies that are organized to judge persons for their behavior during a specific time for a specific event. They have usually been formed as military courts to adjudicate atrocities committed during times of war or civil unrest.

The most famous international tribunals of the twentieth century were the Nuremberg and Tokyo war tribunals that were organized following World War II. The Nuremberg Trials lasted from November 1945 until September 1946 and ended with the conviction of twenty-two defendants, eleven of whom were sentenced to be hanged. The Nuremberg and Tokyo tribunals, although not the first or only war crimes trials, were very important because they established the basis of contemporary international law (Wang, 1995). For example, the Geneva Convention of 1949 was codified using much of the customary law on which the Nuremberg Trials were based, and it now serves as the legal foundation for many supranational cases (Rosenstock, 1994).

Supranational Courts Today

There are currently two major forms of supranational courts dealing with criminal justice–related issues in operation, and a third is in the planning stage. The longest running and most permanent is the **International Court of Justice** (ICJ), located at the Peace Palace in The Hague, Netherlands. The ICJ was established under the original Charter of the United Nations in 1945 and held its first session in April 1946. The ICJ was actually the successor to a judicial body called the Permanent Court of International Justice, which was established by the League of Nations in 1922. As the principle judicial body of the United Nations, the ICJ has fifteen judges, with no more than one from any one country, all of whom are elected by the General Assembly and Security Council of the United Nations. In some instances, the ICJ

can be divided up into smaller chambers of three or more judges to handle the volume of cases (UN Charter).

Also known as the World Court, the ICJ has a dual role: (1) to settle, in accordance with international law, legal disputes submitted to it by the 185 UN member states and neutral parties (Nauru and Switzerland) and (2) to give advisory opinions on legal questions referred to it by international organizations. The decisions of the court are binding—no appeal is available, and all decisions are decided in accordance with international treaties, international conventions, international custom, general principles of law, and, in a few cases, prior judicial decisions and teachings (ICJ, 1998).

Since 1946, the ICJ has delivered over sixty judgments in a number of areas such as maritime issues, non-use of force, international treaties, protection of the environment, and territorial frontiers, as well as at least twenty-three advisory opinions. In one example of an advisory opinion, in 1996, the ICJ concluded that "the threat or use of nuclear weapons would generally be contrary to the rules of international law applicable in armed conflict, and in particular the principles and rules of humanitarian law" (World Court Project UK, 1999).

The second form of supranational courts are the two criminal tribunals that were formed to deal with the atrocities committed during the civil wars in the former Yugoslavia and in Rwanda. In 1992, the UN Security Council, using the powers vested in it in Chapter VII of the UN Charter, established the **International Criminal Tribunal for Yugoslavia** (ICTY). After the outbreak of genocide in Rwanda, the UN Security Council in November 1994 established a second and separate tribunal, the **International Criminal Tribunal for Rwanda** (ICTR). The purpose of both tribunals was to prosecute persons responsible for serious violations of international humanitarian law (Lawyers Committee, 1995, p. iii).

Although the war tribunals in Yugoslavia and Rwanda may have been direct descendants of the trials in Nuremberg and Tokyo, they differ in a number of significant ways. For one, the ICTY and ICTR have been developed with the full support of the international community under the direction of the United Nations. This is both positive and negative. With full support of the United Nations comes acknowledgement by the international community of the legitimacy of the actions taken by the tribunals and acceptance of the results. The problem is that, without full occupation and total victory, it is quite difficult to capture and prosecute all those involved.

Some procedural differences are also present. Within the rules of the current war tribunals, it is not possible to prosecute individuals in absentia. Also, there was no appeal process in Nuremberg, whereas those convicted by the ICTY and the ICTR can appeal their cases to special chambers within the tribunals. Further, the charter for the current war tribunals allows for concurrent jurisdiction in other countries. This means that other nations that agree to follow the procedures outlined by the tribunals can assist in prosecuting and trying the persons responsible for serious violations of international humanitarian law (Lawyers Committee, 1995). Thus, for example, Germany in 1999 tried, convicted, and sentenced to life imprisonment Bosnian Serb Djuradad for his role in the slaying of Bosnian Muslims in June 1992. German courts have tried several cases related to the war in the former Yugoslavia to help reduce the workload on the tribunal at The Hague. German law and the UN Charter on the ICTY allow for courts to adjudicate crimes committed in other countries.

The Legal Jurisdiction of Supranational Courts

Where does international humanitarian law come from, and what gives the courts like the ICJ, ICTY, and ICTR the power to decide the fate of individuals around the world? The answer has three parts. First, the United Nations, as the only international body of power in the world and with support of its member states and the Security Council, provides the initial legal jurisdiction. Without the approval of the UN, there would be no ICJ and no criminal tribunals.

Second, as we mentioned briefly with regard to the ICJ, various international courts gain legal legitimacy and power through the application of international laws that have been developed over time in the form of conventions and treaties. This practice allows the courts to adhere to principles agreed to previously by a number of countries. In the case of the ICTR, the following conventions serve the legal foundation for the prosecution of individuals in violation of international humanitarian law:

> The Geneva Convention of August 1949
>
> The Hague Convention of October 1907
>
> The Convention on the Prevention and Punishment of the Crime of Genocide of December 1948
>
> The Charter of the Military Tribunal of August 1945 (Lawyers Committee, 1995, p. 3)

Under each of these conventions are a number of crimes that fall under the legal jurisdiction of the tribunals. (For a full list of the specific offenses, see the Lawyers Committee, 1995, pp. 4–7). In the cases of Yugoslavia and Rwanda, the tribunals have prosecuted four distinct categories of crimes: grave breaches of the Geneva Conventions of 1949, violations of the laws or customs of war, genocide, and crimes against humanity.

The final source of legal power and legitimacy for the tribunals and other international courts is the general legal principle of *jus cogens,* whereby fundamental norms are recognized on the international level as having status superior to other norms. What this means in practical terms is that, if one country believes it is "in the right," this belief may be acceptable within its own borders. However, if the international community condemns the behavior of that country as illegal, the latter supersedes the former in a court of law.

The principle of *jus cogens* likely evolved from a similar Roman concept of *jus gentium*—a term that describes the law practiced by Roman jurists and later medieval jurists, who stated that basic principles of right reason are applicable to all human relationships across borders. Later, Dutch jurist Hugo Grotius (1583–1645) used this principle as legal authority to develop rules for international law (Mueller, 1997; Rush, 1994). *Jus cogens* is a legal principle that has often been referred to by the ICJ, and it appears to have gained strength in the international legal community (Sunga, 1997).

Future Developments in Supranational Courts

For over fifty years after Nuremberg, many attempts were made to develop a permanent court that would investigate and bring to justice individuals who committed the most serious crimes such as genocide, war crimes, and crimes against humanity. Finally, in July 1998, at a UN Diplomatic Conference in Rome, delegations from 160 countries passed a statute to create a permanent **International Criminal Court** (ICC) at The Hague. The ICC will not enter into force for several years, however, because at least 60 countries need to ratify the treaty. Ultimately, the ICC will serve the same purpose as the current ICTY and ICTR tribunals in that it will have jurisdiction over the most serious crimes of international concern, such as genocide, war crimes, crimes against humanity, and aggression (Lawyers Committee, 1998).

The development of a permanent ICC seems to be a good idea. Among the reasons that have been presented by UN human rights expert Lyal Sunga in support of such a court are the following:

- Crimes under international law that go unchecked hinder international peace, fuel instability and can lead into long-term armed hostilities and war.

- International criminal law cannot be effective unless it is enforced systematically and on a regular basis.

- International instability should not be able to dictate that international law is relative.

- Individuals who commit crimes in violation of international law should always be punished, and this principle should take precedence over other factors such as politics, administrative convenience, or historical accident.

- Ad hoc tribunals like the ICTR and the ICTY are created retrospectively and with some discretion, leaving the question as to whether criminals will be prosecuted and punished all the time.

- Creation of a permanent court would symbolize the international community's determination to enforce international law universally (Sunga, 1997, pp. 329–331).

However, the ideal of a permanent ICC has raised some opposition, most notably the United States. Apparently, the United States is concerned that the proposed treaty would give too much power to the ICC and that U.S. troops and citizens would be vulnerable to politically motivated prosecutions (Onestad, 1997). As of late 1999, discussions were being held among the United States and more than forty other countries in an effort to find a way for the United States to sign the treaty (Associated Press, 1999).

SUMMARY

As we consider the similarities and differences in court structures and procedures in the various systems, it seems clear that the similarities are greater than the differences. In each system, a lower judicial agency, often staffed by laypeople, dispenses justice in minor matters. Serious cases are heard in trial courts of general jurisdiction. In all countries we looked at, the possibility of error at the lower level is handled through the institution of intermediate courts of appeal. A high court of final appeal is at the top of each judicial hierarchy. Courts in all these systems lay claim to impartiality and independence in making decisions, and an opportunity for both sides to be heard is guaranteed in the proceedings.

It is the differences among systems, however, that show the relation among culture, tradition, and legal process. In England, the successful struggle to curtail the powers of the monarchs is reflected in the strong emphasis on procedure and on lay participation through the jury. The continental Civil Law systems of France and Germany, with their specialization of courts and their civil servant judicial personnel, reflect the rational-bureaucratic approach to administration that infuses other aspects of their state apparatus. The judicial system of the People's Republic of China takes a highly centralized form, with both informal and formal mechanisms that assist in educating the citizenry about the Socialist society. In Japan, Western-style judicial process coexists with a premodern emphasis on harmony, consensus, and nonconflictual relationships. In the Islamic society of Saudi Arabia, deep religiosity and devotion to Qur'anic principles dominate the criminal law process, as well as much of family law.

The legal foundation for our supranational courts can be traced to conventions and treaties that were developed over fifty years ago. Recently, tribunals have been developed to deal with wartime atrocities in the former Yugoslavia and in Rwanda. Efforts are being made to expand the idea of supranational courts into a permanent international criminal court.

DISCUSSION QUESTIONS AND EXERCISES

1. What is the difference between judicial independence and judicial impartiality? Which is more important in your opinion?

2. To what extent are laypeople (i.e., not legally trained) used in the court systems of our model countries? Which system uses them the most?

3. What is the role of apology in the criminal process? Is it mainly a Japanese phenomenon?

4. In your class, in small-group discussions, rate from one (worst) to six (best) the court system you would least like to be involved with as a defendant and discuss why. Then compare your results with the other groups.

5. Name one characteristic of the Chinese court system that makes it unique in comparison to other non-Socialist countries? Could this characteristic be implemented in the United States? Why or why not?

6. Pick one of the supranational courts mentioned in the chapter, and search the Web for the current status on the subject.

7. Where do the international tribunals for the former Yugoslavia and for Rwanda, as well as the idea of a permanent international criminal court, acquire their legal legitimacy?

FOR FURTHER READING

Amin, S. (1985). *Middle East Legal Systems.* Glasgow: Royston.

David, R. (1972). *French Law: Its Structure, Sources, and Methodology.* New York: Free Press.

Glendon, M. A., M. Gordon, and C. Osakwe. (1985). *Comparative Legal Traditions.* St. Paul, Minn.: West.

Malekian, F. (1996). *The Concept of Islamic International Criminal Law: A Comparative Study.* Dordrecht: Kluwer Academic Publishers.

Shapiro, M. (1981). *Courts.* Chicago: University of Chicago Press.

Spencer, J. R. (1989). *Jackson's Machinery of Justice in England.* New York: Cambridge University Press.

Sunga, L. S. (1997). *The Emerging System of International Criminal Law.* The Hague: Kluwer Law International.

Tanaka, H. (1976). *The Japanese Legal System.* Tokyo: University of Tokyo Press.

Zander, M. (1989). *A Matter of Justice: The Legal System in Ferment.* Oxford: Oxford University Press.

10 After Conviction: The Sentencing Process

The Purposes of Criminal Sanctions
Sentencing Practices
Corporal punishment
Noncustodial Sanctions
Imprisonment
The Death Penalty
Public Opinion and Sentencing
Summary
Discussion Questions and Exercises
For Further Reading

Key Terms and Concepts

community service
control of freedom
day fines
deterrence
Diyya
electronic monitoring
exile
fincs
flow design
house arrest
incapacitation
jail

laogai
noncustodial sanctions
probation
remand prison
prison
restitution
restorative justice
retribution
rehabilitation
stock design
warnings

Consider the following:

- In 1994, Michael Fay, an 18-year-old Ohio native, was detained in Singapore for defacing automobiles with spray paint and committing other acts of vandalism. Soon after, he was sentenced to be caned with six lashes and to serve four months behind bars; later, the punishment was reduced to four lashes. The caning was carried out in May 1994.

- After being detained incommunicado for three years, Li Hai, a former student at Beijing University, was sentenced in 1997 to nine years in a Chinese prison. He was found guilty of state secrets–related charges for compiling a list of names of Beijing residents who were in prison due to their connection with the 1980s prodemocracy movement (Human Rights Watch, 1998).

- After a seventeen-year investigation, FBI agents in 1996 arrested Ted Kaczynski, called the Unabomber because his targets were airlines and universities. In 1998, he pleaded guilty to federal charges and was sentenced to life in prison without the possibility of parole.

- In September 1999, Samuel Sheinbein, a Maryland teenager, pleaded guilty to the murder, dismemberment, and burning of 19-year-old Alfred Tello, Jr. The case was unique because Sheinbein confessed and was sentenced in an Israeli court for a crime he committed in the United States. Sheinbein fled to Israel immediately after the killing and sought refuge there under a law that said he could not be extradited back to the United States because his father had been born in Israel and therefore he was technically an Israeli citizen. He was sentenced to twenty-four years in an Israeli prison.

In each situation, we see how different countries sentence their criminal offenders. Criminal sentences and the treatment of offenders reflect how a society feels about crime, criminals, and justice. If a country is in the midst of a crime wave and fear of crime is very high, it might be more likely to hand down harsh sentences. Examples of this include the "war on crime" in the United States and the *yanda* campaign in China. Some countries, however, such as those in Scandinavia, which have low rates of violent crime and a high tolerance toward offenders and are more likely to support rehabilitation-based sanctions.

The Sheinbein case is particularly interesting because it represents a situation where an American citizen would much rather be convicted and sentenced in a country other than in the United States. This case is ironic, since the United States was long considered a leader in progressive reforms in sentencing and imprisonment. The penitentiary system itself was an Enlightenment reform that blossomed in the United States in the early nineteenth century as an alternative to death, galleys, forced labor, transportation, and corporal punishment. In addition, much of the stimulus for modern penal reform, including a separate juvenile justice system, probation, parole, and alternative sentencing, came from the United States. Today, however, we look to Western Europe for reform initiatives and progressive modes of sentencing and corrections.

In this chapter, we will look at the varieties of sentencing schemes in various countries. In the next chapter, we will consider the issues and problems surrounding imprisonment.

THE PURPOSES OF CRIMINAL SANCTIONS

What does a society hope to gain from punishing wrongdoers? The classic answer is that one or more of the following should be accomplished:

- **Retribution:** The offender should "pay back" society for the harm he or she has done.
- **Rehabilitation:** The offender should be transformed into a law-abiding person

through programs of medical, psychological, economic, or educational improvement.

- **Deterrence:** The offender, through various devices, such as certainty of punishment or length or severity of punishment, should come to the conclusion that crime is not worth the risk of the resulting punishment.

- **Incapacitation:** The offender, usually through prison or exile, should be denied the opportunity to commit further crimes.

In practice, motives for imposing criminal punishment on offenders are usually mixed. At different times and places, however, one or the other of these purposes has been stressed. During the nineteenth century, the "classical school" of criminologists saw simple retribution, applied equitably, as the major goal of sentencing in much of Europe. In the United States, where rehabilitation as a philosophy of punishment held sway for much of the twentieth century, there was an abrupt swing in sentencing theory and practice during the 1970s toward a more classic retributive approach. During the 1990s, the United States promoted incapacitation, as evidenced by the prison-building boom and longer sentences for drug and violent crimes. In Europe, the philosophy of rehabilitation developed in earnest in the later twentieth century, but now the swing is back to a retributive philosophy. An exception is the Scandinavian countries, where "neoclassicism," as it is called there, developed parallel to the classical movement in the United States.

Non-Western countries seem to have their own ideas about the goals of punishment. In China, it is important that criminal offenders be persuaded to reform not for themselves but for the good of their family, village, and, especially, society. Thus, the official purpose of the criminal sanction has been one of rehabilitation. Islamic justice, according to Shari'a law, has two central purposes: (1) deterrence and (2) protection of the community by reforming offenders (Al-Sagheer, 1994). The practice in Islamic states has varied, depending on a variety of factors, including the influence of Islamic Law within the state apparatus and historical developments in specific countries.

The four purposes of criminal sanctions, as just described, all have to do with what happens to wrongdoers and with their capacity to be changed or to do further damage. From a more global perspective, however, we discover that penal sanctions have had less acknowledged and less legitimate functions in many societies. One of these has been the economic function of providing cheap labor that the society could not afford or could not entice its citizens to do otherwise. Transportation to penal colonies and, sentencing to galleys, Siberian prison camps, and road gangs all had a lot to do with economic development, as well as with penal sanctions (Rusche and Kirchheimer, 1939).

This kind of sanction should not be confused with purely slave labor, such as that used in the United States until 1865, or the importation of Polish people to do slave labor in Germany during World War II. In such cases, there is no pretension to a connection with the penal process. Nor should this kind of sanction be confused with prison labor designed to keep convicts busy and to train them in work skills and habits. Such prison labor may be marginally compared to exploitative use of prisoners, in that it may help pay the costs of imprisonment, as has happened with prison farms in the United States. The purpose of the criminal sanction, however, is not to provide labor for economic development. In today's world, it is an infraction of the standards of the International Labor Organization (an agency of the United Nations) to do so.

Although the implementation of criminal sanctions to provide labor for economic development may seem like a thing of the past, unfortunately, this is not the case. In 1983, an estimated 3 to 4 million prisoners in the former Soviet Union performed forced labor (Committee on Foreign Affairs, 1984, p. 2). More recently, the same issue has arisen with respect to the fruits of Chinese prisoner labor. Prisoners in China are subject to institutions called *laogai* thought to promote "thought reform through labor." In the *laogai,* inmates are required to work at prison farms and factories to support the economic system in China. Even more disturbing, however, are the allegations that over 1,000 Chinese prisoners were executed and then had their organs harvested for financial gain (Wu, 1995).

Another economic function that criminal sanctions may serve is that of social control, providing the kind of working class necessary for an organized, industrial society. In a study comparing crime and justice in Massachusetts and South Carolina in the late eighteenth and early nineteenth centuries, for example, Michael Hindus found a relationship between the development of prisons and the proliferation of misdemeanor crimes and the development of the factory system in Massachusetts. In South Carolina, however, where feudal plantation conditions prevailed, social control was exercised in a less formal and centralized way (Hindus, 1980). More recently, in his classic book about the historical foundation of prisons, David Garland explains how the United States, during the beginning of capitalist development, used prisons as a storage facility for surplus laborers and as a school to spread capitalist values (Garland, 1990). In a similar study, Italian researchers found a correlation in that country between the development of prisons and the social control needs of an industrial society (Melossi and Pavarini, 1981).

An overt economic rationale for criminal processes, especially penal sanctions, is ordinarily beyond the margin of generally accepted notions of legitimacy and is not usually acknowledged by modern governments. Another illegitimate but much-practiced use of criminal sanctions that is also condemned in international law is punishment of political enemies of a regime. This practice is so notorious in some countries, especially those in political turmoil, that we hardly realize that it happens in most countries, even established democracies that supposedly cherish freedom of speech. Often, it is difficult to draw the line between political persecution and simple diligence in carrying out the criminal law. For example, was it political repression or basic law enforcement to imprison antiwar demonstrators who, in defiance of the law, publicly burned their draft cards during the Vietnam War?

Political uses of the criminal law may be tied to religious persecution, especially where a state-sponsored religion believes itself to be threatened by independent religious groups. As described in Chapter 7, many of today's rules of criminal procedure in Common Law systems evolved in response to attempted suppression of religious minorities in England. Although religious fervor is not as likely to lead to criminal sanctions in today's secular nations, as it was in earlier times, the example of countries such as Iran and Pakistan, which apply Islamic Law to promote religious tenets, shows that this practice continues. One famous example is the case of Salman Rushdie, a British novelist who was sentenced to death in absentia in Iran for the crime of apostasy, which is defined as the renunciation of Islam by a Muslim. The continued use in some jurisdictions in the United States of "blue laws," which prohibit working or buying liquor on the Sabbath, remind us that the use of criminal sanctions to further religion is not a thing of the past in this country, either.

As we probe ever deeper into the purpose of criminal sanctions, we find that it becomes an increasingly complex subject, one that does not allow for simple explanations. In most systems, a mixture of social, economic, and political factors is at work and needs to be analyzed to understand the criminal justice process. Unfortunately, the tendency among scholars, as well as the public, is to take one part of the complex whole, such as deterrence, and elevate it to exclusive status as a prescriptive or descriptive element in the criminal sanction process.

SENTENCING PRACTICES

Despite serious abuses that continue today, sentencing practices generally have become more humane over the centuries. We have only to compare the fate of would-be assassins or assassins of rulers in seventeenth-century France, nineteenth-century

United States, and twentieth-century United States to illustrate this. After a crazed Frenchman made an unsuccessful attempt to murder King Louis XV, he was hanged, was cut down while still alive, had his intestines pulled out and roasted before him, and was then pulled apart by four horses, each one tied to a different limb. When Charles Guiteau assassinated President James Garfield in 1881, he was hanged despite the fact that he suffered from delusions and displayed other symptoms of mental illness. On the other hand, when Lynette "Squeaky" Fromme, a follower of the notorious killer and cult leader Charles Manson, attempted to kill President Gerald Ford, she received a life term in a California penitentiary with the possibility of parole after fifteen years. John Hinckley, the delusional young man who attempted to kill President Ronald Reagan, was placed in a mental facility.

It was, in fact, reaction to the excesses of criminal punishment as it had been practiced in Europe that caused the authors of the U.S. Bill of Rights to include in the Eighth Amendment the famous phrase "nor cruel or unusual punishment [shall be] inflicted." This phrase echoes the earlier contents of the English Bill of Rights of 1689, which was passed in reaction to the notoriously cruel penalties imposed by judges loyal to the last two Stuart kings, Charles II and James II.

Charters of human rights, including the UN Universal Declaration of Human Rights, the UN Standard Rules for the Treatment of Prisoners, and the European Convention on Human Rights, outlaw the use of torture and inhumane treatment of prisoners. Although the phrasing in such documents is vague, subject to different interpretations, and often ignored, we can safely say that the rhetoric of criminal punishment, and often its practice, has become more benign throughout much of the world over time.

There is conflicting research as to whether sentencing practices reflect the relative wealth of a society. In a historical and comparative study of criminal justice practices in four major world cities, Robert Gurr (1977, ch. 5) suggests that hu-

mane imprisonment, because of its expense, is a luxury of wealthier nations and that corporal punishment (including death), exile, and swiftly enforced penalties generally are sanctioning possibilities for less-developed societies. Prison farm camps and the hiring out of prison labor under the "convict lease" system, used in some southern states in the United States until World War II, are other examples of the response of impoverished societies to the problem of criminal sentencing.

However, in the Fifth UN Crime and Justice Survey (UNCJS) an analysis of economic indicators and sentencing practices in thirty-four countries did not support the hypotheses of sentencing being related to wealth. Rather, the use of punishment is independent of a country's developmental or economic situation or of regional differences and dependent on the availability and acceptability of the sentencing options (Shinkai and Zvekic, 1999, p. 91).

It is difficult to clearly determine whether one kind of criminal sanction is more or less prevalent in the world today. But if we review the results of the Fifth UNCJS, we can see some general patterns. The survey indicates that the majority of adults in 1994 were punished in the community through methods related to some control in freedom (e.g., probation) and through fines, warnings, and community service. Over one-third of countries in the survey still relied heavily on deprivation of freedom (i.e., incarceration) as the primary sentencing alternative. For a graphic depiction of these results, see Figure 10.1.

This is not to imply that there is no variation among individual countries when it comes to sentencing. In some countries, warnings, fines, and noncustodial sanctions account for up to 70 percent of total sentences (e.g., Slovenia, Japan, Germany, Finland, Austria, Egypt); in others, more than 50 percent of sentences are custodial (e.g., Colombia, Singapore, Moldova). At the same time, some countries show no preference for any one kind of punishment (Zvekic, 1997).

As we examine various sentencing practices, we can place them in four basic categories:

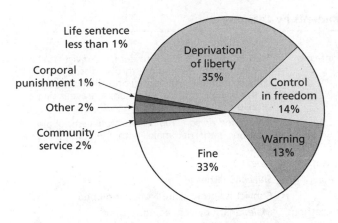

Life sentence less than 1%

Corporal punishment 1%

Other 2%

Community service 2%

Deprivation of liberty 35%

Control in freedom 14%

Warning 13%

Fine 33%

FIGURE 10.1 Types of Punishments Applied to Adult Convicted Persons in Thirty-Four Countries, 1994

Source: *Global Report*, 1999, p. 89. Reprinted with permission of the United Nations.

(1) corporal punishment, (2) noncustodial sanctions, (3) imprisonment, and (4) the death penalty. In the following sections, we will explore these practices in more detail.

CORPORAL PUNISHMENT

Corporal punishments such as flogging, branding, dunking, and maiming have gradually disappeared as official, court-imposed sanctions in most societies. This does not mean that abuse of convicted offenders today does not occur; we all know that such abuse takes place even in the most enlightened societies. The distinction is similar to that between judicially ordered executions and extrajudicial killing of citizens by agents of a government.

One government that still favors the use of corporal punishment, as we saw in the example at the beginning of the chapter, is Singapore. However, the major exception to the gradual disuse of corporal punishment sanctions is found in Islamic countries, where measures of punishment that seem extreme to most Americans can, and sometimes do, take place (Badr-el-Din, 1985; Metz, 1993). Since the Qur'an describes not only forbidden acts but also the penalties for engaging in these acts, societies that are faithful to Islamic Law have little choice but to carry out these penalties. Table 10.1 shows the severity of the punishments

prescribed under Islamic Law. The force of such punishments is mitigated, however, by the fact that the standards of proof are so high that many of them are infrequently carried out. This is so especially in cases involving sexual misconduct, a most serious crime in Islamic Law. People who are guilty of adultery are supposed to be stoned to death. But there must have been a valid confession or four witnesses to the crime. Further, the only witnesses who can be used, according to most interpretations, are male Muslims. Needless to say, convictions for adultery are extremely rare even in countries that follow Shari'a criminal law. It is not uncommon for a year to pass without an execution for adultery.

A Westerner who is appalled by the severity of the punishments prescribed under Islamic Law might also consider the following:

The Hudud *penalties are designed to avoid unreasonable limitations on individual freedom to the extent that they are "bodily penalties." They are executed in limited duration and cause momentarily severe physical pain to the criminal and remain unforgettable to him so that in most cases, he will refrain from future criminal conduct. These penalties contrast with prison sentences which the criminal becomes accustomed to, having experienced them for long periods of time. Thus, imprisonment soon loses its deterrent effect and prisoners lose their sense of responsibility. Often after being released, they return to prison to serve*

Table 10.1 Islamic Crimes, Proofs, and Punishments by Category

Crime	Proof	Punishment
Adultery	4 witnesses or confession	*Married person:* stoning to death. Convict is taken to a barren site. Stones are thrown first by witnesses, then by the quadi and finally by the rest of the community. For a woman, a grave is dug to receive the body.
		Unmarried person: 100 lashes. Maliki school also punishes unmarried males with 1 year in prison or exile.
Defamation	Unsupported accusation of adultery	*Free:* 80 lashes.
		Slave: 40 lashes.
		Convict is lightly attired when whipped.
Apostasy	2 witnesses or confession	*Male:* death by beheading.
		Female: imprisonment until repentance.
Highway robbery	2 witnesses or confession	*With homicide:* death by beheading. The body is then displayed in a crucifixion-like form.
		Without homicide: amputation of right hand and left foot.
		If arrested before commission: imprisonment until repentance.
Use of alcohol	2 witnesses or confession	*Free:* 80 lashes (Shafi'i 40).
		Slave: 40 lashes.
		Public whipping is applied with a stick, using moderate force without raising the hand above the head so as not to lacerate the skin. Blows are spread over the body and are not to be applied to the face and head. A male stands, and a female is seated. A doctor is present. Flogging is inflicted by scholars well versed in Islamic law, so that it is justly meted out.
Theft	2 witnesses or confession	*1st offense:* amputation of hand at wrist by an authorized doctor.
		2nd offense: amputation of second hand at wrist by an authorized doctor.
		3rd offense: amputation of foot at ankle, by an authorized doctor, or imprisonment until repentance.

a longer sentence. Thus execution of the "bodily penalty" allows the criminal to resume his work immediately thereafter; he is also not prevented from supporting himself and his children. Similarly, Islam teaches that to undergo the Hudud punishment is in itself an act of penance and remission after which the offender resumes his normal life as a good citizen. . . .

Thus, despite the hope that imprisonment will have a beneficial effect on society in suppressing crime, law enforcement officials have failed to successfully combat violent crimes, while prisons serve as a training ground for youthful offenders.

By contrast, in Islamic society, the reliance on Hudud penalties brings about peace, stability, and security. When these were abandoned in favor of

Crime	Proof	Punishment
Rebellion	2 witnesses or confession	*If captured:* death.
		If surrendered or arrested: Ta'azir punishment.
		Quesas
Willful murder with weapon	2 witnesses or confession	Death by retaliation by victim's family, compensation (payment of money or property to victim's family), exclusion from inheritance, or pardon.
Voluntary manslaughter	2 witnesses or confession	Fine (to be paid within 3 years); exclusion from inheritance; religious expiation or pardon.
Homicide by misadventure	2 witnesses or confession	Fine; exclusion from inheritance, religious expiation, or pardon.
Homicide by intermediate cause	2 witnesses or confession	Compensation; loss of inheritance.
Bodily harm, intentional	2 witnesses or confession	Retaliation (same harm inflicted as suffered by the victim); or compensation (varies with the value placed on the bodily part).
Bodily harm, unintentional	2 witnesses or confession	Compensation.
		Tesar
Sodomy	4 witnesses or confession	Death by sword, followed by incineration; live burial; or being thrown from a high building and stoned.
Wine importing, exporting, transporting, manufacturing, or selling	2 witnesses or confession	Imprisonment up to 5 years; up to 30 lashes.
Minor offenses (wifely disobedience, insults to others)	2 witnesses or confession	Admonishment by the quadi; reprimand by words and actions; delayed sentence.
Desertion from the military	2 witnesses or confession	Boycott (exclusion from social interaction).
Embezzlement, false testimony	2 witnesses or confession	Public disclosure and stigmatization (display of offender in various sections of city, announcement of the offense and the punishment); fines.
Tax evasion	2 witnesses or confession	Fines, seizure of property.
Varied misdemeanors	2 witnesses or confession	Up to 40 lashes with a stick or unknotted whip.
Recidivists of varied crimes	2 witnesses or confession	Imprisonment, varying from 1 day to life, at the discretion of the quadi.

SOURCE: Lippman, McConville, and Yerushalmi, *Islamic Criminal Law and Procedures,* Praeger Publishers, an imprint of Greenwood Publishing Group, Inc., Westport, CT, 1988, pp. 42–46. © 1988 by the authors. All rights reserved.

foreign theories of penology, Islamic societies experienced increased crime rates. (Mansour, 1982, pp. 201–202)

Mansour goes on to give the example of Saudi Arabia, which was a hotbed of violent crimes and robberies prior to its adoption of the Hudud penalties:

Saudi Arabia is now an example of a country in which theft and highway robberies rarely occur. The number of amputations during the last 25 years (the reign of King Abdel Aziz Al Saud) was only 16. Comparing this number to the number of robberies which took place in Egypt, for instance, we find that 1038 robbery cases were sentenced to imprisonment in 1938, and in 1968 the number was approximately 30,000. . . . The only remedy may be to enforce the sentence of amputation ordained by God in the Qur'an. (p. 201)

However, Mansour ignores important information about changing social conditions in both Saudi Arabia and Egypt. In Saudi Arabia, the establishment of the kingdom centralized power and suppressed warring and anarchic factions in the territory. In Egypt, urbanization, unemployment, and overpopulation have created conditions that typically contribute to higher crime rates. Nevertheless, the argument is a cogent one, especially given the low crime rate in Saudi Arabia (Adler, 1983; Metz, 1993) and the dysfunctional results of imprisonment as it is practiced today.

An interesting point about sanctions under Islamic Law is that imprisonment is considered a proper sanction only for recidivists, people who have not changed as a result of the more direct corporal punishments. Thus, a person who has been convicted of theft for the third or fourth time is sentenced to prison. With the first conviction, one hand is amputated by an authorized doctor; with the second conviction, the other hand is amputated; with the third conviction, however, the penalty may be either amputation of a foot or "imprisonment until repentance" (Lippman, McConville, and Yerushalmi, 1988, p. 42).

One might well ask, "Which is preferable? Twenty years in the state penitentiary or the loss of a hand or foot?" Nevertheless, a certain repugnance for visible violence has made the application of corporal punishment not useful as a criminal sanction in modern Western society.

NONCUSTODIAL SANCTIONS

The search for noncustodial sanctions is as old as the practice of imprisonment itself. **Noncustodial sanctions,** also called alternatives to incarceration, are legal sanctions handed out to offenders that do not require time served in a correctional facility. The call for such alternatives be-

came increasingly intense in the latter part of the nineteenth century, when European criminologists, assessing almost a century of experience with prison as the favored mode of punishment, voiced widespread disillusionment with the practice. Declaring that prison did little to change or rehabilitate offenders, these criminologists directed their attacks mainly at short-term imprisonment of nondangerous offenders. At that time, short-term sentences were by far the punishment of choice for convicted offenders. Franz von Liszt, a leading German criminologist, summed up these sentiments in 1885: "The short prison sentence in its present form is worthless, indeed harmful. It does not deter, it does not improve, it contaminates" (Kalmthout and Tak, 1988, p. 3). Alternatives, including fines and special systems of juvenile justice, were the answer to the dysfunctional aspects of short-term imprisonment, according to von Liszt and other European reformers.

In more modern times, the search for alternatives has both humanitarian and utilitarian motives. From a humanitarian standpoint, minimization of short-term imprisonment of nondangerous offenders increases the possibility of rehabilitation through work programs, counseling, and restitution plans, whereas imprisonment breeds further crime and alienation from conventional society. From a utilitarian standpoint, alternatives alleviate the financial and other problems involved in dealing with an ever-growing prison population, especially in Europe and the United States. For a more inclusive description of the advantages and disadvantages of noncustodial alternatives, we turn to the writings of two prominent international scholars, Matti Jousten and Ugljesa Zvekic:

The arguments for noncustodial sanctions are essentially the mirror image of the arguments against imprisonment. First, they are considered more appropriate for certain types of offenses and offenders. Second, because they avoid "prisonization," they promote integration back into the community, promote rehabilitation, and are therefore more hu-

mane. Third, they are generally less costly than sanctions involving imprisonment. Fourth, by decreasing the prison population, they ease prison crowding and thus facilitate the administration of prisons and the proper correctional treatment of those who remain in prison.

The main arguments against the greater use of noncustodial sanctions are that they are not as effective as sentences of imprisonment in deterring other members of the public from committing offenses, that they do not incapacitate the offender, and that they do not sufficiently demonstrate the reprobation of the offense by society. Put simply, this argument is that noncustodial sanctions are overly lenient. (1994, p. 6)

The call for alternatives to incarceration is heard in much of the industrialized world. A leading agency in promoting alternatives at least since 1976 has been the Council of Europe, which passed a resolution in their favor at that time. The United Nations, in 1980, 1985, and 1990 also promulgated resolutions calling for alternatives to incarceration (Kalmthout and Tak, 1988, pp. 5–6; Jousten and Zvekic, 1994, p. 1).

What are the alternatives? Because each country approaches the issue differently, it would require a book of considerable length to document the many options available today. To keep our discussion within the limits of this chapter, we will focus on the most commonly used alternatives within two general categories: (1) monetary payments and (2) community supervision.

It is important to mention here that our discussion of alternatives to incarceration will only include measures that are implemented subsequent to adjudication. Noncustodial sanctions prior to adjudication, such as pretrial detention, bail, release on recognizance, diversion programs, and related issues (e.g., promoting decriminalization and dealing with social conditions that help create crime), will not be addressed here. (For a full description of these and other forms of community corrections programs, see Clear and Dammer, 1999.)

Monetary Sanctions

Fines. The **fine** is a penalty imposed on a convicted offender by a court or, in some countries, by another arm of the criminal justice system, requiring that he or she pay a specified sum of money. Fines are among the most common noncustodial sanctions in the world. They are used in as many as 95 percent of cases in Japan and in more than 70 percent of cases in most of Western Europe; the percentages are much lower in countries in transition and in the developing world (Zvekic, 1997).

Fines are not popular in the United States as punishment for felonies or serious misdemeanors, despite their extensive use for minor crimes. This is probably because judges have not found them to be very effective as a deterrent to crime or because of the difficulty in collecting the fines. Since judges are not required to assess fines rather than incarceration for many kinds of offenses, including cases of repeat offenders (as it is in Germany), and they have little knowledge about or faith in offenders' ability to pay, they tend to use other options. Nevertheless, fines are often imposed in addition to other sanctions (Hillsman et al., 1987). In any case, many judges perceive conventional fines, which are legislatively determined by the nature of the crime rather than by a combination of this factor and the offender's ability to pay, as discriminatory against the poor.

Fines can serve many benefits for the criminal justice system and for society in general. Government coffers benefit from fines, especially given that fines are inexpensive to administer by the court system. Fines also can lower the numbers of persons in jails and prisons and thus save taxpayers money.

In addition to providing economic benefits, fines can serve the correctional purposes of rehabilitation. When offenders are required to pay fines they can learn to be more financially responsible and can also remain in the community to work and interact with family and friends.

There are two ways that fines can be determined. One is the fixed-sum rate system. In this system, specific offenses are allocated a certain "value," and offenders are fined according to the offenses they commit. This method appears easy to administer and rather equitable. However, not all offenders are able to pay the fines assessed for their crimes. Typically, offenders with more economic resources are able to pay the fines while poorer offenders find themselves in violation of the court order, which can lead to further legal difficulties. A second fine-setting method is called the day fine.

Day Fines. In response to the concern that fines exact a heavier toll on the poor than on the wealthy, Scandinavian countries developed **the day fine** (also called the structured fine), a criminal penalty that is based on the amount of money an offender earns in a day's work. Day fines thus take into account the differing economic circumstances of offenders who have committed the same crime. The amount of the fine is calculated in a two-stage process. First, the number of units of punishment is determined according to the seriousness of the offense and such factors as the offender's prior record. Second, the monetary value of each unit of punishment is established in light of the offender's financial circumstances. Thus, the total penalty—the degree of punishment—should place an equivalent economic burden on offenders of differing means who are convicted of similar offenses. For example, a person making $36,500 a year and sentenced to ten units of punishment would pay $3,650; a person making $3,650 and receiving the same penalty would pay $365.

Day fines have at least two advantages. First, they provide a balance between the crime committed and the offender's ability to pay for the crime. Offenders are required literally to "pay for their crimes" but not beyond what is possible for them financially. This reduces discrimination of sentencing and increases the likelihood of payment. Second, the day fine provides courts and correctional officials with another alternative to in-

Table 10.2 Countries in Europe Using Day Fines and Year of Introduction (if available)

Finland	1921
Sweden	1931
Denmark	1939
Germany	1975
France	1983
Hungary	—
Greece	—
Austria	—
Portugal	—
England	(In 1991, temporarily adopted use of *unit fines,* which are based on a week's income rather than a day's income)

SOURCE: Junger. *Alternatives to Prison Sentences.* The Hague: Kugler Publications. Used with permission.

carceration, one that is more punitive than probation supervision but less harsh than jail or prison.

Some of the countries that have made use of day fines outside Europe are Cuba, Costa Rica, and Bolivia. Finland, which pioneered this penal reform in 1921, uses only day fines. For a summary of the use of day fines in Europe, see Table 10.2.

Day fines are generally not used for minor misdemeanors, because the basic intent is to make them true alternatives to incarceration. The maximum number of days that an individual may be fined varies from country to country: In Denmark it is 60 days, while in Germany it is 360 days. However, few judges in Germany use the maximum number, and the majority of day fines fall between 5 and 30 days (Grebing, 1978). Since it is not possible under German law to imprison someone for less than one month, the day fine in that country serves as a substitute for minimal jail sentences.

Until recently, day fines were not as widely used in the United States as in Europe. As the need for alternatives to incarceration becomes ever greater because of prison crowding, however, the use of day fines is increasing in this country. Day fines often are promoted as a way to improve the use of fines as sanctions in the United States.

However, fines and day fines are not a panacea, and they have been criticized both in countries that have refused to adopt them and in the countries where they are most used. Some claim that fines tend to overpenalize the poor, who still find their living standard appreciably lowered when they have to pay a fine. Day fines tend to be mechanically applied, and they leave little discretion to the sentencing judge. Also, the actual financial circumstances of offenders often are hard to determine, and certain categories of offenders, such as students, housewives, and the unemployed are not amenable to any fine system. Nor does there appear to be a movement toward more equitable and relatively inflation-proof day fine systems. Because of these and other difficulties, countries like France have not adopted a system of day fines, while Mexico and England have abandoned the system.

Restitution and Community Service. **Restitution** technically is when an offender is required or volunteers to participate in community service or to pay money to make reparation for harm resulting from a criminal offense. With restitution, payment is made by the offender and is received by the victim, his or her representative, or a public fund for victims of crime.

The idea of paying crime victims for losses, damage, or injuries is an ancient idea that actually predates formal criminal justice systems. Both the Old Testament of the Bible and the 4,000-year-old Code of Hammurabi state that the offender must repay crime victims "in kind or extent." In ancient times, Babylonian, Greek, Roman, and Jewish law all contained provisions for compensation to be paid by offenders. Our current conceptions about restitution have developed over many centuries. In prehistoric times, people acted on their own to punish others for transgressions against them. But as people began living in large tribes, blood feuds between different groups surfaced, and vigilante groups developed for the purpose of administering punishment. To resolve violent feuds between tribes, the crime victims or their families were given compensation for the

crimes committed against them. Over time, the family's role in the compensation process diminished, and by the thirteenth century, the state (or reigning monarch) had become the offended party in criminal offenses. With this development, the state assumed responsibility for punishing offenders and collecting fines. As time passed, victims became less and less involved in the punishment process. In eighteenth-century England, the concept of restitution resurfaced when philosopher Jeremy Bentham argued that payment of monetary fines was essential to his idea that the punishment should equal the crime (Hudson and Galaway, 1975).

One form of restitution used in Islamic countries is called *Diyya,* which is paid directly to the victim or his or her family as compensation for five different Quesas (felony) crimes. Because *Diyya* is technically a collective responsibility, the offender's family or the government may be asked to pay. Many other rules regulate the payment of *Diyya,* including those related to the offense, religious affiliation, the sex of the victim, and the financial status of the families involved (Jousten and Zvekic, 1994, p. 16).

In **community service,** an offender is asked to personally "pay back" the community by performing a set number of hours of unpaid work for a not-for-profit agency. Community service mixes two historical traditions: (1) ordering offenders to make reparation for crimes and (2) requiring unpaid labor as punishment. Community service as part of restitution can be traced back to ancient times. The sanction also was used in the Middle Ages in Germany, when it was handed out in lieu of other punishments; tasks included building city walls and cleaning canals. In the early seventeenth century, offenders in England were "persuaded" to join the Royal Navy in lieu of more formal punishment. In some cases, they were transferred to English colonies to work as servants for free settlers (McDonald, 1992, p. 184). Reformers in nineteenth-century France mounted a crusade for the use of community service to replace detention for those who had defaulted on fines. Community service as a substitute for paying a fine was codified in Italy in 1889, in Norway in 1902, in Germany in 1924, in Portugal in 1929, and in Switzerland in 1942 (Kalmthout and Tak, 1988, p. 14).

By the late 1970s, community service programs were accepted correctional practice in the United Kingdom, Canada, Australia, New Zealand, and the United States (Hudson and Galaway, 1990). France passed a community service law in 1983 with the intention of reducing short-term prison sentences, but the results were hardly encouraging. Although community service as a sanction was used quite extensively, short-term prison sentences rose by 16 percent between 1983 and 1986. The implication is that these alternatives were being used in addition to the prison option rather than instead of it. Community service in the United States and Great Britain has become a regular sanction, used both as an alternative to incarceration and as a supplement to probation. In many cases, community service is used as a sentence in lower and misdemeanor courts. Traffic, DWI, and juvenile cases are common offenses for which community service is implemented.

Community Supervision

Probation. With **probation,** in lieu of imprisonment the offender is given the chance to remain within the community and demonstrate a willingness to abide by its laws. Probation usually is accompanied by a suspended sentence and includes some form of supervision in the community. Probation sentences may also require the offender to pay restitution to the victim and/or provide free services to the community to compensate for the crime. Further, the probationer may be ordered to attend treatment programs to deal with problems that led to criminal involvement. On the international level, probation is generally referred to as **control of freedom.**

In this country, probation began with the innovative work of John Augustus, a Boston bootmaker who was the first person to stand bail for defendants under authority of the Boston Police Court. Augustus probably borrowed the idea of probation from the British, who in the 1820s combined the Common Law surety and recognizance systems by releasing young offenders into the hands of employers (UNAFEI, 1997, p. 119).

Of all the forms of supervising offenders in the community, probation is the most common. This form of noncustodial sanction is practiced in some form in almost all criminal justice systems in the world, although specific practices may vary considerably. In some jurisdictions, offenders are kept under close supervision to ensure that the conditions of probation are followed and the individuals are properly reintegrated into the community. In others, offenders have very limited contact with their probation officers and receive little or no community support. Variation also exists in terms of who supervises the probationers (volunteers or professionals) and whether a violation of probation conditions automatically leads to revocation and incarceration (Jousten and Zvekic, 1994).

Probation is generally administered by a probation officer employed by the local judiciary. In some cases, probation departments are part of the executive branch of government, run by state or federal organizations. In China, probation is sometimes supervised by the police or by one of the many community units. In Indonesia, it is implemented by the office of the prosecutor (UNAFEI, 1997, p. 232).

In many regions of the world, the use of probation is increasing; in others, its use is declining. According to results in the Fifth UNCJS, probation use increased in 16 countries between 1990 and 1994 and decreased in 11 others. The countries with the highest rates of probation are the United States, Canada, and England. Table 10.3 gives data on the use of probation in 33 countries.

Probation is not only a sanction devised by governments but also a general framework for a series of programs that can be developed to fit the needs of offenders and their communities. As a result, there are very few aspects of probation that are the same around the world. A review of international probation procedures would reveal a diverse set of programs that reflect local cultural norms and political aims and provide a variety of sentencing options (Hamai et al., 1995).

Table 10.3 Annual Probation Rate per 100,000 Population, 1990 and 1994, and Persons on Probation, 1994

	1990 RATE	1994 RATE	PERSONS ON PROBATION	
			ADULT	JUVENILE
Belarus	16.1	50.3	5,212	—
Belgium	35.3	47.9	4,824	—
Bermuda	19.7	34.9	20	2
Bulgaria	8.1	10.1	825	28
Canada	248.6	268.9	78,639	—
Chile	7.0	8.8	1,226	—
Costa Rica	98.3	81.1	2,490	—
Denmark	41.7	32.4	—	—
England and Wales	177.3	217.2	82,908	28,838
Germany	52.8	25.5	11,384	9,413
Hong Kong	53.5	55.1	869	2,472
Indonesia	1.5	.8	1,172	277
Jamaica	27.1	41.6	594	444
Japan	63.8	47.2	5,054	53,815
Latvia	30.4	—	—	—
Lithuania	17.0	9.6	356	0
Macau	60.2	83.3	88	261
Malta	2.0	13.7	31	19
Marshall Islands	13.0	14.8	8	0
Mexico	.3	1.0	938	—
Netherlands	44.3	79.1	—	—
Nicaragua	4.4	4.2	—	—
Northern Ireland	—	75.9	963	275
Catar	—	1.9	—	10
Republic of Korea	21.1	39.0	0	17,237
Republic of Moldova	14.4	10.0	370	65
Russian Federation	—	100.8	—	—
Scotland	80.8	117.1	5,978	32
Slovenia	49.0	35.8	691	4
Sweden	78.2	77.8	6,634	201
USA	655.3	536.2	—	—
Western Samoa	22.0	—	—	—
Portugal	—	.50	—	—

SOURCE: Fifth UN Crime and Justice Survey in *Global Report on Crime and Justice*. United Nations Office for Drug Control and Crime Prevention. Reprinted with permission of the United Nations.

House Arrest. With **house arrest,** offenders are sentenced to terms of incarceration, but they serve those terms in their own homes. Some offenders might, after a time, be allowed to venture out to go to work or to run errands. Others might be allowed to maintain their employment for the entire duration of their sentence. Whatever the details, the concept has as its basic thrust the use of the offender's residence as the place of punishment.

The use of house arrest (also called home confinement, home detention, or home probation) is hardly a novel form of punishment. Throughout history, people have been confined to their homes for violating the laws of the land. These include Galileo, who was confined to his home for making scientific statements contrary to the teachings of the Roman Catholic Church, and, more recently, Lech Walesa in Poland and Winnie Mandela in South Africa. There are at least three kinds of house arrest, which can be best understood in terms of levels of restrictiveness. The lowest level involves a simple curfew, when an offender is required to be home after a certain hour. The next level is when an offender is allowed to be away from home during certain hours of the day for work, school, religious reasons, or counseling sessions; this is often called home confinement. The third, and most punitive, form of house arrest requires the person to be home at all times, unless a special situation arises such as medical or legal appointments (Hofer and Meierhofer, 1987).

The use of house arrest (home probation) has been reported in Australia, Iraq, Thailand, and the United States in connection with electronic monitoring. In addition, Canada, England, and Wales have also utilized electronic monitoring (Jousten and Zvekic, 1994).

Electronic Monitoring. One of the most popular approaches to noncustodial supervision is the use of **electronic monitoring** (EM) to expand the surveillance capacity of supervision. EM was initially developed in 1964 by Harvard University researcher Ralph Schwitzgebel. The original goals of EM were to reduce crime, promote a therapeutic relationship with clients, and provide a humane alternative to incarceration (Schwitzgebel, 1969). The use of EM in the United States dates back to 1983 when a New Mexico judge, inspired by the Spiderman comic strip, placed a probation violator on EM for one month. Other states soon adopted the idea, and by 1993 between 50,000 and 70,000 people were being monitored in all fifty States. At least

1800 federal offenders add to that total (Lilly, 1995).

EM ordinarily is combined with house arrest and is used to enforce its restrictions. However, EM has been utilized in many other ways in corrections. In Los Angeles County, EM has been used for intensive probation supervision (IPS) programs, work furlough–home detention programs, temporary detention of juveniles, gang supervision, narcotic surveillance, and traditional home detention (Zhang, Polakow, and Nidorf, 1995). Other uses include supervision of parolees and pretrial defendants.

Exile. Another time-honored sanction that has assumed various forms throughout recorded history is **exile.** Most of us are familiar with the tales of the Old West in which outlaws were ridden out of town and threatened with being shot on sight if they appeared again. In small tribal communities, banishment frequently was equivalent to a death sentence. Without a sustaining community, subject to attack by enemy peoples and wildlife of various kinds, and at the mercy of the elements, the offender often did not survive exile for very long.

Exile to prison colonies was a widespread practice until the end of the nineteenth century. The terrible conditions of the prison colonies in Australia are described in vivid terms by Robert Hughes in his 1987 book *The Fatal Shore.* The inhabitants of these colonies, often banished there for minor crimes or for political or religious dissent, were subject to extreme abuse, and many did not live long under the harsh conditions. The same can be said for the French prison colonies in Guyana. Transportation of convicts to prison colonies was under attack by reformers throughout the nineteenth century in France. It was gradually abandoned, although the last prisoners did not leave Guyana until 1946 (Wright, 1983, p. 194). England had discontinued transportation in the middle of the nineteenth century.

Exile is rarely used today. When it is implemented, it is usually internal and accompanied by another alternative to incarceration. Such is the case in Italy, where offenders may be sent to a town far from where they committed their crimes but must remain under the supervision of the local police. And the former Soviet Union made extensive use of internal exile. Aleksandr Solzhenitsyn's novel *Cancer Ward* describes internal exile in the Soviet Union. The hero of this novel is a young dissident exiled to remote Tashkent in Kazakhstan, just as Solzhenitsyn himself had been.

Andrei Sakharov, the Nobel Prize winner in physics, was no doubt the best known of recent internal exiles in the Soviet Union. After he became disillusioned with the Soviet regime and was vocally critical of its human rights abuses, Sakharov was convicted of undermining the state and sentenced to exile. Sakharov could not practice his vocation in exile or engage in the kind of political activity that had put him under so much suspicion. In effect, the Soviets removed him from the center of action, thinking (albeit wrongly, since Sakharov generated a lot of concern and publicity even in exile) that he would no longer be able to engage in activities embarrassing to the regime.

Americans, who move frequently and are accustomed to change, may feel that internal exile, with freedom of movement within a prescribed new territory, is not such a terrible punishment. Further, the chances of escaping from such a territory would seem to be quite good. But in reality, in the Soviet Union, that punishment was similar to probation in that the offender had to report periodically to an officer of the court. Moreover, loss of vocation was certainly a severe problem for many individuals in exile. And offenders really had few escape options since all Soviet citizens had to be registered with the police at their place of residence and be prepared to show their identification papers at all times. It would have been next to impossible to take up a new residence in some other area or city without coming to the notice of the neighbors and the authorities.

Restorative Justice. Restoration is in some ways the oldest correctional method, and in other ways the most recent trend. The idea of restoration has its roots in Judeo-Christian religious thought, dating back to ancient Middle Eastern civilization. Religious traditions taught that those who offended against their neighbors could atone for their offenses and be restored to community life if they made reparation for their misdeeds and promised to never repeat them. In fact, penitence, expiation, and forgiveness are central concepts of Judeo-Christian morality.

There is an active modern movement to resurrect these ideals. **Restorative justice** (sometimes called community justice) is an approach that calls for participation by the offender, victim, and community in the sentencing process. Proponents of restorative justice believe that, for the community, victim, and offender to be "restored," the offender must understand the harm caused by the offense, accept responsibility for it, and repair the harm done. To accomplish this, it is imperative that all parties (offender, victim, and community) become involved in the criminal justice process (Pranis, 1993). Restorative justice practices have become very popular in the United States, New Zealand, Canada, and some African countries. (See the accompanying box on page 230 for one example of a restorative justice program for juveniles.)

Warnings. In many countries, especially in Europe, **warnings** are used in a large number of cases. These warnings are provided at the adjudication stage by the judge and usually are accompanied by the threat of incarceration if criminal behavior does not desist. The countries that are most likely to use warnings are Slovenia (73 percent) and Kazakhstan (51 percent) (Zvekic, 1997).

IMPRISONMENT

Imprisonment is today the severest punishment inflicted in most societies. It is also the most problematic of punishments, in that so little other than short-term incapacitation appears to be achieved through its use. It is used almost universally, but there are major differences among criminal justice systems in duration of prison sentences and in prison conditions and programs. In this chapter,

Neighbors, Victims, Offenders Collaborate on Sentencing

MINNEAPOLIS—In the shadow of the city's downtown skyscrapers, a comfortable home sits on a quiet street, opposite a school and a park. It looks nothing like a court of law.

But as often as twice a week, it functions much like a courthouse. In the large living room, criminal offenders admit their guilt, and a punishment is determined and approved, even though no judge, jury, or police officers are present.

This is no kangaroo court. Instead, it's a social experiment by a state with a lengthy pedigree of reform. The aim is to reduce crime, strengthen community bonds, and reduce the caseload in the local criminal justice system, which has struggled in the last decade as Minneapolis began suffering from urban problems that used to plague only other cities.

The concept is called "circle sentencing," and is off to a promising start with support from local prosecutors, judges, and public defenders. Minnesota is the first state to try the idea, which originated among an aboriginal people deep in Canada's Yukon Territory and has now spread to Franklin County in Western Massachusetts.

The process works like this: When a person is convicted in court, a judge can decide to let the community sentence the offender. If the judge turns over the sentencing power to the community, a group of volunteers—anyone from the area can participate—gets together, along with the offender, and sometimes with the victim as well.

So far, several jurisdictions in Minnesota, plus the Mille Lacs band of Chippewa Indians, have used circle sentencing. Most of the cases involve younger offenders and relatively minor cases such as property crimes. Sitting in a circle, the group talks with the offender about the crime, each person explaining why the act is considered an affront to the community. Everyone has a chance to speak, including the offender and the victim, and members of the circle try to elicit an admission of guilt.

"We're trying to get the [offender] to see the light," said Oscar Reed, a volunteer in North Min-

neapolis, a high-crime area that began using circles this year to promote understanding.

The objective at this juncture, advocates for the circle concept said, is to promote healing and understanding for both the community and the offender. Members of the circle want the offender to know the behavior is intolerable, but they also make an effort to understand his or her motivation, whether it's anger, an alcohol or drug problem, or a lack of skills or self-esteem. They try to help the person, if they deem it possible.

"What it's really about is the whole community coming together to take care of its own," said Kay Prannis of the Minnesota Department of Corrections, who brought the concept to the state's attention. "It's very, very important work that has implications for democracy, for sort of re-creating a form of social control that's healthy."

On an unseasonably warm Minneapolis night recently, circle volunteers met at the home-cum-courthouse to decide what should be done with a 10-year-old boy from North Minneapolis, who had been convicted in juvenile court of shooting a pellet gun in public. He has shot the gun at a stop sign, and later at his brother, participants said. The boy's parents also attended.

Volunteers were worried that the boy, who had been hanging out with a tough crowd, was on track to commit more-serious crimes as he moved into his teenage years.

Initially, the boy was sullen and withdrawn. Wearing an ankle bracelet to monitor his whereabouts, he sat on a sofa and wouldn't look anyone in the eye, nor would he admit he had done anything wrong.

"I didn't do it," the boy repeatedly said, looking only at the floor. But the dozen circle volunteers, many of whom came from the immediate neighborhood, gently probed and prodded him for more than an hour.

Gradually, the boy warmed to them and began to admit his guilt, a bit at a time, first admitting

---

we examine sentences to prison. In the next chapter, we will consider penal policies and prison conditions in our model countries.

It is important to note that in this chapter and the next we will use the term *prison* exclusively to

describe any facility used to incarcerate criminal offenders. Technically, at least in the United States, there is a difference between prisons and jails. **Prisons** are used almost exclusively for serious offenders who receive sentences of more than having the gun outside, although he insisted his escapade went unnoticed.

"No one saw me with it," he said.

"Then who called the police?" several volunteers wanted to know.

"I don't know," he replied.

After realizing someone had seen him with the gun outside, he confessed to shooting at a stop sign, before finally conceding he had shot at his younger brother, although he continued to insist that was an accident. By the end of the night, the boy was smiling and animated, and the circle volunteers had gained a measure of trust. Their main goal was not to punish him; they didn't see a juvenile lockup as the solution. Instead, they hoped he would understand why his conduct was unacceptable, and would begin to distance himself from the crowd with which he was associating.

"It's extremely helpful to realize that there are other ways to get to these kids without being punitive," said Alice Lynch, who runs a shelter for battered women and coordinates the North Minneapolis circle program. "We are focusing on the needs of young people and their families, which doesn't happen in the courtroom." But the process isn't only about understanding and rehabilitation. It's also about allowing the community to determine the appropriate punishment, a power that people across the country have sought in recent years. Offenders must agree.

If the initial circle is successful, another circle is scheduled for sentencing. To arrive at a punishment, everyone involved must agree to the proposed sentence, including the offender. This prevents an angry or fearful community from going down the path of vigilantism.

If agreement is reached, the case returns to the judge, who typically approves the sentence. If consensus proves elusive, the community can ask the judge to take back control of the process and sentence the offender. Thus far, sentences have ranged from community service to jail time.

"You're pretty well protected from outrageous conclusions," Prannis said. "If an offender agrees to something outrageous, I would expect the system people to say no."

In one case, an offender found the circle so beneficial, he attended another offender's circle. "One young man completed the circle," Lynch said, "and came to another young man's circle to offer assistance."

Thus far, circles have been used on a small scale, and there are no statistics showing whether they prevent crime. But advocates believe that by connecting with offenders, providing them with support, and getting them help, frayed community bonds can be restored and crime can be reduced.

"We're not going to know about the kids who didn't commit a crime as a result of this process," said Don Johnson, a juvenile prosecutor in Hennepin County, which includes Minneapolis.

Franklin County, Mass., has become the first U.S. area outside Minnesota to give the idea a try.

The county recently completed its first sentencing circle, for an offender from the poverty-stricken community of Orange. The man who was sentenced has benefited enormously from the process, said Lucinda Brown, who recently was hired as community relations coordinator for the county and will oversee the circle process there.

"It is an amazing change, the development we've seen already in his capacity to understand that everything we do has repercussions," she said.

But Brown said the best part is that while the sentence may be an end point for the traditional court system, it is only the beginning for the circle process.

The volunteers who spoke and listened and helped determine the sentence will continue to work with the offender, to help him reconstruct his life.

"I believe in this stuff," said Brown. "We're really making dramatic changes. We're making history."

SOURCE: Siegel, 1999.

one-year; **jails** are facilities that house less serious offenders who are generally sentenced to less than one year or who are awaiting trial or transfer to another institution. We use the term *prison* in these chapters because it is more representative of the kind of terminology used throughout the world. In many countries, due to a lack of financial resources, untried prisoners are not separated from those already convicted. When a country separates inmates, they typically use the term

remand prison to describe the facility used to house unconvicted inmates.

International Prison Data

To assist in the study of international prison data, Roy Walmsley, an English researcher and consultant to the United Nations, compiled the "World Prison Population List" (Walmsley, 1999). The list, which is shown in Table 10.4, gives details on the number of prisoners in 180 countries and territories between the years 1994 and 1998. It shows the differences in the level of imprisonment across the world and provides the information necessary to estimate the world prison population. Derived from a variety of sources, the list specifically includes the number of those incarcerated in remand or prison, the estimated national population, the rate of inmates per 100,000 population, and the date of data compilation. The list does have some limitations including missing data (from about thirty countries or territories), some variability in the dates, and limited information about special categories of offenders such as remand, juvenile, and mentally ill offenders (Walmsley, 1999). Even with its limitations, the list is the best source of international prison data compiled up to this date.

A review of the list indicates that early in the 1990s over 8 million people were in correctional institutions throughout the world as either pretrial (remand) or convicted and sentenced criminals. The countries with the most total number of inmates were the United States (1.7 million) followed by China (1.4 million) and Russia (over 1 million). The highest prison population rate was in Russia (685 per 100,000 people) followed by the United States (645 per 100,000 people). The median number of inmates per 100,000 is about 125, but 65 percent of the countries have rates of 150 or below (Walmsley, 1999).

Walmsley's data provide an excellent source of information for comparisons among countries at one period of time, in what is called **stock design.** But it would be even better if we could study the number of prison admissions over time, in what is called **flow design** (Lynch, 1988). This would allow us to separate the tendency to incarcerate and the length of time served (Reichel, 1999). With this in mind, we address the issue of how international prison rates have changed over time.

Studying changes in prison populations over time is a difficult task. Not all countries are willing to report prison data over time, and those that do often neglect the stock design–flow design methodology. Fortunately, there are some data available that can provide at least some insight into this complicated issue. According to the Fifth UNCJS, of the sixty-five countries that participated in the survey, only thirty showed an increase in total prison population from 1990 to 1994. The other countries in the survey showed more stable prison populations. The countries that showed the greatest increase in imprisonment rates with at least a 100 percent increase, were Belarus, the Czech Republic, and Italy. In contrast, Macau cut its imprisonment rate in half (from 193 to 88 per 100,000) (Shinkai and Zvekic, 1999).

For the longer view of a flow design, we can turn to the data provided by the First, Second, Third, Fourth, and Fifth UNCJSs. Using UN demographic information and prison rate data from the five UNCJSs, we can see that prison rates from 1972 through 1992 increased considerably among industrialized countries and remained relatively stable in developing countries. For a graphic summary of this data, see Figure 10.2.

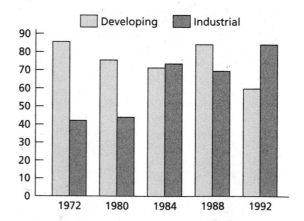

FIGURE 10.2 Incarceration Rates per 100,000 Population over Twenty Years of UN Surveys

Source: *Global Report,* 1999, p. 97. Reprinted with permission of the United Nations.

Table 10.4 World Prison Population List, 1994–1998[a]

Africa[b]	Total in Penal Institutions (including pretrial detainees)	Date	Estimated National Population	Prison Population Rate (per 100,000 population)
Northern Africa				
Algeria	35,737	96	28.6m	125
Egypt	c.40,000	96	64.2m	c.60
Morocco	48,600	97	27.5m	175
Sudan	32,000	97	27.9m	115
Tunisia	23,165	31/12/96	9.2m	250
Western Africa				
Burkina Faso	6,100	31/12/94	10.2m	60
Cape Verde	c.600	97	406,000	c.150
Côte d'Ivoire	12,215	31/12/93	13.55m	90
Ghana	7,076	12/96	18.15m	40
Guinea	c.4,000	97	7.6m	c.55
Mali	4,384	15/1/95	10.6m	40
Mauritania	1,400	97	2.4m	60
Nigeria	c.70,000	96	115.0m	c.60
Senegal	4,653	9/97	8.8m	55
Togo	2,043	6/11/98	4.4m	45
Central Africa				
Cameroon	15,903	97	13.9m	115
Chad	2,521	1/96	6.4m	40
Sao Tome e Principe	99	94	130,000	75
Eastern Africa				
Burundi	9,411	97	6.4m	145
Djibouti	c.650	94	566,000	115
Kenya	41,064	23/10/96	28.9m	140
Madagascar	19,743	1/9/97	15.9m	125
Malawi	6,505	7/98	10.4m	65
Mauritius	3,239	97	1.1m	295
Mozambique	c.4,500	5/94	15.5m	c.30
Rwanda[c]				
Tanzania	38,135	1/8/98	32.2m	120
Uganda	21,971	30/6/98	21.3m	105
Zambia	27,048	94	9.2m	295
Zimbabwe	18,271	3/8/98	11.9m	155
Réunion (France)	1,019	1/10/98	682,000	150
Southern Africa				
Lesotho	4,738	31/12/94	2.0m	235
Namibia	4,397	31/8/98	1.7m	260
South Africa	142,410	31/12/97	44.3m	320
Swaziland	2,221	14/9/98	931,000	240

continued on following page

Table 10.4 continued

Americas	Total in Penal Institutions (including pretrial detainees)	Date	Estimated National Population	Prison Population Rate (per 100,000 population)
North America				
Canada	34,166	97–98	30.0m	115
USA	1,725,842	30/6/97	267.5m	645
Bermuda (UK)	226	31/3/94	63,000	360
Greenland (Denmark)	78	25/8/98	56,000	140
Central America				
Belize	1,118	1/98	229,000	490
Costa Rica	5,495	31/12/96	3.55m	155
El Salvador	8,725	31/12/96	5.9m	150
Guatemala	6,931	31/12/96	11.05m	65
Honduras	9,457	31/12/96	5.9m	160
Mexico	103,262	31/12/96	94.9m	110
Nicaragua	3,692	31/12/96	4.5m	80
Panama	7,322	31/12/96	2.7m	270
Caribbean				
Antigua and Barbuda	225	11/95	65,000	345
Bahamas	1,401	1/98	290,000	485
Barbados	772	1/98	263,000	295
Cuba	c.33,000	97	11.1m	c.300
Dominica	243	12/97	74,000	330
Dominican Republic	11,114	30/6/97	8.1m	135
Grenada	327	1/98	99,000	330
Haiti	2,300	2/96	7.25m	30
Jamaica	3,629	1/98	2.5m	145
St. Kitts and Nevis	109	1/98	43,600	250
St. Lucia	325	1/98	145,000	225
St. Vincent and Grenadines	420	1/98	111,000	380
Trinidad and Tobago	4,715	30/4/98	1.3m	365
Aruba (Netherlands)	223	11/98	89,000	250
Cayman Islands (UK)	210	97	36,600	575
Guadeloupe (France)	706	1/10/98	444,000	160
Martinique (France)	547	1/10/98	392,000	140
Neth. Antilles (Netherlands)	780	11/98	213,000	365
Puerto Rico (U.S.)	14,971	1/10/98	3.8m	395
Virgin Islands (U.S.)	417	31/12/97	117,000	355
South America				
Argentina	43,174	31/12/96	35.35m	120
Bolivia	5,412	31/12/96	7.7m	70
Brazil	167,066	31/12/97	157.1m	105
Chile	27,000	31/12/98	14.8m	c.180

Americas (continued)	Total in Penal Institutions (including pretrial detainees)	Date	Estimated National Population	Prison Population Rate (per 100,000 population)
Colombia	43,000	98	37.7m	115
Ecuador	9,961	31/12/96	11.8m	85
Guyana	1,697	1/98	852,000	200
Paraguay	3,097	31/12/96	5.1m	60
Peru	20,899	95	23.8m	90
Suriname	560	1/98	440,000	125
Uruguay	3,190	95	3.2m	100
Venezuela	25,000	98	23.2m	110
French Guiana/Guyane (France)	3,471	10/98	144,000	240
Asia[d]				
Western Asia				
Israel	10,148	1/1/94	5.4m	190
Jordan	3,749	31/12/93	5.1m	75
Kuwait	1,735	97	1.7m	100
Lebanon	5,000	97	3.1m	160
Qatar	527	31/12/93	540,000	100
Saudi Arabia	7,939[e]	31/12/93	17.2m	45[e]
Syria	14,000	97	15.0m	95
United Arab Emirates[f]				
Yemen	14,000[g]	98	16.9m	95[g]
Central Asia				
Kazakhstan	82,945	1/5/97	16.8m	495
Kyrgyzstan	19,857	1/5/97	4.5m	440
Tajikistan	c.6,000	96	6.3m	c.95
Turkmenistan	c.18,000	98	4.5m	c.400
Uzbekistan	c.60,000	96	23.3m	c.260
South Central Asia				
Bangladesh	44,111	95	120.4m	35
India	231,325	97	960.2m	25
Iran	101,801	31/12/93	65.0m	155
Nepal	6,200	94	21.35m	30
Pakistan	72,700	96	144.5m	50
Sri Lanka	14,090	97	18.3m	75
South Eastern Asia				
Brunei Darussalam	285	29/10/98	313,000	90
Cambodia	2,909	97	10.5m	30
Indonesia	41,699	97	203.5m	20
Malaysia	24,400	12/97	21.2m	115
Myanmar (Burma)	53,195	31/12/93	45.0m	120

continued on following page

Table 10.4 continued

Asia[d] (continued)	Total in Penal Institutions (including pretrial detainees)	Date	Estimated National Population	Prison Population Rate (per 100,000 population)
South Eastern Asia				
Philippines}	35,864	31/12/93	65.5m	55
Philippines}	19,541[h]	97	70.7m	30[h]
Singapore	15,746[i]	97	3.4m	465[i]
Thailand	130,997	30/9/97	59.3m	220
Vietnam	43,000	96	76.2m	55
Eastern Asia				
China	1,410,000	97	1,243.7m	115
Japan	49,414	97	125.6m	40
Korea (Republic of)	70,303	30/6/98	46.1m	155
Mongolia	6,085	31/12/93	2.3m	265
Taiwan	c.31,000	98	20.5m	c.150
Hong Kong (UK)[j]	11,637	97	6.2m	190
Macau (Portugal)	642	97	415,000	155
Europe[k]				
Northern Europe				
Denmark	3,508	6/11/98	5.3m	65
Estonia	4,647	1/7/98	1.45m	320
Finland	2,798	1/9/97	5.1m	55
Iceland	113	1/9/95	270,000	40
Ireland	2,424	1/9/97	3.6m	65
Latvia	10,070	31/12/97	2.45m	410
Lithuana	13,205	1/9/97	3.7m	355
Norway	2,318	1/9/97	4.4m	55
Sweden	5,221	1/9/97	8.85m	60
United Kingdom	(73,545)	(30/9/98)	(59.2m)	(125)
England and Wales	65,906	30/9/98	52.4m	125
Scotland	6,098	30/9/98	5.1m	120
Northern Ireland	1,541	30/9/98	1.7m	90
Guernsey (UK)	64	16/10/98	59,500	110
Jersey (UK)	108	16/10/98	86,500	125
Isle of Man (UK)	82	16/10/98	72,500	115
Southern Europe				
Albania	1,077	1/6/94	3.4m	30
Bosnia and Herzegovina (Federation)	769[l]	31/1/98	2.5m[l]	30
Croatia	2,119	31/12/97	4.5m	45
Greece	5,577	1/9/97	10.5m	55
Italy	49,477	1/9/97	57.5m	85

Europe (continued)	Total in Penal Institutions (including pretrial detainees)	Date	Estimated National Population	Prison Population Rate (per 100,000 population)
Southern Europe				
Macedonia	965	1/9/97	2.0m	50
Malta	190	1/9/96	374,000	50
Portugal	14,336	15/3/98	9.8m	145
San Marino[m]				
Slovenia	752	31/12/97	1.9m	40
Spain	42,827	1/9/97	39.7m	110
Gibraltar (UK)	34	16/10/98	27,000	125
Western Europe				
Austria	6,946	1/9/97	8.1m	85
Belgium	8,342	1/9/97	10.2m	80
France	53,259[n]	1/10/98	58.7m	90
Germany	74,317	1/9/97	82.2m	90
Liechtenstein	18	22/5/94	30,000	60
Luxembourg	431	1/9/96	418,000	105
Monaco[o]				
Netherlands	13,618	1/9/97	15.65m	85
Switzerland	6,259	97	7.1m	90
Europe/Asia				
Armenia	7,608	2/98	3.8m	200
Azerbaijan	24,881	2/7/97	7.7m	325
Cyprus	235[p]	1/9/96	640,000[p]	35
Georgia	7,900	5/97	5.4m	145
Russian Federation	1,009,863	1/1/98	147.0m	685
Turkey	59,275	1/9/97	63.5m	95
Central and Eastern Europe				
Bulgaria	11,814	1/7/98	8.3m	140
Belarus	52,033	31/12/95	10.3m	505
Czech Republic	22,138	22/10/98	10.3m	215
Hungary	13,405	31/12/97	10.1m	135
Moldova	9,812[q]	1/10/96	3.75m[q]	260
Poland	56,596	31/10/98	38.7m	145
Romania	45,121	31/12/97	22.5m	200
Slovakia	7,511	14/1/98	5.4m	140
Ukraine	211,568	1/1/98	51.2m	415
Oceania[r]				
Australia	17,661[s]	97	18.2m	95
Fiji	1,091	97	773,000	140
Kiribati	91	95	70,000	130

continued on following page

Table 10.4 continued

Oceania[r] (continued)	Total in Penal Institutions (including pretrial detainees)	Date	Estimated National Population	Prison Population Rate (per 100,000 population)
Marshall Is.	23	94	52,000	45
New Zealand	5,236	97	3.65m	145
Papua New Guinea	3,728	96	3.75m	100
Solomon Is.	147	97	380,000	40
Tonga	87	94	100,000	85
Vanuatu	89	95	164,000	55
Western Samoa	255	95	165,000	155
American Samoa (U.S.)	102	31/12/97	60,500	170
Cook Is. (NZ)	45	95	20,000	225
French Polynesia (France)	280	1/10/98	220,000	125
Guam (U.S.)	464	31/12/97	146,000	320
New Caledonia (France)	303	1/10/98	197,000	155
Northern Mariana Is. (U.S.)	63	31/12/97	63,500	100

[a]For a complete list of sources of data for each country, see Walmsley, 1999.

[b]No information: N. Africa: Libya; W. Africa: Benin, Gambia, Guinea Bissau, Liberia, Niger, Sierra Leone; C. Africa: Angola, Central African Republic, Congo (Brazzaville), Congo (Kinshasa), Equatorial Guinea, Gabon; E. Africa: Comoros, Eritrea, Ethiopia, Seychelles, Somalia; S. Africa: Botswana.

[c]Some 130,000 people are believed to be held in penal institutions in Rwanda following the genocide in that country, which has created a unique set of circumstances.

[d]No information: W. Asia: Bahrain, Iraq, Oman; S. Central Asia: Afghanistan, Bhutan, Maldive Islands; S. E. Asia: Laos; E. Asia: Korea (Democratic Peoples Republic of North Korea).

[e]Sentenced prisoners only.

[f]Two sources give widely discrepant figures.

[g]Government-managed prisons only.

[h]Does not include those in municipal and provincial prisons.

[i]Almost half of this total are persons held in drug rehabilitation centers.

[j]UK dependency until 30/6/97 when it became a "Special Administrative Region" within China.

[k]No information: S. Europe: Andorra, Yugoslavia.

[l]Excludes Bosnia and Herzegovina (Republika Srpska) with an estimated population of 1.4m.

[m]By agreement with the Italian government, institutions in Italy are used to hold persons imprisoned by San Marino.

[n]Includes 3,202 in penal institutions in French departments and territories in Eastern Africa, the Caribbean and Oceania (figures shown in those sections).

[o]Monaco has one penal institution, for pretrial and short-sentence prisoners only. It held 13 people in 10/98.

[p]Excludes the internationally unrecognised Turkish Republic of Northern Cyprus (TRNC). Including TRNC, the population of Cyprus is believed to have been about 840,000 at the end of 1996, but other sources give a total of about 750,000.

[q]Excludes the internationally unrecognised Transdniestria. Including Transdniestria, the estimated national population of Moldova was 4.4m in mid-1996.

[r]No information: Micronesia (Federated States), Nauru, Palau, Tuvalu.

[s]Average daily population, 1997.

SOURCE: R. Walmsley, World Prison Population List, Research Findings, No. 88, 1999. Adapted with permission.

How does the United States fare in terms of its incarceration rates compared to other countries? Not well. As mentioned previously, the United States has the highest total prison population and the second highest incarceration rate, surpassed only by Russia. However, James Lynch argues that the United States is less punitive in comparison with other Western democracies when the types of crimes are accounted for in the incarceration rates (Lynch, 1993). Lynch reexamined the contention that the United States is the most punitive of the industrialized democracies. He found that time served in prison in the United States is longer than that served in Australia and in England and Wales for similar offenses, except for homicide. The differences between the United States and Canada are also minimal for violent offenses. Lynch points out that Germany gives longer sentences than the United States for both violent crimes and property crimes. However, offenders serve longer sentences for property crimes in the United States than in Australia, Canada, or England (Lynch, 1993, p. 657). Studies of this kind further illustrate the complexity of comparing imprisonment rates across national boundaries and highlight the importance of improved research methodologies.

At this point, it might be interesting to compare the results of the "World Prison Population List" with another data set to find out if the rates in individual countries changed in the mid-1990s. Swiss professor of penology Andre Kuhn has published a partial list of imprisonment rates using a variety of sources that we can utilize for comparison purposes; Table 10.5 gives his findings. Compare the rates of incarceration of different countries to the data in Table 10.4 to determine if any changes are discernible. One example of a considerable increase from 1994 to 1997 would be the United States, which increased its prison population from 574 to 645 per 100,000 population.

There are many theories as to why prison populations have soared recently throughout the world. The most common is that the increase in prison populations is directly related to the increase in the crime rate. However, there is little data to support this assertion. In fact, many researchers have presented evidence that there is little or no relationship between incarceration rates and crime rates (Young and Brown, 1993). More recent data presented in the Fifth UNCJS affirm the contention that sentencing is not significantly related to the crime rate (*Global Report,* 1999, p. 91). Kuhn claims that many countries have adopted criminal justice policies that promote longer sentences, which directly creates

prison population growth. He suggests strategies that would decrease sentence length, such as increased use of parole, use of partially suspended sentences, changes in judges' attitudes and shorter sentences (Kuhn, 1994). Roy Walmsley, in his study of prison populations in eastern and central Europe, offers three reasons there are so many people in prison: (1) laws mandating that certain crimes must be punished by a certain minimum sentence and that recidivists must receive longer sentences than others, (2) the length of sentences, and (3) the limited availability of alternatives to incarceration (Walmsley, 1996).

As with international crime data, there are a number of pitfalls to comparing international prison data. As we noted in Chapter 2, one of the weaknesses of international crime data is that many countries fail to report or underreport their crime data. The same can be said for international prison data. Despite the best attempts by private researchers and international organizations to collect this data, many countries simply fail to respond truthfully or competently to inquiries about prison populations.

Prison data also suffer from a form of nonstandardization when it comes to definitions. The definitional problems involve what counts as a prison and who counts as a prisoner. Some countries include all correctional facilities in the statistics, while others exclude certain types of institutions such as remand facilities (jails) and even special work camps. When counting inmates, some countries may not feel it necessary to include inmates who have yet to be tried. Others may exclude certain groups of inmates because they are "mentally ill." For example, in the Netherlands, those convicted of murder or rape are sent to special mental hospitals run by health authorities (Stern, 1998).

Another larger methodological problem with incarceration figures is that they do not account for sentence length. Rates of incarceration are naturally tied to sentence length, since longer sentences tend to increase the rate at any one time (Kuhn, 1996; Young and Brown, 1993). The United States, for example, with longer sentences

Table 10.5 Incarceration Rates per 100,000 Inhabitants, 1993–1995

Country	Year	Incarceration per 100,000 Inhabitants	Country	Year	Incarceration per 100,000 Inhabitants
Albania	1994	30.0	Luxembourg	1994	109.0
Australia	1994	89.3	Macao	1995	107.1
Austria	1994	85.0	Malaysia	1995	104.2
Bangladesh	1995	37.1	Mexico	1993	97.0
Belarus	1994	445.0	Moldova	1994	275.0
Belgium	1994	64.8	Nepal	1994	33.5
Brazil	1993	84.0	Netherlands	1994	55.0
Brunei Darussalam	1995	109.7	New Zealand	1995	126.8
Bulgaria	1994	95.0	Northern Ireland	1994	117.0
Cambodia	1995	26.0	Norway	1994	62.0
Canada	1994	114.0	Papua New Guinea	1994	106.9
China	1995	103.0	Peru	1993	91.0
Cook Islands	1995	225.0	Philippines	1995	26.2
Croatia	1994	60.0	Poland	1994	162.6
Cyprus	1994	24.7	Portugal	1994	101.0
Czech Republic	1994	181.6	Rumania	1994	195.0
Denmark	1994	72.0	Russia	1993	558.0
Egypt	1993	62.0	Scotland	1994	109.0
England and Wales	1994	96.0	Singapore	1995	287.3
Estonia	1994	270.0	Slovakia	1994	139.0
Fiji	1995	122.7	Slovenia	1994	40.0
Finland	1994	59.0	Solomon Islands	1995	45.5
France	1994	90.3	South Korea	1995	137.3
Germany	1994	83.0	South Africa	1993	368.0
Greece	1994	71.0	Spain	1994	105.9
Hong Kong	1995	207.2	Sri Lanka	1994	68.1
Hungary	1994	128.1	Sweden	1994	66.0
Iceland	1994	38.2	Switzerland	1993	89.4
India	1995	23.5	Thailand	1995	180.5
Indonesia	1993	21.7	Tonga	1994	87.0
Ireland	1994	58.6	Turkey	1994	72.4
Italy	1994	89.7	USA	1994	574.0
Japan	1995	37.2	Ukraine	1994	345.0
Kiribati	1995	130.0	Vanuatu	1994	72.7
Latvia	1994	365.0	Western Samoa	1994	146.3
Lithuania	1994	342.0			

SOURCE: Adapted with permission from Kuhn, 1996. From *European Journal on Criminal Policy and Research* 4:3, p. 47, Kluwer Academic Publishers.

than other countries, will tend to have a higher rate of imprisonment.

Length of sentence is an issue that concerns both the public and correctional policymakers. The clearance rates for many crimes, especially burglary, are generally less than 40 percent, which makes certainty of punishment a deterrence goal that is not easily obtained. Faced with that fact, many individuals would like to increase the deterrence value of prison by increasing the length of prison sentences. This is true in most countries today, as people are increasingly concerned about high crime rates. What constitutes longer sentences is a relative matter, however. At the same time that western European corrections experts have asserted the uselessness of short-term sentences and called for the use of alternatives to these sentences, American prison reformers are looking to European nations as models for short-term sentences and enlightened prison administration. Compared to the long prison sentences often given out in the United States, most nations, including Japan, sentence offenders to relatively short periods of incarceration. In Switzerland, for example, incarceration is divided into three categories: (1) confinement (one to twenty years), (2) prison (three days to three years), and (3) detention (one day to three months). Detention is designed for misdemeanor crimes, but prison sentences even for felonies are extremely short by American standards. The same is true in England, where the maximum nonlife sentence is fourteen years, although sentences have actually been increasing in recent years. Normal sentences range from two years (assault on a police officer, causing bodily harm by furious driving) to five years (wounding or inflicting grievous bodily harm, certain kinds of sexual offenses with minors) (McClean, 1981).

Most Western governments, faced with seemingly intractable crime problems, have been under political pressure to increase sentence lengths. As a result, lengths of sentences and incarceration rates have gone up in recent years even in most western European countries. Compared to the United States, however, these nations still have substantially lower rates of incarceration and shorter sentence lengths.

The incarceration figures also suffer from the fact that the arrest process differs substantially in the countries compared, and it is difficult to give completely analogous definitions. The data serve as a reminder once again that even simple comparisons among countries with respect to some facet of the criminal justice process need to be scrutinized very closely. As with the even more problematic comparative crime rates, careful evaluations of multiple indicators of the extent of the phenomenon are preferable to unidimensional comparisons.

Many researchers have presented possible ways to improve methods of collection and presentation of international prison data. As we have already mentioned, one option is the use of stock designs and flow designs to measure the number of prison admissions over time. Ken Rahim (1986) proposes that the incarceration rate should be determined by dividing the number of persons sentenced to prison by the number convicted during that same year. Finally, Buck and Pease (1993) suggest that we should compare the prison population to the number of prosecutions in the country. Each of these methods might bring us closer to a more precise understanding of international incarceration rates.

Commitment to Mental Hospitals

The issue of accountability for crimes committed was dramatized in the United States when John Hinckley, who attempted to assassinate President Reagan in 1981, was found not guilty by reason of insanity. Hinckley was forcibly committed to a mental hospital, where he will remain until his mental health can be certified by physicians. An earlier assassin, Charles Guiteau, whose attack on President Garfield in 1881 led to the president's death, was by all accounts seriously mentally ill, and indeed the question of his sanity was the focus of his trial. Nevertheless, he was convicted and hanged (Rosenberg, 1968).

These cases exemplify some of the difficulties involved in dealing with certain kinds of offenders and finding appropriate sanctions in their cases. They also exemplify the increasing importance of technical experts, in this case psychiatrists, in developing appropriate outcomes for criminal cases. An important early-nineteenth-century case that documents the growing influence of doctors as opposed to lawyers in the criminal process is that of Pierre Riviere, whose memoirs and case dossier were studied by Michel Foucault and his associates (1975). In that case, Riviere, a peasant youth, killed his mother, brother, and sister with an agricultural tool, imagining that he was doing this to help his father. His generally bizarre behavior throughout his childhood cast serious doubts on his mental health. Although Riviere was sentenced to death, his sentence was finally commuted to life imprisonment as a result of the petition of a group of physicians who maintained that he was not responsible for his actions because of his insanity.

Riviere's case exemplifies consideration of mental illness as a factor in sentencing. Formal recognition of insanity as a defense at trial has been in use in England and the United States at least since 1843, when the famous M'Naughton Rule was established. This rule states that if the accused was incapable of understanding the nature of the act committed at the time it was committed, he or she cannot be held responsible for it. As can be imagined, this rule often raises more questions than it answers about the trial of any particular individual.

The problem with the insanity defense in many cases is that there is so little agreement among experts in psychiatry about the particulars of mental illness and about diagnosis of mental illness. Also, the defendant who is found not guilty by reason of insanity often faces many years of incarceration in a mental hospital, where conditions may be similar to prison, without having a clear limit on his or her term of deprivation of liberty. The further problem of leaving the ultimate judgment about the mental health of a defendant to a jury makes this a fringe area of the criminal process, one in which there seems to be no clear method of achieving justice.

The practice of committing political dissidents to mental hospitals without trial represents a different use of mental hospitals as substitutes for prison. This practice ensures incapacitation of the dissident without risking the publicity or vagaries of the criminal process. Many people believe that this was the fate of Ezra Pound, one of America's premier poets, who supported Fascist Italy in broadcasts from that country during World War II and who thus could have been tried for treason at the end of the war. Instead, he was declared insane and spent many years in St. Elizabeth's Hospital for the mentally ill in Washington, D.C., before he was released and allowed to return to Italy.

The Pound case suggests that political commitment to mental hospitals is possible even in a democratic society. The extensive use of commitment as a substitute for trial and imprisonment was notorious in the former Soviet Union, where large numbers of political dissidents were committed to mental hospitals and forced to undergo painful and debilitating "treatments" that amounted to torture in most cases. This practice was started in the Khrushchev regime in the 1950s, when the Stalinist campaign of terror had been repudiated but political dissidence was still vigorously suppressed. Soviet psychiatrists were implicated in this practice and were excluded for years from international psychiatric associations because of it. The Soviets themselves estimate that mistaken diagnoses occurred in 500–600 cases of political dissidents.

Under Gorbachev, there was some reform in this area in the 1980s. Many of the dissidents who were diagnosed with "creeping schizophrenia" have been released, and the Soviet state renounced its use of this substitute for legal process. The Supreme Soviet passed a law in January 1988 forbidding psychiatric commitment merely for "slandering the state" and restricting its use in cases of anti-Soviet propaganda.

The use of mental hospitals as a means of punishing individuals who have not been tried and sentenced is a deviant practice in the history of criminal process, just as conventional imprisonment without accusation or trial is a deviant practice. However, the fact that commitment is practiced within the umbrella concept of modern medical science makes it particularly troubling. In such cases, ordinary citizens, who otherwise might be closely involved in, or informed about, criminal justice matters, must give way to experts who often act with little accountability to anyone other than their professional peers.

THE DEATH PENALTY

The penalty of death has been a sentencing option since the beginning of civilization. In biblical times, criminals were stoned to death and their bodies hung up as an act of deterrence. Ancient Athenian society restricted the use of the death penalty and actually "humanized" the process by allowing the condemned to drink poison. The Romans used many forms of execution, including burning, stoning, strangulation, drawing and quartering, crucifixion, and, famously, being thrown to the lions. In medieval times, executions were conducted through the use of ordeals, in the belief that God would protect the innocent from extreme physical harm while permitting the guilty to succumb (Johnson, 1988). Hanging, shooting, electrocution, and lethal injection remain the major forms of execution throughout the world although some countries (primarily Islamic nations) still resort to more ancient methods like stoning and crucifixion.

According to the human rights organization Amnesty International, 2,258 persons were officially reported executed in thirty-seven countries and another 4,845 sentenced to death in 1998. The actual number of executions throughout the world is very difficult to determine since some countries do not publish these figures, and others do not give accurate figures. Amnesty International reports that, in 1998, 1,700 executions took place in China, over 100 in the Democratic Republic of Congo, 68 in the United States, and 66 in Iran. Amnesty International has also received unconfirmed reports of hundreds of executions in Iraq (Amnesty International Website, 1999). Other sources indicate that Saudi Arabia is also a world leader in executions with at least 87 in 1999 (*Guardian,* 1999).

According to a 1996 United Nations report, 90 countries retain capital punishment on their statutes, 58 have abolished it, and 14 have abolished it for ordinary crimes. Of the 90 that retain the sanction, 30 have not executed anyone over the last ten years (United Nations, 1996). According to an Amnesty International report, the trend in 1999 was toward an increase in worldwide abolition. The report states that 90 countries have retained the death penalty, 70 have abolished it for all crimes, 13 have abolished it for ordinary crimes, and 23 have exercised de facto abolition—meaning they no longer implement the death penalty in practice although it still exists in the law. Of the 90 countries that retain the death penalty, a lesser number (78) sentenced 3,899 offenders to death in 1998 (Amnesty International Website, 1999).

This means that by the end of 1998 about half of all nations in the world had outlawed the death penalty by law or in practice. In some countries, the possibility of this sentence remains for nonordinary crimes such as crimes in wartime and crimes against humanity. One of the most significant steps was taken by South Africa, which in 1995 scrapped the death penalty. This was significant because prior to abolition, during apartheid, South Africa had carried out hundreds of executions a year. Even some countries with dictatorial governments, such as Libya, have chosen to abolish the death penalty. In 1998, the Libyan People's Congress amended the constitution to outlaw the death penalty, and President Quaddafi thereupon decreed that life imprisonment be substituted for all pending executions (Amnesty International, 1989, p. 31). Among Middle Eastern nations, Israel also does not have the death penalty; the last person executed in that country was the Nazi war criminal Adolf Eichmann, in 1962.

No country in western Europe continues to execute offenders although the death penalty has not been abolished officially in all these countries. Switzerland abolished the death penalty in 1879, restored it in a limited form in 1897, and abolished it again in 1942. Italy abolished the death penalty in 1890, restored it in 1931, and again abolished it in 1944. The last execution for a nonmilitary crime in Italy, however, took place in 1876. France, which since revolutionary times had used the guillotine, abandoned the death penalty in 1981 when the new Socialist government pushed through a law abolishing it (Zimring and Hawkins, 1986). Belgium abolished executions in 1996, and the eastern European nation of Russia has been under serious pressure since joining the Council of Europe to introduce a moratorium on the death penalty (Stern, 1998).

Abolition of the death penalty has also become an important issue for international bodies. The Sixth Protocol to the European Convention on Human Rights abolished the death penalty except in time of war or imminent threat of war, thus reflecting the reality that exists in the European nations. As of 1999, thirty-three European nations had ratified this covenant (Amnesty International Website, 1999). The UN High Commissioner for Human Rights in December 1989 proclaimed in a General Assembly resolution that there should be an "international commitment to abolish the death penalty" and that the abolition of the death penalty would "contribute to enhancement of human dignity and progressive development of human rights" (UN Human Rights Website, 1999).

Criminologists Franklin Zimring and Gordon Hawkins (1986, p. 8) assert that the declining use of executions in some countries is part of a "long-term evolutionary process—the development process of civilization, in fact." Statutory abolition, they tell us, was preceded in each case by long periods in which no one was executed in normal times; in other words, de facto abolition preceded de jure abolition, as Table 10.6 shows. Statutory abolition occurred in these countries

Table 10.6 Year of Last Execution Versus Abolition of Capital Punishment[a]

Country	Year of Last Execution for Civil Crime	Formal Abolition
Netherlands	1860	1870
Belgium[b]	1863	1996
Norway	1875	1905
Italy[c]	1876	1890
Denmark	1892	1930
Sweden	1910	1921
Queensland, Australia	1911	1921
Switzerland[d]	1924	1942
New Zealand[e]	1935	1941

[a]This table excludes executions of collaborators after World War II.

[b]Except for the execution of a soldier in a civil offense in 1918.

[c]Restored in 1931 and again abolished in 1944.

[d]Previously abolished in 1874 with limited restoration in 1879.

[e]Restored in 1950 and again abolished in 1962.

SOURCE: *Royal Commission on Capital Punishment 1949–1953,* Report 340, App. 6 (1953). As printed in Zimring and Hawkins, *Capital Punishment and the American Agenda,* 1986, p. 10. Copyright © 1986 by Cambridge University Press. Reprinted with permission.

despite public opinion in favor of continuing the death penalty.

One may well ask, in the face of these facts, why the United States and Japan, two of the most powerful modern nations in the world, continue to execute offenders. Various opinions exist concerning this phenomenon. Japan entered the company of democratic nations late in its history, according to some, and has not yet achieved the maturity in its criminal process that abolition would signify. The United States, on the other hand, has a history of violence, as reflected in the widespread possession and use of firearms, lynchings, and government-sanctioned brutality in the case of the institution of slavery. Thus, there is greater tolerance for violence, including execution of convicted murderers, and executions serve a ritualistic function that responds to the cultural reality in the country.

Japan does not execute offenders with any degree of haste or enthusiasm. The two Japanese who were executed in 1988 were sentenced to death thirteen and ten years earlier. The Japanese executed no one from 1990 through 1993, and since 1993 less than ten people have been executed. The United States, by contrast, has ignored the international trend away from the death penalty. In 1983, only five people were executed in the United States, but the number climbed to seventy-four in 1997 (Bureau of Justice Statistics, 1998; Human Rights Watch, 1998).

One matter regarding the use of the death penalty that deserves some attention is the way the penalty is carried out. Both historical tradition and technological developments seem to play a role. In earlier times, the goal was to make executions as painful, public, and humiliating as possible. Crucifixions in Rome were just one example of this. The guillotine, so much used during the Reign of Terror following the French Revolution, was supposed to be a more humane form of execution in that it was swift and sure. The electric chair and the gas chamber were "reforms" that came about as a result of new technology. In today's medically oriented society, lethal injection has become the mode of choice for executions in eleven of the thirty-nine American states with the death penalty. The trend toward lethal injections has been bolstered by the case of Florida murderer Anthony Bryan. After the news of a second "botched" execution using the electric chair in Florida, Bryan persuaded the court to postpone his execution and to examine whether electrocution is unconstitutionally cruel. The case will be heard in the year 2000 (Mauro, 1999). Under Islamic Law, the method of execution is prescribed in the Qur'an and depends on the crime and the criminal. The usual penalty for adultery is stoning to death. Most executions in Saudi Arabia, however, are by beheading and are conducted in public. In most countries today, executions are conducted in private within prisons. In China, the method of execution is the firing squad.

The crimes for which one can be executed and the age and mental state of the convicted have narrowed considerably in those countries that still carry out executions. In the past, minor thefts could result in deaths in England, and even children occasionally were executed. As late as the 1970s, rape and even first-degree burglary were still punishable by death in certain states of the United States. Recently, the Supreme Court has upheld laws that allowed people who are mildly retarded and people as young as 16 years old to be executed for their crimes. In fact, the United States is one of six countries that will execute people for acts committed before the age of 18. The others are Iran, Nigeria, Pakistan, Saudi Arabia, and Yemen (Human Rights Watch, 1998)

PUBLIC OPINION AND SENTENCING

In most nations, public opinion with respect to crime and criminals tends to be punitive. There is a general belief that severe sanctions will deter crime and that rising crime rates call for more severe sanctions. And this belief persists even though there is little evidence to support it in democratic societies, which place definite limits on the degree of punishment that can be imposed and the degree of surveillance over the population that can be exercised. With the rise in crime rates in recent decades throughout most of the industrialized world, crime has become a political issue that frequently outranks problems related to the economy or to military threats.

In the United States, surveys of public opinion regarding major social problems have included crime among the top problems for many years. In Great Britain, the Gallup organization has been assessing opinion about social problems since 1944. When asked what the most urgent public problem in the country was, "law and order" was listed by less than 1 percent of the population from 1944 to 1973. Starting in 1973, however, this problem was listed with increasing frequency, rising as high as second (after unemployment) in

1985. This finding must be tempered by the fact that it depends to some degree on the way questions are phrased. In British Gallup polls, as in the United States, the salience of the crime problem was affected by whether the respondents were given a list of problems from which to choose or if they were asked to name the most serious problems without a prompting list. In the former case, law and order were often at the top or near the top; when respondents had to come up with their own list, other social problems tended to dominate (Walker and Hough, 1988).

Public attitudes are important in affecting political decision making in democratic societies. Too often, however, we lack studies that measure finer points of public opinion about sentencing and corrections. Nevertheless, some studies that shed light on this matter have been done in Western nations. In one study of the issue of whether severity of sentence may actually influence public opinion about the severity of particular crimes, no correlation was found between these variables (Walker and Hough, 1988, ch. 3). In Holland, researchers found that punitiveness, or belief in more severe sanctions, was not correlated with personal experiences of victimization or other personal contact with crime. A Canadian study yielded similar results. In this study, punitiveness had its highest correlation with higher income, older age, rural residence, and smaller degree of education. There appeared to be no correlation between punitiveness and either sex, prior victimization, or even fear of crime (Walker and Hough, 1988). More recent research confirms this finding. In an analysis of the 1989 International Criminal Victimization Surveys, it was determined that those who have been victimized show no substantial differences in sentencing preferences (Kuhn, 1992).

Another Canadian study found that public attitudes about sentencing became more "complex as knowledge increased." In Canada, the researchers note, "since 1969 a majority has always thought that sentences were too lenient" (Walker and Hough, 1988, p. 131). But they go on to elaborate:

This simple view, however, does not do justice to the public's actual views. . . . Not only are these views based on inadequate information, but the public is, in fact, much more tolerant of leniency in sentencing (especially of nonviolent offenders) than this simple view would suggest. One-dimensional questions give one-dimensional answers. . . . When asked simple questions about sentencing, especially the sentencing of violent offenders, Canadians seem to react with severity. When asked in a more appropriate way and when provided with more adequate information, it appears that Canadians respond in quite a sensitive manner.

A study in England also suggests that public opinions tend to become more complex when greater knowledge of the actual situation exists. This study found as well that, despite the media's and politicians' claims to the contrary, in England there was not a great deal of dissatisfaction with sentence severity (Walker and Hough, 1988, ch. 7).

One important series of studies that has shed some light on sentencing preferences was jointly conducted by the Ministry of Justice of the Netherlands, the UK Home Office, and UNICRI. The study involved interviewing 130,000 people in some sixty countries about their victimization experiences and about their preferred sentence for a 21-year-old repeat burglar. Forty percent of the respondents chose imprisonment as the most appropriate sentence for the burglar. However, some interesting regional differences surfaced in the data. Over three-quarters of the respondents from Asia and Africa opted for imprisonment. Slightly over half of respondents from North America and Latin America and around one-fourth of Western Europeans favored imprisonment. The next most desired sanction was community service. Half of Western Europeans wanted this sanction while only one-third of Latin Americans and only 10 percent of Asians preferred community service (Zvekic, 1997). Among the conclusions reached from this research were that, except in Asia, support for imprisonment is highest in countries where crime is highest. Further, in countries where noncustodial sanctions are less available, there was less desire to choose them. Finally, the results were in agreement with earlier research (Kuhn, 1992) stating that imprisonment preferences have little to do with personal victimization (Shinkai and Zvekic, 1999).

These various studies suggest that presumed public support for greater punitiveness may be misleading, at least in the areas included. A general question about whether sentences are severe enough usually finds a large majority that wants tougher sentences. This opinion seems to be based on attitudes toward violent and career criminals. Faced with the facts of particular cases, however, people modify their attitudes considerably and present a more complex and multidimensional approach to the matter of appropriateness of sentence. On a more general level, these studies suggest that attitudes toward sentencing are a function of ideology and worldview rather than actual or potential victimization.

Unfortunately, empirical studies of sentencing are all too scarce in most countries, and attitude surveys are particularly rare in societies that have not progressed very far in sophisticated social science or criminological research. In authoritarian societies, especially, in which public opinion does not affect the power structure as immediately as in democratic societies, we have little knowledge about public attitudes toward sentencing practices. In Saudi Arabia or Iran, for example, we do not know if the people support the severe corporal punishments that are typical in the criminal process or if there is some support for a more varied system of punishments.

SUMMARY

It is often said that a society may be judged by its treatment of those who are at the margin. What is generally meant by those at the margin is those who are somehow less able to compete in the conventional life of the society: children, the sick, the aged, the handicapped, and the poor. The criminal process in general and criminal sentences in particular are another gauge by which we measure a society. There is no doubt that many nations have come a long way from the cruel practices that constituted sanctions in earlier centuries. Ideas about human rights, including rights of the convicted, although certainly not honored universally, have achieved a kind of legitimacy through efforts of international organizations and a gradually developing international standard.

Broadly speaking, criminal sanctions have moved over the past 200 years from primary reliance on corporal punishment and transportation, to heavy reliance on conventional imprisonment, to the development of alternative sanctions. The most common of these include probation, fines, day fines, restitution, and community service. The day fine is an innovation designed to deal with the problem of inequity between rich and poor by gearing the fine not only to the crime but also to the capacity of the offender to pay.

Corporal punishment, especially the death penalty, is still widely used, however. In the countries that adhere to the Islamic Law, corporal punishments are preferred to imprisonment, and indeed in these societies imprisonment is a last resort for truly intractable offenders. Although the death penalty has virtually been abolished in western Europe and Latin America, it is still practiced in most other parts of the world, albeit usually on a very limited scale. In the United States, the use of the death penalty has increased dramatically over the past fifteen years. Clauses in some international human rights conventions have outlawed capital punishment.

The philosophy of sentencing also has undergone changes in the past 200 years. In the nineteenth century, the classical school of criminologists spearheaded the move toward rational sentencing linked to the severity of the crime. In the early twentieth century, under the influence of Progressive Movement reformers and with the United States in the lead, the philosophy of sentencing became increasingly rehabilitative. However, over the past thirty years, there has been a backlash against the rehabilitative philosophy, again with the United States in the lead.

The philosophy of sentencing in Socialist countries has always emphasized rehabilitation and the creation of a new Socialist individual who would not commit crimes in a society where class oppression has been eliminated. The practice in these countries has not honored this philosophy, however, and their sanctions systems, at least in China, are characterized by the use of oppressive labor camps in which criminal offenders are mixed with large numbers of political dissidents.

Philosophy of sentencing and sentencing practice are important indicators of the mood of a country and its stage of development. The most troublesome aspect of corrections in many countries, however, remains the administration of actual imprisonment as a form of punishment. This is the topic we will consider in the next chapter.

DISCUSSION QUESTIONS AND EXERCISES

1. Which purpose of criminal sanctioning seems to be predominant in the world today?

2. How do day fines differ from fines typically used in criminal justice sanctioning? Are they a useful alternative?

3. Would exile to Alaska be a better way than prison to handle serious offenders in the United States? What problems would this policy encounter?

4. Why do the United States and Japan continue to use the death penalty when most industrial nations have outlawed it?

5. Search the Internet for an restorative justice program in the United States and a foreign country. Compare the purposes and methods of the two programs.

6. What are the economic benefits of the increased use of incarceration? Do nations today continue to use imprisonment as a tool for increasing national wealth?

FOR FURTHER READING

Bohm, R. M. (1991). *The Death Penalty in America: Current Research.* Cincinnati: Anderson.

Foucault, M. (1977). *Discipline and Punish: The Birth of a Prison.* New York: Pantheon Books.

Garland, D. (1990). *Punishment and Modern Society.* Oxford: Clarendon.

Hamai, K., R. Ville, R. Harris, M. Hough, and U. Zvekic (eds.). (1995). *Probation Around the World: A Comparative Study.* London: Routledge.

Lippman, M., S. McConville, and M. Yerushalmi. (1988). *Islamic Criminal Law and Procedure.* New York: Praeger.

Rusche, G., and O. Kirchheimer. (1939). *Punishment and Social Structure.* New York: Russell and Russell.

Stern, V. (1998). *A Sin Against the Future: Imprisonment in the World.* Boston: Northeastern University Press.

Van Ness, D. W., and K. Heetderks-Strong. (1997). *Restorative Justice.* Cincinnati: Anderson.

Walker, N., and J. Hough (eds.). (1988). *Public Attitudes to Sentencing.* Brookfield, Vt.: Gower.

11 After Conviction: The Problem of Prison

The Evolution of Prison Systems
Penal Policy in the Model Nations
Prison Crowding
Rights of Prisoners
Summary
Discussion Questions
For Further Reading

Key Terms and Concepts

Board of Visitors
Borstals
conjugal visiting
dispersal prisons
freiganger
juges de l'application des peines
juvenile reformatories
legalist perspective
lettres de catchet
parole
prerelease programs
Prison Act of 1976
private prisons
Progressive Movement
public surveillance
Rechtsstaat
reeducation through labor
reform through labor
remand centers
thought reform
work–study schools

Prisons today are symbols of the failure of the criminal justice process to achieve the changes in human attitudes and behavior that would make their use a worthwhile endeavor. The penitentiary movement, launched with high hopes in the late eighteenth century, has not lived up to the expectations of the reformers who conceived it. Indeed, the only two goals of sentencing that prisons seem to achieve are the ones that admit to failure: retribution and incapacitation. The more optimistic goals of rehabilitation and deterrence have not been achieved even in the most progressive, humane, and costly prison systems, in the United States or elsewhere. As measured by recidivism figures, there is little indication that we know how to change people by putting them in prison and subjecting them to various programs of reform.

It may be that depriving people of their freedom is not a good way to teach them to act as proper citizens in countries in which freedom of action and thought are emphasized in governmental and economic ideologies. It may be that no system has really devoted the necessary resources to programs of rehabilitation. Or it may simply be that no programs exist that can change the conditioning patterns that individuals undergo in their earliest years.

Extreme forms of rehabilitation in prison are rarely tried. One extreme form of rehabilitation is the "brainwashing," or "thought reform," that is often used in Chinese corrections as a way of changing people. Brainwashing is a slow process that involves constant study sessions, efforts to confuse the individual, insistence on self-denunciation, and intense group pressure. In effect, an individual's ego strength and sense of individualism are destroyed and then rebuilt to fit the ideological and social needs of the regime. This is, of course, what is attempted in all prison programs; the problem is the limits to which the authorities might be willing to go to make a person conform to society's demands.

For Americans, an interesting tale of thought reform is that of Allyn and Adele Rickett, an American couple who went to China in 1948 as Fulbright scholars (Rickett and Rickett, 1973). The Ricketts were arrested in 1950 and accused of spying for the U.S. government. They had in fact been recruited by American Naval Intelligence to report on events and opinions among the Chinese they knew, but they considered this to be harmless fact-gathering rather than spying. They were separated, and each was subjected to four years of intense study sessions, indoctrination, interrogation, and group discussion. They were released in 1955 and returned to the United States, where they wrote an account of their experience. The peculiar thing about this account, written after their release and therefore voluntary, is the extent to which these two individuals had grown to believe in their own guilt, in the falseness of their own previous values, and in the essential goodness of the Chinese regime. Adele Rickett, looking back on the painful separation from her husband for four years, says, "I feel that it was better that way. . . . If I had been able to see him, I would have thought of little else, and any ideas of reform would have been secondary" (1973, p. 299). She also reflects on the people she saw on the train carrying her south toward her transfer at the border with Hong Kong:

> For three and a half years I had been reading in the newspaper and magazines about the new character of the Chinese people, about the pride, security, and happiness with which they were meeting the problems of modernization and the building of a new society. In prison I had seen this character in action in the examples set by the supervisors and guards, but I had always looked on them as not being particularly typical. . . . But, now, on the train I was viewing people from all walks of life, and the same eagerness and comradeliness were evident all around me. (p. 302)

Despite the Ricketts' account, written shortly after their return, we actually have little evidence that extreme rehabilitation techniques such as brainwashing or behavior modification are effective ways to change behavior or attitudes in the long run. Anthony Burgess's novel *A Clockwork Orange* (1972) is a chilling account of an experiment in behavior modification that forces us to confront the ambiguities involved in this practice. In the story, a violent delinquent undergoes a radical course of behavior modification that makes him unable to commit acts of violence. The results are disastrous in the environment to which he returns after release from prison, and a rapid "deprogramming" process re-creates his original dangerous and asocial character.

THE EVOLUTION OF PRISON SYSTEMS

Alexis de Tocqueville, Charles Dickens, and even Karl Marx spent time in the United States in the second quarter of the nineteenth century. Their purpose was to study the American system of penitentiaries, which had achieved international fame as a major reform of the criminal justice process. Various American reformers hoped that a regime of meditation (the Pennsylvania system) or of silent, controlled work (the Auburn system) would provide a humane way to bring about a change of disposition and lifestyle in convicted criminals. The American prison system developed in response to the arbitrary, often cruel corporal punishments that were inflicted on offenders in previous eras in the hopes that they would deter others from crime. The eighteenth-century English judge who reportedly said, "You are to be hanged not because you have stolen a sheep but in order that others may not steal sheep" (Fox, 1952, p. 11), typified the practice that the reformers hoped to counteract with a system that led to genuine reform of offenders rather than offer a pretense of increased security for others.

The American experiment rapidly became the focus of reform discussions in other countries, and American-style prisons were built even though it soon became evident that the American prisons could not reform offenders or even provide them with humane conditions of incarceration. In France and England, prison systems

began to take the place of transportation of offenders to remote prison colonies. The criminal law was reformed to provide sentences to prison instead of the prevailing corporal punishments and the excessive use of the death penalty for relatively minor crimes. By the middle of the nineteenth century, prison was the accepted aftermath of conviction rather than the exception.

These nineteenth-century prisons actually did not represent the first efforts to deal with crime and punishment through the incarceration of offenders. Workhouses had been extensively used in England and continental Europe during the seventeenth and eighteenth centuries as places of confinement for the destitute, vagrants, and minor criminals. Common gaols served to house men, women, and children awaiting trial and serving short sentences, while individuals who could not pay their debts were confined in debtors' prisons. Since it might take six months for a circuit judge to arrive in town to handle the accumulated cases, many prisoners were in the gaols for a fairly long period. In England, the deplorable conditions in these unheated, unfurnished gaols frequently led to disease and death among prisoners. It was estimated that 25 percent of the prisoners died annually, many from the notorious "gaol fever." And prison warders were compensated by fees from the prisoners themselves. As can be imagined, the more affluent prisoners received better food, clothing, and general treatment than the poor (Fox, 1952; Melossi and Pavarini, 1981).

Periodic reform efforts, most notably by John Howard, prominent Quaker women, and utilitarian philosopher Jeremy Bentham, led to some changes by the early nineteenth century in England. Howard, who was a sheriff and large landowner in Bedfordshire, was horrified when he inspected the prisons of his own county and saw the deplorable conditions that existed there. This experience led him to visit prisons all over England and then in other countries. He published several books describing prison conditions, the first in 1777. Howard, who died of the plague in 1790 while visiting prisons in the Ukraine, provided the impetus for further reformers to attempt to change the English prisons. He has been immortalized in the "John Howard Societies" that continue to this day to work for prison reform in England and the United States.

It was the American experiments, however, that generated the major impetus for reforms at the turn of the nineteenth century. In France, England, and other European countries, the relative merits of the Pennsylvania and Auburn systems were hotly debated. Later, in 1872, the first International Prison Congress, held in London, proclaimed the ideals of rehabilitation and humane treatment for prisoners in the ever-growing number of institutions that were being established.

By the early twentieth century, it was obvious that prisons were not fulfilling their promise and, in fact, were generally as cruel and inhumane as any previous method of punishment. One of the hallmarks of the American **Progressive Movement** of the early twentieth century was the interest in a new approach to corrections: rehabilitation of the individual offender by specialists in corrections. A whole panoply of new or renewed proposals for change, including probation, parole, therapeutic prison regimes, and separate juvenile justice mechanisms became the dominant ideological, if not practical, reform proposals of the movement.

Probation, which allows the offender to remain outside of prison, and **parole,** whereby offenders are released to community supervision after a period of incarceration, were especially important mechanisms for decreasing prison population. They have continued to play this role, even in the post-Progressive or, as the Europeans call it, neoclassical period of disillusionment with rehabilitation efforts. The important point is that the realization that prison neither deters or rehabilitates has led to increasing efforts to find alternatives to incarceration. As explained in the previous chapter, fines have largely replaced imprisonment for minor and even some serious crimes in Germany. Other alternatives, including community service and restitution, are becoming increasingly popular. This is so despite the fact that we are again in a period of reliance on incarceration and on a general hardening of attitudes toward offenders, not only in the United States but also in most other parts of the world, including Europe, Japan, and China.

Incarceration is considered a sanction of last resort for Qur'anic crimes in countries that practice Islamic Law and is not generally used as a postconviction measure for major crimes. Increased concern with secular and religious offenses has led to a greater reliance on the criminal sanctions that do exist, however.

In considering more conventional prison regimes, we find that many of the problems faced in the United States are also endemic in the systems of other countries. These include overcrowding, lack of resources, lack of well-trained staff, and abuse of prisoners. Nevertheless, each country has its own distinctive problems, and there are strong differences among nations that are of particular interest. After describing the penal policies and correctional systems of our model countries, we will address some of the common problems of prison crowding and prisoner rights.

PENAL POLICY
IN THE MODEL NATIONS

There are many cross-national similarities in penal policy among modern nations. Each nation nevertheless also has its distinctive approaches to this matter. Often, these distinctive approaches are historically or culturally based, and we need to look at the factors that resulted in today's organization and practices. An examination of penal policy in our model nations will illustrate some of these similarities and differences.

England and Wales

The English correctional system has experienced major reforms and reorganizations over the past 200 years. Transportation to penal colonies was largely abandoned by the middle of the nineteenth century, overreliance on the death penalty was mitigated, and prison administration was transferred from localities to the central government. Prison became the major recourse for dealing with convicted offenders. Between 1842 and 1848, fifty-four fortress-type prisons were built, containing a total of 11,000 cells (Fox, 1952, p. 38). Many of these prisons continue to hold prisoners to this day. With its present prison population of more than 65,000, however, England has greatly exceeded the capacity of these earlier prisons and has engaged in some prison building since that time, with a new spurt of building now underway.

In the latter part of the nineteenth century, there were continued parliamentary investigations into and debates about the optimal way to deal with convicted offenders. Many of the same arguments about deterrence, rehabilitation, sentence length, and prison regime that are familiar to us today were aired at that time. English prisons, however, were notorious for their rigid regimes and harsh conditions, with prisoners forced to do hard labor and essentially go without amenities. Only later were they permitted a more "comfortable" existence, with a mattress, a few books, and some correspondence with the outside world. According to one author, "For death itself the system had substituted a living death" (Fox, 1952, p. 51).

The twentieth century has seen the same movements of concern, efforts to reform, new ideas, and new failures. Influenced by the Progressive Movement in the United States, some reformers called for less reliance on prison as a way of punishing offenders. The early twentieth century also saw increased concern for juveniles, through the development of both separate court processes and the Borstal training system, which soon became famous as a way of dealing with youthful offenders.

However, England's current correctional system appears to be in a state of crisis, and there seem to be few solutions in sight. The familiar continuum of increased crime, hardening of attitude, crowding of prisons, deterioration of conditions and relationships within prison, and desperate temporary measures to decrease the prison population characterizes the English system today. The crisis is exacerbated by the racial tensions that have followed the influx of immigrants from Britain's former colonies. This influx has created an urban underclass that suffers from severe political, social, and economic disadvantages in English society and is disproportionately represented in the English prisons. The United Kingdom has been the defendant in a number of cases that have been brought to the European Court of Human Rights (ECHR).

Officially, English correctional thought adheres to dual purposes of incapacitation for serious offenders and rehabilitation for lesser offenders. The goal of treatment and rehabilitation for offenders serving time in prison has been pushed aside because of the realities of prison overcrowding and the negative influences of correctional institutions.

Prison administration in England is still under the office of the Home Secretary, who is equivalent to an interior minister in other European countries. Prison policy and administration, however, are directed by the Prison Department, equivalent to the U.S. Bureau of Prisons. The Prison Department is headed by an appointed Prisons Board. Regional directors head the four divisions of the Prison Department.

The number of prisons in England is well over 130 and still growing. There are five types of prisons in England and Wales. **Remand centers,** also called local prisons, hold offenders awaiting trial or sentencing or serving very short sentences; thus, they are similar to the county jail in the United States. Medium-term institutions hold the majority of British inmates, who generally are sentenced to between eighteen months and four years. Long-term prisons house inmates serving more than four years. Highly secure prisons, called **dispersal prisons,** handle high-security and dangerous inmates. A fifth type of institution incarcerates only young offenders. Prison rehabilitation programs are available in the medium- and long-term institutions, but because of crowding, not all programs are available to all inmates.

The two major problems facing the correctional system in England and Wales are prison conditions and prison crowding. Many correctional facilities in England and Wales are antiquated, with deplorable conditions the norm; chamber pots were still in use as toilet facilities in some prisons as late as 1996. The number of prisoners has grown dramatically in recent years. Between 1995 and 1998, the prison population in England and Wales increased from 51,000 to over 65,000 (Walmsley, 1999), and the Home Office estimates that by 2002 the prisons will hold over 71,000 offenders.

To address these problems, the English government began a series of prison expansion projects in the 1990s. The expansion was fueled by the "prison works" slogan adopted by Home Secretary Michael Howard and addressed three main issues: (1) the rise in the use of custodial sanctions by courts, (2) the increase in the length of sentences, and (3) the increase in the time served by those in remand prisons (Ryan and Sim, 1998).

Considerable effort also has been devoted to the development and implementation of noncustodial sanctions in England and Wales. For example, the use of community sentences (e.g., probation) increased from 51,000 in 1990 to over 83,000 in 1994 (HEUNI, 1999, p. 139). The noncustodial options include warnings/admonitions, probation, restitution, community service, fines, curfews, suspended sentences, and a new idea called the combination order, which includes aspects of probation and community service (Terrill, 1999).

Two structures, Borstals and the Boards of Visitors, are important distinguishing characteristics of English corrections. **Borstals,** much copied since their establishment in England in 1908, are detention facilities that segregate youthful offenders with some prospect of reform from adult convicts. Borstal age is generally 16 to 20, and their characteristic organization involves training, edu-

cation, and residence in a "house" system, in which several offenders live in small houses, each with a "head master." Borstals vary in size, degree of security, and sex of the inhabitants, but the basic purposes of providing work training and developing self-respect and self-discipline are common to all. Graduated rewards tied to individual accomplishment are part of the regime, with home leave the highest reward. The system was designed to be nonpunitive but strict, with a large measure of participation by the offenders in determining house rules and other aspects of their lives.

Conceived idealistically and long considered a major reform in corrections for youthful offenders, Borstals today suffer from the same problems of overcrowding, poor conditions, and intractable populations that plague the adult English prisons. Although they are meant to be distinguished from the "young prisoner centers," that handle the more difficult cases, the Borstal concept has lost its momentum. In England today, every effort is made to divert juveniles from courts and prisons through agencies that handle juvenile cases in a nonjudicial, nonincarcerative style.

Boards of Visitors, or visiting committees, represent a way to bring "outsiders" into the prisons to help with problems of administration and discipline. The 135 boards, with an average of fifteen members each, act as an independent watchdog on the prisons, meeting with inmates and staff to safeguard the well-being and rights of all prisoners. Their origins are in nineteenth-century committees set up by judges to inspect the local prisons. The visiting committee of each prison has three duties:

- To visit the prison on a regular basis and no less than once a month. Each member of the committee has the right to visit at any time and to get in touch with any inmate within the institution.

- To hear complaints against prison officials and to make decisions in major disciplinary cases against prisoners.

- To advise the prison administration on matters of procedure, policy, and the like, and to make an annual report to the Home Office on the status of each institution.

The members of the Boards of Visitors are appointed by the Home Secretary, and at least half must be magistrates. These boards represent a distinctly English way of involving nonprofessionals in the criminal justice process. They may be compared to police advisory boards, lay magistrates, and independent lay juries, all structures that do not exist in Continental legal systems. They are particularly important in England as a way of guarding against excesses occurring in prison, because Britain's Official Secrets Act makes it illegal for government employees (in this case, prison employees) to disclose what is going on within their agencies.

The Boards of Visitors have come under attack, however, for several reasons. In the first place, the running of prisons has become the domain of specialized professionals who do not like to have amateurs looking over their shoulders. In the second place, board members are not trusted by many prisoners, who see them as part of the establishment and unlikely to take the side of prisoners against keepers. Indeed, board members do tend to be older, conservative, and oriented toward the prison administration, with which they have a good deal of contact. Thus, today, major prisoner grievances are more often taken up by lawyers and presented to the European Commission on Human Rights than settled through the Boards of Visitors.

France

In the generally dismal worldwide history of treatment of criminal and political offenders, France occupies a place that is at least as undistinguished as England's and, on the record, somewhat worse. Large numbers of real or imagined enemies of the regime were incarcerated without trial in France during the sixteenth and seventeenth centuries through the infamous *lettres de cachet,* which were simply orders of the king that a person be imprisoned indefinitely. Transportation to work colonies and the use of prisoners to man the oars on French naval ships were equivalent to death sentences in most cases, since few prisoners survived the appalling conditions in these places for more than a few years. Imprisonment as a sanction was used chiefly for debtors and for women and juveniles, who were not sent to the galleys. As in England, the prison as we know it was preceded by workhouses that incarcerated not only criminal offenders but also the destitute, who had no other means of survival.

As in England, a great wave of reform sentiment accompanied the Enlightenment of the late eighteenth century, and in the nineteenth century, a series of controversial changes made large-scale imprisonment the major sentencing mode. And in the twentieth century, the same effort was made to emphasize rehabilitation and to introduce certain concomitant sentencing possibilities, such as suspended sentences, that characterized first the American and then the English correctional systems. Probation and parole, however, which played an important role in American corrections throughout the twentieth century, were not used in France until after World War II. In addition, France persisted in the use of transportation of prisoners long after this practice had been phased out in England. In fact, the closing of the final prison colony in Guyana did not occur until 1946 (Wright, 1983, pp. 179, 188).

In the postwar years, France moved from an emphasis on prison reform to a generally harsher philosophy of punishment. A series of prison riots resulting in a number of hostage deaths in the early 1970s led to some abortive reform efforts. The large increase in the crime rate during the 1970s contributed to a repressive mood on the part of the public and the government. Prison leaves and suspended sentences were limited, and harsher sentences were imposed. The Socialist government that came into power in 1981 proposed sweeping reforms of the criminal justice system, including abolition of capital punishment, protections against unwarranted pretrial imprisonment, and concern for prisoner's rights. However, public concern over murders and terrorist bombings soon took precedence over reform sentiments, and the generally hard-line mood intensified. The result has been a steady increase in the prison population.

Correctional services in France are currently under the supervision of the Minister of Justice. The Prison Service takes on a dual role: (1) supervision of individuals sentenced by the courts and (2) the preparation for their return to the community (Minister of Justice, 1998, p. 5).

As of January 1998 in France, there are more than 186 prison institutions, with varying degrees of security, administratively allocated to nine regions. Of these correctional facilities, 67 are prisons for offenders sentenced to more than one year, and 119 are remand prisons that house unconvicted offenders and inmates with less than a one-year sentence. Separate institutional arrangements exist for females, the mentally ill, juveniles, and the aged (Minister of Justice, 1998, p. 17).

The French spend an average of $20,000 (in U.S. dollars) per inmate per year, as compared to the $25,000 average in the United States. Programs of work, education, and vocational training are important in the French penal system. In 1998, over 22,000 inmates worked or received vocational training, and 28,900 followed some course of general education. Other rehabilitation facilities and activities may also be available, including libraries, visitor support groups, religious services, and sports (Minister of Justice, 1999). However, the problem of overcrowding makes it difficult to execute these programs and services with any degree of effectiveness.

Two distinguishing features of the French penal system are the office of corrections judge and the proportion of pretrial detainees. With respect to pretrial detainees, figures show that, of the almost 53,000 inmates in French prisons, over 20,000 are remand (unconvicted or serving less than a one-year sentence) inmates (Minister of Justice, 1999). Although Civil Law nations typically have long pretrial detention while the case is being thoroughly examined, France has acquired a reputation of excessiveness in this area. Many detainees are kept in jail for several years while their cases are being investigated by the examining magistrates.

Prison and jail overcrowding have led to efforts in recent years to cut down on the pretrial populations of these institutions. Pretrial diversion programs are being proposed. Other proposals include a maximum of one year of pretrial detention in less serious cases (those that would result in a sentence of less than five years) for adults and a maximum of one month for juveniles in these cases.

The French have lagged behind the rest of Europe in developing and implementing a range of alternatives to incarceration. Recently, however, efforts have been made to increase their usage. There are primarily four noncustodial sanctions in France: fines, suspended sentence, community service, and probation. As of January 1999, over 130,000 offenders were serving their sentences in the community (Minister of Justice, 1999).

While the rate of pretrial detention continues to be a major problem in France, the office of *juges de l'application des peines* (corrections judges) was instituted in 1958 and strengthened in 1970 and 1972 as a reform of the penal process. Corrections judges are appointed by the government to perform several functions, including determining the actual length of time that a particular prisoner remains in prison or is released on parole. Most interesting, however, is the function of overseeing prison conditions and prison disciplinary procedures. The corrections judges have the responsibility of visiting the prison or prisons in their jurisdictions at least once a month, hearing individual inmate complaints, and keeping informed about prison programs, physical plants, and general conditions. Although this program has met with a good deal of opposition, especially from prison administrators, and can hardly be considered an unqualified success, it represents an effort to make the dark world of

French prisons somewhat more open to outside scrutiny and thereby more accountable to the government and the public. In this sense, the office of corrections judge performs some of the same functions as the Boards of Visitors have served in England for almost a century. At the same time, these officials have a major influence on the actual sentences served by particular inmates.

Germany

Germany, with its federal system of government, administers prisons at the level of the states, or Laender. With the exception of the period of National Socialism, when all German institutions, including corrections institutions, were centralized, each German state has run its own prison system since the creation of the German Empire in 1871. Criminal law and criminal sentences are determined by the national legislature, but their execution occurs independently at the state level. This is part of the peculiar German brand of federalism that we have already encountered in police organization, according to which substantive legislation is framed at the national level and administered at the state level. Within the German states, prison administration falls under the jurisdiction of the Ministry of Justice, with varying kinds of administrative and regional subdivisions.

During the latter eighteenth century, over sixty workhouses incarcerated petty criminals, vagrants, and poor people in the German states (Melossi and Pavarini, 1981, p. 49), but these states soon took part in the early nineteenth-century movement to develop large-scale prisons as the major form of criminal corrections. The infrastructure for the prison system of today was established in the German states prior to the 1871 unification.

For over a century, Germany operated under the postunification penal code of 1871, which itself was based on the Prussian Code of 1851. The Prussian Code was heavily influenced by the repressive French Code of 1810 and the Bavarian Code of 1813. These various codes enshrined the classic philosophy of punishment under law that was prevalent in the nineteenth century. Although there were many amendments to the 1871 code, a complete overhaul did not occur until the Prison Act of 1976.

The **Prison Act of 1976,** formally called the Code on the Execution of Prison Sentences, sets forth all of the principles and methods to be practiced in German correctional facilities. The code proclaims the correctional system goal of rehabilitation and reintegration into society for offenders. At the same time, the code includes provisions for safeguarding certain rights accorded to prisoners, including visiting rights, home leave of up to twenty-one days per year, medical care, and productive paid work. The law sets the pay for prison labor at 5 percent of average outside wages. To be sure, these rights were tempered by the discretionary power of prison administrators to grant or deny them in accordance with particular circumstances, including availability of funds to pay for prison labor. Nevertheless, the law represents a major comprehensive statement of purpose and a major effort to codify the regulations for the German penal system (Dammer, 1996; Feest, 1982).

Although the main correctional philosophy in Germany is rehabilitation, this does not mean that punishment is not within the legal rights of the government. The theoretical support for the legitimization of punishment is found in the "amalgamation document of the goals of punishment," which states that imprisonment (incapacitation), prevention, expiation (retribution), and rehabilitation are all recognized as proper penal sanctions (Feest and Weber, 1998).

There are over 160 prisons in western Germany, but less than 10 of these institutions have a capacity of over 500 prisoners, making Germany quite progressive in terms of prison size (Dammer, 1996). In 1997, over 74,000 offenders were incarcerated in Germany, an increase in the incarceration rate from 80.1 per 100,000 persons in 1990 to 90 in 1997. Most prisons within Germany have various levels of security integrated within the institution. When offenders enter prison, they begin at a high level of security. As they serve their sentences and show progress toward rehabilitation, they can move to a lower security level. Special units within the prisons are used to discipline inmates who repeatedly break the rules or are at risk of hurting themselves or others. Several maximum-security institutions in Germany incarcerate escape-risk inmates, terrorists, and those who have proven to be unmanageable in other institutions.

German prisons are known for their extensive use of rehabilitation programs. In a study of five German prisons, it was determined that at least three features strongly support the rehabilitative philosophy: (1) unique environmental conditions, (2) extensive work and training opportunities, and (3) community integration programs (Dammer, 1996).

Of the unique environmental conditions in German prisons, the physical location and structural design are most obvious. German prisons are almost always located within cities or in nearby suburban communities. Because of a scarcity of unutilized land, the Germans cannot afford to use valuable rural land for correctional institutions. Also, having prisons in cities and nearby towns makes it easier for families to visit and for inmates to utilize the community for home leave, work, and educational opportunities. Prisons in Germany look less like secure correctional institutions and more like factories or hospitals. The belief is that keeping the physical appearance more like that of a factory and creating more "normal" living conditions will promulgate rehabilitation.

German prisons also often provide inmates with extensive work and training opportunities to prevent idleness, reduce institutional costs, and help inmates improve themselves so they can become better citizens upon release.

A third common rehabilitative practice is the frequent use of three community reintegration programs: home leave, conjugal visiting, and half-open release. Home leave is one of the rights included in the 1976 Prison Act that has been increasingly implemented. These leaves are given at the discretion of the authorities in specific prisons, with most of the leaves from low-custody as

opposed to high-custody institutions. Kaiser reports that "in 1979 the average prison inmate received 2.6 vacations" (1984, p. 22).

With the **conjugal visiting** program, inmates can receive private visits from their spouses and children for four hours every two months. They obtain this privilege after being incarcerated for two to three months and lose it only if they violate a serious prison rule or are involved with drugs. Another program that promotes rehabilitation and reintegration is the *freiganger,* or half-open release, program. In this program, inmates who have served at least one-half of their sentence can earn the privilege to leave the institution during the day for school or work and then return to the institution in the evening. The *freiganger* program is primarily utilized with inmates who are approaching their time of release (the last six months of their sentence). In Germany, all inmates must be paroled after serving two-thirds of their sentence unless they do not consent to parole or the warden and prosecutor decide the inmate is likely to commit more crimes. The *freiganger* program is guided by the belief that gradual release will assist in the inmates' successful reintegration into the community. During this period, the inmate reestablishes community and family relationships without the pressures of immediate release. Many state correctional systems in the United States implement programs, called **prerelease programs,** that are similar to the half-open German programs.

We have seen how the British prison system, with its Boards of Visitors, and the French system, with its corrections judges, have dealt with some aspects of inmate grievances. Germany has also addressed this matter, albeit in a somewhat different manner. The Prison Act of 1976 provides for inmate access to courts for any violations of prisoners' rights spelled out in the act. Special court panels are constituted to consider inmate grievances, and appeal to the state high courts is possible. This procedure, which involves litigation, is thus more formal than either the French or the English procedures and has resulted in an increase in court claims involving prisoners' rights. This, in turn, has raised questions about the degree to which the courts will get involved in adjudicating prison conditions, with all the ramifications that such adjudication might have, as we know from our experiences in the United States (Feest, 1982, p. 13).

From the standpoint of comparative criminal justice, we can speculate about the significance of the various ways that the three countries—Britain, France, and Germany—have approached the matter of inmate grievances and prison conditions. England uses lay personnel to visit prisons and hear complaints; France uses a bureaucratic judge to do the same; and Germany deals with the problem through litigation. Inmates can appeal to special courts about their prison conditions based on the Prison Law of 1976. These progressively more formal structures to deal with the same problem may reflect the general legal cultures in these countries. Thus, England, with its pragmatic Common Law system and its emphasis on public involvement in government, uses a system that involves lay supervision. France, which has developed a formidable bureaucratic culture in the light of its history of unstable governments, uses a bureaucratic system. Germany, which has emphasized the notion of a **Rechtsstaat** (rule according to law) since the nineteenth century, deals with its prisoners' rights problem through formal legal channels.

If we compare the use of noncustodial sanctions in England, France, and Germany, we can see that Germany is clearly the leader in the use of such sanctions. Over the past twenty years Germany has tried to follow a policy of reduced use of imprisonment (HEUNI, 1999). In addition to extensive measures to prevent the use of pretrial detention, Germany has implemented community service, fines, day fines, offender-victim mediation, and educational programs for juveniles (United Nations, 1999).

China

The underlying foundation for the correctional system in China is based on two ancient traditions: Confucianism and legalism. As mentioned in previous chapters, Confucianism is a 2,500-year-old idea that essentially states that social harmony can be secured through moral education to bring out the good nature of all. Moral education occurs when the family and community apply social pressure to teach the recalcitrant individual how to conform. Formal legal structures are not necessary for this purpose.

The **legalist perspective,** developed almost 200 years after Confucianism, held that only a firm application of laws and strict punishments could persuade people who are innately evil not to commit crime. Early in the first millennium A.D., these two ideals began to merge, with Confucianism serving as the primary social control mechanism and formal legalism providing support (Bodde and Morris, 1967).

China in the post-1949 Communist era has developed a correctional system that retains remnants of both the Confucian and legalist perspectives. The basic principle of Confucian thought—bringing out the good nature of people and creating change through imposing moral education—has meshed with the Communists' need to reeducate the people in Socialist values. The ancient legalist view promoting the use of strict punishments to punish wrongdoing and prevent crime were also within the philosophical framework of the Communist regime, which believes that punishment and reform go hand in hand.

Over the past fifty years, the government of the People's Republic of China has developed a correctional system that retains, in essence, these two historical perspectives. Informal social control mechanisms like the people's mediation committees (see Chapter 9) support both Confucian and Socialist ideologies in families, neighborhoods, rural areas, work units, and schools. The punishment aspect of the legalist perspective has been fused with the concept of reform and implemented through formal social control mechanisms—also called correctional facilities. There are four main kinds of correctional facilities: (1) detention centers, (2) reeducation-through-labor facilities, (3) reform-through-labor camps, and (4) prisons. The total number of these institutions is in question but has been estimated to be 600 (Chen, 1993).

Detention centers, like jails in the United States, house offenders awaiting sentencing and those serving less than a two-year sentence. Moral education programs and manual labor are commonplace in these institutions.

Reeducation through labor (also called rehabilitation through labor) is both a policy and the name of the kind of correctional facility that incarcerates those who have administrative detention status. **Administrative detention** is a form of punishment in the People's Republic of China that allows authorities to impose fines and incarcerate people without the benefit of a trial. It is technically a noncriminal sanction that can be applied to both youths and adults, and it can include incarceration for up to four years. This policy has provided the legal support for the incarceration of hundreds, and maybe thousands, of persons for their involvement in the Tiananmen Square incident in 1989 (Lawyers Committee, 1994). The kinds of crimes that would warrant incarceration in one of these institutions include disturbing public order, carrying a weapon, breaking and entering, theft, traffic offenses, prostitution, gambling, distributing pornography, and some drug violations (Terrill, 1999).

Reform through labor is also both a policy and the name of the kind of correctional facility for offenders who have been tried and convicted of a criminal offense, in most cases a serious one requiring between one and ten years of incarceration. Nonfelony adult and serious criminals who are not seen as dangerous are placed in these institutions. These camps are the most famous for their forced labor policies and their extreme attempts at thought reform (Wu, 1992). The camps, called *laogai,* are based on the military practice model, and the inmates participate in agricultural or industrial production, construction, or service work (Shaw, 1998).

The fourth kind of correctional facility are prisons, which generally house the more dangerous inmates, including those with a sentence of more than ten years, a life sentence, or sentence of death. These inmates require total separation from society and are usually confined to their cells, perform only simple labor, and receive heavy doses of thought reform.

Two special kinds of correctional facility are designed for juveniles: **work–study schools** and **juvenile reformatories.** Work-study schools are facilities for youths who have caused trouble in schools and committed minor criminal offenses like theft, gambling, or fighting (Bracey, 1988). The juvenile reformatories are for serious juvenile offenders between the ages of 14 and 18, who participate in intensive work and moral education programs (Shaw, 1998).

Labor is an important element of the Chinese correctional system through all the forms of incarceration. Although labor is not formally recognized to be as important as reform and rehabilitation, it constitutes the main activity in many of the prisons, camps, and other facilities. Labor serves a number of purposes in Chinese prisons. Its primary purpose is to augment the education and reform process: Correctional labor teaches work skills, helps inmates pass the time, and also provides financial assistance to the institution (Shaw, 1998, p. 192). In addition, for years, China's leaders have boasted that prison labor is vital to the country's economic growth. They claim that using inmates to staff prison factories that do light assembly work and even to work in coal and asbestos mines contributes funds to the Chinese treasury that can be reinvested in the economy.

However, the financial success of the Chinese *laogai* has been challenged in an extensive study by James Seymour, who argues that prison businesses make "no significant contribution" to the Chinese economy. He claims that an unmotivated work force that is often skilled at sabotage has negated the positive benefits of inmate labor (Seymour and Anderson, 1998).

This is not to imply that labor programs are the only attempts at reform that occur in Chinese prisons. Many reports note that Chinese prisons also provide other kinds of rehabilitation programs. According to Yingyi Situ and Weizheng Liu, juvenile and adult institutions offer a variety of educational methods:

> Political education is used to rehabilitate and reform offenders. Political education includes the study of laws and government regulations. Offenders also obtain moral education in Socialist ideology such as sound work ethic and accepting the ideal of collectivity. Self-criticism and mutual criticism are an important part of the process. Everybody is supposed to confess to his or her crime and make self-criticism in public. Juvenile inmates, as well as adults, may receive cultural education at their own level—from elementary school through college. Vocational education is available in most of the institutions. (1996, p. 133).

Among the most controversial of the "educational" and reform methods used in Chinese correctional facilities are programs that promote **thought reform.** Thought reform, as implied in the quotation from Situ and Liu, includes having inmates confess to their wrongdoing, attack their criminal identity, and construct a new self-image that fits with the beliefs of the Socialist agenda. Other tactics used to encourage thought reform include the study of Socialist doctrine and the constant recitation of important texts. The results of thought reform are exemplified in the story of Allyn and Adele Rickett, presented early in the chapter.

The incarceration figures for China are difficult to determine because China often fails to report such data and does not allow outside scrutiny of their correctional system. It is not known how many persons are detained in China, especially under the guise of "shelter and protection," a policy we discussed in Chapter 8. The large number of work camps (*laogai*) located throughout the vast regions of China, as well as the frequent transfer of inmates between the camps, also makes it very difficult to count inmates. We do know that there are at least 1.4 million inmates in China, with an incarceration rate in 1997 of 115 per 100,000 population (Walmsley, 1999). And we also know from Chinese reports that this number has increased since 1991, when the prison population was 1.2 million.

However, various reports place the number of persons incarcerated in China much higher. Harry H. Wu, a Chinese-American human rights activist who has written extensively about prisons in China based on his own incarceration experiences there, has stated that 4 to 6 million persons are incarcerated in reform-through-labor camps and another 3 to 5 million are in reeducation-through-labor institutions (Wu, 1992).

As a supplement to the extensive informal and formal social control mechanisms, the People's Republic of China also provides five forms of noncustodial sanctions. Probation, called **public surveillance,** can be imposed for from three months to six years and requires that the offender report regularly to the local public security agency. Suspended sentences can be handed out to nondangerous offenders with a sentence of less than three years. Fines are used in special circumstances. Two lesser-used sanctions are restricting offenders' right to vote and confiscating their property (Terrill, 1999, pp. 589–590).

China does not fare well when it comes to complying with international standards for the treatment of offenders. Even the International Committee of the Red Cross has been barred from providing basic humanitarian relief to prisoners (Human Rights Watch Website, 1999). The information on China is limited because the Chinese do not often allow private researchers or international organizations to observe their correctional system. But based on the information we have been able to obtain about the treatment of those incarcerated in China, we can state that the reports are not favorable. (For two excellent sources of information on this issue see Wu, 1996, and Seymour and Anderson, 1998.) In addition to the questionable conditions that are present for convicted criminals in Chinese institutions, what is of equal concern to the international community are the reports claiming that the number of Chinese dissidents who have been incarcerated for reeducation through labor has actually increased in recent years (Amnesty International, 1999).

With the passing by the National People's Congress of the new Prison Law of 1994, the Chinese, at least on paper, have made some significant changes to their correctional system. These include more centralization of administration, more accountability to other aspects of the justice system, more scientifically based approaches to rehabilitation, and more sensitivity to prisoners' rights (Anderson, 1996). At this point, however, it is difficult to determine whether any of these changes have actually been implemented.

Japan

A visitor to Kawagoe Youth Prison near Tokyo reacts first to the beautiful landscaping in the Japanese style, with carefully placed shrubs and trees not only in the large prison yard inside the walls but also in the small courtyard behind the interview rooms, where prisoners are tested, classified, and assigned to work and education programs. Additional facilities include a swimming pool (used chiefly by townspeople, according to a prison official) and a drill ground, where prisoners exercise in military formations under the direction of guards for at least one hour a day.

Of the 1,300 prisoners, about 200 are in the classification center, 195 are awaiting trial, and 160 are enrolled in vocational courses including hairdressing, welding, woodwork, gardening, construction, and carpentry. The remainder of the prisoners are at work in large, hangarlike facilities, each containing a different industry. The industries include auto repair and manufacture of garden ornaments and tatami mats. A correctional official "foreman" in each industry salutes, clicks his heels, and reports on the productivity of his group in clipped military speech. The prisoners work in the industries forty-four hours each week, including four hours on Saturday.

After 5:00 P.M. inmates are confined to their cells, where they also receive their meals. The six-

man cells are neat but rather bare, with futons and tatami mats for bedding stacked in one corner and a television set in the center. There are a few one-man cells, smaller but also furnished with a futon and mat stacked in the corner and a small television receiver, for prisoners who present discipline problems and cannot adjust to the group life of the other cells.

Kawagoe Prison illustrates several facets of Japanese prison life and penal philosophy. There is a strong emphasis on work, with prison administrations contracting to manufacture products or provide services. Prisoners receive some pay for this work, although much of the money earned is used to offset prison maintenance costs. Prison life is also strongly regimented, with little freedom of movement or individual programming once an inmate has been assigned to a particular regime. Prisoners have few rights as such, and Japan does not provide the kind of treatment staff that most European and American prisons have. Correctional staff are trained, however, to emphasize resocialization into the community as one aspect of the prison regime.

The prison population itself consists largely of serious offenders who have resisted conventional Japanese efforts to achieve harmony and conformity without confrontational measures such as court convictions and prison sentences. Approximately 25 percent of prisoners are associated with organized crime groups (Kaiser, 1984, p. 140).

The imprisonment rate is quite low compared to other countries. The population of Japanese prisons in 1997 was 49,414, a rate of 40 per 100,000 population. This represented a slight increase in the prison population from 1992, when 46,000 were incarcerated in Japan, a rate of 36 per 100,000. Interestingly, with the exception of a large increase in the prison population shortly after World War II, the average daily population today is almost the same as in 1945, when there were 53,656 inmates (Research and Training Institute, 1989a, p. 116). By comparison, in the United States, the population has grown from 200,000 total inmates in 1970 to well over 1.2 million people in prisons alone (not including jails, which are included in the Japanese figures). Even taking into account the larger American population, the numbers still reflect an amazing disparity: Japan's prison population rate is 40 per 100,000 inhabitants versus 645 per 100,000 in the United States.

Thus, Japan has so far escaped the staggering problems of prison overcrowding that plague the Western nations we have studied. The relatively small prison population partially reflects the relatively lower crime rates in Japan, but it is also a function of the length and kinds of sentences. Japanese sentences are quite short. In 1988, for example, of the 28,156 offenders admitted to Japanese prisons, 21,468 were sentenced to two years or less (Research and Training Institute, 1989a, p. 120). Only 39 were given life sentences. Parole tends to decrease these sentences even further. Also in 1988, of the 30,328 prisoners released from the Japanese system, 16,540 were released on parole, while the remainder had served their entire sentences. Most parolees had served between 60 percent and 90 percent of their sentences (p. 15).

The Japanese courts are most likely to administer fines, which account for 97 percent of all sanctions for crimes (Terrill, 1999). Also, two-thirds of all defendants sentenced to prison are granted a suspended sentence. As a result of these sentencing practices, fewer offenders are incarcerated, and still fewer receive other traditional noncustodial sanctions like probation. When someone is placed on probation in Japan, he or she is likely to have contact with one of the 52,000 volunteer probation officers who assist the full-time officer in community supervision (Johnson, 1996).

Japanese prisons are administered centrally by a division of the Ministry of Justice called the Correction Bureau. The system is divided into eight regions, with broad decision-making powers existing at the regional level. The prisons themselves are differentiated according to age, sex (less than 2 percent of Japanese prisoners are women), pretrial or postconviction status, and type of prison regime. The Correction Bureau operates 59 adult prisons, 110 detention centers, 3 medical prisons,

2 medical branch prisons, and 8 juvenile prisons (Correction Bureau, 1995).

Inmates in Japanese prisons reportedly are afforded individualized treatment that allows them to become rehabilitated and reintegrated into the community. As in the Chinese system, offenders progress through a system that allows them more privileges and freedoms as they successfully serve their sentence. Success is measured by one's ability to work well in the prison factory or maintenance job, get along with others, abide by prison rules, and otherwise be actively involved in rehabilitation programs. Japanese prisoners receive a small amount of money, the equivalent of about $15 per month, for their work. Because of the industrial arrangements in most prisons, the system actually operates without cost to the Japanese government. One example of a unique rehabilitative program that is practiced in many Japanese correctional facilities is *naikan,* a method of therapy in which individuals use introspection to understand the impact of their behavior on others and that of others on themselves. (For a description of naikan, see the accompanying box on pages 264–266.)

Recent reports on the treatment of offenders in Japanese prisons have not been favorable. Human Rights Watch stated in 1994 that Japanese prisons were overly repressive and restrictive in regime. In particular, they voiced concerns about the limited number of contacts allowed with the outside world and family members (Human Rights Watch, 1995). Amnesty International voiced similar concerns in a more recent report that criticized Japanese prisons for their "cruel, inhuman and degrading treatment through the use of handcuffs and other instruments of restraint, and the imposition of severe penalties for minor infractions of complex prison rules" (Amnesty International, 1998).

In general, Japan seems to pay less attention to, and to provide less resources for, its prison system than most Western countries. Because of the strong emphasis on conformity in Japanese life, prisons are a symptom of failure, and being a prisoner is a particular disgrace for both the inmates

The Practice of Naikan in Japanese Prisons

by Dieter Bindzus, Ph.D., Professor of Law, University of Saarland, Germany

NAIKAN means "to see oneself" (NAI = inner, KAN = observe), in a free translation, "inner self-observation" (introspection). It was developed as a method of therapy fifty years ago in Japan by Ishin Yoshimoto.[1] As a method of treatment, NAIKAN is based on the simple realization that every person sees himself and his environment only from his own point of view, which is inevitably one-sided and incomplete, because this view is determined only by the perceived needs of that individual; this is true even for those individuals who often reflect critically on themselves.[2] It is the aim of the NAIKAN method to facilitate the formation of as complete a picture as possible of a person to himself by helping him to look at himself as an outside observer; that is, to see himself as those around him perceive him, since he is already more than sufficiently familiar with his own perception of himself.[3] The conscious look at himself from the point of view of his environment can have—as is immediately self-evident—only one positive effect; the individual sees himself as he really is and not how he would like to be or how he should be. This leads to the result that the person can learn to accept himself better as an individual and can himself resolve neurotic guilt feelings and behavior patterns. This understanding of oneself which corresponds more closely to reality leads at the same time to a better understanding of the cares and problems of others and makes it possible to overcome one's own conflict with his environment, which, in turn, can be followed by clearer perspectives for the future.[4] The most important change, however, that this more complete understanding brings about—and herein lies its applicability for treatment of prisoners—is the more positive social behavior patterns of those who have undergone NAIKAN treatment, testified by research done on the NAIKAN process.

Seductively simple and not at all expensive, NAIKAN therapy takes about one week to complete and is usually carried through only on a voluntary basis. To begin with, the participants are given a thorough introduction to the objectives and methods of the treatment by the counselor,[5] who does not have any special academic qualifications. After this, the prison inmate who is partici-

pating in the treatment is brought to a single cell, in which he is, as far as possible, isolated from the outside world. The participant receives instructions from the counselor during the sessions, which can last up to sixteen hours a day, to recall his experiences and encounters with the most meaningful personal relationships in his environment—beginning usually with his mother—within a specified period of his lifetime. During the process of NAIKAN treatment the counselor poses three different questions to the participant. The participant is to consider each question in a certain order respective to each meaningful relationship and, in turn, to apply it to a certain period in his life, beginning in the past and usually ending in the present. The questions to be considered are, first of all, "What has this person done that was positive for me?" (these can be quite minor things); secondly, "What has the participant himself done positively for this person?", and thirdly, "What difficulties has the participant posed for this person?", whereby the emphasis is usually placed upon the third question.[6] The question concerning the difficulties this person has posed for the participant is purposefully not asked because the prisoner has normally been preoccupied with this question continuously in the past and such a preoccupation is not NAIKAN, that is, introspection, from the point of view of the outside observer. During the sessions the counselor comes to the participant every hour or so and allows him to report on what he has remembered in the time elapsed. Only if the participant has not been engaged in true introspection: if he has lost himself in accusations and placing blame on the other person, if he deliberately or unconsciously reveals unreadiness to recall a certain period of his lifetime or has not remembered accurately enough, does the counselor intervene in a helpful clarifying manner.

A therapy session which is progressing positively may possibly be broken up several times by phases in which the participant is unable to remember certain things, but progresses towards a slow, step-by-step insight and understanding of his own personality, that is, a decrease in the gap between phantasm and reality concerning himself. Gradually there appear the first signs of a readiness to change his attitudes and behavior towards himself and his surroundings. At this stage the participant is sometimes filled with guilt feelings and feeling of sadness, which, however, bit-by-bit disappear during the course of the therapy through further exercises in recollection and a growing self-awareness and self-acceptance, without serious mental or physical risks for the participant, and finally pass on to a feeling of understanding and responsibility, at first in relation to this one meaningful relationship he has been considering and finally in relation to his whole environment.[7]

Prisoners especially, including the hardened "Yakuzas" (members of the organized underworld) often suffer under negative childhood memories, which have quelled deep in their hearts as a lack of devotion and love. NAIKAN shows relatively quickly, that this is usually an exaggerated subjective assessment, which has, however, often had the negative consequence of becoming the cause of criminal behavior in the prisoners. Unfulfilled expectation of love and nurture with regard to his most personal relationships produce such strong feelings of rejection and hate towards this person that they obscured every possibility of an insight into his self-responsibility. This allows him to believe that others and not himself are the cause of his miserable situation. NAIKAN can help the prisoner to overcome this vicious circle, with its one-sided and purely subjective point of view, by tapping his own inner energies. This proposition, that reflection on his criminal past can convert the prisoner to the rightful path, is anything but new.

The Pennsylvania System, which has influenced correctional systems throughout the world for 150 years, is based on the conviction that by means of strict twenty four hour solitary confinement without any work or occupation other than with the Bible, the prisoner could be brought through reflection to inner conversion, repentance and atonement with God.[8] This system, correct in its point of departure, fails to recognize, however, what experienced prison officials realized soon after the Pennsylvania System was introduced, that the prisoner, when left all by himself, and given his one-sided perception of reality, becomes only more entangled in these feelings of hate and rejection or, less often, in feelings of self-destructive guilt, and that only with guidance could he liberate himself from this predicament.

The NAIKAN method offers the prisoner guidance through the help of the counselor throughout all three steps which are developed respective to each of his meaningful relationships and within these relationships for each progressive period of time. The recollection process in the first step, in which the prisoner has to consider what this person has done for him that was positive, enables the prisoner, when the introduction is correctly applied—as is guaranteed by the presence of the counselor throughout the whole treatment process—to relive the concern and love which he had at one time experienced, but which had in the meantime become covered with debris. Already during this recollection process, a distinct stabilization of the prisoner's frame of mind occurs. This establishes at the same time his ability to confront his negative experiences in life. This is reinforced during the second step of the recollection process, in which the prisoner is to occupy himself with those things which he himself has done that were positive for his person, in spite of the not very positive results. The prisoner reaches the highest degree of insight into his actual state of mind in the third step of the NAIKAN process, in which he must confront the difficulties he has caused to this individual person. Only at this stage is the prisoner ready to accept those negative aspects of life which have already appeared in the foregoing phases of the NAIKAN process—which are, especially among a group of prisoners, particularly abundant and severe. If the prisoner reaches this stage relative to a particular person and a certain period of time which had a decisive meaning for his life—this can come to light at any time during the NAIKAN therapy—he is now able to develop new and more positive patterns of behavior for the future, in particular from his perspective as a prisoner this means that after his release from prison he is able to lead a life of social responsibility without committing crimes.

NAIKAN therapy was introduced into the Japanese prisons and Juvenile Training schools shortly after it was developed by Ishin Yoshimoto.[9] Ryoji Takeda, the first person to scientifically analyze the results of NAIKAN therapy in prisons, estimates that between 1954 and 1975 about 1,000,000 juvenile and adult criminals underwent NAIKAN treatment.[10]

Most of the readers will certainly pose the question at this point, if and to what extent the NAIKAN therapy could also be used in the

continued on following page

continued from previous page

treatment of prisoners in the Western world. From all that we know today the author has formed the opinion that—in the case of Germany for example—a clearly affirmative answer is justified. NAIKAN offers a number of advantages to other forms of therapy presently used in German prisons, such as Gestalt therapy and person-centered psychotherapy (Gesprachspsychotherapie), either as individual or as group therapy, as well as psychoanalysis.

NAIKAN was introduced into Europe as a method of treatment for prisoners for the first time over twenty years ago by Akira Ishii and the author.[11] At that time the answer to the question as to the applicability of the NAIKAN therapy in European prisons was purposefully left open, since Bindzus and Ishii had doubts about the physical and psychological ability of European prisoners to stick through NAIKAN for a one-week period, with daily sessions lasting up to sixteen hours, without a more intense participant-counselor interaction. In the meantime, however, this aspect of NAIKAN therapy has been explicitly tested (if even with modest beginnings) on prisoners in the Federal Republic of Germany, and on criminal drug addicts in Austria.[12]

[1]Cf. David K. Reynolds, "Naikan Therapy" in Raymond J. Corsini (ed.) *Handbuch der Psychotherapie,* Vol. 2, p. 770: Ryoki Takeda, "The Participation of Private Citizens in Crime Prevention—The Case of Naikan-ho in Japan," in UNAFEL, Resource Material Series, Nr. 2 (1971), pp. 145 ff.

[2]Rudimentary see also Reynolds, ibid., p. 772.

[3]Reynolds (ibid., p. 769) seems to have completely misunderstood the objective of Naikan Therapy when he writes, "The therapy explicitly aims at producing a sense of existential guilt." To use the word "guilt" in the sense of the Christian understanding of "original sin," which is not familiar to the Japanese, in connection with Naikan is an obvious mistake, It would have been better for Reynolds to have used the term "consciousness of responsibility."

[4]Reynolds (ibid., p. 774) speaks of a new "perspective on life."

[5]For further discussion see also Reynolds, ibid., p. 774.

[6]Reynolds (ibid., p. 774) even proposes—which however is not acceptable in such unequivocal terms—an exact apportionment of time, by which 20% should be spent on the first and second steps and 60% of the time spent on step three.

[7]Reynolds (ibid., p. 772) goes a bit too far when he speaks of a "catharsis."

[8]Gunther Kaiser, Hans-Jurgen Kerner and Heinz Schoch, *Strafvollzug* (Penal Institutions) 3rd edition, 1982, paragraph 15 (p. 49).

[9]Ryoji Takeda, "The Participation of Private Citizens in Crime Prevention—The Case of Naikan-ho in Japan," in UNAFEL, Resource Materials Series, Nr. 2 (1971), pp. 145 ff.

[10]Ryoji Takeda, "Naikan-ho to innai shogu" (Treatment and Naikan Method in Juvenile Training Schools) in Chubu-kyosei, Vol. 6 (1975).

[11]Dieter Bindzus and Akira Ishii, *Strafvollzug in Japan* (Prisons in Japan), 1977, pp. 76 ff.

[12]For information on the expansion of Naikan as a general method of therapy see Franz Ritter, "The Development of Naikan in Europe" (Japanese) in Compilation of reports presented to the 7th Naikan Congress (Tokyo 1984), pp. 44 ff; Helga Margreiter, "My Experience as Naikan Participant and Counselor" (Japanese) in Compilation of reports presented to the 9th Naikan Congress (Tokyo 1987); David K. Reynolds, "Naikan in the USA" (Japanese) in Compilation of reports to the 7th Naikan Congress (Tokyo 1984), pp. 38 ff.

SOURCE: Bindzus, Dieter, 1997. Reprinted with permission of the author.

and their families. The Japanese believe that the tough methods used in prisons are necessary costs for a safer society (Kristof, 1995). Thus, there is little public involvement in prison conditions, and the correctional process remains an operation that receives little scrutiny.

Saudi Arabia

Prison is not the conventional sentencing recourse in Saudi Arabia that it is in our other model countries, primarily because of the tendency to use other methods, such the corporal punishments outlined in Chapter 10. Neverthe-less, prisons, under the Interior Ministry, do exist to house those awaiting trial and also those intractable offenders who are not deterred by the corporal punishments. A Supreme Council for prisons, chaired by a representative from the Interior Ministry, has been established to conduct studies relevant to improving prisons. This same council has been commissioned to consider the development of alternatives to incarceration, because noncustodial sanctions are almost nonexistent in Saudi Arabia. Terms of imprisonment are sometimes reduced and pardons provided during the religious holiday of Ramadan (United Nations, 1999).

Although incarceration figures for Saudi Arabia are hard to come by, according to one United Nations inquiry, as of January 1994 the Saudi prison population was 7,939, with a rate of 45 per 100,000 population (Walmsley, 1999). It is also very difficult to assess the kind and quality of the correctional facilities in Saudi Arabia because of the lack of available information. This dearth of information is caused by the fact that no international human rights organization has received authorization to conduct a mission to Saudi Arabia for several years (Human Rights Watch, 1998, p. 346).

Saudi correctional theory implies that written rules to regulate the prison system are unnecessary because the rights of prisoners are guaranteed according to Muslim law (Shari'a) (United Nations, 1999, p. 7). The Shari'a forms the basis for all Islamic codes and regulates all principles of the justice system, including corrections. In fact, "justice" is the fundamental principle that governs all actions in Islamic Law, whether by the police, courts, or correctional system.

Westerners sometimes are aghast at the way "justice" is meted out by the Saudis, claiming it is unduly harsh. But the perception of Muslims is different. As explained by Saudi expert Frank Vogel, "What the Saudis might consider obedience to God's direct command, the Westerner often calls arbitrary, capricious, and cruel" (Daniszewski, 1997).

Efforts to persuade the Saudis to comply with various international treaties that outline protections for inmates have been unsuccessful. For example, the Saudis have rejected the 1987 Convention for the Prevention of Torture or Inhumane or Degrading Treatment because it contains articles that would forbid countries to deport or extradite individuals where there is risk of torture (Human Rights Watch, 1998, pp. 345–346). The Saudi rejection of such conventions would imply that they condone such methods.

Based on individual accounts reported to organizations like the Human Rights Watch, we can determine that, by Western standards and those outlined in international prisoners' rights conventions, the imprisonment conditions in Saudi Arabia are quite harsh. The use of arbitrary arrest and incarceration, torture, and corporal and capital punishment have been said to be common in both political and criminal cases in Saudi Arabia (Human Rights Watch, 1998, p. 343). However, until international organizations and private researchers are allowed to visit and conduct studies in Saudi Arabia, much of what we hear about corrections in Saudi Arabia will tend to be negative, judgmental, and lacking in empirical validity.

PRISON CROWDING

Prison crowding is the single most pressing problem faced by major prison systems today, not only in Western countries but also in eastern European and many Third World countries. Although countries like Spain, France, and Germany instituted either amnesties or sentencing changes to decrease the number of persons incarcerated, prison populations have increased dramatically again since then, creating serious overcrowding.

Prison Crowding Data

It is difficult to measure the extent of prison crowding. The most common way is to compare the number of prison beds with the number of prison inmates in a given day. If the number of inmates exceeds the number of beds, then we can conclude that the system is crowded beyond 100 percent capacity (Shinkai and Zvekic, 1999). In a study of forty-one countries, most prisons were at or close to 100 percent capacity. As Table 11.1 shows, the countries with the highest rate of overcrowding are Sudan, the Republic of Korea, and Belarus, and over half of the countries had an increase in the capacity rate between 1990 and 1994.

In England and Wales, the rate of imprisonment per 100,000 population rose from 68 in 1967, to 90 in 1987, to 97 in 1990, and to 125 by 1998 (Walmsley, 1999). Not surprisingly, many prisons in Britain are over capacity. The average

Table 11.1 Occupancy Rates in Prison, 1990 and 1994

	1990	1994
Sudan	1105%	962%
Republic of Korea	475	479
Belarus	83	165
Madagascar	149	156
Portugal	117	123
Hong Kong	136	121
Singapore	—	118
Nicaragua	87	113
Czech Republic	55	109
Chile	127	109
Hungary	64	107
Israel	101	105
England and Wales	101	100
Scotland	83	99
Costa Rica	83	96
Marshall Islands	154	96
Malta	72	96
Denmark	85	93
Bulgaria	119	90
Guyana	100	90
Austria	85	90
Russian Federation	—	89
Latvia	94	88
Northern Ireland	79	84
Finland	86	84
Slovakia	62	83
Liechtenstein	—	82
Republic of Moldova	93	79
Lithuania	68	77
Western Samoa	67	77
Cypress	91	77
Uganda	66	75
Japan	74	71
Kyrgyzstan	—	66
Bermuda	89	63
Croatia	40	60
Slovenia	58	58
Mauritius	52	54
FYRM[a]	38	53
Greece	43	42
Macau	—	39
Kuwait	—	2

[a]Former Yugoslav Republic of Macedonia.

SOURCE: Fifth UNCJS. In *Global Report on Crime and Justice*. Reprinted with permission.

prison sentence in England rose by 25 percent between 1945 and 1961, and by 60 percent between 1961 and 1980. In 1957, England had 122 prisoners serving life terms; in 1981, that figure was 1,626. In 1986, only 28 percent of prisoners had a sentence of longer than four years, but by 1996, that rose to 42 percent. England reduced its prison population from 45,000 in 1981 to 43,000 in 1983; but by 1987, it rose to 50,000, and in 1998, it stood at 65,906 (Walmsley, 1999). To handle the population explosion, 12,500 beds were added between 1981 and 1996 (Stern, 1998).

France in 1981 had 42,000 inmates in a system designed for 28,000. In contrast to 1975, when French prisons contained 180 inmates with life terms, there were 355 such inmates in 1981. By 1987, the population was up to 45,000 and a large program of prison construction was under way (Jenkins, 1987, pp. 17–25). By January 1999, there were over 50,000 beds in French prisons. But the problems of crowding have not been alleviated by this building spree. As of January 1999, there were 52,961 inmates, a rate of 84 per 100,000 population. The crowding problem is a result of the fact that there are only 50,014 actual beds for inmates (Minister of Justice, 1999). The French government responded to prison crowding with amnesty programs in 1981, 1988, and 1995, but in each case there were only temporary reductions in the prison population followed by sharp increases. For example, the 1988 amnesty reduced the prison population to 45,000, only to be followed by the steady increase to the high of almost 55,000 in 1996. The serious prison crowding problem keeps the French prison system in a constant state of crisis (Wright, 1983, ch. 9).

Germany has an incarceration rate similar to that of France, Belgium, and Switzerland—90 per 100,000 inhabitants. However, the total number of prisoners, 74,317, is much higher than in those countries (Walmsley, 1999). Germany's incarceration rate actually decreased between 1983 and 1991, due to two factors. First, during the 1960s and again in the early 1990s, Germany decriminalized a large number of offenses, making them administrative offenses. Second, the Germans have vastly increased their use of fines as a sentencing alternative. Short sentences of less than six months can now be imposed under only very restrictive situations in Germany (HEUNI, 1999). However, over the past ten years, since the reunification of East and West Germany and the opening of the European borders, Germany has seen an increase in its incarceration rates, and the problem of overcrowding has resurfaced. The change is largely due to an increase in the number of adjudicated drug offenders (Dunkel, 1992). The German prison incarceration rate increased from 70 per 100,000 population in 1991, to 86 in 1995, to 90 in 1997.

As mentioned earlier, the incarceration figures for China are commonly believed to be imprecise. We can determine, according to UN data, that there are over 1.4 million inmates in China, with an incarceration rate in 1997 of 115 per 100,000 population (Walmsley, 1999). Given our limited knowledge about prisons in China, it is difficult to determine the extent of the crowding problem. It has been reported, however, that China may have a crowding problem caused by an increase in crime and a general hardening of attitude toward criminals based on *yanda*.

Japan's total prison population increased from 46,000 in 1975 to 55,000 in 1986, despite that country's remarkable success in reducing violent crime. In the late 1980s, the prison population stabilized and even lowered. In 1988, the prison population stood at 54,000 (Research and Training Institute, 1989a), and in 1992, it dropped to 46,000, a rate of 36 per 100,000 people. More recently, the prison population again increased—to 49,414 in 1997, a rate of 40 per 100,000 (Walmsley, 1999). However, with prison space for 64,000 inmates, it does not appear that crowding is a problem in Japan (Stern, 1999, p. 96).

Incarceration numbers from Saudi Arabia are even more difficult to acquire than from China, with the United Nations, Amnesty International, and Humans Rights Watch all unable to secure such data. We do know that as of 1994 the Saudi

prison population was 7,939, a rate of 45 per 100,000 persons (Walmsley, 1999). According to a report given by the Saudi government to the secretary general of the United Nations, there is no prison crowding in Saudi Arabia (United Nations, 1999).

Compared to the United States, with its 1997 incarceration rate of 645 per 100,000 population, its generally long sentences, and its massive increase in prison population (from 200,000 in 1970, to 800,000 in 1990, to 1.7 million in 1997), prison as a sanction is still less prevalent in our model countries. Although we must look at the data with some skepticism, we can safely conclude that U.S. rates of incarceration, despite the large increases in England, France, Germany, China, and Japan, continue to be comparatively very high.

In the United States, to be sure, extensive building programs to relieve prison crowding, and court decisions that have forced prison administrators to deal with poor conditions related to crowding, have existed since the 1970s. Western Europe now seems to be facing the same problems, including some increases in crime rates and the general hardening of attitudes toward criminals.

Effects of Prison Crowding

Consider the following:

- Venezuela has some of the worst prison crowding problems in the world. Its thirty-three prisons, built to house 15,000 inmates, now hold more than 24,000. In 1994, 274 inmates were killed by other inmates in Venezuelan jails. The system largely ignores all minimum standards of hygiene, medical care, and security. According to Joan Mariner of the Human Rights Watch in New York, "every aspect of the system is overloaded and not functioning (*Times,* 1998, p. A30).

- In Brazilian police detention centers, where a large proportion of the country's 180,000 prisoners are held, inmates have been forced to tie themselves to the cell bars to sleep because of the lack of floor space (Human Rights Watch Website, 1999).

■ Violent prison riots in the 1990s at England's Strangeways Prison and earlier riots at Wormwood Scrubs, Albany, Gartree, and Hull were largely the result of conditions related to crowding. Other inmate uprisings occurred in the former East Germany, the Czech Republic, Brazil, Russia, and Venezuela in the 1990s (Stern, 1998, p. 9).

These scenarios are just a few of the hundreds, and maybe thousands, of stories that can be told about the impact of prison crowding in the world today. In general, prison crowding can limit the ability of correctional officials to do their work, increase the potential for violence, and lead to mental and physical health problems for inmates.

According to the Human Rights Watch, violence may be a factor in many prison deaths, but the most common causes of death are the spread of diseases and the subsequent lack of medical care that are promulgated by prison crowding. Communicable diseases such as cholera have contributed to inmate deaths in prisons in Zambia, Malawi, and Mozambique. It is estimated that around 100 (untried) prisoners per year are dying in Nairobi (Kenya) jails from preventable or treatable diseases (Penal Reform International Website, 1999). The spread of tuberculosis throughout prisons in the world, including Russia and some of its former republics, have caused serious health problems there. HIV/AIDS has also exacerbated the disease problem, with grossly disproportionate rates of infection in many correctional facilities (Human Rights Watch Website, 1999). In some cases, inmates acquire HIV/AIDS as a result of sharing dirty needles or having sexual contact with other inmates; in other cases, inmates enter prison with the disease. In 1995, it was estimated that over 27,000 inmates in the U.S. prison system were infected with HIV or AIDS (U.S. Department of Justice, 1995). In 1996, in England and Wales, eighty prisoners were known to have HIV or AIDS (Home Office, 1996). Prisons respond to the problem by a variety of methods, including isolation and restrictions. For example, in Poland, infected prisoners are kept in separate cells and use the bathroom, washroom, and kitchen separately (Platek, 1994). In Brazil, Norway, Germany, India, and England and Wales, policies to combat the spread of AIDS have included the provision of clean needles and condoms to inmates (Stern, 1998, p. 127).

Solutions to Prison Crowding

Responses to prison crowding have varied among countries. The Scandinavian countries and the Netherlands, which have earned a reputation for enlightened penal philosophy, are particularly noteworthy. The average sentence in the Netherlands is less than one month, thus allowing for a large turnover in prison population. Rather than being sent directly to prison, convicted criminals must wait their turn to serve their sentences. And in 1975, an amnesty and a shortening of sentences were used to counteract the large increase in crime and convictions. Likewise, Sweden responded to its prison population problem with a large-scale amnesty in 1983, and measures were taken to cut down on sentencing. In Denmark, which also suffered from a large increase in crime between 1960 and 1980, authorities responded by instituting a program of decriminalization, abolishing indeterminate sentences, and expanding the probation system. Iceland, Finland, and Norway all seem to have minimal problems with crowding due to low incarceration rates of 40, 55, and 55 per 100,000 people, respectively.

In many countries, the answer to the problem of prison crowding has more often than not been simply to build more prisons. This practice has been criticized by a number of academics and social reformers who claim that it is illogical to think that prison can be offered as its own remedy (Foucault, 1979).

Building prisons to reduce the crowding problem has been called the construction strategy (Blumstein, 1995). This policy is the result of a generally more conservative and hard-line attitude toward crime and criminals. Prison building has been a growth industry in many countries, especially the United States and the western European nations, but even the prison explosion cannot keep up with the burgeoning populations. Antiquated fortress prisons built in the nineteenth century continue to be used in Russia, Mexico, England, Germany, and the United States, to name just a few. In some cases, as in Lancaster, old castles in England have been converted to prisons in order to deal with the crush of prisoners. And in 1996, England purchased a large boat from the United States and turned it into a low-security prison (Stern, 1998, p. 280).

One way in which the construction strategy has been advanced in the United States and, more recently, in other countries has been through the development of **private prisons**—correctional institutions operated by private firms on behalf of governments. The first such institution was opened in Pennsylvania in 1975, and by 1997, there were 126 private prisons holding over 70,000 inmates in the United States (Clear and Cole, 2000). The private prison business is dominated by two companies, the Wackenhut Corporation, and the Corrections Corporation of America (CCA). These corporations have formed alliances with businesses throughout the world, and private prisons are now operating in Puerto Rico, Australia, England and Wales, and Canada (Stern, 1998, p. 297).

In addition to the construction approach, Alfred Blumstein (1995) proposes three other ways to address the crowding crisis: the null strategy, the intermediate sanctions strategy, and the prison population reduction strategy. Although Blumstein presents these in a North American context, they can be applied across boundaries; in fact, a number of countries have already implemented them in various forms, as in Scandinavia.

Proponents of the null strategy say that nothing should be done, that prisons should be allowed to become increasingly congested. The hope is that criminals will be deterred by living in such conditions or that a change in the demographics of the crime cohort will resolve prison crowding. Although this may be the cheapest and most politically acceptable approach in the short run, in the long run it may not solve the crowding problems and may lead to some of the problems mentioned previously, such as riots, disease, and general system failure.

Proponents of the intermediate sanctions strategy call for the development of punishments short of incarceration. These punishments, as we discussed in Chapter 10, include probation, fines, community service, restitution, and home confinement. Because of limited prison space, they say, prisons should be used only for violent offenders who have not been deterred by prior punishments.

Finally, proponents of the population reduction strategy call for a two-step process of changing sentencing practices and developing more methods for letting inmates out of prison. With regard to the former, those who determine sentences (legislators) must write laws that limit the use of imprisonment. With regard to the latter, "back-door" strategies such as parole, work release, and good time must be implemented to get offenders out of prison before the end of their terms in order to free space for newcomers (Blumstein, 1998).

Different countries have adopted a variety of strategies to address prison crowding. The problem exists in all regions of the world and has a definite impact on corrections internationally. A mixture of approaches that best suit the needs of a particular correctional system is probably the optimal solution to the problem.

RIGHTS OF PRISONERS

Legal challenges to prison conditions have become common only in the past thirty years, although they did occur earlier. These challenges are especially prominent in the United States, where civil litigation regarding prison conditions has become a major consideration in corrections administration. The legal basis for challenges to prison conditions in the United States comes from the Eighth Amendment of the U.S. Constitution, which states that "excessive bail shall not be required, nor excessive fines imposed, nor cruel and unusual punishments inflicted."

In the international community, legal challenges arise from a number of covenants and conventions. The foundation for these documents is rooted in the UN Universal Declaration of Human Rights, which states that "no one shall be subjected to torture, or cruel, inhuman or degrading treatment or punishment" (Article 5). The declaration, originally proposed in 1948 by the United Nations and subsequently ratified by a large number of nations, was the result of the desire to combat the massive violations of human rights that occurred in World War II. Since then, other international organizations have produced documents that support Article 5, such as the European Convention on Human Rights, the African Charter on Human and People's Rights, and the Inter-American Convention on Human Rights.

In 1955, the United Nations developed what has become the most well-known of prison guidelines, the Standard Minimum Rules for the Treatment of Prisoners. (For a summary of the Standards, see Appendix B.) According to the Human Rights Watch organization, the UN standards have been integrated into the prison laws and regulations of many countries; unfortunately, few if any prison systems observe all their prescriptions (Human Rights Watch Website, 1999).

Other international conventions also specifically address treatment of prisoners, although the actual law resulting from these conventions has not been highly developed. In 1953, the European Convention on Human Rights was developed by the newly formed Council of Europe (1949), which in 1987 revised its own set of prison rules, a more detailed set than the UN standards (Stern, 1998). The 1984 United Nations Convention for the Prevention of Torture, as well as the 1987 Convention for the Prevention of Torture or Inhumane or Degrading Treatment, echoed the concerns expressed by the European Convention on Human Rights. Other regions of the world have also responded with their own documents. The Conference on Security and Cooperation in Europe (CSCE) also emphasizes human rights, including prisoner rights, as do regional human rights conventions in Africa, Asia, and the Americas. Although these different conventions are not confined to prisoners' rights, these rights are of natural concern because of the essential helplessness of imprisoned persons and the fairly easy possibility of violation of the human rights of those who are not in the public eye or not surrounded by community members and family (Kaiser, 1984).

As in the United States, the European courts were slow to get involved in the thorny issues of prison administration. In the first fifteen years of the European Convention (1950–1965), only 4 of 800 prisoner petitions were supported. Nevertheless, certain celebrated cases, such as *Ireland v. United Kingdom* (in which Great Britain agreed to change its practices after certain procedures used in prison interrogations of suspected IRA terrorists were found to violate Article 3), have resulted in greater public attention to these matters.

German courts, following passage of the 1976 Prison Law, have heard numerous complaints about infringements of prisoners' rights, and a body of rules delineating those rights gradually has developed. Thus, for example, the right to refuse treatment has been confirmed by the Federal Constitutional Court, while an appeals court in one state found overcrowding to be a violation of human dignity and ordered that no additional prisoners be confined until some of those in prison were released. This latter case was decided in 1967 and thus predated the German Prison Law of 1976, as well as many cases in the United States that have addressed overcrowding. One of the earliest and most famous of the American cases, *Pugh v. Locke* (406 F. Supp. 318 M.D. Ala.), which concluded that the Alabama prison system violated inmates' rights because of overcrowding and other abuses, was decided in 1976.

Prisoner rights litigation and international agreements regarding human rights do not guarantee that prison conditions will be safe and hu-

World Report: Prison Conditions Around the Globe—Human Rights Watch

Prison massacres, dramatic protests, and violent guard abuse earned occasional news headlines in 1997, but the deplorable daily living conditions that were the plight of the great majority of the world's prisoners passed largely unnoticed. With scant public attention to the topic in most countries, correspondingly little progress was made in rectifying the abuses routinely inflicted in prisons and other places of detention. Many countries, moreover, fostered public ignorance of prison inadequacies by denying human rights groups, journalists, and other outside observers nearly all access to their penal facilities.

Unchecked outbursts of prison violence continued to violate prisoners' right to life. The killings of at least twenty-nine prisoners in a remote jungle facility in Venezuela led the country's Justice Ministry to promise reforms, and its Public Ministry to conduct an extensive investigation of the incident's causes. The Tajikistan government chose to cover up an even bloodier prison massacre. Although information about the events was scarce, reports indicated that the Tajik security forces stormed a prison in the northern city of Khujand, killing over a hundred prisoners. Earlier that week, inmates had rioted and taken several guards hostage to protest life-threatening detention conditions. The Tajik government apparently took no action to punish those responsible for the deaths.

In Morocco's Oukacha prison, twenty-two prisoners were burned alive; they had been crammed together in a cell reportedly built to hold eight. The cause of the fire was not announced, but the country's Justice Ministry did acknowledge that overcrowding might have played a role in the deaths. The most common cause of death in prison was disease, often the predictable results of severe overcrowding, malnutrition, unhygienic conditions, and lack of medical care. A special commission of inquiry, appointed after the death of a prominent businessman in India's high-security Tihar Central Jail, reported that the 10,000 inmates held in that institution endured serious health hazards, including overcrowding, "appalling" sanitary facilities, and a shortage of medical staff. Similar conditions prevailed in the prisons of the former Soviet Union, where tuberculosis continued its comeback. Russia's prosecutor general announced that about 2,000 inmates had died of tuberculosis in the previous year. In Kazakhstan, the disease, including drug-resistant strains, reached epidemic proportions. AIDS also plagued many prison populations.

Inadequate supervision by guards, easy access to weapons, lack of separation of different categories of prisoners, and fierce competition for basic necessities encouraged inmate-on-inmate abuse in many penal facilities. In extreme cases—as in certain Venezuelan prisons with one guard for every 150 prisoners, and an underground trade in knives, guns, even grenades—prisoners killed other prisoners with impunity. Rape, extortion, and involuntary servitude were other frequent abuses suffered by inmates at the bottom of the prison hierarchy.

In contrast, powerful inmates in some facilities in Colombia, India, and Mexico, among others, enjoyed cellular phones, rich diets, and comfortable lodging. With guard corruption rampant in so many prisons around the world, the adage "You get what you pay for" was only too appropriate.

Shielded from public view, and populated largely by the poor, uneducated, and politically powerless, prisons tended to remain hidden sites of human rights abuse. By struggling against this natural tendency toward secrecy and silence, the efforts of numerous local human rights groups around the world—who fought to obtain access to prisons, monitored prison conditions, and publicized the abuses they found—were critical. In some countries, moreover, government human rights ombudspersons, parliamentary commissions, and other monitors helped call attention to abuses.

SOURCE: Clear and Cole, 2000, p. 229.

mane. In fact, a recent United Nations study revealed that a number of countries have been unable to meet the minimal standards outlined by the United Nations in 1955 (United Nations, 1996). (For a graphic description of some abuses in prisons around the globe, see the accompanying box.)

Not coincidentally, countries that are generally more amenable to human rights considerations are the ones that have been in the forefront of protecting prisoners' rights, while those countries that chronically violate the human rights of their citizens typically also pay little attention to prisoners' rights. Nevertheless, the very fact that this issue has become prominent in terms of litigable rights, rather than conventional reform efforts, has led to greater attention to prison conditions and the problems of individual prisoners.

SUMMARY

In the United States and the other countries we have considered, there have been many changes in the correctional systems. Advances have occurred in many countries in the form of improved prison conditions and an increase in the different kinds of rehabilitation programs available. Because of the elusive goals of rehabilitation, however, some countries have become discouraged with it. The result is an increase in the number of prisoners purely for incapacitation purposes. With this goal in mind, correctional systems have become more interested in maintaining a just system, one that is not degrading or inhumane to its clients. Although few countries can claim to have reached even that goal to any degree of satisfaction, we have only to consider the horrors of prisons and corrections as they existed in earlier times, even as recently as the nineteenth century, to conclude that progress has been made, especially in recent decades.

A review of the correctional practices of the model countries reveals a number of similarities. Many systems make some effort to separate serious convicted criminals from the unconvicted and lesser criminals. Most correctional systems have developed some form of classification system that segregates inmates according to time to be served or seriousness of the offense. All of our model correctional system, even China and Saudi Arabia, propose kinds of rehabilitation programs to assist offenders in their reform and reintegration efforts. The quality and kind of these programs vary greatly, however.

One of the major problems facing many correctional systems throughout the world is prison crowding. Almost all of our model countries, with the exception of Japan and perhaps Saudi Arabia, suffer from the effects of this malady. Unfortunately, the "get-tough" attitude toward crime has caused many countries to build more prisons as a solution to the problem. Of the many issues that arise as a result of prison crowding, one of concern to many in the international community, is its effect on inmates' rights. A significant number of documents and international covenants have tried with varying success to standardize the treatment of offenders.

While prison conditions and prison crowding remain a concern, there has been some movement toward the increased use of alternatives to prison, especially probation and fines, in dealing with convicted offenders. Perhaps in the twenty-first century, we will see the development of an "ideal" solution to the prison crisis—such as a pill that will instantly turn an intractable and antisocial offender into a congenial and law-abiding citizen.

DISCUSSION QUESTIONS

1. Based on what you learned about the different rationales for punishment in Chapter 10, which of our model countries seems to believe in rehabilitation? Incapacitation? Retribution?

2. Germany has increased its use of noncustodial sanctions but has also recently experienced an increase in the imprisonment rate. What factors might account for this phenomenon?

3. Why does the United States have a much higher incarceration rate than most other countries?

4. In which of the model countries would you prefer to be incarcerated if convicted of a major crime? Explain.

5. Why has prison building (the construction strategy) not solved the prison crowding problem around the world?

6. In light of China's abuses in the use of incarceration and violations of prisoners' rights, what can be done to influence it to change its policies? What might be some reasons the international community chooses not to come in conflict with China over this issue?

FOR FURTHER READING

Carlie, M. K., and K. I. Minor. (1992). *Prisons Around the World: Studies in International Penology.* Dubuque, Iowa: Brown.

Foucault, M. (1979). *Discipline and Punish.* Harmondsworth, UK: Penguin Books.

Kensey, A., and P. Tournier. (1997). *French Prison Populations: Some Features.* Trans. R. Greenstein. Paris: Minister of Justice.

Melossi, D., and M. Pavarini. (1981). *The Prison and the Factory.* New York: Macmillan.

Seymour, J. D., and R. Anderson. (1998), *New Ghosts, Old Ghosts: Prisons and Labor Reform Camps in China.* Armonk, N.Y.: Sharpe.

Weiss, R. P., and N. South (eds.). (1998). *Comparing Prison Systems: Toward a Comparative and International Penology.* Amsterdam: Gordon and Breach.

Wu, H. H. (1992). *Laogai: The Chinese Gulag.* Boulder, Colo.: Westview Press

Part III Modern Dilemmas in International Criminal Justice

12   Terrorism

The Historical Background of Terrorism
Defining Terrorism
The Goals of Terrorism
The Prevalence of Terrorism
Terrorist Groups
Terrorism in the Model Nations
Responses to International Terrorism
The Future of Terrorism
Summary
Discussion Questions and Exercises
For Further Reading

Key Terms and Concepts

Abu Nidal Organization
agents of biological origin (ABOs)
al-Qaida
Antiterrorism and Effective Death
   Penalty Act
Assassins
Aum Shrinrikyo
Bin Laden
Carlos the Jackal
Delta Force
diaspora
domestic terrorism
Good Friday Accord
Grenzschutzgruppe 9 (GSG–9)
Groupment d'Intervention de la
   Gendarmerie Nationale (GIGN)
Hamas

Hizballah
international terrorism
Japanese Red Army (JRA)
jihad
Palestinian Liberation Organization (PLO)
Paris P/8 Ministerial Conference
Popular Front for the Liberation of Palestine (PFLP)
Provisional Irish Republican Army (PIRA)
Red Army Faction (RAF)
religious terrorism
revolutionary terrorism
Seal Team 6
Special Air Service Regiment (SAS)
state-sponsored terrorism
Thugs
terrorism
Uygurs

Acts of terrorism kill and injure innocent people, often at random and often in large numbers, which makes terrorism a particularly agonizing problem. And because terrorism is generally a political crime, with the perpetrators having political or ideological motives for their actions, the problem of dealing with terrorism lies somewhere between waging war and conducting a law enforcement operation. In our time, international terrorism has become an alarming and frustrating reality that affects the lives of international travelers, as well as of residents of terrorism-prone areas. Plane passengers of today have become so accustomed to passing through security checks at airports that they have forgotten or never knew the days when one could board a plane directly without going through an electronic security barrier and having one's carryon luggage x-rayed. These precautions are the result of large increases in terrorist activities worldwide and of the heightened fear of terrorism.

A few examples of recent international terrorist actions involving Americans will give some idea of the diversity and enormity of the problem:

- In 1988, a bomb was planted on Pan American flight 103. The plane exploded over Lockerbie, Scotland, and all aboard, as well as some citizens of Lockerbie, were killed.

- In 1993, a bomb detonated in the basement garage of the World Trade Center in New York City, killing 6 people and injuring over 1,000.

- In 1996, a truck bomb attack on the U.S. Embassy in Dhahran, Saudi Arabia, killed 19 American soldiers and injured 250 persons.

- In 1998, in Nairobi, Kenya, 291 persons were killed, including 12 Americans, when bombs devastated the U.S. embassy.

In this chapter, we focus on terrorism as a problem for the criminal justice system. We will discuss the background, definition, prevalence, and purposes of terrorism. In addition, we will address terrorism in our model countries and

look at the system responses to the problem. We will conclude our discussion with a look at the future of terrorism.

THE HISTORICAL BACKGROUND OF TERRORISM

Terrorism traditionally has been a tool of groups trying to overthrow a regime but lacking the numbers to do so militarily or legitimately. In the first century A.D., terror and assassination were used by the Jewish Zealots, who opposed Roman rule in Palestine. The Zealots were crushed by the Romans, and the Jews were banished from Palestine, beginning the long period of Jewish life in forced exile, or **diaspora** (Schlagheck, 1988, ch. 2).

In seventh-century India, a group called the **Thugs** was formed; their goal was for their victims "to experience terror and to express it visibly for the pleasure of Kali, the Hindu goddess of terror and destruction" (Rapoport, 1984, p. 660). The Thugs lasted for over seven centuries and killed millions of people using their typical method of execution—hanging (Barghothi, 1996, p. 86). A third group active during the eleventh through thirteenth centuries was the **Assassins,** who supported Islam in the Persian Gulf area, using the dagger and the reward of martyrdom to promote their terrorist objectives (Barghothi, 1996, p. 87).

The term *terrorism* was actually first used during the French Revolution and the Jacobean Reign of Terror of the late 1700s. A century later, a group of Russian terrorists called the Narodnaya Volya used similar tactics in an effort to overthrow the czar. What is important to remember is that each of these "historical" terrorist groups was at least partly successful, and this success undoubtedly influenced the development of modern terrorist organizations. Later in this chapter, we will discuss some of the major terrorist groups that have developed over the past 75 years in more detail.

DEFINING TERRORISM

Terrorism is not easy to define, and at least a hundred definitions have been proposed (Kegley, 1990). Why is it so difficult to reach a consensus on the definition? The central problem involves the larger ideological argument about whether the acts committed are "criminal" or are in the interest of promoting the "greater good." It has been often stated that "one man's terrorist is another man's freedom fighter." Terrorists themselves may not view their activities as illegal or immoral, and they may not believe themselves to be criminals. In fact, they may look upon themselves as martyrs.

The issue is further clouded by a change in status for those who are involved with terrorism. In the 1980s, President Reagan called the African National Congress a terrorist group, but the group subsequently was applauded for the sacrifices it made in the fight to eliminate apartheid in South Africa. Menachem Begin, former Israeli prime minister, was well known in the late 1940s as a leader of the notorious Irgun Zvai Leumi, a terrorist group that worked to speed the departure of the British from Palestine and the establishment of a Jewish state. In that same part of the world, Yasir Arafat, long excoriated as a terrorist, is now the leader of an increasingly moderate element of the Palestine Liberation Organization. These examples illustrate how defining terrorism and deciding who is a terrorist is often an elusive process and is highly sensitive to a number of factors.

For our purposes, we will adopt the definition used by the FBI to explain the phenomenon of **terrorism.** It reads:

The unlawful use of force or violence against persons or property to intimidate or coerce a government, the civilian population, or any segment thereof, in furtherance of political or social objectives. (FBI, 1997)

There are two general types of terrorism: domestic and international. **Domestic terrorism** involves persons or groups committing a terrorist act(s) in their own country. One famous example would be the bombing of the federal building in Oklahoma City by Timothy McVeigh and his associates. Another example occurred in Spain, where the Basque Fatherland and Liberty Movement has used terrorist tactics to overcome Spanish resistance to Basque separatism. A third example took place in Japan, where sarin nerve gas was planted in five trains in the Tokyo subway in 1995 by a Japanese religious cult. **International terrorism** involves citizens or the territory of more than one country. Four examples of international terrorism are provided earlier in the chapter.

THE GOALS OF TERRORISM

What is it that terrorists are trying to achieve? Again, it is not easy to explain the goals of terrorism. In some cases, there are multiple purposes; in others, the goals are not clearly understood even by those involved. In any case, it is important to have some grasp of the reasons behind terrorist activity throughout the globe.

One goal of terrorists is to force the government to respond to their violence in a harsh manner, in the hope that such repression will lead to discontent among the people and ultimately to revolution. In this case, terrorism may be used to destabilize colonial governments and occupation forces. Such terrorism is directed at a specific goal that is easy to articulate and understand, such as overthrow of the current political regime. This kind of terrorism, referred to as **revolutionary terrorism,** often results from the absence of democratic opportunities and ways to petition those in power in a legitimate fashion. The clearest example of this kind of terrorism in the twentieth century involved the efforts of the PLO in Palestine to unseat the Israelis in the Middle East.

Terrorism is also practiced by governments against their own citizens when they wish to protect their own political or economic interests. For example, they may use their power to harass, arrest, torture, or kill alleged enemies of the state.

Governments may also implement covert actions against other countries for political, economic, or military reasons. These activities by governments against their own citizens or other countries are called **state-sponsored terrorism.** An example of this form of terrorism is The Reign of Terror, which sent thousands of French citizens to the guillotine in 1793 and 1794. This was a calculated effort on the part of the revolutionary leaders to suppress opposition, combat increasing instability, and ward off counterrevolutionary threats to the new French state. More recently, Stalin's brutal repression in the former Soviet Union, the wholesale killing of Cambodians by the Khmer Rouge, and state-sanctioned killing and torture of citizens in several South and Central American countries are just a few chilling reminders that governments are frequently guilty of random violence designed to terrorize their own citizens.

Another frequently stated goal of terrorist groups is to promote a certain religious system or protect a set of beliefs within a religion. This kind of terrorism is called **religious terrorism.** A good example of this type of terrorism is the use of **jihad,** or holy war, by Islamic fundamentalists who wish to protect their religion from "creeping secularism and cultural imperialism posed by Western countries such as the United States" (Ali and Bowe, 1988).

Probably the most important goal of most terrorist activity is to generate publicity on a worldwide scale: "Terrorism is not simply what terrorists do, but the effect they create by their actions" (Jenkins, 1978, p. 119). Terrorists want their actions to be publicized to get their message before a larger audience. Because of the horrifying nature of terrorist acts, the media usually oblige and give them extensive coverage. This heightens the sense that we live in an insecure world and might be the victim of random violence at any time. Extensive publicity also enables terrorists to focus attention on the reasons for their actions, which is very important if they wish to initiate any change, gain a reaction from those in power, and even generate some sympathy for their plight. And, given the improvements in technology and world communications, it is not uncommon for videotaped segments of in-progress terrorist activity to be instantaneously broadcast across the world.

Even more unsettling is terrorism that appears to have no clear or immediate goal or that gains publicity through acts that will not further a goal in any evident way. General dissatisfaction with German society seems to inspire most of the serious acts of terrorism encountered by the Germans in recent years. Terrorism in Italy has been a major problem, but it does not have a clear goal other than to vent frustration and create insecurities within the population. Some of the hostage kidnappings in Lebanon have been by unknown groups for unclear reasons. And Pan American flight 103 was sabotaged by then unknown groups and for unarticulated reasons (although the United States has since claimed that the bombing took place at the instigation of Libya, in retaliation for a U.S. bombing raid on Libya in 1986, and suspects have been extradited for trial to Scotland). Such incidents are particularly difficult to understand because they run counter even to the general goal of advertising a cause, the goal that is usually so important in terrorist action.

THE PREVALENCE OF TERRORISM

Despite the seeming pervasiveness of international terrorism today, few incidents actually take place, and the number of people affected is relatively small (Ross, 1991). For example, the number of individuals killed by terrorists in any year is minuscule when compared to homicides in general, accidents, or other causes of death. But the relative smallness of the terrorist enterprise is not an indicator of its importance as an international crime problem. As the word implies, the purpose of terrorist acts is to inspire terror—to make people feel insecure and interrupt their expectations that they will be able to conduct their affairs in a normal manner without taking great precautions.

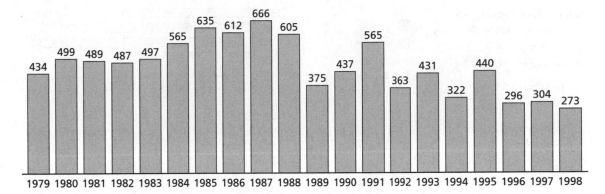

FIGURE 12.1
Total International Terrorist Attacks, 1979–1998

SOURCE: U.S. State Department, 1999.

For a twenty-year period, the number of terrorist incidents increased considerably, from 125 in 1968 to 855 in 1988. However, beginning in 1988, there was a decline in the number of terrorist acts throughout the world, and except for a few years of intense activity, it has steadily declined since that time. For an overview of the total number of international terrorist acts in recent years, see Figure 12.1. Note that, although the number of terrorist attacks has dropped in recent years, the total number of persons killed or wounded in these attacks has increased due to the severity of the incidents. For example, in 1998, terrorist acts were reported to be at their lowest total since 1971. However, the total number of persons killed and wounded in the 273 attacks was at an all-time high of 741 and 5,952, respectively. Most of these deaths and injuries were the result of attacks on the U.S. embassies in Nairobi, Kenya, and in Dar es Salaam, Tanzania (U.S. State Department, 1999). For a graphic depiction of the total casualties in terrorist attacks in 1998, as well as information about the kind of facilities struck and type of terrorist event, see Figure 12.2.

In the United States, terrorist incidents have also declined in number since the early 1980s. In 1982, terrorist acts in the United States reached a high of 51; in 1995, the number dropped to 1, a slight increase from 1994, when no terrorist acts were committed. More recent figures indicate that there were no acts of international terrorism in the United States in 1998 (U.S. State Department, 1999). Figure 12.3 gives a year-by-year breakdown of terrorist acts in the United States from 1980 through 1995.

TERRORIST GROUPS

Literally hundreds of terrorist groups surfaced over the course of the past century. One study published in 1979 estimated that in 1979 there were about 3,000 terrorists in fifty groups worldwide (Kupperman and Trent, 1979, p. 5), but more recent reports place the numbers much higher. The FBI stated in 1993 that in the United States alone there were over forty-five active terrorist groups (FBI, 1993). In his comprehensive text on political crime, Frank Hagan lists thirteen terrorist groups that are related only to the larger PLO movement in Palestine (Hagan, 1997, p. 150). A current and more comprehensive list of terrorist groups is provided by the U.S. State Department, Office of the Coordinator for Counterterrorism, which reports that forty-seven terrorist organizations are active in the world today; Table 12.1 lists these groups.

Total Facilities Struck

Business - 282
Military - 4
Government - 10
Diplomat - 35

Other - 68

_____

Total - 399

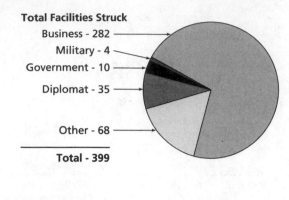

Type of Event

Bombing - 166
Hijacking - 2
Arson - 8
Firebombing - 11

Armed attack - 40

Other - 2

Kidnapping - 44

_____

Total - 273

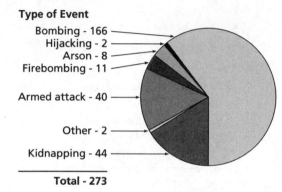

Total Casualties

Government - 19
Military - 23
Business - 49
Diplomat - 153

Other - 6,449

_____

Total - 6,693

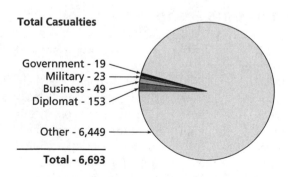

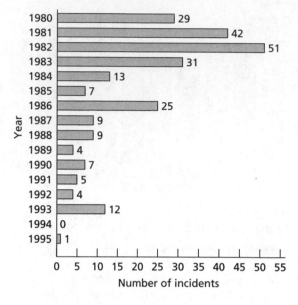

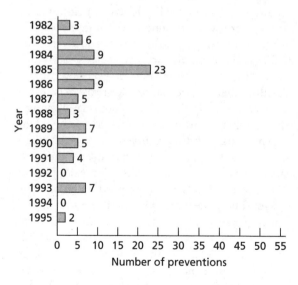

FIGURE 12.2
Total International Attacks, 1998

SOURCE: U.S. State Department, 1999.

FIGURE 12.3
Terrorist Incidents and Preventions in the United
States, 1980–1995

SOURCE: Federal Bureau of Investigation, 1997, p. 2.

Although these figures may not be accurate in an absolute sense, one thing is clear: The numbers of terrorist organizations has increased considerably over the years, and the groups have become a major concern for law enforcement throughout the world. Further, any discussion of these groups is sure to exclude some groups that are problematic and include others that are waning in enthu-

Table 12.1 Foreign Terrorist Organizations, 1997

Abu Nidal Organization (ANO)	Loyalist Volunteer Force (LVF)
Abu Sayyaf Group (ASG)	Manuel Rodriguez Patriotic Front Dissidents (FPMR/D)
Alex Boncayao Brigade (ABB)	Mujahedin-e Khalq Organization (MEK, MKO)
Armed Islamic Group (GIA)	New People's Army (NPA)
Aum Supreme Truth (AUM)	National Liberation Army (ELN)
Aum Shinrikyo (AUM)	Palestine Islamic Jihad—Shaqaqi Faction (PIJ)
Basque Fatherland and Liberty (ETA)	Palestine Liberation Front—Abu Abbas Faction (PLF)
Continuity Irish Republican Army (CIRA)	Party of Democratic Kampuchea
Democratic Front for the Liberation of Palestine—Hawatmeh Faction (DFLP)	Popular Front for the Liberation of Palestine (PFLP)
Devrimici Sol (Revolutionary Left)	Popular Front for the Liberation of Palestine—General Command (PFLP-GC)
Euzkadi Ta Askatasuna (ETA)	Provisional Irish Republican Army (PIRA)
Gama'a al-Islamiyya (Islamic Group, IG)	Qibla and People Against Gangsterism and Drugs (PAGAD)
HAMAS (Islamic Resistance Movement)	Real IRA (RIRA)
Harakat ul-Ansar (HUA)	Revolutionary Armed Forces of Colombia (FARC)
Harakat ul-Mujahidin (HUM)	Revolutionary Organization 17 November (17 November)
Hizballah (Party of God)	Revolutionary People's Liberation Party/Front (DHKP/C)
Irish Republican Army (IRA)	Revolutionary People's Struggle (ELA)
Jamaat ul-Fuqra	Shining Path (Sendero Luminoso, SL)
Japanese Red Army (JRA)	Sikh Terrorism
al-Jihad	Tupac Amaru Revolutionary Movement (MRTA)
Kach	Al Ummah
Kahane Chai	Zviadists
Khmer Rouge	
Kurdistan Workers' Party (PKK)	
Liberation Tigers of Tamil Eelam (LTTE)	

SOURCE: U.S. State Department, 1997.

siasm. Here we will look at two of the most widely publicized and longest-running terrorist groups of the past century, the PLO and IRA, and describe a third group, al-Qaida, that appears to be among the most formidable of the new groups.

Northern Ireland

One of the most protracted conflicts of the twentieth century was the struggle between the English government and the Irish Republican Army (IRA) and, more recently, the **Provisional Irish Republican Army (PIRA)** of Northern Ireland. The "troubles" between England and Ireland are centuries old; the independent Irish Free State, however, was not established until 1920, after years of struggle by the illegal Irish Republican Army, which combined terrorism and guerilla warfare in its battle with England. At that time, England retained the largely Protestant northern counties of Ireland, called Ulster, and gave them special status as an entity within Great Britain. Although this partition of Ireland was vehemently opposed by the newly independent Irish Free State, it continued and developed a certain legitimacy over the years.

Within Ulster, however, the Catholic minority held second-class status, with little political or economic power and a great deal of discriminatory legislation directed against it. During the 1960s, a large civil rights movement began in Ulster, and the often violent disturbances led to a peacekeeping occupation by English military forces. It is from this modern history of struggle that the PIRA developed, breaking off from the Irish Republican Army (IRA—also called the Official Irish Republican Army, or OIRA), which during the years after the partition of Ireland had continued to work toward reunification of the north and south. The IRA tactics, but not its goals, were repudiated by the Republic of Ireland during the postindependence era. Choice of tactics also led to the rupture between the PIRA and the OIRA in the early 1970s. The OIRA now tries to work for peaceful reform, while the PIRA remains a terrorist organization (Moxon-Browne, 1981).

In addition to the PIRA, a number of other splinter groups have surfaced that are willing to terrorize to achieve a reunification of Ireland. Among the most organized and dangerous are the Continuity Irish Republican Army (CIRA), the Irish National Liberation Army (INLA), and, more recently, the Real IRA (RIRA).

The PIRA's aim is to dislodge the British troops from Ulster and unite this area with the Republic. Through bombings in England and attacks on British soldiers in England and Northern Ireland, it hopes to wear down British resistance to unification. Each year there are tragic cases of the murder of civilians and soldiers. In 1990 a terrorist attack against the residence of the British prime minister was narrowly averted, and in 1992 the IRA stepped up its campaign of terror, with frequent bombings and bomb threats.

From September 1994 through February 1996, a cease-fire was observed by the IRA and a truce declared by Great Britain and the Republic of Ireland. In April 1998, feuding Catholic and Protestant parties signed the **Good Friday Accord,** which was a historic agreement outlining a power-sharing arrangement to share multiparty administration of Northern Ireland. As of this writing, the fate of the accord hangs in the balance due to the passing of deadlines for full disarma-ment of the IRA and the lack of acceptance of the document by dissenters such as the PIRA and the RIRA.

Palestine

The history of the conflict in the territory called Palestine is over two thousand years old. Wars have plagued the region and have involved the Assyrians, Babylonians, Persians, Greeks, Romans, Egyptians, Mongols, Turks, and British, as well as the modern Arab nations in the Middle East. The root of the conflict is ownership of territory perceived as the Holy Land by Muslim, Jewish, and Christian settlers (Borders, 1999).

The most recent conflict over the territory has lasted over fifty years, with the main combatants being Muslims and Jews. The conflict began in 1948 when the British government, which had held sovereignty since the end of World War I, relinquished control of the majority of Palestine to the new Jewish state. Since that time, Israel has had a number of armed conflicts with its Arab neighbors, with the Israelis gaining the upper hand because of their economic, military, and political strength. However, in response to the Israeli stranglehold on the region, Muslims have developed a number of terrorist groups, with the parent organization the **Palestinian Liberation Organization (PLO).**

The PLO, formally developed under the guidance of Ahmad Shuqeiri in 1964, originally consisted of a collection of interest groups in the Palestinian region. The main goal of the group was to destroy the Israeli state and re-create an Arab state in the former Palestine. Guided by this philosophy, a number of terrorist organizations were born in the region including militant groups such as the al-Fatah under the direction of Yasir Arafat. Arafat took control of the PLO in 1967 after the Six-Day War, and over the next twenty years, he transformed the organization from a fragmented amalgamation of groups into a united political body that could represent all Palestinians. Arafat was responsible for helping the PLO gain recognition as a legitimate political entity in both the Arab community and the United Nations.

However, over the years, Arafat has lost the support of a number of Palestinian groups that believe he has compromised too much with the Israelis. As a result, splinter groups have surfaced throughout the region to continue the violence against the Israelis, the Americans, and even Arafat's PLO (Simonsen and Spindlove, 2000). Among the most dangerous groups are the Islamic extremist groups such as the Hamas and Hizballah, as well as more formally organized groups such as the Popular Front for the Liberation of Palestine (PFLP) and the Abu Nidal organization.

The **Hizballah,** meaning the "Party of God," is a Shi'ite extremist group that was formed in Lebanon and is dedicated to the creation of an Iranian-style Islamic republic in Lebanon and the removal of all non-Islamic influences from the area. The group is believed to be responsible for a number of terrorist attacks including the bombing of the U.S. Marine barracks in Beirut in 1983, the U.S. embassy annex in Beirut in 1984, and the Israeli embassy in Argentina in 1992 (U.S. State Department, 1999).

Hamas was founded in late 1987 as an outgrowth of the Palestinian branch of the Muslim Brotherhood. With an unknown number of members and tens of thousands of supporters and sympathizers, Hamas has attacked Israeli military and civilian targets, as well as those perceived to be PLO collaborators and rivals. One of the major funding sources for the Hamas is believed to be the Islamic country of Iran.

The **Popular Front for the Liberation of Palestine (PFLP)** is a Marxist-Leninist group founded in 1967 that joined the PLO coalition but broke away in the early 1990s over ideological differences. The group is responsible for a number of terrorist attacks since the early 1970s and is still active in Syria, Lebanon, Israel, and other occupied territories of Palestine. The **Abu Nidal Organization (ANO)** split from the PLO in 1974 and since that time has carried out terrorist attacks in twenty countries, killing al-

most 900 persons. Led by leader Al-Banna, this group is believed to have relocated to Iraq in 1998 (U.S. State Department, 1999).

It is interesting to note how the situation in the Middle East, where splinter groups have surfaced in response to the internal disagreement between the PLO and their Arab counterparts, is similar to the situation in Northern Ireland, where the CIRA, INLA, and RIRA have developed as alternatives to the IRA.

Al-Qaida

The group **al-Qaida,** meaning "the Base," is made up of Sunni Islamic extremists who were originally formed as a group of Arab nationals to fight the Russians during the war in Afghanistan. The group has recently gained in strength and notoriety, developing into one of the major international terrorist organizations thanks to the financial support and leadership of Usama **Bin Laden.** Bin Laden has used his ties with al-Qaida to conduct a worldwide campaign of terrorism. The primary goal of Bin Laden and his supporters is to liberate Palestine, with secondary goals of removing the Saudi ruling family from power and driving Western military forces and their corrupt, Western-oriented governments from predominantly Muslim countries.

Bin Laden and the al-Qaida are believed to have supported and trained thousands of terrorist fighters in Afghanistan, Tajikistan, Bosnia and Herzegovina, Chechnya, Somalia, Sudan, Yemen, the Philippines, Egypt, Libya, Pakistan, and Eritrea. The embassy bombings in Dhahran, Saudi Arabia, and Nairobi, Kenya are believed to be the work of Bin Laden and the al-Qaida.

In addition to the groups and individuals known to have engaged in terrorist activity, seven countries have been designated by the United States as state sponsors of terrorism: Cuba, Iran, Iraq, Libya, North Korea, Sudan, and Syria (U.S. State Department, 1997). Countries are placed on this list if they assist terrorists by providing sanctuary, arms, training, logistic or financial support, or diplomatic facilities. The purpose of this

designation is to promote international cooperation in condemning state-sponsored terrorism
and to bring maximum pressure against those involved, via a range of bilateral and multilateral
sanctions, to discourage them from supporting
terrorism.

TERRORISM IN THE MODEL NATIONS

Each of our model countries has had to deal with
problems of international terrorism in recent
times. Without going into all the details of the
terrorist threat in the model countries, we can
summarize its dimensions.

England

As mentioned previously, the terrorist activities of
the PIRA have lasted for decades and continue to
be a problem for Northern Ireland and the larger
Great Britain. Even the signing of the Good Friday Accord has not totally stemmed the violence
in the region. The splinter terrorist group RIRA
was responsible for two major incidents in 1998.
The first was the exploding of a 500-pound car
bomb outside a courthouse in Omagh that killed
29 persons and injured 330 others; the second
was a bombing in Banbridge that injured 35 persons and damaged 200 homes (U.S. State Department, 1999).

Over the years, Britain has responded to terrorist activities with repressive measures that have
resulted in claims of human rights violations,
chiefly in matters of criminal procedure. Suspected terrorists have been imprisoned without
trial for long periods of time under prison conditions. Searches and seizures without warrants are
common. In 1988, Prime Minister Margaret
Thatcher proposed to Parliament that the right to
protection against self-incrimination be suspended in the case of suspected terrorists. This
300-year-old guarantee that an individual does
not have to testify either before or during his or

her own trial is a mainstay of the adversarial system of criminal procedure. In the United States,
it was written into the Fifth Amendment to the
Constitution and is generally known as the "right
to remain silent." The abrogation of the right not
to testify is a major departure from British constitutional tradition and is an indicator of the des-
peration of the British government in the face of
the Irish terrorist threat.

Britain has begun to work closely with the
United States on counterterrorism issues. In September 1998, the British arrested Khalid a-
Fawwaz, a Saudi Arabian citizen who is wanted
in the United States for conspiring to murder
American citizens between 1993 and 1998 (U.S.
State Department, 1999). This collaborative relationship is important for two reasons. First, there
is mounting evidence that IRA members have in
the past smuggled people, money, and possibly
weapons in and out of the United States via
Canada through Buffalo. Second, London is
known to be the home of a number of organizations with ties to Islamic terrorist groups that are
a threat to American interests, as well as to citizens of Britain. To respond to the threat of
terrorism in their country, the British have developed special antiterrorist organizations that specialize in the detection and apprehension of
terrorist suspects. The most prominent of these
organizations are the Metropolitan (London)
Anti-Terrorist Branch and the **Special Air Service Regiment (SAS).** The latter was originally
formed in World War II to fight the Germans in
North Africa but has since concentrated its efforts
on dealing with the IRA and PIRA (Simonsen
and Spindlove, 2000).

France

From 1986 to 1990, citizens of all nations that
were not part of the then twelve-nation European
Union were required to present visas before crossing the borders into France. In these modern days
of easy tourism in Europe and easy passage across
the borders of the generally small nations of Europe, this visa requirement constituted a major

obstacle to travel, as many Americans discovered. Why, then, would the French inhibit the tourism that makes a major contribution to the French economy?

The answer is terrorism. In the fall of 1986, Paris was unnerved by a series of random terrorist bombings in crowded streets, department stores, and train stations. The French people were outraged and called for government action to protect them against the terrorist threat. President François Mitterand outlined a program of response that included special police action, special courts to deal with terrorists, and visas for foreign nationals entering France. Only the European Union countries, which are guaranteed unimpeded access to each other by treaty, were exempted from the visa requirement. For a country like France, which has traditionally been a haven for political refugees, deposed rulers, and expatriate revolutionaries of both the left and right, this restriction on border passage was a drastic action. Whether as a result of this action or for other reasons, the terrorist bombings ceased.

Certain endemic problems of discontent in France, however, historically have contributed to waves of terrorist activity. There are several reasons France has such a long tradition of terrorism. Among the most prevalent are its geographic location within Europe, the weight of its history, and its involvement with Africa and the Middle East (Bruguiere, 1997).

Prior to the granting of independence to France's colonies in North Africa in the early 1960s, anticolonial attacks were frequent both in France and in Algeria, Tunisia, and Morocco. Right-wing elements in France also resorted to terrorism as a way to keep the government from granting independence to the North African states.

At least two internal ethnic groups, the Bretons and the Corsicans, have engaged in terrorist activity as part of separatist movements. During the 1970s, French government installations in Brittany were common bomb targets. In 1978, the Palace of Versailles on the outskirts of Paris was the scene of a Breton terrorist bomb attack that caused much damage to precious artworks. The French police crackdown on Breton terrorists after this attack, which included the arrest and trial of some of the major leaders of the separatist movement, contributed to the end of this chapter of terrorist activity (Cerny, 1981). It is noteworthy that, in over 300 bombings during the course of fifteen years, the Breton terrorists did not kill a single individual. This is probably a world record for humane terrorism!

Corsica, an island near the coast of Italy, has belonged to France since 1769 and has been a source of nationalist, anti-French feeling for some time. Hundreds of terrorist bombings aimed at winning separation from France and improving economic conditions on Corsica have occurred in the postwar years, both on the island and on the mainland of France. In 1995 alone, over 500 violent actions, including 420 bomb attacks, were attributed to Corsican separatists (Bruguiere, 1997).

Just as in England with the IRA, France's major problem of terrorism has been a domestic one, with its own citizens engaging in these acts for a definite purpose. France has not been immune, however, from the very frightening international terrorism that plagues so many countries today. French citizens have been kidnapped in Lebanon. Palestinian terrorists have struck at airports in France, and PLO members have been killed in France. Armenian nationalist terrorists, as well as Basque separatists, have engaged in assassinations, and a variety of other groups on both the left and right have also been active in France. In 1995, the Armed Islamic Groups, a radical Algerian Islamic organization, committed several terrorist attacks in France (Bruguiere, 1997). They were also blamed for a terrorist attack in 1996 when a bomb on a Paris commuter train detonated, killing four persons and injuring more than eighty.

The variety of groups that seek to make France the place in which to advertise their causes through terrorist activities seems to be quite large. Because of its extensive and efficient transportation system and its geographical location (France borders six countries), France provides an ideal location for European and Middle Eastern terrorist groups to launch their terrorist campaigns. Groups that have used France as a haven for their terrorist activities include the Popular Front for the Liberation of Palestine (PFLP), the PLO, the FLNC (a liberation group of Corsican separatists), and even the Japanese Red Army, which supports the larger Palestine movement (Simonsen and Spindlove, 2000).

One infamous member of the PFLP whose name has become synonymous with terrorism is Ilich Ramirez Sanchez—better known as **Carlos the Jackal.** Ramirez was born in Venezuela in 1949 and in his youth was a member of the Communist Youth Movement. Beginning in the 1960s, he became involved with international terrorism and is believed to be responsible for a number of high-profile incidents, including the Munich Olympic Games massacre in 1972, the kidnapping of eleven OPEC oil ministers in 1975, and the U.S. embassy hostage taking in Iran in the late 1970s (Simonsen and Spindlove, 2000). After hiding for years in several Middle Eastern states, he was finally extradited from Sudan in August 1994, found guilty of killing two policemen in 1997, and sent to a French prison.

To fight the scourge of terrorism, France has implemented special criminal justice measures. One law passed in 1996 makes it illegal under a code called the *association de malfaiteurs* to participate in a formed group or to try to establish a group that has any characteristics of a terrorism organization. The French also have set up special anti-terrorism courts that deal only with these kinds of cases. And, like England and Wales, France has broadened its use of detention of suspects to investigate terrorism cases. One example of this procedure was the 1998 detention of a hundred persons suspected of planning terrorist activities at the World Cup soccer matches (U.S. State Department, 1999).

As a member of the European Union, France has also signed a number of treaties that ensure its cooperation with the other countries relative to judicial assistance, law enforcement assistance, and

extradition of terrorists (Bruguiere, 1997). **The Groupment d'Intervention de la Gendarmerie Nationale (GIGN)** is the police unit that has been developed from within the ranks of National Police (Gendarmerie Nationale) to serve as the law enforcement agency that combats terrorism.

Germany

Terrorism in Germany has assumed a different form than in England or France. In the latter countries, most terrorist activity is directed at ethnic or nationalist goals. The objectives are clear and lend themselves to policy initiatives designed to satisfy their aims. Germany, by contrast, is troubled by a more amorphous, nondirected, even nihilistic brand of internal terrorism. German terrorists share only a general disenchantment with German society and a vague attachment to Marxism. Big business and American military targets, as well as those justice system personnel who were involved in processing terrorists, were the major targets of the **Red Army Faction (RAF),** the major terrorist group operating in the early 1970s. This group was also known as the Baader-Meinhof Gang after two of its leaders, Andreas Baader and Ulrike Meinhof. The leadership of the RAF was effectively destroyed by the German police. Baader and Meinhof both died in prison, ostensibly suicides; other leaders have gradually been captured; and the faction announced its "self-dissolution" in 1998.

Internal terrorist attacks in Germany diminished substantially in the 1980s but resumed in the 1990s with the murder or attempted murder of several government officials. In 1991, for example, Detlef Rohwedder, the head of the Treuhandanstalt, the government agency charged with denationalizing East German industry, was murdered.

In addition to its homegrown terrorists, Germany shares with England and France the unfortunate distinction of having frequently been the target of Middle Eastern terrorist activity that has nothing to do with Germany itself. One of the most horrifying incidents in the generally horrifying history of modern terrorist activity occurred in Munich during the Olympic Games of 1972. Eleven Israeli athletes were taken hostage in the Olympic Village by Palestinian terrorists of the Black September organization, who demanded freedom for Palestinians held in Israeli prisons. At the same time, they wanted to get the hostages out of Germany and demanded that a plane be made available to them. Although the German government initially sought to accommodate the terrorists, it decided to station sharpshooters at the airport in case the lives of the hostages seemed in immediate danger. Through a series of circumstances, the sharpshooters opened fire on the kidnappers, who then killed all the Israeli athletes. A total of seventeen deaths resulted from this incident: the eleven Israeli athletes, five terrorists, and one German police officer (Poland, 1988, p. 132).

In the 1990s, terrorism in Germany was directed more toward groups of foreign immigrants than at government institutions. The people responsible for these acts are members of right-wing and neo-Nazi groups; some called Skinheads. The main goal of these groups is to foster hate campaigns against foreign workers and the increasing number of aliens seeking political asylum in Germany. Some of the right-wing groups, such as the German People's Union (Deutsche Volksunion, or DVP) and Republikaner (Die Republikaner, or REP), have caused havoc but have eluded authorities because they are small in number and avoid using Nazi symbols that would make them easily identified.

The federal police reported that in 1992 there were over 2,000 acts of right-wing violence, a sevenfold increase over 1990. Among the most serious of these incidents were the street assaults and firebombings of hostels and government housing for immigrants in Rostock, Cottbus, Leipzig, and Solingen. Terrorism in Germany has inspired the development of a sophisticated police machinery of surveillance and internal security. Between 1971 and 1978, the German Bundeskriminalamt (the equivalent of the FBI in the

United States) grew tenfold, and new laws were passed to deal with the terrorist threat. These developments have led to serious concern within civil liberties groups about threats to privacy rights and other liberties in Germany. One police tactic that aroused a good deal of alarm is what is called Rasterfahndung (literally, "finding the remainder"). Under this program, police eliminated from suspicion all people who were registered with the police and conducted such "normal" activities as having bank accounts, paying for their electricity with checks rather than cash, and having children registered in school. The "remainder"—that is, those who did not have at least one of these characteristics—were targeted as possible terrorists and subjected to heightened surveillance (Schiller, 1987).

After the 1972 Munich Olympic Games tragedy, the Germans developed the **Grenzschutzgruppe 9 (GSG-9),** which has gained the reputation as one of the top antiterrorism forces in the world. The GSG-9 is split into three groups: The GSG-9/1 handles the majority of counterterrorism activity, the GSG-9/2 is responsible for maritime counterterrorism, and the GSG-9/3 handles airborne counterterrorism (Simonsen and Spindlove, 2000). GSG-9 personnel became famous in 1977 when they performed a dramatic rescue of hostages from a German airliner that was hijacked and landed in Mogadishu, in Somalia. The GSG-9 case is particularly interesting because the others are under the supervision of the Bundesgrenzschutz (border police), who under German law are part of the civilian police apparatus and who are authorized to act as a military agency only in times of war or extreme national emergency. In response to the rightist violence in the 1990s, the government developed a new federal police division to monitor the activities of those groups.

China

The only terrorist group that has any significant presence in China today is the **Uygurs,** a Chinese Muslim minority group that is concentrated in the western region of China. In 1997, a series of bombings and disturbances, during which up to 200 persons were killed, was attributed to Uygur separatists (Simonsen and Spindlove, 2000). As a result of the Uygurs' activities, hotels, airports, and train stations in Beijing and other western China locations were placed on alert against possible bomb attacks (*Journal of Commerce,* 1998). There were some additional bombings or attempted bombings in China during the first half of 1999, including an explosion in Hunan province that killed 8 persons (*New York Times,* 1999).

An interesting issue in China is whether the Communist government is guilty of state-sponsored terrorism for their actions against Chinese citizens. Relatives of victims of the government crackdown in the 1989 Tiananmen Square prodemocracy demonstrations have asked the government to open a criminal investigation into the culpability of government officials, including former Prime Minister Li Peng, in the killing or disappearance of demonstrators. This would be a first for China—trying to hold the government legally responsible for state-sponsored terrorism against its own citizens (Eckholm and Chen, 1999). Similar charges have been made by others, who argue that since the founding of the People's Republic of China there have been numerous instances of state-sponsored terrorism by the Communist regime, including Chairman Mao and his followers, who killed millions during the Great Leap forward and the Cultural Revolution (Heilbrunn, 1998).

Japan

Japan's biggest terrorist concern in the 1970s and into the 1980s was the actions of the **Japanese Red Army (JRA).** Like the German Baader-Meinhof group and its imitators, the JRA is amorphous and pluralistic in organization, generally Marxist in ideology, and unclear in its goals and objectives; a strong streak of anarchy and nihilism pervades this group or groups. Unlike the German terrorists, however, the JRA is engaged in a worldwide campaign of terrorism and has not shown particular preference for operating within Japan. In fact, many JRA members are reported to be living in other countries and acting as mercenaries to promote various political causes.

The most shocking incident that the JRA engaged in was an attack at Lod Airport in Israel in 1972, in which twenty-six people were killed and seventy wounded. The JRA also engaged in aircraft hijacking, both by itself and in conjunction with Palestinian groups. In a dramatic 1973 incident, one JRA member and three Palestinians hijacked a Japan Airlines plane en route from Amsterdam to Tokyo; four days later, the hijackers released the passengers in Benghazi and blew up the plane. These and other terrorist actions by the JRA provoked only a "soft" response from the Japanese government, which gave in to terrorist demands in exchange for the safety of hostages and kidnap victims. In fact, the Japanese have been criticized for advocating peaceful solutions to violent provocations (Wu Dunn, 1997).

Two incidents of terrorism were particularly troubling to the Japanese in the 1990s. In March 1995, the Tokyo subway system was poisoned with sarin gas by a religious cult called **Aum Shrinrikyo.** Membership in the Aum is believed to have grown since the bombing despite the prosecution of cult leaders, including their founder, Shoko Asahara (U.S. State Department, 1999). Then, in 1996, the Japanese ambassador's residence in Peru was attacked, an incident that reminded the Japanese that their increased presence in the international community brings with it the threat of terrorism to Japan's interests and citizens overseas (National Police Agency, 1999).

In response to these terrorist acts, Japanese police officials have become increasingly involved in antiterrorism planning and training. The Japanese Police (NPA) have established the Special Assault Team (SAT) to handle serious terrorist incidents. Also, in 1999, the NPA set up a new section within the agency to develop psychological profiles and study the tendencies of terrorists and hostages to help prepare for future crises. With the 1997 arrest, conviction, and imprisonment of several JRA members in Lebanon and Bolivia, it appears the power of that organization has been seriously reduced.

Saudi Arabia

Terrorism in Saudi Arabia revolves around religious factionalism. This should come as no surprise in a country where religion and religious orthodoxy are major preoccupations. As explained earlier, the prevailing religion in Saudi Arabia derives from the conversion in the late nineteenth century of King Abdul Assiz to the fundamentalist Wahhabi sect, which is tied to the Sunni branch of Islam. One of the deepest divisions within Islam is between Sunnis and Shi'ites. Shi'ite Muslims, under their late spiritual leader, the Ayatollah Khomeini, gained new prominence when they took over the largely secular government in Iran in 1979, replacing it with an Islamic theocracy. Shi'ite Muslims are found in other Middle Eastern countries as well, most notably Iraq, where they represent a large proportion of the population and a strong opposition force to Iraqi leader Saddam Hussein. It is in Iraq, in fact, that the holy city of Najaf, the center of the Shi'ite faith, is located. In Saudi Arabia, Bahrain, Oman, and Yemen in the Arabian peninsula, radical Shi'ites have used terrorist tactics to destabilize the Sunni regimes, spread Shi'ite fundamentalism, and combat secularism and Western (especially Israeli) influences (Kramer, 1987). Ruthlessly suppressed in Iraq, their place of origin, Shi'ite radicals operate dramatically in Lebanon. With the aid of Iran, which hopes to spread Shi'ism to its neighbors, they have engaged in the kidnapping of Westerners and other acts of terrorism, including hijackings and bombings.

Saudi Arabia's most serious incident of domestic terrorism was the 1979 takeover of the Grand Mosque in Mecca by several hundred fundamentalists of the Wahhabi sect. The Saudi National Guard eventually was able to regain control of the mosque, killing most of the radicals in the process. Those who were not killed at the mosque were subsequently executed. At the same time, demon-strations against the Saudi regime by Shi'ite radicals resulted in the deaths of seventeen Shi'ites. While not strictly an act of terrorism, trouble again broke out at the Grand Mosque in 1987 when fundamentalist pilgrims rioted against the Saudi authorities. As was explained in Chapter 5, an entire division of the Saudi police called the Pilgrims and Festivals Police Force deals with the annual pilgrimages to the holy cities; trouble is not unusual during these events (Kostiner, 1987).

In recent years, the most serious act of terrorism in Saudi Arabia was actually directed at the United States. In June 1996, 19 people were killed and 500 wounded when a truck bomb exploded at the U.S. military base near Dhahran. As of 1998, the investigation into the bombing had yet to produce conclusive evidence as to who was responsible. There have been other reports of threats against U.S. interests in Saudi Arabia in the late 1990s, including Bin Laden, who has publicly declared a holy war against U.S. forces in the Arabian peninsula (U.S. State Department, 1999).

Despite these incidents and some other attempts to smuggle armaments to dissident groups in Saudi Arabia, terrorism does not appear to be a major concern of Saudi authorities. This may be because the groups that surface in the quest to destabilize the regime do not appear to be highly organized or to have much connection to each other. In effect, they give voice to vague objections to the westernization and secularization of Saudi Arabia but do not represent a strong current of opposition within the Saudi people as a whole.

To further the reduction of terrorism in the Gulf region, efforts have been made by the Arab League of Nations to develop an antiterrorism accord. Algeria, Bahrain, Egypt, Jordan, Saudi Arabia, the United Arab Emirates, Tunisia, and the newly formed Palestine Authority all ratified a convention in 1999 that binds the signatories "not to order, finance or commit terrorist acts, as well as prevent terrorist crimes and fight against them in accordance with the national laws of each country" (Agence France Press, 1999).

What can we conclude about terrorism in our model countries and worldwide? Although some of the virulent terrorism of the 1970s seems to have subsided in many countries, in others, like Germany, new forms of domestic terrorism have emerged. Terrorism is tenuously in abeyance in Britain, with the long-term impact of the Good Friday Accord still to be determined. One constant has been the terrorism associated with Middle Eastern, and particularly Palestinian, groups, especially the recent growth of Bin Laden and his associates.

RESPONSES TO INTERNATIONAL TERRORISM

Organized responses to international terrorism are not simple matters of crime detection, apprehension, and punishment. The complexity of dealing with crime and criminals across borders, the range of motivations for terrorist activity, and the large number of terrorists and terrorist groups create a plethora of problems for criminal justice and government officials. So, what can be done to stem the tide of international terrorism? Foreign policy concerns, international cooperation strategies, military as opposed to police operations, and adjudication all play a prominent role.

Foreign Policy

For years, the United States accused Libya and its president, Moammar Quaddafi, of sponsoring international terrorism, by providing a haven for terrorists and training and funding them. Libya denied these claims while continuing to engage in provocative acts, such as welcoming plane hijackers and refusing to extradite them. The antagonism between the two countries came to a head in the spring of 1986, when the United States received word that Libyan agents had been behind the bombing of a pub in West Berlin in which two American soldiers were killed. In retaliation, American bombers attacked the coastal areas of Libya, killing some civilians including a daughter of Quaddafi.

Of America's traditional allies, only Great Britain endorsed the American action, although many of these allies had been the victims of Libyan-sponsored terrorist acts. Libya then was accused of masterminding the 1988 explosion that blew up a Pan American jet over Lockerbie, Scotland. In response to the Lockerbie bombing, the United States imposed economic sanctions against Libya, including a ban on oil sales and international travel, and a freeze on Libyan financial assets.

In this case, foreign policy questions and military decisions were inextricably mingled with terrorism control. In other cases, such as in the Middle East and Northern Ireland, efforts have been made to deal with the core issues behind terrorism through foreign policy—which generally means negotiation and compromise. Unfortunately, these efforts often have been for naught and sometimes have actually exacerbated the bad feelings between the parties involved. Dealing with terrorism within the confines of foreign policy may remain the first option, but other responses may be more viable.

International Cooperation Strategies

International cooperation strategies may be allied to diplomatic efforts and may involve criminal justice agency or military cooperation among countries. Often, treaties regarding cooperation and extradition provide the general framework for the strategies. In 1973, for example, Cuba and the United States agreed not to provide sanctuary for airliner hijackers. This agreement, as well as increased airport security measures, put a virtual end to the wave of plane hijackings in the United States in which the hijackers demanded to be taken to Cuba. In addition, resolutions of the United Nations and other international organizations reinforce solidarity against terrorism among large numbers of nations.

There are eleven global and four regional treaties against terrorism. Among the most recent and comprehensive of these is the International Convention for the Suppression of Terrorist

Table 12.2 Twenty-Five Recommendations from the 1996 Paris P/8 Ministerial Conference

1. Strengthen internal cooperation among government agencies that deal with different aspects of counterterrorism.
2. Expand training of counterterrorism personnel.
3. Intensify consultations to improve the capability of governments to respond to terrorist attacks against public transport.
4. Accelerate research, development, and consultation on methods for detecting explosives and for tracing their origins.
5. Act against terrorist front organizations.
6. Prevent terrorist use of electronic or wire communications.
7. Adopt effective legal controls over terrorist devices.
8. Strengthen punishments for terrorist acts.
9. Prosecute terrorists and their supporters.
10. Refrain from supporting terrorists.
11. Accelerate consultations on law enforcement access to encrypted data.
12. Improve travel barriers to terrorists.
13. Prevent terrorist abuse of asylum.
14. Ratify international conventions.
15. Develop and enhance mutual legal assistance procedures.
16. Expand extradition arrangements.
17. Promote an international terrorist bombing convention. Seek ICAO action to establish international bomb detection standards and to heighten airport security.
18. Implement biological weapons controls.
19. Prevent terrorist fundraising.
20. Intensify information exchange on the international movement of funds for terrorist purposes.
21. Adopt regulatory measures to impede the movement of terrorists' funds.
22. Facilitate information exchange via central authorities.
23. Intensify the exchange of basic information on persons and groups suspected of terrorist-linked activities.
24. Intensify the exchange of operational information on suspect persons and groups.
25. Accelerate exchanges of information.

SOURCE: U.S. State Department, 1998.

Bombings adopted by the General Assembly of the UN in January 1997. This convention created universal rules for the use of explosives in public places, strengthened protections for hostages, and broadened the requirements for the extradition of terrorists (U.S. State Department, 1999). Even more recently, in 1999, a UN working group finalized an international convention aimed at cutting off all legal and illegal sources of funding for terrorism. It will come into force after it has been ratified by the legislative bodies of at least twenty-two countries.

At least six major conferences dealt with the issue of international terrorism between 1995 and 1997 in diverse locales such as Nova Scotia, Ottawa, Egypt, Denver, and Paris. The **Paris P/8 (Political 8) Ministerial Conference** on terrorism in July 1996 was especially important because it resulted in the adoption of twenty-five recommendations centering on measures to prevent terrorism by means of border control, improved international cooperation, and regulation of fundraising by terrorists; Table 12.2 lists the twenty-five proposals.

Military and Police Detection and Apprehension Strategies

Detection and apprehension strategies are at the heart of antiterrorist activity. A liberal democracy that values human rights does not have the luxury of massive repressive reactions to incidents of terrorism. Following terrorist attacks, however, an outraged public usually expects the government to take strong measures to prevent further incidents. In general, the use of military agencies to deal with internal terrorist acts is unacceptable in democratic governments. International incidents are another matter, since police departments do not have jurisdiction to operate across borders or to engage in the kind of intelligence operations that are crucial to preventing terrorist acts or tracking down terrorists. The large number of international terrorist operations in today's world of easy transport and communications pose a particularly difficult problem of response. Still, over the years, military agencies, civilian police forces, and intelligence agencies have developed an increasingly sophisticated apparatus of response to terrorism. Many countries have passed laws allowing for extraordinary antiterrorist measures by government authorities.

Because it is the constant target of terrorist attacks near its borders and even within its cities, Israel represents an extreme case of planned response to terrorism. Israeli authorities have a firm policy of refusing to negotiate or give in to terrorist demands. This policy is often honored only in the breach, especially when Israeli soldiers have been captured, but it remains a pillar of Israeli response. Military incursions against known or suspected terrorist bases are a common Israeli response to terrorist incidents. Antiterrorism squads, which themselves practice a form of terrorist assassination, have formed part of the Israeli response, as in the assassination of a PLO vice chairman in Egypt in 1991. Israel has even practiced counterkidnapping, as in the seizure of Muslim clergyman Sheik Obeid.

As we mentioned earlier in our discussion of terrorism in our model countries, many countries plagued by terrorist acts employ special units in both their police and their military to deal with terrorism. They may pass special powers laws that allow for martial law, curfews, and abrogation of certain criminal procedure guarantees such as habeas corpus. This kind of legislation poses serious questions about abuse of civil rights, however. According to Gutteridge, the police are better suited than the military to gather intelligence about terrorist activities because the police have deeper roots in the community than do the military (1986, p. 23). In any case, using the military for domestic matters, as mentioned before, is generally not acceptable other than as a last resort or in severe emergencies. In international cases, by contrast, the military and military intelligence units are more likely to be deeply involved.

The U.S. military has two primary counterterrorism units. The U.S. Army's Combat Applications Group, more commonly known as **Delta Force,** serves mainly as a hostage rescue team. This highly trained, highly respected, and highly selective unit began operating in 1977 under the direction of Colonel Charles Beckwith. Interestingly, the Delta Force is actually under the authority of the president based on Presidential Decision Directive 25, which allows the group to operate on U.S. soil. The Naval Special Warfare Development Group, known as **Seal Team 6,** is responsible for counterterrorism operations in the maritime environment. Since being created in 1980, the group has been deployed in a number of domestic and international operations including the apprehension of Manuel Noriega in 1989.

In addition to the military units, the United States also has at its disposal two primarily civilian units: the FBI's Hostage Rescue Team (HRT) and the CIA's Special Activities Staff (SAS). The HRT team is an elite counterterrorism unit that handles terrorist or hostage situations inside the borders of the United States. The SAS is an elite group whose members are drawn from the ranks of the best of the military, the Delta Force, the Seal Team 6, and the CIA itself. The SAS carries out a number of delicate operations as directed by the president of the United States. Because of the secrecy of its missions, the SAS are probably the least known of the units operating on behalf of the United States.

A great deal of mutual training and exchange of information and communications procedures has been implemented through INTERPOL and other regular and occasional police cooperative programs. The TREVI compact (dealing with terrorism, drugs, and organized crime) has established mutual cooperation among the nations of Europe, while the 1985 Shengen Agreement between Germany, France, Belgium, and Luxembourg allows for "hot pursuit" of offenders across the borders of these countries.

Prevention of terrorist activity through improved technology has also become an important issue in international criminal justice circles. For example, in April 1998, the Political 8 (the United States, Canada, Great Britain, France, Germany, Italy, Russia, and Japan) met in Atlanta to discuss potential terrorist threats and the technological responses to these threats. What emerged was the sharing of information about new technologies that are being used around the world, including explosive and chemical detection sensor systems, information systems security, surveillance systems, and emergency management strategies (Barnes, 1998).

Planning for all kinds of contingencies is a crucial part of dealing with terrorism. Inevitably, however, the handling of a specific incident of terrorism will be an ad hoc affair, depending on the circumstances of the case and requiring rapid decision making about resources, jurisdictions, and actions to be taken.

Experts talk about "soft" responses versus "hard" responses to particular terrorist acts. Soft responses mean giving in to terrorist demands, especially in hostage situations, in exchange for the hostages' safety. Such a soft response is generally considered counterproductive because it encourages further acts of terrorism. Needless to say, the anguish of having hostages in the hands of cruel and reckless individuals makes the soft approach understandable. Even Israel, which has been fairly

consistent in its policy of not negotiating with terrorists or giving in to terrorist demands, has been known to trade prisoners for hostages when members of the Israeli army are taken hostage.

The United States has taken the opposite approach to deal with terrorism activity, one that can be characterized as firm and hard-line. The policy is as follows:

1. Make no concessions to terrorists and strike no deals.

2. Bring terrorists to justice for their crimes.

3. Isolate and apply pressure on states that sponsor terrorism to force them to change their behavior.

4. Assist the counterterrorism capabilities of countries that work with the United States and require assistance (U.S. State Department, 1999).

The United States has also passed a law aimed at deterring future terrorist activity. President Clinton in 1996 signed the **Antiterrorism and Effective Death Penalty Act,** which banned fundraising and financial support for international terrorist organizations, allocated a billion dollars to law enforcement to fight terrorism, created standards for the deportation of suspected terrorists, allowed for the use of the death penalty for international terrorism acts, made it a federal crime to plan terrorist acts, and regulated the production and selling of raw materials to make bombs (Schmalleger, 1999). Based on the recent reduction in the number of international terrorist incidents involving U.S. citizens and interests, the U.S. policies seem to have been successful.

Adjudication

When innocent people are killed by terrorists, emotions run high, and a certain spirit of mob vengeance can develop. Even governments dedicated to the rule of law have difficulty dealing objectively and lawfully with suspected terrorists. Special courts for dealing with terrorists may be proposed, as happened in France in 1986 (even though these courts have been ruled unconstitutional by the French Constitutional Council). A particularly distressing English case was that of the Birmingham Six, a group of Irishmen who were convicted of the 1974 bombing of a pub in Birmingham and given life sentences in prison. In 1991, all six were released after it became clear that the police evidence in the case had been fabricated (*The Economist,* 1991, p. 53).

Unfortunately, terrorist excesses can become an excuse for suspension of rights and development of a repressive paramilitary regime, as happened in Uruguay in 1972. Terrorist leaders may believe that such a development will lead to further support for their own revolutionary causes, but this is seldom the case. In extreme cases, a country may slide into dictatorship and lose whatever traditions of democracy it once may have had.

As we have seen, international terrorism is not simply a problem of crime and punishment. However, we must not lose sight of the fact that terrorist actions are crimes. In dealing with individual terrorists, then, we need to view them as criminals who have committed acts of murder, assault, arson, robbery, and the like rather than as pawns in an international power struggle. Otherwise, the system of crime and punishment in any country, as well as the rule of law, may be seriously diminished.

THE FUTURE OF TERRORISM

In our increasingly technological world, a relatively small number of terrorists potentially can wreak havoc out of all proportion to their numbers. The possibility that a terrorist or terrorist group may obtain a nuclear device increases all the time, as knowledge about their manufacture becomes more available. This would be a far cry from the bomb-carrying anarchist terrorists of the early twentieth century. The poisoning of water and food supplies through chemical alterations, and the use of biological agents to attack large population centers previously have been used

only in time of war, but recently these have become a major concern for antiterrorism authorities. **Agents of biological origin (ABOs)** fall into one of three categories: bacteria, viruses, or toxins (McDonald, 1998). One example of the use of ABOs was the sarin nerve gas attack in the Tokyo subway system in March 1995.

The terrorist threat that probably looms largest in the twenty-first century is cyberterrorism. Potential acts of computer terrorism include hijacking air traffic control systems, infiltrating defense systems, cutting water and power supplies, and disrupting transportation systems. Large international gatherings, like the 2000 Olympics in Sydney, Australia, will also produce a situation vulnerable to terrorism. The possibilities for terrorist mischief in this area seem as endless as the uses for computers themselves.

SUMMARY

The threat of terrorism and the impact of terrorist activity have changed the way people view the world and the way they act on a daily basis. Terrorism is not a new phenomenon, and the general goals have changed little over the past century, but the form and frequency of terrorist activity certainly have been transformed. For over twenty years, the number of terrorist acts increased considerably. In recent years, however, there has been a decline in terrorism in many regions of the world, including our model countries. There appears to have been a concurrent increase in the number of terrorist groups that have surfaced, although they vary considerably in their size and effectiveness. Among the areas of the world that remain as terrorist "hot beds" are the Middle East and Northern Ireland, although terrorist activity in the latter region has been halted by the Good Friday Accord.

Each of our model countries provides some system response to terrorism through the development of either law enforcement or military forces. Other options for dealing with the problem include foreign policy, international cooperation, and adjudication. Although the quantity and quality of counterterrorism measures seem to have had some impact on the incidence of terrorism and the apprehension of terrorists, the problem still remains because of the new and improved methods of spreading terror.

DISCUSSION QUESTIONS AND EXERCISES

1. Why has terrorism been so prevalent in the Middle East in the recent years? In Northern Ireland?

2. What do you believe is the most common goal of terrorists in the world today? Give examples to support your answer.

3. Which of our model countries has the biggest problem with terrorism today?

4. What terrorist group do you believe is the greatest threat to the world today? To the United States?

5. Use the Internet to find out the international terrorism trends for 1999. Which country and region is the most susceptible?

6. Is terrorism a useful way to bring about social change?

7. What do you believe is the best approach to dealing with terrorism?

FOR FURTHER READING

Kushner, H. W. (ed.). (1998). *The Future of Terrorism: Violence in the New Millennium.* Thousand Oaks, Calif.: Sage.

Moors, C., and R. Ward (eds.). (1998). *Terrorism and the New World Order.* Office of International Criminal Justice. Chicago: University of Illinois, Chicago.

Poland, J. (1988). *Understanding Terrorism.* Englewood Cliffs, N.J.: Prentice-Hall.

Rapoport, D. (ed.). (1988). *Inside Terrorist Organizations.* New York: Columbia University Press.

Schlagheck, D. (1988). *International Terrorism.* Lexington, Mass.: Lexington Books.

Simonsen, C. E., and J. R. Spindlove (2000). *Terrorism Today: The Past, the Players, the Future.* Upper Saddle River, N.J.: Prentice-Hall.

Smith, B. L. (1994). *Terrorism in America: Pipe Bombs and Pipe Dreams.* Albany: SUNY Press

13 Transnational Organized Crime and Drug Trafficking

What Is Organized Crime?
The Scope of the Organized Crime Problem
    Worldwide
"Traditional" Criminal Syndicates
"New" Organized Crime Groups
The Organized Drug Trade
Responses to Organized Crime and Drug
    Trafficking
Summary
Discussion Questions
For Further Reading

Key Terms and Concepts

balloon effect
Boryokudan
Cali cartel
certification
Chinese Triad
Colombian drug cartel
integration
international criminal organization (ICO)
Italian Mafia
layering
Medellin cartel
Mexican Federation
money laundering
organized crime
placement
Russian Mafiya
transnational criminal organization (TCO)
Yakuza

M ario Puzo's best-selling novel *The Godfather* and the films that were based on it gave expression to the image of organized crime held by many Americans. A close-knit Italian family and its retainers, headed by a respected patriarch, engage in extortion, the procurement of illicit goods, and violence. Gang warfare erupts in which potential usurpers and others are killed. The victims of this violence are part of the organized crime underworld. Journalistic accounts of organized crime activities, and even autobiographies and biographies of major figures such as Joe Bonano and John Gotti, have reinforced this image.

Organized crime, however, is not that simple or easy to understand. It is a complex phenomenon that is found in many countries and among diverse national and social groups. There may be a parent organization in one country and offshoot organizations in other countries. The Italian crime organizations in Sicily and Naples with their American offshoots are one example. The Chinese secret societies that trade in heroin and have established branches in cities around the world are another. The myriad individual organizations around the world that engage in producing, importing, and exporting illegal drugs are still others.

In this chapter, we will look at the phenomenon of organized crime as a major problem in the administration of justice worldwide. After a general introduction to the concept, the chapter goes on to describe the scope of this problem. We will also examine several "traditional" types of criminal syndicates—the Mafia, the Japanese Yakuza, and the Chinese Triads—as well as three of the "newer" groups that have achieved international prominence—the Russian Mafiya, the Colombian drug cartels, and the Mexican Federation. Finally, we will scrutinize one seemingly intractable global problem involving organized criminality; the trade in narcotics.

WHAT IS ORGANIZED CRIME?

It is often stated in the literature regarding organized crime that an acceptable definition for the term is hard to come by, and none has been accepted with any consensus in the international community. This excerpt from a 1993 United Nations Economic and Social Council document clearly states this view:

> As is the case for highly complex social phenomena, all efforts to formulate an unequivocal and universally accepted definition of organized crime have failed. In fact, the relevant literature contains many different definitions, none having met general acceptance.

For our purposes, we will adopt the simple definition proposed by M. Cherif Bassiouni and Eduardo Vetere: **Organized crime** is the label given to the phenomenon represented by certain groups engaging essentially in violent, profit-motivated criminal activity (1998, p. xxvii). However, at the same time, to fully understand organized crime in the beginning of the twenty-first century, we must keep in mind that it has also become a sophisticated international venture, as well as one that begets violence and generates significant profits. According to a recent report by the European Union on organized crime, the evidence clearly reveals the international dimension of organized crime. The report states that "criminal groups often have a foreign component and . . . national boundaries pose no obstacle to these organizations" (European Union, 1996). Because of the global dimension of organized crime, we can also refer to the groups that participate in this activity as **international criminal organizations (ICOs)** or **transnational criminal organizations (TCOs)** (Richards, 1999, p. 4).

Although organized crime may be defined in various ways and assume different forms in different areas that may or may not transcend borders, it generally has three characteristics wherever it is found. First, all organized crime involves the provision of illegal goods and services. Drugs and gambling are the best examples of goods and services provided, although other illegal activities, such as prostitution, trafficking in illegal liquor, and loan sharking often are controlled by criminal syndicates. Other rackets, such as extortion, and even legitimate enterprises, such as garbage collection, may be a part of a crime syndicate's operations; they are not usually as important, however, as the provision of illegal goods and services.

Not all observers would agree that the provision of illegal goods or services is always a distinguishing characteristic of organized crime. Alan Block (1983) makes a distinction between "enterprise syndicates" and "power syndicates." Enterprise syndicates provide goods and services, while power syndicates seek control and wealth through extortion or "protection" and other types of crime that provide no real services. Enterprise syndicates, as their name suggests, have parallels to corporations, with specialist employees and capital investment. Power syndicates, especially as they existed in the past in Italy and the United States, were involved in social control and thus paralleled government efforts to rule through intimidation and fear of sanctions. Large-scale organized criminals today, however, find that the big profits are in providing illegal commodities, and pure power syndicates have gone into an eclipse.

The second defining characteristic of organized crime is the use or threat of violence to strengthen the organization and intimidate outsiders. The use of violence is designed to strike terror into the hearts of would-be informers, to discourage competition, and to settle old scores. Even when gangsters are involved in legitimate enterprises, they use violence as a way to destroy competition and assure a monopoly for themselves. So-called contract killings, car bombings, and street shoot-outs among gangsters have become a part of American folklore, but the threat of violence is pervasive in organized crime operations in many countries. One sad example is in the tiny Asian country of Macau, where an ongoing war between different factions of the organized crime groups called Triads has led to shootings that have recently left dozens of people dead and wounded.

The third defining characteristic of organized crime is involvement with the political, financial, or industrial establishment. This involvement usually takes the form of bribery or other profit-making schemes to ensure that the crime syndicate is able to operate smoothly in particular areas. An extreme example is the case of Bolivia, where drug lords actually took control of the government during the early 1980s. Maintaining secret bank accounts and "laundering" money through legitimate banks are at best marginally legal practices of organized crime. The scandal revolving around the Bank of New York in 1999 included an operation run by a Russian organized crime group that is believed to have resulted in $10 billion being illegally laundered.

The more common practice is to make large payoffs to police and local political figures in exchange for nonrigorous law enforcement. A recent example of political corruption of a serious magnitude involves Mexico's fugitive state governor, Mario Villanueva, who is believed to have helped drug traffickers and to be the leader himself of a cocaine cartel. Making campaign contributions and getting out the vote for cooperative candidates are other tactics used to ensure smooth operations for crime syndicates.

THE SCOPE OF THE ORGANIZED CRIME PROBLEM WORLDWIDE

Organized crime was originally a local or at most a regional phenomenon. But as we mentioned earlier, it has become an international problem for several reasons. The most significant is the globalization of the world economy, due partly to the fall of the Soviet Union and the switch to a free-market economy in China. These events have been accompanied by a surge in economic independence throughout the world. Concomitant with these economic changes has been an opening of the borders to trade and travel. The amount of commercial trade that transpires over the course of a single year is mind-boggling. Consider this: In 1996, nearly 1.8 million containers moved through the Port of Newark (New Jersey) alone (Cusimano, 2000).

In this context, it's hardly surprising that the illegal trafficking of drugs has become the most widespread international crime problem in history. Also, the considerable advances in technology, such as the Internet and cellular phones, have facilitated international criminal transactions and money laundering. While a sign of relative prosperity and modernity, the economic changes, liberal immigration policies, and the advances in technology have created a wide range of criminal opportunities. The result has been an increase in transnational organized crime in almost every region of the world.

The true scope of organized crime is very difficult to determine. We can only speculate as to how many billions of dollars are accumulated by criminal enterprises, how much government revenue is lost to tax-free trade, how much damage is done to the environment, and how many lives are lost or ruined.

What we do know is that organized crime groups have engaged in a wide range of illegal activities, including, among others, illicit drug trafficking; illegal trafficking in arms, nuclear materials, illegal immigrants, women and children, and body parts; theft and smuggling of vehicles; money laundering; and collaboration in terrorism (Bassiouni and Vetere, 1998, pp. 567–574). For a more detailed list of transnational crimes, most of which feature some level of organized crime involvement, we refer you back to Chapter 1.

What is equally frightening is the impact of the various organized crime activities on society. As stated cogently in a UN Report of the Secretary General in 1993:

> Organized crime is nothing less than a massive attack on the fabric of society affecting practically all of its components at the individual, collective and institution levels. It is also an insidious form of lawlessness, which cynically exploits citizens' rights and constitutional guarantees for the purpose of reducing risk of detection and maximizing impunity. In this manner, organized crime threatens some of the most basic elements of a democratic order. (p. 9)

"TRADITIONAL" CRIMINAL SYNDICATES

"Traditional" criminal syndicates have been established for some time, even for centuries, and have developed distinctive rules, rituals, and operating modes. They are dynamic organizations that often attract what might be called the "entrepreneurial dispossessed"—that is, energetic, capable people to whom legitimate channels of achievement are barred, perhaps because of low social status or a criminal record. Robin Hood and his Merry Men and any number of other historical bandit organizations even have a good deal of legitimacy with the common people in oppressive regimes.

These organizations may have periods of ascendancy and periods of retreat, largely dependent upon the intensity of government efforts to suppress them, but they seem to have a remarkable capacity to endure over time. Three such traditional syndicate types are the Italian Mafia, the Japanese Yakuza, and the Chinese Triad societies.

The Italian Mafia

Italian Mafia loosely refers to Italian networks of organized crime in the United States, much to the chagrin of many Italian-Americans, who believe that the image of the Mafia stereotypes them and sensationalizes the real situation with respect to organized crime among Italians in this country. Nevertheless, there have been important Italian organized crime networks in this country, some of them with ties to Italy, and especially to Sicily.

The true Mafia, however, is a Sicilian phenomenon. It developed in Sicily during the nineteenth century as a combination extortion and social control agency at a time of major social change, when many of the old estates were being broken up and peasants were facing new ways of working the land. Henner Hess, who has studied the Mafia in depth, explains:

> In a time of transition, when the feudal ruling order was in a state of decay and collapse and the

modern bureaucratic state was not able to assume authority and its legitimate monopoly on physical coercion, Mafia violence—from the point of view of the affluent classes—was a necessary force needed to quell disturbances and fill the gap of power in order to maintain estate property. . . . The mafioso was a complex social type. He was a criminal, but a respected man, nevertheless, who performed some useful functions in village society. . . . he would mediate in cases of theft and robbery of cattle; his help was solicited in abductions and kidnappings; and he arranged employment for the relatives of his clients. (1986, p. 115)

Gradually, the mafiosi became entrenched. As the social institutions of the modern state developed, they became more purely criminal in their operations. The Sicilian mafiosi influence on local politics and society did take a hit in August 1997, when one of Italy's most senior leaders, Mario Fabbrocino, was finally arrested after a ten-year search. Later that year, a number of high-ranking mafiosi were convicted of murder (Richards, 1999, p. 7). However, despite the sometimes heroic efforts by Italian police and prosecutors to bring them to trial, the Mafia remains a potent force in Sicilian politics and social life.

Hess also describes the stages of a mafioso's criminal career. Usually coming from an impoverished background, he demonstrates his manhood by performing an act or acts of violence. Rather than becoming an outlaw as a result, he is either not accused or else acquitted by the legal system for his crimes. He then may informally begin to do minor work for a particular Mafia group, gradually working his way into the confidence of the "family." As time passes, the social role of mafioso, with all the respect and fear that it engenders, becomes attached to his name. If he is lucky, enterprising, and clever, he may rise further in the ranks, becoming himself a Mafia chief in his area. To do so, he must usurp power from the leader or beat out rivals for leadership positions that become vacant. He gradually becomes influential in the community, acting as mediator

in disputes, performing helpful acts for his friends and family, and perhaps becoming deeply involved with those in legitimate positions of power (Hess, 1986). Essentially, he and his cohorts form a particular kind of upper class in Sicilian society, repressing through violence and intimidation those who challenge their authority. Eric Hobsbawm, in his book on social banditry, calls the Mafia "a strong-arm rural bourgeoisie" (1981, p. 36). It is from this background of the Sicilian "man of honor" that the Godfather of novelistic fame comes.

This does not mean, however, that the Mafia are the only organized criminals in Italy. Nor does it mean that all organized crime by Italians in the United States is being masterminded in Sicily. The fact is that American organizations have developed, in some cases with similar structures and systems of initiation, in response to American social conditions. Further, organized crime has not always been the province of Italians in the United States, and at present the business seems to be moving away from them to Asian, black, and Hispanic groups, just as Jewish and German gangsters were notorious earlier in the twentieth century. In the past twenty-five years, other ethnic organized crime groups have surfaced in the United States such as the Russian Mafiya, and the Jamaican Posse, as well as Colombian, Panamanian, and Mexican drug organizations.

The rise and decline of certain ethnic groups in the organized crime field in the United States makes for interesting sociological speculation about avenues for entrepreneurial talent for members of immigrant groups who are shut out of mainstream American avenues of success. As these groups gradually become politically and economically more secure, their children become part of the legitimate power structure, and a new group moves into the crime syndicate underworld.

In the United States, in fact, the Mafia is in a stage of decay, largely due to an all-out campaign against it by federal and state law enforcement authorities. It is estimated that over 1,300 Mafia members have been imprisoned (Richards, 1999,

p. 7). The 1992 conviction of syndicate boss John Gotti also seems to have created a major vacuum in organized crime leadership and a further diminution of powers. Authorities estimate that Mafia membership has declined from 5,000 in 1967 to 1,500 in the early 1990s. Of those members, a large majority are affiliated with the five Mafia families in the New York area. There, the Mafia dominates a number of legitimate industries, including garment work, garbage collection, construction, and freight operations at Kennedy airport, in addition to continued operation in illegal enterprises such as loan sharking, narcotics trafficking, and gambling (Burden, 1991).

Yakuza: The Japanese Gangster

Yakuza is the popular term that denotes the many Japanese gangs of organized criminals. The official term for these organized criminals is **Boryokudan.** Each year the Japanese Ministry of Justice publishes an annual report on crime and a compilation of crime statistics. Among the most prominent statistics are those that relate to organized crime. In 1980, police reported that there were 103,955 individuals in 2,487 criminal groups. This represented a rather large decline in the numbers since 1960, at which time there were 5,119 groups with a total membership of 124,763 (Ministry of Justice, 1989). Figures for 1999 show a further decline, with about 81,000 Yakuza, including 20,000 in the largest of the groups, called the Yamaguchigumi (Associated Press, 1999). Different groups tend to specialize in different rackets, and often the roots of today's gangster groups can be traced back several centuries in Japan's history, with the same specialty, such as gambling, having made the group notorious hundreds of years ago. Legal businesses make up about 13 percent of the activities of the Yakuza.

In a country that prides itself on low criminality, the phenomenon of gangsterism and organized crime is especially noteworthy. The peculiar thing by American standards is that so much is known by the police about the nature, makeup, income, and membership of organized crime groups in Japan. Indeed, there is some tolerance of this kind of crime, and a certain amount of camaraderie develops between gangsters and police. Although Japanese gangsters had strong ties with government in earlier times, this is not the case today, with some exceptions among small-town officials.

The crimes that are the province of organized criminals in Japan are similar to those that attract this kind of criminal in the United States: drug sales, prostitution, gambling, and extortion. Gangs tend to specialize in particular activities, with gambling and drug dealing the main basis for particular group activities. In the following passage, Hiroaki Iwai describes the organization of drug dealers:

> Tekiya, *the drug syndicates, were at one time called* yashi *and prepared and sold incense, drugs, and other pharmaceutical products in the nineteenth century. . . . In the tekiya groups, the* chomoto-oyabun *superintends his family. His assistants are known as* cho-waki *(lower-level bosses), and beneath them are the* yaki *(workers, dealers) who, in turn, supervise the* wakaishu *(the apprentices). . . . The first job for a newcomer consists of three years of the lowest apprenticeship, selling his boss's articles and goods for 10 percent of the earnings. In the second stage of his apprenticeship, the wakaishu obtains permission to work independently, buys articles and goods from his boss at near cost with his own capital and retains his total profits from sales. In the final step of his initiation, he may accumulate his own capital and purchases large amounts of goods from special wholesalers. Each stage marks a period of growing independence and responsibility for the initiate and eventual assimilation into the ranks of full-fledged membership. (1986, p. 213)*

The pattern of recruitment and indoctrination into Japan's Yakuza is similar to that for other groups of organized criminals. Gangs are made up of people with few legitimate prospects for wealth or recognition. Often, these are Koreans, who are chronic outsiders in Japan, no matter how many generations they may have lived there.

Clannishness and loyalty are stressed, although the members of the various groups, known as "families," are usually not related. As in other aspects of Japanese society, formal relationships among strata within the groups are highly developed, and succession to leadership roles is also determined through rules and ceremonies rather than sheer force as in some gangs in the United States. Gangsters may be recognized by the tattoos that they receive upon being initiated into their groups, and some gangsters even cut off a finger to demonstrate loyalty to the leader. Gangsters are also known for driving large American cars, usually an anomaly in Japan.

As touched on previously, there is a certain ritual quality to relations between the police and the Yakuza. They are aware of each others' presence as adversaries, but they often cooperate with each other. Walter Ames tells of the time he attended a gangster funeral:

> On the appointed day, I went to a large Buddhist temple in Okayama City with a detective from one of the nearby police stations. Five or six American luxury cars with license plates from various prefectures in western Japan were parked directly in front. Black and white striped funeral bunting was draped on the wall surrounding the temple courtyard, and the diamond-shaped symbol of Japan's largest gangster syndicate, the Yamaguchi gumi (gang), to which the local gang belonged, hung over the gate into the courtyard. Thousands of rings of artificial flowers lined the courtyard and were donated by small businesses, bars and cabarets, city assemblymen, and citizens. The courtyard was filled with hundreds of gangsters from all over western Japan, in dark suits, with closely cropped hair, all wearing black armbands and lapel pins declaring the names of their gangs. Dozens of gangsters were still arriving and were met with loud shouts of greeting (osu!) from the others in the courtyard.
>
> A number of police officers stood across the street from the temple entrance watching the gangsters arrive, most of whom said hello to the police. Several of the gangsters from local gangs walked up to the police officers I was with and jokingly commented that they had carefully parked their cars in parking lots so they would not get parking tickets. The police knew the gangsters by name and bantered with them. (1981, pp. 106–107)

Ames goes on to describe visits he made with police officers to gangster offices and to the ornate homes of local gangsters so that he could interview them. The police always appeared to maintain cordial relations with the gangsters, even joking with them on the occasions when they were brought in for questioning at the police stations (Ames, 1981, p. 107).

If gangster activities become too blatant or violence among gangsters becomes too extreme, there is a police crackdown. At various times, gang activities may have decreased as a result of energetic police action, but the institution of the Yakuza, with its roots in the village societies of earlier eras, is very much entrenched in Japanese society. According to one investigation, by a reporter from the German news magazine *Der Spiegel*, the Yakuza control the allocation and costs of day labor for numbers of businesses and, with little opposition, make huge profits through a system of extortion and bribery. Many of the laborers are illegal immigrants, whose labor is needed by Japanese industry but who, as in the United States, receive substantially less than Japanese workers doing similar jobs. This report also claims that the Yakuza are allied to extreme right-wing political factions and use terror and extortion to intimidate liberals and Socialist factions in Japan (Terzani, 1990). Ames likewise suggests that the police tolerate this kind of behavior by the gangsters because it helps them control left-wing elements (Ames, 1981, p. 108).

Police crackdowns on organized crime do occur, however. Among inmates in Japanese prisons, Yakuza representation increased from 21 percent in 1975 to 30.5 percent in 1988—in actual numbers, an increase of from 7,931 to 13,954. This increase creates problems for prison administrators, who find the Yakuza more intractable and difficult to handle than conventional convicts (Johnson, 1991). A major step in the move to control the Yakuza occurred in 1992 when the government passed the Act for the Prevention of Unlawful Activities by Boryokudan. This law made it illegal for the Yakuza to realize profits from extortion, gambling, and other illegal activities (Richards, 1999, p. 12).

The Yakuza tend to engage in harassment and threats of force rather than in actual violence, since violence makes them more vulnerable to police reaction. They pressure banks to make payoffs or face the threat of massive harassment and paperwork following some supposed mistake in the records of a Yakuza client. Or they buy a few shares of stock in a company and threaten to disrupt the annual stockholder meetings with endless questions if the companies do not come forth with large amounts of money. Thus, for example, after Sony executives refused to pay off the Yakuza, the Sony stockholders' meeting, rather than the usual half-hour, lasted thirteen hours. Such Yakuza actions are not exactly illegal, but in Japan, where a large premium is placed on the appearance of propriety, it can be very unsettling (Terzani, 1990, p. 103).

Some citizens and companies find the Yakuza helpful as a kind of "strong-arm" force to aid in achieving particular goals. For a consideration, the Yakuza may help collect debts for companies that believe efforts to get their money through legal means will be fruitless. Individuals who do not receive sufficient payment from their insurance companies after an accident may also have recourse to the Yakuza (Terzani, 1990, p. 104).

Yakuza activities are not confined to Japan, an unsettling fact for law enforcement officials in other Pacific nations and even in Hawaii and the West Coast of America. Yakuza involvement in the prostitution rackets throughout the Far East is also strong, according to an investigative report. This report claims as well that the Yakuza maintain close ties to Korean government officials, helping the South Korean government in its anti-Communist activities. Further, Yakuza activity is

spreading worldwide, even into Europe (Kaplan and Dubro, 1986, pt. 4) Australia, Costa Rica, and Brazil (Richards, 1999, p. 13).

The picture that emerges is of a strong underground organization or series of organizations that play an important if reprehensible role in Japanese work life and in the more conventional gambling and drug rackets. Despite greater control efforts in recent years, there seems to be little Japanese government emphasis on elimination of the Yakuza comparable to Italian efforts to control or eliminate Mafia influence. Indeed, the Yakuza seem to provide a kind of "safety valve" organization for the outsiders in Japanese society. In effect, these gangster groups channel the Japanese cultural traits of fanatic loyalty and conformity to group norms into illegal enterprises, which are, however, strictly controlled by the leadership.

Chinese Triad Groups

More ancient in origin than the Mafia or the Yakuza groups are the **Chinese Triad** societies. Triads are the premier groups in a web of Chinese secret societies involved in organized crime throughout the Far East and into Europe and the Americas. These societies had their origins among the bandit-heroes who resisted oppression of the masses by the Chinese rulers over several thousand years. The actual history of today's Triad societies, however, is related to efforts to oppose the rule of the Manchus, especially in the nineteenth century. One such group provided the leadership for the abortive and bloody Boxer Rebellion of 1900, which also was directed at elimination of colonial infiltration into China (Posner, 1988, ch. 3).

With the final overthrow of the Manchus in 1911, the Triad societies turned to the trade in opiates and became full-blown crime syndicates rather than rebel groups. Over the years, they have smuggled large amounts of heroin from Southeast Asia into the United States. Gambling is also a major source of income for these groups. Six major Triad societies now exist, as well as many smaller groups throughout the world (Richards, 1999, p. 13). The major center of operations, however, is Hong Kong, where an estimated 57 Triad societies and over 160,000 Triad members are present (Bassiouni and Vetere, 1998, p. 563; Ramsey, 1998). Members of the Chinese Triads located on the southern border of China are also working with the Yakuza to run bars and hotels as legal fronts to launder their illegal earnings (*Kyodo News International,* 1994). Although they are compared to the Mafia and engage in similar enterprises in similar ways, less is known about Triad operations. The groups are highly organized, with close ties to each other, and they engage in formal rituals of initiation and passage (Matherson, 1988).

Triad involvement in politics, like that of the Yakuza in Japan, seems to be largely on the side of right-wing elements. Posner claims that Triad organizations were closely allied to Chiang Kai-shek in his efforts to control mainland China before World War II. After the war, during the Communist takeover in China, many of the gangsters joined the mass of refugees that fled to Hong Kong. There, amid intrigue, rivalry, and gang war, several major Triad organizations became dominant, using extortion to gain money from legitimate businesses and running rackets of their own, including becoming leading actors in the international opium trade. Like other criminal syndicates, they have expanded their operations to include legitimate enterprises. Posner quotes a Hong Kong police executive:

> They've moved into everything from home-decoration firms to fancy hotels to construction companies to car dealerships to licensed casinos. The old Triads wouldn't have thought about legitimate business. But today the Triads make so much money that if they don't invest it in legitimate enterprises, there is no way they can spend it in twenty lifetimes. And most of them are such good businessmen that they make another fortune from their legitimate activities. (1988, p. 43)

Clannishness, a draconian code of silence, and language barriers make the Triads a rather myste-rious force in Chinese communities worldwide. Nevertheless, law enforcement officials are beginning to realize that these groups have created a massive underground economy in illegal goods and services, as well as exerting a large measure of influence on the Chinese communal structure and subculture in many major cities.

"NEW" ORGANIZED CRIME GROUPS

In addition to the traditional organized crime groups just discussed, at least three other major groups have gained considerable influence in the world crime scene today; the Colombian drug cartel, the Russian Mafiya, and the Mexican Federation.

The Colombian Drug Cartel

The most sophisticated and powerful of these groups is the **Colombian drug cartel.** Also called La Empresa Coordinadora because of its business acumen, the Colombian drug cartel is unlike most other TCOs in that it deals primarily with the illegal trade in drugs. It is the predominant group in the cocaine industry and has the criminal and corporate cultures with more success than any organized crime group in history (Bassiouni and Vetere, 1998, p. 565). The Colombian cocaine industry is the Third World's first multinational enterprise and is probably the most profitable business in the world (Salzano and Hartman, 1999). It has been estimated that in 1995 alone the Cali cartel earned more than $8 billion in profits. To gain a perspective, their *profits* were equal to the *total sales* of the Coca-Cola corporation and more than the *combined profits* of General Motors and Wal-Mart (Richards, 1999, p. 18).

The larger Colombian drug cartel actually consists of a number of small organizations (called cartels), with the most powerful being the **Medellin** and **Cali cartels** and, more recently, the Cartel de la Costa. The arrest of numerous Medellin cartel leaders, the death of drug king-pin Pablo Escobar in 1993, and similar fates reached by members of the Cali cartel, have seriously curtailed the drug trafficking activities of the Colombian cartels. However, they still remain a strong force in the trafficking of drugs throughout the world. There are at least a hundred separate drug trafficking organizations in Colombia alone (Holden-Rhodes, 1992). In addition, the Colombian cartels are closely aligned with the coca producers of Peru and Bolivia and, more recently, Mexico. We will discuss the Colombian drug cartel in more detail later in this chapter.

The Russian Mafiya

A second important TCO in the world today is the **Russian Mafiya.** The Russian Mafiya, called the *reketiry* (racketeers), is technically not a "new" group in that it has existed in some form for centuries and for over fifty years provided black market goods for citizens and government officials of the former Soviet Union. But over the past decade, the Russian Mafiya has become among the largest and most powerful TCOs in the world.

Since the collapse of the Communist party, the conditions for organized crime involvement have been ripe in the former Eastern Bloc countries. With the dismantling of the governments came the removal of formal criminal justice systems. Few laws against organized crime activities existed, and the mechanisms for the enforcement of laws were weak or absent. The new Russian Federation started to develop a free-market economy without the rules and regulations necessary to ensure its integrity, efficiency, and effectiveness. And the end of the Cold War made it easier for organized crime groups to engage in transnational criminal activity (Bassiouni and Vetere, 1998). There were over 4,300 organized crime groups in the Russian Federation in 1993 and as many as 5,700 by 1995. Over 200 of these groups are regarded as very sophisticated and are operating on the international level (Johnson, 1995).

Many current Mafiya members in Russia are former KGB agents who were cast adrift in 1991, when the KGB, as well as other USSR governmental agencies, became defunct. Trained in methods of persuasion and violence, possessing knowledge about criminals and criminal activities in Russian society, and, most important, unemployed, the former KGB agents were excellent candidates for integration into the organized crime network. And many took advantage of this opportunity, albeit criminal, to prosper in the new Russian Federation. The Russian Mafiya is currently involved with arms smuggling, prostitution, racketeering, narcotics trafficking, gasoline theft and fraud, car theft, and the illegal export of raw materials from the territories of the Russian Federation (Richards, 1999).

Within Russia, the Mafiya is bound by an eighteen-part "Thieves' Code" (*vorsvskoy zakon*), and each group typically is led by a *pakhan,* or boss. Within each of the groups are cells that specialize in their illegal activities, such as drugs, prostitution, and extortion (www.sgrm.com/Russian.html).

According to FBI Director Louis Freeh, over 200 Russian organized crime groups are operating in the United States in least seventeen cities and fourteen states. The area with the greatest concentration of Russian organized crime is Brighton Beach, New York. Russian crime organizations there are involved with a plethora of illegal activities such as gasoline fraud, medical and counterfeiting fraud, prostitution, and violence linked to criminal activity. Although the growth of Russian organized crime has generated considerable interest in the media and law enforcement community, it is not clear whether the Russian Mafiya in the United States actually resembles other traditional organized crime groups. James Finckenauer and Elin Waring, in their well-researched book *Russian Mafia in America* (1998), propose that this is not the case. They claim that Russian organized crime in the United States does not really conform to the formal definitions of being a "Mafia" or "organized crime." The Russian Mafiya is better described as an uncoordinated amalgamation of groups operating in response to specific criminal opportunities; in many cases, the groups are not even Russian. They are, in fact, different from many newer TCOs in that they lack cohesion and centrality of purpose. Research of this kind is important because, without a true picture of the extent and nature of Russian-related crime, we cannot begin to develop possible solutions to the problem.

The Mexican Federation

The final "new" group for our discussion is the **Mexican Federation.** This drug cartel is similar to the Colombian drug cartel in that its primary business is the distribution of illegal drugs. Some understanding of the Mexican Federation is important to Americans because of the proximity of Mexico to the United States and the impact of the trade in illegal drugs. Four major groups or cartels within the Mexican Federation are primarily responsible for the shipment of heroin, cocaine, and marijuana to the United States: the Gulf, Juarez, Sonora, and Tijuana cartels. Each of these cartels uses extortion, political corruption, and violence to move their drugs within and out of Mexico. Another group, the Amezuqa Organization, is not within the federation but is a major force in the trafficking of methamphetamines throughout America, Canada, and Europe (Richards, 1999).

Law enforcement officials in Mexico and the United States have worked together closely to stem the flow of illegal drugs into America. There have been some successes, as evidenced by a number of arrests and prosecutions of drug kings in the 1990s and a 50 percent hike in drug seizures from 1998 through 1999. But skeptics claim that others have taken the place of those incarcerated and that the increasing number of drug seizures is only an artifact of more and more drugs crossing the border. And efforts by law enforcement officials have resulted in the increased use of violence by organized crime groups. For example, in March 2000, Tijuana's police chief, Alfredo de la Torre, was killed by gunfire after leaving Sunday mass—the second police chief murdered in a

week in Mexico. In addition, the Juarez cartel has placed a $200,000 bounty on an unidentified U.S. federal drug officer, and the murder of Mexican civilians in the Mexican-American border town of Tamaulipas reached an all-time high in 1999. As stated by Jorge Chabet, a drug cartel expert in Mexico City, "Organized crime is willing to take on the government face to face, and it's the government that is losing the battle" (Mandel-Campbell, 2000).

"Second Tier" Groups

Organized crime is not confined to a few major organizations and does not exist in only a few countries. Enterprising criminal groups, often working in tandem with corrupt public officials, can be found worldwide. In addition to the traditional and newer groups discussed here, a number of what has been referred to as "second tier" criminal organizations exist. These groups are smaller yet are highly organized, and they sometimes work in collaboration with the six aforementioned groups. This tier includes organized crime groups in Nigeria, Panama, Jamaica, Puerto Rico, and the Dominican Republic (Richards, 1999, p. 4).

Wherever these lesser organized crime rackets are found, they tend to reflect the peculiar economic and social conditions in those countries rather than concentrating on the better-known targets of conventional organized gangsters: gambling, illegal substances, and prostitution. And the gangs in these areas do not have the historical and cultural cohesion that characterizes many major gangs in the more developed areas.

The situation in the nations of Africa reveals how organized criminality is adapted to local conditions. In these countries, major gang efforts are concentrated in the areas of poaching, smuggling, appropriation of state property, and various black market activities, including speculation in money. The smuggling of coffee, cocoa, diamonds, and emeralds is especially common. In 1973, for example, it was estimated that, of 12,600 tons of coffee produced in Uganda, only

2,600 were exported legally; the rest was diverted by organized criminals and sold illegally (Opolot, 1986). Likewise, a huge illegal trade in elephant tusks is made possible by the slaughter of the animals in Kenya by both native Kenyans and neighboring Somalias organized into criminal gangs. Opolot (1986) suggests that organized crime in Africa has responded to the conditions peculiar to developing nations. These conditions include the introduction of a money economy (which creates an easily exchanged and valuable commodity), political instability, expanding international trade, urbanization, and unemployment.

THE ORGANIZED DRUG TRADE

No doubt the most lucrative and vicious organized crime racket today is the illegal drug trade. The most infamous organized crime groups involved in the illicit drug trade are those already discussed: the Colombian cartels, Chinese Triads, Italian Mafia, Japanese Yakuza, Mexican Federation, and Russian Mafiya, as well as the Jamaican Posse and Nigerian criminal organizations. All these groups today commonly work together to increase their criminal enterprises. One example of the complicity of crime organizations is how drug traffickers and crime syndicates now are partners in crime on an international level. As reported in one 1997 *Washington Post* story, Russian organized crime groups and Colombian drug traffickers are collaborating—with the Colombians delivering cocaine to Europe in exchange for weapons to be used in drug trafficking operations (Farah, 1997). This is just one example of how organized crime groups have joined with drug traffickers to form alliances more powerful than ever before.

The Extent and Impact of the Drug Trade

The actual extent of the international drug trade is impossible to determine, and estimates of the annual revenues generated by drug sales vary greatly. Thomas Constantine, former head of the U.S. Drug Enforcement Agency (DEA), once placed the figure at $500 billion (Constantine, 1995). To put this number in perspective, consider that if it is accurate it would place drug trafficking below only the global arms trade in the rankings of the world's largest industries. Even with a lower estimate of $300 billion, the figure would be the same as that of the global petroleum industry (Cusimano, 2000).

One way to get a grasp on the extent of the drug problem is to study the number of drug seizures reported by law enforcement officials in various countries. This allows us to estimate whether more drugs entered a given country than in the past. For example, a 1997 United Nations report documented the number of countries reporting drug seizures by type from 1980 through 1994. According to that report, the use of marijuana, cocaine, and heroin increased throughout the world while the use of the remaining drugs ebbed and flowed, with an upswing since 1992 (UNDCP, 1997). For a graphic view of this data, see Figure 13.1.

The findings of the UN report are supported by a 1997 U.S. State Department document indicating that the production of opium poppies, from which heroin is produced, increased considerably in Latin America, Southeast Asia, and Southwest Asia over the previous ten years. Similarly, 12,000 more metric tons of coca leaf, the main ingredient in cocaine, were produced in South America in 1996 than in 1987 (U.S. State Department, 1997). We can conclude from these data that the amount of drugs being produced and distributed throughout the world has increased in recent years.

Despite its efforts to deal with both supply by drug dealers and demand by drug consumers, the U.S. government is making little headway in its war on drugs. Although some studies show a drop in the use of cocaine by Americans, others show a slight increase in the use of marijuana and heroin. An estimated $80 billion worth of drug traffic (other estimates are $40 billion and $100 billion), largely controlled by Cubans and South Americans, occurs in this country each year. The

FIGURE 13.1
The Number of Countries
Reporting Seizures, by Drug
Type, 1980–1994

SOURCE: UNDCP, 1997. Reprinted with
permission of the United Nations.

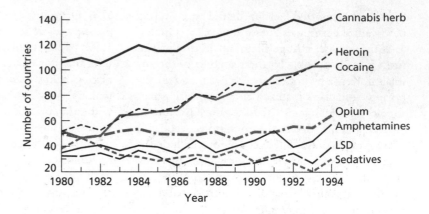

sums of cash that change hands in the various drug transactions and that are "laundered" through legitimate banks and other financial institutions have a major effect on these institutions. The drug trade also provides employment for large numbers of citizens in producer countries, making its control an issue that can have serious adverse effects on the economies of some Third World nations.

Within American cities, drug-related killings and other crimes have reached shockingly high proportions. The portion of the population that is not involved in this criminal underworld and that does not live in the middle of it is usually immune from the full impact of what is happening. There is a tendency to see the increase in violence as being similar to that of the gang wars during Prohibition. In any case, law enforcement and other criminal justice officials live with this crime constantly, and their professional existence is in many ways shaped by it.

The Drug Odyssey

The major sources of narcotic drugs—opium poppies, coca leaves, and marijuana plants—are naturally occurring plants that have long been used as painkillers, tranquilizers, or adjuncts to religious ceremonies in the areas where they are indigenous. Their worldwide use as pleasure-inducing narcotics is the result of increased familiarity and

demand leading to increased production and marketing.

Opium provides an example of a case in which a moralist might well say that the sins of the fathers are being visited upon the children. According to Alan Block and William Chambliss (1981, ch. 2), Turkish traders introduced opium to the rest of Asia in the eighth and ninth centuries. Initially, this was a relatively insignificant trade. During the Age of Exploration, however, when European traders were combing the world for new products and markets, they discovered that opium could be used as a medium for trade. The opium was purchased from the Turks and exchanged with traders in the Far East and southern Asia for spices and silks, which, in turn, were sold in Europe. Opium continued to be used chiefly for medical purposes at that time.

Naturally, it was to the advantage of the traders to increase the use of opium in the East, and India and the British East India Company became major producers and marketers of opium. Opium use as a narcotic became increasingly widespread, especially in China. When the Chinese government attempted to stop the importation of opium in the nineteenth century, Britain seized a number of Chinese ports, including Hong Kong, and defeated the Chinese in what is known as the Opium War. The peace treaty of 1842 ceded Hong Kong to Britain and created certain treaty ports, to which Britain had open access. As a result, British importation of opium into China continued and expanded, despite the fact that opium was still illegal under Chinese law. After Britain won a second opium war in 1856, China was forced to legalize opium smoking and trading. Ironically, Chinese farmers then began to grow their own poppies, and the Chinese government began to tax opium imports, thus resulting in a diminution of British profits from the opium trade (Block and Chambliss, 1981, p. 23). At the same time, farmers in Laos, Burma, and Thailand began to realize that their climate and soil were ideal for growing opium poppies, which brought higher profits than other crops. A flourishing industry was born in those countries.

Famine and war in China during the nineteenth century also caused a large out-migration of Chinese. Many of these emigrants settled in other Asian countries, but a large number came to the United States, where they performed menial labor under poor conditions. The Chinese immigrants brought the habit of smoking opium with them, and the harsh working conditions and poor pay encouraged the search for some kind of escape. And this opium smoking was not discouraged, since it resulted in a docile labor force. Block and Chambliss tell us that opium smoking eventually spread to a larger portion of the American labor force (1981, p. 29).

By the early twentieth century, the United States and other countries had become concerned about the deleterious effects of opium and its derivatives (heroin had been developed as a derivative in 1898). Gradually, these products were criminalized except for the stringently controlled medical use of morphine as a painkiller. By the 1920s, trade in narcotics derived from opium was the province of organized crime syndicates in the United States. As we have seen, it was also in the early twentieth century that the Chinese Triad groups became increasingly prominent in the trade in illegal narcotics derived from the opium plant.

Today, illegal drugs originate in many countries. The primary producer of heroin is Afghanistan, which, along with Iran and Pakistan, makes up what is called the "Golden Crescent." Together with the "Golden Triangle" countries of Laos, Thailand, and Myanmar, they dominate the opium market. Recently, Colombian and Mexican drug organizations, recognizing the lucrative nature of heroin, have begun production and smuggling operations (EPIC, 1998). European countries receive their heroin through the Balkan regions and the former Eastern bloc areas. Heroin for the United States is transported mostly through South America.

Over 98 percent of all cocaine is produced by three Andean countries: Bolivia, Peru, and Colombia (NIJ, 1998). Although most of the cocaine in the United States is transported through Mexico, the Caribbean countries of Haiti, the Dominican Republic, and Puerto Rico increasingly are being used as transit points.

Marijuana is grown in virtually every country in the world including the United States. In fact, it has supplanted regular crops in many African and Central American countries. The United States is mainly supplied with marijuana by Canada, Jamaica, the Philippines, Colombia, and Mexico. For a graphic depiction of the path of illegal drugs into the United States, see Figure 13.2.

Methylenedioxymethamphetamine (MDMA), also called "Ecstasy," has recently been flooding into the United States from the source country of the Netherlands. Canadian, Caribbean, and, recently, Israeli organized crime groups have assisted with the transportation of ecstasy (EPIC, 1999). Methamphetamine, dubbed the "crack of the 90s," has been primarily produced and distributed by the Mexican Federation.

Money Laundering

Throughout this chapter, we have noted how organized crime figures reap significant profits from illegal criminal activities. But one integral aspect of organized crime and drug trafficking yet to be discussed is how the financial benefits of crime are filtered into the pockets of criminals while remaining free of law enforcement detection. This

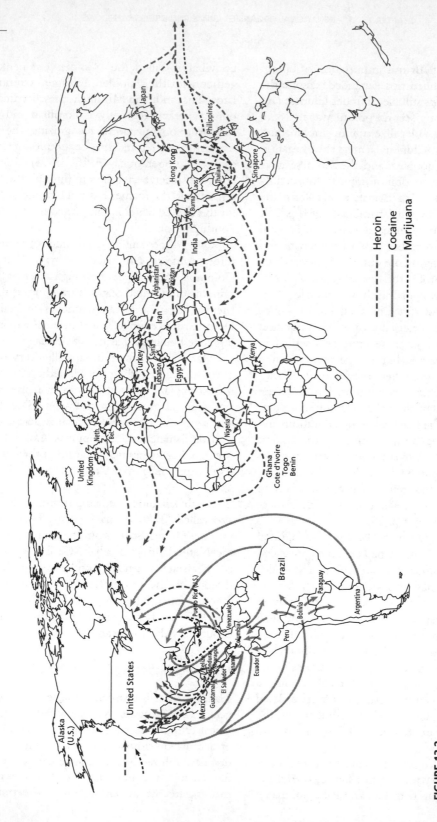

FIGURE 13.2
Drug Routes into the United States

SOURCE: Zawitz, 1994, pp. 47–51.

is done through a process called **money laundering,** whereby the monetary proceeds of criminal activity are converted into funds with an apparent legal source (Manzel, 1996). It is estimated that as much as $600 billion a year is laundered worldwide.

The term *money laundering* suggests a cycle of transactions in which the illegitimate dirty money comes out clean after being processed into a legitimate legal source. Interestingly, however, the term can also be traced back to the Italian Mafia of the 1930s when illegal funds from bootleg liquor were "washed" through cash businesses called "Laundromats." Meyer Lansky, an organized crime accountant, was the first known person in the United States to launder money using foreign (Swiss) bank accounts. Al Capone, the infamous Chicago crime boss, is said to have been the first person to be convicted of laundering money, back in 1931.

International organized crime provides a large array of activities that would require laundering money. These criminal activities include but are not limited to the following:

Drug trafficking

Illegal gambling

Tax fraud and evasion

Theft

Extortion

Counterfeiting

There are actually three steps to money laundering: placement, layering, and integration. *Placement* is the process of moving money from the location of the criminal activity. *Layering* involves the frequent series of money transfers and transactions used to "cover the tracks" of the illegal funds. *Integration* refers to when the money is returned to the regular economy through purchase or investment.

Historically, high-cash-flow businesses—such as restaurants, bars, vending machine companies, and pizza parlors—have been used to launder money. Laundromats, and especially casinos, traditionally have been the purchase choice of legitimate businesses for money laundering. Among the common ways to launder money are buying high-cost goods with cash, converting to a foreign currency, and then transferring them back to a third banking system—keeping the transaction under $10,000, which precludes having to report the transaction to tax authorities. However, with the widespread adoption of computers, the number of ways to launder money has grown beyond comprehension.

Traffic in Narcotics and U.S. Foreign Policy

As a foreign policy issue, the drug trade raises issues about U.S. relations with other countries, especially its South and Central American neighbors. Pressure on foreign leaders to cooperate in the elimination of drug production, as well as foreign aid incentives to do so, fall within the realm of foreign policy aspects of drug control. Matters are complicated by the fact that in some countries the drug industry supports antigovernment guerilla movements. In Peru, for example, the Shining Path, a powerful Maoist guerilla group that controls much of the countryside, supports its efforts through the sale of coca leaves grown by Peruvian peasants. U.S. DEA agents cooperate with the Peruvian antidrug police, supplying helicopters to find coca fields and spraying defoliants to destroy the crop. The use of defoliants is itself a sensitive issue that affects U.S. foreign policy. Permission to engage in antidrug operations in other countries may be tied to the continued provision of U.S. military and economic aid, thus leaving few alternatives other than cooperation for Third World governments.

In Colombia, drug dealers have terrorized the legitimate government through multiple assassinations of judicial and law enforcement personnel engaged in drug control activities. According to one report, U.S. DEA officials in Colombia compare the conditions there to Vietnam during the war. Fears for their employees' safety have caused American businesses to abandon their operations in Colombia and have led the U.S. government to pull dependents out of the country—actions that further weaken an already shaky economy. Police officers, who are paid only $800 a year, are sorely tempted to take payoffs in exchange for providing protection to drug dealers (Ward, 1989).

The United States has called for the extradition of captured Colombian drug "kingpins," and this threat of extradition has led to further violence. The Colombian government, caught between strong U.S. demands for suppression of drug trafficking, economic considerations related to the lucrative drug trade, and a fearsome army of drug dealers, has at great cost managed to check some of the blatant drug trafficking activities of the Medellin cartel. Its major leader, Pablo Escobar Gaviria, turned himself in to the authorities on the condition that he not be extradited. He was later killed by police during an escape attempt. His cousin and third in command, Gustavo Gaviria, as well as his first deputy, Gonzalo Rodriguez Gacha, were killed in shoot-outs with Colombian police (Sutton, 1991).

Internally, police departments throughout the United States are profoundly involved in apprehending drug traffickers. As an international criminal justice issue, however, the drug trade raises questions about sovereignty, international cooperation, jurisdictional boundaries, and political relations between nations in general. Increasing U.S. pressure on other countries leads to claims that the real problem is the consumer demand for drugs in the United States, a demand that is sure to be satisfied by other sources if any one source is cut off.

The Enrique Camarena case illustrates the deep involvement of political and foreign policy issues in drug smuggling into the United States. Camarena, a U.S. DEA special agent, and Mexican captain Alfredo Zavala, who supplied information to the DEA, were both abducted in February 1985 near Guadalajara, Mexico. Frantic efforts by U.S. authorities to find Camarena were met by peculiar resistance and evasion on the part of the Mexican Federal Judicial Police. After a series of bizarre incidents and attempted coverups, the bodies of the two men, who had been tortured and killed in the guest house of a large

Guadalajara residence, were found. The FBI began an exhaustive search for forensic evidence that might lead to detention and prosecution of the killers. Again, there were efforts on the part of some Mexican authorities to conceal evidence and prevent U.S. agents from examining aspects of the crime scene. Only after high-level negotiations between the two nations would the Mexican police allow further investigation. Ultimately, two leading drug lords and twenty-six of their associates were accused of the crime, tried in Los Angeles, convicted, and sentenced to long terms in U.S. prisons. The evidence in the case pointed to payoffs of Mexican authorities to conceal evidence in the case (Malone, 1989).

Further accusations of governmental involvement in the conspiracy to murder Camarena and Zavala and cover up the crime have drawn heated denials from the Mexican government. A TV miniseries about the case resulted in a strong reaction, as this newspaper account shows:

> The broadcast . . . drew bitter condemnation and threats of a possible lawsuit from the Mexican government. Statements by Mexico's Foreign Ministry and congress, the Mexican ambassador to Washington, and consuls in New York, Chicago, Los Angeles, and San Antonio denounced the portrayal of Mexican government police and military officials as "irresponsible," "defamatory," "vile," and "intervention in the country's internal affairs." (Branigan, 1990)

To assist the Mexican government in the fight against drugs, President Clinton in February 1999 earmarked $4 billion to expand legal trade with Mexico to assist in developing the economy and fighting drug trafficking and to develop an FBI program to train police there (Page, 1999). Mexico is also one of the countries that each year is embroiled in the controversial foreign policy issue called **certification.** This policy, developed as part of the Foreign Assistance Act of 1961, allows the president and Congress of the United States to review each year the list of countries believed to support illicit drug trade or production. If a country fails to make progress in its efforts to reduce its drug involvement, it can be denied certi-fication. Without certification, different forms of financial assistance and trade benefits can be with-held. In March 2000, President Clinton granted full certification to twenty of the twenty-six countries on the "questionable" list; only two, Afghanistan and Burma, were denied certification for the second year in a row (INL, 2000).

There is no doubt that the lucrative drug trade taints most of those who come in contact with it, whether they be government officials, major organized crime figures, minor street dis-tributors, or criminal justice personnel. In recent years, collusion between drug dealers and gov-ernment agents has been uncovered in the Philip-pines, Turkey, Mexico, and Colombia (Sutton, 1991). In Mexican prisons, drug dealers have lux-urious quarters while penniless suspected drug users are kept in appallingly overcrowded condi-tions. Matamoros State Prison, for example, which was built to house 250 prisoners, in late 1991 had about 1,500 prisoners, 90 percent of whom were there on drug charges (Olivero, 1991).

Further, the drug trade tends to distort the economies of the countries that are heavily in-volved. The farmers who grow the opium pop-pies, the marijuana, or the coca plants are actually those who benefit least from the lucrative spoils of the drug trade. Nevertheless, even for them, these crops bring in higher cash payments than con-ventional foodstuffs.

RESPONSES TO ORGANIZED CRIME AND DRUG TRAFFICKING

Consider the following:

- General Manuel Noriega, head of Panama's defense forces and virtual leader of Panama, was indicted in the United States as an inter-national drug dealer.
- The U.S. government negotiated with Peru to destroy illegal coca crops in that country through dusting with a lethal herbicide.

- Charles "Lucky" Luciano, a famous crime syndicate boss, was deported to his native Italy after a trial in the United States.
- U.S. agents worked in Mexico to help Mexi-can authorities combat drug smuggling— with tragic results in the case of Enrique Camarena, who was tortured and murdered by gangsters in Mexico.
- Six defendants accused of laundering mil-lions of dollars for the Cali and Juarez drug cartels were tried in a Los Angeles court after a law enforcement operation called "Casablanca" resulted in 150 arrests and seizure of $50 million in assets.

In each of these cases, the United States was working closely with another country to impact the organized crime problem. However, these kinds of legal developments take considerable time, cost significant resources, and often fail as many times as they succeed. Such efforts are complicated by issues of national sovereignty, ju-risdiction, interagency cooperation, and politics involved in such cross-border operations. A per-son wanted in one country may or may not be extradited from another country to face trial. The economy of a poor agricultural region may be seriously affected by drug eradication policies, and political unrest may follow. Law enforcement agents in one country may engage in passive re-sistance to efforts by agents from another country to become involved in local antidrug activities. The individual offender may particularly desire to be tried in a nation where sentences are short or where there is no danger of receiving the death penalty. In many cases, the person brought to jus-tice is just one of many figures involved in the criminal activity, and others immediately take their place in the criminal organization. These are just a few of the many complexities that may arise when we try to arrest, indict, and punish transnational offenders. Does this imply that we should abandon our efforts to bring suspects to justice and stem the tide of organized criminal activity? Hardly. What is more appropriate, how-ever, is to make a concerted effort to closely study the issues at hand, to clearly plan our goals and objectives in attacking the problem, and to implement our methods with efficiency and integrity.

Fortunately, there is not a shortage of ideas about how to reduce transnational organized crime. At this point, we focus on some of the cogent suggestions about how to best deal with the problem of transnational organized crime and its related problem of drug trafficking. This discussion is by no means inclusive of all the possible legal, social, and political means available to deal with this important issue. But it does present some of the current ideas that could help combat transnational organized crime and drug trafficking.

Prevention Strategies

One way to prevent the spread of organized crime is to reduce the opportunities for criminal activity simply by reducing the *demand* for illicit goods. In the case of some goods and services, like drugs, they can be made legally available. Although this alternative is highly controversial, some recent evidence suggests that decriminalization of some forms of drugs can reduce criminality. In an evaluation of the Swiss heroin maintenance program conducted over a three-year period from 1994 to 1997, the results clearly reflected a drop in criminal activity for those in the program. As stated by Martin Killias of the Swiss Institute of Police Science and Criminology, "I know of no other crime prevention program with such a big reduction in theft and other serious crimes" (Nullis, 1997). Unfortunately, other forms of drug demand reduction programs, like the DARE program in the United States, and drug education programs in Scotland have been less successful.

Demand reduction programs for other kinds of criminal activity require more emphasis on the moral education of citizens about crime involvement. The use of the media can be a tremendous resource in this area (Bassiouni and Vertere, 1998, p. 523). Many examples of how moral education can reduce crime were given throughout this book in our discussions of the model countries of Japan, China, and Saudi Arabia.

Another prevention strategy is simply to reduce the *supply* of illegal goods and services. With drugs, this is attempted through eradication and crop substitution programs. At this juncture, it is difficult to ascertain whether these programs have worked to any significant degree. Although national eradication and crop substitution programs can have an impact on illicit cultivation, the **balloon effect** is most often the result. With the balloon effect, when drugs are eliminated in one region, another region will increase production to meet demand.

Crime Control Strategies

A variety of crime control strategies frequently are adopted by many countries to deal with the problems of international organized crime. The most common of these are more laws, stricter laws, and better law enforcement.

A number of countries have developed legislation that either makes it illegal to participate in certain activities or to be a part of an illegal organization, or allows for the confiscation of goods obtained through illegal activity. Special laws in Germany have made it illegal to be involved in gang robbery, management of prostitution, and illicit gambling. Jamaica has a dangerous drug act and a corruption prevention act. The countries of the new Russian Federation have also updated their laws to include provisions against organized crime (Bassiouni and Vetere, 1998, p. 525).

The main idea behind the changing of many laws is to undermine the efforts of criminals who are believed to benefit from legal loopholes. For example, one way to impact organized crime is to develop laws reducing opportunities for money laundering. In the United States, two key statutes in this area are the Money Laundering Control Act of 1986 and the Bank Secrecy Act of 1970 (Richards, 1999). Each of these laws cover the main aspects of money laundering as they pertain to organized criminal activity and allow for relatively easy prosecution of offenders.

Of course, qualified and competent law enforcement personnel are essential to controlling international organized crime. In many developing and politically changing countries, the police lack the basic resources to do their jobs well. Poor training, limited technology, and low pay all increase the risk of organized crime infiltrating and corrupting the police force. Fortunately, there have been positive steps in law enforcement in recent years relative to assisting law enforcement agencies across borders. For example, the FBI has recently opened up branches in Budapest and Moscow to teach law enforcement officials there how better to protect and serve in a region where the police have long been associated with oppression and organized crime is now in control (Page, 1999).

International police organizations also are involved in the effort to fight international organized crime. Most prominent are the recent efforts of EUROPOL and INTERPOL. EUROPOL, as mentioned in Chapter 2, is the European equivalent of INTERPOL. In November 1999, over 120 officials and experts from around the world met in The Hague to develop a comprehensive crime prevention strategy to deal with organized crime.

INTERPOL has strong ties to law enforcement agencies and also works to promote cooperative projects among agencies. Through its Organized Crime and Criminal Activities section, it provides information, stimulates research, and organizes training sessions. It also works with member nations to encourage their legislatures to implement laws designed to combat organized crime (Lavy, 1990).

Cooperation Strategies

Another significant advance in the fight against organized crime and drug trafficking involves the strides made within the international community to coordinate efforts. In addition to increased interagency cooperation, a variety of international treaties and conventions have been adopted to deal with transnational crime issues. The first of these was adopted in 1909, when thirteen countries met in Shanghai to discuss a formal drug control treaty (McAllister, 1991). Since then, many treaties and conventions have been signed and supported by literally hundreds of countries.

In the European Union, the so-called TREVI (terrorism, drugs, organized crime) agreement provides for exchanges of personnel, information, and technology, as well as cooperative work in emergency situations. The European Union also has agreed to outlaw drug money laundering through the banks of its members. The Shengen Group Agreement of 1985, which opened the borders of France, Germany, and the Benelux nations to each other, has resulted in a good deal of cooperation and planning on the part of law enforcement officials.

But probably the most important of these international documents is the 1988 UN Convention Against Illicit Traffic in Narcotic Drugs and Psychotropic Substances. This document, signed in 1990 by eighty-eight nations, includes provisions for extradition in drug cases, increased exchange of information, and increased cooperation in tracking down and eliminating money laundering. Bank secrecy is not allowed as grounds for refusal to cooperate in a money-laundering investigation. In addition to written treaties, the United Nations often sponsors international crime conferences that deal with organized crime issues, among other topics. The United Nations also has developed the Office for Drug Control and Crime Prevention (ODCCP), which oversees two agencies that work to foster cooperation in crime control among different countries; the Center for International Crime Prevention (CICP) and the UN International Drug Control Programme (UNDCP). One example of the fine work by these agencies is their efforts in May 1999 to gain support and funding for the development of a *World Organized Crime Report*. This report will be produced every two years and will provide information to policymakers and the general public on trends in organized crime worldwide and efforts to combat this phenomenon (UNICJRI, 1999).

It is also important at the national level for individual countries to improve coordination efforts. Articulating clear goals and jurisdictional responsibilities within and between the police, courts, and correctional systems can help in this process. For example, in the United States, federal agencies like the FBI and DEA, special task forces, and state and local agencies all deal in some way with issues related to organized crime. Efforts must be made to improve collaboration and share valuable resources.

SUMMARY

This chapter only touches on the intricacies of the organized crime problem, in terms of both its dimensions and the reactions of governments and intergovernmental organizations to this kind of criminality. Organized crime is a wide-ranging phenomenon that is difficult to define and equally difficult to assess in scope. We do know that it is a widespread and growing problem that greatly impacts societies in overt and covert ways. Although there are a few acknowledged "leaders" in the field of organized crime, the field is widening. New groups and new forms of organized crime activity are constantly being introduced.

The major activity of organized crime, drug trafficking, also appears to have reached epidemic proportions. Drug traffickers are becoming more sophisticated, more violent, and more global in influence. The U.S. policy toward drug trafficking has remained firm although the results of these efforts remain unclear.

Responses to organized crime and drug trafficking can be collapsed into three categories: prevention strategies, control strategies, and cooperation strategies. Although advances have been made in all of these areas, their overall impact on the transnational organized crime scene remains suspect.

DISCUSSION QUESTIONS

1. Should the United States try to control drug production at the source through the use of U.S. troops, agents, and money, or should it concentrate on controlling traffic and consumption within the United States?

2. Invite a local FBI agent to your class, and discuss some ways that organized crime may impact your community or city.

3. Is it a sign of progress or concern when organized gangsters become involved in legitimate businesses like selling stocks and collecting garbage? Explain.

4. What might the president and Congress "certify" a country that is obviously a drug-producing nation?

5. Of all the possible responses to organized crime and drug trafficking, which do you believe is the most effective? Why?

FOR FURTHER READING

Bassiouni, M. C., and E. Vetere (eds.). (1998). *Organized Crime: A Compilation of U.N. Documents 1975–1998.* New York: Transnational.

Block, A., and W. Chambliss. (1981). *Organizing Crime.* New York: Elsevier.

Hess, H. (1992). The Traditional Sicilian Mafia: Organized Crime and Repressive Crime. In R. Kelly, *Organized Crime: A Global Perspective.* Totowa, N.J.: Rowman and Littlefield, pp. 113–133.

Kaplan, D., and A. Dubrow. (1986). *Yakusa.* Reading, Mass.: Addison-Wesley.

Posner, G. (1988). *Warlords of Crime.* New York: McGraw-Hill.

Richards, J. R. (1999). *Transnational Criminal Organizations, Cybercrime, and Money Laundering.* Boca Raton, Fla.: CRC Press.

United Nations International Drug Control Programme (UNDCP). (1997). *World Drug Report.* New York: Oxford University Press.

14 Contemporary Influences and Future Developments in Transnational Crime and Justice

Key Terms and Concepts

convergence
corruption
cultural persistence
illegal immigration
smuggling
smuggling of human organs
smuggling of women
software piracy
political and policy-making process

Three forces come together to influence the development of legal and criminal processes in the world today. First is the dynamic of **convergence,** in which laws, policies, and practices of the criminal justice system become more uniform across nations. Second is the dynamic of **cultural persistence,** in which deep-rooted historical, economic, and social realities create adaptations to change that result in the continuance of individualistic systems. Third is the **political and policy-making process,** in which particular governmental regimes that foster particular ideologies stamp the legal system with their own character. These three forces are at work simultaneously at all times; nevertheless, one or the other may dominate in a particular nation at any time. In this brief concluding chapter, we will explore these forces in more detail and also address some of the possible future directions of crime and criminal justice as we enter the twenty-first century.

CONVERGENCE

Many of the descriptions in this book gave evidence of convergence of criminal justice systems. In today's "global village," where transportation and communication systems are highly developed, and national borders are beginning to mean less and less to businesspeople and to workers and travelers, convergence tends to accelerate. The phenomenon of convergence may be analyzed in terms of three categories: (1) imitation/interpenetration, (2) simultaneous development, and (3) supranational regulation.

Imitation or interpenetration of institutions and practices from one people or nation to another is surely as old as warfare, commerce, and travel. Indeed, progress and learning throughout the world have depended on exchanges of ideas and institutions from one society to another. Imitation may be inspired by genuine admiration for the institutions of another society. It may be forced on a society by a conqueror (in which case it is more properly called interpenetration). Or it may be the result of expediency of one kind or another.

Examples of imitation or interpenetration are found in all parts of the world and all aspects of the criminal process. In the latter half of the nineteenth century, the Japanese based their civil code, their criminal code, and their police organization on European models. Today, police departments in countries as varied as Singapore, the United States, Australia, and Norway are borrowing Japanese police structures and practices in the name of "community policing." Numerous countries in Africa, the Near East, and Asia, as well as political subdivisions such as Quebec and Louisiana, have adopted the French Civil Code and/or the French Penal Code, either by choice or because of colonization by the French. Others have chosen to adopt the more recent German Civil Code. U.S. criminal procedure is a direct imitation of the English procedure, or at least of colonial procedure, which came from England. Nineteenth-century American innovations with prisons were promoted in Europe. The Scandinavian system of day fines as an alternative to conventional fines has been widely adopted, most prominently in Germany and, more recently, in the United States. Australia and England and Wales have embarked on the building of private prisons that borrows directly from the American experience.

Simultaneous development of criminal justice institutions is also a natural process, as similar problems develop in a variety of regions. The industrial revolution, with its concomitant urbanization and dislocation of masses of people, fostered the development of metropolitan police departments in both England and the United States at roughly the same time. Modern nations have gone through an evolutionary process in which formal governmental institutions became more specialized and rule bound. Courts as independent and specialized dispute resolution bodies, free from executive influence (and, in fact, free from the "court" of a monarch), developed gradually in Europe throughout the late Middle Ages and Renaissance. Bureaucratization—that is, the development of impersonal rules, merit hiring practices, specialization of effort, and higher educational standards—of criminal justice agencies is a modern development in many countries. Broader criminal procedure protections of the accused have developed in many countries since World War II, partially in response to the excesses of that war and partially in response to renewed concerns for human and civil rights in more recent decades.

Supranational bodies are especially important in fostering convergence. The United Nations supports the protection of human rights, including rights of the accused. Organizations like Amnesty International, Human Rights Watch, and Lawyers Committee for Human Rights pressure governments to adhere to humane standards in treating "prisoners of conscience," that is, political prisoners who have committed no crimes of violence.

Most important, however, are the bodies that have more direct power over the legal process of member nations. In the European Court of Human Rights, the International Court of Justice in The Hague, and the recent war tribunals for the former Yugoslavia and for Rwanda, attempts were made to ensure conformity to transnational conventions and treaties. Inevitably, this process arrives at a certain convergence both of criminal procedure and sanctions rules and of the two families of law involved, the Common Law and the Civil Law. Changes have come about in the adversarial system and, more often, in the inquisitorial system as a result of the supranational body. One example is the new rules for maximum length of pretrial detention of suspects in Civil Law countries like Austria, Italy, and Germany. In this context, Scheingold (1970), writing about the European Court of Justice, describes a model of interpenetration in which "participation in regional decision-making processes will tend to socialize the participants and generate attitudes and behavior which are favorable to the regional system" (p. 28).

INTERPOL and other cooperative international policing and data-gathering agencies also facilitate convergence among systems. Their requests for information encourage standardization of comparative information. Greater uniformity also results from exchanges of information, ar-

rangements for international meetings of criminal justice personnel, development of educational materials, and other cooperative efforts by international agencies.

International compacts are another force for convergence of systems. These compacts may address particular problems, such as terrorism, drug trafficking, extradition, and prison conditions. Their main goal, however, is to impose an international standard for dealing with the problems. Thus, Holland, which does not prosecute narcotics crimes with particular vigor, nevertheless adheres to the international treaties that outlaw drug traffic and call for cooperation among authorities in the various signatory countries. Cuba's involvement in a compact against air piracy in the 1970s virtually halted the practice of hijacking American planes to Cuba.

More subtle factors are also at work in promoting convergence of criminal justice systems and legal processes. Exchange of academics under the Fulbright Scholar program, access to international publications through the widespread use of the Internet, the extensive use of satellites to broadcast television programs and movies across borders—all provide the information necessary for individual countries to look at possible reforms and imitate programs from other systems.

CULTURAL PERSISTENCE

Cultural persistence works to counter the forces of convergence, with varying degrees of success, depending on the circumstances. In the face of pressure for modernism and convergence and for reform, cultural persistence will use the already present historical, economic, and social realities to create adaptations to change.

As a result of cultural persistence two events often occur. One is co-optation of change; the other is reversion to earlier structures for the administration of justice.

Japan is a premier example of co-optation of change. Although Japan imitated Western structures on a seemingly wholesale scale, the end product is a culturally determined system that resembles its progenitors only superficially. Eleanor Westney (1987) describes one aspect of this in her book, aptly entitled *Imitation and Innovation.* Westney examines certain Meiji-era Japanese institutions, including the post office and the police, whose organization was borrowed from Western models. She makes the point that *imitation,* the first stage in developing the new Japanese police, was modified almost immediately by *innovations* (e.g., the *koban* and *chuzaisho*) that made the police a uniquely Japanese entity that in its practices actually had little resemblance to its French precursor. Likewise, setting up Western-style machinery for dispute settlement on a confrontational basis did not obviate the need for uniquely Japanese-style institutions that stressed mediation and conciliation. After World War II, the Japanese adopted an American-style constitution with American-style rights clearly spelled out. Despite this fact, Japanese people do not routinely take their grievances to court. On human rights and even human relations matters, they take their concerns to the Civil Liberties Bureau, an agency that was supposed to support constitutional rights but that actually deals largely with human relations problems. The Supreme Court, which was designed to act independently of the executive and legislature in an American-style separation of powers, has failed to assert itself against the party in power. The same party has been in power since the first postwar elections, so obviously competition for political office in Japan occurs within the Liberal Democratic party rather than between parties. A superficial examination of the legal basis for Japanese institutions of justice would miss most of the subtleties of adaptation because they are not written down; thus, the system must be studied in terms of behavior rather than law.

Japan is not the only example of co-optation of change to conform to deep-seated cultural and historical norms. In the United States, where statutory law has largely replaced the basic Common Law, case precedents continue to be law with a force that amazes the Continental lawyer or judge. Efforts to cut down on rampant discre-

tionary powers of judges and prosecutors are usually absorbed into the complex, pluralistic, and ambiguous matrix that is so typical of American institutions. When Western legal structures were introduced in African colonies, Africans continued to settle a large proportion of cases through the traditional informal dispute resolution structures that had served them in the past.

Co-optation is not the only form that persistence of culture takes. A more extreme form, one that may be ideologically or politically driven, is reversion to structures of an earlier time. The revolution in Iran in the late 1970s, for example, brought about a reversion to strict adherence to fundamentalist Islamic Law after a period of relatively secularized and westernized legal institutions. Other Near Eastern countries are also returning to their traditional religious law, albeit with allowances for commercial transactions through administrative court, as opposed to Shari'a court, supervision. A less extreme example would be the reversion of the post–World War II German police organization to the structures of the Weimar Republic, which were particularly suited to the traditional German brand of federalism.

There is some concern in the international community that the large-scale economic and social problems being experienced by the newly formed Russian Federation will cause some form of reversion. Key political victories by some former members of the Communist party suggest that change may be in the air, but what the changes will be are simply projections at this time.

POLITICAL AND POLICY-MAKING PROCESSES

The opposing forces of modernism and traditionalism generally bring about a gradual change in a nation's criminal justice system. More drastic change can result from energetic political action on the part of rulers. An extreme example of this would be the former Soviet Union's move from a modified Civil Law system to a new kind of system, the one that we have called Socialist Law. Without changing institutions in any radical sense, the purposes of the law and the relation between citizen and legal system were changed dramatically during the time of Communist rule.

More recently, Prime Minister Margaret Thatcher, faced with a continued and intractable threat of terrorism on the part of the Irish Republic Army, convinced Parliament to modify the right to protection against self-incrimination in the case of suspected terrorists. In this situation, she was undermining a painfully developed cornerstone of criminal procedure right within the adversarial system.

Currently, in China, the movement toward *yanda* (strike back) to deal with the apparent rise in crime and social unrest has resulted in modifications of the criminal procedure rules. The crime situation in China has been exacerbated by the opening of the borders due to a shift to a market economy. Another current example is South Africa, where the political decision to eliminate apartheid has created a host of crime problems; this issue will undoubtedly be a main source of concern in the region for at least the near future.

Wars and conquest often have dramatic effects on the system of law and justice in a country. The Norman Conquest of England was solidified by use of the law. Later English kings set up prerogative courts, including equity courts, to assert themselves against the increasingly independent Common Law judges. Equity as a kind of legal procedure remains an integral part of Anglo-Saxon law today. There are myriad examples in which a ruler or ruling party has directly changed or influenced the development of legal and criminal justice processes.

In reviewing the many details of the criminal process in our six model countries, we can see all of these forces at work. A closer understanding of the historical, economic, and cultural traditions helps us understand which structures can be successfully imitated and which are too foreign to have any chance of success in a new culture.

In the end, as homogeneity and cross-cultural similarities grow, as they inevitably will in our shrinking world, we might pause to consider both the positive and the negative aspects of this development. We will perhaps be moving toward universal standards of humanity and decency in the process of maintaining law and order. At the same time, we will be sacrificing much of the native color, individual character, and diversity that makes, in the natural world at least, for a stronger and more interesting environment. The optimal balance between unity and diversity has not yet been found, and it is a significant challenge for future generations.

LOOKING TO THE FUTURE

The number of experts who were confounded by the fall of the Berlin Wall and the dismantling of the Soviet Union indicates that predictions about the future of political systems are at best an art, not a science. Nevertheless, predictions continue to be made.

We have learned that change in political systems is often accompanied by modifications in the legal and criminal justice systems. Among our model nations, it is possible to make some modest claims relating to the near future.

Changes in the Model Nations

The stable democracies of England, France, and Germany, which have a postwar history of increasing concern with due process of law, will probably maintain that concern, despite some serious destabilizing pressures on the justice system. The pressures are related to the ever-larger immigrant populations seeking haven in these countries. Germany is especially at risk here, because of the hundreds of thousands of refugees from eastern Europe, some of them ethnic Germans, who are moving west. Economic and cultural difficulties associated with absorbing these populations lead both to increased crime and to a right-wing backlash that often becomes violent. The criminal justice system becomes the focus for dealing with many of the ensuing problems. We can expect increasing conservatism, more "law and order" campaigns, and some attenuation of civil liberties as a result.

Another factor that will affect the criminal process in these three countries is the ongoing movement toward European integration. As the borders among the countries within the European Union become more open, issues related to jurisdiction, "hot pursuit," and extradition will become even more important, and cooperation among authorities of the various justice systems will become even more crucial. The pressures for convergence of laws and rules, as explained previously, also will increase. We can expect that, despite the language differences, relations among the nations of Europe in criminal justice matters will increasingly resemble relations among the states of the United States.

The tremendous economic and social changes in the People's Republic of China makes prediction, especially about criminal justice matters, extremely tenuous. This situation is further complicated by the inclusion of satellite republics like Tibet and Taiwan in the Chinese political mix. We can predict, however, that as the citizens of China become more accustomed to the individual freedoms that go with a market economy, the issues of democracy and individual rights will come to the forefront. How the Chinese government reacts to these matters will also be closely observed in the international community.

Saudi Arabia provides an interesting field for speculation. Western influences in that nation and commercial development related to oil wealth have so changed the society that it does not seem likely that its justice institutions will remain as solidly Islamic as they have been during the previous history of the country. Although the king has taken some steps toward increased consultation with the people in governing the nation, and a constitution has been promised, change will probably be incremental and related to internal security needs and relations with other Arab countries, among other things.

Japan is another nation that will probably experience important changes in the near future. The vaunted Japanese system of close surveillance of the population through the police system may not be able to withstand the forces of technology and modernization that are beginning to make inroads on the traditional forms. Likewise, individual rights, protected by the Japanese constitution, will probably be asserted with increasing frequency by the "outsiders" in Japan: women, Burakamin, and Koreans. In other words, litigation will be more instrumental in social change than it has been in the past.

In addition to making predictions about our model countries, we can also speculate as to what kinds of criminal activity will be most problematic in the years to come. As with our prior predictions, speculation as to the most problematic of future crimes is also an arbitrary endeavor, especially given that there are undoubtedly numerous crimes that have yet to surface as major concerns for criminal justice officials worldwide. Among the crimes that we exclude from our discussion but that nonetheless are serious are environmental crime, fauna and flora trafficking, theft and trafficking of automobiles, and theft of cultural property. The three general categories of crime that we have chosen for further exploration because of their transnational significance are computer crimes, smuggling, and corruption.

Computer Crime

As we briefly mentioned in Chapter 1, computer crime, also called cybercrime, is crime committed with the use of computers. As the number of legitimate uses of computers rise, so does the chances of their illegitimate use. The FBI's National Computer Crime Squad (NCCS) lists the following general categories of computer crime: violations of or into telephone systems, violations of or into major computer networks, computer privacy violations, industrial espionage, **software piracy** (pirating of licensed software), and other crimes in which computers are the major tool used to commit an offense such as interstate distribution of pornography, cybertheft, and cyberstalking (Richards, 1999, p. 69).

Cybercrime within these categories can now spread from relatively minor acts of consumer fraud to major crimes that paralyze entire financial networks and national security systems. In one 1995 case, in what can be literally described as a "computer crime," armed robbers stole more than $12 million worth of computer chips from a California distributor (Bradford, 1995). That same year, computer expert Kevin Mitnick, known as the "FBI's most wanted hacker," broke into an Internet service provider and stole more than 20,000 credit card numbers. Apparently, economic cybercrime is not unusual if we believe the results of one recent study by the Computer Security Institute, which reported that 64 percent of the companies polled experienced some breech of computer security in 1998 (*Washington Post,* 1999).

Cybercrime of a noneconomic nature can lead to breeches in national security. In 1996 alone, there were approximately 250,000 intrusions into the U.S. Department of Defense computer system. When the e-mail system at the Langley (Virginia) U.S. Air Force Base was attacked by hackers operating in Australia and Estonia, the system was rendered inoperable (Richards, 1999).

As in the latter case, what makes cybercrime even more problematic is the fact that computer networks and the Internet do not recognize international boundaries. Computer attacks can result in the transfer of large amounts of funds, as with cyberbanking fraud, or in the passing of viruses to damage and destroy data. One group of Russian computer hackers in 1994 broke into the computer network of U.S. Citibank and transferred about $10 million to bank accounts in the United States and abroad (Sinuraya, 1999). An infamous example of the distribution of infected software was the Michelangelo virus that was passed throughout the United States in the early 1990s.

Interestingly, there are also media reports of governments using computers to infiltrate and disrupt those seen as adversaries. The Chinese Ministry of Public Security recently was accused of attacking with "e-bombs" the U.S.-based Webmaster of the Falun Gong, the spiritual group that has been a nuisance to Chinese authorities.

In Burma, a military group trying to maintain power is said to be responsible for sending an e-mail virus to political opponents. And the United States was reportedly set up to use cyberstrikes against Serbia in the Kosovo conflict in 1999 (Stroebel, 2000).

The rise in cybercrime has prompted individual countries and international organizations to develop new laws and special law enforcement tactics to tackle the problem. The United States, for example, has no less than forty federal laws applicable to thefts through the use of the computer (Arkin et al., 1988). On the law enforcement front, U.S. Attorney General Janet Reno announced in January 2000 a proposal to form a national cybercrime-fighting network that would promote cooperation and coordination among law enforcement agencies, enabling them to respond quickly to crimes that often cross multiple jurisdictions in a matter of minutes. Specifics for the proposal include the call for a new nationwide computer system for sharing information on crimes ranging from computer hacking to drug trafficking, the creation of a forensic computer lab, and the development of trained computer crime coordinators at law enforcement agencies around the country (*Los Angeles Times,* 2000).

Individual countries have formed agencies specifically authorized to prevent, detect, and investigate cybercrime. For example, in Russia, the Federal Security Bureau, the successor to the KGB, is the main organization that deals with cybercrime. The Japanese have developed a High-Tech Crime Technical Expert Center that will act as a cyberpolice force within the National Police Agency.

Countries have also begun to look at ways of improving transnational cooperation as one of the key steps in reducing cybercrime. The European Union has begun to formulate a system of electronic surveillance to track e-mails, faxes, and cell phone calls from criminals operating across boundaries, as well as empowering law enforcement agencies to work with Internet providers to monitor money laundering and cyberporn (*Wall Street Journal,* 2000). On the global scale, the

Paris–based International Chamber of Commerce is setting up a unit to work with INTERPOL to combat economic cybercrime. The issue of computer-related crimes has also been the subject of international conferences sponsored by the United Nations, including the 1990 Eighth UN Congress at Havana and a 1992 conference in Wurzburg, Germany, that brought together delegates from Africa, Asia, Europe, Latin America, North America, and the Middle East.

Corruption

Corruption can be formally defined as a transaction that enables private actors to gain access to public resources by giving them an unfair advantage, because there is neither transparency nor competition (Della Porta, 1997). Corruption is hardly a new phenomenon. For centuries, entrepreneurs, pirates, and monarchs tried to pilfer financial resources from unsuspecting citizens and governments. But the problem of corruption today in all its forms is much larger in scale and impact. It is currently threatening the balance of world peace and stifling the growth of democracy. The UN Center for International Crime Prevention in its report entitled *Global Programme Against Corruption,* describes the impact of corruption as follows:

> *Nowadays corruption is internationally recognized as a major problem in society, one capable of endangering the stability and security of societies, threatening social, economic and political development and undermining the values of democracy and morality. This holds true at both the domestic level and the international level. Indeed, with the growing globalization of illegal activities, the international dimension of corruption gains in significance. As a result, reducing corruption becomes a priority at both the national and international levels and requires concerted efforts, exchange of experience and a certain degree of standardization.*
> *(United Nations, 1999, p. 6)*

Probably the most infamous and far-reaching corruption case was the Bank of Credit and Commerce (BCCI) scandal that surfaced in the late 1980s. The BCCI was a loose conglomeration of financial establishments in at least seventy countries, including major players in the United States, England, Luxembourg, and the Cayman islands. After a lengthy investigation, it was determined that the BCCI scandal resulted in financial losses in the billions and also involved illegal activities such as drug trafficking, illegal arms smuggling, and extensive money laundering.

There are probably few countries in the world that are not deeply affected by corruption. The Latin American countries of Peru, Guatemala, Mexico, Brazil, Venezuela, Argentina, and, most notably, Colombia have been hard hit by corruption (Passas, 1997). Scandals have also been exposed in the Asian countries of India, South Korea, Thailand, Indonesia, and Japan. In Nigeria, President Olusegun Obasanjo has recently been fighting a series of corruption charges that are causing serious damage to his credibility. The European nations were rocked by the Elf scandal in France, which also has been linked to Germany and the claim that Elf slush funds helped finance former Chancellor Helmut Kohl's political party (Ignatius, 2000). Official corruption in Russia is probably the single biggest reason for that country's tremendous economic struggles and rise in organized crime. One news article revealed that crimes of corruption committed by Russian officials increased by over 35 percent from 1998 to 1999 and more than 21,000 officials have been charged with the crime (Radio Free Europe, 2000). And the United States certainly has not avoided scandals related to corruption. For almost the entire duration of the Clinton administration, there have been charges of improper campaign payments, as well as special privileges given to those involved in the Whitewater affair.

Forms of Corruption. According to the *UN Global Programme Against Corruption,* corruption can be categorized into three major forms: (1) corruption in public administration, (2) business corruption, and (3) high-level corruption. Corruption in public administration mainly involves citizen dealings with government officials, usually on the local or state levels. It can lead to the deterioration of civic culture and provision of local services. Business corruption occurs when private companies interfere with the ethical business practices of medium-sized businesses, undermining fair economic competition and thus giving rise to monopolies and unfair market practices. High-level corruption involves the collaboration of holders of financial, political, and high administrative power. This form of corruption can undermine democratic institutions and rule of law and disrupt economic and political relations (United Nations, 1999, p. 6).

Reasons for Corruption. Although corruption surely develops for many reasons, three general sources can be identified. The first is the growth of economic monopolies or oligopolies in which a few control the majority of any one market. This allows for opportunities for overcharging, low-quality work, and extensive delays. The second is the situation in which a few individuals wield power and are allowed to make the decisions about the kind and quality of work to be done and the recipients of financial contracts or rewards. With no checks and balances on those with the power, corruption will blossom. Finally, a lack of transparency can cause corruption. If an agency, government official, or private corporation is allowed to operate in secrecy, the detection and prevention of corruption becomes extremely difficult (Passas, 1997).

Solutions to Corruption. The reduction or elimination of corruption, as with other forms of transnational crime, often rely on a combination of strategies. Several recommendations have been suggested by international crime expert Phil Williams (1999) to deal with corruption on an international scale:

1. Enhance data collection—more needs to be known about the causes of and prevention of corruption.

2. Improve international cooperation—efforts to combat corruption need to be transnational in scope.

3. Establish conditionality—financial assistance to nations should be contingent on their efforts to combat corruption.

4. Increase technical support—countries throughout the world must share resources and assist each other in training.

5. Elaborate on international conventions—standards must be developed for countries to measure the conduct of officials and their efforts in combating corruption.

Clearly, the struggle against global corruption will be among the most important crime battles of the twenty-first century. The power of those involved is significant, and it will take a concerted and coordinated effort by all reasonably honest governments to stem the tide of this growing problem.

Smuggling

Smuggling refers to a number of illegal activities entailing the illegal movement of some item, person, or persons into or from a country through some means of stealth. There are many variations on smuggling, but we will concentrate on four main forms: (1) smuggling of firearms and nuclear weapons material, (2) smuggling of human organs, (3) smuggling of women, and (4) smuggling of migrants.

It is important to note that the terms *smuggling* and *trafficking* technically are different. Smuggling, as just mentioned, means to bring in or take out by stealth, while trafficking means to carry on in trade. However, because the difference is slight, and for heuristic purposes, we will use the terms interchangeably.

Smuggling of Firearms. The current weapons smuggling issue revolves mainly around the transnational importation of illegal firearms, mostly small arms, by governments and insurgents in war zone regions. Major problems are apparent in Asia, Africa, eastern Europe, Latin America, and the Caribbean—weapons smuggling has led to death and social disorder. One example of the effect of illegal trafficking in firearms can be seen in Africa, where gun trafficking has led to the formation of an army of 120,000 child soldiers (under 18 years old) who actively participate in various armed conflicts (Inter Press Service, 1999).

To better assess the extent of the transnational smuggling of firearms, the United Nations included in a larger survey about firearms regulations a set of questions about firearm smuggling. As of January 1998, sixty-nine countries had returned the surveys. Among the most disturbing findings were that forty-nine countries believed that some illegal import of firearms and ammunition took place. The survey also indicated how the firearms were illegally imported, what kinds of firearms were imported, what their purpose was, and what country they originated in. Among the uses were armed robbery, organized crime, drug trafficking, assault, murder, tribal fights, aid to rebel elements, insurrection, and exchanges for food. Interestingly, most countries responded that they have little or no evidence of the illegal *export* of firearms, components, and ammunition (UN International Study, 1998, p. 78).

Penalties for the serious smuggling of firearms are quite harsh throughout the world. Some countries, including China and Saudi Arabia, may impose the death penalty for such violations of law. Many other countries impose life sentences or sentences of twenty years or more in prison. All the survey respondents indicated that the serious smuggling of guns results in some sentence of imprisonment, often five years or more (UN International Survey, 1998, p. 88).

Efforts are being made by the United Nations and the United States to reduce arms smuggling. The UN has expressed "serious concern" over the issue and has called for efforts to disarm, demobilize, and then reintegrate factions or nations that have been warring with the use of illegal armaments. At the same time, the United States has pushed for a global convention to curb the supply of weapons (Inter Press Service, 1999).

Smuggling of Nuclear Weapons Materials. Another issue related to the smuggling of weapons is the illegal trafficking of nuclear material. Since the fall of the Soviet Union and the dismantling of their nuclear arsenal, this problem has become a major issue of concern for governments throughout the world. The dissolution of that country made large quantities of weapons-usable materials susceptible to theft because of the lessened power of the now defunct State Security Committee (KGB), the Russian Army, and other control mechanisms. The goal of these smugglers is to obtain and then sell the essential radioactive materials like uranium and plutonium to countries or terrorist groups that wish to develop nuclear weapons capabilities. There is evidence that the number of smuggling incidents involving radioactive materials increased over 25 percent between 1992 and 1994 (Williams, 1999).

Smuggling of Human Organs. One of the more recent and troubling developments in illegal trafficking involves the **smuggling of human organs,** which is simply the illegal procurement and/or sale of human organs. The real cause of this form of smuggling is created by the demand for precious organs such as kidneys, hearts, livers, pancreases, and corneas. Many thousands of persons throughout the world are waiting for organ transplants. For example, in the United States, over 20,000 people per year are in need, while in Great Britain, the number exceeds 4,500. Reports in foreign and underground newspapers state that the going price for an illegal kidney is $30,000. Give the high demand and equally high profit margin, transnational criminals have taken advantage of this new market.

Countries that have economic problems are more likely to act as bases for human organ smuggling. India, for example, with its abundance of poor people provides a large source of persons willing to sacrifice a kidney for money. Indonesia, Colombia, Taiwan, the Philippines, and, more recently, countries in eastern Europe and the Balkans have reportedly increased their involvement in human organ smuggling. Even more troubling are the allegations about the collusion of the Chinese government in organ smuggling, with Chinese prisoners being executed and harvested for their organs. For example, Chinese-American human rights activist Harry Wu recently helped to uncover a Chinese organ trafficking ring that tried to sell fifty human kidneys removed from executed Chinese prisoners. As with other forms of transnational crime, efforts are being made by the United Nations to develop international strategies to fight trafficking of humans in all forms.

Smuggling of Women. A major form of smuggling that has grown considerably in recent years, especially in Europe, is the **smuggling of women.** International smuggling/trafficking of women occurs when a woman in a country other than her own is exploited by another person against her will for financial gain (Williams, 1999, p. 225). It happens when women are given passage to a country as legal or illegal immigrants, fall into debt to smugglers, and then are enslaved under threat of violence or coercion into prostitution as they attempt to pay their debt.

Watchdog groups estimate that some 30 million young women have joined the ranks of the global sex trade industry through this form of trafficking since the early 1970s, with the majority from Thailand, Brazil, the Philippines, and, more recently, the former Soviet Union. The women are being brought to a growing number of countries, but they primarily are trafficked to the United States, Australia, Israel, Macau, Germany, Italy, and Austria (Williams, 1999). Reports indicate that another related trend is the provision of young boys and girls as instruments of child prostitution. Costa Rica and the Dominican Republic have been known to provide children for sex as part of tour packages (Shannon, 1999).

Unfortunately, the programs and conventions aimed at solving the problem of smuggling of women have not been adequately developed. One set of recommendations by the International Organization for Migration (IOM) argues for less use of deportation and more use of legal sanctions against those responsible for the exploitation. Such measures would require programs that help women escape from the smugglers, protect them from their violence and coercion, and eventually return them to their homeland (IOM, 1996).

Smuggling of Migrants. Intertwined with human trafficking are problems related to the illegal movement of willful persons across borders, in what is known as **illegal immigration.** Because of the economic deprivation, political instability, and ethnic strife in many countries, many persons are trying to cross borders in the simple hope for a better life. The increasing movement of people has caused governments of desired locations to restrict the flow of immigration. As a result, illegal immigration practices have flourished.

It has been estimated that about 300,000 people are smuggled into western Europe each year (*Economist,* n.d.). Russian migration officials estimate that up to 2 million Asian and African illegals are living in Russia (*Migration News,* 1994). The United States is not immune to illegal immigration; in March 1999 alone, U.S. agents on the Mexican border apprehended a record number of 19,908 migrants trying to cross over into Southern California (Associated Press, 1999). Immigration and Naturalization officials estimate that as of late 1993 there were over 3.4 million illegal residents in the United States, with the majority from Mexico, El Salvador, Guatemala, Canada, and Poland (McDonald, 1997). The total number of illegal immigrants who have crossed borders due to fear or in search of a better opportunity is difficult to determine, but it has probably reached 10 million worldwide (Cusimano, 2000).

Solutions to the problem of illegal immigration are very complicated and hard to come by. Two of the most common are the provision of economic and military aid to source countries, although these have been shown to be only stop-gap measures that fail to address the core issues that cause people to leave their homelands.

As we proceed through the twenty-first century, we can be certain that crime and justice will not be static in our model nations or the other nations of the world. The student of comparative criminal process will have many opportunities to observe changes and evaluate the accuracy of the preceding predictions over the next twenty years. As the justice systems of the nations of Africa, South America, eastern Europe, and southern Asia change, they will also provide fruitful arenas of comparison with the model systems described in this book. The subject remains an open and endlessly fascinating one.

SUMMARY

Underlying factors that influence the criminal justice scene today include convergence, cultural persistence, and political process, all of which help form the main elements within the systems of justice in our model countries and undoubtedly affect others as well. It is difficult to prognosticate as to what will be the major crime issues of concern in the new century. But with the explosion in technology, various forms of computer crimes will surely be a global threat. As the world economy develops, and borders continue to become less important, we will also become more susceptible to different forms of smuggling. Finally, the kind and magnitude of corruption appears to be a growing concern for all those who struggle in the battle against transnational crime.

DISCUSSION QUESTIONS

1. Discuss some examples of convergence for each of the model countries. What forces brought about these changes?

2. With the economic and social changes in China, what would you foresee as some possible changes in the criminal justice system in that country?

3. Of the projected future crimes discussed in the chapter, which do you believe poses the most serious threat to your security? Why?

4. Invite to your class an employee of the Immigration and Naturalization Service to discuss the pressing migration issues that it must deal with on a daily basis. How might these issues be related to transnational crime?

FOR FURTHER READING

Damaska, M. (1986). *The Faces of Justice and State Authority.* New Haven, Conn.: Yale University Press.

Della Porta, D. (1997). Introduction: Democracy and Corruption. In D. Della Porta and Y. Meny (eds.), *Democracy and Corruption in Europe.* London: Pinter Books.

United Nations Commission on Crime Prevention and Criminal Justice. (1999). *Global Programme Against Corruption.* E/Cn.15/1999/CRP.3.

International Organization for Migration. (1996). *Trafficking and Prostitution: The Growing Exploitation of Migrant Women from Central and Eastern Europe.* Geneva: International Organization for Migration.

Schmidhauser, J. (1987). Alternative Conceptual Frameworks in Comparative Cross-National Legal and Judicial Research. In J. R. Schmidhauser (ed.), *Comparative Judicial Systems.* London: Butterworth.

United Nations International Study on Firearms Regulation. (1998). New York: United Nations

Basic Principles
on the Role of Lawyers

These principles were adopted by the Eighth United Nations Congress on the Prevention of Crime and the Treatment of Offenders in Havana, Cuba, on September 7, 1990. The United Nations General Assembly subsequently welcomed these principles in its Resolution 45/121 of December 14, 1990.

Access to Lawyers and Legal Services

1. All persons are entitled to call upon the assistance of a lawyer of their choice to protect and establish their rights and to defend them in all stages of criminal proceedings.

2. Governments shall ensure that efficient procedures and responsive mechanisms for effective and equal access to lawyers are provided for all persons within their territory and subject to their jurisdiction, without distinction of any kind, such as discrimination based on race, colour, ethnic origin, sex, language, religion, political or other opinion, national or social origin, property, birth, economic or other status.

3. Governments shall ensure the provision of sufficient funding and other resources for legal services to the poor and, as necessary, to other disadvantaged persons. Professional associations of lawyers shall co-operate in the organization and provision of services, facilities and other resources.

4. Governments and professional associations of lawyers shall promote programmes to inform the public about their rights and duties under the law and the important role of lawyers in

protecting their fundamental freedoms. Special attention should be given to assisting the poor and other disadvantaged persons so as to enable them to assert their rights and where necessary call upon the assistance of lawyers.

Special Safeguards in Criminal Justice Matters

5. Governments shall ensure that all persons are immediately informed by the competent authority of their right to be assisted by a lawyer of their own choice upon arrest or detention or when charged with a criminal offence.

6. Any such persons who do not have a lawyer shall, in cases in which the interests of justice so require, be entitled to have a lawyer of experience and competence commensurate with the nature of the offence assigned to them in order to provide effective legal assistance, without payment by them if they lack sufficient means to pay for such services.

7. Governments shall further ensure that all persons arrested or detained, with or without criminal charge, shall have prompt access to a lawyer, and in any case not later than forty-eight hours from the time of arrest or detention.

8. All arrested, detained or imprisoned persons shall be provided with adequate opportunities, time and facilities to be visited by and to communicate and consult with a lawyer, without delay, interception or censorship and

in full confidentiality. Such consultations may be within sight, but not within the hearing, of law enforcement officials.

Qualifications and Training

9. Governments, professional associations of lawyers and educational institutions shall ensure that lawyers have appropriate education and training and be made aware of the ideals and ethical duties of the lawyer and of human rights and fundamental freedoms recognized by national and international law.

10. Governments, professional associations of lawyers and educational institutions shall ensure that there is no discrimination against a person with respect to entry into or continued practice within the legal profession on the grounds of race, colour, sex, ethnic origin, religion, political or other opinion, national or social origin, property, birth, economic or other status, except that a requirement, that a lawyer must be a national of the country concerned, shall not be considered discriminatory.

11. In countries where there exist groups, communities or regions whose needs for legal services are not met, particularly where such groups have distinct cultures, traditions or languages or have been the victims of past discrimination, Governments, professional associations of lawyers and educational institutions should take special measures to provide opportunities for candidates from these groups to enter the legal profession and should ensure that they receive training appropriate to the needs of their groups.

Duties and Responsibilities

12. Lawyers shall at all times maintain the honour and dignity of their profession as essential agents of the administration of justice.

13. The duties of lawyers towards their clients shall include:

   a. Advising clients as to their legal rights and obligations, and as to the working of the legal system insofar as it is relevant to the legal rights and obligations of the clients;

   b. Assisting clients in every appropriate way, and taking legal action to protect their interests;

   c. Assisting clients before courts, tribunals or administrative authorities, where appropriate.

14. Lawyers, in protecting the rights of their clients and in promoting the cause of justice, shall seek to uphold human rights and fundamental freedoms recognized by national and international law and shall at all times act freely and diligently in accordance with the law and recognized standards and ethics of the legal profession.

15. Lawyers shall always loyally respect the interests of their clients.

Guarantees for the Functioning of Lawyers

16. Governments shall ensure that lawyers:

   a. Are able to perform all of their professional functions without intimidation, hindrance, harassment or improper interference;

   b. Are able to travel and to consult with their clients freely both within their own country and abroad;

   c. Shall not suffer, or be threatened with, prosecution or administrative, economic or other sanctions for any action taken in accordance with recognized professional duties, standards and ethics.

17. Where the security of lawyers is threatened as a result of discharging their functions, they shall be adequately safeguarded by the authorities.

18. Lawyers shall not be identified with their clients or their clients' causes as a result of discharging their functions.

19. No court or administrative authority before whom the right to counsel is recognized shall refuse to recognize the right of a lawyer to appear before it for his or her client unless that lawyer has been disqualified in accordance with national law and practice in conformity with these principles.

20. Lawyers shall enjoy civil and penal immunity for relevant statements made in good faith in written or oral pleadings or in their professional appearances before a court, tribunal or other legal or administrative authority.

21. It is the duty of the competent authorities to ensure lawyers access to appropriate information, files and documents in their possession or control in sufficient time to enable lawyers to provide effective legal assistance to their clients. Such access should be provided at the earliest appropriate time.

22. Governments shall recognize and respect that all communications and consultations between lawyers and their clients within their professional relationship are confidential.

Freedom of Expression and Association

23. Lawyers like other citizens are entitled to freedom of expression, belief, association and assembly. In particular, they shall have the right to take part in public discussion of matters concerning the law, the administration of justice and the promotion and protection of human rights and to join or form local, national or international organizations and attend their meetings, without suffering professional restrictions by reason of their lawful action or their membership in a lawful organization. In exercising these rights, lawyers shall always conduct themselves in accordance with the law and the recognized standards and ethics of the legal profession.

Professional Associations of Lawyers

24. Lawyers shall be entitled to form and join self-governing professional associations to represent their interests, promote their continuing education and training and protect their professional integrity. The executive body of the professional associations shall be elected by its members and shall exercise its functions without external interference.

25. Professional associations of lawyers shall cooperate with governments to ensure that everyone has effective and equal access to legal services and that lawyers are able, without improper interference, to counsel and assist their clients in accordance with the law and recognized professional standards and ethics.

Disciplinary Proceedings

26. Codes of professional conduct for lawyers shall be established by the legal profession through its appropriate origins, or by legislation, in accordance with national law and custom and recognized international standards and norms.

27. Charges or complaints made against lawyers in their professional capacity shall be processed expeditiously and fairly under appropriate procedures. Lawyers shall have the right to a fair hearing, including the right to be assisted by a lawyer of their choice.

28. Disciplinary proceedings against lawyers shall be brought before an impartial disciplinary committee established by the legal profession, before an independent statutory authority, or before a court, and shall be subject to an independent judicial review.

29. All disciplinary proceedings shall be determined in accordance with the code of professional conduct and other recognized standards and ethics of the legal profession and in the light of these principles.

Appendix B Standard Minimum Rules for the Treatment of Prisoners (Abridged)

Approved by the Economic and Social Council, 31 July 1957 (resolution 633 C I (XXIV)), on the recommendation of the First Congress.

Men and women in detention are to be held in separate facilities; likewise, untried and convicted prisoners, those imprisoned for civil offences and criminal offenders, and youths and adults shall be housed separately.

Cells for individuals should not be used to accommodate two or more persons overnight; dormitory facilities are to be supervised at night.

Prisoners shall be provided with adequate water and toilet articles, and required to keep themselves clean.

Prisoners not allowed to wear their own clothing are to be provided with an adequate and suitable outfit, with provisions for laundry and changes of clothes.

Prisoners outside an institution for an authorized purpose are to be allowed to wear their own clothing.

Every prisoner shall be provided with a separate bed and clean, separate and sufficient bedding.

Wholesome, well-prepared food is to be provided prisoners at usual hours.

Drinking water shall be available whenever needed.

If not employed in outdoor work, every prisoner shall have at least one hour of exercise in the open air, weather permitting.

Young prisoners and others of suitable age and physique are to receive physical and recreational training.

A medical officer with some knowledge of psychiatry is to be available to every institution.

Prisoners requiring specialized treatment are to be transferred to a civil hospital or appropriate facility.

A qualified dental officer shall be available to every prisoner.

Prenatal and postnatal care and treatment are to be provided by women's institutions; where nursing infants are allowed to remain with their mothers, a nursery staffed by qualified persons is needed.

Every prisoner shall be examined by the medical officer shortly after admission; prisoners suspected of contagious diseases are to be segregated.

The medical officer shall see all sick prisoners daily, along with those who complain of illness or are referred to his attention.

The medical officer is to report to the director on prisoners whose health is jeopardized by continued imprisonment and on the quality of the food, hygiene, bedding, clothing and physical regimen of the prisoners.

Every institution shall maintain for the use of prisoners a library with recreational and instructional books.

Transport is to be at the expense of the prison administration, and equal conditions shall obtain for all prisoners.

The administration shall carefully select every grade of personnel and maintain in their minds and the public's the important social service they provide.

To these ends, pay, conditions and benefits shall be suitable to professional and exacting service.

Personnel are to be sufficiently educated, and to receive ongoing courses and training.

As far as possible, personnel should include psychiatric, social work and education professionals.

The director shall be a qualified administrator, retained on a full time basis and residing on the premises or in the immediate vicinity.

Staff personnel are to be able to speak the language of the greatest number of prisoners, and to retain the services of an interpreter when necessary.

In larger institutions, at least one medical officer should reside on the premises or in the immediate vicinity.

In others, a medical officer shall visit daily and reside near enough to be available for emergencies.

Prison officers are to receive physical training in the use of force.

SOURCE: *GLOBAL REPORT,* 1999, PL 106. The original including Part 2 Special Categories, may be found in many United Nations documents, and also at the UNCJIN Website: http://www.ifs.univie.ac.at/~uncjin/uncjin/html. The original document issued from the first United Nations Congress on Prevention of Crime and Treatment of Offenders, 1955. A/CONF/6/C.1/L.1

Appendix C Demographic Summaries

UNITED KINGDOM

Geography

Area:	Total: 244,820 sq. km, slightly smaller than Oregon
	Land: 241,590 sq. km
	Water: 3,230 sq. km
Location:	Western Europe
Border Countries:	West: Ireland
	Southeast: France
Capital:	London
Climate:	Temperate, more than one-half the days are overcast
Terrain:	Primarily rugged hills and low mountains; level to rolling plains in the east and southeast

People

Population:	58,970,119 (July 1998 est.)
Age Distribution:	0–14 years: 19% (male: 5,832,086; female: 5,530,679)
	15–64 years: 65% (male: 19,304,762; female: 19,032,024)
	65 years and older: 16% (male: 3,807,710; female: 5,462,858) (July 1998)
Sex Ratio:	at birth: 1.05 males/female
	under 15 years: 1.05 males/female
	15–64 years: 1.01 males/female
	65 years and older: 0.7 males/female (July 1998)
Growth Rate:	0.25% (1998 est.)
Birth Rate:	12.01 births/1,000 population (1998 est.)
Death Rate:	10.72 deaths/1,000 population (1998 est.)
Life Expectancy at birth:	Total population: 77.19 years
	Male: 74.57 years
	Female: 79.96 years (1998 est.)
Education:	Compulsory—12 years

Literacy: 99% age 15 and over can read and write (1998)

Ethnic Groups: English 81.5%, Scottish 9.6%, Irish 2.4%, Welsh 1.9%, Ulster 1.8%, West Indian, Indian, Pakistani, and other 2.8%

Languages: English, Welsh and Gaelic

Religions: Anglican, Roman Catholic, Muslim, Presbyterian, Methodist, Sihk, Hindu, Jewish

Government

Type: Constitutional monarchy

Branches: Executive: Monarch (Head of State), Prime Minister (Head of Government), cabinet

Legislative: bicameral parliament: House of Commons, House of Lords

Judicial: magistrates' courts, county courts, high courts, appellate courts, House of Lords

Divisions: 47 counties, 7 metropolitan counties, 26 districts, 9 regions and 3 islands areas

Constitution: Unwritten; partly statutes, partly common law and practice

Legal System: Common law tradition; no judicial review

Suffrage: Universal at 18 years of age

Economy

GDP: $1.29 trillion (1997)

GDP per capita: $22,241 (1997)

GDP real growth rate: 3.5% (1997)

Inflation rate: 3.1% (1997)

Labor Force: 28.2 million: Services 68.9%, manufacturing and construction 17.5%, government 11.3%, other 2.3% (1996)

Exports: $268 billion (1997); Commodities: machinery, transport equipment, manufactured goods, petroleum, chemicals; Partners: EU countries, US, Saudi Arabia, Nigeria, Switzerland, South Africa

Imports: $283.5 billion (1997); Commodities: machinery, transport equipment, manufactured goods, foodstuffs, chemicals; Partners: EU countries, US, Japan, Norway, Switzerland

Debt—external: $16.2 billion (June 1992)

Communications

Televisions: 1 television per 2.95 persons (20 million, 1998 est.)

Telephones: 1 telephone per 2.00 persons (29.5 million, 1987 est.)

Radios: 1 radio per 0.84 persons; (70 million, 1998 est.)

Transportation

Railways:	16,878 km (1996)
Highways:	372,000 km (372,000 km paved; 0 km unpaved; 1996 est.)
Waterways:	3,200 km
Airports:	497 (356 paved runways; 141 unpaved runways; 1997 est.)

Transnational Issues

Disputes:
Northern Ireland question with Ireland (historic peace agreement approved April 10, 1998); Gibraltar question with Spain; Argentina claims Falkland Islands (Islas Malvinas); Argentina claims South Georgia and the South Sandwich Islands; Mauritius claims island of Diego Garcia in British Indian Ocean Territory; Rockall continental shelf dispute involving Denmark, Iceland, and Ireland (Ireland and the UK have signed a boundary agreement in the Rockall area); territorial claim in Antarctica (British Antarctic Territory); Seychelles claims Chagos Archipelago in British Indian Ocean Territory

Illicit Drugs:
Gateway country for Latin American cocaine entering the European market; producer of synthetic drugs, precursor chemicals; transshipment point for Southwest Asian heroin; money-laundering center

Sources:
CIA Publications—1998 World Factbook—United Kingdom, [On-Line]. Available: www.cia.gov/cia/publications/factbook/uk.htm

Reichel, Philip L. (1994). *Comparative criminal justice systems, A topical approach.* Englewood Cliffs, New Jersey: Prentice Hall Career and Technology. Pp. 427–428

US Department of State, *Background notes: United Kingdom, August 1998,* [On-Line]. Available: http://www.state.gov/background_notes/ united_kingdom_9808_bgn.html

FRANCE

Geography

Area:
Total: 547,030 sq. km, four fifths the size of Texas
Land: 545,630 sq. km
Water: 1,400 sq. km

Location:
Western Europe

Border Countries:
East: Italy, Switzerland, Germany
North: Luxembourg, Belgium
South: Spain

Capital:
Paris

Climate:
Cool winters and mild summers except along the Mediterranean where there are mild winters and hot summers

Terrain:	Primarily flat plains or rolling hills in the north and west, mountainous in the south (Pyrenees) and east (Alps)

People

Population:	58,804,944 (July 1998 est.)
Age Distribution:	0–14 years: 19% (male: 5,674,417; female: 5,411,685) 15–64 years: 65% (male: 19,243,919; female: 19,182,933) 65 years and older: 16% (male: 3,759,565; female: 5,532,425) (July 1998 est.)
Sex Ratio:	at birth: 1.05 males/female under 15 years: 1.04 males/female 15–64 years: 1.00 males/female 65 years and older: 0.67 males/female (1998 est.)
Growth Rate:	0.31% (1998 est.)
Birth Rate:	11.68 births/1,000 population (1998 est.)
Death Rate:	9.12 deaths/1,000 population (1998 est.)
Life Expectancy at birth:	Total population: 78.51 years Male: 74.6 years Female: 82.62 years (1998 est.)
Education:	Compulsory—10 years
Literacy:	99% age 15 and over can read and write (1998)
Ethnic Groups:	Celtic and Latin with Teutonic, Slavic, North African, Indochinese, Basque minorities
Languages:	French with rapidly declining regional dialects and languages
Religions:	Roman Catholic 90%, Protestant 2%, Jewish 1%, Muslim 1%, unaffiliated 6%

Government

Type:	Republic
Branches:	Executive: president (chief of state), prime minister (head of government) Legislative: bicameral parliament (577 member National Assembly, 319 member Senate) Judicial—Court of Cassation (civil and criminal law), Council of State (administrative court), Constitutional Council (constitutional law)
Divisions:	22 administrative regions subdivided into 96 departments, four overseas departments (Guadeloupe, Martinique, French Guiana, and Réunion), five overseas territories (New Caledonia, French Polynesia, Wallis and Futuna Islands, and French Southern and Antarctic Territories), and two special status territories (Mayotte and St. Pierre and Miquelon).
Constitution:	September 28, 1958. Amended in 1962, 1992 and 1993

Legal System: Civil law system. Review of administrative but not legislative acts.

Suffrage: Universal at 18 years of age

Economy

GDP: $1.32 trillion (1997 est.)

GDP per capita: $22,700 (1997 est.)

GDP real growth rate: 2.3% (1997 est.)

Inflation rate: 2% (1996)

Labor Force: 25 million: Services 66%; industry and commerce 28%, agriculture 6% (1997)

Exports: $275 billion (1997 est.); Commodities: chemicals, electronics, machinery and transportation equipment and parts, aircraft, foodstuffs, iron and steel products, textiles and clothing; Partners: Germany, Italy, UK, Spain, Belgium-Luxembourg, US, Netherlands, Japan, Russia

Imports: $256 billion (1997 est.) Commodities: crude petroleum, electronics, transportation equipment, aircraft, foodstuffs, iron and steel products. Partners: Germany, Italy, US, Belgium-Luxembourg, UK, Spain, Netherlands, Japan, China

Debt—external: $117.6 billion (1996 est.)

Communications

Televisions: 1 television per 2.01 persons (29.3 million, 1993 est.)

Telephones: 1 telephone per 1.68 persons (35 million, 1987 est.)

Radios: 1 radio per 1.20 persons; (49 million, 1993 est.)

Transportation

Railways: 32,027 km (1996)

Highways: 892,500 km (892,500 km paved; 0 km unpaved; 1996 est.)

Waterways: 14,932 km (6,969 km heavily traveled)

Airports: 473 (266 paved runways; 207 unpaved runways; 1997 est.)

Transnational Issues

Disputes: Madagascar claims Bassas da India, Europa Island, Glorioso Islands, Juan de Nova Island, and Tromelin Island; Comoros claims Mayotte; Mauritius claims Tromelin Island; Suriname claims part of French Guiana; territorial claim in Antarctica (Adelie Land); Matthew and Hunter Islands east of New Caledonia claimed by France and Vanuatu

Illicit Drugs: Transshipment point for and consumer of South American cocaine and Southwest Asian heroin

Sources: Bureau of European and Canadian Affairs, U.S. Department of State, *Background Notes: France, March 1998*, [On-Line]. Available: http://www.state.gov/www/background_notes/france_9803_bgn.html
CIA Publications—1998 World Factbook—France, [On-Line]. Available: http://www.cia.gov/cia/publications/factbook/fr.html
Reichel, Philip L. (1994). *Comparative criminal justice systems, A topical approach.* Englewood Cliffs, New Jersey: Prentice Hall Career and Technology. Pp. 408–409

GERMANY

Geography

Area: Total: 356,910 sq. km, slightly smaller than Montana
Land: 349,520 sq. km
Water: 7,390 sq. km

Location: Central Europe

Border Countries: East: Czech Republic, Poland
North: Denmark
West: Netherlands, Belgium, Luxembourg, France
South: Switzerland, Austria

Capital: Berlin

Climate: Cool, cloudy, wet winters and summers; occasional warm tropical wind, relatively high humidity

Terrain: Lowlands in the north, uplands in the center, Bavarian Alps in the south

People

Population: 82,079,454 (July 1998 est.)

Age Distribution: 0–14 years: 16% (male: 6,570,582; female: 6,240,671)
15–64 years: 68% (male: 28,688,052; female: 27,532,099)
65 years and older: 16% (male: 4,866,122; female: 8,181,928)
(July 1998 est.)

Sex Ratio: at birth: 1.06 males/female
under 15 years: 1.05 males/female
15–64 years: 1.04 males/female
65 years and older: 0.59 males/female (1998 est.)

Growth Rate: 0.02% (1998 est.)

Birth Rate: 8.84 births/1,000 population (1998 est.)

Death Rate: 10.77 deaths/1,000 population (1998 est.)

Life Expectancy at birth:	Total population: 76.99 years
	Male: 73.83 years
	Female: 80.33 years (1998 est.)
Education:	Compulsory—10 years
Literacy:	99% age 15 and over can read and write (1998)
Ethnic Groups:	German 91.5%, Turkish 2.4%, Italian 0.7%, Greek 0.4%, Pole 0.4%, other 4.6%
Languages:	German
Religions:	Protestant 38%, Roman Catholic 34%, Muslim 1.7%, unaffiliated or other 26.3%

Government

Type:	Federal Republic
Branches:	Executive: President (titular chief of state), Chancellor (executive head of government)
	Legislative: bicameral parliament
	Judicial: independent, Federal Constitutional Court
Divisions:	16 states
Constitution:	May 23, 1949 known as Basic Law; adopted by united German people October 3, 1990
Legal System:	Civil law system. Judicial review of legislative acts in Federal Constitutional Court
Suffrage:	Universal at 18 years of age

Economy

GDP:	$2.1 trillion (1998)
GDP per capita:	$25,000 (1998)
GDP real growth rate:	2.8% (1998)
Inflation rate:	0.9% (1998)
Labor Force:	38.6 million (1998 average): Services 56%, industry 41%, agriculture 3% (1995)
Exports:	$539 billion (1998); Commodities: Motor vehicles, chemicals, iron and steel products, electrical products, manufactured goods, agricultural products; Partners: France, UK, Italy, Netherlands, Belgium-Luxembourg, Austria, Eastern Europe, US, Japan, OPEC, China
Imports:	$467 billion (1998); Commodities: Food, petroleum products, electrical products, automobiles, clothing, manufactured goods; Partners: France, Netherlands, Italy, Belgium-Luxembourg, UK, Austria, Eastern Europe, US, Japan, China, OPEC
Debt—external:	NA

Communications

Televisions:	1 television per 1.83 persons (44.8 million, 1992 est.)
Telephones:	1 telephone per 1.87 persons (44 million, 1998 est.)
Radios:	1 radio per 1.17 persons; (70 million, 1991 est.)

Transportation

Railways:	43,966 km (1995)
Highways:	633,000 km (627,303 km paved; 5,697 km unpaved; 1996 est.)
Waterways:	5,222 km
Airports:	620 (321 paved runways; 299 unpaved runways; 1997 est.)

Transnational Issues

Disputes: Individual Sudeten German claims for restitution of property confiscated in connection with their expulsion after WWII

Illicit Drugs: Source of precursor chemicals for South American cocaine processors; transshipment point for and consumer of Southwest Asian heroin and hashish, Latin American cocaine, and European-produced synthetic drugs

Sources: Bureau of European Affairs, U.S. Department of State, *Background Notes: Germany, April 1999,* [On-Line]. Available: http://www.state.gov/www/background_notes/germany_9904_bgn.html

CIA Publications—1998 World Factbook—Germany. [On-Line]. Available: http://www.cia.gov/cia/publications/factbook/gm.html

Reichel, Philip L. (1994). *Comparative criminal justice systems, A topical approach.* Englewood Cliffs, New Jersey: Prentice Hall Career and Technology. Pp. 409–410

JAPAN

Geography

Area: Total: 377,835 sq. km, slightly smaller than California
Land: 374,744 sq. km
Water: 3,091 sq. km

Location:	Eastern Asia
Border Countries:	North: Russia
	West: South Korea
Capital:	Tokyo
Climate:	Tropical in the south to cool in the north
Terrain:	Primarily rugged and mountainous

People

Population:	125,931,533 (July 1998 est.)
Age Distribution:	0–14 years: 15% (male: 9,802,921; female: 9,342,254)
	15–64 years: 69% (male: 43,486,840; female: 43,135,979)
	65 years and older: 16% (male: 8,388,242; female: 11,775,297) (July 1998 est.)
Sex Ratio:	at birth: 1.05 males/female
	under 15 years: 1.05 males/female
	15–64 years: 1.01 males/female
	65 years and older: 0.71 males/female (1998 est.)
Growth Rate:	0.2% (1998 est.)
Birth Rate:	10.26 births/1,000 population (1998 est.)
Death Rate:	7.94 deaths/1,000 population (1998 est.)
Life Expectancy at birth:	Total population: 80 years
	Male: 76.91 years
	Female: 83.25 years (1998 est.)
Education:	90% complete high school (March 1999)
Literacy:	99% age 15 and over can read and write (1999)
Ethnic Groups:	Japanese 99.4%, other 0.6% primarily Korean
Languages:	Japanese
Religions:	Shinto and Buddhist 84%, other 16%

Government

Type:	Constitutional monarchy
Branches:	Executive: Prime minister (head of state)
	Legislative: bicameral Diet (House of Representatives and House of Councillors)
	Judicial: Supreme Court, chief justice appointed by emperor, other by cabinet
Divisions:	47 prefectures
Constitution:	May 3, 1947
Legal System:	Civil law system based on the model of Roman law with English-American influence; judicial review of legislative acts in the Supreme Court
Suffrage:	Universal at age 20

Economy

GDP:	$3.797 trillion (1998)
GDP per capita:	$30,100 (1998)

GDP real growth rate:	−2.5% (1998)
Inflation rate:	1.7% (1997)
Labor Force:	67.23 million (March 1997): Trade and services 50%; manufacturing, mining and construction 33%; communications 7%; agriculture, forestry and fishing 6%; government 3%
Exports:	$421 billion (1997); Commodities: motor vehicles, machinery and equipment, electronics, metals and metal products; Partners: US, Southeast Asia, Western Europe, China
Imports:	$339 billion (1997); Commodities: fossil fuels, foodstuffs, machinery and equipment, raw materials; Partners: Southeast Asia, US, Western Europe, China
Debt—external:	NA

Communications

Televisions:	1 television per 1.26 persons (100 million, 1993 est.)
Telephones:	1 telephone per 1.97 persons (64 million, 1987 est.)
Radios:	1 radio per 1.30 persons; (97 million, 1993 est.)

Transportation

Railways:	23,670 km (1994)
Highways:	1.16 million km (859,560 km paved; 300,440 km unpaved; 1996 est.)
Waterways:	1,770 km
Airports:	167 (137 paved runways; 30 unpaved runways; 1997 est.)

Transnational Issues

Disputes:	Islands of Etorofu, Kunashiri, Shikotan, and the Habomai group occupied by the Soviet Union in 1945, now administered by Russia, claimed by Japan; Liancourt Rocks (Takeshima/Tokdo) disputed with South Korea; Senkaku-shoto (Senkaku Islands claimed by China and Taiwan (CIA)
Sources:	Bureau of East Asian and Pacific Affairs, U.S. Department of State, *Background Notes: Japan, March, 1999,* [On-Line]. Available: http://www.state.gov/www/background_notes/japan_0399_bgn.html
	CIA Publications—1998 World Factbook—Japan, [On-Line]. Available: http://www.cia.gov/cia/publications/factbook/ja.html
	Reichel, Philip L. (1994). *Comparative criminal justice systems, A topical approach.* Englewood Cliffs, New Jersey: Prentice Hall Career and Technology. Pp. 414–415

SAUDI ARABIA

Geography

Area:	Total: 1,960,582 sq. km, slightly more than ⅕ the size of the US
	Land: 1,960,582 sq. km
	Water: 0 sq. km
Location:	Middle East
Border Countries:	East: United Arab Emirates, Qatar
	North: Kuwait, Iraq, Jordan
	South: Yemen, South Yemen, Oman
Capital:	Riyadh
Climate:	Harsh, dry desert with extremes of temperature
Terrain:	Primarily uninhabited, sandy desert

People

Population:	20,795,955 (July 1998 est.)
	(note: includes 5,244,058 non-nationals)
Age Distribution:	0–14 years: 43% (male: 4,547,971; female: 4,398,628)
	15–64 years: 55% (male: 6,738,820; female: 4,591,477)
	65 years and older: 2% (male: 268,136; female: 240,923) (July 1998 est.)
Sex Ratio:	at birth: 1.05 males/female
	under 15 years: 1.03 males/female
	15–64 years: 1.46 males/female
	65 years and older: 1.11 males/female (1998 est.)
Growth Rate:	3.41% (1998 est.)
Birth Rate:	37.63 births/1,000 population (1998 est.)
Death Rate:	5.02 deaths/1,000 population (1998 est.)
Life Expectancy at birth:	Total population: 70.03 years
	Male: 68.19 years
	Female: 71.96 years (1998 est.)
Education:	NA
Literacy:	62.8% age 15 and over can read and write (1995 est.)
	male: 73%, female 48% (Sept. 1998)
Ethnic Groups:	Arab 90%, Afro-Asian 10%
Languages:	Arabic
Religions:	Muslim 100%

Government

Type:	Monarchy with a council of ministers
Branches:	Executive: King (chief of state and head of government)

Legislative: none; a Consultative Council with advisory powers was formed in September 1993.

Judicial: Islamic Courts of First Instance and Appeals

Divisions: 13 provinces

Constitution: Governed according to the Shari'a (Islamic Law). Basic Law outlining the government's rights and responsibilities was introduced in 1993

Legal System: Islamic Law system, several secular codes have been introduced; commercial disputes handled by special committees

Suffrage: none

Economy

GDP: $145.9 billion (1997)

GDP per capita: $7,200 (1997)

GDP real growth rate: 7.1 overall; non-oil share 4.5% (1997)

Inflation rate: 0.0% (1997)

Labor Force: 7.2 million (approx. 69% foreign workers) (Sept. 1998): Government 34%, Industry 28%, service and commerce 22%, agriculture 16%

Exports: $54.3 billion (1997 Embassy est.); Commodities: petroleum and petroleum products ($47.3 billion); Partners: Japan, US, South Korea, Singapore, France

Imports: $26.9 billion (1997 Embassy est.); Commodities: foodstuffs, machinery and equipment, chemicals, textiles; Partners: US, United Kingdom, Japan, Germany, Italy, France

Debt—external: NA

Communications

Televisions: 1 television per 4.62 persons (4.5 million, 1993 est.)

Telephones: 1 telephone per 14.24 persons (1.46 million, 1993 est.)

Radios: 1 radio per 4.16 persons; (5 million, 1993 est.)

Transportation

Railways: 1,390 km (1992)

Highways: 162,000 km (69,174 km paved; 92,826 km unpaved; 1996 est.)

Waterways: 0 km

Airports: 202 (70 paved runways; 132 unpaved runways; 1997 est.)

Transnational Issues

Disputes: Large section of boundary with Yemen not defined; location and status of boundary with UAE is not final, de facto boundary reflects 1974 agreement; Kuwaiti ownership of Qaruh and Umm al Maradim islands is disputed by Saudi Arabia; in 1996, agreed with Qatar to demarcate border per 1992 accord; that process is ongoing

Illicit Drugs: Death penalty for traffickers; increased consumption of heroin and cocaine

Sources: Bureau of Near Eastern Affairs, U.S. Department of State, *Background Notes: Saudi Arabia, March, 1999,* [On-Line]. Available: http://www.state.gov/www/background_notes/saudi_0998_bgn.html

CIA Publications—1998 World Factbook—Saudi Arabia, [On-Line]. Available: http://www.cia.gov/cia/publications/factbook/sa.html

Reichel, Philip L. (1994). *Comparative criminal justice systems, A topical approach.* Englewood Cliffs, New Jersey: Prentice Hall Career and Technology. Pp. 422–423

CHINA

Geography

Area: Total: 9,596,960 sq. km, slightly smaller than the US
Land: 9,326,410 sq. km
Water: 270,550 sq. km

Location: Eastern Asia

Border Countries: Northeast: North Korea, Russia
North: Mongolia
Northwest: Russia
West: Kazakhstan, Kyrgyzstan, Tajikistan, Afghanistan, Pakistan
South: India, Nepal, Myanmar, Bhutan, Burma, Laos, Vietnam

Capital: Beijing

Climate: Ranges from tropical in the south to subarctic in the north

Terrain: Primarily mountains, high plateaus, deserts in the west and plains, deltas, and hills in the east

People

Population: 1,236,914,658 (July 1998 est.)

Age Distribution: 0–14 years: 26% (male: 169,347,516; female: 149,897,253)
15–64 years: 68% (male: 431,164,591; female: 404,513,208)
65 years and older: 6% (male: 38,398,920; female: 43,593,170)
(1998 est.)

Sex Ratio: at birth: 1.15 males/female
under 15 years: 1.13 males/female

	15–64 years: 1.07 males/female
	65 years and older: 0.88 males/female (1998 est.)
Growth Rate:	0.83% (1998 est.)
Birth Rate:	15.73 births/1,000 population (1998 est.)
Death Rate:	6.99 deaths/1,000 population (1998 est.)
Life Expectancy at birth:	Total population: 69.59 years
	Male: 68.32 years
	Female: 71.06 years (1998 est.)
Education:	Compulsory—9 years
Literacy:	82% age 15 and over can read and write (1997 est.)
Ethnic Groups:	Han Chinese 91.9%, Zhuang, Uygur, Hui, Yi, Tibetan, Miao, Manchu, Mongol, Buyi, Korean, and other nationalities 8.1%
Languages:	Standard Chinese or Mandarin, Yue, Wu, Minbei, Minnan, Xiang, Gan, Hakka dialects, minority languages
Religions:	Officially atheist, Daoism (Taoism), Buddhism, Muslim, Christian

Government

Type:	Communist party-led state
Branches:	Executive: president, vice president, State Council, premier
	Legislative: unicameral National People's Congress
	Judicial: Supreme People's Court
Divisions:	23 provinces, 5 autonomous regions, and 4 municipalities
Constitution:	Most recent promulgation December 4, 1982
Legal System:	A complete combination of custom and statute, largely criminal law; rudimentary civil code in effect since January 1, 1987; new legal code in effect since January 1, 1980; continuing efforts are being made to improve civil, administrative, criminal and commercial law (CIA)
Suffrage:	Universal at 18 years of age

Economy

GDP:	$890 billion, exchange rate based (1997 est.)
GDP per capita:	$700, exchange rate based (1997 est.)
GDP real growth rate:	8.8% (1997 est.)
Inflation rate:	2.8% (1997 est.)
Labor Force:	699 million: Agriculture and forestry 60%; Industry and commerce 25%; Other 15%
Exports:	$182.7 billion (1997); Commodities: textiles, clothing, electrical machinery, chemicals, footwear, minerals; Partners: Hong Kong, Japan, U.S., South Korea, Germany, Netherlands, Singapore

Imports:	$142.36 billion (1997); Commodities: industrial machinery, chemicals, textiles, iron, steel, electrical equipment, mechanical appliances, mineral fuels, plastics
Debt—external:	$131 billion (1997 est.)

Communications

Televisions:	1 television per 16.49 persons (75 million, 1998 est.)
Telephones:	1 telephone per 13.89 persons (89 million, 1997 est.)
Radios:	1 radio per 5.71 persons; (216.5 million, 1992 est.)

Transportation

Railways:	64,900 km
Highways:	1.18 million km (241,300 km paved; 938,700 km unpaved)
Waterways:	138,600 km (110,600 km navigable)
Airports:	206 (192 with paved runways; 14 with unpaved runways) (1996 est.)

Transnational Issues

Disputes:	Boundary with India in dispute; two disputed sections of the boundary with Russia remain to be settled; most of the boundary with Tajikistan in dispute; 33-km section of boundary with North Korea in the Paektusan (mountain) area is indefinite; involved in a complex dispute over the Spratly Islands with Malaysia, Philippines, Taiwan, Vietnam, and possibly Brunei; maritime boundary dispute with Vietnam in the Gulf of Tonkin; Paracel Islands occupied by China, but claimed by Vietnam and Taiwan; claims Japanese-administered Senkaku-shoto (Senkaku Islands/Diaoyu Tai), as does Taiwan; sections of land border with Vietnam are indefinite
Illicit Drugs:	Major transshipment point for heroin produced in the Golden Triangle; growing domestic drug abuse problem
Web Sites:	Department of State, China homepage at http://www.state.gov/www/current/debate/china.html
	China Internet Information Center homepage at http://www.china news.org
	Chinese Embassy homepage at http://www.china-embassy.org
Sources:	Bureau of East Asian and Pacific Affairs, U.S. Department of State, *Background Notes: China, October 1998,* [On-Line]. Available: http://www.state.gov/www/background_notes/china_1098_bgn.html
	CIA Publications—1998 World Factbook—China, [On-Line]. Available: http://www.cia.gov/cia/publications/factbook/ch.html
	Reichel, Philip L. (1994). *Comparative criminal justice systems, A topical approach.* Englewood Cliffs, New Jersey: Prentice Hall Career and Technology. Pp. 404–405

UNITED STATES

Geography

Area:	Total: 9,629,091 sq. km, slightly larger than China
	Land: 9,158,960 sq. km
	Water: 470,131 sq. km
Location:	North America
Border Countries:	North: Canada
	South: Mexico
Capital:	Washington, D.C.
Climate:	Mostly temperate, but tropical in Hawaii and Florida and arctic in Alaska. Semi-arid in the great plains and arid in the southwest
Terrain:	Vast central plain, mountains in the west, hills and mountains in the east, rugged mountains and broad river valleys in Alaska and volcanic topography in Hawaii

People

Population:	270,311,756 (July 1998 est.)
Age Distribution:	0–14 years: 22% (male: 29,952,220; female: 28,560,357)
	15–64 years: 66% (male: 88,113,895; female: 89,399,501)
	65 years and older: 12% (male: 14,088,571; female: 20,197,212 (July 1998 est.)
Sex Ratio:	at birth: 1.05 males/female
	under 15 years: 1.05 males/female
	15–64 years: 0.99 males/female
	65 years and older: 0.7 males/female (1998 est.)
Growth Rate:	0.87% (1998 est.)
Birth Rate:	14.4 births/1,000 population (1998 est.)
Death Rate:	8.8 deaths/1,000 population (1998 est.)
Life Expectancy at birth:	Total population: 76.13 years
	Male: 72.85 years
	Female: 79.58 years (1998 est.)
Literacy:	97% age 15 and over can read and write (1979 est.)
Ethnic Groups:	white 83.4%, black 12.4%, Asian 3.3%, Amerindian 0.8% (1992)
Languages:	English, Spanish "*spoken by a sizable minority*"
Religions:	Protestant 56%, Roman Catholic 28%, Jewish 2%, other 4%, none 10% (1989)

Government

Type:	Federal republic
Branches:	Executive: President (chief of state and govt.), Vice President, Cabinet
	Legislative: bicameral congress (Senate and House of Representatives)
	Judicial: Supreme Court
Divisions:	50 states, 1 district
Constitution:	September 17, 1787, effective March 4, 1789
Legal System:	Common law tradition; judicial review of legislative acts
Suffrage:	Universal at 18 years of age

Economy

GDP:	$8.083 trillion (1997 est.)
GDP per capita:	$30,200 (1997 est.)
GDP real growth rate:	3.8% (1997)
Inflation rate:	2% (1997)
Labor Force:	136.3 million (includes unemployed) (1997): Managerial and professional 29.1%, technical; sales and administrative support 29.6%; services 13.5%; manufacturing, mining, transportation and crafts 25.1%; agriculture, forestry and fishing 2.7%
Exports:	$625.1 billion (1996); Commodities: motor vehicles, industrial supplies and raw materials, agricultural products, consumer goods; Partners: Canada, Western Europe, Japan, Mexico
Imports:	$822 billion (1996); Commodities; Crude oil and petroleum products, machinery, automobiles, foodstuffs, beverages, consumer goods; Partners: Canada, Western Europe, Japan, Mexico
Debt—external:	$862 billion (1995 est.)

Communications

Televisions:	1 television per 1.26 persons (215 million, 1993 est.)
Telephones:	1 telephone per 1.48 persons (182.558 million, 1987 est.)
Radios:	1 radio per 0.50 persons; (540.5 million, 1992 est.)

Transportation

Railways:	240,000 km (1989)
Highways:	6.42 million km (3,903,360 km paved; 2,516,640 km unpaved; 1996 est.)
Waterways:	41,009 km, exclusive of the Great Lakes
Airports:	14,574 (5,167 paved runways; 9,407 unpaved runways; 1997 est.)

Transnational Issues

Disputes:	Maritime boundary disputes with Canada (Dixon entrance, Beaufort Sea, Strait of Juan de Fuca, Machais Seal Island); US Naval Base at Guantanamo Bay is leased from Cuba and only mutual agreement or US abandonment of the area can terminate the lease; Haiti claims Navassa Island; US has made no territorial claim in Antarctica (but reserved the right to do so) and does not recognize the claims of any other nation; Marshall Islands claim Wake Island
Illicit Drugs:	Consumer of cocaine shipped from Colombia through Mexico and the Caribbean; consumer of heroin, marijuana, and increasingly methamphetamines from Mexico; consumer of high-quality Southeast Asian heroin; illicit producer of cannabis, marijuana, depressants, stimulants, hallucinogens, and methamphetamines; drug money-laundering center
Sources:	*CIA Publications—1998 World Factbook—United States,* [On-Line]. Available: http://www.cia.gov/cia/publications/factbook/us.html
	Reichel, Philip L. (1994). *Comparative criminal justice systems, A topical approach.* Englewood Cliffs, New Jersey: Prentice Hall Career and Technology. Pp. 428–429

Appendix D The World's Legal Systems

This list excludes countries for which no data were available.

Country	Legal System	Country	Legal System
Afghanistan	Islamic & combinations	Chad	Civil
Albania	Civil	Chile	Civil
Algeria	Islamic & combinations	China	Socialist
Andorra	Civil	Colombia	Civil/Common
Angola	Civil	Comoros	Islamic & combinations
Antigua and Barbuda	Common	Congo	Civil
Argentina	Civil/Common	Costa Rica	Civil
Armenia	Civil	Croatia	Civil
Australia	Common	Cuba	Socialist
Austria	Civil	Cyprus	Civil/Common
Azerbaijan	Civil	Czech Republic	Civil
Bahamas	Common	Denmark	Civil
Bahrain	Islamic & combinations	Djibouti	Islamic & combinations
Bangladesh	Common	Dominica	Common
Barbados	Common	Dominican Republic	Civil
Belorussia	Civil	Ecuador	Civil
Belgium	Civil	Egypt	Islamic & combinations
Belize	Common	El Salvador	Civil/Common
Benin	Civil	Equatorial Guinea	Civil
Bhutan	Common	Estonia	Civil
Bolivia	Civil	Ethiopia	Other
Bosnia and Herzegovina	Civil	Fiji	Common
Botswana	Civil	Finland	Civil
Brazil	Civil	France	Civil
Brunei	Islamic & combinations	Gabon	Civil
Bulgaria	Civil	Gambia	Islamic & combinations
Burkina Faso	Civil	Georgia	Civil
Burundi	Civil	Germany	Civil
Cambodia	Other	Ghana	Common
Cameroon	Civil	Greece	Civil
Canada	Civil/Common	Greenland	Civil
Cape Verde	Other	Grenada	Common
Central African Republic	Civil	Guam	Common

Country	Legal System	Country	Legal System
Guatemala	Civil	Mexico	Civil/Common
Guinea	Civil	Micronesia	Other
Guinea-Bissau	Other	Moldavia	Civil
Guyana	Common	Monaco	Civil
Haiti	Civil	Mongolia	Civil
Honduras	Civil/Common	Morocco	Islamic & combinations
Hong Kong	Common	Mozambique	Civil
Hungary	Civil	Namibia	Civil
Iceland	Civil	Nepal	Common
India	Common	Netherlands	Civil
Indonesia	Civil	New Zealand	Common
Iran	Islamic & combinations	Nicaragua	Civil
Iraq	Islamic & combinations	Niger	Civil
Ireland	Common	Nigeria	Islamic & combinations
Israel	Common	Norway	Civil/Common
Italy	Civil	Oman	Islamic & combinations
Ivory Coast	Civil	Pakistan	Islamic & combinations
Jamaica	Common	Palau	Other
Japan	Civil/Common	Panama	Civil
Jordan	Islamic & combinations	Papua New Guinea	Common
Kazakhstan	Civil	Paraguay	Civil
Kenya	Islamic & combinations	Peru	Civil
Kyrgyzstan	Civil	Philippines	Civil/Common
Korea, Dem. Peoples Rep.	Socialist	Poland	Civil
Rep. of Korea	Civil/Common	Portugal	Civil
Kuwait	Islamic & combinations	Puerto Rico	Common
Laos	Socialist	Qatar	Islamic & combinations
Latvia	Civil	Romania	Civil
Lebanon	Civil	Russian Federation	Civil
Lesotho	Civil/Common	Rwanda	Civil
Liberia	Common	Saint Lucia	Common
Libya	Islamic & combinations	Saint Vincent and the Grenadines	Common
Liechtenstein	Civil	San Marino	Civil
Lithuania	Civil	Sao Tome and Principe	Civil
Luxembourg	Civil	Saudi Arabia	Islamic & combinations
"FYRM"	Civil	Senegal	Civil
Madagascar	Civil	Seychelles	Civil/Common
Malawi	Common	Sierra Leone	Common
Malaysia	Common	Singapore	Common
Maldives	Islamic & combinations	Slovakia	Civil
Mali	Civil	Slovenia	Civil
Malta	Civil/Common	Solomon Islands	Common
Marshall Islands	Other	Somalia	Islamic & combinations
Mauritania	Islamic & combinations	South Africa	Civil/Common
Mauritius	Civil/Common		

Country	Legal System	Country	Legal System
Spain	Civil	Uganda	Common
Sri Lanka	Islamic & combinations	Ukraine	Civil
Sudan	Islamic & combinations	United Arab Emirates	Islamic & combinations
Surinam	Civil	United Kingdom	Common
Swaziland	Civil	United States	Common
Sweden	Civil	Uruguay	Civil
Switzerland	Civil	Uzbekistan	Civil
Syria	Islamic & combinations	Vanuatu	Civil/Common
Tadzhikistan	Civil	Vatican City	Civil
Taiwan	Civil/Common	Venezuela	Civil
Tanzania	Common	Vietnam	Socialist
Thailand	Civil/Common	Western Sahara	Other
Togo	Civil	Western Samoa	Common
Trinidad and Tobago	Common	Yemen	Islamic & combinations
Tunisia	Islamic & combinations	Yugoslavia	Civil
Turkey	Civil	Zaire	Civil
Turkmenistan	Civil	Zambia	Common
U.S. Virgin Islands	Common	Zimbabwe	Civil/Commo

SOURCE: Philip Reichel. *Comparative Criminal Justice Systems.* Copyright © 1999. Upper Saddle River, N.J.: Prentice-Hall. Reprinted with permission of the author.

Glossary

Abstract review review whereby advisory opinions rather than judgments are rendered because constitutionality is decided without hearing an actual case that has arisen under a particular law

Abu Nidal terrorist group led by al-Banna, currently located in Iraq, that split from the PLO in 1974 and since that time has carried out terrorist attacks in twenty countries, killing almost 900 persons

Adjudicators individuals who decide the outcome of legal disputes; judges

Administrative detention form of punishment in the People's Republic of China that allows authorities to impose fines and incarcerate people without benefit of a trial for up to four years

Adversarial system procedure used in Common Law countries to determine the truth during adjudication whereby the prosecution and defense compete against each other with a judge ensuring fairness and adherence to the rules

Advocats attorneys in France

Advocates legal representatives, usually lawyers, who present the evidence and the arguments that allow adjudicators to make their decisions

Agents of biological origin (ABOs) bacteria, viruses, or toxins used by terrorists to poison water and food supplies

Al-Qaida group of Sunni Islamic extremists who were originally formed as a group of Arab nationals to fight the Russians during the war in Afghanistan; currently aligned with Bin Laden

Amtsgerichte level of court in Germany that hears minor criminal and civil cases at the local level.

Ancien régime an old judicial body that served the rulers of France at the expense of the people

Annuaire statistique de la justice crime data in France derived from the Directory of Justice data

Antiterrorism and Effective Death Penalty Act legislation signed by President Clinton in 1996 that banned fundraising and financial support for international terrorist organizations, added $1 billion to law enforcement for fighting terrorism, created standards for the deportation of suspected terrorists, allowed the use of the death penalty for international terrorism acts, made a federal crime out of planning terrorism abroad, and regulated the production and sale of raw materials to make bombs

Assassins religious terrorist group that supported Islam in the current Persian Gulf region during the years 1090–1275

Assessors in France, professional judges selected from other courts to sit in on trials and assist the president judge

Assize courts courts in France that hear appeals from lower courts and that have original jurisdiction in major felony cases

Aum Shrinrikyo religious terrorist group in Japan responsible for the March 1995 poisoning of the Tokyo subway system with sarin gas

Balloon effect the effect of drug eradication strategies such that drugs are eliminated from one region only to have production increase in another region to meet demand

Barristers advocates in Great Britain

Basic people's court lowest level of the formal Chinese court system, found in each county and

361

municipal area, that handles most criminal, civil, and economic matters of first instance unless the matter is a special case

Bereitschaftspolizei (Bepo)   German police officers in training who live in barracks and act as civil order police when the situation arises

Bin Laden   the terrorist leader believed to have supported and trained thousands of terrorist fighters in numerous countries

Board of Visitors   committees in England that act as an independent watchdog on the prisons, meeting with inmates and staff to safeguard the well-being and rights of all prisoners and to help with the problems of discipline and administration

Borstals   detention facilities in England that segregate youthful offenders with some prospect of reform from adult convicts

Boryokudan   the official term for the many Japanese gangs of organized criminals

Bundesgerichtshof   the Federal Supreme Court in Germany that handles final appeals in all cases from the lower courts except those involving constitutional interpretation

Bundesrat   the upper house of the legislature in Germany

Bundestag   the lower house and principal chamber of the legislature in Germany

Bundesverfassungsgericht   the German Federal Constitutional Court

Cali cartel   a smaller organization that is part of the Colombian drug cartel

Canon Law   law developed by the Catholic Church that dealt with church and spiritual matters including provisions regulating family life and morals, and rules for church governance

Carlos the Jackal   Ilich Ramirez Sanchez, infamous member of the Popular Front for the Liberation of Palestine, responsible for a number of high-profile terrorist incidents, who is currently residing in a French prison

Certification   U.S. policy that requires countries believed to support illicit drug trade or production to make progress in their efforts to reduce their

drug involvement or forfeit financial assistance and trade benefits from the United States

Challenges for cause   process providing the opportunity for the defense or prosecution to reject potential jurors if there is reason to believe they would not be fair or impartial

Chinese Triad societies   Chinese secret societies that are involved in organized crime throughout the Far East and into the Americas and Europe

Chusai-san   Japanese rural police officers

Chuzaisho   local police post in villages and rural areas of Japan

CICP   United Nations Centre for International Crime Prevention, which administers the United Nations Surveys of Crime and Trends and Operations of Criminal Justice Systems

Civil Law   all law that is not criminal; the body of rules that regulate behavior between individuals that do not involve the potential of criminal sanctions (contracts, torts, wills, property, family matters, commercial law)

Civil Liberties Bureau   a bureau comprised of unpaid commissioners operating in each town and neighborhood in Japan that hears complaints and provides remedies for individuals whose civil liberties have been infringed

Civil order control function   the duty of the police to respond to, supervise, or control two or more citizens in any situation that can disrupt the peace and tranquility of society

Collegial bench   group composed of one to three judges and two to four people's assessors that tries cases in the basic people's, intermediate, and higher people's courts in China

Colombian drug cartel   the largest and predominant group in the illegal cocaine trade industry consisting of a number of smaller organizations

Commercial law   body of law developed in Europe during the Middle Ages regulating the buying and selling of goods and services between cities and nations

Common Law   body of law developed in the eleventh and twelfth centuries in England based on decisions of the judges of the King's Court incorporating Canon Law, feudal custom and Roman Law.

Community policing umbrella term describing programs that serve as collaborative efforts between the police and the public to identify the problems of crime and then involve the public in finding solutions

Community service penalty for criminal actions that requires offenders to personally "pay back" in time and effort, by working for a not-for-profit agency

Comparative Crime Data File (CCDF) compilation of crime data for the period 1900–1972 for five crimes in 110 countries

Comparative criminal justice investigating, evaluating, and comparing the criminal justice processes of more than one country, culture, or institution

Confucian thought the belief that social order can be achieved through moral and political reform, because man is by nature good or capable of goodness; the idea of group consciousness or collectivity is the main force behind motivating people to avoid illegal or immoral activity

Conjugal visiting program in German prisons that allows an inmate private visits from his or her spouse and children for four hours every two months.

Conseil Constitutionnel council in France that considers the constitutionality of legislation before it goes into effect and ensures that elections are conducted properly

Construction strategy policy of building prisons to reduce the crowding problem resulting from a generally more conservative and hard-line attitude toward crime and criminals

Control of freedom term used on the international level to refer to probation

Convergence the dynamic whereby laws, policies, and practices of the criminal justice system become more uniform across nations

Coordinate ideal system that stresses horizontal distribution of authority, an amorphous machinery of justice, and short terms of office with extensive use of lay officials

Correctional court second level of criminal court in France; hears cases somewhat more serious than police courts that result in sentences of up to five years in prison

Council of State apex of the French administrative court system that acts as the primary guarantor of the rights of French citizens

Court an agency with power to settle disputes in a society

Court of Appeals the English court that hears appeal cases from the crown courts and the High Court of Justice

Court of Cassation highest level of appeals court in France; hears appeals from the courts of assizes and appeals

Crown courts trial courts for serious crimes in England

Corpus Juris Civilis body of laws resulting from the compilation and codification of the law in force in the Roman world in the sixth century A.D.; also known as the Institutes of Justinian

Correlates of crime (COC) compilation of crime data and social, economic, and political information relevant to crime for fifty-two nations for 1960–1980

Corruption a transaction that enables private actors to gain access to public resources by giving them an unfair advantage because there is neither transparency nor competition

Council of Ministers the cabinet in France and Saudi Arabia, presided over by the president

Courts of assize in France, the court of original jurisdiction in criminal matters

Crime mapping computer-based information system in which locations of crime are displayed on maps to help develop more information about crime trends and crime prevention design

Criminal justice system the aggregate of all the people and agencies that perform criminal justice functions

Criminal law body of rules that define crimes, set punishments, and provide the procedures for adjudication

Cross-sectional studies research studies that focus on one point in time

Crown Prosecution Service an independent agency, formed in 1986, responsible for prosecuting cases in England

Cultural persistence the dynamic in which deep-rooted historical, economic, and social realities create adaptations to change that result in the continuance of individualistic systems

Cultural Revolution reform period in China under Chairman Mao from 1966 to 1976 with the goal to move Chinese society from socialism to a purer form of communism

Cybercrime crime committed with the use of computers

Dark figure the amount of unknown crime

Day fine criminal penalty based on the amount of income an offender earns in a day's work

Delta Force the U.S. Army's Combat Application Group, which serves mainly as a hostage rescue team

Deputies the 2,800 members of the National People's Congress of China

Deterrence purpose of criminal sanctions or punishment whereby offenders, through various devices such as certainty of punishment or length or severity of punishment, should come to the conclusion that crime is not worth the risk of the resulting punishment

Deviance control function a traditional police mission to reinforce community values and laws, protecting the community against nonconformists and trying to keep violators of community norms under control

Diaspora the long period in ancient Jewish history of forced exile outside of Palestine

Diet the bicameral legislature in Japan consisting of the House of Representatives and House of Councillors

Dispersal prisons high-security prisons in England and Wales that handle dangerous inmates

District courts the level of court in Japan that handles criminal cases that could result in prison terms of more than three years or civil matters valued at greater than 900,000 yen, as well as appeals from the summary courts.

Domestic terrorism the type of terrorism that involves a citizen or group of citizens committing a terrorist act in their own country

Dossier in France, a complete record of the pretrial proceedings that informs the judge, the defense attorney, and others about the testimony of key witnesses and the evidence to be presented

Electronic monitoring an approach to noncustodial supervision that uses electronic monitors to expand the surveillance capacity of supervision; ordinarily is combined with house arrest

Empirical systems case-based law

Ethnocentrism the view that one's own country or culture does things "right" and all other ways are "wrong" or "foreign"

Family courts Japanese courts operating on the same level as district courts and handling most domestic and juvenile cases

Federal Constitution Court the court in Germany that has the final word in cases of basic rights, including some criminal procedure cases, and has important functions in protecting the Basic Law and preserving the federal balance

Federal system of government a government with multiple levels, each with discrete powers

Fines penalties imposed on convicted offenders by a court or, in some countries, by another arm of the criminal justice system, requiring that they pay a specified sum of money

Freiganger a program in German prisons that allows inmates who have served at least one-half of their sentence to leave the institution during the day for school or work and then return to the institution in the evening

Garde a vue the initial questioning period in the French legal system

Gendarmerie Nationale (GN) French police organization operating within the Ministry of Defense that is responsible for rural areas and communities in France with populations of less than 10,000 people

Globalization the process whereby the world has become interdependent in terms of events and the actions of people and governments around the world

Good Friday Accord historic agreement signed in April 1998 by feuding Catholic and Protestant parties in Ireland whereby both parties would share multiparty administration of Northern Ireland

Grand Bench the Supreme Court of Japan, consisting of fifteen members, that deals with matters related to new constitutional rulings and administrative responsibilities including nominating lower-court judges

Grenzschutzgruppe 9 German antiterrorism organization, developed after the 1972 Munich Olympic Games disaster, that has gained the reputation of being one of the top-notch antiterrorism forces in the world

Groupment d'Intervention de la Gendarmerie Nationale (GIGN) French police unit that has been developed from within the ranks of the National Police to serve as the law enforcement agency to combat terrorism

Habeas corpus court order requiring that a prisoner be brought before a judge to explain by what lawful authority he or she is being detained

Hamas terrorist group, founded in late 1987 as an outgrowth of the Palestinian branch of the Muslim Brotherhood, that has attacked Israeli military and civilian targets

Hierarchical ideal refers to systems that are organized around routinization and specialization, with long periods of tenure in office

High Court court in Japan that handles appeals from the summary, district, or family courts, and cases of original jurisdiction in which the person is charged with insurrection or sedition of the government

High Court of Justice in England, the first level of appeal and the court of original jurisdiction for serious civil cases and some criminal cases

Higher people's court the level of the Chinese court system that handles criminal, civil, and economic matters of first instance that may affect the entire province, autonomous region, or municipality, as well as appeals from the intermediate courts,

cases transferred from the lower courts, and cases protested by the procurator

Hizballah Shi'ite extremist terrorist group based in Lebanon and dedicated to the creation of an Iranian-style Islamic republic in Lebanon and the removal of all non-Islamic influences from the area

House arrest incarceration sentence that uses the offender's residence as the place of punishment

House of Lords the highest court in England; handles only cases that address an important point of law involving general public importance

Hudud in Islamic Law, crimes against God that are likely to endanger the social order

Human trafficking the illegal trading of persons across borders against their will for financial gain

Hybrid a legal tradition that combines different aspects of more than one legal tradition

ICVS International Crime Victim Surveys conducted through the coordinated efforts of the Ministry of Justice of the Netherlands and the United Nations Interregional Crime and Justice Research Institute

Illegal immigration the illegal movement of willful persons across borders

Incapacitation a purpose of criminal sanctions or punishment whereby offenders, usually through prison or exile, are kept from committing further crimes

Indigenous law native laws of persons who originate from or live in a particular area

Injunction an order of the court designed to prevent harms that would occur before a case works its way through the regular court system

Inquisitorial system a procedure used in non-adversarial systems to determine the truth during adjudication; characterized by extensive pretrial investigations and interrogations designed to ensure that no innocent person is brought to trial

Integration a step in the money-laundering process that returns the money to the regular economy through purchase or investment

Intermediate people's courts the level of the Chinese court system that handles serious criminal, civil, and economic cases of first instance at the municipal and prefectural levels, serious cases transferred from the basic people's courts, and appeals from the basic people's courts

Intermediate sanctions strategy a policy based on the belief that, because of limited prison space, prisons should be used only for violent offenders who have not been deterred by prior punishments and that punishments short of incarceration should be developed

International Court of Justice the principal judicial body of the United Nations, located in The Hague, Netherlands, with the dual role of setting, in accordance with international law, legal disputes submitted by the 185 UN member states and neutral parties and giving advisory opinions on legal questions referred by international organizations

International crimes crimes against the peace and security of humankind based on international agreements between countries or based on legal precedents developed in history

International Criminal Court a proposed permanent international court with jurisdiction over the most serious crimes of international concern such as genocide, war crimes, crimes against humanity and aggression; voted on by the members of the United Nations and awaiting ratification as of this writing

International criminal justice the study and description of one country's law, criminal procedure, or justice process

International criminal organizations organized criminal groups that have a foreign component or operate across national boundaries

International criminal tribunals courts established by the Security Council of the United Nations with the power to adjudicate charges of international crimes by countries and individuals from conflicts in former Yugoslavia and in Rwanda

International Criminal Tribunal for Rwanda tribunal established in 1994 by the Security Council of the United Nations after the outbreak of genocide in Rwanda

International Criminal Tribunal for Yugoslavia tribunal established in 1992 by the Security Council of the United Nations to deal with the atrocities committed during the civil war in the former Yugoslavia

International terrorism type of terrorism that involves the citizens or territory of more than one country

INTERPOL the International Police Organization, which acts as a clearinghouse for information on offenses and offenders believed to operate across national boundaries

Islamic Law legal tradition in Islamic countries based on the rules of conduct revealed by God with two primary sources: the Shari'a and the Sunnah

Italian Mafia organized crime group developed in Sicily during the nineteenth century as a combination extortion and social control agency; a term loosely applied to networks of organized crime in the United States

Jail facilities used for less serious offenders who are generally sentenced to less than a one-year sentence or for those awaiting trial or transfer to another institution

Japanese Red Army Japanese group engaged in a worldwide campaign of terrorism, with members reportedly living in other countries to act as mercenaries to promote various political causes

Japanese Yakuza a popular term for the many Japanese groups of organized criminals

Jihad a holy war by Islamic fundamentalists who want to protect their religion from "creeping secularism and cultural imperialism posed by Western countries such as the United States"

Judicial impartiality a concept whereby judicial authorities treat parties in court as equals

Judicial independence a principle holding that judges are bound to the law rather than influenced by the desires of those in power; the freedom of judges to make their decisions without any form of outside pressure

Judicial review the power of a court to review actions and legal decisions made by those in the criminal justice system

Juge d'instruction in France, the examining magistrate who is responsible for a complete and impartial investigation of the facts

Juges de l'application des peines corrections judge in France whose functions include determining the actual length of time that a prisoner remains in prison or is released on parole and overseeing prison conditions and prison disciplinary procedures

Jus cogens term used to explain that fundamental norms are recognized on the international level to have a superior status over other norms

Justice of the peace lay judges in small American towns who carry out many legal functions such as traffic violations, some misdemeanors, small civil claims, and some domestic court matters

Juvenile reformatories facilities in China for serious juvenile offenders between the ages of fourteen and eighteen where youths are confined for intensive work and moral education programs

Kidotai civil order police officers in Japan who live in barracks, receive training in crowd control, and use military formations during civil order crises

Koban a local police post in urban areas of Japan

Kontachbereichsbeamter officers assigned to community policing programs, with main functions including contact with the public, crime suppression, traffic control, accident prevention, and assistance to other agencies

Kriminalpolizei (Kripo) German plainclothes police who handle serious crime investigations and matters that require developing a case against a suspect

Laender states in Germany

Landgericht the regional level of court in Germany that hears major criminal and civil cases and appeals from the Amtsgerichte courts

Laogai institutions in China that require inmates to work at prison farms and factories to support the economic system; based on the idea of "thought reform through labor"

Law lords the nine members of the House of Lords, the highest court in England, who hear civil and criminal appeals from the Court of Appeals and a limited number from the High Court

Lay magistrates volunteer judges who are appointed to serve in English courts

Layering the step in the money-laundering process that involves frequent financial transfers and transactions to hide illegally obtained cash

Legal advisors legally trained individuals who work outside the courtroom to advise and instruct individuals who have legal problems or needs, both civil and criminal

Legal pluralism the mixing of more than one system of law within a country or region of a country

Legal scholars individuals who study the law and write on it in legal commentaries and professional journals

Legalist perspective the belief that only a firm application of laws and strict punishments can persuade people who are innately evil not to commit crime; developed in China almost 200 years after Confucianism

Lettres de cachet orders of the king in France during the sixteenth and seventeenth centuries that a person be imprisoned indefinitely

License a general degree received by a student in France upon graduation after three years of study

Longitudinal studies research studies that describe crime trends over time

Magister Master of Law degree received by students in France after completing the fourth year of study and passing a national examination

Magistrate's courts the level of court in England that handles minor crimes and preliminary hearings in major criminal cases

Medellin cartel a smaller organization that is part of the Colombian drug cartel

Médiateur an intermediary agent of the administrative courts who hears minor complaints against the French government and makes recommendations for redress

Mexican Federation an organized crime group of drug cartels operating in Mexico that are primarily responsible for the shipment of heroin, cocaine, and marijuana into the United States

Mixed court a method of adjudication whereby one or more lay judges help a professional judge come to a decision

Monarch a person who is the sole and absolute ruler of a country, such as a king, queen, or emperor

Money laundering the conversion of the monetary proceeds of criminal activity into funds with an apparent legal source

Mubahith the secret police or special investigative police officers of the General Directorate of Investigation in Saudi Arabia that conduct criminal investigations and handle matters pertaining to domestic security and counterintelligence

Mutawa the morals force or religious police that assures that Saudi Arabian citizens live up to the rules of behavior derived from the Qur'an

Naikan a method of therapy used in Japan whereby individuals use introspection to understand the impact of their behavior on others and others on them

Nation any group with a common culture, ethnic, racial, or religious identity

National Crime Survey (NCS) a national survey of more than 100,000 people from 50,000 U.S. households in which people are asked to report anonymously whether they have been the victims of certain crimes over the past year

National Incident-Based Reporting System (NIBRS) an improved version of Uniform Crime Reports, implemented in 1991 by the FBI, that counts each incident reported and collects additional information

National People's Congress theoretically, the highest organ of power in China; meets annually to review and approve major new policy directions, laws, the budget, and major personnel changes

National Police Agency (NPA) the central police organization in Japan, supervised by the National Public Safety Commission, with eight regional police bureaus and a number of special divisions to handle training, research, crime prevention, public safety functions related to the environment and transportation, and matters of national security and multiple jurisdiction

Noncustodial sanctions legal sanctions handed out to offenders that do not require confinement in a correctional facility

Notaries legal advisors in France

Null strategy the policy that prisons should be allowed to become increasingly congested in the hope that criminals will be deterred by living in such conditions or that a change in the demographics of the crime cohort will resolve prison crowding

Oberlandesgericht the top level of the state court system in Germany; primarily hears point of law raised in appeals in the lower courts and holds original jurisdiction in cases of treason and anticonstitutional activity

Ombudsman an individual in Socialist Law systems who hears complaints and ensures that government agents are performing their functions correctly

Organized crime the label given to the phenomenon whereby certain groups engage in essentially violent, profit-motivated criminal activity

PACE the Police and Criminal Evidence Act of 1984 passed by the British Parliament to make arrest and prosecution procedures less cumbersome

Palestinian Liberation Organization (PLO) the parent organization of a number of Arab Muslim terrorist groups fighting the Israelis for control of Palestine

Paris P/8 Ministerial Conference an international conference on terrorism held in July 1996 that resulted in the adoption of twenty-five recommendations centering on measures to prevent terrorism by means of border control, improved international cooperation, and regulation of fundraising by terrorists

Parliament governmental structure in England consisting of the monarch, the House of Lords, and the House of Commons

Parole the practice of releasing offenders to community supervision after a period of incarceration

People mediation committees (PMCs) informal social control mechanism used in China and under the control of the court system

People's assessors ordinary citizens serving on the Chinese collegial bench; must be elected, at least twenty-three years of age, and eligible to vote

Peremptory challenges process that allows the defense or prosecution to remove a juror for no specified reason

Petty Bench　the court of the Supreme Court of Japan, divided into three separate benches of five justices, that handles all legal matters other than those assigned the Grand Bench, including the cases of appellate-level jurisdiction

Placement　the step in the process of money laundering that involves the movement of money from the location of the criminal activity

Plea bargaining　the process whereby the accused agrees to plead guilty in return for various concessions, such as a lesser charge or promise of a lenient sentence

Police Authority Board　in England, a committee made up of local elected officials and judicial officials appointed by the Home Secretary that hears citizen complaints about alleged police abuses and consults about police practices; also involved in hiring local chief constables and setting their compensation

Police courts　the lowest level of trial court in France; handles more than half the criminal cases that arise and issues sentences of no more than two months in jail and fines no greater than $1,000

Police Nationale (PN)　the French police organization within the Ministry of the Interior responsible for Paris and other urban areas

Political and policy-making process　the dynamic whereby governmental regimes that foster particular ideologies stamp the legal system with their own character

Political culture　deep-seated patterns of behavior and thought that have developed over the course of a society's history

Politicized justice　the process whereby the judicial or criminal justice process is perverted in order to achieve particular political objectives

Popular Front for the Liberation of Palestine (PDLP)　Marxist-Leninist group founded in 1967 that joined the PLO coalition but broke away in the early 1990s over ideological differences; is active in Syria, Lebanon, Israel, and other occupied areas of Palestine

Population-reduction strategy　a way of dealing with prison crowding that calls for changing sentencing policies and adopting methods for letting inmates out of prison

Prerelease programs　correctional programs in the United States that permit inmates who achieve a certain status to leave the facility during the day for work or school and return in the evening

Prefect　the head of a province in France selected by the government to enforce the laws

Prefectural police　midlevel police agencies in Japan organized under the Regional Police Bureaus, with local police stations under them, specialized riot police forces living in barracks, and a national police academy

Prefectures　administrative divisions in China and Japan

Prisons　facilities used almost exclusively for serious offenders who receive sentences of more than one year

Prison Act of 1976　code that sets forth all of the principles and methods to be practiced in German correctional facilities

Private law　law that regulates behavior between individuals within the state; also known as Civil Law

Private prisons　correctional institutions operated by private firms on behalf of governments

Probation　the sentence offenders receive when they are convicted of a crime but are allowed to continue to reside in the community, under certain conditions

Procurator　in Civil Law systems, roughly equivalent to the prosecutor in Common Law systems; in Socialist Law systems, the person who prosecutes criminal offenders, supervises the criminal justice system, and ensures that all citizens and state personnel carry out the laws and policies of the state

Professed values　values that are proclaimed as values by the participants in the system

Progressive Movement　early twentieth-century movement calling for a new approach to corrections; focused on rehabilitation of individual offenders by specialists in corrections, probation, parole, on therapeutic prison regimes, and on separate juvenile justice mechanisms

Provisional Irish Republican Army (PIRA) terrorist group in Northern Ireland whose aim is to dislodge the British troops from Ulster and unite this area with the rest of the Republic of Ireland

Public law law that is developed by modern states in their legislatures or through their regulatory process dealing largely with relations between governments and citizens

Public Security police Chinese police organization that provides basic uniformed patrol and twelve other specialized functions including criminal investigations, fire control, border patrols, and regulations of all modes of transportation

Public surveillance probation in China

Quadi Islamic judges who decide cases in the Shari'a courts based on the facts according to their own wisdom and the principles of the religious law

Queen's counsel a group of preeminent barristers who serve as counsel to the British Crown

Quesas in Islamic Law, crimes against others that cause damage to a family's livelihood

Rational systems code-based law

Rechtsanwalte legal advocates in Germany

Rechtsstaat term in Germany that means rule according to law

Red Army Fraction (RAF) a major German terrorist group operating in the early 1970s that engaged in internal terrorism

Reeducation through labor in China, both a policy and a kind of correctional facility that incarcerates those who have administrative detention status whereby they are imprisoned without benefit of a trial

Referendar period of apprenticeship in Germany during which law students rotate among different specialties

Reform through labor in China, both a policy and a place for offenders who have been tried and convicted of a criminal offense, with emphasis on forced labor and extreme attempts at thought reform

Rehabilitation a purpose of criminal sanctions or punishment whereby offenders should be transformed into law-abiding persons through programs of medical, physiological, economic, or educational improvement

Reichsstrafgesetzbuch unified criminal code in Germany, codified during the rule of Bismarck in 1871

Religious terrorism terrorism used to promote a certain religious system or protect a set of beliefs within a religion

Remand centers local facilities in England and Wales that hold offenders awaiting trial or sentencing and those serving very short sentences

Remand prisons facilities used to house unconvicted inmates

Republican government a form of government in which a president is head of the government but the main power remains in the hands of citizens who vote for representatives, who are then responsible to the electorate

Residents' committees public security organizations formed in the early 1950s in China in neighborhoods, workplaces, schools, and rural areas whose purpose was to encourage participation of all citizens in their community and to assist police in maintaining public order

Restitution process whereby an offender is required to or volunteers to pay money or otherwise make reparations for harm resulting from a criminal offense

Restorative justice correctional method that calls for participation by the offender, victim, and community in the sentencing process and allows the offender to atone for the offense and be restored to community life

Retribution purpose of criminal sanctions or punishment asserting that the offender should "pay back" society for the harm done

Revolutionary terrorism form of terrorism that forces a government to respond in a harsh manner in the hopes that such governmental actions will lead to discontent among the people and to revolution

Russian Mafiya organized crime group operating in Russia involved with arms smuggling, prostitution, racketeering, narcotics trafficking, gasoline theft and fraud, car theft, and the illegal export of raw materials from the territories of the Russian Federation

Schoffen lay judges in Germany used extensively in courts of appeal for minor offenses and for first-level criminal offenses

Schutzpolizei (Schupo) the German equivalent of municipal police, who handle all general aspects of law enforcement and simple investigations

Seal Team 6 the U.S. Naval Special Warfare Development Group responsible for counterterrorism operations in the maritime environment

Secular law law that does not pertain to any religion or religious body

Self-report survey research method whereby people are asked to report their own delinquent and criminal acts in an anonymous questionnaire or confidential interview

Shari'a the rules of conduct revealed by God (Allah) to his Prophet (Muhammad) specifying how the people are to live in this world

Shoguns military leaders who exercised absolute rule in Japan during the years of isolation from other cultures from 1603 to 1867

Shura in Saudi Arabia, the Consultative Council, a sixty-member all-male advisory body with no legislative functions

Smuggling the illegal movement of some item, person, or persons, into or from a country through some form of stealth

Smuggling of human organs the illegal procurement and/or selling of human organs

Smuggling of migrants the illegal movement of willful persons across borders

Smuggling of women illegal movement and exploitation of women against their will for financial gain

Socialist Law a family of law with its origins in socialism, a system characterized by the absence of social classes and common ownership of the means of production and livelihood; the emphasis is on communal values at the expense of the individual

Software piracy the crime of pirating licensed software

Solicitors legal advisors in Great Britain

Sovereign state an internationally recognized unit of political authority over a given territory

Special Air Service Regiment the antiterrorist organization in England that specializes in the detection and apprehension of suspected terrorists

Staatsexamen the national bar examination in Germany that follows three and a half years of university education

Standing Committee of the NPC a committee of 135 full-time members including the leading government officials and influential people of the Chinese Communist party with the ability to annul any law or court decision if it contravenes the constitution, statutes, or administrative rules and regulations

Stare decisis literally, "it stands decided"; the principle used in Common Law countries to signify the legal force of precedent

State-sponsored terrorism the form of terrorism practiced by governments against their own citizens or another country in order to protect their own political, economic, or military interests

Stipendiary magistrates in England, professional attorneys who are paid by the state for their work

Summary courts lower-level courts in Japan that have original jurisdiction in minor criminal and civil cases

Supranational courts judicial mechanisms that direct their decisions across borders and supposedly have a higher legal standing than decisions of courts in individual countries

Supreme Court the highest court in Japan that acts as the final court of appeal in civil and criminal cases, handles matters of constitutionality, nominates judges to the lower courts, and supervises the judicial system

Supreme Judicial Council the body that hears final appeals in Saudi Arabia, refers cases back to the court of appeals for reconsideration, and makes regulations and policies for administering the court system

Supreme People's Court the highest court in China that deals with matters of national importance including appeals from the higher people's courts

Terrorism the unlawful use of force or violence against persons or property to intimidate or coerce a government, the civilian population, or any segment thereof, in furtherance of political or social objectives

Thought reform a program in Chinese correctional facilities that requires inmates to confess to their wrongdoing, attack their criminal identity, and reconstruct a new self-image that fits with the beliefs of the Socialist agenda

Thugs terrorist group beginning in seventh-century India whose reign lasted for seven centuries and who executed millions of people

Transnational crimes offenses whose inception, proportion, and/or direct or indirect effects involve more than one country

Transnational criminal organizations organized criminal groups that have a foreign component or that operate across national boundaries

Triangulation the implementation of multiple measures as a way to improve the validity or truthfulness of what one is trying to measure

Ujama a council of religious authorities who are deeply involved in most aspects of Saudi life, especially the administration of criminal justice, and who provide leadership to the *mutawa* or religious police

UNCJS the United Nations Surveys of Crime and Trends and Operations of Criminal Justice Systems; administered by the United Nations Centre for International Crime Prevention and consisting of data from member nations about crime rates and operations of criminal justice systems

Underlying values values that are not openly proclaimed but that nevertheless govern actions within the criminal justice system

Uniform Crime Reports (UCR) crime statistics collected by over 16,000 city, county, and state law enforcement agencies about twenty-nine types of crimes that have been brought to their attention with or without an arrest, and then compiled by the FBI into an annual published report

Unitary government governmental organization in which power is centralized

United Nations Minimal Standard Rules for the Treatment of Prisoners standards developed by the UN that describe the minimum conditions that are acceptable in prisons

Uygurs a Muslim minority group concentrated in the western region of China that is the only terrorist group that has any significant presence in China today

Voir dire the right of the prosecution and defense to ask potential jurors questions in order to decide whether to challenge for cause or peremptorily

Warnings penalties provided at the adjudication stage by the judge and usually accompanied by the threat of incarceration if the criminal behavior does not desist

Work-study schools facilities designed for juveniles who have caused trouble in schools and committed minor criminal offenses in China

Writ of mandamus an order of the court requiring public servants to do the duties that are part of their jobs

Yanda a major anticrime campaign initiated by the Communist party in China in the early 1980s in response to a perceived rise in violent crime

Works Cited

Abel, R. (1987). *The Legal Profession in England and Wales.* Oxford: Basil Blackwell.

Abraham, H. J. (1986). *The Judicial Process: An Introductory Analysis of the Courts of the United States, England, and France,* 5th ed. New York: Oxford University Press

Adler, F., G. O. W. Mueller, and W. S. Laufer. (1994). *Criminal Justice.* New York: McGraw-Hill

Adler, Freda. (1983). *Nations Not Obsessed with Crime.* Littleton, Colo.: Rothman

Agence French Press. (1999). Arab League's Anti-Terrorism Convention Comes into Force. May 11. Website: http://www.justinfo.net/html/news/1874.htm

Ai, Xue. (1989). New "People's Mediation Committee's Organic Rules" Promulgated in China. *Outlook Weekly,* 42: 10

Alderson, J. (1985). Police and the Social Order. In Roach and Thomanek, 1985

Al-Farsy, F. (1986). *Saudi Arabia.* London: Routledge and Kegan Paul

Alford, W. (1995). Tasseled Loafers for Barefoot Lawyers: Transformation and Tension in the World of Chinese Legal Workers. *China Quarterly,* 141: 27

Ali, B. (1985). Islamic Law and Crime: The Case of Saudi Arabia. *International Journal of Comparative and Applied Criminal Justice,* 9: 45–57

Ali, S. R., and J. J. Bowe. (1988). Terrorism in the Middle East. *International Journal of Comparative and Applied Criminal Justice,* 12(1)

Alobied, A. (1989). Police Functions and Organizations in Saudi Arabia. *Police Studies,* 10: 84–88

Al-Sagheer, M. F. (1994). Diya Legislation in Islamic Shari'a and Its Application in the Kingdom of Saudi Arabia. In Zvekic, 1994, pp. 80–94

Alvazzi del Frate, A., et al. (eds.). (1992). *Understanding Crime: Experiences of Crime and Crime Control.* Rome: UNICRI

American Correctional Association (ed.). (1987). *International Corrections: An Overview.* College Park, Md.: American Correctional Association

Ames, W. (1981). *Police and Community in Japan.* Berkeley: University of California Press

Amin, S. A. (1985a). *Islamic Law in the Contemporary World.* Glasgow: Royston

———. (1985b). *Middle East Legal Systems.* Glasgow: Royston

Amnesty International. (1999). *China: Open Letter from Amnesty International to European Union Governments on the Eve of EU-China Human Rights Dialogue.* Report ASA 17/08/99, February 4. Extracted from the Amnesty International Website: http://www.amnesty.org

———. (1989). *Jahresbericht.* Frankfurt-am-Main: Fisher Taschenbuch Verlag

———. (1998). *Japan: Abusive Punishments in Japanese Prisons.* Summary Report ASA 22/04/98, June. Extracted from the Amnesty International Website: http://www.amnesty.org

———. (1997). *Report 1997.* London: Amnesty International

Amnesty International Website. (1999): http://www.amnesty.org/ailib/intcam/dp/dpfacts.htm

Anderson, A. F. (1996). A Perspective on China's New Prison Law. *International Criminal Justice Review,* 6

Archer, D., and R. Gartner. (1984). *Violence and Crime in Cross-National Perspective.* New Haven, Conn.: Yale University Press

Arkin, S., et al. (eds.). (1988). *Prevention and Prosecution of Computer and High Technology Crime.* New York: Bender

Associated Press. (1999). Border Crackdown Blamed for Tension. July 30. World Justice Information Network: http://www.wjin.net/html/news/2367.htm

———. (1999). FBI Reports Drop in Crime Last Year. May 17

———. (1999). Japanese Mob Raising Fears, Concern. April 4. http://www.justinfo.net/html/news/1753.htm

———. (1999). U.S. Seeks Changes to International War Crimes Treaty. Aug. 10

Awad, A. M. (1982). The Rights of the Accused Under Islamic Criminal Procedure. In Bassiouni, 1982

Badr-el-Din, A. (1985). Islamic Law and Crime: The Case of Saudi Arabia. *International Journal of Comparative and Applied Criminal Justice,* 8(2): 45–56

Baker, B. G. (1982). Chinese Law in the Eighties: The Lawyer and the Criminal Process. *Albany Law Review,* 46: 751

Baldwin, J., and M. McConville. (1979). *Jury Trials.* Oxford: Oxford University Press

Barak-Glantz, I., and E. Johnson (eds.). (1983). *Comparative Criminology.* Beverly Hills, Calif.: Sage

Barghothi, J. I. (1996). International Terrorism in Historical Perspective. In Fields and Moore, 1996, pp. 83–97

Barnes, E. (1998). Protecting Public Transportation from Terrorists. *NIJ Journal,* March. U.S. Department of Justice. National Institute of Justice

Bassiouni, M. C. (1979). *The Criminal Justice System of the U.S.S.R.* Springfield, Ill.: Thomas

———. (ed.). (1982). *The Islamic Criminal Justice System.* New York: Oceana

———, and E. Vetere (eds.). (1998). *Organized Crime: A Compilation of U.N. Documents 1975–1998.* New York: Transnational

Bayley, D. H. (1991). Forces of Order: Policing in Modern Japan, 2nd ed. Berkeley: University of California Press

———. (1991). *Forces of Order: The Police in Japan.* Berkeley: University of California Press

———. (1996). Lessons in Order. In Heiner, 1996, pp. 3–14

———. (1985). *Patterns of Policing.* Rutgers, N.J.: Rutgers University Press

Becker, T. L. (1970). *Comparative Judicial Politics.* Chicago: Rand McNally

Bedford, S. (1961). *The Faces of Justice.* New York: Simon and Schuster

Belal, A. A. (1993). Procedural Safeguards in Islamic Law and Islamic Criminal Justice. Paper presented at the 11th International Congress on Criminology, Budapest, Hungary, August

Bellah, R. (1985). *Tokugawa Religion.* New York: Free Press

Bennett, R. (1990). *Correlates of Crime: A Study of 52 Nations, 1960–1984.* Ann Arbor, Mich.: ICPSR

———, and J. P. Lynch. (1990). Does a Difference Make a Difference? Comparing Cross-National Crime Indicators. *Criminology,* 28: 153–181

Bensinger, G. J. (1998). *Justice in Israel: The Criminal Justice System,* 3rd ed. Chicago: Loyola University Press

Benyon, J. (1997). The Developing System of Police Cooperation in the European Union. In McDonald, 1997, pp. 103–122

Berkeley, G. (1969). *The Democratic Policeman.* Boston: Beacon Press

Berman, H. (1963). *Justice in the USSR.* New York: Random House

Bernhardt, K., and P. Huang. (1994). *Civil Law in Qing and Republican China.* Stanford, Calif.: Stanford University Press

Bindzus, D. (1997). Introduction of the Japanese Treatment Program NAIKAN into Western Detention Facilities. Paper presented at the Academy of Criminal Justice Sciences Annual Meeting, Louisville, March

Black's Law Dictionary. (1979). 5th ed. St. Paul, Minn.: West

Block, A. (1983). *East Side, West Side: Organizing Crime in New York, 1930–1950.* New Brunswick, N.J.: Transaction Press

———, and W. Chambliss. (1981). *Organizing Crime.* New York: Elsevier

Blumstein, A. (1995). Prisons. In Wilson and Petersilia, 1995

Bodde, D., and C. Morris. (1967). *Law in Imperial China.* Cambridge, Mass.: Harvard University Press

Borders, E. E. (1999). The Palestinian Quest for Statehood and Security. *Crime and Justice International,* June: 5

Borricand, J. (1999). World Factbook—France: Wf-bcjfra. txt at blackstone.ojp.usdoj.gov

Bottoms, A. E., and I. McClean. (1976). *Defendants in the Criminal Process.* London: Routledge and Kegan Paul

Bracey, D. (1988). Like a Doctor to a Patient, Like a Prison to a Child: Corrections in the People's Republic of China. *The Prison Journal,* 68(1): 24–33

Bradford, T. (1995). $12 Million High-Tech Heist One of Largest Ever. *USA Today,* May 19, p. A3

Branigan, W. (1990). TV Series Stirs Up Debate on Murder of U.S. Drug Agent. *The Washington Post,* reprinted in Raleigh, N.C., *News and Observer,* Jan. 14, 1990, p. A15

Bresler, F. (1993). *INTERPOL.* Toronto: Penguin Books

Bridges, L. (1994). Normalizing Injustice: The Royal Commission on Criminal Justice. *Journal of Law and Society,* 21: 20–38

Brown, B. E., and R. C. Macridis (eds.). (1996). *Comparative Politics: Notes and Readings,* 8th ed. Belmont, Calif.: Wadsworth

Brown, J. (1996). Neighborhood Policing in West Berlin. In Heiner, 1996

Brown, R. M. (1979). Historical Patterns of American Violence. In Graham and Gurr, 1979

Bruguiere, J. L. (1997). International Counterterrorism Cooperation: The French Experience. In UNAFEI: Annual Report for 1996 and Resource Material Series No. 51. Tokyo: United Nations Asian and Far East Institute for the Prevention of Crime and Treatment of Offenders, pp. 309–327

Buck, W., and K. Pease. (1993). Cross-National Incarceration Comparisons Inherently Misleading. *Overcrowded Times,* 4(1): 5–6,17

Buckwalter, J. (ed.). (1990). *International Perspectives on Organized Crime.* Chicago: Office of International Criminal Justice

Burden, O. (1991). The Mafia Under Siege. *CJ International,* April/May: 5

Bureau of Justice Statistics. (1998). Death Penalty Information Center. Washington, D.C.: U.S. Department of Justice

——— . (1994). *Guns and Crime.* Washington, D.C.: U.S. Government Printing Office

——— . (1988). *Report to the Nation on Crime and Justice,* 2nd ed. Washington, D.C.: Department of Justice

——— . (1991). *Violent Crime in the United States.* Washington, D.C.: Department of Justice

Burger, W. (1968). Adversarial and Nonadversarial Systems. Presented at a conference at the Center for the Study of Democratic Institutions, Washington, D.C., November

Burkins, G. (1995). Deadly Crime Wave Engulfs S. Africa Following the End of Apartheid Era. *Buffalo News,* Sept. 24, p. 24

Burmham, R. W. (1997). History of World Crime Surveys, In *Global Report on Crime and Justice,* 1999, p. 2

Byrne, J. M., A. J. Lurigio, and J. Petersilia (eds.). (1992). *Smart Sentencing: The Emergence of Intermediate Sanctions.* Newbury Park, Calif.: Sage

Cao Guanghui. (1995). Bringing Police in Hunan Province to Account: Before and After. *Outlook Weekly Beijing,* 49

Cappelletti, M. (1971). *Judicial Review in the Contemporary World.* New York: Bobbs-Merrill

——— , and W. Cohen. (1979). *Comparative Constitutional Law.* New York: Bobbs-Merrill

Carbonneau, T. (1980). The French Legal Studies Curriculum. *McGill Law Journal,* 25(445). Reprinted in Glendon, Gordon, and Osakwe, 1985, p. 1401

Castberg, A. (1990). *Japanese Criminal Justice.* New York: Praeger

Cerny, P. (1981). France: Non-Terrorism and the Politics of Repressive Tolerance. In Lodge, 1981

Charters, D. (ed.). (1991). *Democratic Response to International Terrorism.* Ardsley-on-Hudson, N.Y.: Transnational

Chen, D. (1993). Inmates' Human Rights in China. *Outlook Weekly,* 9: 8

Chenguang, W., and Z. Xianchu. (1997). *Introduction to Chinese Law.* Hong Kong: Sweet and Maxwell Asia Press

China Law Yearbook. (1997). Beijing: China Law Yearbook Publishing House

CIA. (1999a). World Factbook—Japan: www.cia.gov/cia/publications/factbook/gm.html

——— . (1999b). World Factbook—Germany: www.cia.gov/cia/publications/factbook/ja.html

——— . (1998). World Factbook—United Kingdom: www.cia.gov/cia/publications/factbook/uk.html

Clear, T. R., and G. F. Cole. (2000). *American Corrections.* Belmont, Calif.: West/Wadsworth ITP

Clear, T. R., and H. R. Dammer. (1999). *Managing the Offender in the Community.* Belmont, Calif.: Wadsworth

Clifford, W. (1976). *Crime Control in Japan.* Lexington, Mass.: Lexington Books

Cochran, J. (1987). The Variable Effects of Religiosity on Deviant Behavior. Doctoral dissertation. Ann Arbor: University of Michigan Press

Committee on Foreign Affairs. (1984). *Forced Labor in the Soviet Union.* Subcommittee on Human Rights and International Organizations, 98th Congress, First Session, Nov. 9, 1983. Washington D.C.: U.S. Government Printing Office

Confucius. (1989). *The Analects of Confucius.* A. Waley (trans.). New York: Vantage Books

Conner, A. (1994). Lawyers and the Legal Profession During the Republican Period. In Bernhardt and Huang, 1994

Constantine, T. (1995). Keynote address before the 17th Annual International Asian Crime Conference, Boston, March 8

Cornish, W. R. (1968). *The Jury.* London: Penguin Books

Correction Bureau. (1995). *Correctional Institutions in Japan.* Tokyo: Ministry of Justice

Cusimano, M. K. (ed.). (2000). *Beyond Sovereignty: Issues for a Global Agenda.* New York: Bedford/St. Martin's Press

Damaska, M. (1986). *The Faces of Justice and State Authority.* New Haven, Conn.: Yale University Press

Dammer, H. R. (1996). Rehabilitation in German Prisons. *Journal of Offender Rehabilitation,* 24(1–2): 1–10

Danelski, D. (1971). The Chicago Conspiracy Trial. In T. Becker (ed.). *Political Trials.* Indianapolis, Ind.: Bobbs-Merrill

Daniszewski, J. (1997). Judging the Divine Law of Islam. *Los Angeles Times,* Jan. 31, p. A1

David, R. (1972). *French Law: Its Structure, Sources, and Methodology.* Baton Rouge: Louisiana State University Press

David, R., and J. C. Brierly. (1978). *Major Legal Systems in the World Today.* New York: Free Press

Davidson, R., and Z. Wang. (1996). The Court System in the People's Republic of China with a Case Study of a Criminal Trial. In Ebbe, 1996

———, and J. C. Brierly. (1978). *Major Legal Systems in the World Today.* New York: Free Press

Davis, K. C. (ed.). *Discretionary Justice in Europe and America.* Urbana: University of Illinois Press

Dean, M. (1997). *The Japanese Legal System: Text and Materials.* London: Cavendish

Della Porta, D. (1997). Introduction: Democracy and Corruption. In Della Porta and Meny, 1997

———, and Y. Meny. (eds.). (1997). *Democracy and Corruption in Europe.* London: Pinter Books

Dennis, I. (1995). The Criminal Justice and Public Order Act of 1994: The Evidence Provisions. *Criminal Law Review:* 4–18

Der Spiegel. (1991). Wir brauchen jetzt 'ne Krache. 42: 28–45

Deutch, K. (1996). Systems Theory and Comparative Analysis. In Brown and Macridis, 1996

Doob, A., and J. Roberts. (1988). Public Punitiveness and Public Knowledge of the Facts. In Walker and Hough, 1988

Dunkel, F. (1992). The Development of Drug-Related Crime and Drug Control in Germany. *International Journal of Comparative and Applied Criminal Justice,* 16(1)

Durkheim, E. (1947). *The Division of Labor in Society.* Glencoe, Ill.: Free Press

Dutton, M. (1992). *Policing and Punishment in China: From Patriarchy to "the People."* New York: Cambridge University Press

Ebbe, O. N. I. (ed.). (1996). *Comparative and International Justice Systems.* Newton, Mass.: Butterworth-Heinemann

———. (1996). The Judiciary and Criminal Procedure in Nigeria. In Ebbe, 1996

Eckholm, E., and D. Chen. (1999). Kin of the Dead Seeking Inquiry on Tiananmen Square Incident. *New York Times,* June 1, p. A1

The Economist. (1991). March 2, p. 53

The Economist. (n.d.). The New Trade in Humans, p. 45

Ehrmann, H. (1976). *Comparative Legal Cultures.* Englewood Cliffs, N.J.: Prentice-Hall

El Paso Information Center. (1998). *Worldwide Quarterly Threat.* Washington, D.C.: U.S. Government Printing Office

El Paso Information Center. (1999). *Worldwide Quarterly Threat.* Washington, D.C.: U.S. Government Printing Office

European Union. (1996). *Situation Report on Organised Crime in the EU 1995.* 10555/1/96. Brussels: EU

Fairchild, E. (1988). *German Police.* Springfield, Ill.: Thomas

Fan, Chongyi. (ed.). (1997). *Chinese Criminal Procedural Law.* Beijing: Chinese University Law Publishing House

Fang, B. (1999). China, at 50, on a Long March to Modernity. *U.S. News & World Report,* Oct. 4

Farah, D. (1997). Russian Mob, Drug Cartels Joining Forces. *Washington Post,* Sept. 29, p. A1

Federal Bureau of Investigation. (1997). *Terrorism in the United States, 1995.* Washington, D.C.: U.S. Government Printing Office

Feest, J., and H. M. Weber. (1998). Germany: Ups and Downs in the Resort to Imprisonment—Strategic or Unplanned Outcomes? In Weiss and South, 1998, pp. 233–262

Feest, J. (1982). *Report on the West German Prison System.* Breman: University of Bremen Research Program in Social Problems

Fields, C. B., and R. H. Moore, Jr. (eds.). (1996). *Comparative Criminal Justice: Traditional and Nontraditional Systems of Law and Control.* Prospect Heights, Ill.: Waveland Press

Finckenauer, J. O., and E. J. Waring. (1998). *Russian Mafia in America: Immigration, Culture and Crime.* Boston: Northeastern University Press

Fooner, M. (1989). *INTERPOL.* New York: Plenum Press

Foucault, M. (1979). *Discipline and Punish.* Harmondsworth, UK: Penguin Books

———. (ed.). (1975). *I, Pierre Riviere* . . . Lincoln: University of Nebraska Press

Fourth United Nations Survey of Crime Trends and Operations of Criminal Justice Systems. (1995). A/CONF.169/15/Add.1, 4 April

Fowler, N. (1979). *After the Riots: The Police in Europe.* London: Davis-Poynter

Fox, L. (1952). *English Prisons and Borstal Systems.* London: Routledge and Kegan Paul

Frase, R. (1990). Comparative Criminal Justice as a Guide to American Law Reform: How the French Do It, How Can We Find Out, and Why Should We Care? *California Law Review,* 78: 542–683

———, and T. Weigend. (1992). How the Germans Do It—Comparisons with American Criminal Justice. Paper presented at the American Society of Criminology, New Orleans, November

Frase, R. (1988). In Lock and Frase, 1988, pp. 1–40

Garland, D. (1990). *Punishment and Modern Society.* Oxford: Clarendon

Geck, W. (1977). The Reform of Legal Education in the Federal Republic of Germany. *American Journal of Comparative Law,* 25(86). Reprinted in Glendon, Gordon, and Osakwe, 1985

Gelatt, T. (1991). Lawyers in China: The Past Decade and Beyond. *New York University Journal of International Law and Politics,* 23: 753

Glendon, M. A., M. Gordon, and C. Osakwe. (1985). *Comparative Legal Traditions.* St. Paul, Minn.: West

Global Report on Crime and Justice. (1999). United Nations Office for Drug Control and Crime Prevention, Centre for International Crime Prevention. G. Newman (ed.). New York: Oxford University Press

Graham, J., and B. Bowling. (1996). *Young People and Crime.* Home Office Research Study No. 145, London

Graham, M., and T. R. Gurr (eds.). (1979). *Violence in America.* Beverly Hills, Calif.: Sage

Graham, M. (1983). *Tightening the Reins of Justice in America.* Westport, Conn.: Greenwood Press

Grebing, G. (1978). Die Geldstrafe in rechtvergleichender Darstellung. In Jeschek and Grebing, 1978

Gregory, F. (1985). The British Police System. In Roach and Thomanek, 1985

Griffith, J. (1991). *The Politics of the Judiciary,* 4th ed. Hammersmith, UK: Fontana Press

Grove, N. (1997). *Atlas of World History.* Washington, D.C.: National Geographic Society

The Guardian. (1999). Sept. 30

Guo, J., G. Xiang, W. Zongxian, X. Zhangun, P. Xiaohui, and L. Shuangshuang. (1999). World Factbook of Criminal Justice Systems: China: http://www.ojp.usdoj.gov/bjs/pub/ascii/wfbcjchi.txt

Gurr, T. R. (1976). *Rogues, Rebels, and Reformers.* Beverly Hills, Calif.: Sage

Gutteridge, W. (ed.). (1986). *The New Terrorism.* London: Mansell

Hagan, F. (1997). *Political Crime: Ideology and Criminology.* Needham Heights, Mass.: Allyn and Bacon

Hagan, F. E. (2000). *Research Methods in Criminal Justice and Criminology,* 5th ed. Needham Heights, Mass.: Allyn and Bacon

Haley, J. (1978). The Myth of the Reluctant Litigant. *Journal of Japanese Studies,* 4(2): 359

Hamai, K., R. Ville, R. Harris, M. Hough, and U. Zvekic (eds.). (1995). *Probation Around the World: A Comparative Study.* London: Routledge

Harris, J. F. (1995). UN Anniversary Celebration Opens with Notes of Discord: Clinton Urges Global Effort Against Crime. *Washington Post,* Oct. 23, pp. A1, A12

Hayward, J. E. S. (1983). *Governing France.* London: Weidenfeld and Nicolson

Heather, N., F. Nadelman, and P. O'Hare (eds.). (1993). *Psychoactive Drugs and Harm Reduction: From Faith to Science.* London: Whurr

Heilbrunn, J. (1998). San Francisco Diarist. *New Republic,* June 1, p. 42

Heiner, R. (ed.). (1996). *Criminology: A Cross-Cultural Perspective.* St. Paul, Minn.: West

Herrmann, J. (1987). The Federal Republic of Germany. In Cole, Frankowski, and Gertz, 1987

———. (1976). The German Prosecutor. In Davis, 1976

Hess, H. (1986). The Traditional Sicilian Mafia. In Kelly, 1986

HEUNI. (1999). *Profiles of Criminal Justice Systems in Europe and North America, 1990–1994.* K. Kangaspunta, M. Jousten, N. Ollus, and S. Nevala (eds.). Helsinki: European Institute for Crime Prevention and Control (HEUNI)

Hillsman, B., G. Mahoney, G. Cole, and M. Auchter. (1987). *Fines.* Washington, D.C.: National Institute of Justice

Hindus, M. (1980). *Prison and Plantation.* Chapel Hill: University of North Carolina Press

Hirota, T. (1997). A Day in the Life of a Tokyo Police Officer. In Global Report on Crime and Justice, 1999

Hitchner, D. G., and C. Levine. (1981). *Comparative Government and Politics.* New York: Harper & Row

Hobsbawm, E. (1981). *Bandits.* New York, Pantheon

Hofer, P. J., and B. S. Meierhofer. (1988). *Home Confinement.* Washington, D.C.: Federal Judicial Center

Holdaway, S. (1990). *Recruiting a Multiracial Police Force.* London: H.M.S.O.

Holden-Rhodes, J. F. (1992). *Sharing the Secrets. Open Source Intelligence and the War on Drugs.* Westport, Conn.: Praeger

Holland, K. (1988). Germany. In Waltman and Holland, 1988

Holmes, O. W. (1923). *The Common Law.* Boston: Little, Brown

Home Office. (1996). In NACRO (National Association for Care and Resettlement of Offenders), *Criminal Justice Digest,* 89: 8

Horton, C. (1995). *Policing Policy in France.* London: Policy Studies Institute

Huang, W., and S. Wilson. (1993). Are International Murder Data Valid and Reliable? Some Evidence to Support the Use of Interpol Data. *International Journal of Comparative and Applied Criminal Justice,* 17(1): 77–89

Hudson, J., and B. Galaway. (1990). Community Service: Toward Program Definition. *Federal Probation Magazine,* 54(2): 3–10

——— . (1975). *Considering the Victim.* Springfield, Ill.: Thomas, pp. xix–xx

Human Rights Watch/Asia. (1995). *Prison Conditions in Japan.* New York: Human Rights Watch

Human Rights Watch, China. (1999): http://www.hrw.org/wr2k/Asia-03.htm

Human Rights Watch. (1993). *Global Report on Prisons 1993.* New York: Human Rights Watch, p. xxxi

Human Rights Watch, Saudi Arabia. (1999): http://www.hrw.org/wr2k/ Mena-08.htm

Human Rights Watch Website. (1999): http://www.hrw.org/wk2k/Issues-12.htm

Human Rights Watch. (1998). *World Report 1998.* New York: Yale University Press

Ignatius, D. (2000). Global Corruption Threatens the 21st Century. *Buffalo News,* reprinted in *The Washington Post,* Jan. 9, p. H5

Ingraham, B. (1987). *The Structure of Criminal Procedures.* Westport, Conn.: Greenwood Press

INL (International Narcotics and Law Enforcement Affairs). (2000). *Certification Decisions.* Washington, D.C.: U.S. Government Printing Office

International Court of Justice, 23 March 1998. http://www.un.org/Overview/Organs/icj.html

International Organization for Migration. (1996). Trafficking and Prostitution: The Growing Exploitation of Migrant Women from Central and Eastern Europe. Geneva: International Organization for Migration

INTERPOL. (1997). *International Crime Statistics.* Lyons, France: INTERPOL

Inter Press Service. (1999). Crime Takes Heavy Toll on Colombian Economy According to Report. May 13

Inter Press Service. (1999). U.S. Pushes Arms Trafficking Agreement. July 22. World Justice Information Network: http://www.wjin.net/html/news/2322.htm

Itar-Tass News Agency. (1999). 11,000 Crimes Committed in Leningrad Region in 1999. May 2

Itoh, H. (1988). Japan. In Waltman and Holland, 1988

Iwai, H. (1986). Organized Crime in Japan. In Kelly, 1986

Jackson, D. (1999). *US Criticism of China Rings Hollow in US Prisons. Boston Globe,* March 3

Jenkins, B. (1978). International Terrorism: Trends and Potentialities. *Journal of International Affairs,* 32(1): 115–124

Jenkins, P. (1987). Prison Crowding: A Cross-National Study. In American Correctional Association, 1987

Jeschek, H., and G. Grebing (eds.). (1978). *Die Geldstrafe in deutchen und auslaendischen Recht.* Baden-Baden: Nomos Verlag

Jiahong, H., and J. R. Waltz. (1995). *Criminal Prosecution in the People's Republic of China and the United States: A Comparative Study.* Beijing: China Procuratorial Press

Jiao, A. Y. (1995). Community Policing and Community Mutuality: A Comparative Analysis of American and Chinese Police Reforms. *Police Studies,* 18(3/4)

Jinfeng, D. (1997). Police-Public Relations—A Chinese View. *The Australian and New Zealand Journal of Criminology,* 30(1): 87–94

Johnson, C. Russian Organized Crime. In Williams et al., 1995

Johnson, E. (1991). Yakusa (Criminal Gangs): Characteristics and Management in Prison. *CJ International,* Jan./Feb.

Johnson, E. H. (1996). Japanese Version of Community Corrections: Volunteer Probation Officers and Hostels. In Ebbe, 1996, pp. 185–198

Johnson, H. A. (1988). *History of Criminal Justice.* Cincinnati: Anderson

Johnson, K. (1999). Scotland Yard Confounded by Crisis of Confidence. *USA Today,* Aug. 25

Jordan, M., (1996). Japan's Bar Exam: Would-Be Lawyers Fail, Fail Again. *International Herald Tribune,* Feb. 15, p. 4

Journal of Commerce. (1998). China on Alert Against Muslim Bombings. Feb. 5, p. A3

Journes, C. (1993). The Structure of the French Police System: Is the French Police a National Force? *International Journal of the Sociology of the Law,* 21: 281–287

Jousten, M., and U. Zvekic. (1994). Noncustodial Sanctions: Comparative Overview. In Zvekic, 1994, pp. 1–42

Jousten, M. (1994). Victimology and Victim Policy in Europe. *The Criminologist,* 19(3)

Junger-Tas, J., G. Terlouw, and M. Klien (eds.). (1994). *Delinquent Behavior of Young People in the Western World—First Results of the International Self-Report Delinquency Study.* Amsterdam: Kluger

Juviler, P. (1976). *Revolutionary Law and Order.* New York: Free Press

Kadish, S. H. (ed.). (1983). *Encyclopedia of Crime and Justice,* Vol. 1. New York: Free Press

Kaiser, G. (1984). *Prison Systems and Correctional Laws.* Dobbs Ferry, N.Y.: Transnational Press

Kalish, C. (1988). International Crime Rates. *BJS Special Report.* Washington, D.C.: U.S. Department of Justice, May

Kalmthout, A., and P. Tak. (1988). *Sanctions Systems in the Member States of the Council of Europe—Part I.* Norwell, Mass.: Kluwer Law and Taxation

Kane, H. (2000). Leaving Home: The Flow of Refugees. In Cusimano, 2000

Kaplan, D., and A. Dubro. (1986). *Yakusa.* Reading, Mass.: Addison-Wesley

Karl, D. J. (1991). Islamic Law in Saudi Arabia: What Foreign Attorneys Should Know. *George Washington Journal of International Law and Economics,* 25(1): 131–170

Kegley, C. W. (ed.). (1990). *International Terrorism: Characteristics, Causes, Controls.* New York: St. Martin's Press

Keir, D., and F. Lawson. (1967). *Cases in Constitutional Law,* 5th ed. Oxford: Clarendon Press

Kelly, R. (ed.). (1986). *Organized Crime: A Global Perspective.* Totowa, N.J.: Rowan and Littlefield

Kommers, D. (1976). *Judicial Politics in West Germany.* Beverly Hills, Calif.: Sage

Koshi, G. (1970). *The Japanese Legal Adviser.* Rutland, Vt.: Tuttle

Kostiner, J. (1987). The Rise and Fall of Militant Opposition Movements in the Arabian Peninsula. In Kurz, 1987

Kramer, M. (1987). The Structure of Shi'ite Terrorism. In Kurz, 1987

Kratcoski, P. C. (1999). Policing of Public Order: A World Perspective. *Crime and Justice International,* Nov.: 11

Kristof, N. (1995). Japanese Say No to Crime: Tough Methods, at a Price. *New York Times,* March 14, p. 1

Krose, T. R. (1999). House of Lords Itself Could Fall After Ousters. *USA Today,* Oct. 21, p. A21

Kuhn, A. (1992). Attitudes Toward Punishment. In del Frate et al., 1992

———. (1996). Incarceration Rates: Europe Versus the United States. *European Journal on Criminal Policy and Research,* 4(3): 46–73

———. (1994). What Can We Do About Prison Overcrowding. *European Journal on Criminal Policy and Research,* 2(4): 101–106

Kupperman, R., and D. Trent. (1979). *Terrorism: Threat, Reality, and Response.* Stanford, Calif.: Hoover Institution Press

Kurz, A. (ed.). (1987). *Contemporary Trends in World Terrorism.* New York: Praeger

Kyodo News International. (1994). Japan's Organized Crime Infiltrating South China. Aug. 15

Laing, L., M. Vernon, S. Eldersveld, J. Meisel, and J. Pollock (eds.). (1950). *Sourcebook in European Governments.* New York: Sloane

Langbein, J. (1977). *Comparative Criminal Procedure: Germany.* St. Paul, Minn.: West

Lavy, D. (1990). Interpol's Role in Combating Organized Crime. In Buckwalter, 1990

Lawton, F. (1991). Confession Pressures Must Stop. *CJ International,* 47(2): 23

Lawyers Committee. (1994). *Criminal Justice with Chinese Characteristics.* New York: Lawyers Committee

———. (1998). *Wrongs and Rights: A Human Rights Analysis of China's Revised Criminal Law.* New York: Lawyers Committee

Lawyers Committee for Human Rights. (1994). *Criminal Justice with Chinese Characteristics.* New York: Lawyers Committee for Human Rights

Lawyers Committee for Human Rights. (1998). *Frequently Asked Questions About the International Criminal Court.* New York: Lawyers Committee for Human Rights

Lawyers Committee for Human Rights. (1998). *Lawyers in China: Obstacles to Independence and the Defense of Rights.* New York: Lawyers Committee for Human Rights

Lawyers Committee for Human Rights. (1996). *Opening to Reform?: An Analysis of China's Revised Criminal Procedure Law.* New York: Lawyers Committee for Human Rights

Lawyers Committee for Human Rights. (1995). *Prosecuting War Crimes in the Former Yugoslavia.* New York: Lawyers Committee for Human Rights

Leng, S., and H. Chiu. (1985). *Criminal Justice in Post-Mao China.* Albany: SUNY Press .

Leng, S. (1982). Criminal Justice in Post-Mao China: Some Preliminary Observations. *The Journal of Criminal Law and Criminology,* 73: 204–237

Levy, L. (1969). *Essays on the Making of the Constitution.* New York: Oxford University Press

Lewis, C. (1997). Difficulties in Interpreting and Recording Crime Statistics. In *Global Report on Crime and Justice,* 1999, p. 43

——— . (1999). Police Records of Crime. In *Global Report on Crime and Justice,* 1999, p. 55

Li, Z. (1997). General Introduction of Chinese Police. Speech presented at the 19th Senior Policing Professionalization Conference, Beijing

Liebesny, H. (1975). *The Law of the Near and Middle East.* Albany: SUNY Press

Lilly, J. R. (1995). Electronic Monitoring in the United States. In Tonry and Hamilton, 1995, pp. 112–120

Lippman, M., S. McConville, and M. Yerushalmi. (1988). *Islamic Criminal Law and Procedure,* New York: Praeger

Liu, W., and Situ, Y. (1999). Criminal Courts in China Transition: Inquisitorial Procedure to Adversarial Procedure? *Crime and Justice International,* Feb.: 13–21

Lock, G. L., and R. S. Frase. (1998). *The French Code of Criminal Procedure.* Littleton, Colo.: Rothman

Lodge, J. (ed.). (1981). *Terrorism: A Challenge to the State.* New York: St. Martin's Press

Longworth, R. C. (1990). Perjury, Abuse of Prisoners Lead to Criticism of British Police. *CJ International,* 6(5): 19

López-Ray, M. (1970). *Crime: An Analytical Appraisal.* New York: Praeger

Los Angeles Times. (2000). Clinton Administration Beefs Up Cybercrime-fighting Efforts. Jan. 11. World Justice Information Network: http://www.wjin.net/html/news/3368.htm

Lott, J. R., Jr. (1998). *More Guns, Less Crime.* Chicago: University of Chicago Press

Luban, D. (1988). *Lawyers and Justice.* Princeton, N.J.: Princeton University Press

Lubman, S. (1983). Comparative Criminal Law and Enforcement: China. In Kadish, 1983

Luney, P. (1990). The Judiciary: Its Organization and Status in the Parliamentary System. *Law and Contemporary Problems,* 53(1): 135–162

Lynch, J. (1995). Crime in International Perspective. In Wilson and Petersilia, 1995, pp. 11–38

Lynch, J. P. (1988). A Comparison of Prison Use in England, Canada, West Germany, and the United States: A Limited Test of the Punitive Hypothesis. *Journal of Criminal Law and Criminology,* 79: 180–217

——— . (1993). A Cross-National Comparison of the Length of Custodial Sentences for Serious Crimes. *Justice Quarterly,* 10(4)

Ma, Y. (1995). Crime in China: Characteristics, Causes, and Control Strategies. *International Journal of Comparative and Applied Criminal Justice,* 19(2)

MacCoun, R., A Saiger, J. P. Kahan, and P. Reuter. (1993). Drug Policies and Problems: The Promises and Pitfalls of Cross-national Comparisons. In Heather, Nadelman, and O'Hare, 1993

Malone, M. (1989). The Enrique Camarena Case: A Forensic Nightmare. *FBI Law Enforcement Bulletin,* Sept.

Mandel-Campbell, A. (2000). Blood on the Border. *U.S. News & World Report,* March 13

Mansour, A. (1982). Hudud Crimes. In Bassiouni, 1982

Manzel, T. (1996). A Basic Introduction to the Complex Topic of Money Laundering. *Organized Crime Registry,* Feb. 24

Marenin, O. (ed.). (1996). *Policing Change, Changing Police: International Perspectives.* New York: Garland

Maruta, T. (1989). The Rise and Fall of the Japanese Jury System. Presented at the annual meeting of the Law and Society Association, June

Mason, G. (1999). British Police Embark on Ethnic Recruitment Campaign. *Blue Line Magazine,* Aug./Sept.

Matherson, M. (1988). Chinese Triads: The Oriental Mafia. *CJ International,* May/June

Mauro, T. (1999). Death Penalty on High Court's Minds. *USA Today,* Nov. 15, p. A6

Maxon-Browne, E. (1981). Terrorism in Northern Ireland. In Lodge, 1981

Mayhew, P., P. Elliot, and L. Dowds. (1989). *The 1988 British Crime Survey.* London: H.M.S.O.

McAllister, W. B. (1991). Conflicts of Interest in the International Drug Control System. *Journal of Policy History,* 3(4): 494–517

McClean, I. (1981). *The Crown Court—Pattern of Sentencing.* Chichester and London: Rose

McDonald, D. C. (1992). Punishing Labor Unpaid Community Service as a Criminal Sentence. In Byrne, Lurigio, and Petersilia, 1992

McDonald, F. (1998). Biological Terrorism: The Threat and the Response. In Moors and Ward, 1998

McDonald, W. F. (1997). Crime and Justice in the Global Village: Towards Global Criminology. In McDonald, 1997

———— (ed.). (1997). *Crime and Law Enforcement in the Global Village.* Cincinnati: Anderson

———— . (1997). Illegal Immigration: Crime, Ramifications, and Control (The American Experience). In McDonald, 1997, pp. 65–86

McWhinney, E. (1965). *Judicial Review,* 4th ed. Toronto: University of Toronto Press

———— . (1986). *Supreme Courts and Judicial Lawmaking: Constitutional Tribunals and Constitutional Review.* Dordrect: Martinus Nijhoff

Melossi, D., and M. Pavarini. (1981). *The Prison and the Factory.* New York: Macmillan

Merryman, J. H. (1985). *The Civil Law Tradition.* Stanford, Calif.: Stanford University Press

Metz, H. C. (1993). *Saudi Arabia: A Country Study,* 5th ed. Washington, D.C.: Federal Research Division, Library of Congress

Migration News (Russia). (1994). Dec. 11

Miller, W. (1977). *Cops and Bobbies.* Chicago: University of Chicago Press

Minister of the Interior. (1993). Aspects of the Observed Criminality in France in 1992. Paris: Minister of the Interior

Minister of Justice. (1999). *Key Figures of the Prison Service.* Paris: Central Headquarters of the Prison Service

Minister of Justice. (1998). *The Prison Service in France.* Paris: Central Headquarters of the Prison Service

Ministry of Justice. (1989). *Summary of the White Paper on Crime.* Tokyo: Ministry of Justice

Ministry of Public Security. (1994). *Policing in China.* Beijing: Ministry of Public Security

Moore, R. (1987). Courts, Law, Justice, and Criminal Trials in Saudi Arabia. *International Journal of Comparative and Applied Criminal Justice,* 11(1): 61–67

Moore, R. Jr. (1996). Islamic Legal Systems: Traditional (Saudi Arabia), Contemporary (Bahrain), and Evolving (Pakistan). In Fields and Moore, 1996

Moors, C., and R. Ward. (eds.). (1998). *Terrorism and the New World Order.* Chicago: University of Illinois, Office of International Criminal Justice

Moriyama, T. (1999). Japan. World Factbook of Criminal Justice Website: http://wfbcjjap.txt@blackstone. ojp.usdoj.gov

Morris, N. (1991). *Crime and Crime Control: Past, Present, and Future.* Seoul: Korean Institute of Criminology

Mortimer, John. (1978). *Rumpole of the Bailey.* London: Penguin Books

Morton, F. (1988). Judicial Review in France. *American Journal of Comparative Law,* 36: 89–110

Mueller, G., and F. LePoole-Griffiths. (1969). *Comparative Criminal Procedure.* New York: New York University Press

Mueller, G. O. W., Enforcing International Criminal Justice, In McDonald, 1997, pp. 139–150

Mueller, G. O. W., and F. Adler. (1997). Gauging Transnational Criminality: A New Challenge for the UN Survey of Crime Trends and UNCJS. In *Global Report on Crime and Justice,* 1999, p. 21

———— . (1996). Globalization and Criminal Justice: A Prologue. In Fields and Moore, 1996

Murty, K. S., J. B. Roebuck, and M. A. Almolhem. (1991). Profile of Adult Offenders in Damman Central Prison, Saudi Arabia. *International Journal of Comparative and Applied Criminal Justice,* 15(1): 89–97

Nader, L., and P. Parnell. (1983). Comparative Criminal Law and Enforcement: Preliterate Societies. In Kadish, 1983

Nader, M. M. J. (1990). *Aspects of Saudi Arabian Law.* Riyadh: Nader

Nakone, O. (1973). *Japanese Society.* Tokyo: Tuttle

National Police Agency of Japan. (1999). June 11: http://www.npa.go.jp/keibi2/it6.htm

New York Times. (1999). Police in China Say Fatal Blast Was Pipe Bomb. Jan. 1, p. A6

NIJ (National Institute of Justice). (1998). *Drug Use Forecast 1998.* Office of Justice Programs. Washington, D.C.: U.S. Government Printing Office

Nullis, C. (1997). Swiss Heroin Program Cuts Crime. *Philadelphia Inquirer,* July 11, p. A20

Oberheim, R. (1985). *Gefaengnisueberfuellung.* Frankfurt-am-Main: Lang

O'Donnell, E. (1990). The Shah Bano Case (1985) and the Muslim Women Act. Unpublished master's thesis, Department of Political Science and Public Administration, North Carolina State University

Olivero, J. (1991). The War on Drugs and Mexican Prisons. *CJ The Americas,* April/May

Omestad, T. (1997). The Brief for a World Court. *U.S. News & World Report,* 6 Oct., pp. 52–54

Opolot, J. (1986). Organized Crime As It Emerges in Sections of Africa. In Kelly, 1986

Organic Law for the People's Procuracies. (1979). Foreign Broadcast Service, People's Republic of China, Supp. 019, July

Page, S. (1999). U.S. to Increase Help for Mexico. *USA Today,* Feb. 15, p. A8

Passas, N. (1997). Corruption: An Old Crime in a New World. In *Global Report on Crime and Justice,* 1997, p. 227

Penal Reform International Website. (1999): http://www.penalreform.org

Phillips, C., G. Cox, and K. Pease. (1999). *World Factbook of Criminal Justice Systems: England and Wales.* Website: http://blackstone.ojp.usdoj.gov/bjs/pub/ascii/wfbcjeng.txt

Platek, M. (1994). AIDS in Prisons in Poland. In Thomas and Moerings, 1996

Plucknett, T. (1940). *A Concise History of the Common Law.* London: Butterworth

Poland, J. (1988). *Understanding Terrorism.* Englewood Cliffs, N.J.: Prentice-Hall

Posner, G. (1988). *Warlords of Crime.* New York: McGraw-Hill

Prall, S. (1966). *The Agitation for Law Reform During the Puritan Revolution, 1640–1660.* The Hague: Martinus Nijhoff

Pranis, K. (1993). Restorative Justice: Back to the Future in Criminal Justice. Working paper, Minnesota Citizens Council, Minneapolis

Quah, S., and J. Quah. (1987). *Friends in Blue: The Police and the Public in Singapore.* Singapore: Oxford University Press

Radio Free Europe. (2000). Official Corruption on the Rise in Russia. March 3. World Justice Information Network: http://www.wjin.net/html/news/3708.htm

Rahim, M. A. (1986). *On the Issue of International Comparison of "Prison Population" and "Use of Imprisonment."* Report no. 1986-41. From the Statistics Division, Programs Branch. Ottawa: Ministry of the Solicitor General

Ramsey, K. (1998). Beneath the Dragon's Shadow: Canadian Investigators Face-Off with Hong Kong Triads. *RCMP Gazette,* 60(4)

Rapoport, D. (ed.). (1988). *Inside Terrorist Organizations.* New York: Columbia University Press

Rapoport, D. C. (1984). Fear and Trembling: Terrorism in Three Religious Traditions. *American Political Science Review,* 78: 658–677

Reed, J. S. (1974). *The Enduring South.* Chapel Hill: University of North Carolina Press

Reichel, P. (1999). *Comparative Criminal Justice Systems: A Topical Approach.* Englewood Cliffs, N.J.: Prentice-Hall

Reiner, R. (1985). *The Politics of the Police.* New York: St. Martin's Press

Research and Training Institute. (1989). *Summary of the White Paper on Crime.* Tokyo: Ministry of Justice

Research and Training Institute. (1990). *Summary of the White Paper on Crime.* Tokyo: Ministry of Justice

Reuschemeyer, D. (1973). *Lawyers and Their Society.* Cambridge, Mass.: Harvard University Press

Richards, J. R. (1999). *Transnational Criminal Organizations, Cybercrime, and Money Laundering.* Boca Raton, Fla.: CRC Press

Richards, M. (1996). Policing the Community: An English Perspective. Paper presented at the Annual Meeting of the Academy of Criminal Justice Sciences, Las Vegas, March

Rickett, A., and A. Rickett. (1973). *Prisoners of Liberation.* New York: Doubleday

Roach, J. (1985). The French Police. In Roach and Thomanek, 1985

————, and J. Thomanek (eds.). (1985). *Police and Public Order in Europe.* London: Croom-Helm

Robertson, A. H. (1977). *Human Rights in Europe.* Dobbs Ferry, N.Y.: Oceana

Robinson, L. (1999). Mexican Mayhem. *U.S. News & World Report,* July 12, p. 39

Rojek, D. G. (1996). Changing Directions in Chinese Society. In Fields and Moore, 1996

Rosch, J. (1987). Institutionalizing Mediation. *Law and Society Review,* 21(2)

Rosenberg, C. (1968). *The Trial of the Assassin Guiteau.* Chicago: University of Chicago Press

Rosenstock, R. B. (1994). 1994 McLean Lecture on World Law: The Proposal for an International Court. *University of Pittsburgh Law Review,* 56: 271–282

Ross, J. (1991). The Nature of Contemporary International Terrorism. In Charters, 1991

Ross, J. I. (1996). Policing in the Gulf States: The Effect of the Gulf Conflict. In Marenin, 1996

Rusche, G., and O. Kirchheimer. (1939). *Punishment and Social Structure.* New York: Russell and Russell

Rush, G. E. (1994). *Dictionary of Criminal Justice,* 4th ed. Guilford, Conn.: Dushkin

Ryan, M., and J. Sim. (1998). Power, Punishment and Prisons in England and Wales 1975–1996. In Weiss and South, 1996, pp. 175–205

Salzano, J., and S. W. Hartman. (1999). Organized Crime in Narcotics Trafficking. *Crime and Justice International,* March

Sanad, N. (1991). *The Theory of Crime and Criminal Responsibility in Islamic Law: Shari'a.* Chicago: Office of International Criminal Justice

Sartori, G. (1996). Comparing and Miscomparing. In Brown and Macridis, 1996

Scheingold, S. (1970). *The Law in Political Integration.* Cambridge, Mass.: Harvard University Center for International Relations

Schille, P. (1990). Gesellschaft der Wahnsinnigen. *Der Speigel,* July 31, pp. 86–100

Schiller, D. (1987). Coping with Terrorism: West Germany in the 1970s and 1980s. In Kurz, 1987

Schlagheck, D. (1988). *International Terrorism.* Lexington, Mass.: Lexington Books

Schmallager, F. (1999). *Criminal Justice Today,* 5th ed. Englewood Cliffs, N.J.: Prentice-Hall

Schmidhauser, J. (ed.). (1963). *Constitutional Law in the Political Process.* Chicago: Rand McNally

Schwartz, B. (ed.). (1956). *The Code Napoleon and the Common Law World.* Westport, Conn.: Greenwood Press

Schwitzgebel, R. K. (1969). Issues in the Use of an Electronic Monitoring System with Chronic Recidivists. *Law and Society Review,* 7: 597–611

Sen, S. (1996). Prison Reforms: A Convict Is a Non-Person. *Statesman, Delhi,* Jan. 12

Seymour, J. D., and R. Anderson. (1998). *New Ghosts, Old Ghosts: Prisons and Labor Reform Camps in China.* Armonk, N.Y.: Sharpe

Shannon, S. L. (1999). The Global Sex Trade: Humans as the Ultimate Commodity. *Crime and Justice International,* May: 5

Shapiro, M. (1981). *Courts.* Chicago: University of Chicago Press

Shaw, V. N. (1998). Productive Labor and Thought Reform in Chinese Corrections: A Historical and Comparative Analysis. *The Prison Journal,* 78(2): 186–211

Shelly, L. I. (1981). *Crime and Modernization.* Carbondale: Southern Illinois University Press

Shelly, L. I. (1986). Crime and Modernization Reexamined. *Annales Internationales de Criminologie,* 24: 7–21

Shinkai, H., and U. Zvekic. (1999). Punishment. In *Global Report on Crime and Justice,* 1999, pp. 91–119

Simonsen, C. E., and J. R. Spindlove. (2000). *Terrorism Today: The Past, the Players, the Future.* Upper Saddle River, N.J.: Prentice-Hall

Sinuraya, T. (1999). Cyber Crime Problem Increases. *Crime and Justice International,* June: 10

Situ, Y., and W. Liu. (1996). An Overview of the Chinese Criminal Justice System. In Ebbe, 1996

Skolnick, J., and D. Bayley. (1986). *The New Blue Line.* New York: Free Press

Smykla, J., and W. Selke. (eds.). (1995). *Intermediate Sanctions: Sentencing in the 1990s.* Cincinnati: Anderson

Solomon, P. (1990). The USSR Supreme Court: History, Role, and Future Prospects. *American Journal of Comparative Law,* 38(1): 127–142

Souryal, S. S. (1987). The Religionization of a Society: The Continuing Application of Shariah Law in Saudi Arabia. *Journal for the Scientific Study of Religion,* 26: 249–265

———, and D. W. Potts. (1994). The Penalty of Hand Amputation for Theft in Islamic Justice. *Journal of Criminal Justice,* 22(3): 249–265

Southgate, P. (1995). Alternative Forms of Patrol: Innovations in the UK. Paper presented at the Annual Meeting of the American Society of Criminology, Boston, November

Spader, D. J. (1999). Teaching Comparative Criminal Procedure: Russian Dolls, Color Charts, and Cappuccino. *Journal of Criminal Justice Education,* 10(1)

Spencer, J. R. (1995a). *Jackson's Machinery of Justice in England,* 2nd ed. New York: Cambridge University Press

———. (1995b). Justice English Style. *The World and I,* Aug.: 315–323

Stark, R., L. Kent, and D. P. Doyle. (1982). Religion and Delinquency: The Ecology of a "Lost" Relationship. *Journal of Research in Crime and Delinquency,* 19: 4–24

Stead, P. (1983). *The Police of France*. New York: Macmillan

Stern, V. (1998). *A Sin Against the Future: Imprisonment in the World*. Boston: Northeastern University Press

Stone, B. (1986). *The French Parlements and the Crisis of the Old Regime*. Chapel Hill: University of North Carolina Press

Stroebel, W. P. (2000). A Glimpse of Cyberwarfare. *U.S. News & World Report,* March 13, pp. 32–33

Sunga, L. S. (1997). *The Emerging System of International Criminal Law*. The Hague: Kluwer Law International

Sutherland, E., and D. Cressey. (1974). *Criminology*. New York: Lippincott

Sutton, J. (1991). The War Against Narcotics: A Report from the International Front. *CJ The Americas,* Oct./Nov.

Tanaka, H. (1976). *The Japanese Legal System*. Tokyo: University of Tokyo Press

Tanner, H. (1994). Crime and Punishment in China: 1979–1989. Doctoral dissertation, Columbia University. Ann Arbor, Mich.: UMI Dissertation Services

Terrill, R. J. (1999). *World Criminal Justice Systems: A Survey,* 4th ed. Cincinnati: Anderson

Terzani, T. (1990). Wir sind die Erben der Samurai. *Der Spiegel,* 27: 100–116

Thomanek, J. (1985). Police and Public Order in the Federal Republic of Germany. In Roach and Thomanek, 1985

Thomas, P. A., and M. Moerings (eds.). (1996). *AIDS in Prison*. Dartmouth: Aldershot

The Times. (1998). Even Guards Stay Out of This Prison. Dec. 25, p. A30

Tonry, M. (ed.). (1993). *Crime and Justice: A Review of Research,* Vol. 17. Chicago: University of Chicago Press

————, and R. Hamilton. (eds.). (1995). *Intermediate Sanctions in Overcrowded Times*. Boston: Northeastern University Press

Tunc, A. (1956). The Grand Outlines of the Code. In Schwartz, 1956

Ueno, Hareo. (1986). Maintaining Police Integrity: Japan. *Police Studies,* 9(18)

UNAFEI. (1997). *Annual Report for 1996*. Resource Material Series No. 51. Tokyo: United Nations Asian and Far East Institute for the Prevention of Crime and Treatment of Offenders

UNDCP (United Nations International Drug Control Programme). (1997). Illicit Drug Trafficking: Report of the Secretariat to the Commission on Narcotic Drugs. Document E/CN.7/1997/4

UNICJRI (United Nations Interregional Crime and Justice Research Institute). (1999). Global Studies on Transnational Organized Crime. Center for International Crime Prevention/Office for Drug Control and Crime Prevention. Document E/CN.15/1999/CRP.4

United Nations. (n.d.). Charter of the United Nations and Statute of the International Court of Justice. New York: United Nations Office of Public Information

United Nations Commission on Crime Prevention and Criminal Justice. *Global Programme Against Corruption*. E/Cn.15/1999/CRP.3

United Nations. (1997). Fifth United Nations Survey of Crime Trends and Operations of Criminal Justice Systems. Vienna: Crime Prevention and Criminal Justice Branch

United Nations, Economic and Social Council. (1996). United Nations Standards and Norms in the Field of Crime Prevention and Criminal Justice: Capital Punishment and Implementations of Safeguards Guaranteeing the Protection of Rights of Those Facing the Death Penalty. Report of the Secretary-General, Document E/CN 15/1996/19

United Nations Economic and Social Council. (1993). The Impact of Organized Criminal Activities upon Society at Large: Report of the Secretary General. Document E/CN.15/1993/3

United Nations Human Rights Website (1999): http://www.unhchr.ch/htmlmenu3/b/a_opt2.htm

United Nations International Study of Firearms Regulation. (1998). New York: United Nations

United Nations. (1996). *United Nations Standards and Norms in the Field of Crime Prevention and Criminal Justice: Use and Application of the Standard Minimal Rules for the Treatment of Prisoners*. Economic and Social Council. E/CN15/1996/19

United Nations. (1999). *Use and Application of United Nations Standards and Norms in Crime Prevention and Criminal Justice: Report of the Secretary General*. Economic and Social Council. E/CN.15/1999/7

Upham, F. (1987). *Law and Social Change in Postwar Japan*. Cambridge, Mass.: Harvard University Press

Urabe, N. (1990). Rule of Law and Due Process: A Comparative View of the United States and Japan. *Law and Contemporary Problems,* 53(1): 61–72

U.S. State Department. (1999). Department of State Publication 10610, Office of the U.S. Secretary of State, Office of the Coordinator for Counterterrorism. Website: http://www.state.gov/www/global/terrorism/1998report

U.S. State Department. (1997). *International Narcotics Control Strategy Report*. Washington, D.C.: Government Printing Office, p. 25

U.S. State Department. (1997). Patterns of Global Terrorism: Overview of State-Sponsored Terrorism. Website: http://www.state.gov.www/global/terrorism/1996report

U.S. State Department. (1998). Website: http://www.state.gov.www/global/terrorism/25measures_oct98.html

Van Caenegem, R. (1973). *The Birth of the English Common Law*. Cambridge, Cambridge University Press

Van Dijk, J. (1997). The International Crime Victim Survey (ICVS): Another Count of Crime. In *Global Report on Crime and Justice*, 1999, p. 55

———, and C. Steinmetz. (1988). Pragmatism, Ideology, and Crime Control: Three Dutch Surveys. In Walker and Hough, 1988

Ville, R., U. Zvekic, and J. F. Klaus. (eds.). (1997). *Promoting Probation Internationally*. Proceedings of the International Training Workshop on Probation, July, Valletta, Malta. Rome/London: United Nations Interregional Crime and Justice Research Institute, Publication No. 58

Walker, N., and M. Hough. (1988). *Public Attitudes to Sentencing*. Brookfield, Vt.: Gower

Wall Street Journal. (1991). May 2, pp. 1, 2

Wall Street Journal. (2000). EU Police Push for Cross-Board E-Eavesdropping. Feb. 26. World Justice Information Network: http://www.wjin.net/html/news/3682.htm

Walmsley, R. (1996). Prison Systems in Central and Eastern Europe: Progress, Problems and International Standards. HEUNI Publication Series 29

———. (1999). World Prison Population List. Research Findings, No. 88. London: Home Office Research, Development and Statistics Directorate

Waltman, J., and K. Holland (eds.). (1988). *The Political Role of Law Courts in Modern Democracies*. New York: St. Martin's Press

Wang, M. M. (1995). The International Tribunal for Rwanda: Opportunities for Clarification, Opportunities for Impact. *Columbia Human Rights Law Review*, 27: 177–226

Wang, Z. (1996). The Police System in the People's Republic of China. In Ebbe, 1996

Ward, D. (1989). War with the Drug Cartels. *CJ The Americas*, Dec./Jan.

Washington Post. (1999). U.S. Treasury Department Targets Internet Crime. Oct. 6. World Justice Information Network: http://www.wjin.net/html/news/2803.htm

Watt, I. (1988). *Police Higher Education and Training in the United Kingdom*. Chicago: Office of International Criminal Justice

Weber, M. (1985). *Rechtssoziologie*. Neuwied: Hermann Luchterhand Verlag

Weiss, R. P., and N. South. (eds.). (1998). *Comparing Prison Systems: Toward a Comparative and International Penology*. Gordon and Breach

Westney, E. (1987). *Imitation and Innovation*. Cambridge, Mass.: Harvard University Press

Williams, P. (1999). Emerging Issues: Transnational Crime and Its Control. In *Global Report on Crime and Justice*, 1999, pp. 221–241

Williams, P., C. Florez, J. Deal, and J. Furloni. (eds.). (1995). *Drug Trafficking and National Security*. Boulder, Colo.: Westview Press

Wilmore, J. H. (1936). *A Panorama of the World's Legal Systems*. Washington D.C.: Washington Law Book

Wilson, J. Q., and J. Petersilia (eds.). (1995). *Crime*. San Francisco: ICS Press

Winer, J. M. (1997). International Crime in the New Geopolitics: A Core Threat to Democracy. In McDonald, 1997

Wolfe, N. (1983). Participation in Courts: American Jurors and German Lay Judges. In Barak-Glantz and Johnson, 1983

World Court Project UK, Feb. 6, 1999. Website: http://www.gn.apc.org/wcp/

World Factbook. (1998). Extracted from CIA Website: http://www.cia.gov/cia/publications/factbook/notes.html

Wright, G. (1983). *Between the Guillotine and Liberty*. New York: Oxford University Press

Wu, H. (1995). A Grim Organ Harvest in China's Prisons. *World Press Review*, June: 22–23

Wu, H. H. (1992). *Laogai—The Chinese Gulag*. Boulder, Colo: Westview

———. (1996). *Troublemaker: One Man's Crusade Against China's Cruelty*. New York: Random House

Wu Dunn, S. (1997). Tokyo Fears Nonviolence Is Invitation to Terrorists. *New York Times*, April 24, p. A13

Xiancui, L. (1998). Crime and Policing in China. Paper presented at the Seminar Series of the Australian Institute of Criminology, September, 7

Xiangrui, G. (ed.). (1993). *The Ideal and the Reality of the Rule of Law.* Beijing: China University of Politics and Law Press

Yisheng, D. (1999). Policing Reform in China. *Crime and Justice International,* 15(34)

———, and H. Zu Yaun. (1993). Organization and Function of Public Security Agencies of the People's Republic of China. *Euro Criminology,* 5–6

Young, W., and M. Brown. (1993). Cross-National Comparisons of Imprisonment. In Tonry, 1993, pp. 1–49

Zander, M. (1989). *A Matter of Justice: The Legal System in Ferment.* Oxford: Oxford University Press

Zawitz, M. (1994). *Drugs, Crime, and the Justice System.* Washington, D.C.: Bureau of Justice Statistics

Zhang, L., D. Zhou, S. Messner, A. Liska, M. Krohn, M. J. Liu, and Z. Lou. (1996). Crime Prevention in a Communitarian Society: Bang-Jiao and Tiao-Jie in the People's Republic of China. *Justice Quarterly,* 13(2): 199–222

Zhang, S. X., R. Polakow, and B. J. Nidorf. (1995). Varies Uses of Electronic Monitoring: The Los Angeles County Experience. In Smykla and Selke, 1995

Zimring, F., and G. Hawkins. (1986). *Capital Punishment and the American Agenda.* New York: Cambridge University Press

Zvekic, U. (ed.). (1994). *Alternatives to Imprisonment in Comparative Perspective.* Chicago: Nelson-Hall

———. (1997). International Trends in Non-Custodial Sanctions. In Ville, Zvekic, and Klaus, 1997

Index